TRAVEL WRITING, 1700–1830

DURING the eighteenth century British travellers fanned out to every corner of the world, driven by diverse motives: scientific curiosity, exploration, colonization, trade, diplomacy, and tourism, which began to flourish during this period. Those at home read voraciously in travel literature, which informed curious Britons about their nation's activities overseas. The Empire, already established in the Caribbean and North America, was expanding in India and Africa and founding new outposts in the Pacific. Readers also enjoyed reports of travel closer to home: tours of the Continent and the British Isles themselves, whose beauty spots fuelled the rising fashion for picturesque and sublime scenery. Travel writing fed readers' desire for adventure and exoticism and reinforced their pride in their nation's achievements. It addressed scientific questions and gave philosophers food for thought. Political controversies were fought out in travel books, including the slavery question and the French Revolution debate. Above all, travellers' descriptions of the wider world reveal their perception of themselves. Selected authors include Daniel Defoe, Joseph Addison, Mary Wortley Montagu, Samuel Johnson, James Boswell, James Cook, William Bartram, Mary Wollstonecraft, Dorothy Wordsworth, Walter Scott, Olaudah Equiano, Mungo Park, Ann Radcliffe, Matthew 'Monk' Lewis, and Frances Trollope.

ELIZABETH A. BOHLS is Associate Professor of English at the University of Oregon. She is the author of *Women Travel Writers and the Language of Aesthetics, 1716–1818*, recently translated into Japanese, and of articles on travel writing and the novel. She is currently finishing a book on identity and place in writings from the colonial British Caribbean.

IAN DUNCAN is Professor of English at the University of California, Berkeley. He has edited several works of fiction for Oxford World's Classics, including Walter Scott's *Ivanhoe* and *Rob Roy*. He is completing a book called *Scott's Shadow: The Novel in Romantic Edinburgh* (Princeton University Press).

T0048632

OXFORD WORLD'S CLASSICS

*For over 100 years Oxford World's Classics have brought
readers closer to the world's great literature. Now with over 700
titles—from the 4,000-year-old myths of Mesopotamia to the
twentieth century's greatest novels—the series makes available
lesser-known as well as celebrated writing.*

*The pocket-sized hardbacks of the early years contained
introductions by Virginia Woolf, T. S. Eliot, Graham Greene,
and other literary figures which enriched the experience of reading.
Today the series is recognized for its fine scholarship and
reliability in texts that span world literature, drama and poetry,
religion, philosophy and politics. Each edition includes perceptive
commentary and essential background information to meet the
changing needs of readers.*

OXFORD WORLD'S CLASSICS

Travel Writing
1700–1830
An Anthology

Edited by
ELIZABETH A. BOHLS *and* IAN DUNCAN

With an Introduction by
ELIZABETH A. BOHLS

OXFORD
UNIVERSITY PRESS

OXFORD
UNIVERSITY PRESS

Great Clarendon Street, Oxford OX2 6DP

Oxford University Press is a department of the University of Oxford.
It furthers the University's objective of excellence in research, scholarship,
and education by publishing worldwide in

Oxford New York

Auckland Cape Town Dar es Salaam Hong Kong Karachi
Kuala Lumpur Madrid Melbourne Mexico City Nairobi
New Delhi Shanghai Taipei Toronto

With offices in

Argentina Austria Brazil Chile Czech Republic France Greece
Guatemala Hungary Italy Japan Poland Portugal Singapore
South Korea Switzerland Thailand Turkey Ukraine Vietnam

Oxford is a registered trade mark of Oxford University Press
in the UK and in certain other countries

Published in the United States
by Oxford University Press Inc., New York

Selection and editorial matter © Elizabeth Bohls and Ian Duncan 2005

The moral rights of the authors have been asserted

Database right Oxford University Press (maker)

First published as an Oxford World's Classics paperback 2005
Reissued 2008

British Library Cataloguing in Publication Data

Data available

ISBN 978-0-19-953752-5

9

Library of Congress Cataloging in Publication Data

Data available

Typeset in Ehrhardt
by RefineCatch Limited, Bungay, Suffolk
Printed and bound in Great Britain by Clays Ltd, Elcograf S.p.A.

ACKNOWLEDGEMENTS

THE editors thank their research assistants, Keiko Kagawa and Nick Nace, whose hard work, resourcefulness, and acuity helped bring this project to completion. Gordon Sayre provided invaluable advice about eighteenth-century North American travellers. We are grateful to the staff of the University of Oregon English Department, especially Marilyn Reid and Sheryl Powell, and to staff at the Knight Library at the University of Oregon, the Bancroft and Doe Libraries at the University of California, Berkeley, and the National Library of Scotland. Financial assistance was provided by the Barbara and Carlisle Moore endowment at the Department of English, University of Oregon, and the Committee on Research of the Academic Senate of the University of California, Berkeley. Thanks are due to Gordon Turnbull, General Editor, and the Editorial Committee of the Yale Editions of the Private Papers of James Boswell, for permission to reproduce selections from Boswell's Scottish and Grand Tour journals; to Alice Wilson, at David Higham Associates, and the Hakluyt Society for permission to reprint selections from J. C. Beaglehole's edition of the journals of Captain Cook; to Richard Price and Sally Price for permission to reprint selections from their edition of John Stedman's *Narrative*; and to the Champlain Society for permission to reprint a passage from the 1962 edition of David Thompson's *Narrative*. Ian Duncan thanks Ayşe Agiş for her encouragement and support. Liz Bohls thanks her family (Chris, Natalie, and Cooper Doe) for their great forbearance, and her parents, Mary and Allen Bohls, for starting her travels early. Last, but far from least, we both thank Judith Luna, at Oxford World's Classics, for her apparently inexhaustible good humour and patience.

CONTENTS

Introduction   xiii

Note on the Texts   xxviii

Select Bibliography   xxx

Chronology   xxxvi

TRAVEL WRITING

PART I. EUROPE AND ASIA MINOR

1. CLASSICAL GROUND

JOSEPH ADDISON, *Remarks on Several Parts of Italy* (1705)   5

JOHN GALT, *Letters from the Levant* (1813)   11

2. DEBATING THE TOUR

The Gentleman's Magazine: 'Of Travelling' (1731)   13

THOMAS NUGENT, *The Grand Tour* (1756)   14

RICHARD HURD, *Dialogues on the Uses of Foreign
Travel* (1775)   18

3. SOCIETY AND SENTIMENT

JAMES BOSWELL, *Boswell on the Grand Tour: Germany and
Switzerland* (1764)   20

TOBIAS SMOLLETT, *Travels through France and Italy* (1766)   29

JOHN MOORE, *A View of Society and Manners in Italy* (1781)   32

HESTER LYNCH PIOZZI, *Observations in a Journey through
Italy* (1789)   36

4. REVOLUTIONARY TOURISM

ARTHUR YOUNG, *Travels, during the Years 1787, 1788
and 1789* (1792)   40

HELEN MARIA WILLIAMS, *Letters from France*
(1790–1796)   48

ANN RADCLIFFE, *A Journey made in the Summer of
1794* (1795)   57

CHARLOTTE ANNE EATON, *Narrative of a Residence in
Belgium* (1817)   60

WALTER SCOTT, *Paul's Letters to his Kinsfolk* (1816)   65

5. OFF THE BEATEN TRACK

LADY MARY WORTLEY MONTAGU, 'Embassy Letters'
(1716–1718)   68

LADY ELIZABETH CRAVEN, *A Journey through the Crimea
to Constantinople* (1789)   77

MARY WOLLSTONECRAFT, *Letters Written during a Short
Residence in Sweden, Norway, and Denmark* (1796)   82

PART II. THE BRITISH ISLES

1. THE STATE OF THE NATION

CELIA FIENNES, *The Diary of Celia Fiennes*
(*c.*1685–1703)   97

DANIEL DEFOE, *A Tour through the Whole Island of Great
Britain* (1724–1726)   105

ARTHUR YOUNG, *A Tour in Ireland* (1780)   116

JOHN CARR, *The Stranger in Ireland* (1806)   122

WILLIAM COBBETT, *Rural Rides in the Southern, Western
and Eastern Counties of England* (1822–1826)   126

2. PICTURESQUE TOURISM

THOMAS GRAY, *Journal in the Lakes* (1769)   129

THOMAS WEST, *A Guide to the Lakes* (1784)   132

WILLIAM GILPIN, *Observations on the River Wye* (1782)   137

ANN RADCLIFFE, *Observations during a Tour in the
Lakes* (1795)   140

3. SCOTLAND

MARTIN MARTIN, *A Voyage to St Kilda* (1698)   141

SAMUEL JOHNSON, *A Journey to the Western Islands of
    Scotland* (1775); JAMES BOSWELL, *The Journal of a
    Tour to the Hebrides* (1773)   149

MARY ANN HANWAY, *A Journey to the Highlands of Scotland*
    (1777)   163

DOROTHY WORDSWORTH, *Recollections of a Tour Made in
    Scotland* (1803)   167

JAMES HOGG, 'Malise's Journey to the Trossacks' (from
    The Spy, 1811)   177

PART III. AFRICA

1. THE SLAVE TRADE, 1732–1789

JOHN BARBOT, *A Description of the Coasts of North and
    South Guinea* (1732)   182

JOHN ATKINS, *A Voyage to Guinea, Brasil and the West-Indies*
    (1735)   186

JOHN NEWTON, *Thoughts upon the African Slave Trade* (1788)   191

OLAUDAH EQUIANO, *The Interesting Narrative of the Life of
    Olaudah Equiano* (1789)   196

2. INFANT COLONY, 1794

ANNA MARIA FALCONBRIDGE, *Two Voyages to Sierra
    Leone* (1793)   206

3. EXPLORERS, 1790–1822

JAMES BRUCE, *Travels into Abyssinia, to Discover the Source
    of the Nile* (1790)   220

MUNGO PARK, *Travels in the Interior Districts of Africa* (1799)   227

JOHN BARROW, *Travels into the Interior of Southern
    Africa* (1801)   237

JAMES K. TUCKEY, *Narrative of an Expedition to Explore
    the River Zaire* (1818)   244

WILLIAM J. BURCHELL, *Travels in the Interior of Southern Africa* (1822)   250

PART IV. THE CARIBBEAN

1. NATURAL HISTORY AND AESTHETICS

HANS SLOANE, *A Voyage to the Islands Madera, Barbados, Nieves, S. Christopher and Jamaica* (1707/1725)   258

JAMES HAKEWILL, *A Picturesque Tour of the Island of Jamaica* (1825)   265

2. WORKING TRAVELLERS

JOHN GABRIEL STEDMAN, *Narrative of a Five Years Expedition against the Revolted Negroes of Surinam* (1790)   267

OLAUDAH EQUIANO, *The Interesting Narrative of the Life of Olaudah Equiano* (1789)   280

MARY PRINCE, *The History of Mary Prince, A West Indian Slave* (1831)   285

3. PLANTERS

WILLIAM BECKFORD, *A Descriptive Account of the Island of Jamaica* (1790)   296

MATTHEW GREGORY LEWIS, *Journal of a West India Proprietor* (1834)   303

4. LADIES

JANET SCHAW, *Journal of a Lady of Quality* (1774–1776)   314

MARIA NUGENT, *Journal of a Residence in Jamaica* (1801–1805)   325

PART V. NORTH AMERICA

1. SURVEYORS AND EXPLORERS

JOHN LAWSON, *A New Voyage to Carolina* (1709)   335

GEORGE SHELVOCKE, *A Voyage Round the World by the Way of the Great South Sea* (1726)   338

WILLIAM BYRD, *History of the Dividing Line betwixt Virginia and North Carolina* (1728)   341

WILLIAM BARTRAM, *Travels Through North and South Carolina* (1791)   350

SAMUEL HEARNE, *A Journey from Hudson's Bay to the Northern Ocean* (1795)   363

ALEXANDER MACKENZIE, *Voyages through North America to the Frozen and Pacific Oceans* (1801)   372

DAVID THOMPSON, *Narrative of his Explorations in Western America* (1784–1812)   377

2. MANNERS AND MORALS

ISAAC WELD, *Travels through the States of North America* (1799)   389

JOHN DAVIS, *Travels of Four Years and a Half in the United States of America* (1803)   393

ANNE GRANT, *Memoirs of an American Lady* (1807)   399

WILLIAM COBBETT, *A Year's Residence in the United States of America* (1818)   404

FRANCES TROLLOPE, *Domestic Manners of the Americans* (1832)   407

PART VI. AUSTRALIA AND THE PACIFIC

1. PRIVATEERS, 1680–1744

WILLIAM DAMPIER, *A New Voyage Round the World* (1697–1703)   422

WOODES ROGERS, *A Cruising Voyage Round the World* (1712)   429

RICHARD WALTER AND BENJAMIN ROBINS, *A Voyage Round the World by George Anson* (1748)   434

2. THE COOK EXPEDITIONS, 1768–1780

JAMES COOK, *The Voyage of the Endeavour* (1768–1771)   441

JOSEPH BANKS, *Journal of the Right Hon. Sir Joseph Banks* (1770)   451

GEORGE FORSTER, *A Voyage Round the World* (1777)   454

JAMES COOK, *The Voyage of the Resolution and Adventure*
(1772–1775)   460

JAMES COOK, *The Voyage of the Resolution and Discovery*
(1776–1780)   461

3. COLONIZING NEW SOUTH WALES, 1788–1791

HIRAM WOOD, *The Voyage of Governor Phillip to Botany
Bay* (1790)   465

JOHN HUNTER, *An Historical Journal of Transactions at
Port Jackson* (1793)   467

WATKIN TENCH, *A Complete Account of the Settlement at
Port Jackson* (1793)   470

JOHN NICOL, *The Life and Adventures of John Nicol,
Mariner* (1822)   478

MARY ANN PARKER, *A Voyage Round the World* (1795)   486

4. THE COMING OF THE MISSIONARIES, 1796–1824

WILLIAM WILSON, *A Missionary Voyage to the Southern
Pacific Ocean* (1799)   489

WILLIAM ELLIS, *Narrative of a Tour through Hawaii, or
Owhyhee* (1826)   490

Explanatory Notes   495

INTRODUCTION

An inquisitive traveller should never be without paper, pen, and
ink, in his pocket, because annotations made with lead pencils
are easily obliterated, and thus he is often deprived of the benefit
of his remarks.

Count Leopold Berchtold, *Essay to Direct and Extend the
Inquiries of Patriotic Travellers*, 1789

[L]eading my horse close to the brink, I went behind him, and
pushed him headlong into the water; and then taking the bridle
in my teeth, swam over to the other side. This was the third
creek I had crossed in this manner, since I had left Sego; but
having secured my notes and memorandums in the crown of my
hat, I received little or no inconvenience from such adventures.

Mungo Park, *Travels in the Interior Districts of Africa*, 1799

I am made for travelling.

James Boswell, Grand Tour journal, 1 October 1764

SINCE remote antiquity, for all kinds of reasons, people have left
home and hit the road. Couriers and diplomats, merchants and wor-
shippers crisscrossed the Mesopotamian triangle well before 3000
BC. Even tourists, travelling for pleasure, left graffiti on the Pyramids
by 1500 BC.[1] Very early in history, then, travel and writing con-
verged. Homer's *Odyssey*, the epic of obstacle-ridden travel in search
of home, raises the journey to the status of a symbolic quest—an
'odyssey'—and the traveller to that of archetypal trickster-hero. Early
non-fiction travel writing illustrates the difficulty, continuing through
the ages, of sorting fact from fiction in the genre. The Greek writer
Herodotus gives us a mélange of myth, history, and geography, from
Lydian customs ('the daughters of the common people . . . practise
as whores to collect dowries for themselves') and how much wine
is drunk at the Egyptian festival of Bubastis to the genealogies of
the gods.

Even the guidebook, still a staple of travel writing, made an ancient
début. In the second century AD Pausanias compiled a *Guide to Greece*

---

[1] Lionel Casson, *Travel in the Ancient World* (Baltimore: Johns Hopkins University
Press, 1994), 22, 32.

for Roman tourists, including such attractions as the Acropolis and
the Oracle at Delphi. In the Middle Ages, pilgrims generated an
entire tourist industry with set itineraries and pre-packaged sites.
The history of pilgrimage brings out the multiple, mixed motives
and the moral as well as physical dangers attending even such an
ostensibly pious quest. Sincere devotion mingled with simple wan-
derlust, or the urge to escape one's sodden, smelly cottage after a
long winter. The clergy denounced *curiositas*, the lure of worldly
distractions along the way; hope of sexual adventure no doubt set
more than a few pilgrims in motion. (An eighth-century missionary
asked that matrons and nuns be barred from Continental pilgrimage,
since 'few keep their virtue. There are many towns in Lombardy and
Gaul where there is not a courtesan or a harlot but is of English
stock.') Pilgrims' snobbery and souvenir collections, displaying the
badges they bought at various shrines, provided themes for satirists
in the later Middle Ages.[2] Travel fulfils obligations and enhances
status, but it also feeds dangerous desires. A traveller might come
back transformed—for better or worse—or might not come back
at all.

The Crusades are a second mode of medieval travel that looks
ahead to travel's more recent history. This massive influx of
conquest-obsessed European Christians into the Middle East to con-
front 'Saracens', different in religion and culture from themselves,
prefigures the cultural confrontations of later exploration and colonization. Sir John Mandeville's famous *Travels* (1356)—a book owned
by Leonardo da Vinci, Christopher Columbus, and the early Arctic
explorer Martin Frobisher, among others—looks both backward to
Herodotus's travel mythology, with tales of one-eyed giants, headless
men, and mouthless pygmies, and forward, with a remarkably toler-
ant account of Muslim attitudes and practices. One scholar of medieval travel sees Mandeville as initiating a new attitude: the medieval
paradigms of pilgrimage and crusade gave way to new modes of
engagement with observed experience and curiosity about other
cultures.[3] Along with Marco Polo, another near-mythical medieval
traveller, Mandeville profoundly influenced Christopher Columbus,

---

[2] Ronald C. Finucane, *Miracles and Pilgrims: Popular Beliefs in Medieval England*
(New York: St Martin's, 1977), 40.
[3] Christian K. Zacher, *Curiosity and Pilgrimage: The Literature of Discovery in
Fourteenth-Century England* (Baltimore: Johns Hopkins University Press, 1976), 130–57.

giving travel writing a continuity belied by the newness of Columbus's discovery to European readers.[4]

The period covered by this anthology begins after the 'heroic age' of early modern exploration. Drake circumnavigated the globe, Ralegh 'discovered' Guiana, and Thomas Hariot and John Smith crossed the Atlantic and founded the so-called First Empire, England's colonies in North America and the Caribbean, well before 1700. And they wrote about it: as exploration came to serve royal and mercantile interests in a more organized fashion, reporting became an integral part of it. England got a relatively late start on all this, lagging eight decades behind Spain and Portugal, which helps account for the patriotic, competitive strain in English travel writing exemplified by the great editor Richard Hakluyt in the pioneering collections of voyages that he published starting in 1589.[5]

Some travel reports, of course, were top secret, proprietary documents of great potential value as merchants and governments competed for territories and markets. But those that were published quickly captured an avid readership in England's print market, whose rapid growth was a defining feature of the period covered by this book. Already top sellers in the relatively limited Elizabethan and Stuart book market, travel books continued to dominate the market throughout the eighteenth century as literacy rose and authorship burgeoned.[6] The expansion of the print market changed literary history for ever, bringing with it a new and popular fictional form—the novel—as well as an influx of authors new to print, including many women and middle-class men. A number of these appear in this anthology. Women travellers wrote, though they did not publish their travels as often as did men; women certainly wrote far fewer travel books than novels. And many of the male authors we include can be reckoned middle class, starting with the famously bourgeois journalist, novelist, entrepreneur, and sometime spy Daniel Defoe. Though a number of male travel writers, notably Grand Tourists like Joseph Addison and James Boswell, display the classical education that defined the gentlemanly élite of the day, many

---

[4] Peter Hulme and Tim Youngs, eds., *The Cambridge Companion to Travel Writing* (Cambridge: Cambridge University Press, 2002), 3.

[5] William H. Sherman, 'Stirrings and Searchings (1500–1720)', ibid. 3.

[6] Charles Batten, *Pleasurable Instruction: Form and Convention in Eighteenth-Century Travel Literature* (Berkeley: University of California Press, 1978), 1–3.

others—explorers like Captain Cook or David Thompson or colonists like Watkin Tench—are from a less privileged background. And a few, such as the sailor John Nicol and the slaves Olaudah Equiano and Mary Prince, are downright plebeian.

This brings up an important and somewhat controversial question, central to our selection: who counts as a traveller, or a travel writer? Paul Fussell, editor of *The Norton Book of Travel*, prefers fairly restrictive criteria. 'To constitute real travel', he declares, 'movement from one place to another should manifest some impulse of non-utilitarian pleasure.'[7] Although it could be argued that even the most utilitarian of travellers enjoys such pleasure at some point in the journey, to privilege this element is to skew the definition of travel, and travel writing, in the direction of an aestheticism that is the hallmark of a leisured élite. As the historian James Clifford puts it, 'The traveler, by definition, is someone who has the security and privilege to move about in relatively unconstrained ways. This, at any rate, is the travel myth.'[8] But what about those whose movement is not so free, not so secure? Do sailors, soldiers, servants, slaves, emigrants, exiles, transported convicts, military and diplomatic wives, count as travellers? Fussell's attitude emerges from a passing remark in his introduction to what he calls 'the heyday of travel', the later nineteenth and early twentieth centuries. 'Porters were indispensable then because you carried so much.'[9] 'You', in this view of the world, were never a porter; 'you' were the porter's employer, owner of all the baggage he had to carry.

And of course 'you' were also never a 'native', one of those inhabiting the places the traveller travelled to see. The involuntary travel of 'natives' makes up the mass population movements that define the twentieth and twenty-first centuries: emigrants, immigrants, refugees, diasporas, *Gastarbeiters*, and 'illegal aliens'. Even in the eighteenth century, however, natives travelled too: Omai, the Polynesian brought back to London by Captain Cook in 1774, became a social sensation who met the King and had his portrait painted by Sir Joshua Reynolds. Before Omai, there were the four 'Indian Kings' from New York brought to London in 1710 to meet Queen

---

[7] Paul Fussell, ed., *The Norton Book of Travel* (New York: W. W. Norton, 1987), 21.

[8] James Clifford, *Routes: Travel and Translation in the Late Twentieth Century* (Cambridge, Mass.: Harvard University Press, 1997), 34.

[9] Fussell, *Norton Book of Travel*, 275.

Anne, plead for more military aid to colonists against the French, and be treated to urban amusements including the theatre, cock-fighting, bear-baiting, and a Punch and Judy show.[10] (Not to mention the seventeenth-century Indian Princess Pocahontas, who married a colonist—not Captain John Smith—and ended her days in England.) And Olaudah Equiano's moving account of his kidnapping and enslavement reminds us of a form of mass involuntary travel that shaped the Atlantic world: the slave trade, which during the sixteenth to the nineteenth centuries removed some six million Africans from their homes, transplanting and transforming those who survived the passage to the Americas. Very few of these travellers had the opportunity of getting their stories into print. We have included excerpts from slave autobiographies by Equiano and Mary Prince (the only surviving British slave narrative by a woman slave) partly to encourage readers to reconsider and broaden their understanding of what constitutes travel.

Clearly, authorship was more accessible to members of groups with higher status, and this reality has necessarily shaped our selection. As interesting as it would be to read Omai's impressions of London, he did not write or even dictate them for publication. But we have done our best to include travel writers of varying social ranks and occupations and both sexes. And importantly, we have not necessarily preferred writing that self-consciously foregrounds the writer's personality or persona, that is romantic or ironic or otherwise highly 'literary' in the present-day sense of the term. Rather, we have striven to do justice to the range and diversity of material that was written, published, purchased, and read concerning travel between 1700 and 1830, and the variety of writers who produced it.

Who were they? Some of the most important kinds of travel writer are familiar from the sixteenth and seventeenth centuries: diplomats, merchants, explorers, colonizers, and scientists. Other types were relatively new, either to travel or to writing. Modern tourism began to flourish during this period. We will have more to say about tourism, but first let us run through the more utilitarian types of travel and their impact on travel writing at this time.

If the early modern period saw a shift in the ethos and language of travel writing 'from chivalric adventure to venture capitalism',[11] the

---

[10] Richmond P. Bond, *Queen Anne's American Kings* (Oxford: Clarendon Press, 1952).
[11] Sherman, 'Stirrings and Searchings', 25.

eighteenth century saw mercantile capitalism mature and mesh with national interests in imperial expansion. Parts of the globe still unknown to Europe were explored in search of potential profit, exploitable real estate, scientific knowledge (the Royal Society for the Improving of Natural Knowledge was chartered by the King in 1662), and national as well as personal prestige. We see these intertwined motives in Captain Cook's famous Pacific voyages in the 1770s, the first commissioned by the Admiralty ostensibly for scientific purposes (to observe the transit of Venus from the southern hemisphere), but really to find the mythical Southern Continent and assess its potential for colonization. And soon it was colonized, initially as a dumping ground for Britain's convicts, since North America was no longer available for that purpose. Cook took along scientists and artists to collect, classify, and document his discoveries. The official accounts of his voyages, anxiously awaited by the reading public, were runaway bestsellers—by far the most popular travel books of the age.

Business, exploration, and science came together in other ways in other areas of the world penetrated by the British. The fur trade had opened up large areas of North America during the seventeenth century; the Scottish fur trader Alexander Mackenzie in 1793 was actually the first European to cross the North American continent and reach the Pacific. Native American trappers guided other explorers such as Samuel Hearne and David Thompson to remote reaches of the continent. The grim business of the slave trade, of course, had linked Europe, Africa, and the Caribbean in the so-called Atlantic Triangle since shortly after Columbus's voyage, though the British did not get involved until 1560. The vested interests of slave traders and slave owners colour much or most of the writing about these areas until the 1788 founding of the Association for Promoting the Discovery of the Interior Parts of Africa by twelve members of an exclusive London club. One founding member was Sir Joseph Banks, the amateur botanist who sailed with Cook on his first voyage. Banks went on to become President of the Royal Society for many years, hatching, among other global projects, Captain Bligh's luckless attempt to ship breadfruit plants from Tahiti to the West Indies as a food source for slaves. (After the mutiny on the *Bounty* and his astonishing survival, Bligh made a second, successful expedition.) Banks's scientific contacts crisscrossed the Empire, shipping back specimens for his collections, exemplifying the global reach and interconnection of the British interests served by eighteenth-century travel.

The African Association, as it was known, sponsored expeditions into the interior of the continent by intrepid or foolish explorers such as Mungo Park, whose deservedly famous narrative we excerpt below. The critic Mary Pratt connects interior exploration with natural history as part of a new age of European 'planetary consciousness', ambitiously aiming to fill in all the dark places on the map or classify all existing species.[12] To narrate their part in fulfilling these grand aspirations, however, explorers like Park or John Barrow construct innocuous personae: the benign naturalist, collecting and classifying his herbs (Barrow), or the lone European (Park), at the mercy of his African hosts, whose body becomes a curiosity for their inspection and whose stated motive of mere curiosity for his epic journey makes him a madman in their eyes. Pratt labels this rhetorical stance in travel writing 'anti-conquest'. The imperial agendas that propelled so many British travellers of this period fade into the background, so to speak, in the travel writing they produce, upstaged by science, sentiment, or simply local colour.

Closer to home, tourism—which has come to dominate and deform popular ideas about travel—took root in Britain during the period covered by this book. 'The tourist', James Buzard summarizes, 'is the dupe of fashion, following blindly where authentic travellers have gone with open eyes and free spirits.'[13] That (to echo Clifford) is the tourism myth. 'The tourist', Evelyn Waugh commented caustically in the 1930s, 'is the other fellow.' Most travellers, however, even those who would scorn to think of themselves as tourists, actually move about within predetermined, quite limited circuits and itineraries, 'dictated by political, economic, and intercultural global relations (often colonial, postcolonial, or neocolonial in nature)', and of course by the available infrastructure of transport and accommodation.[14] Though the word 'tourist' came into use in the late eighteenth century, the roots of Continental tourism as an English institution go

[12] Mary Louise Pratt, *Imperial Eyes: Travel Writing and Transculturation* (New York: Routledge, 1992), 28.

[13] James Buzard, *The Beaten Track: European Tourism and the Ways to 'Culture' 1800–1918* (Oxford: Clarendon Press, 1993), 1.

[14] Clifford, *Routes*, 35.

back to the 1600s. The Grand Tour of Europe as a finishing school
for young aristocrats originated under the Tudors. As early as the
reign of Henry VIII, the diplomat Thomas Wyatt brought back from
his Italian travels a novel souvenir: an exciting new poetic form, the
sonnet. In 1642 the first Continental guidebook, James Howell's
Instructions for Forreine Travel, came out and was in demand for a
number of years.[15] Two centuries later, at the end of the period we
cover, the Grand Tour had become available to the bourgeoisie and
was on the verge of being further democratized by railways and
Cook's Tours.

We will have more to say about the Grand Tour, and domestic
tourism, in section introductions. Since 1700, leisure travel—travel
'for pleasure or culture' (*OED*)—has become a widely prevalent
practice (and a bloated industry) whose written records disclose a
great deal about the values, desires, and the very structure of the
modern self. Though we might not go as far as one theorist who
proposes the tourist as the prototypical modern subject,[16] we include
writings by early tourists who tell us as much about themselves and
their home culture as about the places and cultures they visit.
Ambivalence is typical of the tourist: travel can reinforce satisfaction
with England, articulate and strengthen national identity, while at
the same time fulfilling desires for escape, transgression, and the
exotic. In travel accounts such as Charlotte Eaton's *Narrative of a
Residence in Belgium during the Campaign of 1815* and Walter Scott's
Paul's Letters to his Kinsfolk we see the battlefield of Waterloo being
made into a tourist attraction—a profitable commodity for develop-
ers and promoters—within weeks of the battle. This early in the
nineteenth century, then, tourism was a well-established institution,
ritually transforming bourgeois longings and national values into
admission fees and souvenir purchases.

Travel writing as a form or genre is not easy to pin down.
We think of it as having a narrative core, the story of a journey, yet
eighteenth-century travel writing often includes as much impersonal
description as first-person narration. We think of it as non-fiction:

---

[15] Robert Munter and Clyde L. Grose, *Englishmen Abroad: Being an Account of their
Travels in the Seventeenth Century* (Lewiston, NY, and Queenston, Ontario: Edwin
Mellen Press, 1986), 244.

[16] Dean MacCannell, *The Tourist: A New Theory of the Leisure Class* (New York:
Schocken Books, 1976).

travel writers 'claim—and their readers believe—that the journey actually took place, and that it is recorded by the traveler him or herself'.[17] And yet travel writers avail themselves copiously of the devices of fiction and have been labelled liars through the centuries.[18] Fictional voyages were certainly among the bestsellers of the eighteenth century. *Robinson Crusoe* (1719) and *Gulliver's Travels* (1726) both piggybacked on the popularity of non-fiction travel accounts. Swift cleverly satirizes travel writers' often deadpan style and readers' credulity. Defoe, in his fiction as in his travel writing, plods through a long-winded, doggedly concrete re-creation of the circumstances of travel and the features of place. Indeed, many of the century's best-known authors published travel books alongside their other writings (many excerpted here): Addison, Fielding, Sterne, Smollett, Johnson, Boswell, Thomas Gray, Ann Radcliffe, Helen Maria Williams, Mary Wollstonecraft, Walter Scott, and William Wordsworth (as well as his sister Dorothy). Travel was a staple of fictional plots, from the picaresque rambles of Fielding's Tom Jones and Smollett's Roderick Random to the dramatic abductions of Radcliffe's Gothic heroines and the Highland adventures of Scott's Edward Waverley.

Travel writing and the novel overlap in a number of ways. Travel writing was popular before novels: J. Paul Hunter, describing the market niche targeted by early novelists, notes that their title-pages often 'tried to capitalize on the contemporary popularity of travel books by suggesting the similarity of their wares'. One feature shared by the two genres is thematic: like travel writing, the early novel 'is a product of serious cultural thinking about comparative societies and the multiple natures in human nature'. Formally, novels and travel books have in common an enormous flexibility. Both are 'loosely constructed, capable of almost infinite expansion, and susceptible of a great variety of directions and paces'.[19]

Like travel writers, too, early novelists sought ways to cope with being called liars. For example, the narrator of Aphra Behn's *Oroonoko, or the Royal Slave* (1688), set in the South American

---

[17] Barbara Korte, *English Travel Writing from Pilgrimages to Postcolonial Explorations*, trans. Catherine Matthias (New York: St Martin's, 2000), 1.

[18] Percy G. Adams, *Travel Literature and the Evolution of the Novel* (Lexington: University Press of Kentucky, 1983), 81–102.

[19] J. Paul Hunter, *Before Novels: The Cultural Contexts of Eighteenth-Century English Fiction* (New York: W. W. Norton & Company, 1990), 353.

colony of Surinam, protests, 'I was myself an Eye-Witness to a great part, of what you will find here set down.' In her dedication Behn hammers home the claim: 'This is a true story . . . If there be any thing that seems Romantick, I beseech your Lordship to consider, these Countries do, in all things, so far differ from ours, that they produce inconceivable Wonders; at least, they appear so to us, because New and Strange.'[20] She is using the features her book shares with travel writing—the 'Romantick' appeal of New World 'Wonders', a byproduct of geographical and cultural difference—to fend off the accusations of lying that beset the early novel, before fiction writing gained legitimacy. *Oroonoko* is widely considered a generic hybrid, combining elements of travel writing, romance, and novel, to the extent that it was possible to separate these in 1688.[21] Stephen Greenblatt has identified the experience of wonder as 'the central figure in the European response to the New World, the decisive intellectual and emotional experience in the presence of radical difference'.[22] Building on two centuries of European writing about New World wonders, Behn is able to present her fiction as 'strange, therefore true' (whether or not she actually went to Surinam). Much early exploration writing dwells close to *Oroonoko* in a grey zone of the strange, exotic, and wondrous—not independently verifiable, and thus dependent on the force of rhetoric to compel reader belief— although the realm of verifiable factuality in travel writing expanded as the eighteenth century wore on.[23]

Much travel writing also shares with *Oroonoko* its generic and discursive hybridity. Besides the fictional elements of plot and narrating persona, whose prominence and coherence vary widely, travel books often incorporate pockets of historical anecdote, advice to the traveller (on everything from transportation and inns to how to avoid offending the locals), and proto-ethnographic 'manners and customs' description. Natural history was a staple of travel writing even before, but more importantly after the Swedish taxonomist Linnaeus's epochal 1735 publication of *The System of Nature*. His

---

[20] Aphra Behn, *Oroonoko*, ed. Catherine Gallagher (Boston and New York: Bedford/ St Martin's, 2000), 37.

[21] Oddvar Holmesland, 'Aphra Behn's *Oroonoko*: Cultural Dialectics and the Novel', *ELH* 68 (2001), 57.

[22] Stephen Greenblatt, *Marvelous Possessions: The Wonder of the New World* (Chicago: University of Chicago Press, 1991), 14.

[23] Batten, *Pleasurable Instruction*, 5; Korte, *English Travel Writing*, 31.

disciples 'fanned out by the dozens across the globe' to describe, draw, classify, and collect new species.[24] Later in the century, the language of aesthetics, describing the picturesque and sublime in natural and man-made landscape, entered travel writing to become a nearly indispensable convention, as we will see.

In what other ways did English travel writing change between 1700 and 1830? Well before 1700, amid the chaotic variety of the genre, some basic conventions were in place. The most typical form was the 'report' or 'relation', combining a chronological narrative of a journey with topographical and ethnographic descriptions.[25] In the 1660s the Royal Society published instructions for scientific travellers, calling for accurate observation and a sober, unadorned prose style. As early as the 1620s the Grand Tourist, too, was instructed in detail, in print, on the 'things to be seen and observed'.[26] Travel was to educate both the traveller and the reader of travel books. Amid all this edification, it is not surprising that early eighteenth-century travel writing subordinates—often nearly banishes—the traveller–writer's individual, subjective experience.[27] Addison's influential *Remarks on Italy* (1705), excerpted below, typifies the impersonality expected of travel writing throughout at least the first half of the century.[28] Following the Roman critic Horace's famous dictum about poetry, travel writing was expected to delight as well as to teach. The delight, however, was to come from acute observation and judicious reflection, rather than from the kind of autobiographical material that became more conventional in nineteenth-century travel writing. Otherwise a writer risked reviewers' accusations of egotism, a cardinal fault.[29]

When did this change? We hear these strictures both echoed and rejected as Mary Wollstonecraft (herself a reviewer) admits in her 'Advertisement' to *Letters Written during a Short Residence in Sweden, Norway, and Denmark* (1796), 'In writing these desultory letters, I found I could not avoid being continually the first person—"the little hero of each tale". I tried to correct this fault, if it be one, for

---

[24] Pratt, *Imperial Eyes*, 25.

[25] Sherman, 'Stirrings and Searchings', 30.

[26] Francis Bacon, 'Of Travels', in *The Essays of Francis Bacon*, ed. Mary A. Scott (New York: Scribner's, 1908), 80.

[27] Korte, *English Travel Writing*, 31.

[28] Batten, *Pleasurable Instruction*, 13.

[29] Ibid. 39.

they were designed for publication; but in proportion as I arranged my thoughts, my letter, I found, became stiff and affected.'[30] Barbara Korte explains the gradual movement toward greater subjectivity in English travel writing during the last half of the eighteenth century partly through the expansion of the print market, which made information about the Continent more available at home. In response, travel writers 'discovered' new areas, away from the set Grand Tour itinerary—Boswell in Corsica, Brydone in Sicily and Malta, Southey in Portugal, Wollstonecraft in Scandinavia—but also turned to formal and stylistic innovation, even when writing about familiar routes. The increasing value attached to subjective experience in many areas of late eighteenth-century culture, especially philosophy and literature, is well known. It is no accident that travel writing during this time was published more often in the overtly autobiographical forms of journals, diaries, or letters.[31] And we cannot overlook the widespread influence of Laurence Sterne's bestselling travel novel *A Sentimental Journey* (1768), whose protagonist, the mischievously named Parson Yorick, rambles through France on a 'journey of the heart', looking for persons and situations to touch his emotions and educate his moral sense.[32]

Some scholars see a cleft opening up between literary and scientific travel writing during the Romantic period (1790–1820). Barbara Stafford, for instance, sees the 'synthetic merits' of the Enlightenment travel account giving way during the first decades of the nineteenth century to 'the purely entertaining travel book' on the one hand, and on the other 'the instructive guide (the ancestor of the Baedeker volumes)'. Pleasure, she asserts, 'was no longer inextricably tied to instruction'.[33] Nigel Leask, however, disagrees. His recent study sets out to revise the standard account of 'romantic travel writing', which he says 'elevates the importance of one, self-consciously literary, strain of travel writing at the expense of other discourses of travel which were of equal importance'. Although the areas that are Leask's focus in *Curiosity and the Aesthetics of Travel Writing 1770–1840*

[30] Mary Wollstonecraft, *Letters Written during a Short Residence in Sweden, Norway, and Denmark*, ed. Carol Poston (Lincoln: University of Nebraska Press, 1976), 5.

[31] Korte, *English Travel Writing*, 53.

[32] Laurence Sterne, *A Sentimental Journey*, ed. Ian Jack (Oxford: Oxford University Press, 1968), 84.

[33] Barbara Maria Stafford, *Voyage into Substance: Art, Nature, and the Illustrated Travel Account, 1760–1840* (Cambridge, Mass., and London: MIT Press, 1984), 442.

(India and Mexico) are not among those we have chosen to include, his contention that travel writing at least until 1820 continues to struggle 'to integrate . . . personal narrative with "curious" or "precise" observation', to balance 'literary and scientific discourses', deserves to be tested against a wider range of writings.[34]

Our principles of selection in this anthology arose, in the first place, out of our belief that travel as a cultural practice and travel writing as a literary genre cannot be properly understood by segregating domestic from exotic travel. In a period that saw such a dramatic expansion of the British Empire, literate Britons' global consciousness—fostered by reading travel books—shaped their perception of their home island. Conversely, explorers, colonists, and other adventurers carried with them a sense of their home country, often fed to some extent by their reading in domestic travel writing. Thus Dorothy Wordsworth, reaching for terms to describe the Scottish Highlands to English readers in 1803, declares that it 'was an outlandish scene—we might have believed ourselves in North America'. Her brother William labels the filthy house of a Scots boatman 'Hottentotish'.[35] This reiterates, perhaps knowingly, Samuel Johnson's infamous dictum in his *Journey to the Western Islands of Scotland* (excerpted below): 'Till the Union made [the Scots] acquainted with English manners, the culture of their lands was unskillful, and their domestick life unformed; their tables were coarse as the feasts of Eskimeaux, and their houses filthy as the cottages of Hottentots.'[36] Matthew Lewis compares a cove on the Jamaican coast to 'the most beautiful of the views of coves found in "Cook's Voyages" '. Soon after, however, he comes upon 'places resembling ornamental parks in England, the lawns being of the liveliest verdure . . . enriched with a profusion of

---

[34] Nigel Leask, *Curiosity and the Aesthetics of Travel Writing 1770–1840* (Oxford: Oxford University Press, 2002), 6, 7, 9.

[35] 'Hottentot' is a derogatory term for one branch of the Khoisan people of southwest Africa, used more broadly to denote an uncivilized or inferior person. Dorothy Wordsworth, *Recollections of a Tour Made in Scotland*, ed. Carol Kyros Walker (New Haven: Yale University Press, 1997), 87, 92.

[36] Samuel Johnson, *A Journey to the Western Islands of Scotland*, in Peter Levi, ed., *A Journey to the Western Islands of Scotland by Samuel Johnson and The Journal of a Tour to the Hebrides by James Boswell* (New York: Penguin, 1984), 51.

trees majestic in stature and picturesque in their shapes'.[37] Readers
would miss something crucial about the travel writing of this period
without reading domestic and exotic travel side by side.

British men and women went just about everywhere in the eighteenth century: from China to Peru, to Abyssinia, the Canadian Arctic,
Constantinople, New Zealand, and Buckinghamshire. Rather than
attempting to span a planetary range within a single volume, we have
decided to represent discrete areas of particular historical interest.
Our selections are organized geographically; we have chosen areas
that offer a rich variety of writings and pose interesting questions to
the reader. We begin with the Grand Tour, which became during
this period a major institution of knowledge about European civilization and its cultural limits, marked by the outlying Ottoman Empire.
In travel writings about the Near East we find evidence of the discourse that the critic Edward Said famously labelled 'Orientalism'—
a body of powerful and enduring stereotypes—but we also see these
stereotypes called into question.[38] We then turn to the British Isles,
where various discourses of travel writing, including antiquarian,
economic, and aesthetic tourism, played a significant part in consoli-
dating the new sovereign territory of the United Kingdom between
the Acts of Union with Scotland (1707) and Ireland (1801).

The following three sections cover what is known as Britain's
'First Empire', its colonial holdings before the loss of the United
States and large-scale nineteenth-century territorial takeovers in the
African interior and on the Indian subcontinent. Africa is included
as part of the so-called 'Atlantic Triangle', connected by the sea
routes of the slave trade to England and its island colonies in the
Caribbean, although the late eighteenth and early nineteenth centuries also saw the British start to explore the African interior. The
cultural impact of colonial slavery and the political debate over its
abolition pervade travel writing about both Africa and the Caribbean
up to slave emancipation in 1833. English travellers to North
America also comment on slavery, though it takes up less space amid
diverse responses to awesome nature, nascent democracy, and the
Native American presence on the vast continent. Finally, the Pacific
Ocean marks the farthest reach of what is, by the end of the eight-

[37] Matthew Lewis, *Journal of a West India Proprietor* (Oxford: Oxford University
Press, 1999), 99, 104.
[38] Edward Said, *Orientalism* (New York: Random House, 1978).

eenth century, a truly global British influence. Cook's sensational voyages and the colonizing of Australia represent the crowning achievement of centuries of maritime exploration. Writings from these voyages display the mastery that was the aim of scientific travel, but also reveal the resistance and conflict inevitably provoked by such colonial incursions.

We limit our selections to non-fiction prose travel writing, most of it published between 1700 and 1830. Unpublished sources include excerpts from Captain Cook's original journals as well as some unpublished travel letters and journals, especially those by women, who were less likely to venture into public authorship at the time. Most excerpts are fairly short, but in each section longer selections represent authors whose work in the genre is especially interesting. Each of our sections is organized, not necessarily chronologically, but in subsections that make sense for that particular geographical and historical context. An introductory note for each area provides a more detailed account of historical contexts; further geographical and biographical information accompanies the selections themselves.

The value placed on travel writing relative to other literature between 1700 and 1830 was higher than it is today. Widely read by all classes of readers, it helped to shape the global consciousness of subjects at the centre of the expanding British Empire and pervasively influenced other literary genres. Many of these writings have literary value in the traditional sense. But other kinds of value and interest, we believe, are found in first-hand accounts of encounters with radically unfamiliar cultures, peoples, religions, landscapes, and sensibilities. We have chosen these readings to give pleasure to readers like ourselves—armchair adventurers whose imaginations are braced by a salt breeze, whose curiosity embraces the globe and all it contains. Compiling this collection has been more fun than scholars are usually allowed to have. We hope it brings pleasure to its readers as well.

NOTE ON THE TEXTS

TRAVEL writing was as remarkable for its variety as for its fecundity in the long eighteenth century. Perhaps the most miscellaneous of the age's literary activities, it involved not just a range of interests, styles, and genres but also very different contexts of production and reception. The series of letters provided a common format, as it did for much writing in the period. Some writers were professional authors who wrote directly for the press, and for whom the epistolary convention amounted to a more or less fictitious device. Some were reporting back to the governmental or private body that had sponsored the expedition. Others addressed letters to actual correspondents, and others kept private journals, in many cases with an eye to eventual publication, but in many cases not. Some wrote diaries for family consumption, as did Celia Fiennes, or for their own use. Women writers were less likely to venture into public than men, with the result that some of the best travel literature of the period (represented here by Dorothy Wordsworth, Janet Schaw, and Maria Nugent, as well as Fiennes) remained unpublished until a later generation. Other works did not emerge into print until long after they were written. James Boswell, the most famous diarist of the age, mined some of the journals he kept throughout his adult life for published books, such as his *Account of Corsica* and *Life of Johnson*; however, the vast bulk of these journals remained private until the momentous rediscovery of Boswell's papers in the twentieth century. In some cases, too, the published version of a travel book differed substantially from the author's original, due to more than usually intrusive editorial management (such as John Hawkesworth's redaction of the *Endeavour* journals of James Cook and Joseph Banks) if not outright censorship.

Our anthology reflects the miscellaneous provenance as well as styles and formats of eighteenth-century travel-writing. We have modernized spelling and typography (lower-casing initial capitals, removing italics, and adjusting punctuation), in the interests of consistency and accessibility, but have not otherwise attempted to regularize texts according to a single set of editorial principles. In the great majority of cases we have reprinted our selections from editions published in the author's lifetime, or from later editions reliably based on those texts. In the case of works published posthumously, we have reprinted reputable modern editions. (The travel journals of Celia Fiennes and Dorothy Wordsworth await state-of-the-art editorial scholarship.) In several instances, where manuscripts have survived, we have followed scholarly editions of copytexts based on the author's original rather than published versions, such as the letters of Lady Mary Wortley Montagu and Thomas Gray, and the journals of John Stedman's Surinam expedition and Captain Cook's Pacific voyages. (For a comparison of the Cook and Banks originals with Hawkesworth's edition, see the invaluable 'South Seas Anthology' edited by Lamb, Smith, and Thomas, 2000.) David Thompson's remarkable memoir of life at a Hudson's Bay Company trading post was not published until the 1920s; even then one of the more bizarre episodes, which we have included in these pages, did not appear in print until 1962.

Our selections follow the first printing of a text, unless otherwise noted. The place of publication, unless otherwise noted, is London.

SELECT BIBLIOGRAPHY

1. Modern Editions of Works Featured in this Anthology

Anson, George, *A Voyage Round the World*, ed. Glyndwr Williams (London: Oxford University Press, 1974).

Banks, Joseph, *The Endeavour Journal of Joseph Banks, 1768–1771*, ed. J. C. Beaglehole, 2 vols. (Sydney: Angus and Robertson, 1962).

Bartram, William, *Travels, and Other Writings*, ed. Thomas Slaughter (New York: Library of America, 1996).

Boswell, James, *Boswell on the Grand Tour: Germany and Switzerland, 1764*, ed. F. A. Pottle (London: Heinemann, 1953).

—— *Journal of a Tour to the Hebrides with Samuel Johnson, Ll.D., 1773*, ed. F. A. Pottle (London: Heinemann, 1961).

Byrd, William, *The Prose Works of William Byrd of Westover: Narratives of a Colonial Virginian*, ed. Louis B. Wright (Cambridge, Mass.: Harvard University Press, 1966).

Cobbett, William, *Rural Rides in the Southern, Western and Eastern Counties of England*, ed. G. D. H. Cole and M. Cole, 3 vols. (London: Peter Davies, 1930).

Cook, James, *The Journals of Captain Cook on his Voyages of Discovery*, ed. J. C. Beaglehole, 4 vols. (Cambridge: Cambridge University Press, 1955–74).

Dampier, William, *A New Voyage Round the World*, ed. John Masefield, 2 vols. (New York: E. P. Dutton, 1906).

Defoe, Daniel, *A Tour through the Whole Island of Great Britain*, ed. W. R. Owens and P. N. Furbank, 3 vols. (London: Pickering and Chatto, 1991).

Equiano, Olaudah, *The Interesting Narrative and Other Writings*, ed. Vincent Carretta (New York: Penguin, 2003).

Fiennes, Celia, *The Journeys of Celia Fiennes*, ed. Christopher Morris (London: Cresset Press, 1947).

Forster, George, *A Voyage Round the World*, ed. Nicholas Thomas and Oliver Berghof, 2 vols. (Honolulu: University of Hawaii Press, 2000).

Gray, Thomas, *The Correspondence of Thomas Gray*, ed. P. Toynbee and L. Whibley, vol. iii (Oxford: Clarendon Press, 1935).

Hearne, Samuel, *A Journey from Prince of Wales's Fort in Hudson's Bay to the Northern Ocean*, ed. Richard Glover (Toronto: Macmillan, 1958).

Hogg, James, *The Spy*, ed. Gillian Hughes (Edinburgh: Edinburgh University Press, 2000).

Hunter, John, *An Historical Journal of Transactions at Port Jackson and Norfolk Island*, ed. John Bach (Sydney: Angus and Robertson, 1968).

Johnson, Samuel, *A Journey to the Western Islands of Scotland*, ed. Mary Lascelles (New Haven: Yale University Press, 1971).

Lawson, John, *A New Voyage to Carolina*, ed. Hugh Talmadge Lefler (Chapel Hill: University of North Carolina Press, 1967).

Lewis, Matthew Gregory, *Journal of a West India Proprietor*, ed. Judith Terry (Oxford: Oxford University Press, 1999).

Falconbridge, Anna Maria, and Mary Ann Parker, *Maiden Voyages and Infant Colonies: Two Women's Travel Narratives of the 1790s*, ed. Deirdre Coleman (Leicester: Leicester University Press, 1999).

Montagu, Lady Mary Wortley, *Complete Letters*, ed. Robert Halsband, vol. i (Oxford: Clarendon Press, 1965).

Newton, John, *The Journal of a Slave Trader (John Newton) 1750–1754, With Newton's Thoughts upon the African Slave Trade*, ed. Bernard Martin and Mark Spurrell (London: Epworth Press, 1962).

Nicol, John, *The Life and Adventures of John Nicol, Mariner*, ed. Tim Flannery (New York: Grove Press, 1997).

Nugent, Maria, *Lady Nugent's Journal of her Residence in Jamaica from 1801 to 1805*, ed. Philip Wright (Kingston, Jamaica: Institute of Jamaica, 1966).

Park, Mungo, *Travels in the Interior Districts of Africa*, ed. Kate Ferguson Marsters (Durham, NC: Duke University Press, 2000).

Prince, Mary, *The History of Mary Prince, a West Indian Slave*, ed. Sarah Salih (New York: Penguin, 2000).

Schaw, Janet, *Journal of a Lady of Quality*, ed. Evangeline Walker Andrews and Charles Andrews (New Haven: Yale University Press, 1921).

Smollett, Tobias, *Travels through France and Italy*, ed. Frank Felsenstein (Oxford: Oxford University Press, 1979).

Stedman, John Gabriel, *Narrative of a Five Years Expedition against the Revolted Negroes of Surinam*, ed. Richard Price and Sally Price (Baltimore: Johns Hopkins University Press, 1988).

Tench, Watkin, *1788: Comprising a Narrative of the Expedition to Botany Bay and a Complete Account of the Settlement at Port Jackson*, ed. Tim Flannery (Melbourne: Text Publishing Co., 1996).

Thompson, David, *David Thompson's Narrative 1784–1812*, ed. Richard Glover (Toronto: Champlain Society, 1962).

Trollope, Frances, *Domestic Manners of the Americans*, ed. Pamela Neville-Sington (New York: Penguin, 1997).

Wollstonecraft, Mary, *Letters Written during a Short Residence in Sweden, Norway, and Denmark*, ed. Carol H. Poston (Lincoln: University of Nebraska Press, 1976).

Wordsworth, Dorothy, *Recollections of a Tour Made in Scotland*, ed. Carol Kyros Walker (New Haven: Yale University Press, 1997).

2. *Criticism and Contexts*

Adams, Percy G., *Travel Literature and the Evolution of the Novel* (Lexington: University Press of Kentucky, 1983).

Adams, Percy G., *Travelers and Travel Liars* (Berkeley: University of California Press, 1962).

Agorni, Mirella, *Translating Italy for the Eighteenth Century: Women, Translation, and Travel Writing, 1739–1797* (Manchester: St Jerome, 2002).

Aravamudan, Srinivas, *Tropicopolitans: Colonialism and Agency, 1688– 1804* (Durham, NC, and London: Duke University Press, 1999).

Batten, Charles, *Pleasurable Instruction: Form and Convention in Eighteenth-Century Travel Literature* (Berkeley: University of California Press, 1978).

Bauer, Ralph, *The Cultural Geography of Colonial American Literatures: Empire, Travel, Modernity* (Cambridge: Cambridge University Press, 2003).

Black, Jeremy, *The British and the Grand Tour* (London: Croom Helm, 1985).

Blackall, Chris, and Paul Turnbull, *South Seas: Voyaging and Cross-Cultural Encounters in the Pacific, 1760–1800.* <http://southseas.nla.gov.au/>

Bohls, Elizabeth A., *Women Travel Writers and the Language of Aesthetics, 1716–1818* (Cambridge: Cambridge University Press, 1995).

Buzard, James, *The Beaten Track: European Tourism, Literature, and the Ways to 'Culture' 1800–1918* (Oxford: Clarendon Press, 1993).

Chard, Chloe, *Pleasure and Guilt on the Grand Tour: Travel Writing and Imaginative Geography 1600–1830* (Manchester: Manchester University Press, 1999).

—— and Helen Langdon, eds., *Transports: Travel, Pleasure, and Imaginative Geography, 1600–1830* (New Haven: Yale University Press, 1996).

Cheek, Pamela, *Sexual Antipodes: Enlightenment, Globalization, and the Placing of Sex* (Stanford, Calif.: Stanford University Press, 2003).

Clifford, James, *Routes: Travel and Translation in the Late Twentieth Century* (Cambridge, Mass.: Harvard University Press, 1997).

Clark, Steve, ed., *Travel Writing and Empire: Postcolonial Theory in Transit* (London and New York: Zed Books, 1999).

Dekker, George, *The Fictions of Romantic Tourism: Radcliffe, Scott, and Mary Shelley* (Stanford, Calif.: Stanford University Press, 2004).

Duncan, James, and Derek Gregory, eds., *Writes of Passage: Reading Travel Writing* (London and New York: Routledge, 1999).

Edmond, Rod, *Representing the South Pacific: Colonial Discourse from Cook to Gauguin* (Cambridge: Cambridge University Press, 1997).

Edwards, Philip, *The Story of the Voyage: Sea-Narratives in Eighteenth-Century England* (Cambridge: Cambridge University Press, 1994).

Elsner, Jas, and Joan-Pau Rubies, eds., *Voyages and Visions: Towards a Cultural History of Travel* (London: Reaktion Books, 1999).

Foster, Shirley, *Across New Worlds: Nineteenth-Century Women Travelers and their Writings* (New York: Harvester Wheatsheaf, 1990).

—— and Sara Mills, eds., *An Anthology of Women's Travel Writing* (Manchester: Manchester University Press, 2002).

Fulford, Tim, and Carol Bolton, eds., *Travels, Explorations and Empires: Writings from the Era of Imperial Expansion, 1770–1835*, 7 vols. (London: Pickering and Chatto, 2001).

—— and Peter J. Kitson, eds., *Romanticism and Colonialism: Writing and Empire, 1780–1830* (Cambridge: Cambridge University Press, 1998).

Gikandi, Simon, *Maps of Englishness: Writing Identity in the Culture of Colonialism* (New York: Columbia University Press, 1996).

Gilbert, Helen, and Anna Johnston, eds., *In Transit: Travel, Text, Empire* (New York: Peter Lang, 2002).

Gilroy, Paul, *The Black Atlantic: Modernity and Double Consciousness* (Cambridge, Mass.: Harvard University Press, 1993).

Glendening, John, *The High Road: Romantic Tourism, Scotland, and Literature, 1720–1830* (New York: St Martin's Press, 1997).

Grewal, Inderpal, *Home and Harem: Nation, Gender, Empire, and the Cultures of Travel* (Durham, NC: Duke University Press, 1996).

Grove, Richard, *Green Imperialism: Colonial Expansion, Tropical Island Edens, and the Origins of Environmentalism, 1600–1860* (Cambridge: Cambridge University Press, 1996).

Hibbert, Christopher, *The Grand Tour* (London: Thames Methuen, 1987).

Hughes, Robert, *The Fatal Shore: A History of the Transportation of Convicts to Australia, 1787–1868* (London: Collins Harvill, 1987).

Hulme, Peter, *Colonial Encounters: Europe and the Native Caribbean, 1492–1797* (New York: Routledge, 1986).

—— and Neil L. Whitehead, eds., *Wild Majesty: Encounters with Caribs from Columbus to the Present Day. An Anthology* (Oxford: Clarendon Press, 1992).

—— and Tim Youngs, eds., *The Cambridge Companion to Travel Writing* (Cambridge: Cambridge University Press, 2002).

Krise, Thomas W., ed., *Caribbeana: An Anthology of English Literature of the West Indies, 1657–1777* (Chicago: University of Chicago Press, 1999).

Lamb, Jonathan, *Preserving the Self in the South Seas, 1680–1840* (Chicago and London: University of Chicago Press, 2001).

Lamb, Jonathan, Vanessa Smith, and Nicholas Thomas, eds., *Exploration and Exchange: A South Seas Anthology 1680–1900* (Chicago and London: University of Chicago Press, 2000).

Leask, Nigel, *Curiosity and the Aesthetics of Travel Writing, 1770–1840* (Oxford: Oxford University Press, 2002).

Linebaugh, Peter, and Marcus Rediker, *The Many-Headed Hydra: Sailors, Slaves, Commoners, and the Hidden History of the Revolutionary Atlantic* (Boston: Beacon Press, 2000).

MacCannell, Dean, *The Tourist: A New Theory of the Leisure Class* (New York: Schocken Books, 1976).

Marshall, P. J., and Glyndwr Williams, *The Great Map of Mankind: Perceptions of New Worlds in the Age of Enlightenment* (Cambridge, Mass.: Harvard University Press, 1982).

Massey, Doreen, *Space, Place, and Gender* (Minneapolis: University of Minnesota Press, 1994).

Melman, Billie, *Women's Orients: English Women and the Middle East, 1718–1919* (Ann Arbor: University of Michigan Press, 1992).

Mills, Sara, *Discourses of Difference: An Analysis of Women's Travel Writing and Colonialism* (London and New York: Routledge, 1991).

Morgan, Susan, *Place Matters: Gendered Geography in Women's Travel Books about South Asia* (New Brunswick, NJ: Rutgers University Press, 1996).

Neill, Anna, *British Discovery Literature and the Rise of Global Commerce* (Houndmills: Palgrave, 2002).

Nussbaum, Felicity A., *Torrid Zones: Maternity, Sexuality, and Empire in Eighteenth-Century English Narratives* (Baltimore: Johns Hopkins University Press, 1995).

—— ed., *The Global Eighteenth Century* (Baltimore: Johns Hopkins University Press, 2003).

Porter, Dennis, *Haunted Journeys: Desire and Transgression in European Travel Writing* (Princeton: Princeton University Press, 1991).

Pratt, Mary Louise, *Imperial Eyes: Travel Writing and Transculturation* (New York: Routledge, 1992).

Redford, Bruce, *Venice and the Grand Tour* (New Haven: Yale University Press, 1996).

Rediker, Marcus, *Between the Devil and the Deep Blue Sea: Merchant Seamen, Pirates, and the Anglo-American Maritime World, 1700–1750* (Cambridge: Cambridge University Press, 1987).

Richardson, Alan, and Sonia Hofkosh, eds., *Romanticism, Race, and Imperial Culture, 1780–1834* (Bloomington: Indiana University Press, 1996).

Robinson, Jane, *Wayward Women: A Guide to Women Travellers* (New York: Oxford University Press, 1990).

Said, Edward, *Orientalism* (New York: Random House, 1978).

—— *Culture and Imperialism* (New York: Alfred A. Knopf, 1993).

Sherman, Stuart, *Telling Time: Clocks, Diaries, and English Diurnal Form, 1660–1785* (Chicago: University of Chicago Press, 1996).

Spurr, David, *The Rhetoric of Empire: Colonial Discourse in Journalism, Travel Writing, and Imperial Administration* (Durham, NC, and London: Duke University Press, 1993).

Thomas, Nicholas, *Entangled Objects: Exchange, Material Culture and Colonialism in the Pacific* (Cambridge, Mass.: Harvard University Press, 1991).

Turhan, Filiz, *The Other Empire: British Romantic Writings about the Ottoman Empire* (New York: Routledge, 2003).

Turner, Katherine, *British Travel Writers in Europe 1750–1800* (Aldershot and Burlington, Vt.: Ashgate, 2001).

Trumpener, Katie, *Bardic Nationalism: The Romantic Novel and the British Empire* (Princeton: Princeton University Press, 1997).

Viviès, Jean, trans. Claire Davison, *English Travel Narratives in the Eighteenth Century: Exploring Genres* (Aldershot and Burlington, Vt.: Ashgate, 2002).

Williams, Glyndwr, *The Great South Sea: English Voyages and Encounters, 1570–1750* (New Haven: Yale University Press, 1997).

—— *Voyages of Delusion: The Quest for a Northwest Passage* (New Haven: Yale University Press, 2002).

3. Further Reading in Oxford World's Classics

Behn, Aphra, *Oroonoko and Other Writings*, ed. Paul Salzman.

Defoe, Daniel, *Robinson Crusoe*, ed. J. Donald Crowley.

Homer, *The Odyssey*, trans. Walter Shewring, ed. G. S. Kirk.

Johnson, Samuel, *The Major Works*, ed. Donald Greene.

Sterne, Laurence, *A Sentimental Journey and Other Writings*, ed. Tim Parnell and Ian Jack.

Swift, Jonathan, *Gulliver's Travels*, ed. Claude Rawson and Ian Higgins.

Women's Writing 1778–1838, ed. Fiona Robertson.

CHRONOLOGY

1687   Isaac Newton, *Principia Mathematica* (laws of motion, foundation of classical physics).

1688   Aphra Behn, *Oroonoko, or the Royal Slave*.

1688–9 The 'Glorious Revolution': end of Stuart dynastic rule in Britain as Catholic James II flees into exile; accession of William of Orange ensures Protestant establishment.

1690   Defeat of James II's forces at the Battle of the Boyne, Ireland. The Protestant (or Anglo-Irish) Ascendancy: a series of laws passed throughout the eighteenth century displacing Catholic landlords, subordinating the Catholic peasant majority to Protestant landlords and officials, depriving Catholics of civil rights. John Locke, *Essay Concerning Human Understanding* (empiricist epistemology) and *Two Treatises of Government* (political theory).

1694   Bank of England chartered, national debt instituted.

1701   War of Spanish Succession with France begins. Act of Settlement: Protestant succession established.

1702   William III dies, succeeded by Anne.

1707   Act of Union of Scotland and England. Scottish parliament dissolved in return for representation at Westminster and share of full trading privileges and equal customs duties with England. Scotland retains its own legal system and Presbyterian church establishment. 'Great Britain' formed.

1713   War with France ended by Peace of Utrecht, giving England the Asiento (monopoly on providing slaves to Spanish Empire).

1714   Anne dies; George I, Elector of Hanover (Germany), takes the throne.

1715   First Jacobite rising in Scotland: invasion by forces headed by James Edward, son of James II. The rising is defeated and James escapes back to France. Minor rebellions follow over the next few years.

1716–18 Lady Mary Wortley Montagu and her husband Edward travel on a diplomatic posting to Constantinople; Lady Mary brings back smallpox inoculation.

1719   Daniel Defoe, *Robinson Crusoe*.

1721   'South Sea Bubble', speculative scheme for trading stock in
        Pacific ventures, collapses, causing national financial chaos.
        Robert Walpole becomes Prime Minister.

1726   Jonathan Swift, *Gulliver's Travels*.

1727   George I dies, succeeded by his son George II and Queen
        Caroline.

1739   War with Spain ('War of Jenkins' Ear', named after the British
        sea captain whose ear was supposedly cut off by Spanish coast
        guards).

1741–2 Walpole forced to resign.

1740–4 Royal Navy fleet under Commodore George Anson circum-
        navigates the globe.

1744   War with France (War of Austrian Succession).

1745–6 'The Forty-Five': the last and most dramatic Jacobite rising.
        Charles Edward Stuart lands in the Western Highlands, raises
        clans, captures Edinburgh, and marches into England. Jacobite
        army defeated at Culloden. Suppression of Scottish clan system
        begins.

1748   Peace with France (shaky).

1754   London to Manchester journey takes four and a half days.

1755   Samuel Johnson, *Dictionary of the English Language*.

1756–63 Seven Years' War with France, fought in Germany, North
        America and the Indian sub-continent, secures Britain's
        ascendancy as dominant world imperial power (known as
        French and Indian War in US history).

1760   George II dies; succeeded by grandson George III, aged 22.

1761   Irish 'Whiteboy' risings: agrarian unrest in Munster. Followed
        by the Oakboys in Ulster (1763), Steelboys in Ulster (1769–
        70), Dublin riots (1771), and formation of Protestant militias
        (1778–83).

1763   Peace of Paris ends Seven Years' War; Britain gains huge terri-
        tories in North America (Canada) and India.

1764   Chronometer designed by William Harrison enables accurate
        measurement of longitude at sea.

1767–99 First of series of wars between the British East India Company
        and the Sultans of Mysore, culminating in British victory
        at Seringapatam (1799), consolidating British rule in the
        subcontinent.

1768–73   James Bruce travels to the source of the River Nile.

1768–80   Three voyages into the Pacific led by James Cook: *Endeavour* (1768–71), *Resolution* and *Adventure* (1772–5), *Resolution* and *Discovery* (1776–80). Cook is killed in Hawaii in 1779.

1768   Laurence Sterne, *A Sentimental Journey through France and Italy*.

1769   Watt patents the steam engine; Arkwright patents the water frame; Thomas Gray tours the Lake District.

1770   Hargreaves patents the Spinning Jenny (technological advances start Industrial Revolution).

1771   Mansfield Decision: Chief Justice Mansfield rules in Somerset case that slaves leaving their owners on English soil cannot be taken out of England.

1773   Samuel Johnson and James Boswell visit Scotland.

1773–7   William Bartram in Florida.

1775–83   American War of Independence. Adam Smith, *Wealth of Nations* (1776).

1782–3   Ireland: Legislative Independence. Catholic Relief Acts, relaxing earlier penal laws, and trade concessions.

1783   Peace of Versailles ends American war; US independence recognized. Loss of North American colonies (except Canada) leads to increased imperialist activity in India.

1784   India Act, instituting government regulation of the East India Company.

1786   Robert Burns, *Poems, Chiefly in the Scottish Dialect*.

1787   Society for the Suppression of the Slave Trade founded by Wilberforce and Clarkson.

1788   Sir Joseph Banks, President of the Royal Society, forms Association for Promoting the Discovery of the Interior Districts of Africa. London to Manchester journey takes 28 hours with improved roads and transport technology. 'First Fleet' arrives in Australia, founding penal colony at Botany Bay and Port Jackson.

1789   Storming of Bastille prison by crowd; beginning of French Revolution.

1790   Edmund Burke, *Reflections on the Revolution in France* (conservative manifesto). Refutations include Mary Wollstonecraft's *Vindication of the Rights of Men* (1790) and Thomas Paine's *Rights of Man* (1791).

1791	Slave rebellion in French St Domingue (present-day Haiti) that will lead to first black republic.
1792	Wollstonecraft, *Vindication of the Rights of Woman*; bill to abolish slave trade passes House of Commons, defeated in House of Lords.
1793–1802	French Revolutionary War. Accompanied by domestic government repression of Revolution sympathizers (1793–4).
1793	Lord George Macartney leads diplomatic mission to China. William Mackenzie reaches the Canadian Pacific.
1795–7	Mungo Park in the West African interior. He disappears in the course of a second expedition (1804–5).
1797	Ship chartered by London Missionary Society arrives at Tahiti. Naval mutinies at Spithead and the Nore protest poor treatment of seamen.
1798	United Irishmen rising, in sympathy with ideals of French Revolution, suppressed with great slaughter. Thomas Malthus, *Essay on Population*. Wordsworth and Coleridge, *Lyrical Ballads*.
1800–1	Act of Union between England and Ireland. Irish parliament dissolved in return for Irish representation at Westminster, free trade within Britain, protection of Irish Church (i.e. Anglican Protestant) establishment. Catholics promised emancipation but measures resisted by George III; they are still barred from election to parliament, and public office.
1802	Treaty of Amiens: ceasefire with France.
1803–15	Napoleonic War.
1803	Dorothy Wordsworth, William Wordsworth, and Samuel Taylor Coleridge tour Scotland.
1804–6	Meriwether Lewis and William Clark cross the North American continent.
1805	Battle of Trafalgar at sea: Admiral Nelson wins, but dies.
1807	Parliament votes to abolish slave trade.
1811	The Regency: George, Prince of Wales, takes over powers of George III.
1812	Britain at war with US (War of 1812).
1813	Jane Austen, *Pride and Prejudice*.
1814	Walter Scott, *Waverley*. Treaty of Ghent ends war with US.
1815	June 18: Battle of Waterloo (Belgium): Wellington and allies

decisively defeat Napoleon. Britain, Austria and Russia establish league of reactionary regimes across Europe at the Congress of Vienna; Britain consolidates imperial gains at the expense of France, including Trinidad, Malta and the S. African Cape.

1815   George Stephenson patents first steam locomotive.

1818   Mary Shelley, *Frankenstein*.

1819   'Peterloo massacre': government troops fire on working-class crowd, killing 11, wounding 400.

1820   George III dies, George IV assumes throne.

1822–6   William Cobbett, 'Rural rides'.

1829   Catholic Emancipation, lifting many civil disabilities.

1832   First Reform Bill extends franchise, reforms Parliament.

1833   Parliament emancipates slaves in Britain and colonies.

TRAVEL WRITING
1700–1830

PART I

EUROPE AND ASIA MINOR

YOUNG English aristocrats had visited continental Europe since at least the mid-sixteenth century for the purpose of furthering their education: observing foreign courts, learning modern languages, viewing the monuments of classical antiquity. By 1670, when Richard Lassels coined the term in *The Voyage of Italy*, the 'Grand Tour' of France and Italy was an established institution with set itineraries and topics, such as the examination of sites mentioned in Roman literature and the comparison between a glorious past and a degraded present (rehearsed here by Joseph Addison). The Grand Tour became a literary genre in the eighteenth century as it was taken over by authors of the 'middling sort', many of whom disputed its educational value (foreign customs were scarcely a safe medium for the moral formation of British youth) and criticized the folly and extravagance of milords abroad. Resumption of access to the Continent after the Seven Years War (1756–63) marked the terminal decline of the aristocratic tradition of Grand Tourism and the fitful improvement of a commercial infrastructure of recreational travel, which included the publication of travellers' journals and guidebooks as well as more and better roads, inns and coaches. Steam-packets were crossing the Channel by the 1820s, heralds of the industrial apparatus of leisured tourism that would cover Europe in the nineteenth century.

The expanding literary market encouraged more personalized styles of travel writing, which emphasized the subjective discourses of taste and sentiment and accounts of 'manners and morals' over classical learning. Laurence Sterne's hugely influential *A Sentimental Journey through France and Italy* (1768) helped establish travel writing as (arguably) the dominant literary genre of the second half of the eighteenth century, making it a major forum for exploring the resources and limits of sensibility as well as the encounter with other cultures. (Sterne's book is not represented here, on the grounds of its fictionality as well as its ready availability, although it exemplifies the porousness of the border between the novel and travelogue.) Sentiment became a preferred discourse of women travel writers, who began to publish in significant numbers from the 1770s, authorizing their interventions in the largely masculine public domain of taste and opinion. Sentiment also became a medium for heterodox views, including political radicalism. At century's end Helen Maria Williams draws on its tropes to legitimate the ideals of the French

Revolution, while Mary Wollstonecraft modulates the discourses of
sentimental and philosophical travel into the complex mixed mode of
Romantic autobiography.

The French Revolution provided the occasion for a new kind of political tourism. Travellers flocked across the Channel to witness for themselves the cataclysmic events unfolding in France, and their reports fed
the hunger for news back home. Travel writers did not just provide data
for the 'Revolution controversy' that raged in the 1790s: they actively
shaped it. With the outbreak of war and the Terror, however, spectatorial
distance collapsed. Reporters found themselves threatened by the historical forces they had been observing—from Arthur Young, annoyed by
provincial militias in the Revolution's early months, to Wollstonecraft,
forced into hiding while her Girondist friends went to the guillotine, and
Williams, interned as an enemy alien. Ann Radcliffe records the disruption of her Rhineland tour, and of an aesthetic and historical attention to
scenery, by the encroaching war.

Travellers tended to keep to the Grand Tour itinerary, codified in
guidebooks such as Thomas Nugent's: across the Channel via Calais or
Boulogne to Paris, then on to northern Italy by sea (as Smollett went) or
over the Alps (as did Boswell), taking in the high points of Venice, Rome,
and Naples, with side excursions through Germany, the Netherlands, or
Switzerland. Journeys beyond the core itinerary smacked of exploration
and its attendant risks: Barbary corsairs harassed Mediterranean shipping
well into the nineteenth century, while to the east of Venice and Vienna
loomed Christendom's historic antagonist, the Ottoman Empire, now in
its slow decline. Nevertheless some travellers made a name for themselves
writing from further afield in the later decades of the century: Boswell
went to Corsica, Nathaniel Wraxall around the Baltic, Patrick Brydone to
Sicily and Malta. If these destinations were largely unknown to British
readers, others reflected familiar patterns of desire and dread—none more
so than Turkey. In her posthumously published 'Embassy Letters' Lady
Mary Wortley Montagu writes against the grain of western fantasies about
the secret recesses of the harem and *hamam*. The amateur (not to say raffish)
traveller Lady Eliza Craven follows in Lady Mary's tracks to debunk, in
turn, her predecessor's idealizations of beauty and liberty behind the veil.
Meanwhile the northern shores visited by Mary Wollstonecraft, although
closer to Britain, would have struck readers as more remote and barbarous
than Constantinople.

1. CLASSICAL GROUND

JOSEPH ADDISON, *Remarks on Several Parts of Italy, etc. in the Years 1701, 1702, 1703* (1705; from Addison, *Miscellaneous Works*, vol. ii, ed. A. C. Guthkelch, 1914)

Best known as author of the weekly magazine *The Spectator* (1711–12), Joseph Addison (1672–1719) produced an account of Italy that remained definitive for much of the eighteenth century. Before setting out, writes Addison, 'I took care to refresh my memory among the *Classic* Authors, and to make such collections out of them as I might afterwards have occasion for. I must confess it was not one of the least entertainments that I met with in travelling, to examine these several Descriptions, as it were, upon the spot, and to compare the natural face of the country with the Landskips that the Poets have given us of it.' These comparisons fuel a Protestant, nationalist disparagement of modern Italian customs and institutions, although Addison's critique of Catholicism is not without philosophical nuance. A more 'scientific' curiosity justifies morbid experiments at the so-called Grotta del Cane, a set-piece of eighteenth-century Neapolitan tourism.

In my way from Rome to Naples I found nothing so remarkable as the beauty of the country, and the extreme poverty of its inhabitants. It is indeed an amazing thing to see the present desolation of Italy, when one considers what incredible multitudes of people it abounded with during the reigns of the Roman Emperors. And not-withstanding the removal of the Imperial seat, the irruptions of the barbarous nations, the civil wars of this country, with the hardships of its several governments, one can scarce imagine how so plentiful a soil should become so miserably unpeopled in comparison of what it once was.* We may reckon, by a very moderate computation, more inhabitants in the Campania of old Rome, than are now in all Italy. And if we could number up those prodigious swarms that had settled themselves in every part of this delightful country, I question not but that they would amount to more than can be found, at present, in any six parts of Europe of the same extent. This desolation appears no where greater than in the Pope's territories, and yet there are several reasons would make a man expect to see these dominions the best regulated, and most flourishing of any other in Europe. Their Prince is generally a man of learning and virtue, mature in years and experience, who has seldom any vanity or pleasure to gratify at his people's expence, and is neither encumbered with wife, children or mistresses; not to mention the supposed sanctity of his character, which obliges him in a more particular manner to consult the good and happiness of mankind. The direction of church and state are lodged entirely in his own hands, so that his government is naturally free from those principles of faction and division which are mixed in the very composition of most others. His subjects are always ready to fall in with his designs, and are more at his disposal than any others of the most absolute government, as they have a greater veneration for his person, and not only court his favour but his blessing. His country is extremely fruitful, and has good havens both for the Adriatick and Mediterranean, which is an advantage peculiar to himself and the Neapolitans above the rest of the Italians. There is still a benefit the Pope enjoys above all other soveraigns, in drawing great sums out of Spain, Germany, and other countries that belong to foreign Princes, which one would fancy might be no small ease to his own subjects. We may here add, that there is no place in Europe so much frequented by strangers, whether they are such as come out of curiosity, or such who are obliged to attend the court of Rome on several occasions, as are many of the Cardinals and Prelates, that bring considerable sums into the Pope's dominions. But notwithstanding all these promising circumstances, and the long peace that has reigned so many years in Italy, there is not a more miserable people in Europe than the Pope's subjects. His state is thin of inhabitants, and a great part of his soil uncultivated. His subjects are wretchedly poor and idle, and have neither sufficient manufactures, nor traffic to employ them. These ill effects may arise, in a great measure, out of the arbitrariness of the government, but I think they are chiefly to be ascribed to the very genius of the Roman Catholic religion, which here shews it self in its perfection. It is not strange to find a country half unpeopled, where so great a proportion of the inhabitants of both sexes is tied under such vows of chastity, and where at the same time an inquisition forbids all recruits out of any other religion. Nor is it less easy to account for the great poverty and want that are to be met with in a country which invites into it such swarms of vagabonds, under the title of Pilgrims, and shuts up in cloisters such an incredible multitude of young and lusty beggars, who, instead of encreasing the common stock by their labour and industry, lie as a dead weight on their fellow subjects, and consume the charity that ought to support the sickly, old and decrepit. The many hospitals, that are every where erected, serve rather to encourage idleness in the people, than to set them at work; not to mention the great riches which lie useless in churches and religious houses, with the multitude of festivals that must never be violated by trade or business. To speak truly, they are here so wholly taken up with men's souls, that they neglect the good of their bodies; and when, to these natural evils in the government and religion, there arises among them an avaricious Pope, who is for making a family, it is no wonder if the people sink under such a complication of distempers. Yet it is to this humour of nepotism that Rome owes its present splendour and magnificence; for it would have been impossible to have furnished out so many glorious palaces with such a profusion of pictures, statues, and the like ornaments, had not the riches of the people at several times fallen into the hands of many different families, and of particular persons; as we may observe, though the bulk of the Roman people was more rich and happy in the times of the Common-wealth, the city of Rome received all its beauties and embellishments under the Emperors. It is probable the Campania of Rome, as well as other parts of the Pope's territories, would be cultivated much better than it is, were there not such an exorbitant tax on corn, which makes them plough up only such spots of ground as turn to the most advantage: Whereas were the money to be raised on lands, with an exception to some of the more barren parts, that might be tax-free for a certain term of years, every one would turn his ground to the best account, and in a little time perhaps bring more money into the Pope's treasury.

The greatest pleasure I took in my journey from Rome to Naples was in seeing the fields, towns and rivers that have been described by so many classic authors, and have been the scenes of so many great actions; for this whole road is extremely barren of curiosities. It is worth while to have an eye on Horace's voyage to Brundisi, when one passes this way; for by comparing his several stages, and the road he took, with those that are observed at present, we may have some idea of the changes that have been made in the face of this country since his time. If we may guess at the common travelling of persons of quality, among the ancient Romans, from this poet's description of his voyage, we may conclude they seldom went above fourteen

miles a day over the Appian way, which was more used by the noble
Romans than any other in Italy, as it led to Naples, Baïae, and the
most delightful parts of the nation. It is indeed very disagreeable to
be carried in haste over this pavement.

> Minus est gravis Appia tardis.*

Naples

My first days at Naples were taken up with the sight of processions,
which are always very magnificent in the Holy-Week.* It would be
tedious to give an account of the several representations of our
Saviour's death and resurrection, of the figures of himself, the
Blessed Virgin, and the Apostles, which are carried up and down on
this occasion, with the cruel penances that several inflict on themselves, and the multitude of ceremonies that attend these solem-
nities. I saw, at the same time, a very splendid procession for the
accession of the Duke of Anjou to the Crown of Spain,* in which the
Vice-Roy bore his part at the left-hand of Cardinal Cantelmi. To
grace the parade, they exposed, at the same time, the blood of
St Januarius,* which liquefied at the approach of the Saint's head,
though, as they say, it was hard congealed before. I had twice an
opportunity of seeing the operation of this pretended miracle, and
must confess I think it so far from being a real miracle, that I look
upon it as one of the most bungling tricks that I ever saw. Yet it is this
that makes as great a noise as any in the Roman Church, and that
Monsieur Paschal has hinted at among the rest, in his marks of the
true religion.* The modern Neapolitans seem to have copied it out
from one, which was shown in a town of the Kingdom of Naples, as
long ago as in Horace's time.

> Dehinc Gnatia lymphis
> Iratis extructa dedit risusque jocosque,
> Dum flammâ sine thura liquescere limine Sacro
> Persuadere cupit: credat Judæus apella,
> Non ego

> At Gnatia next arrived, we laughed to see
> The superstitious crowd's simplicity,
> That in the sacred temple needs would try
> Without a fire th'unheated gums to fry;
> Believe who will the solemn sham, not I.*

One may see at least that the heathen priesthood had the same kind of secret among them, of which the Roman Catholics are now masters.

I must confess, though I had lived above a year in a Roman Catholic country, I was surprised to see many ceremonies and superstitions in Naples, that are not so much as thought of in France. But as it is certain there has been a kind of secret reformation made, though not publicly owned, in the Roman Catholic church, since the spreading of the Protestant religion, so we find the several nations are recovered out of their ignorance, in proportion as they converse more or less with those of the reformed churches. For this reason the French are much more enlightened than the Spaniards or Italians, on occasion of their frequent controversies with the Huguenots;* and we find many of the Roman Catholic gentlemen of our own country, who will not stick to laugh at the superstitions they sometimes meet with in other nations. . . .

The natural curiosities about Naples are as numerous and extraordinary as the artificial. I shall set them down, as I have done the other, without any regard to their situation. The grotto del Cani* is famous for the poisonous steams which float within a foot of its surface. The sides of the grotto are marked green, as high as the malignity of the vapour reaches. The common experiments are as follows: a dog, that has his nose held in the vapour, loses all signs of life in a very little time; but if carried into the open air, or thrown into a neighbouring lake he immediately recovers, if he is not quite gone. A torch, snuff and all, goes out in a moment when dipped into the vapour. A pistol cannot take fire in it. I split a reed, and laid in the channel of it a train of gunpowder, so that one end of the reed was above the vapour, and the other at the bottom of it; and I found, though the steam was strong enough to hinder a pistol from taking fire in it, and to quench a lighted torch, that it could not intercept the train of fire when it had once begun flashing, nor hinder it from running to the very end. This experiment I repeated twice or thrice, to see if I could quite dissipate the vapour, which I did in so great a measure that one might easily let off a pistol in it. I observed how long a dog was in expiring the first time, and after his recovery, and found no sensible difference. A viper bore it nine minutes the first time we put it in, and ten the second. When we brought it out after the first trial, it took such a vast quantity of air into its lungs that it swelled almost twice as big as before; and it was perhaps on this stock of air that it lived a minute longer the second time. Dr Connor made a discourse in one of the Academies at Rome upon the subject of this grotto, which he has since printed in England.* He attributes the death of animals, and the extinction of lights, to a great rarefaction of the air, caused by the heat and eruption of the steams. But how is it possible for these steams, though in never so great quantity, to resist the pressure of the whole atmosphere? And as for the heat, it is but very inconsiderable. However, to satisfy myself, I placed a thin vial, well stopped up with wax, within the smoke of the vapour, which would certainly have burst in an air rarefied enough to kill a dog, or quench a torch, but nothing followed upon it. However, to take away all further doubt, I borrowed a weather-glass, and so fixed it in the grotto, that the Stagnum* was wholly covered with the vapour, but I could not perceive the quicksilver sunk after half an hour's standing in it. This vapour is generally supposed to be sulphureous, though I can see no reason for such a supposition. He that dips his hand in it finds no smell that it leaves upon it; and though I put a whole bundle of lighted brimstone matches to the smoke, they all went out in an instant, as if immersed in water. Whatever is the composition of the vapour, let it have but one quality of being very gluey or viscous, and I believe it will mechanically solve all the phenomena of the grotto. Its unctuousness will make it heavy, and unfit for mounting higher than it does, unless the heat of the earth, which is just strong enough to agitate, and bear it up at a little distance from the surface, were much greater than it is to rarefy and scatter it. It will be too gross and thick to keep the lungs in play for any time, so that animals will die in it sooner or later, as their blood circulates slower or faster. Fire will live in it no longer than in water, because it wraps it self in the same manner about the flame, and by its continuity hinders any quantity of air or nitre from coming to its succour. The parts of it however are not so compact as those of liquors, nor therefore tenacious enough to intercept the fire that has once caught a train of gunpowder, for which reason they may be quite broken and dispersed by the repetition of this experiment. There is an unctuous clammy vapour that arises from the stum* of grapes, when they lie mashed together in the vat, which puts out a light when dipped into it, and perhaps would take away the breath of weaker animals, were it put to the trial.

JOHN GALT, *Letters from the Levant; Containing Views of the State of Society, Manners, Opinions, and Commerce in Greece and Several of the Principal Islands of the Archipelago* (1813)

A decade or so before making his name as an author of Scottish regional fiction, John Galt (1779–1839) visited the eastern Mediterranean in search of opportunities for circumventing Napoleon's wartime blockade of British trade. Galt's curmudgeonly provincialism yields not only anti-classical humour, mocking the Grand Tour's reverence for antiquity, but a visionary superimposition of modern London upon the 'ruins of empire'.

ATHENS, 1 March 1812

In consequence of finding the antiquities, with the exception of the Parthenon, pretty much in the state in which they have been often enough described, I have resolved not to trouble you with any other account of them, than as they become essential to the illustration of what may occur to me. At first, as every traveller who now comes to Athens must be, I was greatly vexed and disappointed by the dilapidation of the temple of Minerva;* but I am consoled by the reflection that the spoils are destined to ornament our own land, and that, if they had not been taken possession of by Lord Elgin,* they would probably have been carried away by the French.

I cannot describe the modern city of Athens in fewer words than by saying that it looks as if two or three ill-built villages had been rudely swept together at the foot of the north side of the Acropolis, and enclosed by a garden wall, three or four miles in circumference. The buildings occupy about four-fifths of the enclosure; the remainder is ploughed, and sown with barley at present.

The distant appearance of the Acropolis somewhat resembles that of Stirling Castle, but it is inferior in altitude and general effect. As a fortress, it is incapable at present of resisting any rational attack; the Turks, however, consider it a mighty redoubtable place; nay, for that matter, they even think old frail Athens herself capable of assuming a warlike attitude. At the proclamation of the present war against the Russians,* they closed her paralytic gates in a most energetic manner. The following morning, Father Paul of the convent went at daybreak to take the air among the pillars of the temple of Olympian Jove, and arriving at the arch of Hadrian, found them still shut; whereupon he

gave them a kick, and the gates of Athens flew open at the first touch
of his reverence's toe.

EPHESUS, 26 April

While the horses are getting ready, I sit down to give you some
account of what I have seen to recompense me for the trouble of
coming here. . . .

A walk of more than an hour, over broken vaults, and through
nettles and briars, effectually cooled the slight desire which I felt to
look at objects, of which the era, use, and construction, are equally
unknown. The traveller must be far gone in antiquarianism who can
admire the wreck of the aqueduct, or the other shapeless heaps that
constitute the ruins of Ephesus. To save you the trouble of a search,
or the vexation of coming away without accomplishing the objects of
your journey, if you are ever so mad as to visit this place, I ought to
mention that the remains of the ancient city lie principally along the
heights on the West of the modern village; and that those which are
now commonly visited as such, are, in fact, of posterior origin, and
are perhaps wholly Saracenic.

The situation of Ephesus, as it appears at present, is as well calculated to raise a dispute among topographers as any place that I know.
Were I to describe to you only its existing condition—barren rocky
hills behind, and a morass of many miles in extent in front, you
would not hesitate to say that it must have been extremely ill chosen.
But when it is considered that this morass was formed by the inundations of the river having been neglected; that the river, prior to the
stoppage by the bar across its mouth, and which is probably of the
same date as the morass, was navigable to the city; and that the town
stood exactly in that part of the noble and fertile valley of the Castrus,
by which it was enabled to unite, to its maritime advantages, the
convenience of an easy communication with the interior, you will
perhaps, like me, be disposed to think that it may have been very
happily chosen. The marshes round Ephesus are not half so extensive as the levels on the south side of London. Now, were it possible
to imagine the modern Babylon desolated; the ruins of the bridges
interrupting the course of the Thames; scarcely a vestige of all
her thousands of streets and structures remaining; the very site of
St Paul's unknown to the miserable inhabitants of a few hovels, half
hid by the briars and nettles among the ruins—were it indeed

possible to imagine the ruin of London as complete as that of Ephesus—what would then be the state of the low grounds of Vauxhall, Lambeth, and Camberwell, which at present are covered with so many flourishing gardens and terraces? Could they be otherwise than putrid fens, the abodes of reptiles, and the nurseries of pestilence, like those of the plain of Ephesus?

2. DEBATING THE TOUR

The Gentleman's Magazine (vol. 1, 7 August 1731), 'London Journal'

The Gentleman's Magazine, or Monthly Intelligencer, launched by the printer Edward Cave in 1731, was perhaps the most influential of the mid-eighteenth-century English periodicals. The magazine's critique of the Grand Tour attacks its educational pretensions on nationalist, religious, and anti-aristocratic grounds: inadequately supervised jaunts abroad expose young gentlemen to a host of deleterious influences, chief among them Catholic superstition, absolutist despotism, and temptations to libertinism and extravagance.

Of Travelling

Civicus (a Correspondent) discourses on the humour of travelling and residing in foreign countries, of being profuse there, and niggardly at home.

Travelling, at best, is chargeable, and the money we spend abroad is a loss to our country. None ought to travel abroad but on account of business, or for the sake of making observations, and acquiring useful knowledge.

Our travellers are commonly taken from school, or the university, at 17 or 18 years of age, either because the youth hates his studies, or has a rambling head; and is sent abroad before he has made any progress in learning, or knows the constitution of his own country. The consequence of which is, they are immersed in all manner of lewdness and debauchery, and their principles, both religious and political, are corrupted by the intrigues of Irish Romish Priests,* and other emissaries, who swarm in Roman Catholic countries; and if they once pervert them from the religion of their education, will likewise beget in them an aversion to a Protestant prince, and the form of government of their own country.

But if this humour of rambling in the male part of our nation is blameable, it is more unaccountable in the female, considering those shocks to modesty almost inseparable from sea voyages. If, says he, a lady has a fit of the vapours, she must go to Montpelier, Spaw, or Paris. Questions, if the Bath, or Tunbridge, or a journey to York, might not be as effectual a remedy, unless they had a mind for an intrigue with a French dancing master, or a Marquis?

One evil of residing in foreign countries is that the estates and incomes of many English families are principally expended there, to the discouragement of our own tradesmen and manufacturers.

A late edict of the French King to forbid pilgrimaging shows their sense of it. If we consider the acquisitions made to our nation from this humour of travelling, we shall find no equivalent for the expense, except that of saying they have hunted with the King of France's hounds, or dined with some of his court.

The rational design of travelling is to become acquainted with the languages, customs, manners, laws and interests of foreign nations; the trade, manufactures and produce of countries; the situation and strength of towns and cities. Instead of which, we have brought home the French *Coiffure*, the *Robe de Chambre* of the women, and *Toupé* and *Solitaire* of the men; dancing, gaming and masquerades.

Concludes, that he cannot but think it for the benefit of our country to hinder our ladies from being carried abroad, and much for its honour to prevent the exportation of fools.

THOMAS NUGENT, *The Grand Tour. Containing an Exact Description of Most of the Cities, Towns, and Remarkable Places of Europe. Together with a Distinct Account of the Post-Roads and Stages* (1756)

In 1749 Thomas Nugent (1700?–72) published a comprehensive description of Grand Tour itineraries which became a standard guidebook. Nugent's inclusion of a philosophical defence of travel in the preface to the second edition (1756) reflects the controversial status of the Tour at mid-century.

The Preface

Travelling, even in the remotest ages, was reckoned so useful a custom, as to be judged the only means of improving the understanding, and of acquiring a high degree of reputation. This was doubtless the opinion of the Druids, according to Caesar's relation;* since to attain a perfect knowledge of their mysteries, it was customary for them to make a voyage to Britain, from whence their institution is said to have been derived. The first civilized nations had so exalted an idea of those who had been in foreign countries, that they honoured even such as made but short voyages, with the title of philosophers and conquerors. Of this number were the Argonauts.* Such were also Bacchus, Hercules, Ammon,* etc., mere travellers, whom the scriptures call the gods of nations. The most ancient authors distinguish such as had been abroad in the search of knowledge, by the name of sages: hence Maximus Tyrius takes notice that Ulysses was honoured with this title by Homer.* Agreeably to this it has been observed that those who first distinguished themselves in the republic of letters were all travellers, who owed their learning, name and reputation to different peregrinations. At their return, it was the usual practice with them, publicly to recite whatever they had learnt abroad, sometimes adding their own reflections in regard to the advantages that might be derived from a knowledge of the manners, religion, and civil polity of foreign nations. Such were Pythagoras, Zamolxis of Thrace, Zaleucus of Locris, with other travelling philosophers and legislators. Herodotus takes notice of Homer,* that as soon as he had formed the plan of his poem, he thought it incumbent upon him to travel while he was yet in his youth. It has been also an observation drawn from Hippocrates's Epidemics, that this great physician had travelled through all parts of Greece, in order to make his remarks on popular distempers. The emperor Adrian had so great a passion for travelling as to visit every place of which he had heard anything remarkable;* and without any vehicle, but on foot. This was carrying the curiosity of seeing distant countries even farther than that cynic Asclepiades taken notice of by Tertullian, who made the tour of the world on the back of a cow, and lived all the while upon its milk.*

It is by means of such travelling philosophers, that the sciences were first diffused through the several parts of the inhabited globe. And indeed the most ancient writings, either in prose or verse, are nothing more than the relations of travellers. Those who gave the first history of different countries, were generally foreigners, who, at their return to their native soil, published such accounts concerning the history of other nations, as they had learnt during their residence abroad. This may be easily proved by a multitude of examples from Herodotus, Josephus, Eusebius, and others: we find them quoting histories of almost every country, few of which were wrote by the natives. Those travellers did not think it beneath their care to consult stones, metals, barks of trees, and every other monument, whereby they were enabled to acquaint us with many surprising facts, of which the inhabitants themselves had lost all tradition. How many passages are there in Homer, Herodotus, Diodorus Siculus, Strabo, Plutarch, Pausanias, and others, by which we find that great part of the knowledge with which they enriched their writings and instructed posterity, was derived from inscriptions, medals, temples, palaces, statues of great men, and other public monuments?

If travelling was in such high esteem among the ancients, no wonder that the moderns should be fond of imitating their example, and that this excellent custom should so generally obtain in this learned age. It is well known that the voyages made at the latter end of the fifteenth century to both the Indies, raised the reputation of the kings of Spain and Portugal, under whose auspices those voyages were undertaken. And who is it that has not heard of the illustrious names of Christopher Columbus, Americus Vespusius, Sir Francis Drake, Sir Walter Raleigh, Taverner, Chardin, Tournefort, Montfaucon; not to mention in our own times Maupertuis, Condamine, Don George Juan and Antony de Ulloa, the incomparable Mr Dawlins, and the great Lord Anson? To such noble adventurers the public is indebted for those useful discoveries which have contributed to improve the conveniencies and elegancies of life, and to render human society more happy.

Since travelling is therefore allowed to be productive of immense advantages, it cannot be at all surprising that so many writers should have been employed in communicating the observations they made in foreign parts, in order to entertain and instruct their countrymen at home, or to direct them in their travels abroad. If among such a multitude of writings the following work should claim any small share of merit, it is what perhaps may be owing to its particular method, which seems better adapted to the real use of travellers. For how entertaining soever most other accounts may prove to sedentary readers, whose knowledge of the world extends no farther than to imaginary circles and scales, they are generally insufficient to those who want an instructor abroad, as a kind of guide and companion of their travels. On such occasion these afford but little assistance, as they give but a very imperfect description of the different roads, of the nature and price of carriages, the conveniency of accommodations, the knowledge of the several coins, with several other articles too tedious to mention. How far this objection has been removed in the present work, and the utility as well as amusement of travellers have been consulted, will best appear by the following sketch of the whole undertaking.

As some knowledge of geography is necessary to those that travel, I have therefore thought proper to begin each volume with a general description or view of the country through which we intend to steer our journey, describing its situation, extent, climate, soil, seas, rivers, and mountains. From thence I proceed to a view of the inhabitants, giving a detail of their persons, manners, customs, language, learning, arts, and religion. Next comes the commerce of the country, under which article I examine into its rise, progress, and present state; commonly adding, for the sake of such as travel for business, a list of the principal fairs, and of the chief commodities of each town and province. To this succeeds the manner of travelling, where I have taken care to insert not only my own observations during the course of many years travels, but likewise the remarks of every other valuable writer; so that here the reader may expect a good account of the several roads, and of the different carriages as well by water as by land, with their hours of setting out, and respective prices. This introductory part contains also a view of foreign coins, with their reduction to the English standard.

These preliminaries being settled, we enter upon our several journeys, beginning with the capital of each country, and thence directing our course through the different provinces, comprehending the by-roads as well as the direct, till we have visited every place that is any way deserving of a traveller's notice. In regard to the description of the remarkable places, care has been taken to be very exact; for which reason I have availed myself, where my own observations failed me, of the most authentic relations of approved travellers of different nations.

RICHARD HURD, *Dialogues on the Uses of Foreign Travel;*
Considered as a Part of an English Gentleman's Education:
Between Lord Shaftesbury and Mr Locke (1775)

Richard Hurd (1720–1808), clergyman and man of letters, would later be
appointed Bishop of Lichfield and Coventry and tutor to the sons of
George III. Hurd stages the debate over the educational value of
the Grand Tour in an imaginary dialogue between Anthony Ashley
Cooper, first Earl of Shaftesbury (1621–83), and the great empiricist
philosopher John Locke (1632–1704), who had been attached to Shaftesbury's household. Early in the debate Shaftesbury, spokesman for an
aristocratic cosmopolitanism, claims that foreign travel will polish away
the 'idiot PREJUDICES of our home-bred gentlemen'. Hurd draws on
the historical Locke's critique of the Grand Tour in *Some Thoughts
Concerning Education* (1693) for an ironical rebuttal.

MR LOCKE. I hold then that the knowledge of human nature (the
only knowledge, in the largest sense of the expression, deserving a
wise man's regard) can never be well attained but by seeing it under
all its appearances; I mean not merely, or chiefly, in that fair and
well-dressed form it wears amid the arts and embellishments of our
western world; but in its naked simplicity, and even deformities; nay,
under all its disguises and distortions, arising from absurd governments and monstrous religions, in every distant region and quarter
of the globe.

The subject appears to me in that importance that it almost
warms me, an old philosopher as I am, into some emulation of your
Lordship's enthusiasm.

I would say, then, that, to study HUMAN NATURE to purpose, a
traveller must enlarge his circuit beyond the bounds of Europe.
He must go, and catch her undressed, nay quite naked, in North
America, and at the Cape of Good Hope. He may then examine
how she appears cramped, contracted, and buttoned up close in the
strait tunic of Law and Custom, as in China, and Japan. Or, spread
out, and enlarged above her common size, in the loose and flowing
robe of enthusiasm, among the Arabs and Saracens: Or, lastly, as
she flutters in the old rags of worn out policy and civil government, and almost ready to run back naked to the deserts, as on the
Mediterranean coast of Africa.

These, my Lord, are the proper scenes for the philosopher, for the citizen of the world, to expatiate in. The tour of Europe is a paltry thing: a same, uniform, unvaried prospect, which affords nothing but the same polished manners and artificial policies,* scarcely diversified enough to take, or merit our attention.

It is from a wider and more extensive view of mankind that a just estimate is to be made of the powers of human nature. Hence we collect what its genuine faculties are: what ideas and principles, or if any, are truly innate and essential to it: and what changes and modifications it is susceptible of from law and custom.

If you think I impose too great a task on our inquisitive traveller, my next advice is, that he stay at home; read Europe in the mirror of his own country, which but too eagerly reflects and flatters every state that dances before its surface; and, for the rest, take up with the best information he can get from the books and narratives of the best voyagers.

LORD SHAFTESBURY: That is, you discourage him from looking abroad into the world of reason and civility, the most natural state of mankind; and require him to waste his time and observation on slaves, madmen, or savages; states in which reason and civility have no place, and where humanity itself, almost, disappears.

Admirable advice this to come from a philosopher! And still better, to send your disciple to take his information of this unnatural disordered scene from the lying accounts of ignorant, ill-instructed, and gaping tale-tellers.

MR LOCKE: I was afraid, I should not be able to secure to myself the good opinion, which your Lordship was pleased to express of my knowledge of human nature. This mortifying experience puts an end to my adventurous flights, at once; and forces me back again into the narrower walk, which your Lordship seems willing to prescribe to me.

Be it then, as you insist, that an English gentleman's care should be to accomplish himself in the school of reason and civility; to fit himself, in short, for that state which your Lordship dignifies with the name of natural. Still I declare against his European travels.

The manners of each state are peculiar to itself, and best adapted to it. The civility that prevails in some places on the Continent may be more studied and exquisite than ours, but not therefore to be preferred before it. Those refinements have had their birth from

correspondent policies; to which they are well suited, and from
which they receive their whole value. In the more absolute monarchies
of Europe, all are courtiers. In our freer monarchy all should be
citizens. Let then the arts of address and insinuation flourish in
France. Without them, what merit can pretend to success, what
talents open the way to favour and distinction? But let a manlier
character prevail here. We have a prince to serve, not to flatter. We
have a country to embrace, not a court to adore. We have, in a word,
objects to pursue, and interests to promote, from the cares of which
our finer neighbours are happily disburdened.

Let our countrymen then be indulged in the plainness, nay the
roughness of their manners. But let them atone for this defect by
their useful sense, their superior knowledge, their public spirit, and,
above all, by their unpolished integrity.

3. SOCIETY AND SENTIMENT

JAMES BOSWELL, *Boswell on the Grand Tour: Germany and
Switzerland, 1764* (ed. F. A. Pottle; New York, 1953)

In 1764 James Boswell (1740–95), studying civil law at Utrecht, defied the
wishes of his father (the formidable Scottish judge Lord Auchinleck) and
set out on a full-scale Grand Tour which took him from the courts of
Germany to Italy, France, and the little-known isle of Corsica. More
interested in personalities than in art or scenery, Boswell sought out love
affairs and interviews with famous men: Samuel Johnson in London,
Rousseau and Voltaire in France and Switzerland. Boswell turns conversation into a theatre of self-fashioning in which he plays various roles—
gallant, courtier, philosopher, man of feeling, and man of the world—and
tempers his melancholy egoism with a passionate attention to other
people's lives. Boswell's travel journal, unpublished until the twentieth
century, is written mainly in French, mixed with Scots and English.
These excerpts are translated and edited by the great Boswell scholar
Frederick Pottle. In them Boswell attends a royal hunt at Dessau, lobbies
for a decoration at Karlsruhe, and interviews Jean Jacques Rousseau at
Môtiers, Neuchatel, where the philosopher was living under the protection of Frederick the Great following the scandalous reception of *Émile*
and *The Social Contract* (both 1762).

DESSAU: TUESDAY, 25 SEPTEMBER. Like a bold hunter I rose at five. Monsieur de Berenhorst presented me to Prince Diederic, uncle to the reigning Prince.* I found him a tall, comely old man of sixty-two. He was formerly Velt Marischal in the Prussian service. He has loved hunting all his life. He now keeps two packs of good hounds. He is just one of the old Germans, rough and cordial. He took me by the hand, and showed me his stables, and then we went out. The old gentleman went in his open chaise to the rendezvous. The pack consisted of fifty couple. The hunters were pretty numerous, and had a genteel uniform of red and blue. There were a great many noble *cornes de chasse*,* the sound of which roused my blood. The forests of Dessau are magnificent, all of fine oaks, some of which are immensely large. I was mounted on a trusty old white, very quiet, very sure-footed, and by no means slow. For this day, however, I kept by the young Prince Albert,* who cut the wood by neat, pretty roads which are made in different places. A large stag was singled out, and away we went after him. It was the first time that I saw this sport, and a most noble one it is. Macfarlane* would say, 'Then it might be a marquis, for Most Noble is his title.' The chase lasted more than two hours. At last the stag took the Elbe and was half worried, half drowned, half slain by the hunter's *coup de grâce*. The horns then sounded, and we all assembled. The princesses came out of their coach. I must mark a little anecdote not quite according to strict decorum. The Prince's mistress* was in a chaise, just behind the coach. She did not, however, come out.

After we had paid our respects to Prince Diederic on his chase, a collation of cold meat, bread and butter, and wine was served round. In the mean time the deer was skinned and the best pieces of venison laid by. The rest of him was cut to pieces, while the old Prince sat very composedly with his muster-roll, and named all the dogs to see if they were all there. I was vexed that they could not answer to their names, especially as there were several English dogs among them. They were then well whipped in, till their hunger increased almost to fury. The skin and horns were placed above the minced pieces, and then all at once the pack were let loose, and the moment that they attacked the image of the deer, the skin and horns were removed, and they were allowed to devour with full freedom. Prince Diederic then presented me with the stag's foot, saying, 'My dear Sir, this is a mark of distinction.' This pleased me. It shall be laid up

in the museum at Auchinleck,* with an inscription on a plate of gold
or silver, telling that Laird James the Fourth had it in a present from
a German prince with whom he had the honour of hunting, when
upon his travels. We all had oak garlands in our hats, and returned
gaily to Dessau. I recollected my old Edinburgh vapours—Lord
Galloway—'By chase our long-lived fathers earned their food,'* etc.
I resolved to take daily vigorous exercise.

We dined at Court in boots, as the ladies were not with us. At
three I waited on the Countess d'Anhalt, mother to the Count at
Potsdam. She had three daughters, strong, bouncing women. One of
them is very clever. In the evening we all met again at Court. I must
not forget to mention one personage, Captain O'Grady, an Irish
officer in the Saxon service, a good, honest, light-headed fellow. He
keeps a girl at Dessau, and is very much there. At supper this night
he talked a vast deal of bawdy concerning a Mademoiselle Stenix,
who sat near me. I looked grave, and seemed to give no attention to
his discourse, by way of reproving him. At last he said that 'she
would go like a pair of lobster's claws.' This ludicrous idea struck me
so much that I burst out into a fit of laughter, and Master O'Grady
was heartily pleased.

KARLSRUHE: FRIDAY, 16 NOVEMBER. Munzesheim* again carried
me out to ride. It was charming weather. I was lively. I was amused to
hear, 'His Highness loves the girls. He likes something big and fresh
that he can get without pains, for he is modest.'

And now let me record my talents as a courtier. From my earliest
years I have respected the great. In the groves of Auchinleck I have
indulged pleasing hopes of ambition. Since I have been in Germany
it has been my ardent wish to find a prince of merit who might take a
real regard for me, and with whose ennobling friendship I might be
honoured all my life. I pleased myself with thinking that among
the variety of princes whom I intended to visit such a one might be
found. After having been at a number of courts, I had almost given
up my idea. At the last court but one, my utmost wish has been
fulfilled. I have found a grave, a knowing, and a worthy prince.*
He has seen my merit. He has shown me every mark of distinction.
He has talked a great deal with me. Some days ago, I said to him, 'Is
it possible, Sir, that after I am gone from this I may give you any
mark of my gratitude?' He answered, 'I shall write to you sometimes;

I shall be very glad to receive your letters.' The Prince of Baden-Durlach has an order to give. He creates Knights of the Order of Fidelity. They wear a star and a ribbon hanging from their necks. My Lord Wemyss has this order. I fixed my inclination upon it. I was determined if possible to obtain it. When the Prince honoured me so far as to grant me his correspondence, I thought he would surely grant me his order. I asked him once *en passant* if only counts could have it. He said, 'It is enough to be a good gentleman.' Munzesheim had told me that the Prince was a little nice* in giving it. This being my last day here, I was presented to take leave. The Prince said, 'I cannot ask you to stay longer, as I am afraid you would tire.' I said, by no means, but I was a little hurried at present, and would return again and pass a longer time. I then took courage and said, 'Sir, I have a favour to ask of you, a very great favour. I don't know whether I should mention it.' I was quite the courtier, for I appeared modest and embarrassed, when in reality I was perfectly unconcerned. He said, 'What, Sir?' I replied, 'Your Highness told me that a good gentleman might have your Highness's order. Sir, might I presume to ask you that, if I bring you proof of my being a very good gentleman, I may obtain the order?' He paused. I looked at him steadily. He answered, 'I shall think of it.' I said, 'Sir, you have already been so good to me that I flatter myself that I have the merit for obtaining such a favour. As to my rank, I can assure you that I am a very old gentleman' (some days ago I had given his Highness a history of my family) 'and it may sound strange, but, Sir, I can count kindred with my sovereign from my being related to the family of Lennox and the royal family of Stuart. Sir, I am one of your old proud Scots. If you grant me this favour, you will make me happy for life, in adding honour to my family; and I shall be proud to wear in my own country the Order of Fidelity of such a prince.' He seemed pleased. I said, 'I hope, Sir, you do not take amiss my having mentioned this. I was anxious to obtain it, and I thought it was pity to want what I valued so highly, for want of boldness to ask it.' He said, 'Let me have your genealogy attested, and when you return, we shall see.' Oh, I shall have it. I took leave of his Highness with much respect.

I then went to President Gemmingen's, where I heard music and danced and was gay. I have a weakness of mind which is scarcely credible. Here amidst music and dancing I am as cheerful as if nothing had ever vexed me. My mind is like an air-pump which receives and ejects ideas with wonderful facility. Munzesheim went home with me a little. I told him in confidence my proceedings with his sovereign as to the Order. He told me I would obtain it when I returned. I bid him speak plain. He assured me that I might depend upon having it. I supped at the Marshal's table, where I am much liked. It has been observed that the Grand Écuyer has spoken more to me than to any stranger. He is silent and backward. I have put him at his ease, led him on to talk of horses, of which I am, by the by, completely ignorant. But I had address enough to make that conversation go well on.

After supper I took leave of them all very kindly and said, 'Gentlemen, I should be very unhappy at leaving this room if I thought I should not come back,' and upon my word I thought so. Jacob is a most excellent fellow.* I had mentioned to him my wish to have the Order. He wished it as much as I did, and to obtain it said he would walk a certain length, give a certain sum of money, or do some other extravagant thing which I do not remember. When I told him tonight that I was to have it, the fellow was quite over-joyed. I piqued his vanity by saying, 'You shall have a master with a star.'

MÔTIERS: SATURDAY, 15 DECEMBER. At seven in the morning I got on horseback and rode about a league to St Sulpice, where I saw the source of the Reuse, the river which runs through the Val de Travers. It is a prodigious romantic place. I could not determine whether the water gushes in an immediate spring from the rock, or only issues out here, having pierced the mountain, upon which is a lake. The water comes forth with great violence. All around here I saw mountains and rocks as at Hartfell in Annandale. Some of the rocks were in great courses like huge stone walls, along which grew the towering pines which we call pitch firs, and which are much handsomer than the firs of Scotland.

I was full of fine spirits. Gods! Am I now then really the friend of Rousseau? What a rich assemblage of ideas! I relish my felicity truly in such a scene as this. Shall I not truly relish it at Auchinleck? I was quite gay, my fancy was youthful, and vented its gladness in sportive sallies. I supposed myself in the rude world. I supposed a parcel of young fellows saying, 'Come, Boswell, you'll dine with us today?' 'No, gentlemen, excuse me; I'm engaged. I dine today with Rousseau.'

My tone, my air, my native pride when I pronounced this! Temple!*
You would have given half a guinea to see me at that moment. . . .

I then went to Monsieur Rousseau. 'I hope your health is better
today.' ROUSSEAU. 'Oh, don't speak of it.' He seemed unusually gay.
Before dinner we are all so, if not made to wait too long. A keen
appetite gives a vivacity to the whole frame.

I said, 'You say nothing in regard to a child's duties towards
his parents. You tell us nothing of your *Émile's* father.' ROUSSEAU.
'Oh, he hadn't any. He didn't exist.' It is, however, a real pity that
Monsieur Rousseau has not treated of the duties between parents
and children. It is an important and a delicate subject and deserves to
be illustrated by a sage of so clear a judgment and so elegant a soul.

He praised *The Spectator*. He said, 'One comes across allegories in
it. I have no taste for allegories, though your nation shows a great
liking for them.'

I gave him very fully the character of Mr Johnson. He said with
force, 'I should like that man. I should respect him. I would not
disturb his principles if I could. I should like to see him, but from
a distance, for fear he might maul me.' I told him how averse
Mr Johnson was to write, and how he had his levee. 'Ah,' said he, 'I
understand. He is a man who enjoys holding forth.' I told him
Mr Johnson's *bon mot* upon the innovators:* that truth is a cow which
will yield them no more milk, and so they are gone to milk the bull.
He said, 'He would detest me. He would say, "Here is a corrupter: a
man who comes here to milk the bull." '

I had diverted myself by pretending to help Mademoiselle Le
Vasseur* to make the soup. We dined in the kitchen, which was neat
and cheerful. There was something singularly agreeable in this
scene. Here was Rousseau in all his simplicity, with his Armenian
dress, which I have surely mentioned before now. His long coat and
nightcap made him look easy and well.

Our dinner was as follows: I. A dish of excellent soup. 2. A *bouilli*
of beef and veal. 3. Cabbage, turnip, and carrot. 4. Cold pork. 5.
Pickled trout, which he jestingly called tongue. 6. Some little dish
which I forget. The dessert consisted of stoned pears and of chestnuts. We had red and white wines. It was a simple, good repast. We
were quite at our ease. I sometimes forgot myself and became cere-
monious. 'May I help you to some of this dish?' ROUSSEAU. 'No, Sir.
I can help myself to it.' Or, 'May I help myself to some more of that?'

ROUSSEAU. 'Is your arm long enough? A man does the honours of his house from a motive of vanity. He does not want it forgotten who is the master. I should like every one to be his own master, and no one to play the part of host. Let each one ask for what he wants; if it is there to give, let him be given it; otherwise, he must be satisfied without. Here you see true hospitality.' BOSWELL. 'In England, it is quite another matter. They do not want to be at ease; they are stiff and silent, in order to win respect.' ROUSSEAU. 'In France, you find no such gloom among people of distinction. There is even an affect-ation of the utmost liberty, as though they would have you under-stand, "We stand in no fear of losing our dignity." That is a more refined form of self-esteem.'

BOSWELL. 'Well, and do you not share that yourself?' ROUSSEAU. 'Yes, I confess that I like to be respected; but only in matters of importance.' BOSWELL. 'You are so simple. I expected to find you quite different from this: the Great Rousseau. But you do not see yourself in the same light as others do. I expected to find you enthroned and talking with a grave authority.' ROUSSEAU. 'Uttering oracles? Ha! Ha! Ha!' BOSWELL. 'Yes, and that I should be much in awe of you. And really your simplicity might lay you open to criti-cism; it might be said, "Monsieur Rousseau does not make himself sufficiently respected." In Scotland, I assure you, a very different tone must be taken to escape from the shocking familiarity which is prevalent in that country. Upon my word, I cannot put up with it. Should I not be justified in forestalling it by fighting a duel with the first man who should treat me so, and thus live at peace for the rest of my life?' ROUSSEAU. 'No. That is not allowable. It is not right to stake one's life on such follies. Life is given us for objects of import-ance. Pay no heed to what such men say. They will get tired of talking to a man who does not answer them.' BOSWELL. 'If you were in Scotland, they would begin at the very start by calling you Rousseau; they would say, "Jean Jacques, how goes it?" with the utmost famil-iarity.' ROUSSEAU. 'That is perhaps a good thing.' BOSWELL. 'But they would say, "Poh! Jean Jacques, why do you allow yourself all these fantasies? You're a pretty man to put forward such claims. Come, come, settle down in society like other people." And they would say it to you with a sourness which I am quite unable to imitate for you.' ROUSSEAU. 'Ah, that's bad.'

There he felt the thistle, when it was applied to himself on the tender part. It was just as if I had said, 'Hoot, Johnnie Rousseau man, what for hae ye sae mony figmagairies?* Ye're a bonny man indeed to mauk siccan a wark; set ye up. Canna ye just live like ither fowk?' It was the best idea could be given in the polite French language of the rude Scots sarcastical vivacity.

BOSWELL. 'I have leanings towards despotism, let me tell you. On our estate, I am like an ancient laird, and I insist on respect from the tenants.' ROUSSEAU. 'But when you see an old man with white hair, do you, as a young man, have no feelings at all? Have you no respect for age?' BOSWELL. 'Yes. I have even on many occasions been very affable. I have talked quite freely with the tenants.' ROUSSEAU. 'Yes, you forgot yourself, and became a man.' BOSWELL. 'But I was sorry for it afterwards. I used to think, "I have lowered myself." ' ROUSSEAU. 'Ha! Ha! Ha!' . . .

ROUSSEAU. 'Do you like cats?' BOSWELL. 'No.' ROUSSEAU. 'I was sure of that. It is my test of character. There you have the despotic instinct of men. They do not like cats because the cat is free and will never consent to become a slave. He will do nothing to your order, as the other animals do.' BOSWELL. 'Nor a hen, either.' ROUSSEAU. 'A hen would obey your orders if you could make her understand them. But a cat will understand you perfectly and not obey them.' BOSWELL. 'But a cat is ungrateful and treacherous.' ROUSSEAU. 'No. That's all untrue. A cat is an animal that can be very much attached to you; he will do anything you please out of friendship. I have a cat here. He has been brought up with my dog; they play together. The cat will give the dog a blow with his tail, and the dog will offer him his paw.' (He described the playing of his dog and cat with exquisite eloquence, as a fine painter draws a small piece.) He put some vict- uals on a trencher, and made his dog dance round it. He sung to him a lively air with a sweet voice and great taste. 'You see the ballet. It is not a gala performance, but a pretty one all the same.' I think the dog's name was Sultan. He stroked him and fed him, and with an arch air said, 'He is not much *respected*, but he gets well looked after.' . . .

MADEMOISELLE. 'Sir, your man is calling for you to start.' Monsieur Rousseau embraced me. He was quite the tender Saint- Preux.* He kissed me several times, and held me in his arms with elegant cordiality. Oh, I shall never forget that I have been thus. ROUSSEAU. 'Good-bye. You are a fine fellow.' BOSWELL. 'You have shown me great goodness. But I deserved it.' ROUSSEAU. 'Yes. You are malicious; but 'tis a pleasant malice, a malice I don't dislike. Write and tell me how you are.' BOSWELL. 'And you will write to me?' ROUSSEAU. 'I know not how to reach you.' BOSWELL. 'Yes, you shall write to me in Scotland.' ROUSSEAU. 'Certainly; and even at Paris.' BOSWELL. 'Bravo! If I live twenty years, you will write to me for twenty years?' ROUSSEAU. 'Yes.' BOSWELL. 'Good-bye. If you live for seven years, I shall return to Switzerland from Scotland to see you.' ROUSSEAU. 'Do so. We shall be old acquaintances.' BOSWELL. 'One word more. Can I feel sure that I am held to you by a thread, even if of the finest? By a hair?' (Seizing a hair of my head.) ROUSSEAU. 'Yes. Remember always that there are points at which our souls are bound.' BOSWELL. 'It is enough. I, with my melancholy, I, who often look on myself as a despicable being, as a good-for-nothing creature who should make his exit from life—I shall be upheld for ever by the thought that I am bound to Monsieur Rousseau. Good-bye. Bravo! I shall live to the end of my days.'* ROUSSEAU. 'That is undoubtedly a thing one must do. Good-bye.'

Mademoiselle accompanied me to the outer door. Before dinner she told me, 'Monsieur Rousseau has a high regard for you. The first time you came, I said to him, "That gentleman has an honest face. I am sure you will like him."' I said, 'Mademoiselle is a good judge.' 'Yes,' said she, 'I have seen strangers enough in the twenty-two years that I have been with Monsieur Rousseau, and I assure you that I have sent many of them packing because I did not fancy their way of talking.' I said, 'You have promised to let me have news of you from time to time.' 'Yes, Sir.' 'And tell me what I can send you from Geneva. Make no ceremony.' 'Well, if you will, a garnet necklace.'

We shook hands cordially, and away I went to my inn. My eldest landlady looked at me and said, 'Sir, I think you are crying.' This I retain as a true elogium of my humanity. I replied, '[No.] Yet I am unhappy to leave Monsieur Rousseau. I will see you again in seven years.' I got a-horseback and rode by the house of Monsieur Rousseau. Mademoiselle waited for me at the door, and cried, '*Bon voyage*; write to us.' Good creature. I rode gravely to Yverdon contemplating how this day will appear to my mind some years hence. I was received cordially by my gallant Baron and my amiable Madame de Brackel; yet did my spirits sink pretty low. No wonder after such a high flow.

TOBIAS SMOLLETT, *Travels through France and Italy,
containing Observations of Character, Customs, Religion,
Government, Police, Commerce, Arts, and Antiquities* (1766)

Tobias Smollett (1721–71) offers no less intensely subjective a mode of
travel writing than his fellow countryman Boswell, although their cases are
otherwise very different. Smollett was a middle-aged professional writer
who went abroad, accompanied by his wife, in search of relief from ill
health and various domestic, financial, and political troubles. The exuberantly cranky tenor of Smollett's observations made *Travels through France
and Italy* notorious—so steeped in 'spleen and jaundice', mocked Sterne
in *A Sentimental Journey*, as to be 'nothing but the account of his miserable feelings'. The following excerpt (from Letter IX) reminds us that
he was also a major novelist, the author of *Roderick Random* (1748) and
Humphry Clinker (1771).

We set out from Lyons early on Monday morning, and as a robbery
had been a few days before committed in that neighbourhood, I
ordered my servant to load my musquetoon with a charge of eight
balls. By the bye, this piece did not fail to attract the curiosity and
admiration of the people in every place through which we passed.
The carriage no sooner halted, than a crowd immediately surrounded the man to view the blunderbuss, which they dignified with
the title of *petit canon*. At Nuys in Burgundy, he fired it in the air, and
the whole mob dispersed, and scampered off like a flock of sheep. In
our journey hither, we generally set out in a morning at eight o'clock,
and travelled till noon, when the mules were put up and rested a
couple of hours. During this halt, Joseph* went to dinner, and we
went to breakfast, after which we ordered provision for our refreshment in the coach, which we took about three or four in the afternoon, halting for that purpose, by the side of some transparent
brook, which afforded excellent water to mix with our wine. In this
country I was almost poisoned with garlic, which they mix in their
ragouts, and all their sauces; nay, the smell of it perfumes the very
chambers, as well as every person you approach. I was also very sick
of beccaficas, grieves,* or thrushes, and other little birds, which are
served up twice a day at all ordinaries on the road. They make their
appearance in vine-leaves, and are always half raw, in which condition the French choose to eat them, rather than run the risk of losing
the juice by over-roasting. . . .

One day perceiving a meadow on the side of the road, full of a flower which I took to be the crocus, I desired my servant to alight and pull some of them. He delivered the musquetoon to Joseph, who began to tamper with it, and off it went with a prodigious report, augmented by an echo from the mountains that skirted the road. The mules were so frightened that they went off at the gallop; and Joseph, for some minutes, could neither manage the reins, nor open his mouth. At length he recollected himself, and the cattle were stopped, by the assistance of the servant, to whom he delivered the musquetoon, with a significant shake of the head. Then alighting from the box, he examined the heads of his three mules, and kissed each of them in his turn. Finding they had received no damage, he came up to the coach, with a pale visage and staring eyes, and said it was God's mercy he had not killed his beasts. I answered, that it was a greater mercy he had not killed his passengers; for the muzzle of the piece might have been directed our way as well as any other, and in that case Joseph might have been hanged for murder. 'I had as good be hanged (said he) for murder, as be ruined by the loss of my cattle.' This adventure made such an impression upon him that he recounted it to every person we met; nor would he ever touch the blunderbuss from that day. I was often diverted with the conversation of this fellow, who was very arch and very communicative. Every afternoon, he used to stand upon the foot-board, at the side of the coach, and discourse with us an hour together. Passing by the gibbet of Valencia, which stands very near the highroad, we saw one body hanging quite naked, and another lying broken on the wheel. I recollected, that Mandrin* had suffered in this place, and calling to Joseph to mount the foot-board, asked if he had ever seen that famous adventurer. At mention of the name of Mandrin, the tear started in Joseph's eye, he discharged a deep sigh, or rather groan, and told me he was his dear friend. I was a little startled at this declaration; however, I concealed my thoughts, and began to ask questions about the character and exploits of a man who had made such noise in the world.

He told me Mandrin was a native of Valencia, of mean extraction: that he had served as a soldier in the army, and afterwards acted as *maltotier*, or tax-gatherer: that at length he turned *contrebandier*, or smuggler, and by his superior qualities, raised himself to the command of a formidable gang, consisting of five hundred persons well armed with carbines and pistols. He had fifty horse for his troopers, and three hundred mules for the carriage of his merchandise. His headquarters were in Savoy: but he made incursions into Dauphiné, and set the *maréchaussée* at defiance. He maintained several bloody skirmishes with these troopers, as well as with other regular detachments, and in all those actions signallized himself by his courage and conduct. Coming up at one time with fifty of the *maréchaussée*, who were in quest of him, he told them very calmly, he had occasion for their horses and acoutrements, and desired them to dismount. At that instant his gang appeared, and the troopers complied with his request, without making the least opposition. Joseph said he was as generous as he was brave, and never molested travellers, nor did the least injury to the poor; but, on the contrary, relieved them very often. He used to oblige the gentlemen in the country to take his merchandise, his tobacco, brandy, and muslins, at his own price; and; in the same manner, he laid the open towns under contribution. When he had no merchandise, he borrowed money of them upon the credit of what he should bring when he was better provided. He was at last betrayed, by his wench, to the colonel of a French regiment, who went with a detachment in the night to the place where he lay in Savoy, and surprised him in a wood-house, while his people were absent in different parts of the country. For this intrusion, the court of France made an apology to the king of Sardinia, in whose territories he was taken. Mandrin being conveyed to Valencia, his native place, was for some time permitted to go abroad, under a strong guard, with chains upon his legs; and here he conversed freely with all sorts of people, flattering himself with the hopes of a pardon, in which, however, he was disappointed. An order came from court to bring him to his trial, when he was found guilty, and condemned to be broke on the wheel. Joseph said he drank a bottle of wine with him the night before his execution. He bore his fate with great resolution, observing that if the letter which he had written to the King had been delivered, he certainly should have obtained his Majesty's pardon. His executioner was one of his own gang, who was pardoned on condition of performing this office. You know that criminals broke upon the wheel are first strangled, unless the sentence imports, that they shall be broke alive. As Mandrin had not been guilty of cruelty in the course of his delinquency, he was indulged with this favour. Speaking to the executioner, whom he had

formerly commanded, 'Joseph (dit il) je ne veux pas que tu me
touche, jusqu'à ce que je sois raid mort.' 'Joseph, said he, thou shalt
not touch me till I am quite dead.'—Our driver had no sooner
pronounced these words than I was struck with a suspicion that he
himself was the executioner of his friend Mandrin. On that suspicion, I exclaimed, 'ah! ah! Joseph!' The fellow blushed up to the
eyes, and said, *oui, son nom était Joseph aussi bien que le mien*, 'yes, he
was called *Joseph*, as I am.' I did not think proper to prosecute the
inquiry; but did not much relish the nature of Joseph's connections.
The truth is, he had very much the looks of a ruffian; though, I must
own, his behaviour was very obliging and submissive.

JOHN MOORE, *A View of Society and Manners in Italy; with
Anecdotes relating to some Eminent Characters. By a Gentleman,
who resided several Years in those Countries* (1781), *Letter VI*

John Moore (1729–1802), another Scotsman, took the Grand Tour in a
professional rather than amateur capacity, as tutor to successive Dukes
of Hamilton, 1772–8. Moore's books based on his travels set a new tone
for continental tourism—liberal, sceptical, well-informed without being
pedantic. (Moore also wrote novels, including *Zeluco*, 1786.) Moore plays
with the new vocabulary of Scottish Enlightenment aesthetic theory and
mocks the conventional taste of the 'connoisseur', a figure associated with
the Grand Tour.

VENICE

I was led, in my last, into a very particular (and I wish you may not
have also found it a very tedious) description of St Mark's Place.
There is no help for what is past, but, for your comfort, you have
nothing of the same kind to fear while we remain here; for there is
not another square, or *place*, as the French with more propriety call
them, in all Venice. To compensate, however, for their being but
one, there is a greater variety of objects to be seen at this one, than in
any half dozen of the squares, or places, of London or Paris.

After our eyes had been dazzled with looking at pictures, and
our legs cramped with sitting in a gondola, it is no small relief, and
amusement, to saunter in the Place of St Mark.

The number and diversity of objects which there present

themselves to the eye, naturally create a very rapid succession of ideas.* The sight of the churches awakens religious sentiments, and, by an easy transition, the mind is led to contemplate the influence of superstition. In the midst of this reverie, Nero's four horses appear,* and carry the fancy to Rome and Constantinople. While you are forcing your way, sword in hand, with the heroic Henry Dandelo,* into the capital of Asia, Adam and Eve stop your progress, and lead you to the garden of Eden.* You have not long enjoyed a state of innocence and happiness in that delightful paradise, till Eve

> her rash hand in evil hour
> Forth reaching to the fruit, she plucks, she eats.*

After that unfortunate repast, no more comfort being to be found there, you are glad to mount St Mark's winged lion, and fly back to the Ducal palace,* where you will naturally reflect on the rise and progress of the Venetian state, and the various springs of their government. While you admire the strength of a constitution which has stood firm for so many ages, you are appalled at the sight of the lion's mouth gaping for accusations;* and turning with horror from a place where innocence seems exposed to the attacks of hidden malice, you are regaled with a prospect of the sea, which opens your return to a country of *real* freedom, where justice rejects the libel of the hidden accuser, and dares to try, condemn, and execute *openly*, the highest, as well as the lowest, delinquent.

I assure you I have, more than once, made all this tour, standing in the middle of St Mark's square; whereas, in the French places, you have nothing before your eyes but monuments of the monarch's vanity, and the people's adulation; and in the greater part of the London squares, and streets, what idea can present itself to the imagination, beyond that of the snug neatness and conveniency of substantial brick houses?

I have been speaking hitherto of a morning saunter; for in the evening there generally is, on St Mark's Place, such a mixed multitude of Jews, Turks, and Christians; lawyers, knaves, and pick-pockets; mountebanks, old women, and physicians; women of quality, with masks; strumpets barefaced; and, in short, such a jumble of senators, citizens, gondoliers, and people of every character and condition, that your ideas are broken, bruised, and dislocated in the crowd, in such a manner that you can think, or reflect, on nothing; yet this being a state of mind which many people are fond of, the place never fails to be well attended, and, in fine weather, numbers pass a great part of the night there. When the piazza is illuminated, and the shops, in the adjacent streets, lighted up, the whole has a brilliant effect; and as it is the custom for the ladies, as well as the gentlemen, to frequent the casinos and coffee-houses around, the Place of St Mark answers all the purposes of either Vauxhall or Ranelagh.*

It is not in St Mark's Place that you are to look for the finest monuments of the art of Titian, or the genius of Palladio;* for those you must visit the churches and palaces: but if you are inclined to make that tour, you must find another Cicerone,* for I shall certainly not undertake the office. I do not pretend to be a competent judge of painting or architecture; I have no new remarks to make on those subjects, and I with to avoid a hackneyed repetition of what has been said by others. . . .

But if you are violently bent upon being thought a man of very refined taste, there are books in abundance to be had, which will put you in possession of all the terms of technical applause, or censure, and furnish you with suitable expressions for the whole climax of sensibility. As for myself, I was long ago taught a lesson, which made a deep impression on my mind, and will effectually prevent me from every affectation of that kind. Very early in life, I resided above a year at Paris, and happened one day to accompany five or six of our countrymen, to view the pictures in the Palais Royal.* A gentleman who affected an enthusiastic passion for the fine arts, particularly that of painting, and who had the greatest desire to be thought a connoisseur, was of the party. He had read the lives of the painters, and had the Voyage Pittoresque de Paris* by heart. From the moment we entered the rooms he began to display all the refinements of his taste; he instructed us what to admire, and drew us away with every sign of disgust when we stopped a moment at an uncelebrated picture. We were afraid of appearing pleased with anything we saw, till he informed us whether or not it was worth looking at. He shook his head at some, tossed up his nose at others; commended a few, and pronounced sentence on every piece, as he passed along, with the most imposing tone of sagacity. 'Bad, that Caravaggio is too bad indeed, devoid of all grace; but here is a Caracci that makes amends; how charming the grief of that Magdalen! The Virgin, you'll observe, gentlemen, is only fainting, but the Christ is quite dead. Look at the arm, did you ever see any thing so dead?—Aye, here's a Madonna, which they tell you is an original, by Guido; but anybody may see that it is only a tolerable copy. Pray, gentlemen, observe this St Sebastian, how delightfully he expires: don't you all feel the arrow in your hearts? I'm sure I feel it in mine. Do let us move on; I should die with agony if I looked any longer.'

We at length came to the St John, by Raphael,* and here this man of taste stopped short in an ecstasy of admiration. One of the company had already passed it, without minding it, and was looking at another picture; on which the connoisseur bawled out—'Good God, Sir! what are you about?' The honest gentleman started, and stared around to know what crime he had been guilty of.

'Have you eyes in your head, Sir?' continued the connoisseur. 'Don't you know St John when you see him?'

'St John!' replied the other, in amazement. 'Aye, Sir, St John the Baptist, *in propria persona.*'

'I don't know what you mean, Sir,' said the gentleman, peevishly.

'Don't you?' rejoined the connoisseur; 'then I'll endeavour to explain myself. I mean St John in the wilderness, by the divine Raffaelle Sanzio da Urbino, and there he stands by your side. Pray, my dear Sir, will you be so obliging as to bestow a little of your attention on that foot? Does it not start from the wall? Is it not perfectly out of the frame? Did you ever see such colouring? They talk of Titian; can Titian's colouring excel that? What truth, what nature in the head! To the eloquence of the antique, here is joined the simplicity of nature.'

We stood listening in silent admiration, and began to imagine we perceived all the perfections he enumerated; when a person in the Duke of Orleans' service came and informed us, that the original, which he presumed was the picture we wished to see, was in another room; the Duke having allowed a painter to copy it. That which we had been looking at was a very wretched daubing, done from the original by some obscure painter, and had been thrown, with other rubbish, into a corner; where the Swiss had accidentally discovered it, and had hung it up merely by way of covering the vacant space on the wall, till the other should be replaced.

How the connoisseur looked on this trying occasion, I cannot say. It would have been barbarous to have turned an eye upon him. I stepped into the next room, fully determined to be cautious in deciding on the merit of painting; perceiving that it was not safe, in this science, to speak even from the book.

HESTER LYNCH PIOZZI, *Observations and Reflections Made in the Course of a Journey through France, Italy, and Germany* (1789)

Hester Lynch Piozzi (1741–1821) left for Italy with her second husband, Gabriel Piozzi, six weeks after their marriage in 1784. She had moved in literary circles patronized by her first husband, the wealthy brewer Henry Thrale, and her friends—most vehemently among them Samuel Johnson—condemned her union with a foreign music teacher. The Italian journey was as much an escape as it was an extended or belated honeymoon. Piozzi makes the Tuscan city-state of Lucca, passed over in most Grand Tour itineraries, a model of the 'Golden Age' sought by Enlightenment travellers. (Other examples in the present anthology range from Martin Martin's St Kilda to Captain Cook's Tahiti.) Piozzi's 'fairy commonwealth' is a political utopia, a miniature republic miraculously unruffled by the storms of history.

Lucca

From the headquarters of painting, sculpture, and architecture then, where art is at her acme,* and from a people polished into brilliancy, perhaps a little into weakness, we drove through the celebrated vale of Arno; thick hedges on each side us, which in spring must have been covered with blossoms and fragrant with perfume; now loaded with uncultivated fruits; the wild grape, raspberry, and azaroli,* inviting to every sense, and promising every joy. This beautiful and fertile, this highly-adorned and truly delicious country carried us forward to Lucca, where the panther sits at the gate,* and liberty is written up on every wall and door. It is so long since I have seen the word, that even the letters of it rejoice my heart; but how the panther came to be its emblem, who can tell? Unless the philosophy we learn from old Lilly in our childhood were true, *nec vult panthera domari.**

   That this fairy commonwealth should so long have maintained its independency is strange; but Howel* attributes her freedom to the active and industrious spirit of the inhabitants, who, he says, resemble a hive of bees, for order and for diligence. I never did see a place so populous for the size of it: one is actually thronged running up and down the streets of Lucca, though it is a little town enough for a capital city to be sure; larger than Salisbury though, and prettier than Nottingham, the beauties of both which places it unites with all the charms peculiar to itself.

The territory they claim, and of which no power dares attempt to dispossess them, is much about the size of Rutlandshire* I fancy; surrounded and apparently fenced in on every side by the Apennines as by a wall, that wall a hot one, on the southern side, and wholly planted over with vines, while the soft shadows which fall upon the declivity of the mountains make it inexpressibly pretty; and form, by the particular disposition of their light and shadow, a variety which no other prospect so confined can possibly enjoy.

This is the Ilam gardens* of Europe; and whoever has seen that singular spot in Derbyshire belonging to Mr Port has seen little Lucca in a convex mirror. Some writer calls it a ring upon the finger of the Emperor, under whose protection it has been hitherto preserved safe from the Grand Duke of Tuscany* till these days, in which the interests of those two sovereigns, united by intimacy as by blood and resemblance of character, are become almost exactly the same.

A Doge, whom they call the *Principe*, is elected every two months; and is assisted by ten senators in the administration of justice.

Their armoury is the prettiest plaything I ever yet saw, neatly kept, and capable of furnishing twenty-five thousand men with arms. Their revenues are about equal to the Duke of Bedford's I believe, eighty or eighty-five thousand pounds sterling a year; every spot of ground belonging to these people being cultivated to the highest pitch of perfection that agriculture, or rather gardening (for one cannot call these enclosures fields), will admit: and though it is holiday time just now, I see no neglect of necessary duty. They were watering away this morning at seven o'clock, just as we do in a nursery-ground about London, a hundred men at once, or more, before they came home to make themselves smart, and go to hear music in their best church,* in honour of some saint, I have forgotten who; but he is the patron of Lucca, and cannot be accused of neglecting his charge, that is certain.

This city seems really under admirable regulations; here are fewer beggars than even at Florence, where however one for fifty in the states of Genoa or Venice do not meet your eyes. And either the word liberty has bewitched me, or I see an air of plenty without insolence, and business without noise, that greatly delight me. Here is much cheerfulness too, and gay good-humour; but this is the season of devotion at Lucca, and in these countries the ideas of devotion and diversion are so blended, that all religious worship seems connected with, and to me now regularly implies, a festive show.

Well, as the Italians say, 'Il mondo è bello perche è variabile.'* We English dress our clergymen in black, and go ourselves to the theatre in colours. Here matters are reversed, the church at noon looked like a flower-garden, so gaily adorned were the priests, confrairies,* etc., while the opera-house at night had more the air of a funeral, as everybody was dressed in black: a circumstance I had forgotten the meaning of, till reminded that such was once the emulation of finery among the persons of fashion in this city, that it was found conveni-ent to restrain the spirit of expense, by obliging them to wear con-stant mourning: a very rational and well-devised rule in a town so small, where everybody is known to everybody; and where, when this silly excitement to envy is wisely removed, I know not what should hinder the inhabitants from living like those one reads of in the Golden Age; which, above all others, this climate most resembles, where pleasure contributes to soothe life, commerce to quicken it, and faith extends its prospects to eternity. Such is, or such at least appears to me this lovely territory of Lucca: where cheap living, free government, and genteel society may be enjoyed with a tranquillity unknown to larger states; where there are delicious and salutary baths a few miles out of town, for the nobility to make *villeggiatura** at; and where, if those nobility were at all disposed to cultivate and communicate learning, every opportunity for study is afforded.

Some drawbacks will however always be found from human felicity. I once mentioned this place with warm expectations of delight, to a Milanese lady of extensive knowledge, and every elegant accomplishment worthy her high birth, the Contessa Melzi Resta. 'Why yes,' said she, 'if you would find out the place where common sense stagnates, and every topic of conversation dwindles and per-ishes away by too frequent or too unskilful touching and handling, you must go to Lucca. My ill health sent me to their beautiful baths one summer, where all the faculties of my body were restored, thank God, but those of my soul were stupefied to such a degree that at last I was fit to keep no other company but Dame Lucchesi* I think; and our talk was soon ended, heaven knows, for when they had once asked me of an evening, what I had for dinner? and told me how many pair of stockings their neighbours sent to the wash, we had done.'

This was a young, a charming, a lively lady of quality; full of curiosity to know the world, and of spirits to bustle through it; but had she been battered through the various societies of London and Paris for eighteen or twenty years together, she would have loved Lucca better, and despised it less. 'We must not look for whales in the Euxine Sea,' says an old writer;* and we must not look for great men or great things in little nations to be sure, but let us respect the innocence of childhood, and regard with tenderness the territory of Lucca: where no man has been murdered during the life or memory of any of its peaceful inhabitants; where one robbery alone has been committed for sixteen years; and the thief hanged by a Florentine executioner borrowed for the purpose, no Lucchese being able or willing to undertake so horrible an office, with terrifying circumstances of penitence and public reprehension: where the governed are so few in proportion to the governors; all power being circulated among four hundred and fifty nobles, and the whole country producing scarcely ninety thousand souls. A great boarding-school in England is really an infinitely more licentious place; and grosser immoralities are every day connived at in it than are known to pollute this delicate and curious commonwealth, which keeps a council always subsisting, called the *Discoli*, to examine the lives and conduct, professions, and even health of their subjects: and once a year they sweep the town of vagabonds, which till then are caught up and detained in a house of correction, and made to work, if not disabled by lameness, till the hour of their release and dismission. I wondered there were so few beggars about, but the reason is now apparent; these we see are neighbours, come hither only for the three days gala.

I was wonderfully solicitous to obtain some of their coin, which carries on it the image of no earthly prince; but his head only who came to redeem us from general slavery on the one side, Jesus Christ; on the other, the word *Libertas*.

Our peasant-girls here are in a new dress to me; no more jewels to be seen, no more pearls; the finery of which so dazzled me in Tuscany: these wenches are prohibited such ornaments it seems. A muslin handkerchief, folded in a most becoming manner, and starched exactly enough to make it wear clean four days, is the head-dress of

Lucchese lasses, it is put on turban-wise, and they button their
gowns close, with long sleeves *à la Savoyarde*; but it is made often of
a stiff brocaded silk, and green lapels, with cuffs of the same colour;
nor do they wear any hats at all, to defend them from a sun which
does undoubtedly mature the fig and ripen the vine, but which, by
the same excess of power, exalts the venom of the viper, and gives
the scorpion means to keep me in perpetual torture for fear of his
poison, of which, though they assure us death is seldom the consequence among *them*, I know his sting would finish me at once,
because the gnats at Florence were sufficient to lame me for a
considerable time.

The dialect has lost much of the guttural sound that hurt one's ear
at the last place of residence; but here is an odd squeaking accent,
that distinguishes the Tuscan of Lucca.

The place appropriated for airing, showing fine equipages, etc. is
beautiful beyond all telling; from the peculiar shadows on the mountains. They make the bastions of the town their Corso,* but none
except the nobles can go and drive upon one part of it. I know not
how many yards of ground is thus set apart, sacred to sovereignty;
but it makes one laugh.

Our inn here is an excellent one, as far as I am concerned; and the
salad-oil green, like Irish usquebaugh,* nothing was ever so excellent.
I asked the French valet who dresses our hair, '*Si ce n'etait pas une
republique mignonne?*'— '*Ma foy, madame, je la trouve plus tôt la republique des rats et des souris,*'* replies the fellow, who had not slept all
night, I afterwards understood, for the noise those troublesome
animals made in his room.

4. REVOLUTIONARY TOURISM

ARTHUR YOUNG, *Travels, during the Years 1787, 1788 and
1789. Undertaken more particularly with a View of ascertaining
the Cultivation, Wealth, Resources and National Prosperity, of
the Kingdom of France* (1792)

Arthur Young (1741–1820), experimental farmer and agricultural writer,
made his reputation with a series of travel books assessing economic conditions in the countryside of England and Ireland (1768–80). His visits to

France coincided with the crisis of the old regime and the outbreak of revolution.

BRITTANY: 28–31 AUGUST 1788. The 28th, return to Carentan; and the 29th, pass through a rich and thickly enclosed country, to Coutances, capital of the district called the Cotentin. They build in this country the best mud houses and barns I ever saw, excellent habitations, even of three stories, and all of mud, with considerable barns and other offices. The earth (the best for the purpose is a rich brown loam) is well kneaded with straw; and being spread about four inches thick on the ground, is cut in squares of nine inches, and these are taken with a shovel and tossed to the man on the wall who builds it; and the wall built, as in Ireland, in layers, each three feet high, that it may dry before they advance. The thickness about two feet. They make them project about an inch, which they cut off layer by layer perfectly smooth. If they had the English way of whitewashing, they would look as well as our lath and plaster, and are much more durable. In good houses the doors and windows are in stone work.—20 miles.

The 30th. A fine sea view of the Isles of Chausée, at five leagues distant; and afterwards Jersey, clear at about forty miles, with that of the town of Grandval* on a high peninsula: entering the town, every idea of beauty is lost; a close, nasty, ugly, ill built hole: market day, and myriads of triflers, common at a French market. The bay of Cancalle, all along to the right, and St Michael's rock rising out of the sea, conically, with a castle on the top, a most singular and picturesque object.—30 miles.

The 31st. At Pont Orsin, enter Bretagne; there seems here a more minute division of farms than before. There is a long street in the episcopal town of Doll, without a glass window; a horrid appearance. My entry into Bretagne gives me an idea of its being a miserable province.—22 miles.

1 SEPTEMBER. To Combourg, the country has a savage aspect; husbandry not much further advanced, at least in skill, than among the Hurons, which appears incredible amidst inclosures; the people almost as wild as their country, and their town of Combourg one of the most brutal filthy places that can be seen; mud houses, no windows, and a pavement so broken as to impede all passengers, but ease none—yet here is a chateau, and inhabited; who is this Mons. de

Chateaubriant,* the owner, that has nerves strung for a residence amidst such filth and poverty? Below this hideous heap of wretchedness is a fine lake, surrounded by well wooded enclosures. Coming out of Hedé, there is a beautiful lake belonging to Mons. de Blassac, intendant of Poictiers, with a fine accompaniment of wood. A very little cleaning would make here a delicious scenery. There is a chateau, with four rows of trees, and nothing else to be seen from the windows in the true French style. Forbid it, taste, that this should be the house of the owner of that beautiful water; and yet this Mons. de Blassac has made at Poictiers the finest promenade in France! But that taste which draws a straight line, and that which traces a waving one, are founded on feelings and ideas as separate and distinct as painting and music—as poetry or sculpture. The lake abounds with fish, pike to 36lb. carp to 24lb. perch 4lb. and tench 5lb. To Rennes the same strange wild mixture of desert and cultivation, half savage, half human.—31 miles.

PARIS: 8–9 JUNE 1789. In this dilemma it is curious to remark the *feelings* of the moment. It is not my business to write memoirs of what passes, but I am intent to catch, as well as I can, the opinions of the day most prevalent. While I remain at Paris, I shall see people of all descriptions, from the coffee-house politicians to the leaders in the states; and the chief object of such rapid notes as I throw on paper will be to catch the ideas of the moment; to compare them afterwards with the actual events that shall happen, will afford amusement at least. The most prominent feature that appears at present is that an idea of common interest and common danger does not seem to unite those who, if not united, may find themselves too weak to oppose the common danger that must arise from the people being sensible of a strength the result of *their* weakness. The king, court, nobility, clergy, army, and parliament, are nearly in the same situation. All these consider, with equal dread, the ideas of liberty, now afloat; except the first, who, for reasons obvious to those who know his character, troubles himself little, even with circumstances that concern his power the most intimately. Among the rest, the feeling of danger is common, and they would unite, were there a head to render it easy, in order to do without the states at all. That the commons themselves look for some such hostile union as more than probable appears from an idea which gains ground, that they will find it necessary should the other two orders continue to unite with them in one chamber, to declare themselves boldly the representatives of the kingdom at large, calling on the nobility and clergy to take their places—and to enter upon deliberations of business without them, should they refuse it. All conversation at present is on this topic, but opinions are more divided than I should have expected. There seem to be many who hate the clergy so cordially that rather than permit them to form a distinct chamber would venture on a new system, dangerous as it might prove.

The 9th. The business going forward at present in the pamphlet shops of Paris is incredible. I went to the Palais Royal to see what new things were published, and to procure a catalogue of all. Every hour produces something new. Thirteen came out today, sixteen yesterday, and ninety-two last week. We think sometimes that Debrett's or Stockdale's shops at London are crowded, but they are mere deserts, compared to Desein's, and some others here, in which one can scarcely squeeze from the door to the counter. The price of printing two years ago was from 27 liv. to 30 liv. per sheet, but now it is from 60 liv. to 80 liv. This spirit of reading political tracts, they say, spreads into the provinces, so that all the presses of France are equally employed. Nineteen-twentieths of these productions are in favour of liberty, and commonly violent against the clergy and nobility; I have today bespoke many of this description that have reputation; but enquiring for such as had appeared on the other side of the question, to my astonishment I find there are but two or three that have merit enough to be known. Is it not wonderful, that while the press teems with the most levelling and even seditious principles, that if put in execution would overturn the monarchy, nothing in reply appears, and not the least step is taken by the court to restrain this extreme licentiousness of publication. It is easy to conceive the spirit that must thus be raised among the people. But the coffee-houses in the Palais Royal present yet more singular and astonishing spectacles; they are not only crowded within, but other expectant crowds are at the doors and windows, listening *à gorge deployé** to certain orators, who from chairs or tables harangue each his little audience: the eagerness with which they are heard, and the thunder of applause they receive for every sentiment of more than common hardiness or violence against the present government, cannot easily be imagined. I am all amazement at the ministry permitting such nests and hot-beds of sedition and revolt, which disseminate amongst the people, every hour, principles that by and by must be opposed with vigour, and therefore it seems little short of madness to allow the propagation at present.

MARS-LA-TOUR: 12 JULY 1789. Walking up a long hill, to ease my mare, I was joined by a poor woman, who complained of the times, and that it was a sad country; demanding her reasons, she said her husband had but a morsel of land, one cow, and a poor little horse, yet they had a *franchar* (42 lb.) of wheat, and three chickens, to pay as a quit-rent to one Seigneur; and four *franchar* of oats, one chicken and 1*s.* to pay to another, besides very heavy tailles and other taxes. She had seven children, and the cow's milk helped to make the soup. But why, instead of a horse, do not you keep another cow? Oh, her husband could not carry his produce so well without a horse; and asses are little used in the country. It was said, at present, that something was to be done by some great folks for such poor ones, but she did not know who nor how, but God send us better, *car les tailles et les droits nous écrasent:**—This woman, at no great distance might have been taken for sixty or seventy, her figure was so bent, and her face so furrowed and hardened by labour—but she said she was only twenty-eight. An Englishman who has not travelled cannot imagine the figure made by infinitely the greater part of the countrywomen in France; it speaks, at the first sight, hard and severe labour: I am inclined to think that they work harder than the men, and this, united with the more miserable labour of bringing a new race of slaves into the world, destroys absolutely all symmetry of person and every feminine appearance. To what are we to attribute this difference in the manners of the lower people in the two kingdoms? To GOVERNMENT.—23 miles.

STRASBOURG: 21 JULY 1789. *Night*—I have been witness to a scene curious to a foreigner; but dreadful to Frenchmen that are considerate. Passing through the square of the *hotel de ville,** the mob were breaking the windows with stones, notwithstanding an officer and a detachment of horse was in the square. Perceiving that their numbers not only increased, but that they grew bolder and bolder every moment, I thought it worth staying to see what it would end in, and clambered on to the roof of a row of low stalls opposite the building, against which their malice was directed. Here I beheld the whole commodiously. Perceiving that the troops would not attack them, except in words and menaces, they grew more violent, and furiously attempted to beat the door in pieces with iron crows; placing ladders to the windows. In about a quarter of an hour, which gave time for the assembled magistrates to escape by a back door, they burst all open, and entered like a torrent with a universal shout of the spectators. From that minute a shower of casements, sashes, shutters, chairs, tables, sofas, books, papers, pictures, etc., rained incessantly from all the windows of the house, which is seventy or eighty feet long, and which was then succeeded by tiles, skirting boards, bannisters, frame-work, and every part of the building that force could detach. The troops, both horse and foot, were quiet spectators. They were at first too few to interpose, and, when they became more numerous, the mischief was too far advanced to admit of any other conduct than guarding every avenue around, permitting none to go to the scene of action, but letting every one that pleased retire with his plunder; guards being at the same time placed at the doors of the churches, and all public buildings. I was for two hours a spectator at different places of the scene, secure myself from the falling furniture, but near enough to see a fine lad of about 14 crushed to death by something as he was handing plunder to a woman, I suppose his mother, from the horror pictured in her countenance. I remarked several common soldiers, with their white cockades, among the plunderers, and instigating the mob even in sight of the officers of the detachment. There were amongst them people so decently dressed, that I regarded them with no small surprise: they destroyed all the public archives; the streets for some way around strewed with papers; this has been a wanton mischief; for it will be the ruin of many families unconnected with the magistrates.

L'ISLE-SUR-LE-DOUBS: 26–7 JULY 1789. For twenty miles to Lisle sur Daube, the country nearly as before; but after that, to Baume les Dames, it is all mountainous and rock, much wood, and many pleasing scenes of the river flowing beneath. The whole country is in the greatest agitation; at one of the little towns I passed, I was questioned for not having a cockade of the *tiers etat.** They said it was ordained by the *tiers*, and, if I was not a Seigneur, I ought to obey. *But suppose I am a Seigneur, what then, my friends?*—What then? they replied sternly, why, be hanged; for that most likely is what you deserve. It was plain this was no moment for joking: the boys and girls began to gather, whose assembling has everywhere been the preliminaries of mischief; and if I had not declared myself an Englishman, and ignorant of the ordinance, I had not escaped very well. I immediately bought a cockade, but the hussy pinned it into my hat so loosely, that before I got to Lisle it blew into the river, and I was again in the same danger. My assertion of being English would not do. I was a Seigneur, perhaps in disguise, and without doubt a great rogue. At this moment a priest came into the street with a letter in his hand: the people immediately collected around him, and he then read aloud a detail from Befort, giving an account of M. Necker's passing,* with some general features of news from Paris, and assurances that the condition of the people would be improved. When he had finished, he exhorted them to abstain from all violence; and assured them they must not indulge themselves with any ideas of impositions being abolished; which he touched on as if he knew that they had got such notions. When he retired, they again surrounded me, who had attended to the letter like others; were very menacing in their manner; and expressed many suspicions: I did not like my situation at all, especially on hearing one of them say that I ought to be secured till somebody would give an account of me. I was on the steps of the inn, and begged they would permit me a few words; I assured them, that I was an English traveller, and to prove it, I desired to explain to them a circumstance in English taxation, which would be a satisfactory comment on what Mons. l'Abbé had told them, to the purport of which I could not agree. He had asserted that the impositions must be paid as heretofore: that the impositions must be paid was certain, but not as heretofore, as they might be paid as they were in England. Gentlemen, we have a great number of taxes in England, which you know nothing of in France; but the *tiers etat*, the poor do not pay them; they are laid on the rich; every window in a man's house pays; but if he has no more than six windows, he pays nothing; a Seigneur, with a great estate, pays the *vingtièmes* and *tailles*,* but the little proprietor of a garden pays nothing; the rich for their horses, their voitures, and their servants, and even for liberty to kill their own partridges, but the poor farmer nothing of all this: and what is more, we have in England a tax paid by the rich for the relief of the poor; hence the assertion of Mons. l'Abbé, that because taxes existed before they must exist again did not at all prove that they must be levied in the same manner; our English method seemed much better. There was not a word of this discourse they did not approve of; they seemed to think that I might be an honest fellow, which I confirmed, by crying, *vive le tiers, sans impositions,** when they gave me a bit of a huzza, and I had no more interruption from them. My miserable French was pretty much on a par with their own *patois*. I got, however, another cockade, which I took care to have so fastened as to lose it no more. I do not half like travelling in such an unquiet and fermenting moment; one is not secure for an hour beforehand.—35 miles.

The 27th. To Besançon; the country mountain, rock, and wood, above the river; some scenes are fine. I had not arrived an hour before I saw a peasant pass the inn on horseback, followed by an officer of the *guard bourgeois*, of which there are 1200 here, and 200 under arms, and his party-coloured detachment, and these by some infantry and cavalry. I asked why the militia took the *pas* of the king's troops? *For a very good reason*, they replied, *the troops would be attacked and knocked on the head, but the populace will not resist the milice.* This peasant, who is a rich proprietor, applied for a guard to protect his house, in a village where there is much plundering and burning. The mischiefs which have been perpetrated in the country, towards the mountains and Vesoul, are numerous and shocking. Many chateaus have been burnt, others plundered, the seigneurs hunted down like wild beasts, their wives and daughters ravished, their papers and titles burnt, and all their property destroyed: and these abominations not inflicted on marked persons, who were odious for their former conduct or principles, but an indiscriminating blind rage for the love of plunder. Robbers, galley-slaves, and villains of all denominations have collected and instigated the peasants to commit all sorts of outrages. Some gentlemen at the table d'hôte informed me that letters were received from the Maconais, the Lyonais, Auvergne, Dauphiné, etc. and that similar commotions and mischiefs were perpetrating every where; and that it was expected they would pervade the whole kingdom. The backwardness of France is beyond credibility in everything that pertains to intelligence. From Strasbourg hither, I have not been able to see a newspaper. Here I asked for the *Cabinet Littéraire*? None. The gazettes? At the coffee-house. Very easily replied; but not so easily found. Nothing but the *Gazette de France*; for which at this period, a man of common sense would not give one *sol*. To four other coffee-houses; at some no paper at all, not even the *Mercure*; at the Café Militaire, the *Courier de l'Europe* a fortnight old; and well dressed people are now talking of the news of two or three weeks past, and plainly by their discourse know nothing of what is passing. The whole town of Besançon has not been able to afford me a sight of the *Journal de Paris*, nor of any paper that gives a detail of the transactions of the states; yet it is the capital of a province, large as half a dozen English counties, and containing 25,000 souls—with strange to say! the post coming in but three times a week. At this eventful moment, with no licence, nor even the least restraint on the press, not one paper established at Paris for circulation in the provinces, with the necessary steps taken by *affiche*, or *placard*,* to inform the people in all the towns of its establishment. For what the country knows to the contrary, their deputies are in the Bastille, instead of the Bastille being razed; so the mob plunder, burn, and destroy, in complete ignorance: and yet, with all these shades of darkness, these clouds of tenebrity, this universal mass of ignorance, there are men every day in the states, who are puffing themselves off for the FIRST NATION IN EUROPE! the GREATEST PEOPLE IN THE UNIVERSE! as if the political juntos or literary circles of a capital constituted a people; instead of the universal illumination of knowledge, acting by rapid intelligence on minds prepared by habitual energy of reasoning to receive, combine, and comprehend it. That this dreadful ignorance of the mass of the people, of the events that most intimately concern them, is owing to the old government, no one can doubt; it is however curious to remark that, if the nobility of other provinces are hunted like those of Franche Compté, of which there is little reason to doubt, that whole order of men undergo a proscription, suffer like sheep, without making the least effort to resist the attack.

HELEN MARIA WILLIAMS, *Letters from France* (1790–1796)

Helen Maria Williams (1761–1827), poet and dissenter, shared the euphoria with which most liberal Britons greeted the French Revolution. Accompanied by her sister Cecilia, she travelled to Paris in July 1790 to witness the anniversary celebrations of the fall of the Bastille. Over the next few years Williams published a series of *Letters from France* extolling the Revolution in the teeth of increasing British hostility. Following the execution of Louis XVI and the onset of war with Britain (1793), Williams saw her Girondist (moderate) friends outmanœuvred and persecuted by the rival Jacobin party. After a spell in prison she fled with her family to Switzerland in June 1794. Williams's subsequent volumes of letters deplore the Jacobin Terror as a betrayal of the Revolution's founding principles, which she continued to defend.

Letters Written in France, in the Summer 1790, to a Friend in England.
Containing Various Anecdotes Relative to the French Revolution; and
Memoirs of Mons. and Madame de F— (1790), Letter II

I promised to send you a description of the Federation;* but it is not to be described! One must have been present, to form any judgment of a scene, the sublimity of which depended much less on its external magnificence than on the effect it produced on the minds of the spectators. 'The people, sure, the people were the sight!'* I may tell you of pavilions, of triumphal arches, of altars on which incense was burnt, of two hundred thousand men walking in procession; but how am I to give you an adequate idea of the behaviour of the spectators? How am I to paint the impetuous feelings of that immense, that exulting multitude? Half a million of people assembled at a spectacle which furnished every image that can elevate the mind of man; which connected the enthusiasm of moral sentiment with the solemn pomp of religious ceremonies; which addressed itself at once to the imagination, the understanding, and the heart.

The Champ de Mars* was formed into an immense amphitheatre round which were erected forty rows of seats, raised one above another with earth, on which wooden forms were placed. Twenty days labour, animated by the enthusiasm of the people, accomplished what seemed to require the toil of years. Already in the Champ de Mars the distinctions of rank were forgotten; and, inspired by the same spirit, the highest and lowest orders of citizens gloried in taking up the spade, and assisting the persons employed in a work on which the common welfare of the State depended. Ladies took the instruments of labour in their hands, and removed a little of the earth, that they might be able to boast that they also had assisted in the preparations at the Champ de Mars; and a number of old soldiers were seen voluntarily bestowing on their country the last remains of their strength . . .

In the streets, at the windows, and on the roofs of the houses, the people, transported with joy, shouted and wept as the procession passed. Old men were seen kneeling in the streets, blessing God that they had lived to witness that happy moment. The people ran to the doors of their houses, loaded with refreshments, which they offered to the troops; and crowds of women surrounded the soldiers, and holding up their infants in their arms, and melting into tears, promised to make their children imbibe, from their earliest age, an inviolable attachment to the principles of the new constitution. . . .

The procession, which was formed with eight persons abreast, entered the Champ de Mars beneath the triumphal arches, with a discharge of cannon. The deputies placed themselves round the inside of the amphitheatre. Between them and the seats of the spectators, the national guard of Paris were ranged; and the seats round the amphitheatre were filled with four hundred thousand people. The middle of the amphitheatre was crowded with an immense multitude of soldiers. The National Assembly* walked towards the pavilion, where they placed themselves with the King, the Queen, the Royal Family, and their attendants; and opposite this group, rose in perspective the hills of Passy and Chaillot, covered with people. The standards, of which one was presented to each department of the kingdom, as a mark of brotherhood, by the citizens of Paris, were carried to the altar, to be consecrated by the bishop. High mass was performed, after which Mons. de la Fayette,* who had been appointed by the king Major-General of the Federation, ascended the altar, gave the signal, and himself took the national oath. In an instant every sword was drawn, and every arm lifted up. The King pronounced the oath, which the President of the National Assembly repeated, and the solemn words were re-echoed by six hundred thousand voices; while the Queen raised the Dauphin* in her arms, showing him to the people and the army. At the moment the consecrated banners were obscured, the sun, which had been displayed, by frequent showers in the course of the morning, burst forth; while the people lifted their eyes to heaven, and called upon the Deity to look down and witness the sacred engagement into which they entered. A respectful silence was succeeded by the cries, the shouts, the acclamations of the multitude: they wept, they embraced each other, and then dispersed.

You will not suspect that I was an indifferent witness of such a scene. Oh, no! this was not a time in which the distinctions of country were remembered. (It was the triumph of humankind; it was man asserting the noblest privilege of his nature; and it required but the common feelings of humanity, to become in that moment a citizen of the world.) For myself, I acknowledge that my heart caught with enthusiasm the general sympathy; my eyes were filled with tears: and I shall never forget the sensations of that day, 'while memory holds her seat in my bosom'.*

The weather proved very unfavourable during the morning of the Federation; but the minds of the people were too much elevated by ideas of moral good, to attend to the physical evils of the day. Several heavy showers were far from interrupting the general gaiety. The people, when drenched by the rain, called out, with exultation, rather than regret, 'Nous sommes mouillés à la nation.'* Some exclaimed, 'La révolution Française est cimentée avec de l'eau, au lieu de sang.'* The national guard, during the hours which preceded the arrival of the procession, amused the spectators *d'une danse ronde*,* and with a thousand whimsical and playful evolutions, highly expressive of that gaiety which distinguishes the French character. I believe none but Frenchmen would have diverted themselves, and half a million of people who were waiting in expectation of a scene the most solemn upon record, by circles of ten thousand men galloping *en danse ronde*. But if you are disposed to think of this gaiety with the contempt of superior gravity, for I will not call it wisdom, recollect that these dancers were the very men whose bravery formed the great epocha of French liberty; the heroes who demolished the towers of the Bastille, and whose fame will descend to the latest posterity.

Such was the admirable order with which this august spectacle was conducted, that no accident interrupted the universal festivity. All carriages were forbidden during that day, and the entrances to the Champ de Mars were so numerous that half a million of people were collected together without a crowd.

Letter IV

Before I suffered my friends at Paris to conduct me through the usual routine of convents, churches, and palaces, I requested to visit the Bastille;* feeling a much stronger desire to contemplate the ruins of that building than the most perfect edifices of Paris. When we got into the carriage, our French servant called to the coachman, with an air of triumph, 'A la Bastille—mais nous n'y resterons pas.'* We drove under that porch which so many wretches have entered never to repass, and, alighting from the carriage, descended with difficulty into the dungeons, which were too low to admit of our standing upright, and so dark that we were obliged at noon-day to visit them with the light of a candle. We saw the hooks of those chains by which the prisoners were fastened, round the neck, to the walls of their cells; many of which, being below the level of the water, are in a constant state of humidity; and a noxious vapour issued from them, which more than once extinguished the candle, and was so insufferable that it required a strong spirit of curiosity to tempt one to enter. Good God! And to these regions of horror were human creatures dragged at the caprice of despotic power. What a melancholy consideration, that

> Man! proud man,
> Dressed in a little brief authority,
> Plays such fantastic tricks before high heaven,
> As make the angels weep.*

There appears to be a greater number of these dungeons than one could have imagined the hard heart of tyranny itself would contrive; for, since the destruction of the building, many subterraneous cells have been discovered underneath a piece of ground which was enclosed within the walls of the Bastille, but which seemed a bank of solid earth before the horrid secrets of this prison-house were disclosed. Some skeletons were found in these recesses, with irons still fastened on their decaying bones.

After having visited the Bastille, we may indeed be surprised that a nation so enlightened as the French submitted so long to the oppressions of their government; but we must cease to wonder that their indignant spirits at length shook off the galling yoke.

Those who have contemplated the dungeons of the Bastille, without rejoicing in the French revolution, may, for aught I know, be very respectable persons, and very agreeable companions in the hours of prosperity; but if my heart were sinking with anguish, I should not fly to those persons for consolation. Sterne says* that a man is incapable of loving one woman as he ought who has not a sort of an affection for the whole sex; and as little should I look for particular sympathy from those who have no feelings of general philanthropy.

If the splendour of a despotic throne can only shine like the radiance of lightning, while all around is involved in gloom and horror, in the name of heaven let its baleful lustre be extinguished forever. May no such strong contrast of light and shade again exist in the political system of France! But may the beams of liberty, like the beams of day, shed their benign influence on the cottage of the peasant, as well as on the palace of the monarch! May Liberty, which for so many ages past has taken pleasure in softening the evils of the bleak and rugged climates of the North, in fertilizing a barren soil, in clearing the swamp, in lifting mounds against the inundations of the tempest, diffuse her blessings also on the genial land of France, and bid the husbandman rejoice under the shade of the olive and the vine!

Letters Containing a Sketch of the Politics of France, From the Thirty-first of May 1793, till the twenty-eighth of July 1794, and of the Scenes which have Passed in the Prisons of Paris (1795), *Letter I*

Williams and her mother and sister were imprisoned in October 1793, in the state of emergency that followed the assassination of Marat, but released the following month. In April 1794 the Committee of Public Safety issued a decree expelling foreigners from the capital.

While far along the moral horizon of France the tempest became every hour more black and turbulent, the spring, earlier and more profuse of graces than in the climate of England, arose in its unsullied freshness, and formed a contrast at which humanity sickened. The lovely environs of Paris are not, like those of London, so encumbered with houses and buildings that you must travel ten or twelve miles from town to find the country, but, the moment you have passed the barriers of the city, present you with all the charming variety of vine-clad hills, and fields, and woods, and lawns. Immediately after our release from prison we quitted our apartments in the centre of the town, and tried to shelter ourselves from observation in an habitation situated in the most remote part of the faubourg Germain. From thence a few minutes' walk led us to the country. But we no longer dared, as we had done the preceding year, to forget awhile the horrors of our situation by wandering occasionally amidst the noble parks of St Cloud, the wild woods of Meudon, or the elegant gardens of Bellevue, all within an hour's ride of Paris. Those seats, once the residence of fallen royalty, were now haunted by vulgar despots, by revolutionary commissaries, by spies of the

police, and sometimes by the sanguinary decemvirs* themselves.
Often they held their festive orgies in those scenes of beauty, where
they dared to cast their polluting glance on nature, and tread with
profane steps her hallowed recesses. Even the revolutionary jury
used sometimes on a decade,* the only day of suspension from their
work of death, to go to Marly or Versailles; and, steeped as they were
to the very lips in blood, without being haunted by the mangled
spectres of those whom they had murdered the preceding day, they
saw nature in her most benign aspect, pleading the cause of humanity and mercy, and returned to feast upon the groans of those whom
they were to murder on the morrow.

Those regions of decorated beauty being now forbidden ground,
we confined our walks to some pasturage lands near the town, which
were interspersed with a few scattered hamlets, and skirted by hills,
and were so unfrequented that we heard no sounds except the sheep-
bell, and the nightingales, and saw no human figure but an old peasant with a white beard, who together with a large black dog took care
of the flock. It was in these walks that the soul, which the scenes of
Paris petrified with terror, melted at the view of the soothing landscape, and that the eye was lifted up to heaven with tears of resignation mingled with hope. I have no words to paint the strong feeling
of reluctance with which I always returned from our walks to Paris,
that den of carnage, that slaughter-house of man. How I envied the
peasant his lonely hut! For I had now almost lost the idea of social
happiness. My disturbed imagination divided the communities of
men but into two classes, the oppressor and the oppressed; and peace
seemed only to exist with solitude.

On the 15th of Germinal* (the beginning of April), the committee
of public safety,* or rather of public extermination, caused a law to
be passed, ordering all the former nobility and strangers to leave Paris
within ten days, under the penalty of being put out of the law; which
meant that, if found in Paris after that period, they were to be led to
the scaffold without a trial, as soon as their persons were identified.
This law, to which my family and myself were subject, was a part of
the plan of general proscription that Robespierre had formed against
nobles and foreigners and which he was now impatient to put in
force. We were ordered by the decree, after choosing the place of our
retreat, to present ourselves at the revolutionary committee of our
respective sections, who delivered to each of us not a passport, but

what was called a pass, on which was written a declaration that we left Paris in conformity to the law of the 26th of Germinal. Thus were we condemned to wander into the country with this pass, which was the mark of Cain* upon our foreheads, and which under pain of imprisonment we were to deposit at the municipality where we bent our course; and we were also condemned to present ourselves every twenty-four hours before the municipality and inscribe our names on a list, which was to be dispatched every decade to the committee of public safety. And lest the country municipalities should mistake the intentions of the committee, and treat particular individuals with lenity upon their producing testimonies of their attachment to the cause of the revolution, these devoted victims were ordered by a decree to burn every certificate of civism* of which they might happen to be in possession. We chose for the place of our retreat a little village half a mile distant from Marly, and with hearts overwhelmed with anguish bade adieu to my sister, who, being married to a Frenchman, was exempted from the law; and we were once more driven from our home, not to return under the penalty of death. Our neighbours came weeping to our gate to take leave of us; and the poor, who were the only class which now dared to utter a complaint, murmured loudly at the injustice of the decree. We were obliged to pass the square of the revolution, where we saw the guillotine erected, the crowd assembled for the bloody tragedy, and the gens d'armes on horseback, followed by victims who were to be sacrificed, entering the square. Such was the daily spectacle which had succeeded the painted shows, the itinerant theatres, the mountebank, the dance, the song, the shifting scenes of harmless gaiety, which used to attract the cheerful crowd as they passed from the Tuilleries to the Champs Elysées.

When we reached the barrier we were stopped by a concourse of carriages filled with former nobles, and were obliged to wait till our passes were examined in our turn. The procession at the gate was singular and affecting. Most of the fugitives having, like ourselves, deferred their departure till the last day, and it being the forfeiture of our heads to be found in Paris the day following, the demand for carriages was so great, and the price exacted by those who let them out, and who knew the urgency of the case, so exorbitant, that a coach or chariot was a luxury which fell only to the lot of a favoured few. The greater number were furnished with cabriolets,* which seemed from their tottering condition somewhat emblematical of decayed nobility; and many who found even these crazy vehicles too costly, journeyed in the carts which transported their furniture, seated upon the chairs they were conveying to their new abodes.

We reached our little dwelling at the hour of sunset. The hills were fringed with clouds, which still reflected the fading colours of the day; the woods were in deep shadow; a soft veil was thrown over nature, and objects indistinctly seen were decorated by imagination with those graces which were most congenial to the feelings of the moment. The air was full of delicious fragrance, and the stillness of the scene was only disturbed by sounds the most soothing in nature, the soft rustling of the leaves, or the plaintive notes of the wood-pigeon. The tears which the spectacle of the guillotine had petrified with horror, now flowed again with melancholy luxury. Our habitation was situated within a few paces of the noble park of Marly; and the deserted alleys overgrown with long grass—the encumbering fragments of rock, over which once fell the mimic cascades, whose streams no longer murmur—the piles of marble which once formed the bed of crystal basins—the scattered machinery of the jets d'eaux, whose sources are dried—the fallen statues—the defaced symbols of feudality—the weeds springing between the stone steps of the ascent to the deserted palace—the cobwebbed windows of the gay pavilions, were all in union with that pensiveness of mind which our present circumstances naturally excited. And here, where we could see nothing of Paris but the distant dome of the Pantheon, we should have been less unhappy, if we had not too well known that the committee of public safety had not sent nobles and foreigners into the country to enjoy the freshness of rural gales, or the beauty of the opening spring, but as the first step towards a general proscription; and as we passed every evening through the park of Marly, in order to appear before the municipality, that appalling idea 'breathed a browner horror over the woods'.* We were again rescued from the general danger by the two benevolent commissaries of the revolutionary committee of our section, who when they came to conduct us to prison had treated us with so much gentleness, who had afterwards reclaimed us of the administration of police, and who now, unsolicited and even unasked, went to the committee of public safety, declared they would answer for us with their lives, and caused us to be put into requisition; a form which enabled us to return to

Paris, and thus snatched us from the class of the suspected and the proscribed. To their humanity we probably owe our existence; and I shall ever recollect with gratitude that noble courage which led them amidst the cruel impulse of revolutionary government, the move-ment of which was accelerated as it went on, to pause and succour the unfortunate.

ANN RADCLIFFE, *A Journey made in the Summer of 1794, through Holland and the Western Frontier of Germany, with a Return down the Rhine* (1795)

Ann Radcliffe (1764–1823) became famous for her Gothic romances set in France and Italy, adorned with lavish descriptions of sublime landscape. Radcliffe's tour through Holland and Germany, her first trip abroad, coincided with the publication of her masterpiece *The Mysteries of Udolpho* (1794). She and her husband William travelled as far as Mainz, intending to reach Switzerland, but were forced to turn back by obstructive officials. As they retrace their route down the Rhine, the travellers find themselves hurrying to escape the tide of war between France and the Dutch and Austrian allies, in a nocturnal voyage that might have featured in one of Radcliffe's own novels.

Cologne

Now we began to experience the inconveniences of its neighbour-hood to the seat of war, some of which had appeared at Bonn from the arrival of families who could not be lodged in the former place. We were no sooner within the gates than the throng of people and carriages in a city, which only a few weeks before was almost as silent as gloomy, convinced us we should not find a very easy welcome. The sentinels, when they made the usual enquiry as to our inn, assured us that there had been no lodgings at the Hotel de Prague for several days, and one of them followed us, to see what others we should find. Through many obstructions by military and other carriages, we, however, reached this inn, and were soon convinced that there could be no room, the landlord showing us the chaises in which some of his guests slept, and his billiard table already laden with beds for others. There was so much confusion meanwhile in the adjoining square that, upon a slight assurance, we could have believed the French to be within a few miles of the city, and have taken refuge on the opposite bank of the Rhine.

At length, our host told us that what he believed to be the worst room in the place was still vacant, but might not be so half an hour longer. We followed his man to it, in a distant part of the city, and saw enough in our way of parties taking refreshment in carriages, and gentlemen carrying their own baggage, to make us contented with a viler cabin than any person can have an idea of, who has not been out of England. The next morning we heard from the mistress of it how fortunately we had been situated, two or three families having passed the night in the open market-place, and great numbers in their carriages.

The occasion of this excessive pressure upon Cologne was the entry of the French into Brussels,* their advances towards Liege, and the immediate prospect of the siege of Maestricht, all which had dispeopled an immense tract of territory of its wealthier inhabitants, and driven them, together with the French emigrants, upon the confines of Holland and Germany. The Austrian hospitals having been removed from Maestricht, five hundred waggons, laden with sick and wounded, had passed through Cologne the day before. The carriages on the roads from Maestricht and Liege were almost as close as in a procession, and at Aix la Chapelle, where these roads meet, there was an obstruction for some hours. While we were at Cologne, another detachment of hospital waggons arrived, some hundreds of which we had the misfortune to see, for they passed before our window. They were all uncovered, so that the emaciated figures and ghastly countenances of the soldiers, laid out upon straw in each, were exposed to the rays of a burning sun, as well as to the fruitless pity of passengers; and, as the carriages had no springs, it seemed as if these half-sacrificed victims to war would expire before they could be drawn over the rugged pavement of Cologne. Any person who had once witnessed such a sight, would know how to estimate the glories of war, even though there should be a mercenary at every corner to insult his unavoidable feelings and the eternal sacredness of peace with the slander of disaffection to his country.

We had some thoughts of resuming our course by land from this place, but were now convinced that it was impracticable, seeing the number of post-horses which were engaged, and judging of the crowds of travellers, that must fill the inns on the road. Our watermen from Mainz were, however, not allowed to proceed lower, so that we had to comply with the extortions of others, and to give nine louis for a boat from Cologne to Nijmegen. Having, not without some difficulty, obtained this, and stored it with provisions, we again embarked on the Rhine, rejoicing that we were not, for a second night, to make part of the crowd on shore.

Cologne, viewed from the river, appears with more of ancient majesty than from any other point. Its quays, extending far along the bank, its lofty ramparts, shaded with old chestnuts, and crowned by many massy towers, black with age; the old gateways opening to the Rhine, and the crowd of steeples, overtopping all, give it a venerable and picturesque character. But, however thronged the city now was, the shore without was silent and almost deserted; the sentinels, watching at the gates and looking out from the ramparts, or a few women gliding beneath, wrapped in the nun-like scarf, so melancholy in its appearance and so generally worn at Cologne, were nearly the only persons seen.

The shores, though here flat, when compared with those to the southward, are high enough to obstruct the view of the distant mountains, that rise in the east; in the south, the wild summits of those near Bonn were yet visible, but, after this faint glimpse, we saw them no more.

About two miles below Cologne, the west bank of the Rhine was covered with hospital waggons and with troops, removed from them, for the purpose of crossing the river, to a mansion converted by the Elector into an hospital. About a mile lower, but on the opposite bank, is Muhlheim, a small town in the dominions of the Elector Palatine, which, in the beginning of the present century, was likely to become a rival of Cologne. A persecution of the Protestant merchants of the latter place drove them to Muhlheim, where they erected a staple, and began to trade with many advantages over the mother city; but the pusillanimity of the Elector Palatine permitted them to sink under the jealousy of the Colonese merchants; their engines for removing heavy goods from vessels to the shore were ordered to be demolished; and the commerce of the place has since consisted chiefly in the exportation of grain. . .

After Dormagen, a small town very slightly provided with the means of benefiting itself by the river, we came opposite to Zons, the fortifications of which are so far preserved, as that the boatmen on the Rhine are required to stop before them and give an account of their cargoes.

We were listening to an old French song, and had almost forgotten the chance of interruption from any abuses of power, when the steersman called to us in a low, but eager voice, and enquired whether we would permit him to attempt passing the castle, where, if we landed, we might probably be detained an hour, or, if the officer was at supper, for the whole night. By the help of twilight and our silence, he thought it possible to glide unnoticed under the opposite bank, or that we should be in very little danger, if the sentinels should obey their order for firing upon all vessels that might attempt to pass. The insolent tediousness of a German custom-house, and the probable wretchedness of inns at such a place as this, determined us in favour of the man's proposal; we were silent for a quarter of an hour; the men withheld their oars; and the watchful garrison of Zons saw us not, or did not think a boat of two tons burthen could be laden with an army for the conquest of Germany.

CHARLOTTE ANNE EATON, *Narrative of a Residence in Belgium during the Campaign of 1815; and of a Visit to the Field of Waterloo, by an Englishwoman* (1817)

Charlotte Anne Eaton (née Waldie, 1788–1859), accompanied by her brother John and younger sister Jane, visited Waterloo on 15 July 1815, nearly a month after the defeat of Napoleon's army on 18 June by allied forces under the Duke of Wellington and Marshal Blücher. The field, still grisly with the remains of slaughter, is already turning into 'classical ground' to compare with Marathon or Philippi—and into a tourist attraction.

From the spot where we now stood I cast my eyes on every side, and saw nothing but the dreadful and recent traces of death and devastation. The rich harvests of standing corn, which had covered the scene of action we were contemplating, had been beaten into the earth, and the withered and broken stalks, dried in the sun, now presented the appearance of stubble, though blacker and far more bare than any stubble land.

In many places the excavations made by the shells had thrown up the earth all around them; the marks of horses' hoofs, that had plunged ankle deep in clay, were hardened in the sun; and the feet of men, deeply stamped into the ground, left traces where many a deadly struggle had been. The ground was ploughed up in several places with the charge of the cavalry, and the whole field was literally covered with soldiers' caps, shoes, gloves, belts, and scabbards, broken feathers battered into the mud, remnants of tattered scarlet cloth, bits of fur and leather, black stocks and haversacks, belonging to the French soldiers, buckles, packs of cards, books, and innumerable papers of every description. I picked up a volume of Candide;* a few sheets of sentimental love-letters, evidently belonging to some French novel; and many other pages of the same publication were flying over the field in much too muddy a state to be touched. One German Testament, not quite so dirty as many that were lying about, I carried with me nearly the whole day; printed French military returns, muster rolls, love-letters and washing bills; illegible songs, scattered sheets of military music, epistles without number in praise of 'l'Empereur, le Grand Napoléon', and filled with the most confident anticipations of victory under his command, were strewed over the field which had been the scene of his defeat. The quantities of letters and of blank sheets of dirty writing paper were so great that they literally whitened the surface of the earth.

The road to Genappe, descending from the front of the British position, where we were now standing, passes the farm-house of La Haye Sainte, and ascends the opposite height, on the summit of which stands 'La Belle Alliance', which was occupied by the French. We walked down the hill to La Haye Sainte—its walls and slated roofs were shattered and pierced through in every direction with cannon shot. We could not get admittance into it, for it was completely deserted by its inhabitants. Three wounded officers of the 42d and 92d regiments were standing here to survey the scene: they had all of them been wounded in the battle of the 16th. One of them had lost an arm, another was on crutches, and the third seemed to be very ill. Their carriage waited for them, as they were unable to walk. After some conversation with them, we proceeded up the hill to the hamlet of La Belle Alliance. The principal house on the left side of the road was pierced through and through with cannon balls, and the offices behind it wore a heap of dust from the fire of the British artillery. Notwithstanding the ruinous state of the house, it was filled with inhabitants. Its broken walls, 'its looped and windowed wretchedness', might indeed defend them sufficiently well 'from seasons such as these', when the soft breezes and the bright beams of summer played around it—but against 'the pelting of the storm',* it would afford them but a sorry shelter. It was immediately to be repaired; but I rejoiced that it yet remained in its dilapidated state.

The house was filled with vestiges of the battle. Cuirasses, helmets, swords, bayonets, feathers, brass eagles, and crosses of the Legion of Honour, were to be purchased here. The house consisted of three rooms, two in front, and a very small one behind. On the opposite side of the road is a little cottage, forming part of the hamlet of La Belle Alliance; and at a short distance, by the way side, is another low-roofed cottage, which was pointed out to us as the place where Buonaparte breakfasted on the morning of the battle. Farther along this road, but not in sight, was the village of Planchenoit, which was the headquarters of the French on the night of the 17th.

We crossed the field from this place to Château Hougoumont, descending to the bottom of the hill, and again ascending the opposite side. Part of our way lay through clover; but I observed that the corn on the French position was not nearly so much beaten down as on the English, which might naturally be expected, as they attacked us incessantly, and we acted on the defensive, until that last, general, and decisive charge of our whole army was made, before which theirs fled in confusion. In some places patches of corn nearly as high as myself were standing. Among them I discovered many a forgotten grave, strewed round with melancholy remnants of military attire. While I loitered behind the rest of the party, searching among the corn for some relics worthy of preservation, I beheld a human hand, almost reduced to a skeleton, outstretched above the ground, as if it had raised itself from the grave. My blood ran cold with horror, and for some moments I stood rooted to the spot, unable to take my eyes from this dreadful object, or to move away: as soon as I recovered myself, I hastened after my companions, who were far before me, and overtook them just as they entered the wood of Hougoumont. Never shall I forget the dreadful scene of death and destruction which it presented. The broken branches were strewed around; the green beech leaves fallen before their time, and stripped by the storm of war, not by the storm of nature, were scattered over the surface of the ground, emblematical of the fate of the thousands who had fallen on the same spot in the summer of their days. The return of spring will dress the wood of Hougoumont once more in vernal beauty, and succeeding years will see it flourish:

> But when shall spring visit the mouldering urn,
> Oh! when shall it dawn on the night of the grave!*

The trunks of the trees had been pierced in every direction with cannon-balls. In some of them, I counted the holes where upwards of thirty had lodged: yet they still lived, they still bore their verdant foliage, and the birds still sang amidst their boughs. Beneath their shade, the harebell and violet were waving their slender heads; and the wild raspberry at their roots was ripening its fruit. I gathered some of it with the bitter reflection that amidst the destruction of human life these worthless weeds and flowers had escaped uninjured. . . .

Melancholy were the vestiges of death that continually met our eyes. The carnage here had indeed been dreadful. Amongst the long grass lay remains of broken arms, shreds of gold lace, torn epaulets, and pieces of cartridge-boxes; and upon the tangled branches of the brambles fluttered many a tattered remnant of a soldier's coat. At the outskirts of the wood, and around the ruined walls of the Château, huge piles of human ashes were heaped up, some of which were still smoking. The countrymen told us that, so great were the numbers of the slain, that it was impossible entirely to consume them. Pits had been dug, into which they had been thrown, but they were obliged to be raised far above the surface of the ground. These dreadful heaps were covered with piles of wood, which were set on fire, so that underneath the ashes lay numbers of human bodies unconsumed. . . .

At the garden gate I found the holster of a British officer, entire, but deluged with blood. In the inside was the maker's name, Beazley and Hetse, No. 4, Parliament-street. All around were strewed torn epaulets, broken scabbards, and sabretaches stained and stiffened with blood—proofs how dreadfully the battle had raged. The garden and courts were lined during the engagement with Nassau troops,* as sharpshooters, who did great execution.

A poor countryman, with his wife and children, inhabited a miserable shed amongst these deserted ruins. This unfortunate family had only fled from the spot on the morning of the battle. Their little dwelling had been burnt, and all their property had perished in the flames. They had scarcely clothes to cover them, and were destitute of everything. Yet the poor woman, as she told me the story of their distresses, and wept over the baby that she clasped to her breast, blessed heaven that she had preserved her children. She seemed most grateful for a little assistance, took me into her miserable habitation, and gave me the broken sword of a British officer of infantry (most probably of the Guards) which was the only thing she had left; and which, with some other relics before collected, I preserved as carefully as if they had been the most valuable treasures.

It is a remarkable circumstance that amidst this scene of destruction, and surrounded on all sides by the shattered walls and smoking piles of 'this ruined and roofless abode',* the little chapel belonging to the Château stood uninjured. Its preservation appeared to these simple peasants an unquestionable miracle; and we felt more inclined to respect than to wonder at the superstitious veneration with which they regarded it. No shot nor shell had penetrated its consecrated walls; no sacrilegious hand had dared to violate its humble altar, which was still adorned with its ancient ornaments and its customary care. A type of that blessed religion to which it was consecrated, it stood alone, unchanged, amidst the wreck of earthly greatness—as if to speak to our hearts, amidst the horrors of the tomb, the promises of immortality; and to recall our thoughts from the crimes and sorrows of earth to the hopes and happiness of heaven. The voice of the Divinity himself within his holy temple seemed to tell us that those whom we lamented here, and who in the discharge of their last and noblest duty to their country had met on the field of honour 'the death that best becomes the brave', should receive in another and a better world their great reward! Blackened piles of human ashes surrounded us; but I felt that though 'the dust returns to the earth, the spirit returns unto Him that gave it'.*

The countryman led me to one of these piles within the gates of the court belonging to the Château, where, he said, the bodies of the British Guardsmen who had so gallantly defended it had been burnt as they had been found, heaped in death. I took some of the ashes and wrapped them up in one of the many sheets of paper that were strewed around me; perhaps those heaps that then blackened the surface of this scene of desolation are already scattered by the winds of winter, and mingled unnoticed with the dust of the field; perhaps the few sacred ashes which I then gathered at Château Hougoumont are all that is now to be found upon earth of the thousands who fell upon this fatal field!

WALTER SCOTT, *Paul's Letters to his Kinsfolk* (1816), *Letter IX*

Walter Scott (1770–1832) had just begun to take Europe by storm with his great series of historical novels (*Waverley*, 1814; *Guy Mannering*, 1815) when he visited France and Belgium in the summer of 1815. *Paul's Letters to his Kinsfolk*, a lightly fictionalized travelogue, records Scott's tour of Waterloo on 9 August. The 'reliques of minstrelsy' Scott brings back from the field recall his first literary success as an editor of traditional Scottish ballads.

I should now, my dear sister, give you some description of the celebrated field of Waterloo. But although I visited it with unusual advantages, it is necessary that I should recollect how many descriptions have already appeared of this celebrated scene of the greatest event of modern times, and that I must not weary your patience with a twice-told tale. Such and so numerous have been the visits of English families and tourists, as to enrich the peasants of the vicinity by the consequences of an event which menaced them with total ruin. The good old Flemish housewife, who keeps the principal cabaret at Waterloo, even when I was there, had learnt the value of her situation, and charged three prices for our coffee, because she could gratify us by showing the very bed in which the *Grand Lord*** slept the night preceding the action. To what extremities she may have since proceeded in taxing English curiosity, it is difficult to conjecture. To say truth, the honest Flemings were at first altogether at a loss to comprehend the eagerness and enthusiasm by which their English visitors were influenced in their pilgrimages to this classic spot. Their country has been long the scene of military operations, in which the inhabitants themselves have seldom felt much personal interest. With them a battle fought and won is a battle forgotten, and the peasant resumes his ordinary labours after the armies have left his district, with as little interest in recollecting the conflict, as if it had been a thunder-storm which had passed away. You may conceive, therefore, the grave surprise with which these honest pococur-antés* viewed the number of British travellers of every possible description, who hastened to visit the field of Waterloo. . . .

A more innocent source of profit has opened to many of the poor people about Waterloo, by the sale of such trinkets and arms as they collect daily from the field of battle; things of no intrinsic value, but upon which curiosity sets a daily increasing estimate. These memorials, like the books of the Sybils, rise in value as they decrease in number. Almost every hamlet opens a mart of them as soon as English visitors appear. Men, women, and children rushed out upon us, holding up swords, pistols, carabines, and holsters, all of which were sold when I was there *à prix juste*,* at least to those who knew how to drive a bargain. I saw a tolerably good carabine bought for five francs; to be sure there went many words to the bargain, for the old woman to whom it belonged had the conscience at first to ask a gold Napoleon for it, being about the value it would have borne in Birmingham. Crosses of the Legion of Honour were in great request, and already stood high in the market. I bought one of the ordinary sort for forty francs. The eagles which the French soldiers wore in front of their caps, especially the more solid ornament of that description which belonged to the Imperial Guards, were sought after, but might be had for a few sous. But the great object of ambition was to possess the armour of a cuirassier, which at first might have been bought in great quantity, almost all the wearers having fallen in that bloody battle. The victors had indeed carried off some of these cuirasses to serve as culinary utensils, and I myself have seen the Highlanders frying their rations of beef or mutton upon the breast-plates and back-pieces of their discomfited adversaries. But enough remained to make the fortunes of the people of St John, Waterloo, Planchenoit, etc. When I was at La Belle Alliance I bought the cuirass of a common soldier for about six francs; but a very handsome inlaid one, once the property of a French officer of distinction, which was for sale in Brussels, cost me four times the sum. As for the casques, or head pieces, which by the way are remarkably handsome, they are almost introuvable,* for the peasants immediately sold them to be beat out for old copper, and the purchasers, needlessly afraid of their being reclaimed, destroyed them as fast as possible.

The eagerness with which we entered into these negotiations, and still more the zeal with which we picked up every trifle we could find upon the field, rather scandalized one of the heroes of the day,* who did me the favour to guide me over the field of battle, and who considered the interest I took in things which he was accustomed to see scattered as mere trumpery upon many a field of victory, with a feeling that I believe made him for the moment heartily ashamed of his company. I was obliged to remind him that as he had himself gathered laurels on the same spot, he should have sympathy, or patience at least, with our more humble harvest of peach-stories, filberts, and trinkets. Fortunately the enthusiasm of a visitor, who went a bow-shot beyond us, by carrying off a brick from the house of La Belle Alliance, with that of a more wholesale amateur, who actually purchased the door of the said mansion for two gold Napoleons, a little mitigated my military friend's censure of our folly, by showing it was possible to exceed it. I own I was myself somewhat curious respecting the use which could be made of the door of La Belle Alliance, unless upon a speculation of cutting it up into trinkets, like Shakespeare's mulberry tree.*

A relique of greater moral interest was given me by a lady, whose father had found it upon the field of battle. It is a manuscript collection of French songs, bearing stains of clay and blood, which probably indicate the fate of the proprietor. One or two of these romances I thought pretty, and have since had an opportunity of having them translated into English, by meeting at Paris with one of our Scottish men of rhyme. . . .*

I have taken more pains respecting these poems than their intrinsic poetical merit can be supposed to deserve, either in the original or the English version; but I cannot divide them from the interest which they have acquired by the place and manner in which they were obtained, and therefore account them more precious than any of the other remains of Waterloo which have fallen into my possession.

Had these reliques of minstrelsy, or anything corresponding to them in tone and spirit, been preserved as actual trophies of the fields of Cressy and Agincourt,* how many gay visions of knights and squires and troubadours, and *sirventes* and *lais*, and courts of Love,* and usages of antique chivalry, would the perusal have excited! Now, and brought close to our own times, they can only be considered as the stock in trade of the master of a regimental band; or at best we may suppose the compilation to have been the pastime of some young and gay French officer, who, little caring about the real merits of the quarrel in which he was engaged, considered the war by which the fate of Europe was to be decided only as a natural and animating

exchange for the pleasures of Paris. Still the gallantry and levity of
the poetry compels us to contrast its destined purpose, to cheer
hours of mirth or of leisure, with the place in which the manuscript
was found, trampled down in the blood of the writer, and flung away
by the hands of the spoilers, who had stripped him on the field of
battle. I will not, however, trouble you with any further translations
at present; only to do justice to my gallant Troubadour, I will subjoin
the original French in the postscript to this letter. It is a task of some
difficulty; for accurate orthography was not a quality of the original
writer, and I am myself far from possessing a critical knowledge of
the French language, though I have endeavoured to correct his most
obvious errors.

5. OFF THE BEATEN TRACK

LADY MARY WORTLEY MONTAGU, *'Embassy Letters'*
(1716–18; from *The Complete Letters of Lady Mary Wortley
Montagu*, vol. i, ed. Robert Halsband; Oxford, 1965)

Lady Mary Wortley Montagu (1689–1762) travelled through eastern
Europe to Constantinople with her husband Edward on his appointment
as ambassador to the Sublime Porte, 1716–18. Lady Mary prepared
assiduously for the journey, reading just about all the sources available on
Ottoman history and civilization. She seems to have intended her letters,
addressed to various correspondents, for publication, and they came out
after her death in 1763, despite attempts by her family to suppress them.
Our excerpts, taken from the original manuscript (edited by Robert
Halsband), show Lady Mary dressing for court at Vienna, preparing for
her journey to the east, visiting the baths in Sofia (Bulgaria was then part
of the Ottoman Empire) and donning her Turkish costume.

To LADY MAR,*
VIENNA, 14 September 1716

Though I have so lately troubled you (dear Sister) with a long letter,
yet I will keep my promise in giving you an account of my first going
to Court.

In order to that ceremony, I was squeezed up in a gown and adorned
with a gorget and the other implements thereunto belonging: a

dress very inconvenient, but which certainly shows the neck and shape to great advantage. I cannot forbear in this place giving you some description of the fashions here, which are more monstrous and contrary to all common sense and reason than 'tis possible for you to imagine. They build certain fabrics of gauze on their heads about a yard high consisting of 3 or 4 storeys fortified with numberless yards of heavy ribbon. The foundation of this structure is a thing they call a bourlé, which is exactly of the same shape and kind, but about 4 times as big, as those rolls our prudent milk maids make use of to fix their pails upon. This machine they cover with their own hair, which they mix with a great deal of false, it being a particular beauty to have their heads too large to go into a moderate tub. Their hair is prodigiously powdered to conceal the mixture, and set out with 3 or 4 rows of bodkins, wonderfully large, that stick 2 or 3 inches from their hair, made of diamonds, pearls, red, green and yellow stones, that it certainly requires as much art and experience to carry the load upright as to dance upon May Day with the garland. Their whalebone petticoats out-do ours by several yards circumference and cover some acres of ground. You may easily suppose how much this extraordinary dress sets off and improves the natural ugliness with which God Almighty has been pleased to endow them all generally. Even the lovely Empress herself is obliged to comply in some degree with these absurd fashions, which they would not quit for all the world. . . .

I had audience the next day of the Empress Mother,* a princess of great virtue and goodness, but who piques herself so much on a violent devotion, she is perpetually performing extraordinary acts of penance without having ever done any thing to deserve them. She has the same number of maids of honour, whom she suffers to go in colours, but she herself never quits her mourning, and sure nothing can be more dismal than the mournings here, even for a brother. There is not the least bit of linen to be seen: all-black crepe instead of it, the neck, ears and side of the face covered with a plaited piece of the same stuff; and the face that peeps out in the midst of it looks as if it were pilloried. The widows wear over and above, a crepe forehead cloth, and in this solemn weed go to all the public places of diversion without scruple.

The next day I was to wait on the Empress Amalia* who is now at her palace of retirement half a mile from the town. I had there the pleasure of seeing a diversion wholly new to me, but which is the common amusement of this Court. The Empress herself was seated on a little throne at the end of a fine alley in her garden, and on each side of her ranged 2 parties of her ladies of honour with other young ladies of quality, headed by the 2 young Archduchesses, all dressed in their hair, full of jewels, with fine light guns in their hands, and at proper distances were placed 3 oval pictures which were the marks to be shot at. The first was that of a Cupid filling a bumper of burgundy, and the motto, 'tis easy to be valiant here; the 2nd, a Fortune holding a garland in her hand, the motto, for her whom fortune favours; the 3rd was a sword with a laurel wreath on the point, the motto, here is no shame to the vanquished. Near the Empress was a gilded trophy wreathed with flowers and made of little crooks on which were hung rich Turkish handkerchiefs, tippets, ribbons, laces etc. for the small prizes. The Empress gave the first with her own hand, which was a fine ruby ring set round with diamonds, in a gold snuffbox. There was for the 2nd a little Cupid set with brilliants, and besides these a set of fine china for a tea table enchased in gold, Japan trunks, fans, and many gallantries of the same nature. All the men of quality at Vienna were spectators, but only the ladies had permission to shoot, and the Archduchess Amalia carried off the first prize. I was very well pleased with having seen this entertainment, and I don't know but it might make as good a figure as the prize shooting in the Æneid if I could write as well as Virgil.* This is the favourite pleasure of the Emperor, and there is rarely a week without some feast of this kind, which makes the young ladies skilful enough to defend a fort, and they laughed very much to see me afraid to handle a gun.

My dear Sister, you will easily pardon an abrupt conclusion. I believe by this time you are ready to fear I would never conclude at all.

To LADY MAR,
VIENNA, 16 January 1717

I am now, dear Sister, to take leave of you for a long time and of Vienna for ever, designing tomorrow to begin my journey through Hungary in spite of the excessive cold and deep snows which are enough to damp a greater courage than I am mistress of, but my principle of passive obedience carries me through everything. I have had my audiences of leave of the Empresses. His imperial Majesty was pleased to be present when I waited on the reigning Empress, and after a very obliging conversation both their imperial Majesties invited me to take Vienna in my road back, but I have no thoughts of enduring over again so great a fatigue. . . .

The ladies of my acquaintance have so much goodness for me, they cry whenever they see me, since I am determined to undertake this journey, and indeed I am not very easy when I reflect on what I am going to suffer. Almost everybody I see frights me with some new difficulty. Prince Eugene* has been so good to say all things he could to persuade me to stay till the Danube is thawed that I may have the convenience of going by water, assuring me that the houses in Hungary are such as are no defence against the weather and that I shall be obliged to travel 3 or 4 days between Buda and Esseek* without finding any house at all, through desert plains covered with snow, where the cold is so violent many have been killed by it. I own these terrors have made a very deep impression on my mind because I believe he tells me things truly as they are, and nobody can be better informed of them. . . .

Adieu, dear Sister. This is the last account you will have from me of Vienna. If I survive my journey you shall hear from me again. I can say with great truth in the words of Moneses,* I have long learnt to hold myself at nothing, but when I think of the fatigue my poor infant must suffer, I have all a mother's fondness in my eyes and all her tender passions in my heart.

P.S. I have writ a letter to my Lady——* that I believe she won't like, and upon cooler reflection, I think I had done better to have let it alone, but I was downright peevish at all her questions and her ridiculous imagination that I have certainly seen abundance of wonders that I keep to myself out of mere malice. She is angry that I won't lie like other travellers. I verily believe she expects I should tell her of the Anthropophagi [and] men whose heads grow below their shoulders.* However, pray say something to pacify her.

To LADY——
ADRIANOPLE,* 1 April 1717

I am now got into a new world where everything I see appears to me a change of scene, and I write to your Ladyship with some content of mind, hoping at least that you will find the charm of novelty in my letters and no longer reproach me that I tell you nothing extraordinary. I won't trouble you with a relation of our tedious journey, but I must not omit what I saw remarkable at Sophia, one of the most beautiful towns in the Turkish Empire and famous for its hot baths that are resorted to both for diversion and health. I stopped here one day on purpose to see them. Designing to go incognito, I hired a Turkish coach. These voitures are not at all like ours, but much more convenient for the country, the heat being so great that glasses would be very troublesome. They are made a good deal in the manner of the Dutch coaches, having wooden lattices painted and gilded, the inside being painted with baskets and nosegays of flowers, intermixed commonly with little poetical mottos. They are covered all over with scarlet cloth, lined with silk and very often richly embroidered and fringed. This covering entirely hides the persons in them, but may be thrown back at pleasure and the ladies peep through the lattices. They hold 4 people very conveniently, seated on cushions, but not raised.

In one of these covered wagons I went to the Bagnio* about 10 o'clock. It was already full of women. It is built of stone in the shape of a dome with no windows but in the roof, which gives light enough. There was 5 of these domes joined together, the outmost being less than the rest and serving only as a hall where the portress stood at the door. Ladies of quality generally give this woman the value of a crown or 10 shillings, and I did not forget that ceremony. The next room is a very large one, paved with marble, and all round it raised 2 sofas of marble, one above another. There were 4 fountains of cold water in this room, falling first into marble basins and then running on the floor in little channels made for that purpose, which carried the streams into the next room, something less than this, with the same sort of marble sofas, but so hot with steams of sulphur proceeding from the baths joining to it, 'twas impossible to stay there with one's clothes on. The 2 other domes were the hot baths, one of which had cocks of cold water turning into it to temper it to what degree of warmth the bathers have a mind to.

I was in my travelling habit which is a riding dress, and certainly appeared very extraordinary to them, yet there was not one of 'em that showed the least surprise or impertinent curiosity, but received me with all the obliging civility possible. I know no European court where the ladies would have behaved themselves in so polite a manner to a stranger.

I believe in the whole there were 200 women and yet none of those disdainful smiles or satiric whispers that never fail in our assemblies when anybody appears that is not dressed exactly in fashion. They repeated over and over to me, Uzelle, pek uzelle,* which is nothing but, charming, very charming. The first sofas were covered with cushions and rich carpets, on which sat the ladies, and on the 2nd their slaves behind 'em, but without any distinction of rank by their dress, all being in the state of nature, that is in plain English, stark naked, without any beauty or defect concealed, yet there was not the least wanton smile or immodest gesture amongst 'em. They walked and moved with the same majestic grace which Milton describes of our General Mother.* There were many amongst them as exactly proportioned as ever any goddess was drawn by the pencil of Guido or Titian,* and most of their skins shiningly white, only adorned by their beautiful hair divided into many tresses hanging on their shoulders, braided either with pearl or ribbon, perfectly representing the figures of the Graces. I was here convinced of the truth of a reflection that I had often made, that if 'twas the fashion to go naked, the face would be hardly observed. I perceived that the ladies with the finest skins and most delicate shapes had the greatest share of my admiration, though their faces were sometimes less beautiful than those of their companions. To tell you the truth, I had wickedness enough to wish secretly that Mr Gervase* could have been there invisible. I fancy it would have very much improved his art to see so many fine women naked in different postures, some in conversation, some working, others drinking coffee or sherbet, and many negligently lying on their cushions while their slaves (generally pretty girls of 17 or 18) were employed in braiding their hair in several pretty manners. In short, 'tis the women's coffee house, where all the news of the town is told, scandal invented, etc. They generally take this diversion once a week, and stay there at least 4 or 5 hours without getting cold by immediately coming out of the hot bath into the cool room, which was very surprising to me. The lady that seemed the most considerable amongst them entreated me to sit by her and would fain have undressed me for the bath. I excused myself with some difficulty, they being all so earnest in persuading me. I was at last forced to open my skirt and show them my stays, which satisfied 'em very well, for I saw they believed I was so locked up in that machine that it was not in my own power to open it, which contrivance they attributed to my husband. I was charmed with their civility and beauty and should have been very glad to pass more time with them, but Mr W[ortley] resolving to pursue his journey the next morning early, I was in haste to see the ruins of Justinian's church,* which did not afford me so agreeable a prospect as I had left, being little more than a heap of stones.

Adieu, Madam. I am sure I have now entertained you with an account of such a sight as you never saw in your life and what no book of travels could inform you of. 'Tis no less than death for a man to be found in one of these places.

To Lady Mar,
1 April 1717

I wish to God (dear Sister) that you was as regular in letting me have the pleasure of knowing what passes on your side of the globe as I am careful in endeavouring to amuse you by the account of all I see that I think you care to hear of. You content yourself with telling me over and over that the town is very dull. It may possibly be dull to you when every day does not present you with something new, but for me that am in arrear at least 2 months' news, all that seems very stale with you would be fresh and sweet here; pray let me into more particulars. I will try to awaken your gratitude by giving you a full and true relation of the novelties of this place, none of which would surprise you more than a sight of my person as I am now in my Turkish habit, though I believe you would be of my opinion that 'tis admirably becoming. I intend to send you my picture; in the mean time accept of it here.

The first piece of my dress is a pair of drawers, very full, that reach to my shoes and conceal the legs more modestly than your petticoats. They are of a thin rose colour damask brocaded with silver flowers, my shoes of white kid leather embroidered with gold. Over this hangs my smock of a fine white silk gauze edged with embroidery. This smock has wide sleeves hanging half way down the arm and is closed at the neck with a diamond button, but the shape and colour of the bosom very well to be distinguished through it. The Antery is a waistcoat made close to the shape, of white and gold damask, with very long sleeves falling back and fringed with deep gold fringe, and should have diamond or pearl buttons. My caftan of the same stuff with my drawers is a robe exactly fitted to my shape and reaching to my feet, with very long straight falling sleeves. Over this is the girdle of about 4 fingers broad, which all that can afford have entirely of diamonds or other precious stones. Those that will not be at that expense have it of exquisite embroidery on satin, but it must be fastened before with a clasp of diamonds. The Curdée is a loose robe they throw off or put on according to the weather, being of a rich brocade (mine is green and gold) either lined with ermine or sables; the sleeves reach very little below the shoulders. The head-dress is composed of a cap called Talpock,* which is in winter of fine velvet embroidered with pearls or diamonds and in summer of a light shining silver stuff. This is fixed on one side of the head, hanging a little way down with a gold tassel and bound on either with a circle of diamonds (as I have seen several) or a rich embroidered handkerchief. On the other side of the head the hair is laid flat, and here the ladies are at liberty to show their fancies, some putting flowers, others a plume of heron's feathers, and, in short, what they please, but the most general fashion is a large bouquet of jewels made like natural flowers, that is, the buds of pearl, the roses of different coloured rubies, the jessamines of diamonds, jonquils of topazes, etc., so well set and enamelled 'tis hard to imagine anything of that kind so beautiful. The hair hangs at its full length behind, divided into tresses braided with pearl or ribbon, which is always in great quantity.

I never saw in my life so many fine heads of hair. I have counted 110 of these tresses of one lady's, all natural; but it must be owned that every beauty is more common here than with us. 'Tis surprising to see a young woman that is not very handsome. They have naturally the most beautiful complexions in the world and generally large black eyes. I can assure you with great truth that the Court of England (though I believe it the fairest in Christendom) cannot show so many beauties as are under our protection here. They generally shape their eyebrows, and the Greeks and Turks have a custom of putting round their eyes on the inside a black tincture that at a distance or by candle-light, adds very much to the blackness of them. I fancy many of our ladies would be overjoyed to know this secret, but 'tis too visible by day. They dye their nails rose colour; I own I cannot enough accustom myself to this fashion to find any beauty in it.

As to their morality or good conduct, I can say like Harlequin, 'tis just as 'tis with you,* and the Turkish ladies don't commit one sin the less for not being Christians. Now I am a little acquainted with their ways, I cannot forbear admiring either the exemplary discretion or extreme stupidity of all the writers that have given accounts of 'em. 'Tis very easy to see they have more liberty than we have, no woman of what rank soever being permitted to go in the streets without 2 muslins, one that covers her face all but her eyes and another that hides the whole dress of her head and hangs half-way down her back; and their shapes are wholly concealed by a thing they call a Ferigée, which no woman of any sort appears without. This has straight sleeves that reaches to their fingers' ends and it laps all round 'em, not unlike a riding hood. In Winter 'tis of cloth, and in Summer, plain stuff or silk. You may guess how effectually this disguises them, that there is no distinguishing the great lady from her slave, and 'tis impossible for the most jealous husband to know his wife when he meets her, and no man dare either touch or follow a woman in the street.

This perpetual masquerade gives them entire liberty of following their inclinations without danger of discovery. The most usual method of intrigue is to send an appointment to the lover to meet the lady at a Jew's shop, which are as notoriously convenient as our Indian Houses,* and yet even those that don't make that use of 'em do not scruple to go to buy penn'orths and tumble over rich goods, which are chiefly to be found amongst that sort of people. The great ladies seldom let their gallants know who they are, and 'tis so difficult to find it out that they can very seldom guess at her name they have corresponded with above half a year together. You may easily imagine the number of faithful wives very small in a country where they have nothing to fear from their lovers' indiscretion, since we see so many that have the courage to expose themselves to that in this world and all the threatened punishment of the next, which is never preached to the Turkish damsels. Neither have they much to apprehend from the resentment of their husbands, those ladies that are rich having all their money in their own hands, which they take with 'em upon a divorce with an addition which he is obliged to give 'em. Upon the whole, I look upon the Turkish women as the only free people in the Empire. The very Divan* pays a respect to 'em, and the Grand Signor himself, when a Bassa* is executed, never violates the privileges of the Harem (or women's apartment) which remains unsearched entire to the widow. They are queens of their slaves, which the husband has no permission so much as to look upon, except it be an old woman or 2 that this lady chooses. 'Tis true their law permits them 4 wives, but there is no instance of a man of quality that makes use of this liberty, or of a woman of rank that would suffer it. When a husband happens to be inconstant (as those things will happen) he keeps his mistress in a house apart and visits her as privately as he can, just as 'tis with you. Amongst all the great men here I only know the Tefterdar (i.e. treasurer) that keeps a number of she slaves for his own use (that is, on his own side of the house, for a slave once given to serve a lady is entirely at her disposal) and he is spoken of as a libertine, or what we should call a rake, and his wife won't see him, though she continues to live in his house.

Thus you see, dear Sister, the manners of mankind do not differ so widely as our voyage writers would make us believe. Perhaps it would be more entertaining to add a few surprising customs of my own invention, but nothing seems to me so agreeable as truth, and I believe nothing so acceptable to you. I conclude with repeating the great truth of my being, dear Sister, etc.

LADY ELIZABETH CRAVEN, *A Journey through the Crimea to Constantinople; in a series of letters from the Right Honorable Elizabeth Lady Craven, to his Serene Highness the Margrave of Brandenbourg, Anspach and Bareith* (Dublin, 1789), Letters XXXIV, XLIX, and LVI

When Elizabeth Craven (1750–1828) published her *Journey*, an account of a tour made in 1785–6, it fanned the flames of scandal that followed her separation from Lord Craven in 1781. At several points in the book she inveighs against a false Lady Craven—her husband's mistress—who is circulating on the Continent. The letters are addressed to her lover, the Margrave of Anspach, whom she was finally able to marry (following the deaths of both their spouses) in 1791. The book is also notable for an attack on Lady Mary Wortley Montagu's *Embassy Letters*. Backed up by Lady Mary's daughter Lady Bute, Craven claimed in a later edition of the *Journey* that they were the work of a male forger.

MOSCOW, 29 February 1786

I left my coach at Petersburgh, and hired for myself and my small suite the carriages of the country, called Kibitkas; they are exactly like cradles, the head having windows to the front which let down; I can sit or lie down, and feel in one like a great child, very comfortably defended from the cold by pillows and blankets. These carriages are upon sledges, and where the road is good, this conveyance is comfortable and not fatiguing, but from the incredible quantity of sledges that go constantly upon the track of snow, it is worn in tracks like a road; and from the shaking and violent thumps the carriage receives, I am convinced the hardest head might be broken. I was overturned twice; the postillions I fancy are used to such accidents; for they get quietly off their horse, set the carriage up again, and never ask if the traveller is hurt. Their method of driving is singular: they sit behind three horses that are harnessed abreast—a shrill whistling noise, or a savage kind of shriek is the signal for the horses to set off, which they do full gallop and when their pace slackens, the driver waves his right hand, shrieks or whistles, and the horses obey. I am told the whip is unmercifully used in the stables; I observed a postillion never strikes a horse in driving; which caused my astonishment at their being so tractable to the raising of a hand only. I would never advise a traveller to set out from Petersburgh as I have, just at the end of the carnival;* he might with some reason suppose it is a religious duty for the Russian peasant to be drunk; in most villages I saw a sledge loaded with young men and women in such a manner, that four horses would have been more proper to draw it than one, which wretched beast was obliged to fly with this noisy company up and down the village, which is generally composed of houses in straight rows on each side of the public road. The girls are dressed in their holiday-clothes, and some are beautiful, and do not look less so from various coloured handkerchiefs tied over their forehead in a becoming and *pittoresque* manner. There is one particular piece of roguery practised after this diversion upon travellers, which ought to be put an end to: the horse employed upon these festive occasions is generally upon the point of death; and the first posthorse that is wanted, that horse is harnessed to a kibitka in his place, because a traveller is obliged to pay the value of any horse that dies in his service. I had one that died thus, though I remonstrated upon his being put to the collar, seeing that he was dying—but unless I could have armed six servants with good cudgels, my arguments were as fruitless as those employed at the next post, to prove how unreasonable it was, that I should pay a great deal of money for a dead horse, that was dying when he was put to the carriage.

The Russian peasant is a fine, stout, straight, well-looking man; some of the women, as I said before, are uncommonly pretty; but the general whiteness of their teeth is something that cannot be conceived; it frequently happened that all the men of the village were in a circle round my carriages—and rows of the most beautiful oriental pearl cannot be more regular and white than their teeth. It is a matter of great astonishment to me, how the infants outlive the treatment they receive, till they are able to crawl into the air; there is a kind of space or *entresol* over every stove, in which the husband, wife, and children lie the greatest part of the day, and where they sleep at night—the heat appeared to me so great that I have no conception how they bear it; but they were as much surprised at me for seeking a door or window in every house I was obliged to go into, as I could possibly be at their living in a manner without air. The children look all pale and sickly, till they are five or six years old. The houses and dresses of the peasants are by no means uncomfortable; the first is generally composed of wood, the latter of sheep-skins; but trees laid horizontally one upon another makes a very strong wall, and the climate requires a warm skin for clothing. It might appear to English minds that a people who are in a manner the property of their lord, suffer many of the afflictions that attend slavery; but the very circumstance of their persons being the property insures them the indulgence of their master for the preservation of their lives; and that master stands between them and the power of a despotic government or a brutal soldiery. Beside, my dear Sir, the invaluable advantage which these peasants have, as in paying annually a very small sum each, and cultivating as many acres of land as he thinks fit, his fortune depends entirely upon his own industry; each man only pays about the value of half-a-guinea a year. If his lord would raise this tax too high, or make their vassals suffer, misery and desertion would ruin his fortune, not theirs; it is true that a lord is obliged to give one man as a recruit yearly out of such a number, but it is one out of three or four hundred; so that notwithstanding this great empire is said not to be populated in proportion to the extent of it, when you reflect what a number of troops the Empress has, and these kept up by this method, the Russian people must be more numerous than strangers may imagine, in travelling through this

country. It is very amusing to me to reflect, without prejudices of
any kind, upon the ridiculous ideas of liberty and property that our
English common people have.

PALAIS DE FRANCE, PERA,* 7 May 1786

Monsieur de Choiseul proposed to the Ambassadors' wives and me
to go and see the Capitan Pacha's* country seat; accordingly we set
out with several carriages, and about a league from Constantinople,
towards Romelia,* we arrived there: The house and plantations about
it are new and irregular. The Ambassadors and the rest of the male
party were suffered to walk in the garden; but the Ministers' wives
and myself were shown into a separate building from the house,
where the ground floor was made to contain a great quantity of
water, and looked like a large clean cistern. We then were led up
stairs, and upon the landing-place, which was circular, the doors of
several rooms were open. In some there was nothing to be seen, in
others two or three women sitting close together; in one, a pretty
young woman, with a great quantity of jewels on her turban, was
sitting almost in the lap of a frightful negro woman; we were told she
was the Captain Pacha's sister-in-law; she looked at us with much
surprise; and at last, with great fear, threw herself into the arms of
the black woman, as if to hide herself. We were called away into a
larger room than any we had seen, where the Capitan Pacha's wife, a
middle-aged woman, dressed with great magnificence, received us
with much politeness; many women were with her, and she had by
her a little girl, dressed as magnificently as herself, her adopted
child. She made an excuse for not receiving us at the door, as she was
dining with her husband when we arrived. Coffee, sherbet, and
sweetmeats were offered, and we hastened to take our leave, as our
cavaliers were cooling their heels in the garden.

You can conceive nothing so neat and clean to all appearance as
the interior of this Harem; the floors and passages are covered with
matting of a close and strong kind; the colour of the straw or reeds
with which they are made is a pale straw. The rooms had no other
furniture than the cushions, which lined the whole room, and those,
with the curtains, were of white linen. As the Turks never come
into the room, either men or women, with the slippers they walk
abroad with there is not a speck of sand or dirt within doors. I am
femmelette enough to have taken particular notice of the dress,

which, if female envy did not spoil everything in the world of women, would be graceful. It consists of a petticoat and vest, over which is worn a robe with short sleeves; the one belonging to the lady of the house was of satin, embroidered richly with the finest colours, gold and diamonds. A girdle under that, with two circles of jewels in front, and from this girdle hangs an embroidered hand-kerchief. A turban with a profusion of diamonds and pearls seemed to weigh this lady's head down; but what spoiled the whole was a piece of ermine, that probably was originally only a cape, but each woman increasing the size of it, in order to be more magnificent than her neighbour, they now have it like a great square plaister* that comes down to the hips; and these simple ignorant beings do not see that it disfigures the *tout ensemble* of a beautiful dress. The hair is separated in many small braids hanging down the back, or tied up to the point of the turban on the outside. I have no doubt but that nature intended some of these women to be very handsome, but white and red ill applied, their eyebrows hid under one or two black lines—teeth black by smoking, and an universal stoop in the shoul-ders, made them appear rather disgusting than handsome. The last defect is caused by the posture they sit in, which is that of a tailor, from their infancy.

The black powder with which they line their eyelids gives their eyes likewise a harsh expression. Their questions are as simple as their dress is studied——Are you married? Have you children? Have you no disorder? Do you like Constantinople? The Turkish women pass most of their time in the bath or upon their dress; strange pastimes! The first spoils their persons, the last disfigures them. The frequent use of hot baths destroys the solids, and these women at nineteen look older than I am at this moment. They endeavour to repair by art the mischief their constant soaking does to their charms; but till some one, more wife than the rest, finds out the cause of the premature decay of that invaluable gift, beauty, and sets an example to the rising generation of a different mode of life, they will always fade as fast as the roses they are so justly fond of.

Our gentlemen were very curious to hear an account of the Harem, and when we were driving out of the courtyard, a messenger from the Harem came running after us, to desire the carriages might be driven round the court two or three times, for the amusement of the Capitan Pacha's wife and the Harem, that were looking through

the blinds; this ridiculous message was not complied with, as you
may imagine; and we got home, laughing at our adventures.

ATHENS

The baths here are very well contrived to stew the rheumatism out of
a person's constitution—but how the women can support the heat of
them is perfectly inconceivable. The Consul's wife, Madame
Gaspari, and I went into a room which precedes the bath, which
room is the place where the women dress and undress, sitting like
tailors upon boards. There were above fifty; some having their hair
washed, others dyed, or plaited; some were at the last part of their
toilet, putting with a fine gold pin the black dye into their eyelids; in
short, I saw here Turkish and Greek nature, through every degree of
concealment, in her primitive state—for the women sitting in the
inner room were absolutely so many Eves—and as they came out
their flesh looked boiled. These baths are the great amusement of the
women, they stay generally five hours in them; that is in the water
and at their toilet together—but I think I never saw so many fat
women at once together, nor fat ones so fat as these. There is much
art and coquetry in the arrangement of their dress—the shift particularly, which closes by hooks behind between the shoulders; after it is
fastened round the waist, there is a species of stay or corset, that I had
no idea of, but which to whom melted down as these were, was
perfectly necessary. We had very pressing solicitations to undress and
bathe, but such a disgusting sight as this would have put me in an ill
humour with my sex in a bath for ages. Few of these women had fair
skins or fine forms—hardly any—and Madame Gaspari tells me that
the encomiums and flattery a fine young woman would meet with in
these baths would be astonishing. I stood some time in the doorway
between the dressing-room and the bath, which last was circular,
with niches in it for the bathers to sit in; it was a very fine room with a
stone dome, and the light came through small windows at the top.

MARY WOLLSTONECRAFT, *Letters Written during a Short
Residence in Sweden, Norway, and Denmark* (1796)

After publishing her *Vindication of the Rights of Woman* (1792) the radical
writer Mary Wollstonecraft (1759–97) spent over two years in revolutionary

Paris, where she bore a child by the American adventurer Gilbert Imlay. Their relationship quickly deteriorated, and Wollstonecraft attempted suicide after her return to London in the spring of 1795. In June she travelled to Scandinavia to look after Imlay's business interests, accompanied only by her infant daughter Fanny and her French maid Marguerite. Wollstonecraft's *Letters*, addressed to her faithless lover, proved to be her most popular book. She combines the 'sentimental' manner with an inquiry into the customs and politics of these rough northern countries. Our extracts record her arrival in Sweden and passage to the coast of Norway.

Letter I

Eleven days of weariness on board a vessel not intended for the accommodation of passengers have so exhausted my spirits, to say nothing of the other causes, with which you are already sufficiently acquainted, that it is with some difficulty I adhere to my determination of giving you my observations, as I travel through new scenes, whilst warmed with the impression they have made on me.

The captain, as I mentioned to you, promised to put me on shore at Arendall,* or Gothenburg, in his way to Elsinor; but contrary winds obliged us to pass both places during the night. In the morning, however, after we had lost sight of the entrance of the latter bay, the vessel was becalmed; and the captain, to oblige me, hanging out a signal for a pilot, bore down towards the shore.

My attention was particularly directed to the lighthouse; and you can scarcely imagine with what anxiety I watched two long hours for a boat to emancipate me—still no one appeared. Every cloud that flitted on the horizon was hailed as a liberator, till approaching nearer, like most of the prospects sketched by hope, it dissolved under the eye into disappointment.

Weary of expectation, I then began to converse with the captain on the subject; and, from the tenor of the information my questions drew forth, I soon concluded, that, if I waited for a boat, I had little chance of getting on shore at this place. Despotism, as is usually the case, I found had here cramped the industry of man. The pilots being paid by the king, and scantily, they will not run into any danger, or even quit their hovels, if they can possibly avoid it, only to fulfil what is termed their duty. How different is it on the English coast, where, in the most stormy weather, boats immediately hail you, brought out by the expectation of extraordinary profit.

Disliking to sail for Elsinor, and still more to lie at anchor, or cruise about the coast for several days, I exerted all my rhetoric to prevail on the captain to let me have the ship's boat; and though I added the most forcible of arguments, I for a long time addressed him in vain.

It is a kind of rule at sea not to send out a boat. The captain was a good-natured man; but men with common minds seldom break through general rules. Prudence is ever the resort of weakness; and they rarely go as far as they may in any undertaking, who are determined not to go beyond it on any account. If, however, I had some trouble with the captain, I did not lose much time with the sailors; for they, all alacrity, hoisted out the boat, the moment I obtained permission, and promised to row me to the lighthouse.

I did not once allow myself to doubt of obtaining a conveyance from thence round the rocks—and then away for Gothenburg—confinement is so unpleasant.

The day was fine; and I enjoyed the water till, approaching the little island, poor Marguerite, whose timidity always acts as a feeler before her adventuring spirit, began to wonder at our not seeing any inhabitants. I did not listen to her. But when, on landing, the same silence prevailed, I caught the alarm, which was not lessened by the sight of two old men, whom we forced out of their wretched hut. Scarcely human in their appearance, we with difficulty obtained an intelligible reply to our questions—the result of which was that they had no boat, and were not allowed to quit their post, on any pretence. But they informed us that there was at the other side, eight or ten miles over, a pilot's dwelling; two guineas tempted the sailors to risk the captain's displeasure, and once more embark to row me over.

The weather was pleasant, and the appearance of the shore so grand, that I should have enjoyed the two hours it took to reach it, but for the fatigue which was too visible in the countenances of the sailors who, instead of uttering a complaint, were, with the thoughtless hilarity peculiar to them, joking about the possibility of the captain's taking advantage of a slight westerly breeze, which was springing up, to sail without them. Yet, in spite of their good humour, I could not help growing uneasy when the shore, receding, as it were, as we advanced, seemed to promise no end to their toil. This anxiety increased when, turning into the most picturesque bay I ever saw, my eyes sought in vain for the vestige of a human habitation. Before I could determine what step to take in such a dilemma, for I could not bear to think of returning to the ship, the sight of a barge relieved me, and we hastened towards it for information. We were immediately directed to pass some jutting rocks when we should see a pilot's hut.

There was a solemn silence in this scene, which made itself be felt. The sun-beams that played on the ocean, scarcely ruffled by the lightest breeze, contrasted with the huge, dark rocks, that looked like the rude materials of creation forming the barrier of unwrought space, forcibly struck me; but I should not have been sorry if the cottage had not appeared equally tranquil. Approaching a retreat where strangers, especially women, so seldom appeared, I wondered that curiosity did not bring the beings who inhabited it to the windows or door. I did not immediately recollect that men who remain so near the brute creation, as only to exert themselves to find the food necessary to sustain life, have little or no imagination to call forth the curiosity necessary to fructify the faint glimmerings of mind which entitles them to rank as lords of the creation. Had they either, they could not contentedly remain rooted in the clods they so indolently cultivate.

Whilst the sailors went to seek for the sluggish inhabitants, these conclusions occurred to me; and, recollecting the extreme fondness which the Parisians ever testify for novelty, their very curiosity appeared to me a proof of the progress they had made in refinement. Yes; in the art of living—in the art of escaping from the cares which embarrass the first steps towards the attainment of the pleasures of social life.

The pilots informed the sailors that they were under the direction of a lieutenant retired from the service, who spoke English; adding that they could do nothing without his orders; and even the offer of money could hardly conquer their laziness, and prevail on them to accompany us to his dwelling. They would not go with me alone which I wanted them to have done, because I wished to dismiss the sailors as soon as possible. Once more we rowed off, they following tardily, till, turning round another bold protuberance of the rocks, we saw a boat making towards us, and soon learnt that it was the lieutenant himself, coming with some earnestness to see who we were.

To save the sailors any further toil, I had my baggage instantly removed into his boat; for, as he could speak English, a previous parley was not necessary; though Marguerite's respect for me could hardly keep her from expressing the fear, strongly marked on her countenance, which my putting ourselves into the power of a strange man excited. He pointed out his cottage; and, drawing near to it, I was not sorry to see a female figure, though I had not, like Marguerite, been thinking of robberies, murders, or the other evil which instantly, as the sailors would have said, runs foul of* a woman's imagination.

On entering, I was still better pleased to find a clean house, with some degree of rural elegance. The beds were of muslin, coarse it is true, but dazzlingly white; and the floor was strewed over with little sprigs of juniper (the custom, as I afterwards found, of the country), which formed a contrast with the curtains and produced an agreeable sensation of freshness, to soften the ardour of noon. Still nothing was so pleasing as the alacrity of hospitality—all that the house afforded was quickly spread on the whitest linen. Remember I had just left the vessel where, without being fastidious, I had continually been disgusted. Fish, milk, butter, and cheese, and I am sorry to add brandy, the bane of this country, were spread on the board. After we had dined, hospitality made them, with some degree of mystery, bring us some excellent coffee. I did not then know that it was prohibited.

The good man of the house apologized for coming in continually, but declared that he was so glad to speak English, he could not stay out. He need not have apologized; I was equally glad of his company. With the wife I could only exchange smiles; and she was employed observing the make of our clothes. My hands, I found, had first led her to discover that I was the lady. I had, of course, my quantum of reverences; for the politeness of the north seems to partake of the coldness of the climate, and the rigidity of its iron sinewed rocks. Amongst the peasantry, there is, however, so much of the simplicity of the golden age* in this land of flint—so much overflowing of heart, and fellow-feeling, that only benevolence, and the honest sympathy of nature, diffused smiles over my countenance when they kept me standing, regardless of my fatigue, whilst they dropped courtesy after courtesy.

The situation of this house was beautiful, though chosen for convenience. The master being the officer who commanded all the pilots on the coast, and the person appointed to guard wrecks, it was necessary for him to fix on a spot that would overlook the whole bay. As he had seen some service, he wore, not without a pride I thought becoming, a badge to prove that he had merited well of his country. It was happy, I thought, that he had been paid in honour; for the stipend he received was little more than twelve pounds a year. I do not trouble myself or you with the calculation of Swedish ducats. Thus, my friend, you perceive the necessity of perquisites. This same narrow policy runs through everything. I shall have occasion further to animadvert on it.

Though my host amused me with an account of himself, which gave me an idea of the manners of the people I was about to visit, I was eager to climb the rocks to view the country, and see whether the honest tars had regained their ship. With the help of the lieutenant's telescope I saw the vessel underway with a fair though gentle gale. The sea was calm, playful even as the most shallow stream, and on the vast basin I did not see a dark speck to indicate the boat. My conductors were consequently arrived.

Straying further, my eye was attracted by the sight of some heart's ease that peeped through the rocks. I caught at it as a good omen, and going to preserve it in a letter that had not conveyed balm to my heart, a cruel remembrance suffused my eyes; but it passed away like an April shower. If you are deep read in Shakespeare, you will recollect that this was the little western flower tinged by love's dart, which 'maidens call love in idleness'.* The gaiety of my babe was unmixed; regardless of omens or sentiments, she found a few wild strawberries more grateful than flowers or fancies.

The lieutenant informed me that this was a commodious bay. Of that I could not judge, though I felt its picturesque beauty. Rocks were piled on rocks, forming a suitable bulwark to the ocean. Come no further, they emphatically said, turning their dark sides to the waves to augment the idle roar. The view was sterile: still little patches of earth, of the most exquisite verdure, enamelled with the sweetest wild flowers, seemed to promise the goats and a few straggling cows luxurious herbage. How silent and peaceful was the scene. I gazed around with rapture, and felt more of that spontaneous pleasure which gives credibility to our expectation of happiness than I had for a long, long time before. I forgot the horrors I had witnessed in France,* which had cast a gloom over all nature, and suffering the enthusiasm of my character, too often, gracious God!

damped by the tears of disappointed affection, to be lighted up afresh, care took wing while simple fellow feeling expanded my heart.

To prolong this enjoyment, I readily assented to the proposal of our host to pay a visit to a family, the master of which spoke English, who was the drollest dog in the country, he added, repeating some of his stories, with a hearty laugh.

I walked on, still delighted with the rude beauties of the scene; for the sublime often gave place imperceptibly to the beautiful,* dilating the emotions which were painfully concentrated.

When we entered this abode, the largest I had yet seen, I was introduced to a numerous family; but the father, from whom I was led to expect so much entertainment, was absent. The lieutenant consequently was obliged to be the interpreter of our reciprocal compliments. The phrases were awkwardly transmitted, it is true; but looks and gestures were sufficient to make them intelligible and interesting. The girls were all vivacity, and respect for me could scarcely keep them from romping with my host, who, asking for a pinch of snuff, was presented with a box, out of which an artificial mouse, fastened to the bottom, sprung. Though this trick had doubt-less been played time out of mind, yet the laughter it excited was not less genuine.

They were overflowing with civility; but to prevent their almost killing my babe with kindness, I was obliged to shorten my visit; and two or three of the girls accompanied us, bringing with them a part of whatever the house afforded to contribute towards rendering my supper more plentiful; and plentiful in fact it was, though I with difficulty did honour to some of the dishes, not relishing the quan-tity of sugar and spices put into everything. At supper my host told me bluntly that I was a woman of observation, for I asked him *men's questions*.

The arrangements for my journey were quickly made; I could only have a car with post-horses, as I did not choose to wait till a carriage could be sent for to Gothenburg. The expense of my journey, about one or two and twenty English miles, I found would not amount to more than eleven or twelve shillings, paying, he assured me, generously. I gave him a guinea and a half. But it was with the greatest difficulty that I could make him take so much, indeed anything for my lodging and fare. He declared that it was next to robbing me, explaining how much I ought to pay on the road. However, as I was positive, he took the guinea for himself; but, as a condition, insisted on accompanying me, to prevent my meeting with any trouble or imposition on the way.

I then retired to my apartment with regret. The night was so fine, that I would gladly have rambled about much longer; yet recollecting that I must rise very early, I reluctantly went to bed: but my senses had been so awake, and my imagination still continued so busy, that I sought for rest in vain. Rising before six, I scented the sweet morning air; I had long before heard the birds twittering to hail the dawning day, though it could scarcely have been allowed to have departed.

Nothing, in fact, can equal the beauty of the northern summer's evening and night; if night it may be called that only wants the glare of day, the full light, which frequently seems so impertinent; for I could write at midnight very well without a candle. I contemplated all nature at rest; the rocks, even grown darker in their appearance, looked as if they partook of the general repose, and reclined more heavily on their foundation.—What, I exclaimed, is this active principle which keeps me still awake?—Why fly my thoughts abroad when everything around me appears at home? My child was sleeping with equal calmness—innocent and sweet as the closing flowers.— Some recollections, attached to the idea of home, mingled with reflections respecting the state of society I had been contemplating that evening, made a tear drop on the rosy cheek I had just kissed; and emotions that trembled on the brink of ecstasy and agony gave a poignancy to my sensations, which made me feel more alive than usual.

What are these imperious sympathies? How frequently has melancholy and even misanthropy taken possession of me, when the world has disgusted me, and friends have proved unkind. I have then considered myself as a particle broken off from the grand mass of mankind;—I was alone, till some involuntary sympathetic emotion, like the attraction of adhesion, made me feel that I was still a part of a mighty whole, from which I could not sever myself—not, perhaps, for the reflection has been carried very far, by snapping the thread of an existence which loses its charms in proportion as the cruel experience of life stops or poisons the current of the heart. Futurity, what hast thou not to give to those who know that there is such a thing as

happiness! I speak not of philosophical contentment, though pain
has afforded them the strongest conviction of it.

After our coffee and milk, for the mistress of the house had been
roused long before us by her hospitality, my baggage was taken forward in a boat by my host, because the car could not safely have been
brought to the house.

The road at first was very rocky and troublesome; but our driver
was careful, and the horses accustomed to the frequent and sudden
acclivities and descents; so that, not apprehending any danger, I
played with my girl, whom I would not leave to Marguerite's care, on
account of her timidity.

Stopping at a little inn to bait the horses, I saw the first countenance in Sweden that displeased me, though the man was better
dressed than anyone who had as yet fallen in my way. An altercation
took place between him and my host, the purport of which I could
not guess, excepting that I was the occasion of it, be it what it would.
The sequel was his leaving the house angrily; and I was immediately
informed that he was the custom-house officer. The professional had
indeed effaced the national character, for living as he did with these
frank hospitable people, still only the exciseman appeared—the
counterpart of some I had met with in England and France. I was
unprovided with a passport, not having entered any great town. At
Gothenburg I knew I could immediately obtain one, and only the
trouble made me object to the searching my trunks. He blustered for
money; but the lieutenant was determined to guard me, according to
promise, from imposition.

To avoid being interrogated at the town-gate, and obliged to go in
the rain to give an account of myself, merely a form, before we could
get the refreshment we stood in need of, he requested us to descend,
I might have said step, from our car, and walk into town.

I expected to have found a tolerable inn, but was ushered into a
most comfortless one; and, because it was about five o'clock, three
or four hours after their dining hour, I could not prevail on them to
give me anything warm to eat.

The appearance of the accommodations obliged me to deliver one
of my recommendatory letters, and the gentleman, to whom it was
addressed, sent to look out for a lodging for me whilst I partook of
his supper. As nothing passed at this supper to characterize the
country, I shall here close my letter.

Letter VI

[Wollstonecraft crosses the Skagerrak, from Sweden to Norway.]

The sea was boisterous; but, as I had an experienced pilot, I did not apprehend any danger. Sometimes, I was told, boats are driven far out and lost. However, I seldom calculate chances so nicely— sufficient for the day is the obvious evil!*

We had to steer amongst islands and huge rocks, rarely losing sight of the shore, though it now and then appeared only a mist that bordered the water's edge. The pilot assured me that the numerous harbours on the Norway coast were very safe, and the pilot-boats were always on the watch. The Swedish side is very dangerous, I am also informed; and the help of experience is not often at hand, to enable strange vessels to steer clear of the rocks which lurk below the water, close to the shore.

There are no tides here, nor in the cattegate;* and, what appeared to me a consequence, no sandy beach. Perhaps this observation has been made before; but it did not occur to me till I saw the waves continually beating against the bare rocks, without ever receding to leave a sediment to harden.

The wind was fair, till we had to tack about in order to enter Laurvig,* where we arrived towards three o'clock in the afternoon. It is a clean, pleasant town, with a considerable iron-work, which gives life to it.

As the Norwegians do not frequently see travellers, they are very curious to know their business, and who they are—so curious that I was half tempted to adopt Dr Franklin's plan,* when travelling in America, where they are equally prying, which was to write on a paper, for public inspection, my name, from whence I came, where I was going, and what was my business. But if I were importuned by their curiosity, their friendly gestures gratified me. A woman, coming alone, interested them. And I know not whether my weariness gave me a look of peculiar delicacy; but they approached to assist me, and enquire after my wants, as if they were afraid to hurt, and wished to protect me. The sympathy I inspired, thus dropping down from the clouds in a strange land, affected me more than it would have done, had not my spirits been harassed by various causes—by much thinking—musing almost to madness—and even by a sort of weak melancholy that hung about my heart at parting with my daughter for the first time.

You know that as a female I am particularly attached to her—I feel more than a mother's fondness and anxiety, when I reflect on the dependent and oppressed state of her sex. I dread lest she should be forced to sacrifice her heart to her principles, or principles to her heart. With trembling hand I shall cultivate sensibility, and cherish delicacy of sentiment, lest, whilst I lend fresh blushes to the rose, I sharpen the thorns that will wound the breast I would fain guard—I dread to unfold her mind, lest it should render her unfit for the world she is to inhabit. Hapless woman! what a fate is thine!

But whither am I wandering? I only meant to tell you that the impression the kindness of the simple people made visible on my countenance increased my sensibility to a painful degree. I wished to have had a room to myself; for their attention, and rather distressing observation, embarrassed me extremely. Yet, as they would bring me eggs, and make my coffee, I found I could not leave them without hurting their feelings of hospitality.

It is customary here for the host and hostess to welcome their guests as master and mistress of the house.

My clothes, in their turn, attracted the attention of the females; and I could not help thinking of the foolish vanity which makes many women so proud of the observation of strangers as to take wonder very gratuitously for admiration. This error they are very apt to fall into; when arrived in a foreign country, the populace stare at them as they pass: yet the make of a cap, or the singularity of a gown, is often the cause of the flattering attention, which afterwards supports a fantastic superstructure of self-conceit.

Not having brought a carriage over with me, expecting to have met a person where I landed, who was immediately to have procured me one, I was detained whilst the good people of the inn sent round to all their acquaintance to search for a vehicle. A rude sort of *cabriole** was at last found, and a driver half drunk, who was not less eager to make a good bargain on that account. I had a Danish captain of a ship and his mate with me: the former was to ride on horseback, at which he was not very expert, and the latter to partake of my seat. The driver mounted behind to guide the horses, and flourish the whip over our shoulders; he would not suffer the reins out of his own hands. There was something so grotesque in our appearance that I could not avoid shrinking into myself when I saw a gentleman-like man in the group which crowded round the door to observe us. I could have broken the driver's whip for cracking to call the women and children together; but seeing a significant smile on the face, I had before remarked, I burst into a laugh, to allow him to do so too,—and away we flew. This is not a flourish of the pen; for we actually went on full gallop a long time, the horses being very good; indeed I have never met with better, if so good, post-horses, as in Norway; they are of a stouter make than the English horses, appear to be well fed, and are not easily tired.

I had to pass over, I was informed, the most fertile and best cultivated tract of country in Norway. The distance was three Norwegian miles, which are longer than the Swedish. The roads were very good; the farmers are obliged to repair them; and we scampered through a great extent of country in a more improved state than any I had viewed since I left England. Still there was sufficient of hills, dales, and rocks, to prevent the idea of a plain from entering the head, or even of such scenery as England and France afford. The prospects were also embellished by water, rivers, and lakes, before the sea proudly claimed my regard; and the road running frequently through lofty groves, rendered the landscapes beautiful, though they were not so romantic as those I had lately seen with such delight.

It was late when I reached Tonsberg; and I was glad to go to bed at a decent inn. The next morning, the 17th of July, conversing with the gentlemen with whom I had business to transact, I found that I should be detained at Tonsberg three weeks; and I lamented that I had not brought my child with me.

The inn was quiet, and my room so pleasant, commanding a view of the sea, confined by an amphitheatre of hanging woods, that I wished to remain there, though no one in the house could speak English or French. The mayor, my friend,* however, sent a young woman to me who spoke a little English, and she agreed to call on me twice a day, to receive my orders, and translate them to my hostess.

My not understanding the language was an excellent pretext for dining alone, which I prevailed on them to let me do at a late hour; for the early dinners in Sweden had entirely deranged my day. I could not alter it there, without disturbing the economy of a family where I was as a visitor; necessity having forced me to accept of an invitation from a private family, the lodgings were so incommodious.

Amongst the Norwegians I had the arrangement of my own time; and I determined to regulate it in such a manner that I might enjoy as much of their sweet summer as I possibly could; short, it is true; but 'passing sweet'.*

I never endured a winter in this rude clime; consequently it was not the contrast, but the real beauty of the season which made the present summer appear to me the finest I had ever seen. Sheltered from the north and eastern winds, nothing can exceed the salubrity, the soft freshness of the western gales. In the evening they also die away; the aspen leaves tremble into stillness, and reposing nature seems to be warmed by the moon, which here assumes a genial aspect: and if a light shower has chanced to fall with the sun, the juniper, the underwood of the forest, exhales a wild perfume, mixed with a thousand nameless sweets that, soothing the heart, leave images in the memory which the imagination will ever hold dear.

Nature is the nurse of sentiment,—the true source of taste;—yet what misery, as well as rapture, is produced by a quick perception of the beautiful and sublime, when it is exercised in observing animated nature, when every beauteous feeling and emotion excites responsive sympathy, and the harmonized soul sinks into melancholy, or rises to ecstasy, just as the chords are touched, like the aeolian harp agitated by the changing wind. But how dangerous is it to foster these sentiments in such an imperfect state of existence; and how difficult to eradicate them when an affection for mankind, a passion for an individual, is but the unfolding of that love which embraces all that is great and beautiful.

When a warm heart has received strong impressions, they are not to be effaced. Emotions become sentiments; and the imagination renders even transient sensations permanent, by fondly retracing them. I cannot, without a thrill of delight, recollect views I have seen, which are not to be forgotten,—nor looks I have felt in every nerve which I shall never more meet. The grave has closed over a dear friend, the friend of my youth,* still she is present with me, and I hear her soft voice warbling as I stray over the heath. Fate has separated me from another, the fire of whose eyes, tempered by infantine tenderness, still warms my breast; even when gazing on these tremendous cliffs, sublime emotions absorb my soul. And, smile not, if I add that the rosy tint of morning reminds me of a suffusion, which will never more charm my senses, unless it reappears on the cheeks of my child. Her sweet blushes I may yet hide in my bosom, and she is still too young to ask why starts the tear, so near akin to pleasure and pain?

I cannot write any more at present. Tomorrow we will talk of Tonsberg.

PART II

THE BRITISH ISLES

THE nonconformist gentlewoman Celia Fiennes kept a memoir of her travels in the last years of the seventeenth century which affords us the most comprehensive view of the condition of England between William Camden's topographical survey *Britannia* (1586) and Daniel Defoe's *A Tour through the Whole Island of Great Britain* (1724–6). Fiennes's patriotic justification for domestic tourism and her interest in the 'productions and manufactures of each place' anticipate the claims with which Defoe would advertise his more systematic travelogue two decades later. If Fiennes was the amateur traveller and writer *par excellence*, Defoe turned travel writing into a professional enterprise, a formal survey and accounting of the national stock. His survey of the multinational state created at the 1707 Treaty of Union between England and Scotland founded a distinctively modern genre of 'economic tourism'. Breaking with the antiquarian tradition of Camden, Defoe highlights trade and industry as the foundations of an imperial greatness located in Britain's future rather than its past. The economic tour, surveying the state of the nation from the viewpoint of a Whig and (subsequently) Radical commitment to progress and reform, would remain a staple of modern domestic travel writing. Notable later examples are represented in this anthology by Arthur Young, writing from Ireland, and William Cobbett, scrutinizing the widening gap between property-holders and the labouring poor wrought by the economic and social transformations of the countryside.

A conspicuous trend of leisured tourism emerged in the 1770s, linked to the opening up of the mountainous interiors of Great Britain (Wales, the Lake District, Scotland) and a new discourse of aesthetic categories, the 'picturesque', trained on wild forms of landscape. Domestic tourism provided at once an aesthetic preparation for the Grand Tour (theorized here by Thomas West) and its nationalist, middle-class substitute. Towards the end of the century the Scottish Highlands began to eclipse Westmorland and Cumberland as the premier British site for picturesque tourism. English attitudes to Scotland oscillated between metropolitan contempt and Romantic longing, the expressive tendencies of 'economic' and 'picturesque' tourism, with the latter gaining force in the decades after 1745. Armed Highlanders had threatened the British government, not just their Lowland neighbours, in the last, tragic Jacobite rising; military repression was followed by a legislative dismantling of the clan system and the collapse of local economies. By the early 1770s Samuel Johnson and James Boswell acknowledged that they had come 'too late to see what we had expected, a people of peculiar appearance, and a system of antiquated life'. Tourists came to admire the lochs and glens as the natives left, boarding emigrant ships to North America (in the most familiar scenario).

The century closed with the legislative absorption of Ireland, most troubled of the internal British colonies, into the political body of the nation in a second Act of Union (1801). Ireland, however, was not Scotland, and travellers would be hard put to dismiss the social symptoms of under-development, erupting in the risings of 1798 and 1803, to a romantic past.

1. THE STATE OF THE NATION

CELIA FIENNES, *The Diary of Celia Fiennes* (c.1685–1703; from *Through England on a Side-Saddle, in the Time of William and Mary. Being the Diary of Celia Fiennes*, ed. Emily W. Griffiths, 1888)

Celia Fiennes (1662–1741), granddaughter of the first Lord Saye and Sele, criss-crossed England on horseback between 1684 and c.1703, ostensibly 'to regain my health by variety and change of air and exercise'. Her memoir of her travels, kept for family reading and not published until 1888, gives a vivid account of a still largely unenclosed countryside with few and primitive roads. Fiennes visits 'Spaws', medicinal watering-places or spas, increasingly popular in the later seventeenth century; her visit to Bath (c.1687) antedates by a few years the town's fashionable develop-ment. A northern excursion takes her from Carlisle to the wild tract of the Scottish Border.

To the Reader

As this was never designed, so not likely to fall into the hands of any but my near relations, there needs not much to be said to excuse or recommend it. Something may be diverting and profitable though not to gentlemen that have travelled more about England, stayed longer in places, might have more acquaintance and more opportun-ity to be informed. My journeys as they were begun to regain my health by variety and change of air and exercise, so whatever pro-moted that was pursued; and those informations of things as could be obtained from inns *en passant*, or from some acquaintance, inhabitants of such places could furnish me with for my diversion, I thought necessary to remark: that as my bodily health was promoted my mind should not appear totally unoccupied, and the collecting it together remain for my after conversation (with such as might be inquisitive after such and such places) to which might have recourse; and as most I converse with knows both the freedom and easiness I speak and write as well as my defect in all, so they will not expect exactness or politeness in this book, though such embellishments might have adorned the descriptions and suited the nicer taste.

Now thus much without vanity may be asserted of the subject, that if all persons, both ladies, much more gentlemen, would spend some of their time in journeys to visit their native land, and be curious to inform themselves and make observations of the pleasant prospects, good buildings, different produces and manufactures of each place, with the variety of sports and recreations they are adapt to, would be a sovereign remedy to cure or preserve from these epidemic diseases of vapours, should I add laziness?—it would also form such an idea of England, add much to its glory and esteem in our minds and cure the evil itch of overvaluing foreign parts; at least furnish them with an equivalent to entertain strangers when amongst us, or inform them when abroad of their native country, which has been often a reproach to the English, ignorance and being strangers to themselves. Nay the ladies might have matter not unworthy their observation, so subject for conversation, within their own compass in each county to which they relate, and thence study now to be serviceable to their neighbours especially the poor among whom they dwell, which would spare them the uneasy thoughts how to pass away tedious days, and time would not be a burden when not at a card or dice table, and the fashions and manners of foreign parts less minded or desired. But much more requisite is it for gentlemen in giving service of their country at home or abroad, in town or country, especially those that serve in Parliament to know and inform themselves the nature of land, the genius of the inhabitants, so as to promote and improve manufacture and trade suitable to each and encourage all projects tending thereto, putting in practice all laws made for each particular good, maintaining their privileges, procuring more as requisite; but to their shame it must be owned many if not most are ignorant of anything but the name of the place for which they serve in Parliament; how then can they speak for or promote their good or redress their grievances. But now I may be justly blamed to pretend to give account of our constitution, customs, laws, lect,* matters far above my reach or capacity, but herein I have described what have come within my knowledge either by view and reading, or relation from others which according to my conception have faithfully rehearsed.

Bath

Another journey to the Bath, from Newtontony* to Warminster 18 miles a good road town and good way; thence to Breackly* 5 mile a deep clay way, we passed over one common of some miles' length on a narrow causeway that a coach can scarce pass, all pitched with slates and stones—our coach was once wedged in the wheel in the stones that several men were forced to lift us out; it's made only for packhorses which is the way of carriage in those parts. The common is so moorish their feet and wheels would sink in, so no going there—thence to Philip Norton 3 miles a very neat stone built village. Thence you pass a good way between 2 stone walls to the Bath, 5 mile down a very steep hill and stony, a mile from the town scarce any passing and there descends a little current of water continually from the rocks. The ways to the Bath are all difficult, the town lies low in a bottom and its steep ascents all ways out of the town. The houses are indifferent, the streets of a good size well pitched. There are several good houses built for lodgings that are new and adorned, and good furniture, the baths in my opinion makes the town unpleasant, the air so low, encompassed with high hills and woods. There is 5 baths the hot bath the most hot springs—it's but small and built all round, which makes it the hotter—out of it runs the water into a bath called the Le Pours.

The third bath is called the Cross Bath which is something bigger than the former and not so hot; the Cross in the middle has seats round it for the gentlemen to sit, and round the walls are arches with seats for the ladies, all stone and the seat is stone and if you think the seat is too low they raise it with a cushion as they call it, another stone, but indeed the water bears you up that the seat seems as easy as a down cushion. Before the arch the ladies use to have a laced toilet hung up on the top of the arch and so to shelter their heads even to the water if they please. You generally sit up to the neck in

water, this Cross Bath is much the coolest and is used mostly in the
heat of summer; there are galleries round the top that the company
that does not bathe that day walks in and looks over into the bath on
their acquaintance and company—there are such a number of guides
to each bath of women to wait on the ladies, and of men to wait on
the gentlemen, and they keep their due distance. There is a serjeant
belonging to the baths that all the bathing time walks in galleries and
takes notice order is observed and punishes the rude, and most
people of fashion send to him when they begin to bathe, then he
takes particular care of them and compliments you every morning
which deserves its reward at the end of the season. When you would
walk about the bath I use to have a woman guide or two to lead me
for the water is so strong it will quickly tumble you down, and then
you have 2 of the men guides go at a distance about the bath to
clear the way. At the sides of the arches are rings that you may hold
by and so walk a little way, but the springs bubble up so fast and so
strong and are so hot up against the bottoms of one's feet, especially
in that they call the kitchen in the bath, which is a great cross with
seats in the middle and many hot springs rise there. The King's
Bath is very large, as large as the rest put together, in it is the hot
pump that persons are pumped at for lameness or on their heads for
palsies. I saw one pumped, they put on a broad brimmed hat with the
crown cut out so as the brims cast off the water from the face; they
are pumped in the bath, one of the men guides pumps—they have
twopence I think for 100 pumps. The water is scalding hot out of the
pump, the arms or legs are more easily pumped. The ladies go into
the bath with garments made of a fine yellow canvas, which is stiff
and made large with great sleeves like a parson's gown; the water fills
it up so that it's borne off that your shape is not seen, it does not
cling close as other linen, which looks sadly in the poorer sort that
go in their own linen. The gentlemen have drawers and waistcoats of
the same sort of canvas, this is the best linen, for the bath water will
change any other yellow. When you go out of the bath you go within
a door that leads to steps which you ascend by degrees that are in the
water, then the door is shut which shuts down into the water a good
way, so you are in a private place where you still ascend several more
steps and let your canvas drop off by degrees into the water, which
your women guides take off, and the mean time your maids fling a
garment of flannel made like a nightgown with great sleeves over

your head, and the guides take the tail and so pull it on you. Just as you rise the steps, and the other garment drops off so you are wrapped up in the flannel and your nightgown on the top, and your slippers and so you are set in chair which is brought into the room which are called slips, and there are chimneys in them, you may have fires. These are in several parts of the sides of the bath for the convenience of persons going in and out of the bath decently, and at the top of the stairs stands a woman that lays a woollen cloth for you to set your bare foot, and also to give you attendance. The chairs you go in are a low seat and with frames round and over your head and all covered inside and out with red baize and a curtain drawn before of the same which makes it close and warm; then a couple of men with staves takes and carries you to your lodging and sets you at your bedside where you go to bed and lie and sweat some time as you please. Your own maids and the maids of the house gets your fire and wait on you till you rise to get out of your sweat. All the baths has the same attendance. The Queen's Bath is bigger than the other three but not and near so big as the King's, which do run into each other and is only parted by a wall and at one place a great arch where they run into each other. The Queen's Bath is a degree hotter than the Cross Bath and the King's Bath much hotter. These have all galleries round and the pump is in one of these galleries at the King's Bath which the company drinks of; it's very hot and tastes like the water that boils eggs, has such a smell, but the nearer the pump you drink it, the hotter and less offensive and more spiritous. The baths are all emptied as soon as the company goes out, which is about 10 or 11 of the clock in the morning; then by sluices they empty at once the bath so it fills again. I have seen all the springs bubble up as thick out of the ground when the baths have been empty. The bottom is gravel. So they will be full for the evening if company would go in again, if so they empty them again at night and they are filled against the morning and there will be such a white scum on the bath which the guides goes and skims off clean before any company goes in; if they go in while this scum is on it gives them the bath mantle as they call it, makes them break out into heat and pimples; the like will be on them if they go into the bath before they have purged, especially in the hotter bath. The place for diversion about the Bath is either the walks in that they call the King's Mead which is a pleasant green meadow, where are walks round and cross it, no place for coaches, and indeed there is little use of a coach only to bring and carry the company from the Bath for the ways are not proper for coaches.

The town and all its accommodations is adapted to the bathing and drinking of the waters and to nothing else; the streets are well pitched and clean kept and there are chairs as in London to carry the better sort of people in visits, or if sick or infirm and is only in the town, for it's so encompassed with high hills few care to take the air on them.

[Carlisle to the Scottish Border]

I walked round the walls and saw the river which twists and turns itself round the grounds, called the Emount,* which at 3 or 4 miles off is flowed by the sea. The other river is the Essex which is very broad and ebbs and flows about a mile or two off. There remains only some of the walls and ruins of the Castle, which does show it to have been a very strong town formerly. The walls are of a prodigious thickness and vast great stones, it's moated round and with draw-bridges. There is a large market place with a good cross and hall and is well supplied as I am informed with provision at easy rate, but my landlady notwithstanding ran me up the largest reckoning for almost nothing; it was the dearest lodging I met with and she pretended she could get me nothing else; so for 2 joints of mutton and a pint of wine and bread and beer I had a 12 shilling reckoning, but since I find though I was in the biggest house in town I was in the worst accommodation, and so found it, and a young giddy landlady that could only dress fine and entertain the soldiers. From hence I took a guide the next day and so went for Scotland and rode 3 or 4 mile by the side of this River Emount, which is full of very good fish. I rode sometimes on a high ridge over a hill, sometimes on the sands, it turning and winding about that I went almost all the way by it and saw them with boats fishing for salmon and trout, which made my journey very pleasant. Leaving this river I came to the Essex which is very broad and hazardous to cross even when the tide is out, by which it leaves a broad sand on each side, which in some places is unsafe, made me take a good guide which carried me about and across some part of it here, and some part in another place it being deep in the channel where I did cross which was in sight of the mouth of the river that runs into the sea. On the sand before the water was quite gone from it I saw a great bird which looked almost black picking up fish and busking in the water, it looked like an eagle and by its dimensions could scarce be any other bird. Thence I went into Scotland over the River Serke which is also flowed by the sea, but in the summer time is not so deep but can be passed over—though pretty deep but narrow. It affords good fish, but all here about which are called borderers seem to be very poor people which I impute to their sloth. Scotland this part of it is a low marshy ground where they cut turf and peat for the fuel, though I should apprehend the sea might convey coals to them. I see little that they are employed besides fishing which makes provision plentiful or else their cutting and carving turf and peat, which the women and great girls barelegged does lead a horse which draws a sort of carriage, the wheels like a dung-pot and hold about 4 wheelbarrows. These people though with naked legs are yet wrapped up in plodds,* a piece of woollen like a blanket, or else riding hoods—and this when they are in their houses. I took them for people which were sick, seeing 2 or 3 great wenches as tall and big as any woman sat hovering between their bed and chimney corner, all idle doing nothing or at least was not settled to any work though it was nine of the clock when I came thither, having gone 7 long miles that morning. This is little market town called Adison Bank;* the houses look just like the booths at a fair. I am sure I have been in some of them that were tolerable dwellings to these. They have no chimneys, their smoke comes out all over the house and there are great holes in the sides of their houses which lets out the smoke when they have been well smoked in it. There is no room in their houses but is up to the thatch and in which are 2 or 3 beds, even to their parlours and buttery, and notwithstanding the cleaning of their parlour for me I was not able to bear the room; the smell of the hay was a perfume and what I rather chose to stay and see my horses eat their provender in the stable than to stand in that room for I could not bring myself to sit down. My landlady offered me a good dish of fish and brought me butter in a lairdly dish with the clapbread,* but I could have no stomach to eat any of the food they should order, and finding they had no wheaten bread I told her I could not eat their clapped out bread, so I bought the fish she got for me which was full cheap enough, ninepence for two pieces of salmon half a one near a yard long, and a very large trout of an amber colour, so drinking without eating some of their wine which was exceeding good claret which they stand conveniently for to have from France, and indeed it was the best and truest French wine I have drank this seven year and very clear, I had the first tapping of the little vessel and it was very fine. Then I went up to their church which looks rather like some little house built of stone and brick such as our ordinary people in a village live in. The doors were and the seats and pulpit was in so disregarded a manner that one would have thought there was no use of it, but there is a parson which lives just by, whose house is the best in the place, and they are all fine folks in their Sunday clothes. I observe the churchyard is full of gravestones pretty large with coats of arms, and some had a coronet on the escutcheons cut in the stone. I saw but one house that looked like a house about a quarter of a mile, which was some gentleman's that was built 2 or 3 rooms and some over them of brick and stone. The rest were all like barns or huts for cattle. This is threescore miles from Edinburgh and the nearest town to this place is 18 miles, and there would not have been much better entertainment or accommodation, and their miles are so long in these countries made me afraid to venture, lest after a tedious journey I should not be able to get a bed I could lie in. It seems there are very few towns except Edinburgh, Aberdeen and Kerk* which can give better treatment to strangers, therefore for the most part persons that travel there go from one nobleman's house to another. Those houses are all kind of castles and they live great though in so nasty a way as all things are in even those houses one has little stomach to eat or use anything, as I have been told by some that has travelled there, and I am sure I met with a sample of it enough to discourage my progress farther in Scotland. I attribute it wholly to their sloth for I see they sit and do little. I think there were one or two at last did take spinning in hand at a lazy way. Thence I took my fish to carry it to a place for the English to dress it and repassed the Serke and the River Essex and there I saw the common people men women and children take off their shoes, and holding up their clothes wade through the rivers when the tide was out, and truly some there were that when they come to the other side put on shoes and stockings and had fine plodds cast over them and their garb seemed above the common people; but this is their constant way of travelling from one place to another—if any river to pass they make no use of bridges and have not many.

DANIEL DEFOE, *A Tour through the Whole Island of*
Great Britain (1724–6)

Daniel Foe (1660–1731), a tallow chandler's son, dignified his name when
he became a professional author in 1703. He travelled throughout England
as a merchant in the 1680s and then to the west of England and Scotland
as an undercover agent gathering intelligence for Robert Harley, Earl of
Oxford, during the negotiations leading to the Treaty of Union. Defoe's
Tour, a synthesis of many journeys (not all of which he made himself),
celebrates the new 'Great British Empire' and the basis of its prosperity in
a modernizing mercantile economy. We reprint Defoe's apology for travel
writing, his revisionist account of the 'wonders of the Peak' in Derbyshire,
and the narrative of his trek across the Pennines to the cloth-
manufacturing district of Halifax.

Vol. i (1724), Preface

If this work is not both pleasant and profitable to the reader, the
author most freely and openly declares the fault must be in his
performance, and it cannot be any deficiency in the subject.

As the work itself is a description of the most flourishing and
opulent country in the world, so there is a flowing variety of materials;
all the particulars are fruitful of instructing and diverting objects.

If novelty pleases, here is the present state of the country described,
the improvement, as well in culture,* as in commerce, the increase of
people, and employment for them: also here you have an account of
the increase of buildings, as well in great cities and towns, as in the
new seats and dwellings of the nobility and gentry; also the increase
of wealth, in many eminent particulars.

If antiquity takes with you, though the looking back into remote
things is studiously avoided, yet it is not wholly omitted, nor any
useful observations neglected; the learned writers on the subject of
antiquity* in Great Britain have so well discharged themselves, that
we can never over-value their labours, yet there are daily farther
discoveries made, which give future ages, room, perhaps not to
mend, yet at least to add to what has been already done.

In travelling through England, a luxuriance of objects presents
itself to our view. Wherever we come, and which way soever we look,
we see something new, something significant, something well worth
the traveller's stay, and the writer's care; nor is any check to our
design, or obstruction to its acceptance in the world, to say the like

has been done already, or to panegyric upon the labours and value of those authors who have gone before, in this work. A complete account of Great Britain will be the work of many years, I might say ages, and may employ many hands. Whoever has travelled Great Britain before us, and whatever they have written, though they may have had a harvest, yet they have always, either by necessity, ignorance or negligence passed over so much, that others may come and glean after them by large handfuls.

Nor could it be otherwise, had the diligence and capacities of all who have gone before been greater than they are; for the face of things so often alters, and the situation of affairs in this great British Empire gives such new turns, even to Nature itself, that there is matter of new observation every day presented to the traveller's eye.

The fate of things gives a new face to things, produces changes in low life, and innumerable incidents; plants and supplants families, raises and sinks towns, removes manufactures and trade; great towns decay, and small towns rise; new towns, new palaces, new seats are built every day; great rivers and good harbours dry up, and grow useless; again, new ports are opened, brooks are made rivers, small rivers navigable ports; and harbours are made where none were before, and the like.

Several towns, which antiquity speaks of as considerable, are now lost and swallowed up by the sea, as Dunwich in Suffolk for one; and others, which antiquity knew nothing of, are now grown considerable. In a word, new matter offers to new observation, and they who write next, may perhaps find as much room for enlarging upon us as we do upon those that have gone before.

The author says that indeed he might have given his pen a loose here to have complained how much the conduct of the people diminishes the reputation of the island, on many modern occasions, and so we could have made his historical account a satire upon the country, as well as upon the people; but they are ill friends to England, who strive to write a history of her nudities, and expose, much less recommend, her wicked part to posterity; he has rather endeavoured to do her justice in those things which recommend her, and humbly to move a reformation of those which he thinks do not; in this he thinks he shall best pay the debt of a just and native writer, who, in regard to the reader, should conceal nothing which ought to be known, and in regard to his country, expose nothing which ought to be concealed.

A description of the country is the business here, not descanting upon the errors of the people; and yet, without boasting, we may venture to say, we are at least upon a level with the best of our neighbours, perhaps above them in morals, whatever we are in their pride; but let that stand as it does till times mend; 'tis not, I say, the present business.

The observations here made, as they principally regard the present state of things, so, as near as can be, they are adapted to the present taste of the times. The situation of things is given not as they have been, but as they are; the improvements in the soil, the product of the earth, the labour of the poor, the improvement in manufactures, in merchandises, in navigation, all respects the present time, not the time past.

In every county something of the people is said, as well as of the place, of their customs, speech, employments, the product of their labour, and the manner of their living, the circumstances as well as situation of the towns; their trade and government; of the rarities of art, or nature; the rivers, of the inland and river navigation; also of the lakes and medicinal springs, not forgetting the general dependence of the whole country upon the City of London, as well for the consumption of its produce, as the circulation of its trade.

The preparations for this work have been suitable to the author's earnest concern for its usefulness; seventeen very large circuits, or journeys, have been taken through divers parts separately, and three general tours over almost the whole English part of the island; in all which the author has not been wanting to treasure up just remarks upon particular places and things, so that he is very little in debt to other men's labours, and gives but very few accounts of things, but what he has been an eye-witness of himself.

Besides these several journeys in England, he has also lived some time in Scotland, and has travelled critically over great part of it; he has viewed the north part of England, and the south part of Scotland five several times over; all which is hinted here, to let the readers know what reason they will have to be satisfied with the authority of the relation, and that the accounts here given are not the produce of a cursory view, or raised upon the borrowed lights of other observers. . . .

But after all that has been said by others, or can be said here, no description of Great Britain can be what we call a finished account, as no clothes can be made to fit a growing child; no picture carry the likeness of a living face; the size of one, and the countenance of the other always altering with time, so no account of a kingdom thus daily altering its countenance can be perfect.

Even while the sheets are in the press, new beauties appear in several places, and almost to every part we are obliged to add appendixes, and supplemental accounts of fine houses, new undertakings, buildings, etc., and thus posterity will be continually adding; every age will find an increase of glory. And may it do so, till Great Britain as much exceeds the finest country in Europe as that country now fancies they exceed her.

Vol. iii (1726), Letter I

A little on the other side of Wirksworth begins a long plain called Brassington Moor, which reaches full twelve miles in length another way, *viz.* from Brassington to Buxton. At the beginning of it on this side from Wirksworth, it is not quite so much. The Peak people, who are mighty fond of having strangers showed everything they can, and of calling everything a wonder, told us here of another high mountain, where a giant was buried, and which they called the Giant's Tomb.

This tempted our curiosity, and we presently rode up to the mountain in order to leave our horses, dragoon-like, with a servant, and to clamber up to the top of it, to see this Giant's Tomb. Here we missed the imaginary wonder, and found a real one, the story of which I cannot but record, to show the discontinued part of the rich world how to value their own happiness, by looking below them, and seeing how others live, who yet are capable of being easy and content, which content goes a great way towards being happy, if it does not come quite up to happiness. The story is this:

'As we came near the hill, which seemed to be round, and a precipice almost on every side, we perceived a little parcel of ground hedged in, as if it were a garden. It was about twenty or thirty yards long, but not so much broad, parallel with the hill, and close to it; we saw no house, but, by a dog running out barking, we perceived some people were thereabout and presently after we saw two little children, and then a third run out to see what was the matter. When we came close up we saw a small opening, not a door, but a natural opening into the rock, and the noise we had made brought a woman out with a child in her arms, and another at her foot. *NB*. The biggest of these five was a girl, about eight or ten years old.

'We asked the woman some questions about the tomb of the giant upon the rock or mountain. She told us there was a broad flat stone of a great size lay there, which, she said, the people called a grave-stone; and, if it was, it might well be called a giant's, for she thought no ordinary man was ever so tall, and she described it to us as well as she could, by which it must be at least sixteen or seventeen foot long; but she could not give any farther account of it, neither did she seem to lay any stress upon the tale of a giant being buried there, but said, if her husband had been at home he might have shown it to us. I snatched at the word, at home! Says I, good wife, why, where do you live. Here, Sir, says she, and points to the hole in the rock. Here! says I; and do all these children live here too? Yes, Sir, says she, they were all born here. Pray how long have you dwelt here then? said I. My husband was born here, said she, and his father before him. Will you give me leave, says one of our Company, as curious as I was, to come in and see your house, Dame? If you please, Sir, says she, but 'tis not a place fit for such as you are to come into, calling him, your Worship, forsooth; but that by the by. I mention it, to show that the good woman did not want manners, though she lived in a den like a wild body.

'However, we alighted and went in: there was a large hollow cave, which the poor people by two curtains hanged cross, had parted into three rooms. On one side was the chimney, and the man, or perhaps his father, being miners, had found means to work a shaft or funnel through the rock to carry the smoke out at the top, where the Giant's Tombstone was. The habitation was poor, 'tis true, but things within did not look so like misery as I expected. Everything was clean and neat, though mean and ordinary. There were shelves with earthen-ware, and some pewter and brass. There was, which I observed in particular, a whole flitch or side of bacon hanging up in the chimney, and by it a good piece of another. There was a sow and pigs running about at the door, and a little lean cow feeding upon a green place just before the door, and the little enclosed piece of ground I mentioned was growing with good barley, it being then near harvest.

'To find out whence this appearance of substance came, I asked the poor woman, what trade her husband was? She said, he worked in the lead mines. I asked her how much he could earn a day there? She said, if he had good luck he could earn about fivepence a day, but that he worked by the dish (which was a term of art I did not understand, but supposed, as I afterward understood it was, by the great, in proportion to the ore, which they measure in a wooden bowl, which they call a dish). I then asked, what she did? She said, when she was able to work she washed the ore. But, looking down on her children, and shaking her head, she intimated, that they found her so much business she could do but little, which I easily granted must be true. But what can you get at washing the ore, said I, when you can work? She said, if she worked hard she could gain threepence a day. So that, in short, here was but eightpence a day when they both worked hard, and that not always, and perhaps not often, and all this to maintain a man, his wife, and five small children, and yet they seemed to live very pleasantly, the children looked plump and fat, ruddy and wholesome; and the woman was tall, well shaped, clean, and (for the place) a very well looking, comely woman; nor was there anything looked like the dirt and nastiness of the miserable cottages of the poor; though many of them spend more money in strong drink than this poor woman had to maintain five children with.

'This moving sight so affected us all that, upon a short conference at the door, we made up a little lump of money, and I had the honour to be almoner for the company; and though the sum was not great, being at most something within a crown, as I told it into the poor woman's hand, I could perceive such a surprise in her face that, had she not given vent to her joy by a sudden flux of tears, I found she would have fainted away. She was some time before she could do anything but cry; but after that was abated, she expressed herself very handsomely (for a poor body) and told me, she had not seen so much money together of her own for many months.

'We asked her if she had a good husband. She smiled, and said, yes, thanked God for it, and that she was very happy in that, for he worked very hard, and they wanted for nothing that he could do for them, and two or three times made mention of how contented they were. In a word, it was a lecture to us all, and that such, I assure you, as made the whole company very grave all the rest of the day. And if it has no effect of that kind upon the reader, the defect must be in my telling the story in a less moving manner than the poor woman told it herself.'

From hence enquiring no farther after the giant, or his tomb, we went, by the direction of the poor woman, to a valley on the side of a rising hill, where there were several grooves, so they call the mouth of the shaft or pit by which they go down into a lead mine; and as we were standing still to look at one of them, admiring how small they were, and scarce believing a poor man that showed it us, when he told us that they went down those narrow pits or holes to so great a depth in the earth; I say, while we were wondering, and scarce believing the fact, we were agreeably surprised with seeing a hand, and then an arm, and quickly after a head, thrust up out of the very groove we were looking at. It was the more surprising as not we only, but not the man that we were talking to, knew anything of it, or expected it.

Immediately we rode closer up to the place, where we see the poor wretch working and heaving himself up gradually, as we thought, with difficulty; but when he showed us that it was by setting his feet upon pieces of wood fixed cross the angles of the groove like a ladder, we found that the difficulty was not much; and if the groove had been larger they could not either go up or down so easily, or with so much safety, for that now their elbows resting on those pieces as well as their feet, they went up and down with great ease and safety.

Those who would have a more perfect idea of those grooves, need do no more than go to the Church of St Paul's, and desire to see the square wells which they have there to go down from the top of the church into the very vaults under it, to place the leaden pipes which carry the rain water from the flat of the roof to the common-shore,* which wells are square, and have small iron bars placed cross the angles for the workmen to set their feet on, to go up and down to repair the pipes; the manner of the steps are thus described:

When this subterranean creature was come quite out, with all his furniture about him, we had as much variety to take us up as before; and our curiosity received full satisfaction without venturing down, as we were persuaded to by some people, and as two of our company were inclined to do.

First, the man was a most uncouth spectacle; he was clothed all in leather, had a cap of the same without brims, some tools in a little basket which he drew up with him, not one of the names of which we could understand but by the help of an interpreter. Nor indeed could we understand any of the man's discourse so as to make out a whole sentence; and yet the man was pretty free of his tongue too.

For his person, he was lean as a skeleton, pale as a dead corpse, his hair and beard a deep black, his flesh lank, and, as we thought, something of the colour of the lead itself, and being very tall and very lean he looked, or we that saw him ascend *ab Inferis*,* fancied he looked like an inhabitant of the dark regions below, and who was just ascended into the world of light.

Besides his basket of tools, he brought up with him about three quarters of a hundredweight of ore, which we wondered at, for the man had no small load to bring, considering the manner of his coming up; and this indeed made him come heaving and struggling up, as I said at first, as if he had great difficulty to get out; whereas it was indeed the weight that he brought with him.

If any reader thinks this, and the past relation of the woman and the cave, too low and trifling for this work, they must be told that I think quite otherwise; and especially considering what a noise is made of wonders in this country, which, I must needs say, have nothing in them curious, but much talked of, more trifling a great deal. See Cotton's *Wonders of the Peak*, Hobbes's *Chatsworth*,* and several others; but I shall make no more apologies. I return to our subterranean apparition.

We asked him how deep the mine lay which he came out of. He answered us in terms we did not understand, but our interpreter, as above, told us it signified that he was at work 60 fathoms deep, but that there were five men of his party, who were, two of them, eleven fathoms, and the other three, fifteen fathoms deeper. He seemed to regret that he was not at work with those three, for that they had a deeper vein of ore than that which he worked in, and had a way out at the side of the hill, where they passed without coming up so high as he was obliged to do.

If we blessed ourselves before, when we saw how the poor woman and her five children lived in the hole or cave in the mountain, with the giant's grave over their heads, we had much more room to reflect how much we had to acknowledge to our Maker, that we were not appointed to get our bread thus, one hundred and fifty yards under ground, or in a hole as deep in the earth as the cross upon St Paul's Cupolo is high out of it. Nor was it possible to see these miserable people without such reflections, unless you will suppose a man as stupid and senseless as the horse he rides on. But to leave moralizing to the reader, I proceed.

We then looked on the ore, and got the poor man's leave to bring everyone a small piece of it away with us, for which we gave him two small pieces of better metal, called shillings, which made his heart glad; and, as we understood by our interpreter, was more than he could gain at sixty fathoms under ground in three days; and we found soon after the money was so much that it made him move off immediately towards the alehouse, to melt some of it into good Pale Derby; but, to his farther good luck, we were gotten to the same alehouse before him; where, when we saw him come, we gave him some liquor too, and made him keep his money, and promise us to carry it home to his family, which they told us lived hard by.

Vol. iii, Letter I

[Defoe crosses the Pennines at Blackstone Edge and descends to Halifax.]

It was, as I say, calm and clear, and the sun shone when we came out of the town of Rochdale; but when we began to mount the hills, which we did within a mile, or little more, of the town, we found the wind began to rise, and the higher we went the more wind; by which I soon perceived that it had blown before, and perhaps all night upon the hills, though it was calm below; as we ascended higher it began to snow again, that is to say, we ascended into that part where it was snowing, and had, no doubt, been snowing all night, as we could easily see by the thickness of the snow.

It is not easy to express the consternation we were in when we came up near the top of the mountain; the wind blew exceeding hard, and blew the snow so directly in our faces, and that so thick, that it was impossible to keep our eyes open to see our way. The ground also was so covered with snow that we could see no track, or when we were in the way, or when out; except when we were showed it by a frightful precipice on one hand, and uneven ground on the other; even our horses discovered their uneasiness at it; and a poor spaniel dog that was my fellow traveller, and usually diverted us with giving us a mark for our gun, turned tail to it and cried.

In the middle of this difficulty, and as we began to call to one another to turn back again, not knowing what dangers might still be before us, came a surprising clap of thunder, the first that ever I heard in a storm of snow, or, I believe, ever shall; nor did we perceive any lightning to precede the thunder, as must naturally be the case; but we supposed the thick falling of the snow might prevent our sight.

I must confess I was very much surprised at this blow; and one of our company would not be persuaded that it was thunder, but that it was some blast of a coal-pit, things which do sometimes happen in the country, where there are many coal mines. But we were all against him in that, and were fully satisfied that it was thunder, and, as we fancied, at last we were confirmed in it, by hearing more of it at a distance from us.

Upon this we made a full stop, and coming altogether, for we were then three in company, with two servants, we began to talk seriously of going back again to Rochdale; but just then one of our men called out to us, and said he was upon the top of the hill, and could see over into Yorkshire, and that there was a plain way down on the other side. . . .

From Blackstone Edge to Halifax is eight miles, and all the way, except from Sowerby to Halifax, is thus up hill and down; so that, I suppose, we mounted to the clouds and descended to the water level about eight times, in that little part of the journey.

But now I must observe to you that after having passed the second hill and come down into the valley again, and so still the nearer we came to Halifax, we found the houses thicker, and the villages greater in every bottom; and not only so, but the sides of the hills, which were very steep every way, were spread with houses, and that very thick; for the land being divided into small enclosures, that is to say, from two acres to six or seven acres each, seldom more; every three or four pieces of land had a house belonging to it.

Then it was I began to perceive the reason and nature of the thing, and found that this division of the land into small pieces, and scattering of the dwellings, was occasioned by, and done for the convenience of the business which the people were generally employed in, and that, as I said before, though we saw no people stirring without doors, yet they were all full within; for, in short, this whole country, however mountainous, and that no sooner we were down one hill but we mounted another, is yet infinitely full of people; those people all full of business; not a beggar, not an idle person to be seen, except here and there an alms-house, where people ancient, decrepit, and past labour, might perhaps be found; for it is observable that the people here, however laborious, generally live to a great age, a certain testimony to the goodness and wholesomeness of the country, which is, without doubt, as healthy as any part of England; nor is the health of the people lessened, but helped and established by their being constantly employed, and, as we call it, their working hard; so that they find a double advantage by their being always in business.

This business is the clothing trade, for the convenience of which the houses are thus scattered and spread upon the sides of the hills, as above, even from the bottom to the top; the reason is this: such has been the bounty of nature to this otherwise frightful country, that two things essential to the business, as well as to the ease of the people are found here, and that in a situation which I never saw the like of in any part of England; and, I believe, the like is not to be seen so contrived in any part of the world; I mean coals and running water upon the tops of the highest hills. This seems to have been directed by the wise hand of Providence for the very purpose which is now served by it, namely, the manufactures, which otherwise could not be carried on; neither indeed could one fifth part of the inhabitants be supported without them; for the land could not maintain them. After we had mounted the third hill, we found the country, in short, one continued village, though mountainous every way, as before; hardly a house standing out of a speaking distance from another, and (which soon told us their business) the day clearing up, and the sun shining, we could see that almost at every house there was a tenter,* and almost on every tenter a piece of cloth, or kersie, or shalloon,* for they are the three articles of that country's labour; from which the sun glancing, and, as I may say, shining (the white reflecting its rays) to us, I thought it was the most agreeable sight that I ever saw, for the hills, as I say, rising and falling so thick, and the valleys opening sometimes one way, sometimes another, so that sometimes we could see two or three miles this way, sometimes as far another; sometimes like the streets near St Giles's, called the Seven Dials;* we could see through the glades almost every way round us, yet look which way we would, high to the tops, and low to the bottoms, it was all the same; innumerable houses and tenters, and a white piece upon every tenter.

But to return to the reason of dispersing the houses, as above; I found, as our road passed among them, for indeed no road could do otherwise, wherever we passed any house we found a little rill or gutter of running water; if the house was above the road, it came from it, and crossed the way to run to another; if the house was below us, it crossed us from some other distant house above it, and at every considerable house was a manufactory or work-house, and as they could not do their business without water, the little streams were so parted and guided by gutters or pipes, and by turning and dividing the streams, that none of those houses were without a river, if I may call it so, running into and through their work-houses.

ARTHUR YOUNG, *A Tour in Ireland; With General Observations on the Present State of that Kingdom: Made in the years 1776, 1777, and 1778, and brought down to the end of 1779* (1780; from *Arthur Young's Tour in Ireland (1776–1779)*, ed. Arthur Wollaston Hutton, London, 1892)

Arthur Young gave a definitive account of the nation's agriculture in a series of 'farmer's tours' through England and Wales in the late 1760s and 1770s. Young's visit to Ireland in 1776–9 brought the first systematic survey of that country, and a vigorous criticism of the political and social order that condemned the mass of its (rural, Catholic) population to poverty. Young's accounts of Pakenham and Waterford are followed by a general reflection on the condition of the 'labouring poor'.

PAKENHAM, CO. WESTMEATH: JULY 1776. In conversation with Lord Longford I made many enquiries concerning the state of the lower classes, and found that in some respects they were in good circumstances, in others indifferent; they have, generally speaking, such plenty of potatoes, as always to command a bellyful; they have flax enough for all their linen, most of them have a cow and some two, and spin wool enough for their clothes; all a pig, and numbers of poultry, and in general the complete family of cows, calves, hogs, poultry, and children, pig together in the cabin; fuel they have in the utmost plenty; great numbers of families are also supported by the neighbouring lakes; which abound prodigiously with fish; a child with a packthread and a crooked pin, will catch perch enough in an hour for the family to live on the whole day, and his Lordship has seen 500 children fishing at the same time, their being no tenaciousness in the proprietors of the lands about a right to the fish; besides perch, there is pike upwards of five feet long, bream, tench, trout of 10 lb. and as red as a salmon, and fine eels; all these are favourable circumstances, and are very conspicuous in the numerous and healthy families among them.

Reverse the medal: they are ill clothed, and make a wretched appearance, and what is worse, are much oppressed by many who make them pay too dear for keeping a cow, horse, etc. They have a practice also of keeping accounts with the labourers, contriving by that means, to let the poor wretches have very little cash for their year's work. This is a great oppression, farmers and gentlemen keeping accounts with the poor is a cruel abuse: so many days work for a cabin—so many for a potato garden—so many for keeping a horse—and so many for a cow, are clear accounts which a poor man can understand well; but farther it ought never to go; and when he has worked out what he has of this sort, the rest of his work ought punctually to be paid him every Saturday night. Another circumstance mentioned was the excessive practice they have in general of pilfering. They steal everything they can lay their hands on—and I should remark, that this is an account which has been very generally given me: all sorts of iron, hinges, chains, locks, keys, etc.—gates will be cut in pieces, and conveyed away in many places as fast as built; trees as big as a man's body, and that would require ten men to move, gone in a night. Lord Longford has had the new wheels of a car stolen as soon as made. Good stones out of a wall will be taken for a fire-hearth, etc., though a breach is made to get at them. In short, everything, and even such as are apparently of no use to them—nor is it easy to catch them, for they never carry their stolen goods home, but to some bog-hole. Turnips are stolen by car loads; and two acres of wheat plucked off in a night. In short, their pilfering and stealing is a perfect nuisance! How far it is owing to the oppression of law aimed solely at the religion of these people, how far to the conduct of the gentlemen and farmers, and how far to the mischievous disposition of the people themselves, it is impossible for a passing traveller to ascertain. I am apt to believe that a better system of law and management would have good effects. They are much worse treated than the poor in England, are talked to in more opprobrious terms, and otherwise very much oppressed.

Left Pakenham Hall.

Two or three miles from Lord Longford's, in the way to Mullingar, the road leads up a mountain, and commands an exceeding fine view of Loch Derrevaragh, a noble water eight miles long, and from two miles to half a mile over; a vast reach of it, like a magnificent river, opens as you rise the hill. Afterwards I passed under the principal mountain, which rises abruptly from the lake into the boldest outline imaginable; the water there is very beautiful, filling up the steep vale formed by this and the opposite hills.

WATERFORD: OCTOBER 1776. To Sir William Osborne's, three miles the other side Clonmell. From a character so remarkable for intelligence and precision, I could not fail of meeting information of the most valuable kind. This gentleman has made a mountain improvement which demands particular attention, being upon a principle very different from common ones.

Twelve years ago he met with a hearty looking fellow of forty, followed by a wife and six children in rags, who begged. Sir William questioned him upon the scandal of a man in full health and vigour, supporting himself in such a manner: the man said he could get no work: *Come along with me, I will show you a spot of land upon which I will build a cabin for you, and if you like it you shall fix there.* The fellow followed Sir William, who was as good as his word: he built him a cabin, gave him five acres of a heathy mountain, lent him four pounds to stock with, and gave him, when he had prepared his ground, as much lime as he would come for. The fellow flourished; he went on gradually; repaid the four pounds, and presently became a happy little cottar: he has at present twelve acres under cultivation, and a stock in trade worth at least £80; his name is John Conory.

The success which attended this man in two or three years, brought others, who applied for land, and Sir William gave them as they applied. The mountain was under lease to a tenant, who valued it so little that, upon being reproached with not cultivating, or doing something with it, he assured Sir William that it was utterly impracticable to do anything with it, and offered it to him without any deduction of rent. Upon this mountain he fixed them; gave them terms as they came determinable with the lease of the farm, so that everyone that came in succession had shorter and shorter tenures; yet are they so desirous of settling that they come at present, though only two years remain for a term.

In this manner Sir William has fixed twenty-two families, who are all upon the improving hand, the meanest growing richer; and find themselves so well off that no consideration will induce them to work for others, not even in harvest: their industry has no bounds; nor is the day long enough for the revolution of their incessant labour. Some of them bring turf to Clonmell, and Sir William has seen Conory returning loaded with soap ashes.

He found it difficult to persuade them to make a road to their village, but when they had once done it, he found none in getting cross roads to it, they found such benefit in the first. Sir William has continued to give them whatever lime they come for; and they have desired 1,000 barrels among them for the year 1766, which their landlord has accordingly contracted for with his lime-burner, at 11*d.* a barrel. Their houses have all been built at his expense, and done by contract at £6 each, after which they raise what little offices they want for themselves.

Sir William being prejudiced against the custom of burning land, insisted that they should not do it, which impeded them for some time; but upon being convinced that they could not go on well without it, he relaxed, and since that they have improved rapidly. He has informed them that, upon the expiration of the lease, they will be charged something for the land, and has desired that they will mark out each man what he wishes to have; they have accordingly run divisions, and some of them have taken pieces of 30 or 40 acres: a strong proof that they find their husbandry beneficial and profitable. He has great reason to believe that nine-tenths of them were White-boys,* but are now of principles and practice exceedingly different from the miscreants that bear that name. The lime Sir William gives them for the first breaking up, and the quantity they choose is 40 barrels an acre, so that all the expense is £6 for the house, and £1 16*s.* 8*d.* an acre for the land they improve. He has little doubt but they will take the whole mountain among them, which consists of 900 acres. Their course of tillage is,

1. Potatoes on the burning, generally turks (clustered) and great crops. 2. Rye. 3. Oats.

Their cattle are feeding on the mountain in the day, but of nights they house them in little miserable stables. All their children are employed regularly in their husbandry, picking stones, weeding, etc., which shows their industry strongly; for in general they are idle about all the country. The women spin.

Too much cannot be said in praise of this undertaking. It shows that a reflecting penetrating landlord can scarcely move without the power of creating opportunities to do himself and his country service. It shows that the villainy of the greatest miscreants is all situation and circumstance: EMPLOY, don't *hang* them. Let it not be in the slavery of the cottar system, in which industry never meets its reward, but by giving property, teach the value of it; by giving them the fruit of their labour, teach them to be laborious. All this Sir William Osborne has done, and done it with effect, and there probably is not an honester set of families in the county than those which he has formed from the refuse of the Whiteboys.

Of the Labouring Poor: Oppression

A landlord in Ireland can scarcely invent an order which a servant labourer or cottar dares to refuse to execute. Nothing satisfies him but an unlimited submission. Disrespect or any thing tending towards sauciness he may punish with his cane or his horsewhip with the most perfect security; a poor man would have his bones broke if he offered to lift his hand in his own defence. Knocking down is spoken of in the country in a manner that makes an Englishman stare. Landlords of consequence have assured me that many of their cottars would think themselves honoured by having their wives and daughters sent for to the bed of their master; a mark of slavery that proves the oppression under which such people must live. Nay, I have heard anecdotes of the lives of people being made free with, without any apprehension of the justice of a jury. But let it not be imagined that this is common; formerly it happened every day, but law gains ground. It must strike the most careless traveller to see whole strings of cars whipped into a ditch by a gentleman's footman, to make way for his carriage; if they are overturned or broken in pieces, no matter, it is taken in patience; were they to complain they would perhaps be horsewhipped. The execution of the laws lies very much in the hands of justices of the peace, many of whom are drawn from the most illiberal class in the kingdom. If a poor man lodges a complaint against a gentleman, or any animal that chooses to call itself a gentleman, and the justice issues out a summons for his appearance, it is a fixed affront, and he will infallibly be called out. Where MANNERS are in conspiracy against LAW, to whom are the oppressed people to have recourse? It is a fact that a poor man having a contest with a gentleman must—but I am talking nonsense, they know their situation too well to think of it; they can have no defence but by means of protection from one gentleman against another, who probably protects his vassal as he would the sheep he intends to eat.

The colours of this picture are not charged. To assert that all these cases are common would be an exaggeration; but to say that an unfeeling landlord will do all this with impunity is to keep strictly to truth: and what is liberty but a farce and a jest if its blessings are received as the favour of kindness and humanity, instead of being the inheritance of RIGHT?

Consequences have flowed from these oppressions which ought long ago to have put a stop to them. In England we have heard much of Whiteboys, Steelboys, Oakboys, Peep-of-day-boys, etc.* But these various insurgents are not to be confounded, for they are very different. The proper distinction in the discontents of the people is into Protestant and Catholic. All but the Whiteboys were among the manufacturing Protestants in the north: the Whiteboys Catholic labourers in the south. From the best intelligence I could gain, the riots of the manufacturers had no other foundation, but such variations in the manufacture as all fabrics experience, and which they had themselves known and submitted to before. The case, however, was different with the Whiteboys; who, being labouring Catholics, met with all those oppressions I have described, and would probably have continued in full submission, had not very severe treatment in respect of tithes, united with a great speculative rise of rents about the same time, blown up the flame of resistance; the atrocious acts they were guilty of made them the object of general indignation, Acts were passed for their punishment which seemed calculated for the meridian of Barbary; this arose to such a height that by one they were to be hanged under certain circumstances without the common formalities of a trial, which, though repealed the following sessions, marks the spirit of punishment; while others remain yet the law of the land, that would, if executed, tend more to raise than quell an insurrection. From all which it is manifest that the gentlemen of

Ireland never thought of a radical cure, from overlooking the real cause of the disease, which in fact lay in themselves, and not in the wretches they doomed to the gallows. Let them change their own conduct entirely, and the poor will not long riot. Treat them like men who ought to be as free as yourselves: put an end to that system of religious persecution which for seventy years has divided the kingdom against itself; in these two circumstances lies the cure of insurrection; perform them completely, and you will have an affectionate poor, instead of oppressed and discontented vassals.

A better treatment of the poor in Ireland is a very material point to the welfare of the whole British Empire. Events may happen which may convince us fatally of this truth. If not, oppression must have broken all the spirit and resentment of men. By what policy the Government of England can for so many years have permitted such an absurd system to be matured in Ireland is beyond the power of plain sense to discover.

JOHN CARR, *The Stranger in Ireland; or, A Tour in the Southern and Western Parts of that Country, in the year 1805* (1806)

John Carr (1772–1832), a London barrister and author, visited Ireland after publishing several European travel books; during his stay in Dublin he was knighted by the Lord-Lieutenant. Writing in the immediate aftermath of the 1801 Union, Carr offers an upbeat view of peasant life, and seeks to soften memories of the recent United Irishmen rising—put down with terrible slaughter—by evoking a general historical condition of melancholy ruin and decay.

The following little anecdote will prove that magnanimity is also an inmate of an Irish cabin. During the march of a regiment, the Honourable Captain P—, who had the command of the artillery baggage, observing that one of the peasants, whose car and horse had been pressed for the regiment, did not drive as fast as he ought, went up to him and struck him: the poor fellow shrugged up his shoulders, and observed there was no occasion for a blow, and immediately quickened the pace of his animal. Some time afterwards, the artillery officer having been out shooting all the morning, entered a cabin for the purpose of resting himself, where he found the very peasant whom he had struck, at dinner with his wife and family: the man, who was very large and powerfully made, and whose abode was solitary, might have taken fatal revenge upon the officer, instead of which, immediately recognizing him, he chose the best potato out of his bowl, and, presenting it to his guest, said, 'There, your honour, oblige me by tasting a potato, and I hope it is a good one, but you should not have struck me, a blow is hard to bear.'

In the neighbourhood we saw the arbutus or strawberry tree in great perfection, and many fine myrtles growing in the open air. Wherever we moved in the course of our Wicklow tour, we were equally surprised to find such excellent roads, and no turnpikes. The cabins which lay in our route were also neat, generally whitewashed, and an air of comfort and plenty breathed throughout; before each door were the finest pigs and poultry. The peasant and his wife were tolerably well dressed; and their children, of which every cabin has a bountiful quota, looked fat, fresh, and ruddy. Here, as in every part of Ireland which I visited, a dog was almost always one of the inmates of every cabin. The association seemed to be formed by sympathy, and fidelity appeared to be the common principle which bound the master and his favourite.

An Irish cabin, in general, is like a little antediluvian ark; for husband, wife, and children, cow and calf, pigs, poultry, dog, and frequently cat, repose under the same roof in perfect amity. A whimsical calculation sometime since ascertained, that in eighty-seven cabins there were one hundred and twenty full grown pigs, and forty-seven dogs. The rent of a cabin and potato plot in the country of Wicklow and neighbourhood is from one to two guineas; the family live upon potatoes and butter-milk six days in the week, and instead of 'an added pudding', the Sabbath is generally celebrated by bacon and greens. In those parts I found the price of potatoes to be eight shillings and fourpence the barrel (twenty stone to the barrel) and three quarts of butter-milk for a penny. The price of labour was sixpence halfpenny per day.

Insufficiency of provision, which operates so powerfully against marriage in England, is not known or cared about in Ireland; there the want of an establishment never affects the brain of the enamoured rustic. Love lingers only until he can find out a dry bank, pick a few sticks, collect some furze and fern, knead a little mud with straw, and raise a hut about six feet high, with a door to let in the light and let out the smoke; these accomplished, the happy pair, united by their priest, enter their sylvan dwelling, and a rapid race of chubby boys and girls soon proves by what scanty means life can be sustained and imparted.

Upon an average, a man, his wife, and four children will eat thirty-seven pounds of potatoes a day. A whimsical anecdote is related of an Irish potato.* An Englishman, seeing a number of fine florid children in a cabin, said to the father: 'How do your countrymen contrive to have so many fine children?' 'By Jasus it is the potato, Sir,' said he.

Three pounds of good mealy potatoes are more than equivalent to one pound of bread. It is worthy of remark to those who live well, without reflecting upon the condition of others to whom Providence has been less bountiful, that one individual who subsists upon meat and bread consumes what would maintain five persons who live on bread alone, and twelve who subsist on potatoes; and if such individual keeps a horse, he maintains an animal for his pleasures, for whose subsistence more land is necessary than for that of his master.

In China the men are said to have nearly eaten out the horses, and hence it is usual for travellers to be carried along the high roads to the greatest distances by men. The mode of planting potatoes is as follows: the potato is cut into several pieces, each of which has an eye: these are spread on ridges of about four or five feet wide, which are covered with mould, dug from furrows on each side, of about half the breadth of the ridge. When they dig out the potatoes in autumn, they sow the ridge, immediately before digging, with bere,* and shelter the crop in a pit, piled up so as to form a sloping roof. Potatoes are said to be very propitious to fecundity; and I have been told that some investigators of political economy, enamoured with the fructifying qualities of the precious vegetable, have clothed it with political consequence; and in Ireland have regarded it like Cadmus's teeth,* as the prime source of population; so that hereafter, the given number of potatoes necessary to the due proportion of vital fluid being found, it will only be necessary to have due returns of the potato crops, in order to ascertain the average number of little girls and boys, which have for the last year increased the circle of society. It has been considered that the cultivation of rice was the most favourable to population, not only on account of its nutrition, but because it employed a great number of men, and scarcely any part of the work could be done by horses; but it has been since admitted that more persons can subsist upon potatoes. I am ready to acknowledge the nutritious quality of the potato, and that it may be sufficient for the purposes of mere existence with an Irish rustic, who having little to do, does little: but an enlightened and experienced medical friend of mine assured me that it could not supply the frame with its necessary support under the pressure of violent exercise. A workman in an iron-foundry would not be able to endure the fatigue of his duty for three hours together, if he had no other food than potatoes. . . .

At Rathdrum we took fresh horses and proceeded to Glendaloch (or Glendalough), or the Seven Churches, about five miles off, which had I not seen, I should have deeply regretted. The whole scene, soon after we quitted Rathdrum, became altered: one might have supposed that an ocean had separated Glendaloch from Avonmore. We found ourselves surrounded by vast mountains covered with brown heath, or more sable peat, whose hard and gloomy summits the rays of the sun, beginning to be obscured, shone upon without brightening: the whole was desolate, gloomy, and sublime. 'Your honour,' said our driver, upon our observing that one of his horses plunged, 'that mare is always very unasy in going down hill.' Immediately after we passed a dark avenue of trees, which led to the ruins of a mansion burnt in the rebellion: it stood at the foot of a mountain; some of the walls, blackened by smoke, remained. The garden was overrun with briars and brambles; not a solitary rose-tree was to be seen, and the plantation was a wilderness. As we gazed upon the melancholy scene, the clouds gathered over our heads: all was silent and mournful. The vast and gloomy glen before us, in the year 1798, afforded shelter and concealment, for a short time, to a body of twenty-five thousand rebels under the command of Dwyer and Hoult.* The ruins which we saw marked the residence of a family which, having excited the vengeance of those miserable and deluded beings, were obliged to fly for their lives. Imagination depicted the torches of the frantic mob shooting a frightful gleam through the trees; and now it beheld the crackling blaze of the devoted pile, reddening the sable scenery below, and the murky clouds above, until it sunk amidst the yell of the misguided incendiaries.

Near this melancholy monument of insurrectional fury a barrack has been erected, for the purpose of preventing this place from again affording protection to rebels. Passing the barrack, which is stuccoed

white, and is wholly out of unison with the dusky scenery in which it
is placed, the dark and lofty round tower of Glendaloch, which
means the valley of the two lakes, just appeared rising from a plain;
whilst behind were stupendous mountains, half-covered with mist
and cloud. This awful spot was formerly an episcopal see, and a well-
inhabited city, till about 1214, when it was annexed to the diocese of
Dublin. Upon its religious edifices falling into decay, it became a
place of refuge to outlaws and robbers; and it was not until 1472 that
a peaceable and perfect surrender was made of it to the Archbishop
of Dublin by friar Dennis White, who had long usurped that see in
opposition to the regal authority. Since that period Glendaloch has
become a dreary desert. The venerable remains of this city reminded
me of the words of Ossian. 'Why dost thou build the hall, son of the
winged days? Thou look'st from thy towers today; yet a few years,
and the blast of the desert comes: it howls in thy empty court.'*

WILLIAM COBBETT, *Rural Rides* (1822–6; from *Rural Rides
in the Southern, Western and Eastern Counties of England*, vol. i,
ed. G. D. H. Cole and M. Cole, 1930)

William Cobbett (1763–1835), journalist, farmer, and MP, became
Britain's most influential Radical voice after his return from the United
States in 1819. Cobbett travelled throughout southern England, reporting
on the state of agriculture and the working poor under a regime (as he saw
it) corrupted by finance capital, in the decade preceding the 1832 Reform
Bill. The first series of 'Rural Rides' was published in *Cobbett's Weekly
Political Register* from 1822 to 1826 and reissued in book form in 1830.
The following excerpts contrast relatively flourishing conditions in
Hertfordshire and Buckinghamshire with the squalor of northern Kent.

KENSINGTON: 24 JUNE 1822. Set out at four this morning for
Redbourn, and then turned off to the westward to go to High
Wycombe, through Hempstead and Chesham. The wheat is good all
the way. The barley and oats good enough till I came to Hempstead.
But the land along here is very fine: a red tenacious flinty loam upon
a bed of chalk at a yard or two beneath, which, in my opinion, is the
very best corn land that we have in England. The fields here, like
those in the rich parts of Devonshire, will bear perpetual grass.
Any of them will become upland meadows. The land is, in short,

excellent, and it is a real corn-country. The trees from Redburne to Hempstead are very fine; oaks, ashes, and beeches. Some of the finest of each sort, and the very finest ashes I ever saw in my life. They are in great numbers, and make the fields look most beautiful. No villainous things of the fir-tribe offend the eye here. The custom is in this part of Hertfordshire (and I am told it continues into Bedfordshire) to leave a border round the ploughed part of the fields to bear grass and to make hay from, so that, the grass being now made into hay, every corn field has a closely mowed grass walk about ten feet wide all round it, between the corn and the hedge. This is most beautiful! The hedges are now full of the shepherd's rose, honeysuckles, and all sorts of wild flowers; so that you are upon a grass walk, with this most beautiful of all flower gardens and shrubberies on your one hand, and with the corn on the other. And thus you go from field to field (on foot or on horseback), the sort of corn, the sort of underwood and timber, the shape and size of the fields, the height of the hedge-rows, the height of the trees, all continually varying. Talk of pleasure-grounds indeed! What, that man ever invented, under the name of pleasure-grounds, can equal these fields in Hertfordshire? This is a profitable system too; for the ground under hedges bears little corn, and it bears very good grass. Something, however, depends on the nature of the soil: for it is not all land that will bear grass, fit for hay, perpetually; and, when the land will not do that, these headlands would only be a harbour for weeds and couch-grass, the seeds of which would fill the fields with their mischievous race. Mr TULL has observed upon the great use of headlands.* It is curious enough that these headlands cease soon after you get into Buckinghamshire. At first you see now-and-then a field *without* a grass headland; then it comes to now-and-then a field *with* one; and, at the end of five or six miles, they wholly cease. . . .

Chesham is a nice little town, lying in a deep and narrow valley, with a stream of water running through it. All along the country that I have come, the labourers' dwellings are good. They are made of what they call brick-nog; that is to say, a frame of wood, and a single brick thick, filling up the vacancies between the timber. They are generally covered with tile. Not pretty by any means; but they are good; and you see here, as in Kent, Sussex, Surrey and Hampshire, and, indeed, in almost every part of England, that most interesting of all objects, that which is such an honour to England, and that which distinguishes it from all the rest of the world, namely, those neatly kept and productive little gardens round the labourers' houses, which are seldom unornamented with more or less of flowers. We have only to look at these to know what sort of people English labourers are; these gardens are the answer to the Malthuses and the Scarletts.* Shut your mouths, you Scotch Economists; cease bawling, Mr Brougham, and you Edinburgh Reviewers,* till *you* can show us something, not like, but approaching towards a likeness of *this!*

The orchards all along this country are by no means bad. Not like those of Herefordshire and the north of Kent; but a great deal better than in many other parts of the kingdom. The cherry-trees are pretty abundant and particularly good. There are not many of the merries, as they call them in Kent and Hampshire; that is to say, the little black cherry, the name of which is a corruption from the French, *merise*, in the singular, and *merises* in the plural. I saw the little boys, in many places, set to keep the birds off the cherries, which reminded me of the time when I followed the same occupation, and also of the toll that I used to take in payment. The children are all along here, I mean the little children, locked out of the doors, while the fathers and mothers are at work in the fields. I saw many little groups of this sort; and this is one advantage of having plenty of room on the outside of a house. I never saw the country children better clad, or look cleaner and fatter than they look here, and I have the very great pleasure to add that I do not think I saw three acres of potatoes in this whole tract of fine country, from St Albans to Redbourn, from Redbourn to Hempstead, and from Hempstead to Chesham.

CANTERBURY: THURSDAY AFTERNOON, 4 SEPTEMBER. When I got upon the corn land in the Isle of Thanet, I got into a garden indeed.* There is hardly any fallow; comparatively few turnips. It is a country of corn. Most of the harvest is in; but there are some fields of wheat and of barley not yet housed. A great many pieces of lucerne, and all of them very fine. I left Ramsgate to my right about three miles, and went right across the island to Margate; but that place is so thickly settled with stock-jobbing cuckolds, at this time of the year, that, having no fancy to get their horns stuck into me, I turned away to my left when I got within about half a mile of the town. I got to a little

hamlet, where I breakfasted; but could get no corn for my horse, and
no bacon for myself! All was corn around me. Barns, I should think,
two hundred feet long; ricks of enormous size and most numerous;
crops of wheat, five quarters to an acre, on the average; and a public-
house without either bacon or corn! The labourers' houses, all along
through this island, beggarly in the extreme. The people dirty, poor-
looking; ragged, but particularly *dirty*. The men and boys with dirty
faces, and dirty smock-frocks, and dirty shirts; and, good God! what
a difference between the wife of a labouring man here, and the wife
of a labouring man in the forests and woodlands of Hampshire and
Sussex! Invariably have I observed that the richer the soil, and the
more destitute of woods; that is to say, the more purely a corn
country, the more miserable the labourers. The cause is this, the
great, the big bull frog grasps all. In this beautiful island every inch
of land is appropriated by the rich. No hedges, no ditches, no commons, no grassy lanes: a country divided into great farms; a few trees
surround the great farm-house. All the rest is bare of trees; and the
wretched labourer has not a stick of wood, and has no place for a pig
or cow to graze, or even to lie down upon. The rabbit countries are
the countries for labouring men. There the ground is not so valuable.
There it is not so easily appropriated by the few. Here, in this island,
the work is almost all done by the horses. The horses plough the
ground; they sow the ground; they hoe the ground; they carry the
corn home; they thresh it out; and they carry it to market: nay, in this
island, they *rake* the ground; they rake up the straggling straws and
ears; so that they do the whole, except the reaping and the mowing.
It is impossible to have an idea of anything more miserable than the
state of the labourers in this part of the country.

2. PICTURESQUE TOURISM

THOMAS GRAY, *Journal in the Lakes* (1769; from *The
Correspondence of Thomas Gray*, vol. iii, ed. P. Toynbee and
L. Whibley, Oxford, 1935)

Thomas Gray (1716–71), poet and scholar, kept a journal of his 1769 tour
of the Westmorland Lakes in the form of letters to his friend Thomas

Wharton. Published in a posthumous edition of Gray's poems (1775), the *Journal in the Lakes* made the region a test-site for the new aesthetic vocabulary of 'the picturesque'.

2–3 OCTOBER 1769. Dined by two o'clock at the Queen's Head, and then straggled out alone to the parsonage, fell down on my back across a dirty lane with my glass* open in one hand, but broke only my knuckles: stayed nevertheless, and saw the sun set in all its glory.

3 OCTOBER. Wind at SE, a heavenly day. Rose at seven, and walked out under the conduct of my landlord to Borrowdale; the grass was covered with a hoar-frost, which soon melted, and exhaled in a thin blueish smoke. Crossed the meadows obliquely, catching a diversity of views among the hills over the lake and islands and changing prospect at every ten paces, left Cockshut and Castle Hill (which we formerly mounted) behind me, and drew near the foot of Walla Crag, whose bare and rocky brow, cut perpendicularly down above 400 feet, as I guess, awfully overlooks the way: our path here tends to the left, and the ground gently rising, and covered with a glade of scattering trees and bushes on the very margin of the water, opens both ways the most delicious view, that my eyes ever beheld. Behind you are the magnificent heights of Walla Crag; opposite lie the thick hanging woods of Lord Egremont, and Newland Valley with green and smiling fields embosomed in the dark cliffs; to the left the jaws of Borrowdale, with that turbulent chaos of mountain behind mountain rolled in confusion; beneath you, and stretching far away to the right, the shining purity of the lake, just ruffled by the breeze enough to show it is alive, reflecting rocks, woods, fields, and inverted tops of mountains, with the white buildings of Keswick, Crosthwait Church, and Skiddaw for a background at distance. Oh Doctor! I never wished more for you; and pray think, how the glass played its part in such a spot, which is called Carf-close-reeds: I choose to set down these barbarous names, that anybody may enquire on the place, and easily find the particular station, that I mean. This scene continues to Barrow-gate, and a little farther, passing a brook called Barrow-beck, we entered Borrowdale. The crags named Lodore Banks now begin to impend terribly over your way; and more terribly, when you hear, that three years since an immense mass of rock tumbled at once from the brow, and barred all access to the dale (for this is the only road) till they could work their way

through it. Luckily no one was passing at the time of this fall; but down the side of the mountain and far into the lake lie dispersed the huge fragments of this ruin in all shapes and in all directions. Something farther we turned aside into a coppice, ascending a little in front of Lodore waterfall. The height appears to be about 200 feet, the quantity of water not great though (these three days excepted) it had rained daily in the hills for near two months before: but then the stream was nobly broken, leaping from rock to rock, and foaming with fury. On one side a towering crag, that spired up to equal, if not overtop, the neighbouring cliffs (this lay all in shade and darkness); on the other hand a rounder broader projecting hill shagged with wood and illumined by the sun, which glanced sideways on the upper part of the cataract. The force of the water wearing a deep channel in the ground hurries away to join the lake. We descended again, and passed the stream over a rude bridge. Soon after we came under Gowder Crag, a hill more formidable to the eye and to the apprehension than that of Lodore. The rocks atop, deep-cloven perpendicularly by the rains, hanging loose and nodding forwards, seem just starting from their base in shivers: the whole way down and the road on both sides is strewed with piles of the fragments strangely thrown across each other and of a dreadful bulk. The place reminds one of those passes in the Alps, where the guides tell you to move on with speed, and say nothing, lest the agitation of the air should loosen the snows above, and bring down a mass, that would overwhelm a caravan. I took their counsel here and hastened on in silence.

> Non ragioniam di lor; ma guarda, e passa!*

4 OCTOBER 1769. Wind E, clouds and sunshine, and in the course of the day a few drops of rain. Walked to Crow Park, now a rough pasture, once a glade of ancient oaks, whose large roots still remain on the ground, but nothing has sprung from them. If one single tree had remained, this would have been an unparalleled spot, and Smith* judged right, when he took his print of the lake from hence, for it is a gentle eminence, not too high, on the very margin of the water and commanding it from end to end, looking full into the gorge of Borrowdale. I prefer it even to Cockshut Hill, which lies beside it, and to which I walked in the afternoon: it is covered with young trees both sown and planted, oak, spruce, scotch-fir, etc: all

which thrive wonderfully. There is an easy ascent to the top, and
the view far preferable to that on Castle Hill (which you remember)
because this is lower and nearer to the lake: for I find all points
that are much elevated spoil the beauty of the valley, and make its
parts (which are not large) look poor and diminutive. While I was
here, a little shower fell, red clouds came marching up the hills
from the east, and part of a bright rainbow seemed to rise along the
side of Castle Hill.

From hence I got to the parsonage a little before sunset, and saw
in my glass a picture, that if I could transmit to you, and fix it in all
the softness of its living colours, would fairly sell for a thousand
pounds. This is the sweetest scene I can yet discover in point of
pastoral beauty. The rest are in a sublimer style.

THOMAS WEST, *A Guide to the Lakes* (1784)

In 1778 Thomas West (1720–79) published a guidebook that laid out routes
for the tourist and specified the most favourable 'stations' from which
picturesque views might be taken. West's preface to the 1784 edition,
reprinted here, provides a justification for leisure travel in general, and
domestic tourism in particular, and specifies the optical technologies that
may assist the picturesque tourist.

Since persons of genius, taste, and observation began to make the
tour of their own country, and to give such pleasing accounts of
the natural history, and improving state of the northern parts of the
kingdom, the spirit of visiting them has diffused itself among the
curious of all ranks.

Particularly, the taste for one branch of a noble art* (cherished
under the protection of the greatest of kings and best of men) in
which the genius of Britain rivals that of ancient Greece and modern
Rome, induces many to visit the lakes of Cumberland, Westmorland,
and Lancashire; there to contemplate, in Alpine scenery, finished in
nature's highest tints, the pastoral and rural landscape, exhibited in
all their styles, the soft, the rude, the romantic, and the sublime; and
of which perhaps like instances can nowhere be found assembled in
so small a tract of country. What may be now mentioned as another
inducement to visit these natural beauties is the goodness of the
roads, which are much improved since Mr Gray made his tour in

1765, and Mr Pennant his, in 1772.* The gentlemen of these counties have set a precedent worthy of imitation in the politest parts of the kingdom, by opening, at private expense, carriage roads for the ease and safety of such as visit the country; and the public roads are equally properly attended to. And if the entertainment at some of the inns be plain, it is accompanied with an easy charge, neatness, and attention. When the roads are more frequented, the inns may perhaps be more elegantly furnished and expensive; but the entertainment must remain much the same, as the viands at present are not excelled in any other quarter of the empire.

The design of the following sheets, is to encourage the taste of visiting the lakes, by furnishing the traveller with a Guide; and for that purpose, the writer has here collected and laid before him, all the select stations and points of view, noticed by those authors who have last made the tour of the lakes, verified by his own repeated observations. He has also added remarks on the principal objects as they appear viewed from different stations; and such other incidental information as he judged would greatly facilitate and heighten the pleasure of the tour, and relieve the traveller from the burden of those tedious enquiries on the road, or at the inns, which generally embarrass, and often mislead.

The local knowledge here communicated, will not however injure, much less prevent the agreeable surprise that attends the first sight of scenes that surpass all description, and of objects which will always affect the spectator in the highest degree.

Such as wish to unbend the mind from anxious cares, or fatiguing studies, will meet with agreeable relaxation in making the tour of the lakes. Something new will open itself at the turn of every mountain, and a succession of ideas will be supported by a perpetual change of objects, and a display of scenes behind scenes, in endless perspective. The contemplative traveller will be charmed with the sight of the sweet retreats that he will observe in these enchanting regions of calm repose, and the fanciful may figuratively review the hurry and bustle of busy life (in all its gradations) in the variety of unshaded rills that hang on the mountainsides, the hasty brooks that warble through the dell, or the mighty torrents precipitating themselves at once with thundering noise from tremendous, rocky heights; all pursuing one general end, their increase in the vale, and their union in the ocean.

Such as spend their lives in cities, and their time in crowds will here meet with objects that will enlarge the mind, by contemplation, and raise it from nature to nature's first cause. Whoever takes a walk into these scenes must return penetrated with a sense of the creator's power in heaping mountains upon mountains, and enthroning rocks upon rocks. And such exhibitions of sublime and beautiful objects cannot but excite at once both rapture and reverence.

When exercise and change of air are recommended for health, the convalescent will find the latter here in the purest state, and the former will be the concomitant of the tour. The many hills and mountains of various heights, separated by narrow vales, through which the air is agitated and hurried on, by a multiplicity of brooks and mountain torrents, keep it in constant circulation, which is known to add much to its purity. The water is also as pure as the air, and on that account recommends itself to the valetudinarian.

As there are few people, in easy circumstances, but may find a motive for visiting this extraordinary region, so more especially those who intend to make the continental tour should begin here; as it will give in miniature an idea of what they are to meet with there, in traversing the Alps and Apennines; to which our northern mountains are not inferior in beauty of line, or variety of summit, number of lakes, and transparency of water; not in colouring of rock, or softness of turf, but in height and extent only. The mountains here are all accessible to the summit, and furnish prospects no less surprising, and with more variety, than the Alps themselves. The tops of the highest Alps are inaccessible, being covered with everlasting snow, which commencing at regular heights above the cultivated tracts, or wooded and verdant sides, form indeed the highest contrast in nature. For there may be seen all the variety of climate in one view. To this however we oppose the sight of the ocean from the summit of all the higher mountains as it appears intersected with promontories, decorated with islands, and animated with navigation; which adds greatly to the perfection and variety of all grand views.

Those who have traversed the Alps, visited the lake of Geneva, and viewed Mont Blanc, the highest of the glaciers, from the valley of Chamonix, in Savoy, may still find entertainment in this domestic tour. To trace the analogy and differences of mountainous countries furnishes the observant traveller with amusement; and the travelled visitor of the Cumbrian lakes and mountains will not be disappointed of pleasure in this particular.

This Guide will also be of use to the artist who may purpose to copy any of these views and landscapes, by directing his choice of station, and pointing out the principal objects. Yet it is not presumed positively to decide on these particulars, but only to suggest hints that may be adopted, or rejected, at his pleasure.

The late Mr Gray was a great judge of landscapes, yet whoever makes choice of his station at the three mile stone from Lancaster, on the Hornby road, will fail in taking one of the finest afternoon rural views in England. The station he points out is a quarter of a mile too low, and somewhat too much to the left. The more advantageous station, as I apprehend, is on the south side of the great, or Queen's road, a little higher than where Mr Gray stood; for there the vale is in full display, including a longer reach of the river, and the wheel of Lune, forming a high crowned isthmus, fringed with tall trees, that in time past was the solitary site of a hermit. A few trees, preserved on purpose by the owner, conceal the nakedness of Caton moor on the right, and render the view complete.

By company from the south, the lakes may be best visited by beginning with Haws Water, and ending with Coniston Water, or vice versa. Mr Gray began his tour with Ullswater, but did not see all the lakes. Mr Pennant proceeded from Coniston Water to Windermere Water, etc. but omitted Ulls and Haws Waters. Mr Gray was too late in the season for enjoying the beauties of prospect and rural landscape in a mountainous country for in October the dews lie long on the grass in the morning, and the clouds descend soon in the evening, and conceal the mountains. Mr Pennant was too early in the spring, when the mountains were mantled with snow, and the dells were darkened with impenetrable mist; hence his gloomy description of the beautiful and romantic vale of St John, in his journey from Ambleside to Keswick. Flora displays few of her charms early in May, in a country that has been chilled by seven winter months.

The best season for visiting the lakes is from the beginning of June to the end of August. During these months the mountains are decked in all the trim of summer vegetation, and the woods and trees, which hang on the mountainsides, and adorn the banks of the lakes, are robed in every variety of foliage and summer bloom. In August nature has given her highest tints to all her colours on the enamelled plain and borders of the lakes. These are also the months favourable to botanic studies. Some rare plants are then only to be found; such as delight in Alpine heights, or such as appear in ever-shaded dells, or gloomy vales. . . .

[West lists different itineraries for viewing the Lakes.]

This Guide shall therefore take up the company at Lancaster, and attend them in the tour to all the lakes; pointing out (what only can be described) the permanent features of each scene . . . the vales, the dells, the groves, the hanging woods, the scattered cots, the deep mountains, the impending cliff, the broken ridge, etc. Their accidental beauties depend upon a variety of circumstances; light and shade, the air, the winds, the clouds, the situation with respect to objects, and the time of the day. For though the ruling tints be permanent, yet the green and gold of the meadow and vale, and the brown and purple of the mountain, the silver grey of the rock, and the azure hue of the cloud-topped pike,* are frequently varied in appearance, by an intermixture of reflection from wandering clouds, or other bodies, or a sudden stream of sunshine that harmonizes all the parts anew. The pleasure therefore arising from such scenes is in some sort accidental.

To render the tour more agreeable, the company should be provided with a telescope, for viewing the fronts and summits of inaccessible rocks, and the distant country, from the tops of the high mountains Skiddaw and Helvellyn.

The landscape mirror* will also furnish much amusement in this tour. Where the objects are great and near, it removes them to a due distance, and shews them in the soft colours of nature, and in the most regular perspective the eye can perceive, or science demonstrate.

The mirror is of the greatest use in sunshine; and the person using it ought always to turn his back to the object that he views. It should be suspended by the upper part of the case, and the landscape will then be seen in the glass, by holding it a little to the right or left (as the position of the parts to be viewed require) and the face screened from the sun. A glass of four inches, or four inches and a half diameter is a proper size.

The mirror is a plano-convex glass, and should be the segment of a large circle; otherwise distant and small objects are not perceived in it; but if the glass be too flat, the perspective view of great and near

William Gilpin

William Gilpin

137

objects is less pleasing, as they are represented too near. These inconveniences may be provided against by two glasses of different convexity. The dark glass answers well in sunshine; but on cloudy and gloomy days the silver foil is the better.

Whoever uses spectacles upon other occasions must use them in viewing landscapes in these mirrors.

WILLIAM GILPIN, *Observations on the River Wye, and Several Parts of South Wales, etc., Relative Chiefly to Picturesque Beauty; made in the Summer of 1770* (1782)

William Gilpin (1724–1804) produced the most influential analysis of the forms of landscape according to 'the rules of picturesque beauty' in a series of books covering the Wye Valley, the Lake District, the Scottish Highlands, and other regions of the British Isles, as well as a set of essays, *On Picturesque Beauty; On Picturesque Travel; and On Sketching Landscape* (1792). The relative accessibility of the Wye Valley, on the South Wales border, made it a popular tourist destination. Gilpin's description casts light on its most famous literary monument, William Wordsworth's poem 'Lines, Written above Tintern Abbey' (1798).

Such is the situation of Tintern Abbey. It occupies a gentle eminence in the middle of a circular valley, beautifully screened on all sides by woody hills; through which the river winds its course; and the hills, closing on its entrance, and on its exit, leave no room for inclement blasts to enter. A more pleasing retreat could not easily be found. The woods and glades intermixed; the winding of the river; the variety of the ground; the splendid ruin, contrasted with the objects of nature; and the elegant line formed by the summits of the hills, which include the whole; make all together a very enchanting piece of scenery. Everything around breathes an air so calm, and tranquil; so sequestered from the commerce of life, that it is easy to conceive a man of warm imagination, in monkish times, might have been allured by such a scene to become an inhabitant of it.

No part of the ruins of Tintern is seen from the river, except the abbey-church. It has been an elegant Gothic pile; but it does not make that appearance as a *distant* object, which we expected. Though the parts are beautiful, the whole is ill-shaped. No ruins of the tower are left, which might give form, and contrast to the walls, and buttresses, and other inferior parts. Instead of this, a number of gable-ends hurt the eye with their regularity; and disgust it by the vulgarity of their shape. A mallet judiciously used (but who durst use it?) might be of service in fracturing some of them; particularly those of the cross isles, which are not only disagreeable in themselves, but confound the perspective.

But were the building ever so beautiful, encompassed as it is with shabby houses, it could make no appearance from the river. From a stand near the road, it is seen to more advantage.

But if Tintern Abbey be less striking as a distant object, it exhibits, on a nearer view (when the whole together cannot be seen, but the eye settles on some of its nobler parts) a very enchanting piece of ruin. Nature has now made it her own. Time has worn off all traces of the rule: it has blunted the sharp edges of the chisel; and broken the regularity of opposing parts. The figured ornaments of the east window are gone; those of the west window are left. Most of the other windows, with their principal ornaments, remain.

To these are superadded the ornaments of time. Ivy, in masses uncommonly large, has taken possession of many parts of the wall; and gives a happy contrast to the grey-coloured stone, of which the building is composed. Nor is this undecorated. Mosses of various hues, with lichens, maidenhair, penny-leaf, and other humble plants, overspread the surface; or hang from every joint, and crevice. Some of them were in flower, others only in leaf; but, all together, they give those full-blown tints, which add the richest finishing to a ruin.

Such is the beautiful appearance which Tintern Abbey exhibits on the outside, in those parts, where we can obtain a near view of it. But when we enter it, we see it in most perfection: at least, if we consider it as an independent object, unconnected with landscape. The roof is gone: but the walls, and pillars, and abutments, which supported it, are entire. A few of the pillars indeed have given way; and here and there, a piece of the facing of the wall: but in cor-respondent parts, one always remains to tell the story. The pavement is obliterated: the elevation of the choir is no longer visible: the whole area is reduced to one level; cleared of rubbish; and covered with neat turf, closely shorn; and interrupted with nothing but the noble columns, which formed the aisles, and supported the tower.

When we stood at one end of this awful piece of ruin and surveyed

the whole in one view—the elements of air, and earth, its only covering, and pavement; and the grand, and venerable remains, which
terminated both—perfect enough to form the perspective, yet
broken enough to destroy the regularity; the eye was above measure
delighted with the beauty, the greatness, and the novelty of the
scene. More picturesque it certainly would have been, if the area,
unadorned, had been left with all its rough fragments of ruin scattered round; and bold was the hand that removed them: yet as the
outside of the ruin, which is the chief object of picturesque curiosity,
is still left in all its wild, and native rudeness; we excuse—perhaps
we approve—the neatness, that is introduced within. It *may* add to
the beauty of the scene—to its novelty it undoubtedly does.

Among other things in this scene of desolation, the poverty and
wretchedness of the inhabitants were remarkable. They occupy little
huts, raised among the ruins of the monastery; and seem to have no
employment but begging: as if a place, once devoted to indolence,
could never again become the seat of industry. As we left the abbey,
we found the whole hamlet at the gate, either openly soliciting alms;
or covertly, under the pretence of carrying us to some part of the
ruins, which each could show; and which was far superior to anything which could be shown by anyone else. The most lucrative
occasion could not have excited more jealousy and contention.

One poor woman we followed, who had engaged to show us the
monk's library. She could scarce crawl; shuffling along her palsied
limbs, and meagre, contracted body, by the help of two sticks. She led
us, through an old gate, into a place overspread with nettles, and
briars; and pointing to the remnant of a shattered cloister, told us, that
was the place. It was her own mansion. All indeed she meant to tell us,
was the story of her own wretchedness; and all she had to show us was
her own miserable habitation. We did not expect to be interested: but
we found we were. I never saw so loathsome a human dwelling. It was
a cavity, loftily vaulted, between two ruined walls; which streamed
with various-coloured stains of unwholesome dews. The floor was
earth; yielding, through moisture, to the tread. Not the merest utensil,
or furniture of any kind, appeared, but a wretched bedstead, spread
with a few rags, and drawn into the middle of the cell, to prevent its
receiving the damp, which trickled down the walls. At one end was an
aperture, which served just to let in light enough to discover the
wretchedness within. When we stood in the midst of this cell of

misery, and felt the chilling damps, which struck us in every direction, we were rather surprised that the wretched inhabitant was still alive than that she had only lost the use of her limbs.

The country about Tintern Abbey has been described as a solitary, tranquil scene: but its immediate environs only are meant. Within half a mile of it are carried on great iron-works, which introduce noise and bustle into these regions of tranquillity.

ANN RADCLIFFE, *Observations during a Tour in the Lakes of Lancashire, Westmorland, and Cumberland* (1795)

Radcliffe resorted to the Lakes after war interrupted her Rhineland tour. Writing in full awareness that this landscape has been turned into literature, she trumps the aesthetic language refined by West and Gilpin by commenting on its failure to capture the sublime dynamism of landscape. The apology licenses Radcliffe's own virtuoso performance of scenic description, richly inlaid with allusions to its literary tradition.

It is difficult to spread varied pictures of such scenes before the imagination. A repetition of the same images of rock, wood and water, and the same epithets of grand, vast and sublime, which necessarily occur, must appear tautologous, on paper, though their archetypes in nature, ever varying in outline, or arrangement, exhibit new visions to the eye, and produce new shades of effect on the mind. It is difficult also, where these delightful differences have been experienced, to forbear dwelling on the remembrance, and attempting to sketch the peculiarities which occasioned them. The scenery at the head of Ullswater is especially productive of such difficulties, where a wish to present the picture, and a consciousness of the impossibility of doing so, except by the pencil, meet and oppose each other. . . .

The effect of a stormy evening upon the scenery was solemn. Clouds smoked along the fells, veiling them for a moment, and passing on to other summits; or sometimes they involved the lower steeps, leaving the tops unobscured and resembling islands in a distant ocean. The lake was dark and tempestuous, dashing the rocks with a strong foam. It was a scene worthy of the sublimity of Ossian, and brought to recollection some touches of his gloomy pencil.

'When the storms of the mountains come, when the north lifts the waves on high, I sit by the sounding shore, etc.'*

A large hawk, sailing proudly in the air, and wheeling among the stormy clouds, superior to the shock of the gust, was the only animated object in the upward prospect. We were told that the eagles had forsaken their eyries in this neighbourhood and in Borrowdale, and are fled to the isle of Man; but one had been seen in Patterdale, the day before, which, not being at its full growth, could not have arrived from a great distance.

We returned to our low-roofed habitation, where, as the wind swept in hollow gusts along the mountains and strove against our casements, the crackling blaze of a wood fire lighted up the cheerfulness, which, so long since as Juvenal's time, has been allowed to arise from the contrast of ease against difficulty. *Suave mari magno, turbantibus aequora ventis;** and, however we might exclaim,

> be my retreat
> Between the groaning forest and the shore,
> Beat by the boundless multitude of waves!

it was pleasant to add,

> Where ruddy fire and beaming tapers join
> To cheer the gloom.*

3. SCOTLAND

MARTIN MARTIN, *A Voyage to St Kilda* (1698)

Celia Fiennes returned from her foray across the Border repelled by Scottish indigence and squalor; at roughly the same time Martin Martin (1660–1718), a native of the Isle of Skye, marvelled to find a remnant of the Golden Age on distant St Kilda. Martin accompanied the minister of Harris, John Campbell, on his annual visit to the island in 1697. Martin provided the first and last anthropologically detailed account of these most remote of the Hebridean islands: the 'organic community' he records with such fascination would not survive the coming of smallpox in 1724, which reduced the population from about 200 to 30.

The inhabitants, I must tell you, run no small danger in the quest of the fowls* and eggs, insomuch that I fear it would be thought an hyperbole to relate the inaccessibleness, steepness, and height, of those formidable rocks which they venture to climb. I myself have seen some of them climb up the corner of a rock with their backs to it, making use only of their heels and elbows, without any other assistance; and they have this way acquired a dexterity in climbing beyond any I ever yet saw; necessity has made them apply themselves to this, and custom has perfected them in it; so that it is become familiar to them almost from their cradles, the young boys of three years old being to climb the walls of their houses: their frequent discourses of climbing, together with the fatal end of several in the exercise of it, is the same to them, as that of fighting and killing is with soldiers, and so is become as familiar and less formidable to them, than otherwise certainly it would be. I saw two young men, to whose share the lots fell in June last, for taking the nest of a hawk (which was in a high rock above the sea) bringing home the hawks in a few minutes, without any assistance at all.

Their dogs are likewise very dextrous in climbing and bringing out from their holes those fowls which build their nests far underground, such as the scraber, puffinet, etc., which they carry in their teeth to their masters, letting them fall upon the ground before them, though asleep.

The inhabitants speak the Irish tongue* only; they express themselves slowly but pertinently; and have the same language with those of Harris and other isles, who retain the Irish in its purity.

Their habit anciently was of sheepskins, which has been worn by several of the inhabitants now living; the men at this day wear a short doublet reaching to their waist, about that a double plait of plaid, both ends joined together with the bone of a fulmar; this plaid reaches no further than their knees, and is above the haunches girt about with a belt of leather; they wear short caps of the same colour and shape with the capuchins, but shorter; and on Sundays they wear bonnets; some of late have got breeches, and they are wide and open at the knees; they wear cloth stockings, and go without shoes in the summer-time; their leather is dressed with the roots of tormentil.*

The women wear upon their heads a linen dress, straight before, and drawing to a small point behind below the shoulders, a foot and an half in length, and a lock of about sixty hairs hanging down each cheek, reaching to their breasts, the lower end tied with a knot; their plaid, which is the upper garment, is fastened upon their breasts with a large round buckle of brass in form of a circle; the buckle anciently worn by the stewards' wives were of silver, but the present steward's wife makes no use of either this dress or buckle. The women inhabiting this isle wear no shoes nor stockings in the summertime; the only and ordinary shoes they wear are made of the necks of solan geese, which they cut above the eyes, the crown of the head serves for the heel, the whole skin being cut close at the breast, which end being sewed, the foot enter into it, as into a piece of narrow stocking; this shoe does not wear above five days, and if the down side be next the ground, then not above three or four days; but, however, there is plenty of them; some thousands being catched, or, as they term it, stolen every March.

Both sexes wear coarse flannel shirts, which they put off when they go to bed; they thicken their clothes upon flakes, or mats of hay twisted and woven together in small ropes; they work hard at this employment, first making use of their hands, and at last of their feet; and when they are at this work, they commonly sing all the time, one of their number acting the part of a prime chantress, whom all the rest follow and obey.

They put the faces of their dead towards the east when they bury them, and bewail the death of their relations excessively, and upon those occasions make doleful songs, which they call laments. Upon the news of the late Mack-Leod's death,* they abandoned their houses, mourning two days in the field; they kill a cow, or sheep, before the interment, but if it be in the spring, this ceremony then is delayed, because the cattle are at that time poor and lean, but, however, they are to be killed as soon as ever they become fat.

Their ordinary food is barley and some oat-bread baked with water; they eat all the fowls, already described, being dried in their stone-houses,* without any salt or spice to preserve them; and all their beef and mutton is eaten fresh, after the same manner they use the giben, or fat of their fowls; this giben is by daily experience found to be a sovereign remedy for the healing of green wounds; it cured a cancer in an inhabitant of the isle of Lewis, and a fistula in one Nicholson of Skye, in St Marie's Parish; this was performed by John Mack-Lean, surgeon there. They boil the sea-plants, dulse, and slake,* melting the giben upon them instead of butter, and upon the roots of silver-weed and dock boiled, and also with their scurvy-grass stoved,* which is very purgative, and here it is of an extraordinary breadth. They use this giben with their fish, and it is become the common vehicle that conveys all their food down their throats. They are undone for want of salt, of which as yet they are but little sensible; they use no set times for their meals, but are determined purely by their appetites.

They use only the ashes of sea-ware* for salting their cheese, and the shortest (which grows in the rocks) is only used by them, that being reckoned the mildest.

Their drink is water, or whey, commonly: they brew ale but rarely, using the juice of nettle-roots, which they put in a dish with a little barley-meal dough; these sowens (*i.e.* flummery)* being blended together, produce good yeast, which puts their wort into a ferment, and makes good ale, so that when they drink plentifully of it, it disposes them to dance merrily.

They preserve the solan geese in their pyramids for the space of a year, slitting them in the back, for they have no salt to keep them with. They have built above five hundred stone pyramids for their fowls, eggs, etc.

We made particular enquiry after the number of solan geese consumed by each family the year before we came here, and it amounted to twenty-two thousand six hundred in the whole island, which they said was less than they ordinarily did, a great many being lost by the badness of the season, and the great current into which they must be thrown when they take them, the rock being of such an extraordinary height that they cannot reach the boat.

There is one boat sixteen cubits long, which serves the whole commonwealth; it is very curiously divided into apartments proportionable to their lands and rocks; every individual has his space distinguished to an hair's breadth, which his neighbour cannot encroach so much as to lay an egg upon it.

Every partner in summer provides a large turf to cover his space of the boat, thereby defending it from the violence of the sun, which (in its meridian height) reflects most vehemently from the sea, and rock, upon which the boat lies; at the drawing of it up, both sexes are employed pulling a long rope at the fore-end; they are determined in uniting their strength, by the cryer, who is therefore excepted from being obliged to draw the boat.

There is but one steel and tinder-box in all this commonwealth; the owner whereof fails not upon every occasion of striking fire in the lesser isles, to go thither, and exact three eggs, or one of the lesser fowls from each man as a reward for his service; this by them is called the fire-penny, and this capitation is very uneasy to them; I bid them try their crystal with their knives, which when they saw it did strike fire, they were not a little astonished, admiring at the strangeness of the thing, and at the same time accusing their own ignorance, considering the quantity of crystal growing under the rock of their coast. This discovery has delivered them from the fire-penny tax, and so they are no longer liable to it.

They have likewise a pot-penny tax, which is exacted in the same manner as the fire-penny was, but is much more reasonable; for the pot is carried to the inferior isles for the public use; and is in hazard of being broken; so that the owners may justly exact upon this score, since any may venture his pot when he pleases. When they have bestowed some hours in fowling about the rocks, and caught a competent number, they sit down near the face of it to refresh themselves, and in the mean time, they single out the fattest of their fowls, plucking them bare, which they carry home to their wives, or mistresses, as a great present, and it is always accepted very kindly from them, and could not otherwise be, without great ingratitude, seeing these men ordinarily expose themselves to very great danger, if not hazard their lives, to procure those presents for them.

In the face of the rock, south from the town, is the famous stone, known by the name of the mistress-stone; it resembles a door exactly; and is in the very front of this rock, which is twenty or thirty fathom perpendicular in height, the figure of it being discernible about the distance of a mile; upon the lintel of this door, every bachelor-wooer is by an ancient custom obliged in honour to give a specimen of his affection for the love of his mistress, and it is thus: he is to stand on his left foot, having the one half of his sole over the rock, and then he draws the right foot further out to the left, and in this posture bowing, he puts both his fists further out to the right foot; and then after he has performed this, he has acquired no small reputation, being always after it accounted worthy of the finest mistress in the world: they firmly believe that this achievement is always attended with the desired success.

This being the custom of the place, one of the inhabitants very gravely desired me to let him know the time limited by me for trying of this piece of gallantry before I designed to leave the place, that he might attend me; I told him this performance would have a quite contrary effect upon me, by robbing me both of my life and mistress at the same moment; but he was of a contrary opinion, and insisted on the good fortune attending it; but I must confess all his arguments were too weak to make me attempt the experiment.

They take their measures in going to the lesser islands from the appearance of the heavens; for when it is clear or cloudy in such a quarter, it is a prognostic of wind or fair weather; and when the waves are high on the east point of the bay, it is an infallible sign of a storm, especially if they appear very white, even though the weather be at that time calm.

If the waves in the bay make a noise as they break before they beat upon the shore, it is also an infallible forerunner of a west wind; if a black cloud appears above the south side of the bay, a south wind follows some hours afterwards. It is observed of the sea betwixt St Kilda and the isles Lewis, Harris, etc., that it rages more with a north wind, than when it blows from any other quarter. And it is likewise observed to be less raging with the south wind than any other.

They know the time of the day by the motion of the sun from one hill or rock to another; upon either of these the sun is observed to appear at different times; and when the sun does not appear, they measure the day by the ebbing and flowing of the sea, which they can tell exactly, though they should not see the shore for some days together; their knowledge of the tides depends upon the changes of the moon, which they likewise observe, and are very nice in it.

They use for their diversion short clubs and balls of wood; the sand is a fair field for this sport and exercise, in which they take great pleasure and are very nimble at it; they play for some eggs, fowls, hooks, or tobacco; and so eager are they for victory, that they strip themselves to their shirts to obtain it: they use swimming and diving, and are very expert in both.

The women have their assemblies in the middle of the village, where they discourse of their affairs, but in the mean time employing their distaff, and spinning in order to make their blankets; they sing and jest for diversion, and in their way, understand poetry, and make rhymes in their language. Both men and women are very courteous; as often as they passed by us every day, they saluted us with their ordinary compliment of 'God save you'; each of them making their respective courtesies.

Both sexes have a great inclination to novelty; and, perhaps, anything may be thought new with them that is but different from their way of managing land, cattle, fowls, etc. A parcel of them were always attending the minister and me, admiring our habit, behaviour; and, in a word, all that we did or said was wonderful in their esteem; but above all, writing was the most astonishing to them; they cannot conceive how it is possible for any mortal to express the conceptions of his mind in such black characters upon white paper. After they had with admiration argued upon this subject, I told them that within the compass of two years or less, if they pleased, they might easily be taught to read and write, but they were not of the opinion that either of them could be obtained, at least by them, in an age.

The officer in his embassy in July last travelled so far as to land on the continent next to Skye, and it was a long journey for a native of St Kilda so to do, for scarce any of the inhabitants ever had the opportunity of travelling so great a way into the world.

They observed many wonderful things in the course of their travels; but they have a notion that Mack-Leod's family is equivalent to that of an Imperial Court, and believe the king to be only superior to him; they say his lady wore such a strange Lowland dress that it was impossible for them to describe it; they admired glass windows hugely, and a looking-glass to them was a prodigy; they were amazed when they saw cloth hangings upon a thick wall of stone and lime, and condemned it as a thing very vain and superfluous.

They reckon the year, quarter, and month, as generally is done all Britain over. They compute the several periods of time by the lives of the proprietors and stewards, of whose greatest actions they have a tradition, of which they discourse with as great satisfaction as any historian reflecting on the Caesars, or greatest generals in the world.

They account riding one of the greatest pieces of grandeur here upon earth, and told me with a strange admiration, that Mack-Leod did not travel on foot, as they supposed all other men did, and that they had seen several horses kept on purpose by him for riding.

One of their number, landing in the isle of Harris, enquired who was the proprietor of those lands? They told him, that it was Mack-Leod, which did not a little raise his opinion of him; this man afterwards, when he was in the isle of Skye, and had travelled some miles there, one day standing upon an eminence, and looking round about him, he fancied he saw a great part of the world, and then enquired to whom those lands did belong, and when one of the company had acquainted him, that Mack-Leòd was master of those lands also, the St Kilda man lifting up his eyes and hands to Heaven, cried out with admiration, 'O Mighty Prince, who art Master of such vast territories!' This he expressed so emphatically in the Irish language that the saying from that time became a proverb whenever anybody would express a greatness and plenitude of power.

One of the things they wondered most at was the growth of trees; they thought the beauty of the leaves and branches admirable, and how they grew to such a height above plants was far above their conception: one of them, marvelling at it, told me that the trees pulled him back as he travelled through the woods: they resolved once to carry some few of them on their backs to their boats, and so to take them to St Kilda, but upon second thoughts, the length of the journey, being through the greatest part of the isle of Skye, deterred them from this undertaking, for though they excel others in strength, yet they are very bad travellers on foot, they being but little used to it.

One of their number having travelled in the Isle of Skye, to the south part of it, thought this a prodigious journey; and seeing in the opposite continent the shire of Inverness, divided from Skye only by a narrow sea, enquired of the company, if that was the border of England.

One of the St Kilda men, after he had taken a pretty large dose of *aqua-vitae*,* and was become very heavy with it, as he was falling into a sleep, and fancying it was to have been his last, expressed to his companions the great satisfaction he had in meeting with such an easy passage out of this world; 'for', said he, 'it is attended with no kind of pain'. In short, their opinion of foreign objects is as remote from the ordinary sentiments of other mankind, as they are themselves from all foreign converse.

I must not omit acquainting the reader that the account given of the seamen's rudeness to the inhabitants has created great prejudices in them against seamen in general; and though I endeavoured to bring them into some good opinion of them, it will not be, I hope, improper here to deliver the terms upon which the inhabitants are resolved to receive strangers, and no otherwise; they will not admit of any number exceeding ten, and those too must be unarmed, for else the inhabitants will oppose them with all their might; but if any number of them, not exceeding that abovesaid, come peaceably, and with good designs, they may expect water and fire gratis, and what else the place affords, at the easiest rates in the world.

The inhabitants of St Kilda are much happier than the generality of mankind, as being almost the only people in the world who feel the sweetness of true liberty: what the condition of the people in the Golden Age is feigned by the poets to be, that theirs really is, I mean, in innocency and simplicity, purity, mutual love and cordial friendship, free from solicitous cares, and anxious covetousness; from envy, deceit, and dissimulation; from ambition and pride, and the consequences that attend them. They are altogether ignorant of the vices of foreigners, and governed by the dictates of reason and Christianity, as it was first delivered to them by those heroic souls whose zeal moved them to undergo danger and trouble to plant religion here in one of the remotest corners of the world.

There is this only wanting to make them the happiest people in this habitable globe, *viz.*, that they themselves do not know how happy they are, and how much they are above the avarice and slavery of the rest of mankind. Their way of living makes them contemn gold and silver, as below the dignity of human nature; they live by the munificence of Heaven; and have no designs upon one another, but such as are purely suggested by justice and benevolence.

SAMUEL JOHNSON, *A Journey to the Western Islands of Scotland* (1775); James Boswell, *The Journal of a Tour to the Hebrides with Samuel Johnson, LL.D.* (1773; ed. F. A. Pottle, 1961)

A young and enthusiastic James Boswell befriended Samuel Johnson (1709–84), England's most famous man of letters, in London in 1763. Soon Boswell was urging Johnson to accompany him on a tour to the Hebrides, reviving the fascination inspired in Johnson by a childhood reading of Martin Martin. The two men went to Scotland in the late summer and autumn of 1773, riding north from Edinburgh to Inverness and then westward through the Great Glen and across the mountains to the coast. Johnson published *A Journey to the Western Islands of Scotland* two years later. In his masterpiece of philosophical tourism Johnson ana-lyses the disintegration of traditional Highland society and attacks the authenticity of James Macpherson's translations of the Gaelic bard 'Ossian', which founded the Romantic image of Scotland as a lost world of ghosts and heroes. Boswell edited his journal of their tour after Johnson's death (it was published in 1785), as a preview of the full-scale biography he was planning. While Johnson makes his travelogue the occasion for a wide-ranging inquiry into the nature of historical change, Boswell dramatizes a Scottish Enlightenment ethos of sociability and conversation. In the following excerpts, Johnson pauses on the verge of the Highlands to reflect on British imperial history; both travellers describe their encounter with an old woman on the banks of Loch Ness; Boswell narrates a quarrel and its sequel; Johnson deplores 'the laxity of Highland conversation'; but finds an emblem of hope for the future in Edinburgh.

Johnson: 'Inverness'

Inverness was the last place which had a regular communication by high roads with the southern counties. All the ways beyond it have, I believe, been made by the soldiers in this century. At Inverness therefore Cromwell, when he subdued Scotland,* stationed a garrison, as at the boundary of the Highlands. The soldiers seem to have incorporated afterwards with the inhabitants, and to have peopled the place with an English race; for the language of this town has been long considered as peculiarly elegant.

Here is a castle, called the castle of Macbeth, the walls of which are yet standing. It was no very capacious edifice, but stands upon a rock so high and steep, that I think it was once not accessible, but by the help of ladders, or a bridge. Over against it, on another hill, was a fort built by Cromwell, now totally demolished; for no faction of Scotland loved the name of Cromwell, or had any desire to continue his memory.

Yet what the Romans did to other nations, was in a great degree done by Cromwell to the Scots; he civilized them by conquests, and introduced by useful violence the arts of peace. I was told at Aberdeen that the people learned from Cromwell's soldiers to make shoes and to plant kail.

How they lived without kail, it is not easy to guess. They cultivate hardly any other plant for common tables, and when they had not kail they probably had nothing. The numbers that go barefoot are still sufficient to show that shoes may be spared. They are not yet considered as necessaries of life; for tall boys, not otherwise meanly dressed, run without them in the streets; and in the islands the sons of gentlemen pass several of their first years with naked feet.

I know not whether it be not peculiar to the Scots to have attained the liberal, without the manual arts, to have excelled in ornamental knowledge, and to have wanted not only the elegancies, but the conveniencies of common life. Literature soon after its revival found its way to Scotland, and from the middle of the sixteenth century, almost to the middle of the seventeenth, the politer studies were very diligently pursued. The Latin poetry of *Deliciae Poetarum Scotorum* would have done honour to any nation, at least till the publication of May's *Supplement** the English had very little to oppose.

Yet men thus ingenious and inquisitive were content to live in total ignorance of the trades by which human wants are supplied, and to supply them by the grossest means. Till the Union made them acquainted with English manners, the culture of their lands was unskilful, and their domestic life unformed; their tables were coarse as the feasts of Eskimos, and their houses filthy as the cottages of Hottentots.

Since they have known that their condition was capable of improvement, their progress in useful knowledge has been rapid and uniform. What remains to be done they will quickly do, and then wonder, like me, why that which was so necessary and so easy was so long delayed. But they must be for ever content to owe to the English that elegance and culture, which, if they had been vigilant and active, perhaps the English might have owed to them.

Here the appearance of life began to alter. I had seen a few women with plaids at Aberdeen; but at Inverness the Highland manners are common. There is I think a kirk, in which only the Erse language* is used. There is likewise an English chapel, but meanly built, where on Sunday we saw a very decent congregation.

We were now to bid farewell to the luxury of travelling, and to enter a country upon which perhaps no wheel has ever rolled. We could indeed have used our post-chaise one day longer, along the military road to Fort Augustus, but we could have hired no horses beyond Inverness, and we were not so sparing of ourselves, as to lead them, merely that we might have one day longer the indulgence of a carriage.

At Inverness therefore we procured three horses for ourselves and a servant, and one more for our baggage, which was no very heavy load. We found in the course of our journey the convenience of having disencumbered ourselves, by laying aside whatever we could spare; for it is not to be imagined without experience how, in climbing crags, and treading bogs, and winding through narrow and obstructed passages, a little bulk will hinder, and a little weight will burden; or how often a man that has pleased himself at home with his own resolution will, in the hour of darkness and fatigue, be content to leave behind him everything but himself.

Johnson: 'Loch Ness'

Near the way, by the water side, we espied a cottage. This was the first Highland hut that I had seen; and as our business was with life and manners, we were willing to visit it. To enter a habitation without leave seems to be not considered here as rudeness or intrusion. The old laws of hospitality still give this licence to a stranger.

A hut is constructed with loose stones, ranged for the most part with some tendency to circularity. It must be placed where the wind cannot act upon it with violence, because it has no cement; and where the water will run easily away, because it has no floor but the naked ground. The wall, which is commonly about six feet high, declines from the perpendicular a little inward. Such rafters as can be procured are then raised for a roof, and covered with heath, which makes a strong and warm thatch, kept from flying off by ropes of twisted heath, of which the ends, reaching from the centre of the thatch to the top of the wall, are held firm by the weight of a large stone. No light is admitted but at the entrance, and through a hole in the thatch, which gives vent to the smoke. This hole is not directly over the fire, lest the rain should extinguish it; and the smoke therefore naturally fills the place before it escapes. Such is the general structure of the houses in which one of the nations of this opulent and powerful island has been hitherto content to live. Huts however are not more uniform than palaces; and this which we were inspecting was very far from one of the meanest, for it was divided into several apartments; and its inhabitants possessed such property as a pastoral poet might exalt into riches.

When we entered, we found an old woman boiling goat's-flesh in a kettle. She spoke little English, but we had interpreters at hand; and she was willing enough to display her whole system of economy. She has five children, of which none are yet gone from her. The eldest, a boy of thirteen, and her husband, who is eighty years old, were at work in the wood. Her two next sons were gone to Inverness to buy 'meal', by which oatmeal is always meant. Meal she considered as expensive food, and told us that in spring, when the goats gave milk, the children could live without it. She is mistress of sixty goats, and I saw many kids in an enclosure at the end of her house. She had also some poultry. By the lake we saw a potato-garden, and a small spot of ground on which stood four shucks, containing each twelve sheaves of barley. She has all this from the labour of their own hands, and for what is necessary to be bought, her kids and her chickens are sent to market.

With the true pastoral hospitality, she asked us to sit down and drink whisky. She is religious, and though the kirk is four miles off, probably eight English miles, she goes thither every Sunday. We gave her a shilling, and she begged snuff; for snuff is the luxury of a Highland cottage.

Boswell: Monday, 30 August 1773

This day we were to begin our equitation, as I said, for *I* would needs make a word too. We might have taken a chaise to Fort Augustus. But we could not find horses after Inverness, so we resolved to begin here to ride. We should have set out at seven. But one of the horses needed shoeing; the smith had got drunk the night before at a wedding and could not rise early; so we did not get off till nine. We had three horses for Mr Johnson, myself, and Joseph,* and one which carried our portmanteaus; and two Highlanders who walked with us, John Hay and Lauchlan Vass. Mr Johnson rode very well.

A little above Inverness, I fancy about three miles, we saw just by the road a very complete Druid's temple; at least we took it to be so. There was a double circle of stones, one of very large ones and one of smaller ones. Mr Johnson justly observed that to go and see one is only to see that it is nothing, for there is neither art nor power in it, and seeing one is as much as one would wish.

It was a delightful day. Loch Ness, and the road upon the side of it, between birch trees, with the hills above, pleased us much. The scene was as remote and agreeably wild as could be desired. It was full enough to occupy our minds for the time.

To see Mr Johnson in any new situation is an object of attention to me. As I saw him now for the first time ride along just like Lord Alemoor,* I thought of *London, a Poem*, of the *Rambler*, of *The False*

*Alarm,** and I cannot express the ideas which went across my imagination.

A good way up the Loch, I perceived a little hut with an oldish woman at the door of it. I knew it would be a scene for Mr Johnson. So I spoke of it. 'Let's go in,' said he. So we dismounted, and we and our guides went in. It was a wretched little hovel, of earth only, I think; and for a window had just a hole which was stopped with a piece of turf which could be taken out to let in light. In the middle of the room (or space which we entered) was a fire of peat, the smoke going out at a hole in the roof. She had a pot upon it with goat's flesh boiling. She had at one end, under the same roof but divided with a kind of partition made of wands, a pen or fold in which we saw a good many kids.

Mr Johnson asked me where she slept. I asked one of the guides, who asked her in Erse. She spoke with a kind of high tone. He told us she was afraid we wanted to go to bed to her. This coquetry, or whatever it may be called, of so wretched a like being was truly ludicrous. Mr Johnson and I afterwards made merry upon it. I said it was he who alarmed the poor woman's virtue. 'No, sir,' said he. 'She'll say, "There came a wicked young fellow, a wild young dog, who I believe would have ravished me had there not been with him a grave old gentleman who repressed him. But when he gets out of the sight of his tutor, I'll warrant you he'll spare no woman he meets, young or old."' 'No,' said I. 'She'll say, "There was a terrible ruffian who would have forced me, had it not been for a gentle, mild-looking youth, who, I take it, was an angel."'

Mr Johnson would not hurt her delicacy by insisting to 'see her bedchamber', like Archer in *The Beaux' Stratagem.** But I was of a more ardent curiosity, so I lighted a piece of paper and went into the place where the bed was. There was a little partition of wicker, rather more neatly done than the one for the fold, and close by the wall was a kind of bedstead of wood with heath upon it for a bed; and at the foot of it I saw some sort of blankets or covering rolled up in a heap. The woman's name was Fraser. So was her husband's. He was a man of eighty. Mr Fraser of Balnain allows him to live in this hut and to keep sixty goats for taking care of his wood. He was then in the wood. They had five children, the oldest only thirteen. Two were gone to Inverness to buy meal. The rest were looking after the goats. She had four stacks of barley, twenty-four sheaves in each. They had a few fowls. They will live all the spring without meal upon milk and curd, etc., alone. What they get for their goats, kids, and hens maintains them. I did not observe how the children lay.

She asked us to sit down and take a dram. I saw one chair. She said she was as happy as any woman in Scotland. She could hardly speak any English, just detached words. Mr Johnson was pleased at seeing for the first time such a state of human life. She asked for snuff. It is her luxury. She uses a great deal. We had none, but gave her sixpence apiece. She then brought out her whisky bottle. I tasted it, and Joseph and our guides had some. So I gave her sixpence more. She sent us away with many prayers in Erse.

Boswell: Wednesday, 1 September

We came to a rich green valley, comparatively speaking, and stopped at Auchnashiel, a kind of rural village, a number of cottages being built together, as we saw all along in the Highlands. We passed many many miles today without seeing a house, but only little summer-huts or *shielings*. Ewan Campbell, servant to Mr Murchison, factor to the Laird of MacLeod in Glenelg, ran along with us today. He was a fine obliging little fellow. At this Auchnashiel, we sat down on a green turf seat at the end of a house, and they brought us out two wooden dishes of milk. One of them was frothed like a syllabub. I saw a woman preparing it with such a stick as is used for chocolate, and in the same manner. That dish fell to my share; but I put by the froth and took the cream with some wheat-bread which Joseph had brought for us from Fort Augustus. Mr Johnson imagined my dish was better than his, and desired to taste it. He did so, and was convinced that I had no advantage over him. We had there in a circle all about us, men, women and children, all Macraes, Lord Seaforth's people. Not one of them could speak English. I said to Mr Johnson 'twas the same as being with a tribe of Indians. 'Yes,' said he, 'but not so terrifying.' I gave all who chose it snuff and tobacco. Governor Trapaud had made us buy a quantity at Fort Augustus* and put them up in small parcels. I also gave each person a bit of wheat-bread, which they had never tasted. I then gave a penny apiece to each child. I told Mr Johnson of this, upon which he called for change for a shilling, and declared that he would distribute among the children. Upon this there was a great stir: not only did some children come running down from neighbouring huts, but I observed one black-headed man, who had been among us all along, coming carrying a very young child. Mr Johnson then ordered the children to be drawn up in a row, and he distributed his copper and made them and their parents all happy. The poor Macraes, whatever may be their present state, were much thought of in the year 1715, when there was a line in a song,

> And aw' the brave McCraas is coming.

There was great diversity in the faces of the circle around us. Some were as black and wild in their appearance as any American savages whatever. One woman was as comely as the figure of Sappho, as we see it painted. We asked the old woman, the mistress of the house where we had the milk (which, by the by, Mr Johnson told me, for I did not observe it myself, was built not of turf but of stone), what we should pay. She said, what we pleased. One of our guides asked her in Erse if a shilling was enough. She said, 'Yes.' But some of the men bid her ask more. This vexed me, because it showed a desire to impose upon strangers, as they knew that even a shilling was high payment. The woman, however, honestly persisted in her first price. So I gave her half-a-crown. Thus we had one good scene of uncommon life to us. The people were very much pleased, gave us many blessings, and said they had not had such a day since the old Laird of MacLeod's time.

Mr Johnson was much refreshed by this repast. He was pleased when I told him he would make a good chief. He said if he were one, he would dress his servants better than himself, and knock a fellow down if he looked saucy to a Macdonald in rags.* But he would not treat men as brutes. He would let them know why all of his clan were to have attention paid to them. He would tell his upper servants why, and make them tell the others.

We rode on well till we came to the high mountain called the Rattachan, by which time both Mr Johnson and the horses were a good deal fatigued. It is a terrible steep to climb, notwithstanding the road is made slanting along. However, we made it out. On the top of it we met Captain MacLeod of Balmeanach (a Dutch officer come from Skye) riding with his sword slung about him. He asked, 'Is this Mr Boswell?' which was a proof that we were expected. Going down the hill on the other side was no easy task. As Mr Johnson was a great weight, the two guides agreed that he should ride the horses alternately. Hay's were the two best, and Mr Johnson would not ride but upon one or other of them, a black or a brown. But as Hay complained much after ascending the Rattachan, Mr Johnson was prevailed with to mount one of Vass's greys. As he rode upon it downhill, it did not go well, and he grumbled. I walked on a little before, but was excessively entertained with the method taken to keep him in good humour. Hay led the horse's head, talking to Mr Johnson as much as he could; and just when Mr Johnson was uttering his displeasure, the fellow says, 'See such pretty goats.' Then *whu!* he whistled, and made them jump. Little did he conceive what Mr Johnson was. Here was now a common ignorant horse-hirer imagining that he could divert, as one does a child, *Mr Samuel Johnson!* The ludicrousness, absurdity, and extraordinary contrast between what the fellow fancied and the reality was as highly comic as anything that I ever witnessed. I laughed immoderately, and must laugh as often as I recollect it.

It grew dusky; and we had a very tedious ride for what was called five miles, but I am sure would measure ten. We spoke none. I was riding forward to the inn at Glenelg;* that I might make some kind of preparation, or take some proper measures, before Mr Johnson got up, who was now advancing in silence, with Hay leading his horse. Mr Johnson called me back with a tremendous shout, and was really in a passion with me for leaving him. I told him my intentions. But he was not satisfied, and said, 'Do you know, I should as soon have thought of picking a pocket as doing so.' 'I'm diverted with you,' said I. Said he, 'I could never be diverted with incivility.' He said doing such a thing made one lose confidence in him who did it, as one could not tell what he would do next. I justified myself but lamely to him. But my intentions were not improper. I wished to be forward to see if Sir A. Macdonald* had sent his boat; and if not, how we were to sail, and how we were to lodge, all which I thought I could best settle myself, without his having any trouble. To apply his great mind to minute particulars is wrong. It is like taking an immense balance, such as you see on a quay for weighing cargoes of ships, to weigh a guinea. I knew I had neat little scales which would do better. That his attention to everything in his way, and his uncommon desire to be always in the right, would make him weigh if he knew of the particulars; and therefore it was right for me to weigh them and let him have them only in effect. I kept by him, since he thought I should.

As we passed the barracks at Bernera, I would fain have put up there; at least I looked at them wishfully, as soldiers have always everything in the best order. But there was only a sergeant and a few men there. We came on to the inn at Glenelg. There was nothing to give the horses, so they were sent to grass with a man to watch them. We found that Sir Alexander had sent his boat to a point which we had passed, at Kintail, or more properly at the King's house—that it had waited several days till their provisions ran short, and had returned only this day. So we had nothing to say against that Knight. A lass showed us upstairs into a room raw and dirty; bare walls, a variety of bad smells, a coarse black fir greasy table, forms of the same kind, and from a wretched bed started a fellow from his sleep like Edgar in *King Lear*: 'Poor Tom's a-cold.'*

The landlord was one Munro from Fort Augustus. He pays £8 to MacLeod for the shell of the house, and has not a bit of land in lease. They had no bread, no eggs, no wine, no spirits but whisky, no sugar but brown grown black. They prepared some mutton-chops, but we would not have them. They killed two hens. I made Joseph broil me a bit of one till it was black, and I tasted it. Mr Johnson would take nothing but a bit of bread, which we had luckily remaining, and some lemonade which he made with a lemon which Joseph had for him, and he got some good sugar; for Mr Murchison, factor to MacLeod in Glenelg, sent us some, with a bottle of excellent rum, letting us know he was very sorry that his servant had not come and informed him before we passed his house; that we might have been there all night, and that if he were not obliged to set out early next day for Inverness, he would come down and wait upon us.

I took some rum and water and sugar, and grew better; for after my last bad night I hoped much to be well this, and being disappointed, I was uneasy and almost fretful. Mr Johnson was calm. I said he was so from vanity. 'No,' said he, ''tis from philosophy.' It was a considerable satisfaction to me to see that the Rambler could practise what he nobly teaches.

I resumed my riding forward, and wanted to defend it. Mr Johnson was still violent upon that subject, and said, 'Sir, had you gone on, I was thinking that I should have returned with you to Edinburgh and then parted, and never spoke to you more.'

I sent for fresh hay, with which we made beds to ourselves, each in a room equally miserable. As Wolfe said in his letter from Quebec, we had 'choice of difficulties'.* Mr. Johnson made things better by comparison. At Macqueen's last night he observed that few were so well lodged in a ship. Tonight he said we were better than if we had been upon the hill. He lay down buttoned up in his greatcoat. I had my sheets spread on the hay, and having stripped, I had my clothes and greatcoat and Joseph's greatcoat laid upon me, by way of blankets. Joseph lay in the room by me, upon a bed laid on the floor.

THURSDAY, 2 SEPTEMBER. I had slept ill. Mr Johnson's anger had affected me much. I considered that, without any bad intention, I might suddenly forfeit his friendship. I was impatient to see him this morning. I told him how uneasy he had made me by what he had said. He owned it was said in passion; that he would not have done it; that if he had done it, he would have been ten times worse than me. That it would indeed, as I said, be 'limning in water', should such sudden breaks happen (or something to that effect); and said he, 'Let's think no more on't.' BOSWELL. 'Well then, sir, I shall be easy. Remember, I am to have fair warning in case of any quarrel. You are never to spring a mine upon me. It was absurd in me to believe you.' JOHNSON. 'You deserved about as much as to believe it from night to morning.' Mr MacLeod of Drynoch, to whom we had a letter from Kenneth Macaulay, breakfasted with us.

A quarter before nine we got into a boat for Skye. It rained much when we set off, but cleared up as we advanced. One of the boatmen who spoke English said that a mile at land was two miles at sea. I then said to him that from Glenelg to Armadale in Skye, which was our sail this morning and is called twelve, was only six miles. But this he could not understand. 'Well,' said Mr Johnson, 'never talk to me of the native good sense of the Highlanders. Here is a fellow who calls one mile two, and yet cannot comprehend that twelve such miles make but six.' It was curious to think that now at last Mr Johnson and I had left the mainland of Scotland and were sailing to the Hebrides, one of which was close in our view; and I had besides a number of youthful ideas, that is to say, ideas which I have had from my youth about the Isle of Skye. We were shown the land of Moidart where Prince Charles first landed.* That stirred my mind.

Johnson: 'Skye. Armidel'

As we sat at Sir Alexander's table, we were entertained, according
to the ancient usage of the North, with the melody of the bagpipe.
Everything in those countries has its history. As the bagpiper was
playing, an elderly gentleman informed us that in some remote
time, the Macdonalds of Glengary having been injured, or offended
by the inhabitants of Culloden, and resolving to have justice or
vengeance, came to Culloden on a Sunday where, finding their
enemies at worship, they shut them up in the church, which they set
on fire; and this, said he, is the tune that the piper played while they
were burning.

Narrations like this, however uncertain, deserve the notice of a
traveller, because they are the only records of a nation that has no
historians, and afford the most genuine representation of the life and
character of the ancient Highlanders.

Under the denomination of 'Highlander' are comprehended in
Scotland all that now speak the Erse language, or retain the primitive
manners, whether they live among the mountains or in the islands;
and in that sense I use the name, when there is not some apparent
reason for making a distinction.

In Skye I first observed the use of brogues, a kind of artless shoes,
stitched with thongs so loosely, that though they defend the foot
from stones, they do not exclude water. Brogues were formerly made
of raw hides, with the hair inwards, and such are perhaps still used in
rude and remote parts; but they are said not to last above two days.
Where life is somewhat improved, they are now made of leather
tanned with oak bark, as in other places, or with the bark of birch, or
roots of tormentil, a substance recommended in defect of bark,
about forty years ago, to the Irish tanners, by one to whom the
parliament of that kingdom voted a reward. The leather of Sky is not
completely penetrated by vegetable matter, and therefore cannot be
very durable.

My inquiries about brogues gave me an early specimen of Highland information. One day I was told that to make brogues was a
domestic art, which every man practised for himself, and that a pair
of brogues was the work of an hour. I supposed that the husband
made brogues as the wife made an apron, till next day it was told me
that a brogue-maker was a trade, and that a pair would cost half a
crown. It will easily occur that these representations may both be

true, and that, in some places, men may buy them, and in others, make them for themselves; but I had both the accounts in the same house within two days.

Many of my subsequent inquiries upon more interesting topics ended in the like uncertainty. He that travels in the Highlands may easily saturate his soul with intelligence, if he will acquiesce in the first account. The Highlander gives to every question an answer so prompt and peremptory, that scepticism itself is dared into silence, and the mind sinks before the bold reporter in unresisting credulity; but, if a second question be ventured, it breaks the enchantment; for it is immediately discovered, that what was told so confidently was told at hazard, and that such fearlessness of assertion was either the sport of negligence, or the refuge of ignorance.

If individuals are thus at variance with themselves, it can be no wonder that the accounts of different men are contradictory. The traditions of an ignorant and savage people have been for ages negligently heard, and unskilfully related. Distant events must have been mingled together, and the actions of one man given to another. These, however, are deficiencies in story, for which no man is now to be censured. It were enough, if what there is yet opportunity of examining were accurately inspected, and justly represented; but such is the laxity of Highland conversation that the inquirer is kept in continual suspense, and by a kind of intellectual retrogradation, knows less as he hears more.

Johnson: Edinburgh

We now returned to Edinburgh, where I passed some days with men of learning, whose names want no advancement from my commemoration, or with women of elegance, which perhaps disclaims a pedant's praise.

The conversation of the Scots grows every day less unpleasing to the English; their peculiarities wear fast away; their dialect is likely to become in half a century provincial and rustic, even to themselves. The great, the learned, the ambitious, and the vain, all cultivate the English phrase, and the English pronunciation, and in splendid companies Scotch is not much heard, except now and then from an old lady.

There is one subject of philosophical curiosity to be found in Edinburgh, which no other city has to show; a college of the deaf and dumb, who are taught to speak, to read, to write, and to practise arithmetic, by a gentleman whose name is Braidwood.* The number which attends him is, I think, about twelve, which he brings together into a little school, and instructs according to their several degrees of proficiency.

I do not mean to mention the instruction of the deaf as new. Having been first practised upon the son of a Constable of Spain, it was afterwards cultivated with much emulation in England, by Wallis and Holder, and was lately professed by Mr Baker,* who once flattered me with hopes of seeing his method published. How far any former teachers have succeeded, it is not easy to know; the improvement of Mr Braidwood's pupils is wonderful. They not only speak, write, and understand what is written, but if he that speaks looks towards them, and modifies his organs by distinct and full utterance, they know so well what is spoken, that it is an expression scarcely figurative to say, they hear with the eye. That any have attained to the power mentioned by Burnet,* of feeling sounds, by laying a hand on the speaker's mouth, I know not; but I have seen so much that I can believe more; a single word, or a short sentence, I think, may possibly be so distinguished.

It will readily be supposed by those that consider this subject, that Mr Braidwood's scholars spell accurately. Orthography is vitiated among such as learn first to speak, and then to write, by imperfect notions of the relation between letters and vocal utterance; but to those students every character is of equal importance; for letters are to them not symbols of names, but of things; when they write they do not represent a sound, but delineate a form.

This school I visited, and found some of the scholars waiting for their master, whom they are said to receive at his entrance with smiling countenances and sparkling eyes, delighted with the hope of new ideas. One of the young ladies had her slate before her, on which I wrote a question consisting of three figures, to be multiplied by two figures. She looked upon it, and quivering her fingers in a manner which I thought very pretty, but of which I know not whether it was art or play, multiplied the sum regularly in two lines, observing the decimal place; but did not add the two lines together, probably disdaining so easy an operation. I pointed at the place where the sum total should stand, and she noted it with such expedition as seemed to show that she had it only to write.

It was pleasing to see one of the most desperate of human calamities capable of so much help: whatever enlarges hope will exalt courage; after having seen the deaf taught arithmetic, who would be afraid to cultivate the Hebrides?

Such are the things which this journey has given me an opportunity of seeing, and such are the reflections which that sight has raised. Having passed my time almost wholly in cities, I may have been surprised by modes of life and appearances of nature that are familiar to men of wider survey and more varied conversation. Novelty and ignorance must always be reciprocal, and I cannot but be conscious that my thoughts on national manners are the thoughts of one who has seen but little.

MARY ANN HANWAY, *A Journey to the Highlands of Scotland. With Occasional Remarks on Dr Johnson's Tour. By a Lady* (1777)

Mary Ann Hanway, née Vergy (*c.*1755–*c.*1824), published four novels between 1798 and 1814. Her early, anonymous *Journey to the Highlands of Scotland* accuses Johnson of pedantry and fault-finding. Hanway combines the 'sentimental' style made popular by Sterne with a pose of aristocratic amateurism—defensive ruses of the female author venturing into public.

Preface

The following letters are selected from a correspondence begun, continued, and completed, upon motives of amusement, invitation, and tenderness. I took up the pen, indeed, to prove what will, I believe, be found universally true upon all human occasions. Meditating an excursion into the interior parts of the kingdom of Scotland, I had scarcely lost sight of the towers of London, even at the end of my first stage, before I felt that, according to Mr Pope,

Self-love, and social is the same.*

We may transport our persons, I perceive, to the remotest regions of the earth: from Caledonia we may direct our rambles into the deserts of Arabia, but the mind still remains untravelled, and clings fondly to that dear, and domestic circle whom we have left over our own firesides, and whose prayers and wishes are for ever on the wing to keep pace with our migrations. As the chaise therefore ran rapidly along, bearing me every moment farther from the scene of my accustomed conversation, and the beloved objects, by whose ingenuity they were supported, I resolved to make my journey in some measure compensate the fatigue of undertaking it. This first suggested to me those pleasures which are allowed even to absence, the pleasures of the pen; accordingly, I resolved to travel rather critically than casually, rather to accommodate my friends with information than merely to gratify the greediness of vacant curiosity. The consequences were, I did not suffer the postilion to indulge his professional passion, to pass briskly through any parts of cultivated country, or rattle rapidly over the pavement of towns, that were fertile of remark, but ordered him to go sentimentally. In a word, I rode pencil in hand, employing myself in drawing a sketch of the landscape, whether of hill or valley, morass or mountain, as it lay before me; a task not the less agreeable for its abounding in novelties; or for the various prospects which rewarded it. To this vanity, indeed, may be attributed the spirit which resisted the inconvenience of sometimes travelling over heaths of almost immeasurable sterility: but to these, a gayer and fairer complexion of country always succeeded, which, seconded by the hospitality everywhere shown to me and to my party, a hospitality, which marks the characteristic feature of the kingdom, not only made amends for those occasional glooms which seemed to breathe the spirit of melancholy from the surrounding barrenness, but gave to the whole that sort of chequer-work, which inevitably mixes with every business, and every pleasure, in the circumscribed journey of Life. On my return to London, after I had reciprocally given and received the embraces of welcome, I was not a little surprised (and I am woman enough to own, not a little pleased) to find those running papers which were trusted to the post, very favourably received by those to whom they were addressed. Nay, how shall I escape betraying the symptoms of vanity, when I further observe that Lady —— had taken the pains, by the clue which the knowledge of my connections gave her, to obtain copies from every other correspondent, and to put the little bundle, thus affectionately collected, into the hands of a literary gentleman?

Letter VI

INVERARY, 14 August 1775

I have been for some days past, my Lord, on a pleasant tour through
the Western Highlands. This is written from Inverary, the seat of
the present Duke of Argyle,* but which was originally the property
of the Campbell family, and after that, inhabited by the wonderful
and whimsical Colin,* who is reported to have set fire to his house to
gratify his ambition of displaying to a friend the grandeur of his
equipage in the field. This superb modern building was begun by the
late Duke, and finished by the present;* it stands in a park surrounded by immense hills, planted, to their summit, with firs. Loch
Fyne, an arm of the sea, rolls close to the town, which is all
re-building with stone by the Duke; and will, when finished, make a
handsome appearance. The castle is genteelly furnished in the
present taste, and from the number of bedchambers, is capable of
entertaining a numerous train; which provision, indeed, the gloominess of the situation must render very necessary; for, they tell me, it
rains here eleven months out of the twelve, which, I think, may be
easily accounted for, from its near affinity to the sea, and the mountains that surround it; for, as a learned and elaborate traveller,* in his
usual pomp of phraseology with great scrupulosity of minute
investigation observes, 'where there are many mountains, there will
always be much rain, and the torrents pouring down into the intermediate spaces, seldom find so ready an outlet, as not to stagnate, till
they have broken the texture of the ground.' The philosophy as well
as the philology of this passage, is, to be sure, very profound, and
means, pretty near as much, as many other parts of this investigator's
visionary journey: not that I mean, my Lord, invidiously to rob the
gentleman of the praises due to him for several *real* discoveries
which are scattered through his publication: such, for instance, as
that, 'mountainous countries are not passed without difficulty; that,
climbing is not always necessary; that, what is not mountain is commonly bog, through which bogs, the way must be picked with caution.' These ingenious and important informations, have, I perceive,
already attracted the ridicule of our acute English critics, and, as the
subject hath fallen in my way, I could not help joining the chorus of
ironical approbation for the edifying remarks of the great D. J——,
of whom, however, I must take leave at present, not without a

promise to return again soon, and bend a keener eye, upon his volume of vacancy.* The castle of Inverary is in a bottom, the great fault of all their houses in this country; for you do not know you are near any inhabited place, till you find your chaise at their gates. We have, unfortunately, been favoured with a specimen of the weather natural to the place, having been unable to walk out, for some of the heaviest rains I ever saw. I began to tremble—Heaven forgive me! lest the world was once more destined to be destroyed by a deluge; even now, my Lord, it is pouring down in torrents. We shall quit it tomorrow, 'nothing loth',* without penetrating any farther into the Highlands, this way, and return by the same road we came, which is, to me, not a displeasing one, though the major part that travel are of a contrary opinion. I cannot better describe it than by saying, it strikes a pleasing gloominess that I do not dislike, being so new to me, who have only been used to bowl away upon a turnpike road in England. It is called Glencroe: the road has been rendered good by the soldiers; it lies in a glen between immense mountains, that rear their black and naked tops much above the clouds. I saw some horses that appeared cropping a miserable mouthful, half way to the top, which, from their height, did not appear bigger than spaniels. My wonder was what the brutes could possibly find to eat; but a Scotch horse is not the nicest animal in the world, and will live anywhere. Perhaps, they have sufficient sagacity of instinct, to imitate the frugal maxims of their masters; and the pampered English horses, and English riders, are not far enough North, and too much accustomed to the softening luxuries of the South, to adopt that general habit of economy, which, from the highest to the lowest order of men is here the characteristic. I must not forget to tell you, there is a continuation of natural cascades falling all the way, which gives a grandeur and sparkling splendour to the scene, which render it awfully delightful. There is something exquisite to me, even in the cadence of a cascade: as I listened to it in this captivating spot, I really felt my imagination expand, and if I had anything of the bard in my composition, this would have been the moment of inspiration. Alas! my dear Lord, the Muse would not come at my bidding, and I was obliged to recur to the description of one whom the Muse more highly favoured. His cascade is so like mine at Glencroe, and so much better painted than I could have painted it, that I scruple not to invite your acceptance of a transcription; though as I trust wholly to memory, not having the book with me, I may perhaps transcribe incorrectly.*

DOROTHY WORDSWORTH, *Recollections of a Tour Made in Scotland, AD 1803* (ed. J. C. Shairp, Edinburgh, 1894)

Dorothy Wordsworth (1771–1855) visited Scotland with her elder brother William and their friend Samuel Taylor Coleridge in August and September 1803, travelling in a one-horse Irish 'jaunting car'—which in practice meant going much of the way on foot. Their route took them from their home at Keswick up across the south-west of Scotland to Loch Lomond, whence they ventured into the relatively little-known hill and lake country of the Trossachs. (Seven years later, Walter Scott would make the Trossachs world-famous as the scenery of *The Lady of the Lake*.) Our excerpts show the travellers crossing the 'inhabited solitudes' of Lanarkshire; exploring Loch Lomond from their base at the hamlet of Luss; and returning from a day's hike to their hosts, the Macfarlanes, at Glengyle on Loch Katrine.

SATURDAY, 20 AUGUST. Our road carried us down the valley, and we soon lost sight of Leadhills, for the valley made a turn almost immediately, and we saw two miles, perhaps, before us; the glen sloped somewhat rapidly—heathy, bare, no hut or house. Passed by a shepherd, who was sitting upon the ground, reading, with the book on his knee, screened from the wind by his plaid, while a flock of sheep were feeding near him among the rushes and coarse grass— for, as we descended we came among lands where grass grew with the heather. Travelled through several reaches of the glen, which somewhat resembled the valley of Menock on the other side of Wanlockhead; but it was not near so beautiful; the forms of the mountains did not melt so exquisitely into each other, and there was a coldness, and, if I may so speak, a want of simplicity in the surface of the earth; the heather was poor, not covering a whole hillside; not in luxuriant streams and beds interveined with rich verdure; but patchy and stunted, with here and there coarse grass and rushes. But we soon came in sight of a spot that impressed us very much. At the lower end of this new reach of the vale was a decayed tree, beside a decayed cottage, the vale spreading out into a level area which was one large field, without fence and without division, of a dull yellow colour; the vale seemed to partake of the desolation of the cottage, and to participate in its decay. And yet the spot was in its nature so dreary that one would rather have wondered how it ever came to be tenanted by man, than lament that it was left to waste and solitude. Yet the encircling hills were so exquisitely formed that it was impossible to conceive anything more lovely than this place would have been if the valley and hill-sides had been interspersed with trees, cottages, green fields, and hedgerows. But all was desolate; the one large field which filled up the area of the valley appeared, as I have said, in decay, and seemed to retain the memory of its connexion with man in some way analogous to the ruined building; for it was as much of a field as Mr King's best pasture scattered over with his fattest cattle.

We went on, looking before us, the place losing nothing of its hold upon our minds, when we discovered a woman sitting right in the middle of the field, alone, wrapped up in a grey cloak or plaid. She sat motionless all the time we looked at her, which might be nearly half an hour. We could not conceive why she sat there, for there were neither sheep nor cattle in the field; her appearance was very melancholy. In the meantime our road carried us nearer to the cottage; though we were crossing over the hill to the left, leaving the valley below us, and we perceived that a part of the building was inhabited, and that what we had supposed to be *one* blasted tree was eight trees, four of which were entirely blasted; the others partly so, and round about the place was a little potato and cabbage garth, fenced with earth. No doubt, that woman had been an inhabitant of the cottage. However this might be, there was so much obscurity and uncertainty about her, and her figure agreed so well with the desolation of the place, that we were indebted to the chance of her being there for some of the most interesting feelings that we had ever had from natural objects connected with man in dreary solitariness.

We had been advised to go along the *new* road, which would have carried us down the vale; but we met some travellers who recommended us to climb the hill, and go by the village of Crawfordjohn as being much nearer. We had a long hill, and after having reached the top, steep and bad roads, so we continued to walk for a considerable way. The air was cold and clear—the sky blue. We walked cheerfully along in the sunshine, each of us alone, only William had the charge of the horse and car, so he sometimes took a ride, which did but

poorly recompense him for the trouble of driving. I never travelled
with more cheerful spirits than this day. Our road was along the side
of a high moor. I can always walk over a moor with a light foot; I
seem to be drawn more closely to nature in such places than anywhere else; or rather I feel more strongly the power of nature over
me, and am better satisfied with myself for being able to find enjoyment in what unfortunately to many persons is either dismal or
insipid. This moor, however, was more than commonly interesting;
we could see a long way, and on every side of us were larger or
smaller tracts of cultivated land. Some were extensive farms, yet in
so large a waste they did but look small, with farm-houses, barns,
etc., others like little cottages, with enough to feed a cow, and supply
the family with vegetables. In looking at these farms we had always
one feeling. Why did the plough stop there? Why might not they as
well have carried it twice as far? There were no hedgerows near the
farms, and very few trees. As we were passing along, we saw an old
man, the first we had seen in a Highland bonnet, walking with a staff
at a very slow pace by the edge of one of the moorland cornfields; he
wore a grey plaid, and a dog was by his side. There was a scriptural
solemnity in this man's figure, a sober simplicity which was most
impressive. Scotland is the country above all others that I have seen,
in which a man of imagination may carve out his own pleasures.
There are so many *inhabited* solitudes, and the employments of the
people are so immediately connected with the places where you find
them, and their dresses so simple, so much alike, yet, from their
being folding garments, admitting of an endless variety, and falling
often so gracefully.

After some time we descended towards a broad vale, passed one
farm-house, sheltered by fir trees, with a burn close to it; children
playing, linen bleaching. The vale was open pastures and corn-fields
unfenced, the land poor. The village of Crawfordjohn on the slope of
a hill a long way before us to the left. Asked about our road of a man
who was driving a cart; he told us to go through the village, then
along some fields, and we should come to a 'herd's house by the burn
side'. The highway was right through the vale, unfenced on either
side; the people of the village, who were making hay, all stared at us
and our carriage. We inquired the road of a middle-aged man,
dressed in a shabby black coat, at work in one of the hay fields; he
looked like the minister of the place, and when he spoke we felt

assured that he was so, for he was not sparing of hard words, which, however, he used with great propriety, and he spoke like one who had been accustomed to dictate. Our car wanted mending in the wheel, and we asked him if there was a blacksmith in the village. 'Yes,' he replied, but when we showed him the wheel he told William that he might mend it himself without a blacksmith, and he would put him in the way; so he fetched hammer and nails and gave his directions, which William obeyed, and repaired the damage entirely to his own satisfaction and the priest's, who did not offer to lend any assistance himself; not as if he would not have been willing in case of need; but as if it were more natural for him to dictate, and because he thought it more fit that William should do it himself. He spoke much about the propriety of every man's lending all the assistance in his power to travellers, and with some ostentation or self-praise. Here I observed a honeysuckle and some flowers growing in a garden, the first I had seen in Scotland. It is a pretty cheerful-looking village, but must be very cold in winter; it stands on a hillside, and the vale itself is very high ground, unsheltered by trees.

Left the village behind us, and our road led through arable ground for a considerable way, on which were growing very good crops of corn and potatoes. Our friend accompanied us to show us the way, and Coleridge and he had a scientific conversation concerning the uses and properties of lime and other manures. He seemed to be a well-informed man; somewhat pedantic in his manners; but this might be only the difference between Scotch and English.

WEDNESDAY, 24 AUGUST. Came to a bark hut by the shores, and sat for some time under the shelter of it. While we were here a poor woman with a little child by her side begged a penny of me, and asked where she could 'find quarters in the village'. She was a travelling beggar, a native of Scotland, had often 'heard of that water', but was never there before. This woman's appearance, while the wind was rustling about us, and the waves breaking at our feet, was very melancholy: the waters looked wide, the hills many, and dark, and far off—no house but at Luss. I thought what a dreary waste much this lake be to such poor creatures, struggling with fatigue and poverty and unknown ways!

We ordered tea when we reached the inn, and desired the girl to light us a fire; she replied, 'I dinna ken whether she'll gie fire', meaning her mistress. We told her we did not wish her mistress to give fire, we only desired her to let *her* make it and we would pay for it. The girl brought in the tea-things, but no fire, and when I asked if she was coming to light it, she said 'her mistress was not varra willing to gie fire'. At last, however, on our insisting upon it, the fire was lighted: we got tea by candle-light, and spent a comfortable evening. I had seen the landlady before we went out, for, as had been usual in all the country inns, there was a demur respecting beds, not withstanding the house was empty, and there were at least half-a-dozen spare beds. Her countenance corresponded with the unkindness of denying us a fire on a cold night, for she was the most cruel and hateful-looking woman I ever saw. She was overgrown with fat, and was sitting with her feet and legs in a tub of water for the dropsy—probably brought on by whisky-drinking. The sympathy which I felt and expressed for her, on seeing her in this wretched condition—for her legs were swollen as thick as mill-posts—seemed to produce no effect; and I was obliged, after five minutes' conversation, to leave the affair of the beds undecided. Coleridge had some talk with her daughter, a smart lass in a cotton gown, with a bandeau round her head, without shoes and stockings. She told Coleridge with some pride that she had not spent all her time at Luss, but was then fresh from Glasgow.

It came on a very stormy night; the wind rattled every window in the house, and it rained heavily. William and Coleridge had bad beds, in a two-bedded room in the garrets, though there were empty rooms on the first floor, and they were disturbed by a drunken man, who had come to the inn when we were gone to sleep.

[The travellers ascend one of the islands in Loch Lomond.]

THURSDAY, 25 AUGUST. We had not climbed far before we were stopped by a sudden burst of prospect, so singular and beautiful that it was like a flash of images from another world. We stood with our backs to the hill of the island, which we were ascending, and which shut out Ben Lomond entirely, and all the upper part of the lake, and we looked towards the foot of the lake, scattered over with islands without beginning and without end. The sun shone, and the distant hills were visible, some through sunny mists, others in gloom with patches of sunshine; the lake was lost under the low and distant hills, and the islands lost in the lake, which was all in motion with travelling fields of light, or dark shadows under rainy clouds. There are many hills, but no commanding eminence at a distance to confine the prospect, so that the land seemed endless as the water.

What I had heard of Loch Lomond, or any other place in Great Britain, had given me no idea of anything like what we beheld: it was an outlandish scene—we might have believed ourselves in North America. The islands were of every possible variety of shape and surface—hilly and level, large and small, bare, rocky, pastoral, or covered with wood. Immediately under my eyes lay one large flat island, bare and green, so flat and low that it scarcely appeared to rise above the water, with straggling peat-stacks and a single hut upon one of its out-shooting promontories—for it was of a very irregular shape, though perfectly flat. Another, its next neighbour, and still nearer to us, was covered over with heath and coppice-wood, the surface undulating, with flat or sloping banks towards the water, and hollow places, cradle-like valleys, behind. These two islands, with Inch-ta-vanach, where we were standing, were intermingled with the water, I might say interbedded and interveined with it, in a manner that was exquisitely pleasing. There were bays innumerable, straits or passages like calm rivers, landlocked lakes, and, to the main water, stormy promontories. The solitary hut on the flat green island seemed unsheltered and desolate, and yet not wholly so, for it was but a broad river's breadth from the covert of the wood of the other island. Near to these is a miniature, an islet covered with trees, on which stands a small ruin that looks like the remains of a religious house; it is overgrown with ivy, and were it not that the arch of a window or gateway may be distinctly seen, it would be difficult to believe that it was not a tuft of trees growing in the shape of a ruin, rather than a ruin overshadowed by trees. When we had walked a little further we saw below us, on the nearest large island, where some of the wood had been cut down, a hut, which we conjectured to be a bark hut. It appeared to be on the shore of a little forest lake, enclosed by Inch-ta-vanach, where we were, and the woody island on which the hut stands.

Beyond we had the same intricate view as before, and could discover Dumbarton rock with its double head. There being a mist over it, it had a ghost-like appearance—as I observed to William and Coleridge, something like the Tor of Glastonbury from the Dorsetshire hills. Right before us, on the flat island mentioned before, were several small single trees or shrubs, growing at different distances from each other, close to the shore, but some optical delusion had detached them from the land on which they stood, and they had the appearance of so many little vessels sailing along the coast of it. I mention the circumstance, because, with the ghostly image of Dumbarton Castle, and the ambiguous ruin on the small island, it was much in the character of the scene, which was throughout magical and enchanting—a new world in its great permanent outline and composition, and changing at every moment in every part of it by the effect of sun and wind and mist and shower and cloud, and the blending lights and deep shades which took place of each other, traversing the lake in every direction. The whole was indeed a strange mixture of soothing and restless images, of images inviting to rest, and others hurrying the fancy away into an activity still more pleasing than repose. Yet, intricate and homeless, that is, without lasting abiding-place for the mind, as the prospect was, there was no perplexity; we had still a guide to lead us forward.

Wherever we looked, it was a delightful feeling that there was something beyond. Meanwhile, the sense of quiet was never lost sight of; the little peaceful lakes among the islands might make you forget that the great water, Loch Lomond, was so near; and yet are more beautiful, because you know that it is so: they have their own bays and creeks sheltered within a shelter. When we had ascended to the top of the island we had a view up to Ben Lomond, over the long, broad water without spot or rock; and, looking backwards, saw the islands below us as on a map. This view, as may be supposed, was not nearly so interesting as those we had seen before. We hunted out all the houses on the shore, which were very few: there was the village of Luss, the two gentlemen's houses, our favourite cottages, and here and there a hut; but I do not recollect any comfortable-looking farm-houses, and on the opposite shore not a single dwelling. The whole scene was a combination of natural wildness, loveliness, beauty, and barrenness, or rather bareness, yet not comfortless or cold; but the whole was beautiful. We were too far off the more distant shore to distinguish any particular spots which we might have regretted were not better cultivated, and near Luss there was no want of houses.

After we had left the island, having been so much taken with the beauty of the bark hut and the little lake by which it appeared to stand, we desired the boatman to row us through it, and we landed at the hut. Walked upon the island for some time, and found out sheltered places for cottages. There were several woodman's huts, which, with some scattered fir-trees, and others in irregular knots, that made a delicious murmuring in the wind, added greatly to the romantic effect of the scene. They were built in the form of a cone from the ground, like savages' huts, the door being just large enough for a man to enter with stooping. Straw beds were raised on logs of wood, tools lying about, and a forked bough of a tree was generally suspended from the roof in the middle to hang a kettle upon. It was a place that might have been just visited by new settlers. I thought of Ruth and her dreams of romantic love:

> And then he said how sweet it were,
> A fisher or a hunter there,
> A gardener in the shade,
> Still wandering with an easy mind,
> To build a household fire, and find
> A home in every glade.*

We found the main lake very stormy when we had left the shelter of the islands, and there was again a threatening of rain, but it did not come on. I wanted much to go to the old ruin, but the boatmen were in a hurry to be at home. They told us it had been a stronghold built by a man who lived there alone, and was used to swim over and make depredations on the shore,—that nobody could ever lay hands on him, he was such a good swimmer, but at last they caught him in a net. . . .

I have said so much of this lake that I am tired myself, and I fear I must have tired my friends. We had a pleasant journey to Tarbet; more than half of it on foot, for the road was hilly, and after we had climbed one small hill we were not desirous to get into the car again, seeing another before us, and our path was always delightful, near the lake, and frequently through woods. When we were within about half a mile of Tarbet, at a sudden turning looking to the left, we saw a very craggy-topped mountain amongst other smooth ones; the rocks on the summit distinct in shape as if they were buildings raised up by man, or uncouth images of some strange creature. We called out with one voice. 'That's what we wanted!' alluding to the frame-like uniformity of the side-screens of the lake for the last five or six miles. As we conjectured, this singular mountain was the famous Cobbler, near Arrochar. Tarbet was before us in the recess of a deep, large bay, under the shelter of a hill. When we came up to the village we had to inquire for the inn, there being no signboard. It was a well-sized white house, the best in the place. We were conducted up-stairs into a sitting-room that might make any good-humoured travellers happy—a square room, with windows on each side, looking, one way, towards the mountains, and across the lake to Ben Lomond, the other.

SATURDAY, 27 AUGUST. We returned, of course, by the same road. Our guide repeated over and over again his lamentations that the day was so bad, though we had often told him—not indeed with much hope that he would believe us—that we were glad of it. As we walked along he pulled a leafy twig from a birch-tree, and, after smelling it, gave it to me, saying, how 'sweet and halesome' it was, and that it was pleasant and very halesome on a fine summer's morning to sail under the banks where the birks are growing. This reminded me of the old Scotch songs, in which you continually hear of the 'pu'ing the birks'. Common as birches are in the north of England, I believe their sweet smell is a thing unnoticed among the peasants. We returned again to the huts to take a farewell look. We had shared our food with the ferryman and a traveller whom we had met here, who was going up the lake, and wished to lodge at the ferry-house, so we offered him a place in the boat. Coleridge chose to walk. We took the same side of the lake as before, and had much delight in visiting the bays over again; but the evening began to darken, and it rained so heavily before we had gone two miles that we were completely wet. It was dark when we landed, and on entering the house I was sick with cold.

The good woman had provided, according to her promise, a better fire than we had found in the morning; and indeed when I sate down in the chimney-corner of her smoky biggin'* thought I had never been more comfortable in my life. Coleridge had been there long enough to have a pan of coffee boiling for us, and having put our clothes in the way of drying, we all sat down, thankful for a shelter. We could not prevail upon the man of the house to draw near the fire, though he was cold and wet, or to suffer his wife to get him dry clothes till she had served us, which she did, though most willingly, not very expeditiously. A Cumberland man of the same rank would not have had such a notion of what was fit and right in his own house, or if he had, one would have accused him of servility; but in the Highlander it only seemed like politeness, however erroneous and painful to us, naturally growing out of the dependence of the inferiors of the clan upon their laird; he did not, however, refuse to let his wife bring out the whisky-bottle at our request: 'She keeps a dram,' as the phrase is; indeed, I believe there is scarcely a lonely house by the wayside in Scotland where travellers may not be accommodated with a dram. We asked for sugar, butter, barley-bread, and milk, and with a smile and a stare more of kindness than wonder, she replied, 'Ye'll get that,' bringing each article separately.

We caroused our cups of coffee, laughing like children at the strange atmosphere in which we were: the smoke came in gusts, and spread along the walls and above our heads in the chimney, where the hens were roosting like light clouds in the sky. We laughed and laughed again, in spite of the smarting of our eyes, yet had a quieter pleasure in observing the beauty of the beams and rafters gleaming between the clouds of smoke. They had been crusted over and varnished by many winters, till, where the firelight fell upon them, they were as glossy as black rocks on a sunny day cased in ice. When we had eaten our supper we sate about half an hour, and I think I had never felt so deeply the blessing of a hospitable welcome and a warm fire. The man of the house repeated from time to time that we should often tell of this night when we got to our homes, and interposed praises of this, his own lake, which he had more than once, when we were returning in the boat, ventured to say was 'bonnier than Loch Lomond'.

Our companion from the Trossachs, who it appeared was an Edinburgh drawing-master going during the vacation on a pedestrian tour to John o' Groat's House, was to sleep in the barn with William and Coleridge, where the man said he had plenty of dry hay. I do not believe that the hay of the Highlands is often very dry, but this year it had a better chance than usual: wet or dry, however, the next morning they said they had slept comfortably. When I went to bed, the mistress, desiring me to 'go ben',* attended me with a candle, and assured me that the bed was dry, though not 'sic as I had been used to'. It was of chaff; there were two others in the room, a cupboard and two chests, on one of which stood the milk in wooden vessels covered over; I should have thought that milk so kept could not have been sweet, but the cheese and butter were good. The walls of the whole house were of stone unplastered. It consisted of three apartments,—the cow-house at one end, the kitchen or house in the middle, and the spence* at the other end. The rooms were divided, not up to the rigging, but only to the beginning of the roof, so that there was a free passage for light and smoke from one end of the house to the other.

I went to bed some time before the family. The door was shut between us, and they had a bright fire, which I could not see; but the light it sent up among the varnished rafters and beams, which crossed each other in almost as intricate and fantastic a manner as I have seen the under-boughs of a large beech-tree withered by the depth of the shade above, produced the most beautiful effect that can be conceived. It was like what I should suppose an underground cave or temple to be, with a dripping or moist roof, and the moon-light entering in upon it by some means or other, and yet the colours were more like melted gems. I lay looking up till the light of the fire faded away, and the man and his wife and child had crept into their bed at the other end of the room. I did not sleep much, but passed a comfortable night, for my bed, though hard, was warm and clean: the unusualness of my situation prevented me from sleeping. I could hear the waves beat against the shore of the lake; a little 'syke' close to the door made a much louder noise; and when I sate up in my bed I could see the lake through an open window-place at the bed's head. Add to this, it rained all night. I was less occupied by remembrance of the Trossachs, beautiful as they were, than the vision of the Highland hut, which I could not get out of my head. I thought of the Fairyland of Spenser, and what I had read in romance at other times, and then, what a feast would it be for a London pantomime-maker, could he but transplant it to Drury Lane, with all its beautiful colours!

JAMES HOGG, 'Malise's Journey to the Trossacks' (from *The Spy*, No. 40, 1 June 1811, pp. 397–402)

James Hogg (1770–1835), erstwhile shepherd and farmer in the Scottish Borders, came to Edinburgh in 1810 determined to make his living as an author. Hogg's weekly magazine *The Spy* (much of which he wrote himself) offers a satirical view of the Edinburgh literary establishment. Hogg does not spare his friend Walter Scott, whose metrical romance *The Lady of the Lake*, published to sensational acclaim the previous year, had already gone into nine editions. Hogg pokes fun at the Romantic Scotland fashioned for a modern tourist industry by his brother poet. In 1824 he would write the novel for which he is best known today, *The Private Memoirs and Confessions of a Justified Sinner*.

The whole of the scenery around Callander and Strathgartney is interesting, and to the man who has traversed the flat extent of the eastern counties of Britain, where the verge of the horizon is always resting on something level with, or below his eye, the frowning brows of Ben Ledi (the hill of God), with the broken outline of the mountains, both to the east and the westward, have a peculiarly pleasing effect. Still as you advance, the scenery improves, and in the vicinity of the Bridge of Turk, it is highly picturesque, and yields little in variety to the celebrated Trossacks. From the top of Lanrick Mead, the muster place of the Clan-Alpine,* which is a small detached hill at the junction of the water of Glen Finlas with Loch Venachar, the general effect of the view is more noble and better contrasted, than from any other spot I alighted upon in the Strath.

I had here a conversation of considerable length with an old crusty Highlander, with whose remarks I was highly amused. He asked me frankly where I came from? And what my business was in that country? And on my informing him, that I was going to take a view of the Trossacks, he said that I was right to do so, else I would not be in the fashion, but it was a sign, I was too idle, and had very little to do at home; but that a Mr Scott had put all the people mad by printing a *lying poem*, about a man that never existed—'What the d—was to be seen about the Trossacks, more than in an hundred other places? A few rocks and bushes, nothing else.' He gave me the outlines of the story of the Lady of the Lake, with great exactness, and added several improvements of his own. I asked him if there was any truth in it at all; or, if it was wholly a fiction? He said, there was once indeed a man who skulked and defended himself in and about Loch Ketturin; that an old Gaelic song, related almost the same story, but that Mr Scott had been quite misled with regard to the names—he was mistaken about them altogether. He translated some parts of the song into English, which were not much illustrative of any story; he, however, persisted in asserting that the stories were fundamentally the same.

He told me further, that Mr Burrel intended to build a bower in the lonely Isle of Loch Ketturin, in which he meant to place the prettiest girl that could be found in Edinburgh, during the summer months to personate the *Lady of the Lake*—that she was to be splendidly dressed in the Highland tartans, and ferry the company over to the island. That Robert MacLean, a weaver at the Bridge of Turk, was to be the Goblin of Corrie-Uriskin,* and had already procured the skin of a monstrous shaggy black goat, which was to form a principal part of his dress while in that capacity; that in fact interest and honour both combined to induce MacLean to turn a goblin this very summer; for in a conversation which he had with two ladies, high in rank, last year, he informed them with great seriousness, that the goblin actually haunted the den occasionally to this day, at stated periods, and if they were there on such a day, at such an hour, he would forfeit his ears if they did not see him; they promised to him that they would come, and reward him with a large sum of money if he fulfilled his engagement; that of course Robert was holding himself in readiness to appear himself in case this only surviving brownie, whom they suppose to have been once the king of the whole tribe, should neglect to pay his periodical visit to that lonely seat of his ancient regal court. . . .

About one o'clock, I reached Mr Stuart the guide's house, the name of which I never can either pronounce or spell, and was informed by his mother that he was not at home. I was not in the least sorry on that account, for I wished to lose myself in the Trossacks alone; to have no interruption in my contemplations; but to converse only with nature, please myself with wondering at her wildest picture, and wonder why I was pleased.

After having tasted plentifully of old Mrs Stuart's Highland cheer, I set out with a heart bounding with joy, to put my scheme in execution. I traced every ravine and labyrinth that winded around the rocky pyramids; climbed every insulated mass, and thunder-splintered pinnacle, fantastic as the cones of the gathering thunder-cloud, and huge as the ancient pile that was reared on the valley of Shinar.* Mr Scott has superseded the possibility of ever more pleasing, by a second description of the Trossacks, but in so doing he has certainly added to the pleasure arising from a view of them. Whoever goes to survey the Trossacks, let him have the 11th, 12th, and 13th divisions of the first canto of the *Lady of the Lake* in his heart; a little Highland whisky in his head; and then he shall see the most wonderful scene that nature ever produced. If he goes without any of these necessary ingredients, without one verse of poetry in his mind, and 'Without a drappie in his noddle', he may as well stay at home; he will see little, that shall either astonish or delight him, or if it even do the one, shall fail of accomplishing the other. The fancy must be aroused, and the imagination and spirits exhilarated in order that he may enjoy these romantic scenes and groves of wonder with the proper zest. This is no chimera, Sir, I can attest its truth from experience. I once went with a friend to view the Craig of Glen-Whargen in Nithsdale—it was late before we reached it; we were hungry and wearied, having fished all day; it was no rock at all!—the Cat-Craig at the back of our house was much more striking! It was a mere trifle; we sat down by a well at its base; dined on such provisions as we had, and by repeated applications to a bottle full of whisky, emptied it clean out. The rock continued to improve; we drank out of the bottle alternately, and in so doing were obliged to hold up our faces towards the rock of Glen-Whargen. It was so grand and sublime, that it was not without an effort we could ever bring our heads back to their natural position. Still as the whisky diminished the rock of Glen-Whargen increased in size and magnificence; and by the time the bottle was empty, we were fixed to the spot in amazement at that stupendous pile; and both of us agreed that it was such a rock as never was looked upon by man!

PART III

AFRICA

ENGLISHMEN first came to Africa in search of slaves. In 1562 John Hawkins carried the first shipload of slaves to the Caribbean in an English cargo-carrier. The Portuguese had established trading posts on the west coast of Africa before 1500; English, French, and Dutch interest in the area rose around the mid-sixteenth century. By 1700 Africa was well established as one corner of the so-called 'Atlantic Triangle Trade'. European goods went to Africa to be traded for slaves, who were shipped across the Atlantic to the Caribbean (the infamous Middle Passage) to be sold so that the ships could move sugar and other tropical commodities back eastward to England and Europe. By this time England led the world in the trafficking of slaves, tens of thousands of whom laboured in the sugar colonies of the West Indies. Through most of the eighteenth century the slave trade was not just respectable, but seemed a vital ingredient of national prosperity. No one but a few Quakers spoke out against it before the 1760s. By the 1780s, the peak years of the trade, when the abolitionist movement got organized, the politics of slavery began to be fought out in travel writing with the help of slaves like Olaudah Equiano who could contribute a first-hand view. The slave trade was abolished in 1807, but British slave emancipation was not complete until 1838.

By the late eighteenth century British knowledge of Africa was still limited to a thin strip of coast, but that would soon change. In 1788 twelve influential Londoners, led by Sir Joseph Banks, President of the Royal Society, who in his youth had sailed to the South Seas with Captain Cook, formed the Association for Promoting the Discovery of the Interior Districts of Africa (known as the African Association). They sponsored explorers, who began to 'penetrate' the continent (this often-used verb hints at the sexualized, masculinist perspective of much exploration discourse), taking immense risks to provide the Empire with data bearing on the potential for colonizing the interior: geography, resources, natives. Exploration narratives harness the discourses of natural history and sentiment in the service of 'imperial eyes' (Mary Pratt's phrase). The project of interior exploration continued, of course, into the later nineteenth century with such famous explorers as Burton, Speke, Stanley, and Livingstone. Our selections illustrate this imperial project while making clear explorers' vulnerability to the harsh terrain and their debt to their African hosts—who could be generous and helpful or manipulative and coercive, depending on their interests and their perception of the British intruders.

1. THE SLAVE TRADE, 1732–1789

JOHN BARBOT, *A Description of the Coasts of North and South Guinea* (1732); from Awnsham Churchill, ed., *A Collection of Voyages and Travels, Some Now First Printed from Original Manuscripts, Others Now First Published in English* (1746), vol. v

Jean or John Barbot (1655–1712) was a French Huguenot who made two slaving voyages to West Africa in the 1670s and 1680s. Barbot fled to England to escape French persecution of Protestants; his account, written first in French and later in English, was not published until after his death, when it appeared as part of the Churchill brothers' collection of voyages and travels. Barbot's was the most massive and influential work on West Africa available to the eighteenth-century reader. To his own observations he added material from other writers, in particular the Dutchman Bosman's *New and Accurate Description of the Coast of Guinea* (1704). Our selections give his perspective on the life of the Gold Coast slave trader and advise Europeans how to avoid being cheated when dealing with Africans for gold.

[Guinea fatal to Europeans]

These things considered, it is no wonder that the coast of Guinea should yearly consume so many Europeans living ashore; especially if we consider their way of living, being utterly unprovided of what should comfort and nourish them; having wretched medicines, unskilful surgeons, and no support of nourishing diet and restoratives. The common sort, at best, can get nothing but fish, and some dry lean hens; and were they able to pay for better, it is not to be had; for all the oxen, cows, sheep and poultry, are lean, tough, and dry; nothing being good but spoon-meats.* As for the chief officers, they are commonly pretty well supported with better food; as either having it sent by their friends in Europe, or buying it of European ships that trade on the coast, or else receiving presents of good poultry, salt meat, French and Madeira wine, neats' tongues, gammons, all sorts of pickles, preserves, fruit, sweet oil, fine flour, choice brandy, etc.

with good fresh medicines and restoratives. Besides, they are not obliged to be exposed to all sorts of weather, either to the scorching air of the day or cold evening-dew; nor to hard labour, or going from one place to another in canoes; or, which is worse, passing over bars, and the breaking of the sea, wherein, as I have said before, there is a hazard besides that of drowning; or if they have occasion to do this sometimes, they are presently shifted and comforted with restoratives: whereas the common sort, especially canoe men, labourers and soldiers, are exposed to all sorts of fatigues and hardships upon every command, without those comforts and supports which officers have. Besides all this, they are generally men of no education or principles, void of foresight, careless, prodigal, addicted to strong liquors, as palm-wine, brandy and punch, which they will drink to excess, and then lie down on the bare ground in the open air, at the cool of the evening, without any other covering but a single shirt; nay some, and perhaps no small number, are over fond of the black women, whose natural hot and lewd temper soon wastes their bodies, and consumes that little substance they have: though such prostitutes are to be had at a very inconsiderable rate, yet having thus spent their poor allowance, those wretched men cannot afford to buy themselves convenient sustenance, but are forced to feed on bread, oil, and salt, or, at best, to feast upon a little fish. Thus 'tis not to be admired that they fall into several distempers, daily exposing their lives to danger, very many being carried off through these excesses, in a very deplorable condition, by fevers, fluxes, colics, consumptions, asthmas, smallpox, coughs, and sometimes worms and dropsies: of all which diseases I shall say more in another place.

But it is not only the inferior sort who are guilty of this irregular course of life; there are too many of the officers and heads, who, the greater their salaries and profits are, the more eager they are to spend them extravagantly, in excessive drinking, and other vices, never minding to keep something by them to procure fresh provisions at all times for their support. Nay, some of them run so deep in debt, to gratify their disorderly appetites, that their pay is stopped, or made over by bond, before it becomes due; so that several, who do not die there, return home as empty in the purse as they first went out: and it very seldom happens that any make their fortunes, except the commanders in chief of forts, who have the best opportunity of laying up; or those who make no account of the solemn oaths they have taken, not to trade for their own proper account, directly or indirectly; which oath is generally administered to every person employed by any of the African companies in Europe. Yet many of them openly profess they went not thither for bare wages; and I fear the number of such is not small in every nation.

[A method 'to discover false gold']

Another method to prevent being cheated in gold, especially on shipboard, though not altogether to be depended on, but only in general, is nicely to observe the behaviour of the Blacks, which I have done myself; for generally a cheat, who knows his gold is false and counterfeit, is very impatient, uneasy and in haste to be gone, under some colour or other, besides he commonly bids a higher price than usual for goods, and takes them in a hurry without too much examination; and if not found out, will paddle away to shore with the goods, as fast as his canoe can carry him. Nay, I have observed some of them to stand trembling and quaking, whilst their gold was upon trial; and such their behaviour is a sufficient indication to suspect some fraud, especially when there is a crowd of dealers, for then they expect to find the better opportunity of imposing on the purchasers, and then the European factor ought to be nicest in examining every parcel of gold. When I met with any such knaves, and had discovered the cheat by trial, I always used them very roughly, even to cocking of an unloaded pistol at their breast, or else threatened to throw their false gold overboard, which deterred many of them from offering the like to me again. On the other hand, a Black who knows his gold is pure and fine, appears always calm, stands hard about the price of goods, and is curious in examining every piece, whether it is truly good in its sort.

There is another sure way to try gold, which may be used by merchants and is very plain, by twenty-four artificial needles, made with alloy of metals from the lowest sort of gold to the finest of twenty-four carats fine, having exact rules for valuing of it, according to the degrees of fineness or coarseness.

I will further add this advice to all seafaring men, trading on that coast aboard ships, that when they see many Blacks come aboard together, to trade with gold, they admit but two or three at most, into the great cabin, or any other part of the ship, at one time, and always keep about them four or five of their own men to be upon the watch, lest the Blacks embezzle any goods; that so they and their goldsmith, if there be one aboard, as commonly there is aboard French ships, may have leisure to examine the nature of the gold: for it is common there for one Black, most of those on the coast being factors or brokers for the inland people, to have twenty or more several small parcels of gold, wrapped in rags, or in little leather bags, to purchase goods for so many several persons; and those parcels must be all examined one after another, which takes a long time: and if they admit of a crowd of Blacks about them, they cannot so well examine all their different parcels, so as to be sure they take none but what is good. Besides that the Blacks, when in a crowd, are always prating together.

Take heed of such as come with rush baskets, as I have seen five or six of them together, with every one such a basket, which are generally designed to conceal what they can steal. So those who talk much and make a noise are to be suspected, and it may be observed they will never agree to any price of goods; for the Blacks being generally inclined to steal from one another, make much less scruple of robbing the Europeans, alleging for their excuse, that the Europeans are rich and they poor. Therefore they think it a less crime in themselves to rob us, when an opportunity offers, than for an European to steal from them: and in one respect they may be said to be in the right, since Europeans have the law of God for their guide, which commands them not to steal, which is unknown to the Blacks, who have no other law but that of nature.

Another rule I observed, was to keep in the great cabin, where I used to trade with the Blacks, only one single price of each sort of my goods, for a sample; and when I had struck a bargain with a Black, I sent him with my note to the storekeeper, specifying the quantity and quality of the goods he had contracted to pay for.

Another method to be used in ships is severely to punish any Black that has been taken stealing; for though the person so served does not perhaps much value a few blows he may receive, yet it is a great disgrace among themselves, not on account of the heinousness of the crime of stealing, most of them being ready enough and well inclined to do the same, when an opportunity offers, but because he is scoffed at by his countrymen for being so unskilful as to be taken in the fact.

I have also observed, that those Blacks who had been pretty well drubbed with a knotted rope's end, were afterwards more tractable and better to deal with; which makes out that they are like spaniels, that the more you beat them the more they love you.

In this manner, as I have said above, our business was done orderly and safely, without trouble, or confusion, and at night I entered all my notes in my book of sale, and weighed all the gold I had received that day in the lump, to see whether it answered the particulars for which it was received, and also caused it to be entered in the same book by my under-factor,* observing to keep the said gold in separate boxes, that at my return into France I might have the judgement of the officers of the mint at Paris, or elsewhere, to know which of the chief places of trade on the Gold Coast afforded the finest, and which the worst gold.

[European fraud]

I shall conclude this long discourse of gold with an observation I often made there; which is, that many Europeans, who so loudly exclaim against the perfidiousness and deceitful nature of the Blacks, in offering false gold in trade, never consider that on the other hand they are themselves guilty of a notorious cheat and fraud, in using two sorts of weights there, the heavier to receive gold by, and the lighter to pay it away again, which is frequently practised by too many, and is a great dishonour to Christianity, being contrary to the golden rule, *To do as we would be done by*. Such base dealing rather serves to confirm those pagans in their ill principles, instead of endeavouring to convert them. But self-interest and covetousness, which is called the root of all evil, are vices too common to all the corrupt race of mankind, either Christians or pagans. But Christians ought to remember the words of St Paul, to the Roman Christians in his days, on the like occasion: Romans 2: 24. *That for their evil practices the name of God is blasphemed among the Gentiles*. And that *double weights and double measures are an abomination to God*: Leviticus 19: 36 and Proverbs 11: 1.

JOHN ATKINS, *A Voyage to Guinea, Brasil and the West-Indies; In His Majesty's Ships, the SWALLOW and WEYMOUTH* (1735).

John Atkins (1685–1757), naval surgeon, sailed for the coast of Guinea on a 1721 Navy expedition to put down coastal piracy. The ships visited

Sierra Leone, Whydah (Ouidah, on the so-called Slave Coast, present-day Benin), and Elmina (on the Gold Coast, present-day Ghana), and captured 270 pirates and £10,000 in gold dust. After his return, Atkins turned to authorship: in 1732 he published *The Navy Surgeon*, a treatise on surgery, and in 1735 *A Voyage to Guinea, Brasil and the West-Indies*. Our selections observe slave traders at work and give Atkins's impression of the local authorities with whom he deals.

The slaves, when brought here, have chains put on, three or four linked together, under the care of their *Gromettas*,* till opportunity of sale; and then go at about 15 pounds a good slave, allowing the buyer 40 or 50 per cent advance on his goods.

As these slaves are placed under lodges near the owner's house, for air, cleanliness, and customers' better viewing them, I had every day the curiosity of observing their behaviour, which with most of them was very dejected. Once, on looking over some of old Cracker's* slaves, I could not help taking notice of one fellow among the rest, of a tall, strong make, and bold, stern aspect. As he imagined we were viewing them with a design to buy, he seemed to disdain his fellow-slaves for their readiness to be examined, and as it were scorned looking at us, refusing to rise or stretch out his limbs, as the master commanded; which got him an unmerciful whipping from Cracker's own hand, with a cutting manatee strap,* and had certainly killed him but for the loss he himself must sustain by it, all which the Negro bore with magnanimity, shrinking very little, and shedding a tear or two, which he endeavoured to hide as though ashamed of. All the company grew curious at his courage, and wanted to know of Cracker how he came by him; who told us that this same fellow, called Captain Tomba, was a leader of some country villages that opposed them, and their trade, at the River Nunes; killing our friends there, and firing their cottages. The sufferers this way, by the help of my men (says Cracker), surprised, and bound him in the night, about a month ago, he having killed two in his defence, before they could secure him, and from thence he was brought hither, and made my property. . . .

The king who commands here has the name of Pedro; he lives about five miles up the river, a sample of Negro majesty.

As there is a *dashee** expected before ships can wood and water here, it was thought expedient to send the royal perquisite up by embassy (a lieutenant and purser) who, being in all respects equal to the trust, were dismissed with proper instructions, and, being arrived at the king's town, they were ushered or thrust in by some of the courtiers into the common Palaaver-Room* (to wait the king's dressing, and coming from his palace), his public audience being ever in the presence of the people. After waiting an hour, King Pedro came attended by a hundred naked nobles, all smoking, and a horn blowing before them. The king's dress was very antic: he had a dirty, red baize gown on, chequered with patchwork of other colours, like a jack pudding,* and a fellow to bear the train, which was a narrow slip of Culgee* tacked to the bottom of the gown. He had an old black full-bottomed wig, uncombed; an old hat not half big enough, and so set considerably behind the fore-top, that made his meagre face like a scarecrow; coarse shoes and stockings, unbuckled and untied, and a brass chain of 20 lib.* at least about his neck.

To this figure of a man, our modern ambassadors in their holiday suits fell on their knees, and might have continued there till this time, for what Pedro cared: he was something surprised indeed, but took it for the fashion of their country, and so kept making instant motions for the dashee. This brought them from their knees, as the proper attitude for presenting it; consisting in a trading gun, two pieces of salt ship-beef, a cheese, a bottle of brandy, a dozen of pipes, and two dozen of congees.* But Pedro, who understood the present better than the bows, did not seem pleased when he saw it; not for any defect in the magnificence, but they were such things as he had not present occasion for; asking some of their clothes and to take those back again, particularly their breeches, sullied a little with kneeling in the spittle; but on a palaaver with his ministers, the present was accepted, and the officers dismissed back with a glass of palm-wine and *Attee, ho* (the common way of salutation with thumbs and fingers mixed, and snapping off).

To smooth the king into a good opinion of our generosity, we made it up to his son, Tom Freeman; who, to show his good nature, came on board uninvited, bringing his flageolet,* and obliging us with some wild notes. Him we dressed with an edged hat, a wig, and a sword, and gave a patent* upon a large sheet of parchment, creating him Duke of Sefthos, affixing all our hands, and the impress of a butter mark on putty.

This was taken so kindly by the father that he sent us a couple of goats in return, and his younger son Josee for further marks of our favour; whom we dignified also, on a small consideration, with the title of Prince of Baxos. Several indeed had been titled, but none so eminently as by patent before; which procured us the entire good-will of the king; suffering us at any time to haul our seine in the river, where we catched good store of mullets, soles, bump noses, and rock-fish; and to go up to their villages unmolested.

In one of these towns, some others of us paid a visit to His Majesty, whom we found at a palace built as humble as a hog-sty; the entrance was narrow like a porthole, leading into what we may call his court-yard, a slovenly little spot, and two or three huts in it, which I found to be the apartment of his women. From this we popped through another short portico, and discovered him on the left hand, upon a place without his house, raised like a tailor's shop board, and smok-ing with two or three old women (the favourite diversion of both sexes). His dress and figure, with the novelty of ours, created mutual smiles which held a few minutes, and then we took leave with the *Attee, ho.* . . .

We met the *Robert* of Bristol, Captain Harding, who sailed from Sierra Leone before us, having purchased thirty slaves, whereof Cap-tain Tomba mentioned there was one; he gave us the following mel-ancholy story. That this Tomba, about a week before, had combined with three or four of the stoutest of his countrymen to kill the ship's company and attempt their escapes, while they had a shore to fly to, and had near effected it by means of a woman slave who, being more at large, was to watch the proper opportunity. She brought him word one night that there were no more than five white men upon the deck, and they asleep, bringing him a hammer at the same time (all the weapons that she could find) to execute the treachery. He encouraged the accomplices what he could, with the prospect of liberty, but could now at the push engage only one more and the woman to follow him upon deck. He found three sailors sleeping on the forecastle, two of which he presently dispatched, with single strokes upon the temples; the other rousing with the noise, his com-panions seized; Tomba coming soon to their assistance, and murder-ing him in the same manner. Going after to finish the work, they found, very luckily for the rest of the company, that these other two of the watch were with the confusion already made awake, and upon their guard, and their defence soon awaked the master underneath them, who, running up and finding his men contending for their

lives, took a hand-spike,* the first thing he met with in the surprise,
and redoubling his strokes home upon Tomba, laid him at length flat
upon the deck, securing them all in irons.

The reader may be curious to know their punishment. Why,
Captain Harding weighing the stoutness and worth of the two slaves,
did, as in other countries they do by rogues of dignity, whip and
scarify them only; while three others, abettors but not actors, nor of
strength for it, he sentenced to cruel deaths, making them first eat
the heart and liver of one of them killed. The woman he hoisted up
by the thumbs, whipped, and slashed her with knives before the
other slaves till she died. . . .

We who buy slaves say we confer a good, removing them to a
better state both of temporals* and spirituals; the latter, few have the
hypocrisy (among us) to own, and therefore I shall only touch on the
former.

They live indeed, according to our European phrase, very poor
and mean, destitute almost of the common necessaries of life; but
never starve, that is peculiar to trading republics; then who is judge
of their wants, themselves, or we? Or what does poorness mean?
More than a sound, to signify we have that which another does not
want. Do not many men in politer nations renounce the world for
cloisters and deserts, and place a greater happiness in preserving
their innocence, than enjoying even the necessaries of life; nay, often
ravished with the neglect of them? Wherever therefore contentment
can dwell, though under the meanest circumstances, it is a barbarous
corruption to style such poor, for they have everything they desire,
or, which is much the same, are happily ignorant of any thing more
desirable.

To remove Negroes then from their homes and friends, where
they are at ease, to a strange country, people, and language, must be
highly offending against the laws of natural justice and humanity;
and especially when this change is to hard labour, corporal punishment, and for masters they wish at the D—l.

We are accessories by trade to all that cruelty of their countrymen
which has subjected them to the condition of slaves, little better in
our plantations than that of cattle; the rigour of their usage having
made some hundreds of them at Jamaica run away into barren mountains, where they choose to trust Providence with their subsistence,
rather than their fellow-Christians (now) in the plantations.

Slaves differ in their goodness; those from the Gold Coast are accounted best, being cleanest limbed, and more docible by our settlements than others; but then they are, for that very reason, more prompt to revenge, and murder the instruments of their slavery, and also apter in the means to compass it.

To windward they approach in goodness as is the distance from the Gold Coast; so, as at Gambia, or Sierra Leone, to be much better than at any of the interjacent places.

To leeward from thence, they alter gradually for the worse; an Angolan Negro is a proverb for worthlessness; and they mend (if we may call it so) in that way, till you come to the Hottentots,* that is, to the southernmost extremity of Africa.

JOHN NEWTON, *Thoughts upon the African Slave Trade* (1788)

John Newton (1725–1807), son of a sea captain, went to sea aged 10 and was pressed into the navy as a teenager. He deserted, was captured and flogged (navy discipline was notorious), but then exchanged to a slave-trading vessel. Newton eventually rose to captain in the trade, and from 1750 to 1756 kept a journal of his voyages to Africa. His conversion from freethinking to Christianity did not deter him from slave trading, but ill health forced him to quit in 1756. In 1764 Newton was ordained in the Church of England and published an autobiography, *An Authentic Narrative*. By then he had doubts about the morality of the slave trade: 'I was sometimes shocked with an employment that was perpetually conversant with chains, bolts and shackles.' In 1788 he published *Thoughts upon the African Slave Trade*. Though not strictly classifiable as travel writing, these passages draw from his experience to describe conditions on slave ships. Newton later testified before Parliament against the slave trade, when abolition came up for a vote in 1792 but did not pass.

Thus much concerning the first evil, the loss of seamen and subjects, which the nation sustains by the African slave trade.

There is a second, which either is, or ought to be, deemed of importance, considered in a political light: I mean, the dreadful effects of this trade upon the minds of those who are engaged in it. There are, doubtless, exceptions; and I would willingly except myself. But in general, I know of no method of getting money, not even that of robbing for it upon the highway, which has so direct a tendency to efface the moral sense, to rob the heart of every gentle and humane disposition, and to harden it, like steel, against all impressions of sensibility.

Usually, about two-thirds of a cargo of slaves are males. When a hundred and fifty or two hundred stout men, torn from their native land, many of whom never saw the sea, much less a ship, till a short space before they had embarked; who have, probably, the same natural prejudice against a white man, as we have against a black; and who often bring with them an apprehension they are bought to be eaten: I say, when thus circumstanced, it is not to be expected that they will tamely resign themselves to their situation. It is always taken for granted that they will attempt to gain their liberty if possible. Accordingly, as we dare not trust them, we receive them on board from the first as enemies; and, before their number exceeds, perhaps, ten or fifteen, they are all put in irons; in most ships, two and two together. And frequently, they are not thus confined, as they might most conveniently stand or move, the right hand and foot of one to the left of the other, but across; that is, the hand and foot of each one the same side, whether right or left, are fettered together: so that they cannot move either hand or foot, but with great caution, and with perfect consent. Thus they must sit, walk, and lie, for many months (sometimes for nine or ten), without any mitigation or relief, unless they are sick.

In the night, they are confined below; in the daytime (if the weather be fine) they are upon deck; and as they are brought by pairs, a chain is put through a ring upon their irons, and this likewise locked down to the ring-bolts, which are fastened, at certain intervals, upon the deck. These, and other precautions, are no more than necessary; especially as, while the number of slaves increases, that of the people who are to guard them is diminished, by sickness, or death, or by being absent in the boats: so that, sometimes, not ten men can be mustered, to watch, night and day, over two hundred, besides having all the other business of the ship to attend.

That these precautions are so often effectual is much more to be wondered at, than that they sometimes fail. One unguarded hour, or minute, is sufficient to give the slaves the opportunity they are always waiting for. An attempt to rise upon the ship's company brings on instantaneous and horrid war: for, when they are once in motion, they are desperate; and where they do not conquer, they are seldom quelled without much mischief and bloodshed on both sides. . . .

Hitherto, I have considered the condition of the men slaves only. From the women, there is no danger of insurrection, and they are carefully kept from the men; I mean from the black men. But in what I have to offer, on this head, I am far from including every ship. I speak not of what is universally, but of what is too commonly, and I am afraid, too generally, prevalent.

I have already observed that the captain of an African ship, while upon the coast, is absolute in his command; and if he be humane, vigilant, and determined, he has it in his power to protect the miserable; for scarcely anything can be done on board the ship, without his permission or connivance. But this power is too seldom exerted in favour of the poor women slaves.

When we hear of a town taken by storm, and given up to the ravages of an enraged and licentious army, of wild and unprincipled Cossacks, perhaps no part of the distress affects a feeling mind more than the treatment to which the women are exposed. But the enormities frequently committed in an African ship, though equally flagrant, are little known *here*, and are considered *there*, only as matters of course. When the women and girls are taken on board a ship, naked, trembling, terrified, perhaps almost exhausted with cold, fatigue, and hunger, they are often exposed to the wanton rudeness of white savages. The poor creatures cannot understand the language they hear, but the looks and manner of the speakers are sufficiently intelligible. In imagination, the prey is divided, upon the spot, and only reserved till opportunity offers. Where resistance or refusal would be utterly in vain, even the solicitation of consent is seldom thought of. But I forbear. This is not a subject for declamation. Facts like these, so certain and so numerous, speak for themselves. Surely, if the advocates for the slave trade attempt to plead for it, before the wives and daughters of our happy land, or before those who have wives or daughters of their own, they must lose their cause.

Perhaps some hard-hearted pleader may suggest, that such treatment would indeed be cruel, in Europe: but the African women are negroes, savages, who have no idea of the nicer sensations which obtain among civilized people. I dare contradict them in the strongest terms. I have lived long, and conversed much, amongst these supposed savages. I have often slept in their towns, in a house filled with goods for trade, with no person in the house but myself, and with no other door than a mat; in that security, which no man in his senses would expect in this civilized nation, especially in this metropolis, without the precaution of having strong doors, strongly locked and bolted. And with regard to the women, in Sherbro,* where I was most acquainted, I have seen many instances of modesty, and even delicacy, which would not disgrace an English woman. Yet, such is the treatment which I have known permitted, if not encouraged, in many of our ships—they have been abandoned, without restraint, to the lawless will of the first comer.

Accustomed thus to despise, insult, and injure the slaves on board, it may be expected that the conduct of many of our people to the natives, with whom they trade, is, as far as circumstances admit, very similar; and it is so. They are considered as a people to be robbed and spoiled with impunity. Every art is employed to deceive and wrong them. And he who has most address in this way, has most to boast of.

Not an article that is capable of diminution or adulteration, is delivered genuine, or entire. The spirits are lowered by water. False heads are put into the kegs that contain the gunpowder; so that, though the keg appears large, there is no more powder in it, than in a much smaller. The linen and cotton cloths are opened, and two or three yards, according to the length of the piece, cut off, not from the end, but out of the middle, where it is not so readily noticed.

The natives are cheated, in the number, weight, measure, or quality of what they purchase, in every possible way: and, by habit and emulation, a marvellous dexterity is acquired in these practices. And thus the natives in their turn, in proportion to their commerce with the Europeans, and (I am sorry to add) particularly with the English, become jealous, insidious, and revengeful. . . .

The state of slavery among these wild barbarous people, as we esteem them, is much milder than in our colonies. For as, on the one hand, they have no land in high cultivation, like our West India plantations, and therefore no call for that excessive, unintermitted labour, which exhausts our slaves; so, on the other hand, *no man is permitted to draw blood even from a slave.* If he does, he is liable to a strict inquisition; for the Purrow* laws will not allow a private individual to shed blood. A man may sell his slave, if he pleases; but he may not wantonly abuse him. The laws, likewise, punish some species of theft with slavery; and in cases of adultery, which are very common, as polygamy is the custom of the country, both the woman, and the man who offends with her, are liable to be sold for slaves, unless they can satisfy the husband, or unless they are redeemed by their friends.

Among these unenlightened blacks, it is a general maxim, that if a man steals, or breaks a moveable, as a musket, for instance, the offence may be nearly compensated by putting another musket in its place: but offences, which cannot be repaired in kind, as adultery, admit of no satisfaction, till the injured person declares that he is satisfied. So that, if a rich man seduces the wife of a poor man, he has it in his power to change places with him; for he may send for every article in his house, one by one, till he says, 'I have enough.' The only alternative is personal slavery.

I suppose bribery and influence may have their effects in Guinea, as they have in some other countries; but their laws in the main are wise and good, and, upon the whole, they have considerable operation; and therefore, I believe many of the slaves purchased in Sherbro, and probably upon the whole Windward coast, are convicts, who have forfeited their liberty, by breaking the laws of their country.

But I apprehend that the neighbourhood of our ships, and the desire of our goods, are motives which often push the rigour of the laws to an extreme which would not be exacted, if they were left to themselves.

But slaves are the staple article of the traffic; and though a considerable number may have been born near the sea, I believe the bulk of them are brought from far. I have reason to think that some travel more than a thousand miles before they reach the sea-coast. Whether there may be convicts amongst these likewise, or what pro-portion they may bear to those who are taken prisoners in war, it is impossible to know.

I judge, the principal source of the slave trade, is, the wars which prevail among the natives. Sometimes these wars break out between those who live near the sea. The English, and other Europeans, have been charged with fomenting them; I believe (so far as concerns the windward coast) unjustly. That some would do it, if they could, I doubt not; but I do not think they can have opportunity. Nor is it needful they should interfere. Thousands, in our own country, wish for war, because they fatten upon its spoils.

Human nature is much the same in every place, and few people will be willing to allow that the negroes in Africa are better than themselves. Supposing, therefore, they wish for European goods, may not they wish to purchase them from a ship just arrived? Of course, they must wish for slaves to go to market with; and if they have not slaves, and think themselves strong enough to invade their neighbours, they will probably wish for war. And if once they wish for it, how easy it is to find, or to make, pretexts for breaking an inconvenient peace; or (after the example of greater heroes, of Christian name) to make depredations, without condescending to assign any reasons.

I verily believe that the far greater part of the wars, in Africa, would cease, if the Europeans would cease to tempt them, by offering goods for slaves. And though they do not bring legions into the field, their wars are bloody. I believe the captives reserved for sale are fewer than the slain.

I have not sufficient data to warrant calculation, but, I suppose, not less than one hundred thousand slaves are exported, annually, from all parts of Africa, and that more than one-half of these are exported in English bottoms.

If but an equal number are killed in war, and if many of these wars are kindled by the incentive of selling their prisoners; what an annual accumulation of blood must there be, crying against the nations of Europe concerned in this trade, and particularly against our own!

I have often been gravely told, as a proof that the Africans, however hardly treated, deserve but little compassion, that they are a people so destitute of natural affection that it is common among them for parents to sell their children, and children their parents. And, I think, a charge of this kind is brought against them by the respectable author of *Spectacle de la Nature*.* But he must have been misinformed. I never heard of one instance of either, while I used the Coast.

OLAUDAH EQUIANO, *The Interesting Narrative of the Life of Olaudah Equiano, or Gustavus Vassa, the African. Written by Himself* (1789)

Olaudah Equiano (Gustavus Vassa) (1745?–1797) writes that he was born in present-day Nigeria, kidnapped by slave traders at the age of 11, and brought to Virginia, where he was bought by a navy officer and fought in the Seven Years War (1757–63). In 1762 he was sold to a ship's captain, who took him to the West Indies (see Part IV, the Caribbean section). He bought his freedom in 1766 and returned to London, but not for long, sailing to the Mediterranean and West Indies with the merchant marine and even joining a 1773 Arctic expedition. His career as an activist began before the publication of his *Interesting Narrative*; in 1783 he called abolitionist Granville Sharp's attention to the slave ship *Zong*, whose captain drowned 132 slaves to collect insurance money. Equiano's book was a success, with nine British editions in the author's lifetime. He died a rich man, leaving £950 (£75,000 or $120,000 today) to his daughter. Evidence recently discovered by Vincent Carretta suggests he may have been born in South Carolina, not Africa. If this early Afro-British writer invented rather than reclaimed an African identity, his literary achievement, Carretta comments, has been underrated. Our selections recount his kidnapping and journey as a captive from the African interior to the coast, where he tells of boarding a slave ship and enduring the Middle Passage.

I have already acquainted the reader with the time and place of my birth. My father, besides many slaves, had a numerous family, of which seven lived to grow up, including myself and a sister, who was the only daughter. As I was the youngest of the sons, I became, of course, the greatest favourite with my mother, and was always with her; and she used to take particular pains to form my mind. I was trained up from my earliest years in the arts of agriculture and war: my daily exercise was shooting and throwing javelins; and my mother adorned me with emblems, after the manner of our greatest warriors. In this way I grew up till I was turned the age of eleven, when an end was put to my happiness in the following manner. Generally, when the grown people in the neighbourhood were gone far in the fields to labour, the children assembled together in some of the neighbours' premises to play; and commonly some of us used to get up a tree to look out for any assailant, or kidnapper, that might come upon us; for they sometimes took those opportunities of our parents' absence to attack and carry off as many as they could seize. One day, as I was watching at the top of a tree in our yard, I saw one of those people come into the yard of our next neighbour but one, to kidnap, there being many stout young people in it. Immediately, on this, I gave the alarm of the rogue, and he was surrounded by the stoutest of them, who entangled him with cords, so that he could not escape till some of the grown people came and secured him. But, alas! ere long it was my fate to be thus attacked, and to be carried off, when none of the grown people were nigh. One day, when all our people were gone out to their works as usual, and only I and my dear sister were left to mind the house, two men and a woman got over our walls, and in a moment seized us both; and, without giving us time to cry out, or make resistance, they stopped our mouths, tied our hands, and ran off with us into the nearest wood: and continued to carry us as far as they could, till night came on, when we reached a small house, where the robbers halted for refreshment, and spent the night. We were then unbound, but were unable to take any food; and, being quite overpowered by fatigue and grief, our only relief was some sleep, which allayed our misfortune for a short time. The next morning we left the house, and continued travelling all the day. For a long time we had kept the woods, but at last we came into a road which I believed I knew. I had now some hopes of being delivered; for we had advanced but a little way before I discovered some people at a distance, on which I began to cry out for their assistance; but my cries had no other effect than to make them tie me faster, and stop my mouth, and then they put me into a large sack. They also stopped my sister's mouth, and tied her hands; and in this manner we proceeded till we were out of the sight of these people. When we went to rest the following night they offered us some victuals; but we refused them; and the only comfort we had was in being in one another's arms all that night, and bathing each other with our tears. But, alas! we were soon deprived of even the smallest comfort of weeping together. The next day proved a day of greater sorrow than I had yet experienced; for my sister and I were then separated, while we lay clasped in each other's arms. It was in vain that we besought them not to part us: she was torn from me, and immediately carried away, while I was left in a state of distraction not to be described. I cried and grieved continually; and for several days I did not eat anything but what they forced into my mouth. At length, after many days travelling, during which I had often changed masters, I got into the hands of a chieftain, in a very pleasant country. This man had two wives and some children, and they all used me extremely well, and did all they could to comfort me; particularly the first wife, who was something like my mother. Although I was a great many days' journey from my father's house, yet these people spoke exactly the same language with us. This first master of mine, as I may call him, was a smith, and my principal employment was working his bellows, which were the same kind as I had seen in my vicinity. They were in some respects not unlike the stoves here in gentlemen's kitchens; and were covered over with leather; and in the middle of that leather a stick was fixed, and a person stood up, and worked it, in the same manner as is done to pump water out of a cask with a hand-pump. I believe it was gold he worked, for it was of a lovely bright yellow colour, and was worn by the women on their wrists and ankles. I was there I suppose about a month, and they at last used to trust me some little distance from the house. This liberty I used in embracing every opportunity to inquire the way to my own home: and I also sometimes, for the same purpose, went with the maidens, in the cool of the evenings, to bring pitchers of water from the springs for the use of the house. I had also remarked where the sun rose in the morning, and set in the evening, as I had travelled along; and I had observed that my father's house was towards the rising of the sun. I therefore determined to seize the first opportunity of making my escape, and to shape my course for that quarter; for I was quite oppressed and weighed down by grief after my mother and friends; and my love of liberty, ever great, was strengthened by the mortifying circumstance of not daring to eat with the free-born children, although I was mostly their companion. . . .

Soon after this my master's only daughter and child by his first wife sickened and died, which affected him so much that for some time he was almost frantic, and really would have killed himself had he not been watched and prevented. However, in a small time afterwards he recovered, and I was again sold. I was now carried to the left of the sun's rising, through many dreary wastes and dismal woods, amidst the hideous roarings of wild beasts. The people I was sold to used to carry me very often, when I was tired, either on their shoulders or on their backs. I saw many convenient well-built sheds along the roads, at proper distances, to accommodate the merchants and travellers, who lay in those buildings along with their wives, who often accompany them; and they always go well armed.

From the time I left my own nation I always found somebody that understood me till I came to the sea coast. The languages of different nations did not totally differ, nor were they so copious as those of the Europeans, particularly the English. They were therefore easily learned; and, while I was journeying thus through Africa, I acquired two or three different tongues. In this manner I had been travelling for a considerable time, when one evening, to my great surprise, whom should I see brought to the house where I was but my dear sister. As soon as she saw me she gave a loud shriek, and ran into my arms. I was quite overpowered; neither of us could speak, but, for a considerable time, clung to each other in mutual embraces, unable to do anything but weep. Our meeting affected all who saw us; and indeed I must acknowledge, in honour of those sable destroyers of human rights, that I never met with any ill treatment, or saw any offered to their slaves, except tying them, when necessary, to keep them from running away. When these people knew we were brother and sister they indulged us to be together; and the man, to whom I supposed we belonged, lay with us, he in the middle, while she and I held one another by the hands across his breast all night; and thus for a while we forgot our misfortunes in the joy of being together: but even this small comfort was soon to have an end; for scarcely had the fatal morning appeared, when she was again torn from me for ever! I was now more miserable, if possible, than before. The small relief which her presence gave me from pain was gone, and the wretchedness of my situation was redoubled by my anxiety after her fate, and my apprehensions lest her sufferings should be greater than mine, when I could not be with her to alleviate them. Yes, thou dear partner of all my childish sports! thou sharer of my joys and sorrows! happy should I have ever esteemed myself to encounter every misery for you, and to procure your freedom by the sacrifice of my own. Though you were early forced from my arms, your image has been always riveted in my heart, from which neither time nor fortune have been able to remove it: so that, while the thoughts of your sufferings have damped my prosperity, they have mingled with adversity, and increased its bitterness. To that heaven which protects the weak from the strong, I commit the care of your innocence and virtues, if they have not already received their full reward; and if your youth and delicacy have not long since fallen victims to the violence of the African trader, the pestilential stench of a Guinea ship, the seasoning in the European colonies, or the lash and lust of a brutal and unrelenting overseer.

I did not long remain after my sister. I was again sold, and carried through a number of places, till, after travelling a considerable time, I came to a town called Tinmah, in the most beautiful country I had yet seen in Africa. It was extremely rich, and there were many rivulets which flowed through it; and supplied a large pond in the centre of the town, where the people washed. Here I first saw and tasted cocoa nuts, which I thought superior to any nuts I had ever tasted before; and the trees, which were loaded, were also interspersed amongst the houses, which had commodious shades adjoining, and were in the same manner as ours, the insides being neatly plastered and whitewashed. Here I also saw and tasted for the first time sugar-cane. Their money consisted of little white shells, the size of the finger nail: they are known in this country by the name of *core*.* I was sold here for one hundred and seventy-two of them by a merchant who lived and brought me there. I had been about two or three days at his house, when a wealthy widow, a neighbour of his, came there one evening, and brought with her an only son, a young gentleman about my own age and size. Here they saw me; and, having taken a fancy to me, I was bought of the merchant, and went home with them. Her house and premises were situated close to one of those rivulets I have mentioned, and were the finest I ever saw in Africa: they were very extensive, and she had a number of slaves to attend her. The next day I was washed and perfumed, and when meal-time came, I was led into the presence of my mistress, and ate and drank before her with her son. This filled me with astonishment: and I could scarce help expressing my surprise that the young gentleman should suffer me, who was bound,* to eat with him who was free; and not only so, but that he would not at any time either eat or drink till I had taken first, because I was the eldest, which was agreeable to our custom. Indeed everything here, and all their treatment of me, made me forget that I was a slave. The language of these people resembled ours so nearly that we understood each other perfectly. They had also the very same customs as we. There were likewise slaves daily to attend us, while my young master and I, with other boys, sported with our darts and bows and arrows, as I had been used to do at home. In this resemblance to my former happy state I passed about two months, and I now began to think I was to be adopted into the family, and was beginning to be reconciled to my situation, and to forget by degrees my misfortunes, when all at once the delusion vanished; for, without the least previous knowledge, one morning early, while my dear master and companion was still asleep, I was awakened out of my reverie to fresh sorrow, and hurried away even among the uncircumcised.*

Thus, at the very moment I dreamed of the greatest happiness, I found myself most miserable: and it seemed as if fortune wished to give me this taste of joy only to render the reverse more poignant. The change I now experienced was as painful as it was sudden and unexpected. It was a change indeed from a state of bliss to a scene which is inexpressible by me, as it discovered to me an element I had never before beheld, and till then had no idea of, and wherein such instances of hardship and cruelty continually occurred as I can never reflect on but with horror.

All the nations and people I had hitherto passed through resembled our own in their manners, customs and language: but I came at length to a country, the inhabitants of which differed from us in all those particulars. I was very much struck with this difference, especially when I came among a people who did not circumcise, and ate without washing their hands. They cooked also in iron pots, and had European cutlasses and cross bows, which were unknown to us, and fought with their fists among themselves. Their women were not so modest as ours, for they ate, and drank, and slept with their men. But, above all, I was amazed to see no sacrifices or offerings among them. In some of those places the people ornamented themselves with scars, and likewise filed their teeth very sharp. They wanted sometimes to ornament me in the same manner, but I would not suffer them; hoping that I might some time be among a people who did not thus disfigure themselves, as I thought they did . . .

The first object which saluted my eyes when I arrived on the coast was the sea, and a slave-ship, which was then riding at anchor, and waiting for its cargo. These filled me with astonishment, which was soon converted into terror, which I am yet at a loss to describe, nor the then feelings of my mind. When I was carried on board I was immediately handled, and tossed up, to see if I were sound, by some of the crew; and I was now persuaded that I had gotten into a world of bad spirits, and that they were going to kill me. Their complexions too differing so much from ours, their long hair, and the language they spoke, which was very different from any I had ever heard, united to confirm me in this belief. Indeed, such were the horrors of my views and fears at the moment that, if ten thousand worlds had been my own, I would have freely parted with them all to have exchanged my condition with that of the meanest slave in my own country.

When I looked round the ship too, and saw a large furnace of copper boiling, and a multitude of black people of every description chained together, every one of their countenances expressing dejection and sorrow, I no longer doubted of my fate, and, quite overpowered with horror and anguish, I fell motionless on the deck and fainted. When I recovered a little, I found some black people about me, who I believed were some of those who brought me on board, and had been receiving their pay; they talked to me in order to cheer me, but all in vain. I asked them if we were not to be eaten by those white men with horrible looks, red faces, and long hair? They told me I was not; and one of the crew brought me a small portion of spirituous liquor in a wine glass; but, being afraid of him, I would not take it out of his hand. One of the blacks therefore took it from him and gave it to me, and I took a little down my palate, which, instead of reviving me, as they thought it would, threw me into the greatest consternation at the strange feeling it produced, having never tasted any such liquor before. Soon after this, the blacks who brought me on board went off, and left me abandoned to despair. I now saw myself deprived of all chance of returning to my native country, or even the least glimpse of hope of gaining the shore, which I now considered as friendly: and I even wished for my former slavery in preference to my present situation, which was filled with horrors of every kind, still height-ened by my ignorance of what I was to undergo. I was not long suffered to indulge my grief; I was soon put down under the decks, and there I received such a salutation in my nostrils as I had never experienced in my life; so that with the loathsomeness of the stench, and crying together, I became so sick and low that I was not able to eat, nor had I the least desire to taste anything. I now wished for the last friend, Death, to relieve me; but soon, to my grief, two of the white men offered me eatables; and, on my refusing to eat, one of them held me fast by the hands, and laid me across, I think, the windlass,* and tied my feet, while the other flogged me severely. I had never experienced anything of this kind before; and although, not being used to the water, I naturally feared that element the first time I saw it; yet, nevertheless, could I have got over the nettings, I would have jumped over the side, but I could not; and, besides, the crew used to watch us very closely who were not chained down to the decks, lest we should leap into the water; and I have seen some of these poor African prisoners most severely cut for attempting to do so, and hourly whipped for not eating. This indeed was often the case with myself. In a little time after, amongst the poor chained men, I found some of my own nation, which in a small degree gave ease to my mind. I inquired of these what was to be done with us? They gave me to understand we were to be carried to these white people's country to work for them. I then was a little revived, and thought, if it were no worse than working, my situation was not so desperate: but still I feared I should be put to death, the white people looked and acted, as I thought, in so savage a manner; for I had never seen among any people such instances of brutal cruelty; and this not only shown towards us blacks, but also to some of the whites themselves. One white man in particular I saw, when we were permitted to be on deck, flogged so unmercifully with a large rope near the fore-mast, that he died in consequence of it; and they tossed him over the side as they would have done a brute. This made me fear these people the more; and I expected nothing less than to be treated in the same manner. I could not help expressing my fears and apprehensions to some of my countrymen: I asked them if these people had no country, but lived in this hollow place the ship? They told me they did not, but came from a distant one. 'Then,' said I, 'how comes it in all our country we never heard of them?' They told me, because they lived so very far off. I then asked where were their women? Had they any like themselves! I was told they had. 'And why', said I, 'do we not see them?' They answered, because they were left behind. I asked how the vessel could go? They told me they could not tell; but that there were cloths put upon the masts by the help of the ropes I saw, and then the vessel went on; and the white men had some spell or magic they put in the water when they liked in order to stop the vessel. I was exceedingly amazed at this account, and really thought they were spirits. I therefore wished much to be from amongst them, for I expected they would sacrifice me: but my wishes were vain; for we were so quartered that it was impossible for any of us to make our escape. While we stayed on the coast I was mostly on deck; and one day, to my great astonishment, I saw one of these vessels coming in with the sails up. As soon as the whites saw it, they gave a great shout, at which we were amazed; and the more so as the vessel appeared larger by approaching nearer. At last she came to an anchor in my sight, and when the anchor was let go, I and my countrymen who saw it were lost in astonishment to observe the vessel stop; and were now convinced it was done by magic. Soon after this the other ship got her boats out, and they came on board of us, and the people of both ships seemed very glad to see each other. Several of the strangers also shook hands with us black people, and made motions with their hands, signifying, I suppose, we were to go to their country; but we did not understand them. At last, when the ship we were in had got in all her cargo, they made ready with many fearful noises, and we were all put under deck, so that we could not see how they managed the vessel. But this disappointment was the least of my sorrow. The stench of the hold while we were on the coast was so intolerably loathsome that it was dangerous to remain there for any time, and some of us had been permitted to stay on the deck for the fresh air; but now that the whole ship's cargo were confined together, it became absolutely pestilential. The closeness of the place, and the heat of the climate, added to the number in the ship, which was so crowded that each had scarcely room to turn himself, almost suffocated us. This produced copious perspirations, so that the air soon became unfit for respiration, from a variety of loathsome smells, and brought on a sickness among the slaves, of which many died, thus falling victims to the improvident avarice, as I may call it, of their purchasers. This wretched situation was again aggravated by the galling of the chains, now become insupportable; and the filth of the necessary tubs,* into which the children often fell, and were almost suffocated. The shrieks of the women, and the groans of the dying, rendered the whole a scene of horror almost inconceivable. Happily perhaps for myself I was soon reduced so low here that it was thought necessary to keep me almost always on deck; and from my extreme youth I was not put in fetters. In this situation I expected every hour to share the fate of my companions, some of whom were almost daily brought upon deck at the point of death, which I began to hope would soon put an end to my miseries. Often did I think many of the inhabitants of the deep much more happy than myself; I envied them the freedom they enjoyed, and as often wished I could change my condition for theirs. Every circumstance I met with served only to render my state more painful, and heighten my apprehensions, and my opinion of the cruelty of the whites.

2. INFANT COLONY, 1794

ANNA MARIA FALCONBRIDGE, *Two Voyages to Sierra Leone,*
during the Years 1791–2–3, in a Series of Letters (1793)

Anna Maria Falconbridge set off with her husband, the abolitionist
Alexander Falconbridge, for Sierra Leone in 1791 to rescue the colony of
free blacks shipped from London four years previously by the abolitionist
'Committee for the Relief of the Black Poor'. This colonizing scheme had
had problems from the start. Olaudah Equiano, hired as commissary, was
dismissed for blowing the whistle on corruption. By 1791, sixty of 411
settlers remained, burned out of their homes by a local chieftain. As agent
of the Sierra Leone Company, Falconbridge needed to negotiate with
native brokers and deal tactfully with white slave traders. But tact does not
seem to have been his strong point, and his wife (writing after his death
and her remarriage) does not conceal this. Her book indicts the company
as she tries to vindicate the actions of both her husbands. Our selections
thematize imprisonment, starting with Anna Maria's feelings at viewing
convict hulks bound for Botany Bay. Her husband's reluctance to accept
favours from slave traders leaves his wife a virtual prisoner aboard ship.
By the time she sailed home from her second voyage in 1793 with her
new husband, via Jamaica, she had distanced herself from Falconbridge's
abolitionist views.

LONDON, 5 January 1791

The time draws nigh when I must bid adieu to my native land,
perhaps for ever! The thoughts of it damps my spirits more than you
can imagine, but I am resolved to summon all the fortitude I can,
being conscious of meriting the reproaches of my friends and relations for having hastily married as I did contrary to their wishes, and
am determined rather than be an encumbrance on them, to accompany my husband even to the wilds of Africa, whither he is now
bound, and meet such fate as awaits me in preference to any possible
comfort I could receive from them.

Mr Falconbridge is employed by the St George's Bay Company* to
carry out some relief for a number of unfortunate people, both blacks
and whites, whom government sent to the river Sierra Leone, a few
years since, and who in consequence of having had some dispute
with the natives are scattered through the country, and are just now,
as I have been told, in the most deplorable condition.

He (Mr Falconbridge) is likewise to make some arrangements for collecting those poor creatures again, and forming a settlement which the company have in contemplation to establish, not only to serve them, but to be generally useful to the natives. . . .

This is all the information I can give you at present, respecting my intended voyage, but as it is an unusual enterprise for an English woman to visit the coast of Africa; and as I have ever flattered myself with possessing your friendship, you will no doubt like to hear from me, and I therefore intend giving you a full and circumstantial account of every thing that does not escape my notice, till I return to this blessed land, if it pleases him who determines all things, that should be the case again.

I have this instant learnt that we set off tomorrow for Gravesend, where the ship is lying, ready to sail; should we put into any port in the channel, I may probably write you if I am able, but must now bid you adieu.

SPITHEAD, 12 January 1791

I did not experience any of those fears peculiar to my sex upon the water; and the only inconvenience I found was a little sea sickness, which I had a right to expect, for you know this is my first voyage.

There is one circumstance, which I forbode will make the remainder of our voyage unpleasant.

The gentlemen whom Mr Falconbridge is employed by are for abolishing the slave trade:* the owners of this vessel are of that trade, and consequently the Captain and Mr. Falconbridge must be very opposite in their sentiments.

They are always arguing, and both are warm in their tempers, which makes me uneasy, and induces me to form the conjectures I do; but perhaps that may not be the case.

I have not been on shore at Portsmouth, indeed it is not a desirable place to visit: I was once there, and few people have a wish to see it a second time.

The only thing that has attracted my notice in the harbour is the fleet with the convicts for Botany Bay,* which are wind bound, as well as ourselves.

The destiny of such numbers of my fellow creatures has made what I expect to encounter set lighter upon my mind than it ever did before; nay, nothing could have operated a reconciliation so effectually; for as the human heart is more susceptible of distress conveyed by the eye, than when represented by language however ingenuously pictured with misery, so the sight of those unfortunate beings, and the thoughts of what they are to endure, have worked more forcibly on my feelings than all the accounts I ever read or heard of wretchedness before.

I must close this which is the last, in all probability, you will receive from me, till my arrival in Africa; when, if an opportunity offers, I shall make a point of writing to you.

BANCE ISLAND, 10 February 1791

We sailed the very day I wrote you from Portsmouth, and our passage was unusually quick, being only eighteen days from thence to this place.

The novelty of a ship ploughing the trackless ocean in a few days became quite familiar to me; there was such a sameness in every thing (for some birds were all we saw the whole way) that I found the voyage tiresome, notwithstanding the shortness of it.

You will readily believe my heart was gladdened at the sight of the mountains of Sierra Leone, which was the land we first made.

Those mountains appear to rise gradually from the sea to a stupendous height, richly wooded and beautifully ornamented by the hand of nature, with a variety of delightful prospects.*

I was vastly pleased while sailing up the river, for the rapidity of the ship through the water afforded a course of new scenery almost every moment, till we cast anchor here. Now and then I saw the glimpse of a native town, but from the distance and new objects hastily catching my eye, was not able to form a judgment or idea of any of them; but this will be no loss, as I may have frequent opportunities of visiting some of them hereafter.

As soon as our anchor was dropped, Captain McLean saluted Bance Island with seven guns, which not being returned I enquired the cause, and was told that the last time the *Duke of Buccleugh** came out, she, as is customary, saluted, and on the fort returning the compliment, a wad was drove by the force of the sea breeze upon the roof of one of the houses (which was then of thatch) set fire to the building, and consumed not only the house but goods to a large amount.

When the ceremony of saluting was over, Captain McLean and

Mr W. Falconbridge went on shore; but it being late in the evening, I continued on board till next day.

Here we met the *Lapwing* cutter.* She sailed some time before us from Europe, and had been arrived two or three weeks.

The master of her, and several of the people to whose assistance Mr Falconbridge is come, and who had taken refuge here, came to visit us.

They represented their sufferings to have been very great; that they had been treacherously dealt with by one King Jemmy, who had drove them away from the ground they occupied, burnt their houses, and otherwise divested them of every comfort and necessary of life; they also threw out some reflections against the agent of this island; said he had sold several of their fellow sufferers to a Frenchman, who had taken them to the West Indies.

Mr Falconbridge, however, was not the least inclined to give entire confidence to what they told us; but prudently suspended his opinion until he had made further enquiries.

Those visitors being gone, we retired to bed—I cannot say to rest; the heat was so excessive that I scarcely slept at all.

The following day we received a polite invitation to dine on shore, which I did not object to, although harassed for want of sleep the night before.

At dinner the conversation turned upon the slave trade: Mr Falconbridge, zealous for the cause in which he is engaged, strenuously opposed every argument his opponents advanced in favour of the *abominable* trade: the glass went briskly round, and the gentlemen growing warm, I retired immediately as the cloth was removed.

The people on the island crowded to see me; they gazed with apparent astonishment—I suppose at my dress, for white women could not be a novelty to them, as there were several among the unhappy people sent out here by government, one of whom is now upon the island.

Seeing so many of my own sex, though of different complexions from myself, attired in their native garbs, was a scene equally new to me, and my delicacy, I confess, was not a little hurt at times.

Many among them appeared of superior rank, at least I concluded so from the preferable way in which they were clad; nor was I wrong in my conjecture, for upon enquiring who they were, was informed one was the woman or mistress of Mr. ——, another of Mr. B——, and so on: I then understood that every gentleman on the island had his lady.

While I was thus entertaining myself with my new acquaintances, two or three of the gentlemen left their wine and joined me; among them was Mr B——, the agent; he in a very friendly manner begged I would take a bed on shore.

I thanked him, and said, if agreeable to Mr Falconbridge, I would have no objection: however, Falconbridge objected, and gave me for reason that he had been unhandsomely treated, and was determined to go on board the *Lapwing*, for he would not subject himself to any obligation to men possessing such diabolical sentiments.

It was not proper for me to contradict him at this moment, as the heat of argument and the influence of an over portion of wine had quickened and disconcerted his temper; I therefore submitted without making any objection to come on board this tub of a vessel, which in point of size and cleanliness comes nigher a hog-trough than anything else you can imagine.

Though I resolved to remonstrate the first seasonable opportunity, and to point out the likelihood of endangering my health, should he persist to keep me in so confined a place.

This remonstrance I made the next morning, after passing a night of torment, but to no purpose; the only consolation I got was—as soon as the settlers could be collected, he would have a house built on shore, where they were to be fixed.

I honestly own my original resolution of firmness was now warped at what I foresaw I was doomed to suffer, by being imprisoned, for God knows how long, in a place so disgusting as this was, in my opinion, at that time.

Conceive yourself pent up in a floating cage, without room either to walk about, stand erect, or even to lie at length; exposed to the inclemency of the weather, having your eyes and ears momently offended by acts of indecency, and language too horrible to relate— add to this a complication of filth, the stench from which was continually assailing your nose, and then you will have a faint notion of the *Lapwing* cutter.

However, upon collecting myself, and recollecting there was no remedy but to make the best of my situation, I begged the master (who slept upon deck in consequence of my coming on board) to have the cabin thoroughly cleaned and washed with vinegar;

entreated Falconbridge to let me go on shore while it was doing, and hinted at the indecencies I saw and heard, and was promised they would be prevented in future.

With these assurances I went on shore, not a little elated at the reprieve I was to enjoy for a few hours.

The gentlemen* received me with every mark of attention and civility; indeed, I must be wanting in sensibility, if my heart did not warm with gratitude to Messrs. Ballingall and Tilly, for their kind-nesses to me: the latter gentleman I am informed will succeed to the agency of the island; he is a genteel young man, and I am told, very deservedly, a favourite with his employers.

Mr Falconbridge this day sent a message to Elliotte Griffiths, the secretary of Naimbana, who is the King of Sierra Leone, acquainting him with the purport of his mission, and begging to know when he may be honoured with an audience of his Majesty.

In the evening he received an answer, of which the following is a copy:

ROBANA TOWN

KING Naimbana's compliments to Mr Falconbridge, and will be glad to see him tomorrow.

(Signed)

A. E. GRIFFITHS, Sec.

Such an immediate answer from a King, I considered a favourable omen, and a mark of condescension in his Majesty, but the result you shall hear by and by; in the mean while, I must tell you what passed the remainder of the day at Bance Island, and give, as far as my ideas will allow me, a description of this factory.*. . . .

We now returned to the factory, or as it is otherwise called Bance Island House.

This building at a distance has a respectable and formidable appearance; nor is it much less so upon a nearer investigation: I suppose it is about one hundred feet in length, and thirty in breadth, and contains nine rooms, on one floor, under which are commodious large cellars and store rooms: to the right is the kitchen, forge, etc. and to the left other necessary buildings, all of country stone, and surrounded with a prodigious thick lofty wall.

There was formerly a fortification in front of those houses, which was destroyed by a French frigate during the last war; at present several pieces of cannon are planted in the same place, but without embrasures or breast-work; behind the great house is the slave yard, and houses for accommodating the slaves.

Delicacy, perhaps, prevented the gentlemen from taking me to see them; but the room where we dined looks directly into the yard.

Involuntarily I strolled to one of the windows a little before dinner, without the smallest suspicion of what I was to see; judge then what my astonishment and feelings were, at the sight of between two and three hundred wretched victims, chained and parcelled out in circles, just satisfying the cravings of nature from a trough of rice placed in the centre of each circle.

Offended modesty rebuked me with a blush for not hurrying my eyes from such disgusting scenes; but whether fascinated by female curiosity, or whatever else, I could not withdraw myself for several minutes—while I remarked some whose hair was withering with age, reluctantly tasting their food—and others thoughtless from youth, greedily devouring all before them; be assured I avoided the prospects from this side of the house ever after. . . .

[Next morning on shore]

After setting nigh half an hour, Naimbana made his appearance, and received us with seeming good will: he was dressed in a purple embroidered coat, white satin waistcoat and breeches, thread stockings, and his left side emblazoned with a flaming star; his legs to be sure were harlequined,* by a number of holes in the stockings, through which his black skin appeared.

Compliments ended, Mr Falconbridge acquainted him with his errand, by a repetition of what he wrote the day before: and complained much of King Jemmy's injustice, in driving the settlers away, and burning their town.

The King answered through Elliotte (for he speaks but little English) that Jemmy was partly right—the people had brought it on themselves; they had taken part with some Americans, with whom Jemmy had a dispute, and through that means drew the ill will of this man upon them, who had behaved, considering their conduct, as well as they merited; for he gave them three days notice before he burned their town, that they might remove themselves and all their effects away; that he (Naimbana) could not prudently re-establish them, except by consent of all the Chiefs—for which purpose he must call a court or palaver;* but it would be seven or eight days before they could be collected; however he would send a summons to the different parties directly, and give Falconbridge timely advice when they were to meet.

Falconbridge perceived clearly nothing was to be effected without a palaver, and unless the King's interest was secured his views would be frustrated, and his endeavours ineffectual; but how this was to be done, or what expedient to adopt, he was at a loss for.

He considered it impolitic to purchase his patronage by heavy presents, lest the other great men might expect the same; and he had it not in his power to purchase them all in the same way, as the scanty cargo of the *Lapwing* would not admit of it.

At length, trusting that the praiseworthy purposes he was aiming at insured him the assistance of the King of Kings, he resolved to try what good words would do.

Having prefaced his arguments with a small donation of rum, wine, cheese, and a gold laced hat (which Naimbana seemed much pleased with) Falconbridge began by explaining what advantages would accrue to his Majesty, and to all the inhabitants round about, by such an establishment as the St George's Bay Company were desirous of making; the good they wished to do—their disinterestedness in point of obtaining wealth, and concluded by expostulating on the injustice and imposition of dispossessing the late settlers of the grounds and houses they occupied, which had been honestly and honourably purchased by Captain Thompson of the Navy, in the name of our gracious Sovereign, his Britannic Majesty.

That it was unusual for Englishmen to forgo fulfilling any engagements they made; and they held in detestation every person so disposed.

He then entreated the King would use all his might to prevent any unfavourable prejudices which a refusal to reinstate the settlers, or to confirm the bargain made with Captain Thompson, might operate against him in the minds of his good friends the King of England and the St George's Bay Company.

The King said he liked the English in preference to all white men, though he considered every white man as a rogue, and consequently saw them with a jealous eye; yet, he believed the English were by far the honestest, and for that reason, notwithstanding he had received more favours from the French than the English, he liked the latter much best.

He was decidedly of opinion that all contracts or agreements between man and man however disadvantageous to either party should be binding; but observed, he was hastily drawn in to dispose of land to Captain Thompson, which in fact he had not a right to sell, because says he, 'this is a great country, and belongs to many people—where I live belongs to myself—and I can live where I like; nay, can appropriate any unhabited land within my dominions to what use I please; but it is necessary for me to obtain the consent of my people, or rather the head man of every town, before I sell any land to a white man, or allow strangers to come and live among us.

'I should have done this you will say at first. Granted—but as I disobliged my subjects by suffering your people to take possession of the land without their approbation, from which cause I was not able to protect them, unless I hazarded civil commotions in my country; and as they have been turned away—it is best now—they should be replaced by the unanimous voice of all interested.

'I am bound from what I have heretofore done, to give my utmost support; and if my people do not acquiesce, it shall not be my fault.'

Here Falconbridge, interrupting the King, said—'The King of the English will not blame your people, but load yourself with the stigma; it is King Naimbana who is ostensible* to King George—and I hope, King, you will not fall out with your good friend.'

This being explained by Mr Secretary Elliotte, his Majesty was some moments silent—then clasping Falconbridge in his arms, told him, 'I believe you and King George are my good friends—do not fear, have a good heart, I will do as much as I can for you.'

They then shook hands heartily, and Naimbana retired, I suppose to his Pegininee* woman's house, but presently returned dressed in a suit of black velvet, except the stockings, which were the same as before.

I often had an inclination to offer my services to close the holes: but was fearful lest my needle might blunder into his Majesty's leg, and start the blood, for drawing the blood of an African king, I am informed, whether occasioned by accident or otherwise, is punished with death: the dread of this only prevented me. . . .

Having seen all the raree-shows* of Robana town, we returned to the Queen's house to dinner, which was shortly after put on a table covered with a plain calico cloth, and consisted of boiled and broiled fowls, rice, and some greens resembling our spinach.

But I should tell you, before dinner Naimbana again changed his dress for a scarlet robe embroidered with gold.

Naimbana, Elliotte, Falconbridge, and myself, only set down; the Queen stood behind the King eating an onion I gave her, a bite of which she now and then indulged her royal consort with: silver forks were placed on the King's plate, and mine, but no where else.

The King is rather above common height, but meagre withal; the features of his face resemble a European more than any black I have seen; his teeth are mostly decayed, and his hair, or rather wool, bespeaks old age, which I judge to be about eighty; he was seldom without a smile on his countenance, but I think his smiles were suspicious.

He gave great attention while Falconbridge was speaking, for though he does not speak our language, he understands a good deal of it; his answers were slow, and on the whole tolerably reasonable.

The Queen is of a middle stature, plump and jolly; her temper seems placid and accommodating; her teeth are bad, but I dare say she has otherwise been a good looking woman in her youthful days.

I suppose her now to be about forty-five or six, at which age women are considered old here.

She sat on the King's right hand, while he and Falconbridge were in conversation; and now and then would clap her hands, and cry out *Ya hoo*, which signifies, that's well or proper.

She was dressed in the country manner, but in a dignified style, having several yards of striped taffeta wrapped round her waist, which served as a petticoat; another piece of the same was carelessly thrown over her shoulders in form of a scarf; her head was decorated with two silk handkerchiefs; her ears with rich gold ear-rings, and her neck with gaudy necklaces; but she had neither shoes nor stockings on.

Clara* was dressed much after the same way, but her apparel was not quite of such good materials as the Queen's. Mr Elliotte apologized after dinner, that for want of sugar they could not offer tea or coffee.

The tide serving, and approaching night obliged us to re-embark and return to this place.

On the whole I was much pleased with the occurrences of the day; indeed, methinks, I hear you saying, 'Why the weak mind of this giddy girl will be quite intoxicated with the courtesy and attention paid her by such great folks'; but believe me, to whatever height of self-consequence I may have been lifted by aerial fancies, overpouring sleep prevailed, and clouding all my greatness—I awoke next morning without the slightest remains of fancied importance. . . .

[Granville Town, Sierra Leone, 13 May 1791]

Falconbridge now had effected the grand object; he was next to collect and settle the miserable refugees: no time was to be lost in accomplishing this; the month of February was nearly spent, only three months of dry weather remained for them to clear their land, build their houses, and prepare their ground for a crop to support them the ensuing year . . .

I never did, and God grant I never may again, witness so much misery as I was forced to be a spectator of here. Among the outcasts were seven of our country women,* decrepit with disease, and so disguised with filth and dirt, that I should never have supposed they were born white; add to this, almost naked from head to foot; in short, their appearance was such as I think would extort compassion from the most callous heart; but I declare they seemed insensible to shame, or the wretchedness of their situation themselves; I begged they would get washed, and gave them what clothes I could conveniently spare. Falconbridge had a hut appropriated as a hospital, where they were kept separate from the other settlers, and by his attention and care, they recovered in a few weeks.

I always supposed these people had been transported as convicts, but some conversation I lately had with one of the women has partly undeceived me. She said, the women were mostly of that description of persons who walk the streets of London, and support themselves by the earnings of prostitution; that men were employed to collect and conduct them to Wapping,* where they were intoxicated with liquor, then inveigled on board of ship, and married to black men, whom they had never seen before; that the morning after she was married, she really did not remember a syllable of what had happened over night, and when informed, was obliged to inquire who was her husband? After this, to the time of their sailing, they were amused and buoyed up by a prodigality of fair promises, and great expectations which awaited them in the country they were going to: 'Thus,' in her own words, 'to the disgrace of my mother country, upwards of one hundred unfortunate women were seduced from England to practise their iniquities more brutishly in this horrid country.'

Good heaven! How the relation of this tale made me shudder; I questioned its veracity, and enquired of the other women who exactly corroborated what I had heard; nevertheless, I cannot altogether reconcile myself to believe it; for it is scarcely possible that the British Government, at this advanced and enlightened age, envied and admired as it is by the universe, could be capable of exercising or countenancing such a Gothic* infringement on human liberty.

[Falconbridge returned to England in September 1791 and departed again for Sierra Leone in December of that year. During her second sojourn there, her husband died and she married an American employee of the Sierra Leone Company, Isaac DuBois. Here she writes of her return voyage. London, 11 October 1793:]

We embarked and sailed on the ninth of June; nothing could have reconciled me to the idea of taking my passage in a slave ship, but Mr —— being with me, for I always entertained most horrid notions of being exposed to indelicacies, too offensive for the eye of an English woman, on board these ships; however, I never was more agreeably disappointed in my life. In the centre of the ship a barricade was run across, to prevent any communication between the men and women; the men and boys occupied the forward part, and the women and girls, the after, so I was only liable to see the latter, who were full as well habited as they would have been in Africa, and I had very comfortable apartments in the round house,* where I could retire, when I chose to be alone.

Having heard such a vast deal of the ill treatment to slaves during the middle passage, I did not omit to make the nicest* observations in my power, and was I to give upon oath what those observations were, I would declare I had not the slightest reason to suspect any inhumanity or malpractice was shown towards them, through the whole voyage; on the contrary, I believe they experienced the utmost kindness and care, and after a few days, when they had recovered from sea sickness, I never saw more signs of content and satisfaction, among any set of people, in their or any other country. We had not our complement of slaves by one-third, consequently there was an abundance of room for them. Regularly every day their rooms were washed out, sprinkled with vinegar, and well dried with chafing dishes of coal; during this operation the slaves were kept on deck, where they were allowed to stay the whole day (when the weather would permit) if they liked it; in the morning before they came up, and in the evening, after they retired to rest, our deck was always scrubbed and scoured so clean that you might eat off it.

Their provisions were excellent, consisting of boiled rice and English beans, sometimes separate, sometimes mixed, cleanly dressed, and relished with a piece of beef, salt fish, or palm oil, the latter seemed generally to have the preference; a superabundance of this was their constant breakfast and supper; between the two meals each slave had a large brown biscuit, and commonly a dram of rum. Great attention was paid the sick of which, however, there were few, a mess of mutton, fowl, or some fresh meat, was daily prepared for them, and we arrived in Jamaica on the 13th of July, with the loss only of one boy who was ill before we left the coast, and the remainder of the cargo in much higher health than when they had embarked.

Whether slaves are equally well treated in common, I cannot pretend to say, but when one recollects how much the masters are interested in their well doing, it is natural to suppose such is the case, for self-interest so unalterably governs the human heart, that it alone must temper the barbarity of any man, and prevent him from committing violence on, or misusing his own property, and every cargo of slaves is more or less that of the ship's master's.

A few days before our arrival at Kingston, Mr W——lb——ce and Tom Paine* were burnt in effigy. It would have hurt me had I seen the former coupled with such an incendiary, and thus exposed to public ignominy; for, in my conscience I believe he was impelled by too keen notions of humanity, and too zealous a desire of doing good, to take so active a part as he has done for the abolition.

For a length of time I viewed the slave trade with abhorrence— considering it a blemish on every civilized nation that countenanced or supported it, and that this, our happy enlightened country was more especially stigmatized for carrying it on, than any other; but I am not ashamed to confess, those sentiments were the effect of ignorance, and the prejudice of opinion, imbibed by associating with a circle of acquaintances bigoted for the abolition, before I had acquired information enough to form any independent thoughts upon the subject, and so widely opposite are my ideas of the trade from what they were that I now think it in no shape objectionable either to morality or religion, but on the contrary consistent with both, while neither are to be found in unhappy Africa; and while three fourths of that populous country come into the world, like hogs or sheep, subject, at any moment, to be robbed of their lives by the other fourth, I say, while this is the case, I cannot think the slave trade inconsistent with any moral, or religious law. In place of invading the happiness of Africa, [it] tends to promote it, by pacifying the murdering, despotic chieftains of that country, who only spare the lives of their vassals from a desire of acquiring the manufactures of this and other nations, and by saving millions from perdition, whose future existence is rendered comfortable by the cherishing hands of Christian masters, who are not only restrained from exercising any improper or unjust cruelties over their slaves, by the fear of reciprocal injury, but by the laws of the land, and their religious tenets.

All the slaves I had an opportunity of seeing in Jamaica seemed vastly well satisfied, their conditions appeared to be far preferable to what I expected, and they discovered more cheerfulness than I ever observed the Blacks show in Africa, unless roused by liquor. . . .

How very few of our labouring poor can boast, when their mortal bodies become tenants of the grave, that their children have such certain provision secured them, and probably thousands and thousands of themselves may go supperless to bed this very night, and rise tomorrow, not knowing where to get a breakfast, or without the means of acquiring a morsel of bread to allay the gnawings of hunger—whether then are their situations, or those of slaves, having Christian masters, most preferable? The question, in my opinion, requires but little consideration.

Pray do not misinterpret my arguments, and suppose me a friend to slavery or wholly an enemy to abolishing the slave trade; lest you should, I must explain myself—by declaring from my heart I wish freedom to every creature formed by God, who knows its value, which cannot be the case with those who have not tasted its sweets; therefore, most assuredly, I must think favourably of the slave trade, while those innate prejudices, ignorance, superstition, and savageness, overspread Africa; and while the Africans feel no conviction by continuing it, but remove those errors of nature, teach them the purposes for which they were created, the ignominy of trafficking in their own flesh, and learn them to hold the lives of their fellow mortals in higher estimation, or even let me see a foundation laid, whereupon hopes itself may be built of their becoming proselytes to the doctrine of Abolition; then, no person on earth will rejoice more earnestly to see that trade suppressed in every shape; nor do I apprehend it would be impracticable, or even difficult to effect it, for I still admit what I said upwards of two years ago, to be strictly just— 'That Nature has not endowed the Africans with capacities less susceptible of improvement and cultivation, than any other part of the human race,'—and I am sure they thirst for literature; therefore, if seminaries were established on different parts of the coast, and due attention paid to the morals and manners of the rising generation, I do not question but their geniuses would ripen into ideas congenial with our own; and that posterity would behold them, emerged from that vortex of disgrace, in which they have been overwhelmed since time immemorial, establishing social, political, and commercial connections throughout the globe, and even see them blazing among the *literati* of their age.

3. EXPLORERS, 1790–1822

JAMES BRUCE, *Travels between the Years 1768 and 1773, Through Part of Africa, Syria, Egypt, and Arabia into Abyssinia, to Discover the Source of the Nile* (1790)

James Bruce (1730–94) was a Scottish laird whose profits from coal mining helped finance his travels. In 1762 Bruce became Consul-General at Algiers; he left the consulate in disarray, but learnt Arabic and gained an acquaintance with Muslim culture. In 1768 he set off to discover the Ethiopian source of the Nile, which (although Bruce refused to admit this) was not really unknown: Europeans had visited it, and one wrote a description that Bruce probably read. None the less, reaching it was no mean feat with Ethiopia in political chaos. Bruce was an impressive figure, six foot four, wearing Arab dress and speaking fluent Arabic. He ingratiated himself with local leaders, including Ethiopia's most powerful warlord, the ageing but ruthless Ras Michael. Our selections include Bruce's description of a 'Polyphemus banquet', a passage that led British readers to doubt the authenticity of his account. Later, reaching his goal, he experiences at first elation and then melancholy.

Consistent with the plan of this work, which is to describe the manners of the several nations through which I passed, good and bad, as I observed them, I cannot avoid giving some account of this Polyphemus banquet,* as far as decency will permit me; it is part of the history of a barbarous people; whatever I might wish, I cannot decline it.

In the capital, where one is safe from surprise at all times, or in the country or villages, when the rains have become so constant that the valleys will not bear a horse to pass them, or that men cannot venture far from home through fear of being surrounded and swept away by temporary torrents, occasioned by sudden showers on the mountains; in a word, when a man can say he is safe at home, and the spear and shield are hung up in the hall, a number of people of the best fashion in the villages, of both sexes, courtiers in the palace, or citizens in the town, meet together to dine between twelve and one o'clock.

A long table is set in the middle of a large room, and benches beside it for a number of guests who are invited. Tables and benches the Portuguese introduced amongst them; but bull hides, spread upon the ground, served them before, as they do in the camp and country now. A cow or a bull, one or more, as the company is numerous, is brought close to the door, and his feet strongly tied. The skin that hangs down under his chin and throat, which I think we call the dew-lap in England, is cut only so deep as to arrive at the fat, of which it totally consists, and, by the separation of a few small blood-vessels, six or seven drops of blood only fall upon the ground. They have no stone, bench, nor altar upon which these cruel assassins lay the animal's head in this operation. I should beg his pardon indeed for calling him an assassin, as he is not so merciful as to aim at the life, but, on the contrary, to keep the beast alive till he be totally eaten up. Having satisfied the Mosaical law,* according to his conception, by pouring these six or seven drops upon the ground, two or more of them fall to work; on the back of the beast, and on each side of the spine, they cut skin-deep; then putting their fingers between the flesh and the skin, they begin to strip the hide of the animal half way down his ribs, and so on to the buttock, cutting the skin wherever it hinders them commodiously to strip the poor animal bare. All the flesh on the buttocks is cut off then, and in solid, square pieces, without bones, or much effusion of blood; and the prodigious noise the animal makes is a signal for the company to sit down to table.

There are then laid before every guest, instead of plates, round cakes, if I may so call them, about twice as big as a pan-cake, and something thicker and tougher. It is unleavened bread of a sourish taste, far from being disagreeable, and very easily digested, made of a grain called teff. It is of different colours, from black to the colour of the whitest wheat-bread. Three or four of these cakes are generally put uppermost, for the food of the person opposite to whose seat they are placed. Beneath these are four or five of ordinary bread, and of a blackish kind. These serve the master to wipe his fingers upon; and afterwards the servant for bread to his dinner.

Two or three servants then come, each with a square piece of beef in their bare hands, laying it upon the cakes of teff, placed like dishes down the table, without cloth or any thing else beneath them. By this time all the guests have knives in their hands, and their men have the large crooked ones, which they put to all sorts of uses during the time of war. The women have small clasped knives, such as the worst of the kind made at Birmingham, sold for a penny each.

The company are so ranged that one man sits between two women; the man with his long knife cuts a thin piece, which would be thought a good beef-steak in England, while you see the motion of the fibres yet perfectly distinct, and alive in the flesh. No man in Abyssinia, of any fashion whatever, feeds himself, or touches his own meat. The women take the steak and cut it length-ways like strings, about the thickness of your little fingers, then crossways into square pieces, something smaller than dice. This they lay upon a piece of the teff bread, strongly powdered with black pepper, or Cayenne pepper, and fossile-salt; they then wrap it up in the teff bread like a cartridge.

In the mean time, the man having put up his knife, with each hand resting upon his neighbour's knee, his body stooping, his head low and forward, and mouth open, very like an idiot, turns to the one whose cartridge is first ready, who stuffs the whole of it into his mouth, which is so full that he is in constant danger of being choked. This is a mark of grandeur. The greater the man would seem to be, the larger piece he takes in his mouth; and the more noise he makes in chewing it, the more polite he is thought to be. They have, indeed, a proverb that says, 'Beggars and thieves only eat small pieces, or without making a noise.' Having dispatched this morsel, which he does very expeditiously, his next female neighbour holds forth another cartridge, which goes the same way, and so on till he is satisfied. He never drinks till he has finished eating; and, before he begins, in gratitude to the fair ones that fed him, he makes up two small rolls of the same kind and form; each of his neighbours open their mouths at the same time, while with each hand he puts their portion into their mouths. He then falls to drinking out of a large handsome horn; the ladies eat till they are satisfied, and then all drink together, 'Vive la Joye et la Jeunesse!'* A great deal of mirth and joke goes round, very seldom with any mixture of acrimony or ill-humour.

All this time the unfortunate victim at the door is bleeding indeed, but bleeding little. As long as they can cut off the flesh from his bones, they do not meddle with the thighs, or the parts where the great arteries are. At last they fall upon the thighs likewise; and soon after the animal, bleeding to death, becomes so tough that the canni-bals, who have the rest of it to eat, find very hard work to separate the flesh from the bones with their teeth like dogs.

In the mean time, those within are very much elevated; love lights all its fires, and every thing is permitted with absolute freedom. There is no coyness, no delays, no need of appointments or retire-ment to gratify their wishes; there are no rooms but one, in which they sacrifice both to Bacchus and to Venus.* The two men nearest the vacuum a pair have made on the bench by leaving their seats, hold their upper garment like a screen before the two that have left the bench; and, if we may judge by sound, they seem to think it as great a shame to make love in silence as to eat. Replaced in their seats again, the company drink the happy couple's health; and their example is followed at different ends of the table, as each couple is disposed. All this passes without remark or scandal, not a licentious word is uttered, nor the most distant joke upon the transaction.

[In the next excerpt Bruce is close to reaching the source of the Blue Nile, the goal of his journey.]

He* then carried me round to the south side of the church, out of the grove of trees that surrounded it. 'This is the hill,' says he, looking archly, 'that, when you was on the other side of it, was between you and the fountains of the Nile; there is no other. Look at that hillock of green sod in the middle of that watery spot; it is in that the two fountains of the Nile are to be found: Geesh* is on the face of the rock where yon green trees are. If you go the length of the fountains, pull off your shoes, as you did the other day, for these people are all Pagans, worse than those that were at the ford; and they believe in nothing that you believe, but only in this river, to which they pray every day, as if it were God; but this perhaps you may do likewise.' Half undressed as I was by loss of my sash, and throwing my shoes off, I ran down the hill, towards the little island of green sods, which was about two hundred yards distant; the whole side of the hill was thick grown over with flowers, the large bulbous roots of which appearing above the surface of the ground, and their skins coming off on treading upon them, occasioned me two very severe falls before I reached the brink of the marsh; I after this came to the island of green turf, which was in form of an altar, apparently the work of art, and I stood in rapture over the principal fountain which rises in the middle of it.

It is easier to guess than to describe the situation of my mind at that moment—standing in that spot which had baffled the genius, industry, and inquiry, of both ancients and moderns, for the course of near three thousand years. Kings had attempted this discovery at the head of armies, and each expedition was distinguished from the last, only by the difference of the numbers which had perished, and agreed alone in the disappointment which had uniformly, and without exception, followed them all. Fame, riches, and honour, had been held out for a series of ages to every individual of those myriads these princes commanded, without having produced one man capable of gratifying the curiosity of his sovereign, or wiping off this stain upon the enterprise and abilities of mankind, or adding this desideratum for the encouragement of geography. Though a mere private Briton, I triumphed here, in my own mind, over kings and their armies; and every comparison was leading nearer and nearer to presumption, when the place itself where I stood, the object of my vain-glory, suggested what depressed my short-lived triumph. I was but a few minutes arrived at the sources of the Nile, through numberless dangers and sufferings, the least of which would have overwhelmed me, but for the continual goodness and protection of Providence; I was, however, but then half through my journey, and all those dangers which I had already passed, awaited me again on my return. I found a despondency gaining ground fast upon me, and blasting the crown of laurels I had too rashly woven for myself. I resolved, therefore, to divert, till I could, on more solid reflection, overcome its progress.

I saw Strates* expecting me on the side of the hill. 'Strates,' said I, 'faithful squire! come and triumph with your Don Quixote,* at that island of Barataria, where we have most wisely and fortunately brought ourselves! come, and triumph with me over all the kings of the earth, all their armies, all their philosophers, and all their heroes!' 'Sir,' says Strates, 'I do not understand a word of what you say, and as little what you mean: you very well know I am no scholar. But you had much better leave that bog; come into the house, and look after Woldo; I fear he has something further to seek than your sash, for he has been talking with the old devil-worshipper ever since we arrived.' 'Did they speak secretly together,' said I. 'Yes, sir, they did, I assure you.' 'And in whispers, Strates!' 'Every syllable; but for that,' replied he, 'they need not have been at the pains; they under-stand one another, I suppose, and the devil, their master, under-stands them both; but as for me, I comprehend their discourse no more than if it was Greek, as they say. Greek!' says he, 'I am an ass; I should know well enough what they said if they spoke Greek.' 'Come,' said I, 'take a draught of this excellent water, and drink with me a health to his majesty King George III and a long line of princes.' I had in my hand a large cup made of a coconut shell, which I procured in Arabia, and which was brim-full. He drank to the king speedily and cheerfully, with the addition of, 'Confusion to his enemies,' and tossed up his cap with a loud huzza. 'Now, friend,' said I, 'here is to a more humble, but still a sacred name, here is to— Maria!' He asked if that was the Virgin Mary? I answered, 'In faith, I believe so, Strates.' He did not speak, but only gave a humph of disapprobation. . . .

The night of the 4th,* that very night of my arrival, melancholy reflections upon my present state, the doubtfulness of my return in safety, were I permitted to make the attempt, and the fears that even this would be refused, according to the rule observed in Abyssinia with all travellers who have once entered the kingdom; the con-sciousness of the pain that I was then occasioning to many worthy individuals, expecting daily that information concerning my situation which it was not in my power to give them; some other thoughts, perhaps, still nearer the heart than those, crowded upon my mind, and forbade all approach of sleep.

I was, at that very moment, in possession of what had, for many years, been the principal object of my ambition and wishes: indifference, which, from the usual infirmity of human nature, follows, at least for a time, complete enjoyment, had taken place of it. The marsh, and the fountains, upon comparison with the rise of many of our rivers, became now a trifling object in my sight. I remembered that magnificent scene in my own native country, where the Tweed, Clyde, and Annan, rise in one hill; three rivers, as I now thought, not inferior to the Nile in beauty, preferable to it in the cultivation of those countries through which they flow; superior, vastly superior to it in the virtues and qualities of the inhabitants, and in the beauty of its flocks crowding its pastures in peace, without fear of violence from man or beast. I had seen the rise of the Rhine and Rhone, and the more magnificent sources of the Soane; I began, in my sorrow, to treat the inquiry about the source of the Nile as a violent effort of a distempered fancy:

> What's Hecuba to him, or he to Hecuba,
> That he should weep for her?*

Grief, or despondency, now rolling upon me like a torrent; relaxed, not refreshed, by unquiet and imperfect sleep, I started from my bed in the utmost agony; I went to the door of my tent; every thing was still; the Nile, at whose head I stood, was not capable either to promote or to interrupt my slumbers, but the coolness and serenity of the night braced my nerves, and chased away those phantoms that, while in bed, had oppressed and tormented me.

It was true that numerous dangers, hardships, and sorrows had beset me through this half of my excursion; but it was still as true, that another Guide, more powerful than my own courage, health, or understanding, if any of these can be called man's own, had uniformly protected me in all that tedious half; I found my confidence not abated, that still the same Guide was able to conduct me to my now wished-for home: I immediately resumed my former fortitude, considering the Nile indeed as no more than rising from springs, as all other rivers do, but widely different in this, that it was the palm for three thousand years held out to all the nations in the world as a *detur dignissimo*,* which, in my cool hours, I had thought was worth the attempting at the risk of my life, which I had long either resolved to lose, or lay this discovery, a trophy in which I could have no competitor, for the honour of my country, at the feet of my sovereign, whose servant I was.

MUNGO PARK, *Travels in the Interior Districts of Africa* (1799)

Mungo Park (1771–1805), born on a Scottish farm, studied medicine in Edinburgh. His interest in botany (and no doubt an itch to see the world) took him to London to see his brother-in-law, who knew Sir Joseph Banks. Banks's African Association hired Park to explore West Africa. He was to start at the mouth of the Gambia River, travel inland to the Niger to see which direction it flowed, and bring back information about the country, its resources, and its people. Of the three men the Association had previously sponsored, one turned back and two died. This did not deter Park, who set off in 1795 and returned two years later, having determined that the Niger flowed east. His book, predictably, was a bestseller. Our selections begin with Park's account of his confinement at Benowm (1796), where he is held captive by nomadic Moors; escaping, he is grateful for a humble woman's hospitality. Later he is again robbed, stripped, and left in the desert. After his return from his epic journey, Park went home to Scotland, married, and set up practice as a doctor. Offered the chance to lead another government-sponsored expedition along the Niger in 1804, he left his wife and children and set off again. This larger expedition was a disaster almost from the start. A few letters remain; all we know of Park's death is that he and the remaining few of his party died on the Niger late in 1805.

[March 1796: Park is held captive by the Moorish chieftain Ali at Benowm.]

18 MARCH. Four Moors arrived from Jarra with Johnson my interpreter, having seized him before he had received any intimation of my confinement; and bringing with them a bundle of clothes that I had left at Daman Jumma's house, for my use in case I should return by the way of Jarra. Johnson was led into Ali's* tent and examined; the bundle was opened, and I was sent for, to explain the use of the different articles. I was happy, however, to find that Johnson had committed my papers to the charge of one of Daman's wives. When I had satisfied Ali's curiosity respecting the different articles of

apparel, the bundle was again tied up, and put into a large cow-skin bag, that stood in a corner of the tent. The same evening Ali sent three of his people to inform me, that there were many thieves in the neighbourhood, and that to prevent the rest of my things from being stolen, it was necessary to convey them all into his tent. My clothes, instruments, and everything that belonged to me, were accordingly carried away; and though the heat and dust made clean linen very necessary and refreshing, I could not procure a single shirt out of the small stock I had brought along with me. Ali was however disappointed, by not finding among my effects the quantity of gold and amber that he expected; but to make sure of everything, he sent the same people, on the morning following, to examine whether I had anything concealed about my person. They, with their usual rudeness, searched every part of my apparel, and stripped me of all my gold, amber, my watch, and one of my pocket compasses; I had fortunately, in the night, buried the other compass in the sand; and this, with the clothes I had on, was all that the tyranny of Ali had now left me.

The gold and amber were highly gratifying to Moorish avarice, but the pocket compass soon became an object of superstitious curiosity. Ali was very desirous to be informed, why that small piece of iron, the needle, always pointed to the Great Desert; and I found myself somewhat puzzled to answer the question. To have pleaded my ignorance would have created a suspicion that I wished to conceal the real truth from him; I therefore told him that my mother resided far beyond the sands of Sahara, and that whilst she was alive the piece of iron would always point that way, and serve as a guide to conduct me to her, and that if she was dead it would point to her grave. Ali now looked at the compass with redoubled amazement; turned it round and round repeatedly; but observing that it always pointed the same way, he took it up with great caution and returned it to me, manifesting that he thought there was something of magic in it, and that he was afraid of keeping so dangerous an instrument in his possession.

20 MARCH. This morning a council of chief men was held in Ali's tent respecting me: their decisions, though they were all unfavourable to me, were differently related by different persons. Some said that they intended to put me to death; others that I was only to lose

my right hand; but the most probable account was that which I received from Ali's own son, a boy about nine years of age, who came to me in the evening, and, with much concern, informed me that his uncle had persuaded his father to put out my eyes which they said resembled those of a cat, and that all the Bushreens* had approved of this measure. His father however, he said, would not put the sentence into execution until Fatima the queen, who was at present in the north, had seen me.

21 MARCH. Anxious to know my destiny, I went to the king early in the morning; and as a number of Bushreens were assembled, I thought this a favourable opportunity of discovering their intentions. I therefore began by begging his permission to return to Jarra; which was flatly refused: his wife, he said, had not yet seen me, and I must stay until she came to Benowm, after which I should be at liberty to depart; and that my horse, which had been taken away from me the day after I arrived, should be again restored to me. Unsatisfactory as this answer was, I was forced to appear pleased; and as there was little hope of making my escape, at this season of the year, on account of the excessive heat, and the total want of water in the woods, I resolved to wait patiently until the rains had set in, or until some more favourable opportunity should present itself—but *hope deferred maketh the heart sick*.* This tedious procrastination from day to day, and the thoughts of travelling through the Negro kingdoms in the rainy season, which was now fast approaching, made me very melancholy; and having passed a restless night, I found myself attacked in the morning by a smart fever. I had wrapped myself close up in my cloak, with a view to induce perspiration, and was asleep when a party of Moors entered the hut, and with their usual rudeness pulled the cloak from me. I made signs to them that I was sick, and wished much to sleep; but I solicited in vain: my distress was matter of sport to them, and they endeavoured to heighten it, by every means in their power. This studied and degrading insolence, to which I was constantly exposed, was one of the bitterest ingredients in the cup of captivity; and often made life itself a burden to me. In those distressing moments I have frequently envied the situation of the slave; who, amidst all his calamities, could still possess the enjoyment of his own thoughts; a happiness to which I had, for some time, been a stranger. Wearied out with such continual insults, and perhaps a

little peevish from the fever, I trembled lest my passion might unawares overleap the bounds of prudence, and spur me to some sudden act of resentment, when death must be the inevitable consequence. . . .

About this time, all the women of the camp had their feet, and the ends of their fingers, stained of a dark saffron colour. I could never ascertain whether this was done from motives of religion, or by way of ornament. The curiosity of the Moorish ladies had been very troublesome to me ever since my arrival at Benowm; and on the evening of the 25th (whether from the instigation of others, or impelled by their own ungovernable curiosity, or merely out of frolic, I cannot affirm) a party of them came into my hut, and gave me plainly to understand that the object of their visit was to ascertain, by actual inspection, whether the rite of circumcision extended to the Nazarenes (Christians) as well as to the followers of Mahomet. The reader will easily judge of my surprise at this unexpected declaration; and in order to avoid the proposed scrutiny, I thought it best to treat the business jocularly. I observed to them that it was not customary in my country to give ocular demonstration in such cases, before so many beautiful women; but that if all of them would retire, except the young lady to whom I pointed (selecting the youngest and handsomest), I would satisfy her curiosity. The ladies enjoyed the jest, and went away laughing heartily; and the young damsel herself to whom I had given the preference (though she did not avail herself of the privilege of inspection) seemed no way displeased at the compliment; for she soon afterwards sent me some meal and milk for my supper.

28 MARCH. This morning a large herd of cattle arrived from the eastward; and one of the drivers, to whom Ali had lent my horse, came into my hut with the leg of an antelope as a present, and told me that my horse was standing before Ali's tent. In a little time Ali sent one of his slaves to inform me that, in the afternoon, I must be in readiness to ride out with him, as he intended to show me to some of his women.

About four o'clock, Ali, with six of his courtiers, came riding to my hut, and told me to follow them. I readily complied. But here a new difficulty occurred: the Moors, accustomed to a loose and easy dress, could not reconcile themselves to the appearance of my nankeen breeches,* which they said were not only inelegant, but, on account of their tightness, very indecent; and as this was a visit to ladies, Ali ordered my boy to bring out the loose cloak which I had always worn since my arrival at Benowm, and told me to wrap it close round me. We visited the tents of four different ladies, at every one of which I was presented with a bowl of milk and water. All these ladies were remarkably corpulent, which is considered here as the highest mark of beauty. They were very inquisitive, and examined my hair and skin with great attention; but affected to consider me as a sort of inferior being to themselves, and would knit their brows, and seem to shudder, when they looked at the whiteness of my skin. In the course of this evening's excursion, my dress and appearance afforded infinite mirth to the company, who galloped round me as if they were baiting a wild animal; twirling their muskets round their heads, and exhibiting various feats of activity and horsemanship, seemingly to display their superior prowess over a miserable captive.

[Park has escaped from the Moors and intends to continue his search for the Niger.]

It is impossible to describe the joy that arose in my mind, when I looked around and concluded that I was out of danger. I felt like one recovered from sickness; I breathed freer; I found unusual lightness in my limbs; even the desert looked pleasant; and I dreaded nothing so much as falling in with some wandering parties of Moors, who might convey me back to the land of thieves and murderers, from which I had just escaped.

I soon became sensible, however, that my situation was very deplorable; for I had no means of procuring food, nor prospect of finding water. . . .

A little before sunset, having reached the top of a gentle rising, I climbed a high tree, from the topmost branches of which I cast a melancholy look over the barren wilderness, but without discovering the most distant trace of a human dwelling. The same dismal uniformity of shrubs and sand everywhere presented itself, and the horizon was as level and uninterrupted as that of the sea.

Descending from the tree, I found my horse devouring the stubble and brushwood with great avidity; and as I was now too faint to attempt walking, and my horse too much fatigued to carry me, I thought it but an act of humanity, and perhaps the last I should

ever have it in my power to perform, to take off his bridle and let
him shift for himself; in doing which I was suddenly affected with
sickness and giddiness; and falling upon the sand, felt as if the hour
of death was fast approaching. 'Here then,' thought I, 'after a short
but ineffectual struggle, terminate all my hopes of being useful in my
day and generation: here must the short span of my life come to an
end.' I cast (as I believed) a last look on the surrounding scene, and
whilst I reflected on the awful change that was about to take place,
this world with its enjoyments seemed to vanish from my recollection. Nature, however, at length resumed its functions; and on
recovering my senses, I found myself stretched upon the sand, with
the bridle still in my hand, and the sun just sinking behind the trees.
I now summoned all my resolution, and determined to make another
effort to prolong my existence. And as the evening was somewhat
cool, I resolved to travel as far as my limbs would carry me, in hopes
of reaching (my only resource) a watering-place. . . . About this time
I was agreeably surprised by some very vivid flashes of lightning,
followed by a few heavy drops of rain. In a little time the sand ceased
to fly, and I alighted, and spread out all my clean clothes to collect
the rain, which at length I saw would certainly fall. For more than an
hour it rained plentifully, and I quenched my thirst, by wringing and
sucking my clothes.

There being no moon, it was remarkably dark, so that I was
obliged to lead my horse, and direct my way by the compass, which
the lightning enabled me to observe. In this manner I travelled, with
tolerable expedition, until past midnight, when the lightning becoming more distant, I was under the necessity of groping along, to the
no small danger of my hands and eyes. About two o'clock my horse
started at something, and looking round, I was not a little surprised
to see a light at a short distance among the trees, and supposing it to
be a town, I groped along the sand in hopes of finding corn-stalks,
cotton, or other appearances of cultivation, but found none. As I
approached, I perceived a number of other lights in different places,
and began to suspect that I had fallen upon a party of Moors. However, in my present situation, I was resolved to see who they were, if I
could do it with safety. I accordingly led my horse cautiously towards
the light, and heard by the lowing of the cattle, and the clamorous
tongues of the herdsmen, that it was a watering-place, and most
likely belonged to the Moors. Delightful as the sound of the human

voice was to me, I resolved once more to strike into the woods, and rather run the risk of perishing of hunger, than trust myself again in their hands; but being still thirsty, and dreading the approach of the burning day, I thought it prudent to search for the wells, which I expected to find at no great distance. In this pursuit I inadvertently approached so near to one of the tents as to be perceived by a woman, who immediately screamed out. Two people came running to her assistance from some of the neighbouring tents, and passed so very near to me that I thought I was discovered; and hastened again into the woods.

About a mile from this place, I heard a loud and confused noise somewhere to the right of my course, and in a short time was happy to find it was the croaking of frogs, which was heavenly music to my ears. I followed the sound, and at daybreak arrived at some shallow muddy pools, so full of frogs that it was difficult to discern the water. The noise they made frightened my horse, and I was obliged to keep them quiet, by beating the water with a branch until he had drank. Having here quenched my thirst, I ascended a tree, and the morning being calm, I soon perceived the smoke of the watering-place which I had passed in the night; and observed another pillar of smoke east-southeast, distant 12 or 14 miles. Towards this I directed my route, and reached the cultivated ground a little before eleven o'clock; where seeing a number of Negroes at work planting corn, I inquired the name of the town; and was informed that it was a Foulah village, belonging to Ali, called Shrilla. I had now some doubts about entering it; but my horse being very much fatigued, and the day growing hot, not to mention the pangs of hunger which began to assail me, I resolved to venture; and accordingly rode up to the Dooty's* house, where I was unfortunately denied admittance, and could not obtain even a handful of corn, either for myself or horse. Turning from this inhospitable door, I rode slowly out of the town, and perceiving some low scattered huts without the walls, I directed my route towards them; knowing that in Africa, as well as in Europe, hospitality does not always prefer the highest dwellings. At the door of one of these huts, an old motherly-looking woman sat, spinning cotton; I made signs to her that I was hungry, and inquired if she had any victuals with her in the hut. She immediately laid down her distaff, and desired me, in Arabic, to come in. When I had seated myself upon the floor, she set before me a dish of kouskous, that had been left the preceding night, of which I made a tolerable meal; and in return for this kindness I gave her one of my pocket-handkerchiefs; begging at the same time, a little corn for my horse, which she readily brought me.

Overcome with joy at so unexpected a deliverance, I lifted up my eyes to heaven, and whilst my heart swelled with gratitude, I returned thanks to that gracious and bountiful Being, whose power had supported me under so many dangers, and had now spread for me a table in the wilderness.

Whilst my horse was feeding, the people began to assemble, and one of them whispered something to my hostess, which very much excited her surprise. Though I was not well acquainted with the Foulah language, I soon discovered that some of the men wished to apprehend and carry me back to Ali; in hopes, I suppose, of receiving a reward. I therefore tied up the corn; and lest anyone should suspect I had run away from the Moors, I took a northerly direction, and went cheerfully along, driving my horse before me, followed by all the boys and girls of the town. When I had travelled about two miles, and got quit of all my troublesome attendants, I struck again into the woods, and took shelter under a large tree where I found it necessary to rest myself; a bundle of twigs serving me for a bed, and my saddle for a pillow. . . .

25 AUGUST. I departed from Kooma, accompanied by two shepherds, who were going towards Sibidooloo. The road was very steep and rocky, and as my horse had hurt his feet much in coming from Bammakoo,* he travelled slowly and with great difficulty; for in many places the ascent was so sharp, and the declivities so great, that if he had made one false step, he must inevitably have been dashed to pieces. The shepherds, being anxious to proceed, gave themselves little trouble about me or my horse, and kept walking on at a considerable distance. It was about eleven o'clock, as I stopped to drink a little water at a rivulet (my companions being near a quarter of a mile before me), that I heard some people calling to each other, and presently a loud screaming, as from a person in great distress. I immediately conjectured that a lion had taken one of the shepherds, and mounted my horse to have a better view of what had happened. The noise, however, ceased; and I rode slowly towards the place from whence I thought it had proceeded, calling out; but without receiving any answer. In a little time, however, I perceived one of the

shepherds lying among the long grass near the road; and though I could see no blood upon him, I concluded he was dead. But when I came close to him, he whispered to me to stop; telling me that a party of armed men had seized upon his companion, and shot two arrows at himself, as he was making his escape. I stopped to consider what course to take, and looking round, saw at a little distance a man sitting upon the stump of a tree: I distinguished also the heads of six or seven more, sitting among the grass, with muskets in their hands. I had now no hopes of escaping, and therefore determined to ride forward towards them. As I approached them, I was in hopes they were elephant hunters; and by way of opening the conversation, inquired if they had shot anything; but without returning an answer, one of them ordered me to dismount; and then, as if recollecting himself, waved with his hand for me to proceed. I accordingly rode past, and had with some difficulty crossed a deep rivulet, when I heard somebody holloa; and looking behind, saw those I had taken for elephant hunters running after me, and calling out to me to turn back. I stopped until they were all come up; when they informed me, that the king of the Foulahs had sent them on purpose to bring me, my horse, and every thing that belonged to me, to Fooladoo; and that therefore I must turn back, and go along with them. Without hesitating a moment, I turned round and followed them, and we travelled together near a quarter of a mile, without exchanging a word; when coming to a dark place in the wood, one of them said, in the Mandingo language, this place will do; and immediately snatched my hat from my head. Though I was by no means free of apprehension, yet I resolved to show as few signs of fear as possible, and therefore told them that unless my hat was returned to me, I should proceed no further. But before I had time to receive an answer, another drew his knife, and seizing upon a metal button which remained upon my waistcoat, cut it off, and put it into his pocket. Their intentions were now obvious; and I thought that the easier they were permitted to rob me of everything, the less I had to fear. I therefore allowed them to search my pockets without resistance, and examine every part of my apparel, which they did with the most scrupulous exactness. But observing that I had one waistcoat under another, they insisted that I should cast them both off; and at last, to make sure work, they stripped me quite naked. Even my half boots (though the sole of one of them was tied on to my foot with a broken bridle-rein) were minutely inspected. Whilst they were examining the plunder, I begged them, with great earnestness, to return my pocket compass; but when I pointed it out to them, as it was lying on the ground, one of the banditti, thinking I was about to take it up, cocked his musket and swore that he would lay me dead upon the spot, if I presumed to put my hand upon it. After this, some of them went away with my horse, and the remainder stood considering whether they should leave me quite naked, or allow me something to shelter me from the sun. Humanity at last prevailed: they returned me the worst of the two shirts, and a pair of trousers; and as they went away, one of them threw back my hat, in the crown of which I kept my memorandums; and this was probably the reason they did not wish to keep it. After they were gone, I sat for some time, looking around me with amazement and terror. Whichever way I turned, nothing appeared but danger and difficulty. I saw myself in the midst of a vast wilderness, in the depth of the rainy season; naked and alone; surrounded by savage animals, and men still more savage. I was five hundred miles from the nearest European settlement. All these circumstances crowded at once on my recollection; and I confess that my spirits began to fail me. I considered my fate as certain, and that I had no alternative but to lie down and perish. The influence of religion, however, aided and supported me. I reflected that no human prudence, or foresight, could possibly have averted my present sufferings. I was indeed a stranger in a strange land, yet I was still under the protecting eye of that Providence who has condescended to call himself the stranger's friend. At this moment, painful as my reflections were, the extraordinary beauty of a small moss, in fructification, irresistibly caught my eye. I mention this to show from what trifling circumstances the mind will sometimes derive consolation; for though the whole plant was not larger than the top of one of my fingers, I could not contemplate the delicate conformation of its roots, leaves, and capsula, without admiration. Can that Being (thought I), who planted, watered, and brought to perfection, in this obscure part of the world, a thing which appears of so small importance, look with unconcern upon the situation and sufferings of creatures formed after his own image? Surely not! Reflections like these, would not allow me to despair. I started up, and disregarding both hunger and fatigue, travelled forwards, assured that relief was at hand; and I was not disappointed. In a

short time I came to a small village, at the entrance of which I
overtook the two shepherds who had come with me from Kooma.
They were much surprised to see me; for they said they never
doubted that the Foulahs, when they had robbed, had murdered me.
Departing from this village, we travelled over several rocky ridges,
and at sunset arrived at Sibidooloo, the frontier town of the kingdom
of Manding.

JOHN BARROW, *An Account of Travels into the Interior of
Southern Africa in the Years 1797 and 1798* (1801)

John Barrow (1764–1848) accompanied Lord George Macartney on his
famous diplomatic mission to China in 1793, after which Barrow published *Travels in China* (1804) and served as Macartney's private secretary
on a mission to the Cape of Good Hope. Sent out to survey the colony
and reconcile the Xhosa inhabitants with the Dutch colonists, or Boers,
Barrow covered over a thousand miles on foot, horseback, and covered
wagon. He later became Second Secretary of the Admiralty, a post he
occupied for forty years. In this position he influenced government-
sponsored exploration in Africa and (his particular interest) the Arctic. He
founded the Royal Geographical Society in 1830. Our selections narrate
an expedition intended to 'bring about a conversation with' San leaders.
Against his instructions, Barrow's Boer companions open fire; he tries to
patch things up with gifts. He later expresses regret and recommends a
change in policy by the colonial government.

In the course of our long hunting excursions, several kraals,* or dwell-
ing-places of Bosjesmans,* had been seen, but all of them deserted;
and from many circumstances it was evident that most of them had
recently been evacuated. Their inhabitants, no doubt, had fled at the
appearance of so large a party of Europeans, which they could consider in no other light than that of an enemy. The commandant now
announced to his people that for a time all hunting parties must be
suspended, and that the same regular order and obedience to commands should be observed as in their usual expeditions. He assured
us that unless this plan was adopted we might pass through the heart
of the Bosjesmans' country without seeing a human creature, as there
was little doubt of their being already well apprised of our approach.
This in fact was the principal object of our present journey, that

we might be eye-witnesses of the manner in which the farmers conducted their expeditions against these miserable set of beings. I thought it, however, a necessary step to make a previous stipulation with the commandant, that the extent of hostilities against these savages should be that of surrounding one of their kraals; that after this had been done we should act only on the defensive; and he was enjoined to deliver to his people a most serious charge not to fire a single shot unless it should be found absolutely necessary for their own personal security; for that the sole object of our journey was to bring about, if possible, a conversation with some of the chiefs of this people. On these conditions, a party, consisting of six farmers and as many Hottentots,* were ordered out after sunset to reconnoitre. . . .

The following morning, at daybreak, one of the scouting party, attended by a Hottentot, returned with intelligence that they had discovered from a high hill several fires at the bottom of a narrow defile about twenty miles to the eastward. In consequence of this information we remained still at our encampment the whole day, and at night proceeded towards the place where the fires had been seen. Previous to this movement the colonists prepared themselves for the enterprise by singing three or four hymns out of William Sluiter, and drinking each a glass of brandy.

Travelling slowly along, and without noise, till about one o'clock, we halted the waggons, and, taking the other hymn and glass of brandy, mounted horse and advanced towards the hill, where the rest of the reconnoitring party lay concealed, in order to observe the motions of the Bosjesmans. . . .

About two o'clock in the morning we joined the scouting party at the base of this mountain. They and their horses had been exposed the whole of the preceding day to the scorching rays of the sun, not having dared to move from the spot lest they should be discovered and cut off by the Bosjesmans; and they had but just returned from giving their horses a little water, near fifteen miles off, in the Sea-Cow river. They gave information that during the day vast numbers of the savages had appeared upon the plain digging up roots: that they came from different quarters, and in so many groups that they concluded there must be several hordes in the neighbourhood of this spot: that the nearest, which it was the intention to surprise, was within two or three miles.

Having halted here a couple of hours, in order to arrive at the mouth of the defile, in which the kraal was situated, just at the first dawn of day, the march was continued in solemn silence. As we entered the defile it was perceived that at the opposite extremity a hill stretched across, admitting a pass on either side; the party there-fore divided into three companies in order to possess all the passes; and they again closed together slowly towards the hill, at the foot of which the horde was supposed to lie. A Hottentot, having ascended one of the heights, waved his hat as a signal of discovery, and then pointed to the spot where the horde was situated. We instantly set off on full gallop, and in a moment found ourselves in the middle of the kraal. Day was but just beginning to break; and by the faint light I could discover only a few straw-mats, bent each between two sticks, into a semicircular form; but our ears were stunned with a horrid scream like the war-hoop of savages; the shrieking of women and the cries of children proceeded from every side. I rode up with the commandant and another farmer, both of whom fired upon the kraal. I immediately expressed to the former my very great surprise that he, of all others, should have been the first to break a condition which he had solemnly promised to observe, and that I had expected from him a very different kind of conduct. 'Good God!' he exclaimed, 'have you not seen a shower of arrows falling among us?' I certainly had seen neither arrows nor people, but had heard enough to pierce the hardest heart; and I peremptorily insisted that neither he nor any of his party should fire another shot. In justification of their conduct they began to search on the ground for the arrows, a search in which they were encouraged to continue, in order to give the poor wretches a little time to scramble away among the detached fragments of rocks and the shrubbery that stood on the side of the heights. On their promises I could place no sort of dependence, knowing that, like true sportsmen when game was sprung, they could not withhold their fire. Of this I was presently convinced by the report of a musket on the opposite side of the hill; and, on riding round the point, I perceived a Bosjesman lying dead upon the ground. It appeared that as one of our party, who could speak their language, was endeavouring to prevail upon the savages to come down from the heights, this Bosjesman had stolen close to him behind a rock, and was taking deliberate aim with his drawn bow, which another of the colonists perceiving, levelled his musket and shot him dead. It had been hoped the affair would happily have been accomplished without the shedding of human blood, and that the views of the expedition would have met with no interruption from an accident of such a nature. They soon perceived, however, that there was no attempt to pursue them up the heights, which could easily have been done; but that on the contrary the party had laid down their arms and turned their horses out to graze. Upon this, in a short space of time, several little children came down upon the plain. Among these we distributed some biscuits and other trifles, and then suffered them to return: presently afterwards the women and young girls, to the number of thirty or forty, came towards us, not without symptoms of fear. These being treated in the same manner, were sent back to desire their husbands would also come down in order to receive a present of tobacco. The men, however, had less confidence in the Christians than the women. They hovered a long time round the summit of the hill, doubting what step they should take; and the women had gone and returned, at least a dozen times, before they were able to prevail upon one man to descend; and when at last he ventured to come down, he approached us half-laughing, half-crying, trembled and acted just like a frightened child. A large piece of tobacco was immediately given to him, and he was sent back to his companions to let them know there was also a present for each of them. Three others mustered resolution to come down to us, but no more chose to venture themselves. The manner indeed in which their village was attacked was certainly not calculated to inspire them with much confidence. On the contrary, it was so directly hostile as perfectly to justify their shooting a volley of arrows among us, which was afterwards found to be the case, as the commandant had asserted. The conclusion of the business, however, must have appeared to them very different from what, on former occasions, they had always experienced, when those who escaped from immediate death were incessantly pursued and fired upon, and their wives and children seized and carried away into slavery. In this instance they were well treated, and left at full liberty to remain with us or to depart. The women all stayed behind; but three of the men accompanied us to the waggons, where they continued for several days. We had wished to speak with the captain or chief of the horde, but they assured us there was no such person; that everyone was master of his own family, and acted entirely without control, being at liberty to remain with, or quit, the society as it might best suit them.

Little satisfactory could be obtained from those who returned with us to the waggons. They insisted on their innocence, by asserting that their horde, so long as they had composed a part of it, had never committed depredations on the colonists, but had always remained about the spot we found them, where they subsisted by the chase, and upon the roots of the earth. Appearances certainly were much in their favour; no bones nor horns of animals were found near the horde; no skins but those of young elands, springboks, tigers, and jackals. One woman in the whole party had a single sheep's skin thrown over her shoulders, which was very industriously pointed out by the farmers as a proof of their having suffered from this horde.

Before the men were sent away from the waggons a large present was made to each of tobacco, beads, knives, flints, and steels; and they were desired to tell all their countrymen they should happen to see, that whenever they should desist from stealing the cattle of the colonists, and should come to any of the farm-houses without bow and arrows, or other weapons, and say they were in want, as many or more sheep should be given to them than they could possibly obtain by plunder: that our present journey into their country was for no other intention than to give them an opportunity of putting a final stop to all expeditions against them, if, by a change of conduct, they were inclined to avail themselves of it; and they were assured that not a single shot would have been fired upon their horde had they not first discharged their arrows upon the farmers. Having remained with us very contentedly for a few days, they returned to their kraal highly pleased with the treatment they had met with, and with the presents they had received.

The horde or kraal consisted of five-and-twenty huts, each made of a small grass-mat bent into a semicircle, and fastened down between two sticks; open before, but closed behind with a second mat. They were about three feet high and four feet wide, and the ground in the middle was dug out like the nest of an ostrich; a little grass strewed in this hollow served as their bed, in which they seemed to have lain coiled round in the manner of some quadrupeds. It appeared that it was customary for the elderly men to have two wives, one old and past child-bearing, and the other young; that no degree of consanguinity prevented a matrimonial connection, except between brothers and sisters, parents and children. One of these miserable huts served for a whole family. The population of the horde was calculated to amount to about a hundred and fifty persons. They possessed no sort of animals except dogs, which, unlike those of the Kaffers,* were remarkably fat. . . .

The men were entirely naked, and most of the women nearly so. Their only covering was a belt of springbok's skin, with the part that was intended to hang before cut into long threads like those before mentioned to be worn by some of the Hottentot women; but the filaments were so small and thin that they answered no sort of use as a covering; nor indeed did the females, either old or young, seem to feel any sense of shame in appearing before us naked. Whether in the confusion and hurry they had scrambled among the rocks before they had time to adjust this their only dress, or whether they were indifferent about concealing any particular part of their bodies, their aprons happened to be very carelessly put on. The fringed part of some was hanging behind; of others, on the exterior part of the thigh; and some had fallen down as low as the knee. Yet they were not entirely without some notions of finery. A few had caps made of the skins of asses, in form not unlike helmets; and bits of copper, or shells, or beads, were hanging in the neck, suspended from their little curling tufts of hair. All the men had the cartilage of the nose bored, through which they wore a piece of wood or a porcupine's quill.

Whether considered as to their persons, turn of mind, or way of life, the Bosjesmans are certainly a most extraordinary race of people. In their persons they are extremely diminutive. The tallest of the men measured only four feet nine inches, and the tallest woman four feet four inches. About four feet six inches is said to be the middle size of the men, and four feet that of the women. One of these that had several children measured only three feet nine inches. Their color, their hair, and the general turn of their features, evidently denote a common origin with the Hottentots, though the latter, in point of personal appearance, has the advantage by many degrees. The Bosjesmans, indeed, are amongst the ugliest of all human beings. The flat nose, high cheek-bones, prominent chin, and concave visage, partake much of the apeish character, which their keen eye, always in motion, tends not to diminish. . . .

The temper of a Bosjesman is widely different from that of a Hottentot who lives in the colony. The latter, for a life of indolence, would barter all that he possessed in the world; a state of inactivity would be to the former intolerable. The powers of the mind, in one, are languid, and difficulty brought into action; in the other, they seem capable of great exertion. Their mechanical skill appeared in their arrows, which were finished with great neatness; in the baskets placed in the rivers for the purpose of taking fish, ingeniously contrived, and very well executed; in the mats of grass, of which their huts were composed; and in their imitations of different animals, designed on the smooth faces of the rocks. . . .

It were greatly to be wished that the peasantry would see the policy of putting an end to their expeditions against this miserable people, and adopt in their place a lenient mode of treatment. They might not perhaps succeed in reclaiming them at once from their rooted habits of life; but their hatred towards the colonists, which aims at their lives, might certainly be abated. The first step towards it would be to abolish the inhuman practice of carrying into captivity their women and children. This, in fact, is the 'lethalis arundo'* that rankles in their breasts, and excites that spirit of vengeance which they perpetually denounce against the Christians. The condition of those who are made prisoners by the farmers is, in fact, much worse than that of slavery; for, not being transferable property, they have no claims upon their interest. . . .

Forty years ago, it appears from living testimony, the Bosjesmans frequented the colony boldly and openly, begged, and stole, and were troublesome, just as the Kaffers now are; but they never attempted the life of anyone. They proceeded not to this extremity until the government had unwisely and unjustly suffered the peasantry to exercise an unlimited power over the lives of those who were taken prisoners. It failed, at the same time, to fix any bounds to the extent of the expeditions made against them, which certainly ought not to go beyond the limits of the colony. Nothing could be more unwarrantable, because cruel and unjust, than the attack made by our party upon the kraal; and the only palliation it could admit of is the consideration of the end it was meant to answer. The poor wretches were peaceably sleeping under their humble covering of mats, and in the heart of their own country, far removed from the boundary of the colony. The inroads of these savages would much more effectually be checked by charging them boldly, whenever they should be known to have passed the limits, but not to pursue them into their own country. This, however, would not answer the object of the farmer, which is that of procuring children. To attend his numerous flocks and herds, he must have many people; and Hottentots are now so scarce that a sufficient number is not to be had! These, too, must be paid wages; but the poor Bosjesman has nothing except his sheep-skin and his meat.

JAMES K. TUCKEY, *Narrative of an Expedition to Explore the River Zaire, Usually Called the Congo, in Southern Africa, in 1816, Under the Direction of Captain J. K. Tuckey, R.N.* (1818)

James K. Tuckey (1776–1816), an Irishman, joined the Royal Navy as a teenager and was made lieutenant at the age of 24. He served in India and led an expedition to New South Wales before spending nearly ten years in Verdun as a French prisoner of war. He married a fellow prisoner, had several children, and wrote a book, *Marine Geography and Statistics* (1815). Whether because of his aptitude as a geographer or as recompense for his years in prison—and despite a history of chronic liver disease— Tuckey got command of an expedition to explore the Congo. Leaving a store ship in the lower river, Tuckey's vessel, the *Congo*, pushed upriver to the falls. He led a land party above them, but his health collapsed and he had to turn back; he died 'of exhaustion, rather than of disease', writes the editor of his *Narrative*. Our selections include part of the Admiralty instructions to the expedition, signed by Barrow, Tuckey's memo to his crew, and the final section of his journal.

[Admiralty instructions]

It is almost unnecessary to observe to you, how important it will be to keep a journal of your proceedings . . . You should be as circumstantial as possible in describing, in your own, the general appearance of the country, its surface, soil, animals, vegetables, and minerals; everything that relates to the population; the peculiar manners, customs, language, government, and domestic economy of the various tribes of people through which you will probably have to pass.

The following, however, will be among the most important subjects on which it will be more immediately your province, assisted by your officers, to endeavour to obtain information.

The general nature of the climate as to heat, cold, moisture, winds, rains, and periodical seasons. The temperature regularly registered from Fahrenheit's thermometer, as observed at two or three periods of the day.

The direction of the mountains, their names, general appearance as to shape, whether detached or continuous in ranges.

The main branches of rivers, their names, direction, velocity, breadth, and depth.

The animals, whether birds, beasts, or fishes, insects, reptiles, etc. distinguishing those animals that are wild, from those that are domesticated.

The vegetables, and particularly those that are applicable to any useful purposes. . . .

Minerals, any of the precious metals or stones; how used, and how valued, by the natives.

The description and characteristic difference of the several tribes of people.

The occupations and means of subsistence. . . .

A circumstantial account of such articles, if any, as might be advantageously imported into Great Britain, or her colonies, and those which would be required by the natives in exchange for them.

The state of the arts or manufactures, and their comparative perfection in different tribes.

A vocabulary of the language spoken by every tribe. . . .

The condition of the people, as far as can be ascertained; what protection the chief, or the laws afford them; what is the state of slavery among them: whether wars are carried on for the purpose of making slaves: how their prisoners are treated; how disposed of; and every possible information that can be collected, as to the manner and extent to which the slave trade is conducted with Europeans: who those Europeans are; where residing: how their agents are employed; what the articles of barter are; in what manner the slaves are brought down to the coast, etc. . . .

The genius and disposition of the people, as to talent, mental and bodily energy, habits of industry or idleness, love, hatred, hospitality, etc. The nature of their amusements, their diseases, and remedies, etc.

Their religion, and objects of worship, their religious ceremonies; and the influence of religion on their moral character and conduct.

A description of the manners, appearance and condition of any Mahomedans* that may be found in any of the tribes in southern Africa.

What written or traditionary records may exist among the latter; any facsimiles of their written character, or copies of any drawings or paintings they may have attempted would be desirable.

[Tuckey's memo to his crew]

As we were now approaching the scene of action, I thought it right to issue to the officers and naturalists the following memorandum of regulations for our conduct while in the country. . . .

'Though we are not to expect to find in the natives of Africa, even in the most remote region, that state of savage nature which marks the people of other newly discovered countries, with whom the impulse of the moment is the only principle of action, it is nevertheless highly necessary to be guarded in our intercourse with them; that, by showing we are prepared to resist aggression, we may leave no hope of success, or no inducement to commit it.

'In doing this, it is, however, by no means necessary to exhibit marked appearance of suspicion, which would probably only serve to induce the hostility it seemed to fear; it is, on the contrary, easy to combine the shew of being guarded, with marks of the greatest confidence. . . .

'Although we may expect to find the idea of property fully known to all the people we shall have intercourse with, it is not to be the less expected that they will be addicted to theft, the punishment of which in savages has been one of the most frequent causes of the unhappy catastrophes that have befallen navigators; it is therefore urgently advised, not to expose anything unnecessarily to the view of the natives, or to leave any object in their way that may tempt their avidity. . . .

'A great cause of the disputes of navigators with uncivilized people is in unauthorized freedoms with their females; and hence every species of curiosity or familiarity with them, which may create jealousy in the men, is to be strictly avoided; taking it for granted, that, in a state of society where the favours of the women are considered as a saleable or transferable commodity by the men, the latter will be the first to offer them.

'As one of the objects of the expedition is to view and describe manners, it will be highly improper to interrupt, in any manner, the ceremonies of the natives, however they may shock humanity or create disgust; and it is equally necessary, in the pursuits of the different naturalists, to avoid offending the superstitions of the natives in any of their venerated objects.'

[Tuckey's journal]

12 SEPTEMBER. With great difficulty got a foomoo* and four of his boys to go down for two fathoms* each, paid beforehand, and a canoe to ferry us across the creek to Condo Yango. A long palaver about a pig detained us till nine o'clock. Discovered that the barometer was stolen. Purchased ten fowls for empty bottles. Found the river so greatly risen that the creeks we had crossed in our way upwards were now filled, and we were obliged to go high up and cross them on fallen trees.

At noon we dined at the brook Sooloo Looanzaza, and at three encamped at Cainga to wait for Dawson, who was obliged to be supported by two men. I now found that besides the barometer we had lost our silver spoons, great coat, remnant of cloth, etc. In the night we were driven out of the tent by ants.

13 SEPTEMBER. This morning we found that our bearers had gone off during the night, and left us in the lurch. Got a foomoo and four men of Cainga to go on, for two fathoms each; ascended the Mango Enzooma hill, the highest yet passed, covered with fern; and the transition from it between the mica and clay slate.

At eleven reached the brook Looloo: at three got to Keilinga, where we could procure nothing by purchase. Here we found the Mafook of Inga, who informed us that a goat which we were carrying was fetished* at Inga, and that we must not carry it there on any account, dead or alive, or even a bit of its skin; we therefore exchanged it for two fowls, which we left for Dawson's use, and pushed on.

At five we arrived at Inga, where the Inga men had reported that one half of us had been drowned in canoes, and the rest killed by black bushmen. Greeted with Izacalla moudela by the people, but greatly shocked on learning the deaths and sickness on board the Congo.

14 SEPTEMBER. Sent off Mr Hawkey with ten men and as many loads of baggage: though ill myself, I intended to proceed; but Dr Smith and two of our people are too ill to be moved; remained therefore this day, and passed it most miserably.

After dark, the corporal of marines arrived with intelligence of Galwey's death. I passed a miserable and sleepless night, and at daylight mustered the boys with the intention of proceeding; but after paying them two fathoms each, the usual price, they refused to go without receiving three. Gave them three; being very weak myself and wishing to get on before the sun became too hot, I set off with Dr Smith, leaving Mr Hawkey behind to bring on the people; at noon he joined me, and from him I learnt that he had a terrible business to get the people off.

Four of the bearers of the sick men ran away and carried off a canteen of brandy and a case of preserved meat: a squabble for salt. Could not get a single fowl for eight bunches of beads. Terrible march; worse to us than the retreat from Moscow.*

Arrived at Cooloo at five p.m. Hospitality of these people. Got a goat from the Chenoo,* fowls and eggs; all ran cheerfully to assist us; brought us grass for our beds; water; wood for our fire.

At dark Dawson arrived; Inga men left him on the return of the people. Butler did not come in. Passed a good night; it rained hard, but the tent kept it out.

15 SEPTEMBER. At daylight sent two men to wait for Butler. Dr Smith very ill; Dawson better.

Having arranged everything for the men, I set off at eight a.m., leaving Mr Hawkey to bring up the sick. Reached the river at eleven. Thank God for his great mercies in bringing me on thus far!

Found no canoes; waited till two o'clock, when I learnt that the Chenoo of Bibbi, in whose district the landing place is, had forbidden his people to furnish any more canoes; according to some, on account of the commanding officer on board the Congo having ill treated one of the canoe men, who went down with the sick; while others said it was because he was not paid his customs for using his landing place; and I was told I must send my interpreter to him with a present before any canoes would be given. As I knew this would occupy the whole of the next day in palavering, and as Dr Smith, Dawson, and Butler, were so very ill, that an hour's delay in reaching the ship might prove fatal, I seized all the canoes, and a foomoo.

16 SEPTEMBER. Unable at daylight to procure any canoe men, I set off with our own people, and at 3 p.m. reached the Congo.

Terrible report of the state on board: coffins. . . .

17 SEPTEMBER. At daylight sent off all the sick in double boats, as well as the people who had been up with me, to the transport; hired fifteen black men to assist in taking the Congo down the river below Fetish rocks. The river bordered by a level plain, four miles deep, to hills of little elevation. Good place for a settlement.

Mangroves commence at the east end of Tall Trees island.

Muddiness of water and red colour begins at the . . . land, which latter is a bar of sand covered with clay, and under water when the river is at its height.

Extraordinary quiet rise of the river shows it, I think, to issue chiefly from some lake, which had received almost the whole of its water from the north of the line.

Commencement of its rise was first observed above Yellala, on the 1st of September; on the 17th of September, at Tall Trees it had risen seven feet, but the velocity was not at all increased.

Hypothesis confirmed. The water . . .

Mistaken idea of anchoring ships out of the current for any length of time; the current always creating a current of air.

Palm wine in the dry season only. Palm trees, when two years old, begin to give out wine.

18 SEPTEMBER. Reached the transport; found her people all in health; her decks crowded with goats, fowls, pigeons, pumpkins, plantains, flaskets of palm wine; in short, the greatest appearance of abundance.

The difference of atmosphere perceptible between this place and Embomma. Fresh sea breezes.

Mangrove trees fit for?

No fish but cat-fish. Few hippopotami below Yellala.

Quartz sand in vast quantities on the banks of the river; must come from a great distance.

Maucaya . . . child, child-birth.

Different foods fetished. Children fetished for eating the food which their fathers had been forbidden to eat. Women fetished for eating meat the same day that it is killed—with the men. When a man applies to a Gangam* for a domestic fetish, he is at the same time instructed from what foods he must abstain; some from fowls, others from plantains.

Lindy N'Congo resides at Banza Congo, far inland to the south.

In war the Chenoo of Embomma musters 1,000 muskets; fire into the enemies' houses at night. Cut off the heads of the prisoners and burn the bodies. All the women sent away before a war is begun. Some Foomoo makes up the business, and each party keeps the trophies, and puts up with the losses. All the men of a Chenooship obliged to go to war. Commanded by the Macaya, next brother to the Chenoo, and civil magistrate; Mambouk, relative of the Chenoo, war minister.

Chenoo of Inga dead, blind man substituted.

Dress. Old men, long thin aprons; young men, cat-skins; tiger cat most valuable; each costs a piece; common cat skins at Embomma for six fathoms.

Canoes made of *camba fuma* (bombax).

Spoons, and mouthpieces of pipes made of *lemanzao*, and *pacabanda*.

Flocks of flamingos going to the south denote the approach of the rains.

WILLIAM J. BURCHELL, *Travels in the Interior of Southern Africa* (1822)

William Burchell (1782?–1863) was a schoolmaster and botanist on the Atlantic island of St Helena. There he met the Dutch governor of the Cape, who helped launch his expedition (1810–16) to explore South Africa and document its natural history. In Cape Town Burchell equipped a wagon and hired ten Khoikhoin (called Hottentots), his sole companions and assistants on his travels, all of whom he replaced along the way. He learned the Afrikaans language: 'To be qualified for judging of the character of these inhabitants', he writes, 'it is not enough to have mingled with the better part of society; the Boors [Boers] must be heard, the Hottentots must be heard, and the slaves must be heard.' Burchell trekked well over a thousand miles, north-east from Cape Town into the interior and down to the Indian Ocean, drawing and collecting all the way. Not content with one continent, in 1825 he set out across South America, but had to go home to take care of his ailing mother. In our selections Burchell expresses aesthetic disappointment at the village of Klaarwater and narrates negotiations with a village chief over the sale of a gun.

1 OCTOBER 1811. I accompanied the three missionaries round the village, to take a cursory view of the different parts of it; the huts of

the Hottentots; their own dwellings; the house for religious meetings and school instruction; their storehouse, and their garden. When I considered that this little community, and the spot on which I stood, were nearly eight hundred miles deep in the interior of Africa, I could not but look upon every object of their labours with double interest; and received, at that moment, a pleasure, unalloyed by the knowledge of a single untoward circumstance. The Hottentots peeped out of their huts to have a look at me; and I fancied they appeared glad at having one more white man amongst them.

I paid a visit to my fellow-travellers, Mrs Anderson and Mrs Kramer, to whom I was under obligation for much friendly attention during our journey; and found them in their cottages, busily employed in arranging and disposing of the stores they had brought from the Cape. They were assisted in their domestic work by Hottentot women, very cleanly dressed in clothes of European fashion and materials. . . .

From the moment when I decided on making Klaarwater in my way to the interior, I naturally endeavoured to form, in my own mind, some picture of it; and I know not by what mistake it arose, that I should conceive the idea of its being a picturesque spot* surrounded by trees and gardens, with a river running through a neat village, where a tall church stood, a distant beacon to mark that Christianity had advanced thus far into the wilds of Africa. But the first glance now convinced me how false may oftentimes be the notions which men form of what they have not seen. The trees of my imagination vanished, leaving nothing in reality but a few which the missionaries themselves had planted; the church sunk to a barn-like building of reeds and mud; the village was merely a row of half a dozen reed cottages; the river was but a rill; and the situation an open, bare, and exposed place, without any appearance of a garden, excepting that of the missionaries.

It would be very unfair towards those who have devoted themselves to a residence in a country, where they are cut off from communication with civilized society, and deprived of all its comforts, to attribute this low state of civilization and outward improvement, to a want of solicitude on their part. Their continual complaint, indeed, was of the laziness of the Hottentots, and of the great difficulty there had always been in persuading them to work, either on the buildings or in the garden; and in this complaint there was too much truth.

My disappointment at the appearance of the place arose from expecting, perhaps, too much. Yet, notwithstanding its discouraging appearance, this colony of Hottentots, and its different outposts, is a field in which the seeds of civilization and religion may be sown with a probability of success; but I will not say that this is to be accomplished without expense, or without the employment of proper and reasonable means, and the adopting of some plan grounded on a knowledge of human nature.

Our whole party being now finally assembled at the termination of our long journey, we all, on this occasion, dined together; and the school-room was found to be the only place large enough for the purpose. A dinner that would have become a table in Cape Town was served up; and two or three Hottentot women, who formed part of their domestic establishment, waited on us in a very attentive and proper manner. The circumstance of our being the only white people in this part of the world, and all seated round the same table, together with the idea of our being in the heart of a wilderness, and surrounded only by savage nations, created in me some peculiar feelings, and a strange interest in every thing that was passing, and in all that I saw about me.

[Here Burchell is negotiating with Chief Mattivi of Litakun village over Mattivi's request to buy a gun, which Burchell very much does not want to sell him.]

13 JULY 1812. When they had drunk all the coffee, they seemed inclined to enter into conversation. Mattivi commenced by saying, that Mulihában his father, a short time before he died, had desired him to be kind to all his brothers, and to take every care of them; that they were numerous, and all depended on him for protection. He then remarked that Mulihában was always a great friend to white men. To which I replied: Yes, I had already heard that he was, and that the white men would therefore lament, on receiving the news of his death; but that when I should inform them that Mattivi was equally their friend, they would rejoice again, and white men would again come to see him.

These remarks, and a few others of the same kind, were made in a desultory manner, and appeared to have no mutual connection, nor any particular object: they were merely meant as an introduction to another more important subject which, it seems, had occupied their thoughts long before my arrival, and had been a matter of national consultation. It had previously pressed so much on their minds that it had evidently been resolved to make it the very first point of discussion, as soon as I had reached their town. The Chief, therefore, informed me that since Afrikaander* had now supplied the Bamuchárs with guns, he could no longer consider himself safe in this part of the country, unless he could procure similar arms; and that as soon as this most desirable object was obtained, he intended to remove his town and all his people nearer towards the Gariep, to the spot where it stood at the time of his birth. He expressed himself highly displeased with the Klaarwater people, because they had hitherto refused to sell him any of their muskets; but that now I was come among them, they expected I should be their friend and should let them have one of mine, as they saw I had many, and could therefore easily spare one out of so great a number.

So unexpected a demand, and of such a nature, for it had more the character of a demand than of a request, and made on the very moment of my arrival, was a circumstance exceedingly unpleasant, as the earnestness with which it was made convinced me at once of the difficulty of the situation in which it placed me. I had no more than just muskets enough to arm all my men, and three even of these belonged to the Hottentots themselves, who had preferred bringing their own guns as being more accustomed to them. It was putting into the hands of this people a weapon which in the event of any future misunderstanding would be used against ourselves; so that we might lose our lives by the very instrument which we had brought for the purpose of defending them: besides which, ammunition would also be required. If I refused giving it, I must run the risk of its being taken either by force or by stealth. I had but an instant for reflection; my answer must follow the question. I resolved not to grant his request; although I foresaw that my refusal would produce some unpleasant consequences.

I therefore replied that I had no more than one for each of my men, and that if I were to give up any, some of my own people must go unarmed, which, as he well knew, was a thing not to be ventured in travelling through a country inhabited by *Baróba* (Bushmen); that as we were but very few in number, we had the greater necessity for retaining our arms for our own defence; that they were not all my own, and must be taken back to the colony again; that besides this, he saw that we had no food but what was procured by hunting, and must be well aware that we had in these countries, no other means of support, consequently that our lives depended on our guns, which was not the case with them, as they had abundance of corn, milk, and cattle. And I concluded by assuring him that I felt the most friendly sentiments towards him and all his people, otherwise I should not have come to see him; that if I had more muskets than were wanted, I would willingly let him have one, but that it was impossible to think of disarming my own men.

All these arguments, which they must have had discernment enough to think perfectly reasonable, appeared to have no effect in inducing them to relinquish their demand. They continued to talk on the subject, with the same confidence as though they had not heard what I had said; and both Mattivi and Mollemmi were most importunate in urging their request. . . .

16 JULY 1812. Early in the morning four oxen were produced for my acceptance. By their following up the affair so closely, and by their pertinaciously endeavouring to make me receive a payment before-hand, I perceived that their intention was to establish a claim to have immediate possession of their purchase. I had now put it out of my power to break off the negotiation by a peremptory refusal to part with any of my arms; because I had consented, though under a remote condition, to let them have a musket. There was no plea left, by which I could save my gun, but that of objecting to the price; and though it was barely probable that they would relinquish it on that account, I should at least gain, as some compensation, a greater strength in oxen, a point on which no small share of our future safety and success depended: for, to have hinted that it was intended as a present would leave me no excuse for withholding it when it should be discovered that I was not returning to the place appointed for receiving it. This plea, they must have been well aware, might now be urged on reasonable grounds.

On my objecting therefore to the four oxen, as being but half its value, they replied that they had learnt from the people of Klaarwater that a musket might be purchased in the Colony for that price. They appeared however resolved to have it on their own terms; and there is little doubt that they were emboldened to act in this manner by observing the symptoms of fear which the looks and behaviour of my own men had, from the first hour of our arrival, but more especially during these transactions, too visibly betrayed.

Mattivi and his chieftains now appeared in serious debate; while I sat in the midst of them, totally ignorant of what resolutions they were forming. At this moment Speelman, Philip, and Gert came, and in great trepidation, begged me to leave the circle. I saw so much alarm in their countenances, that I was led to suppose that they had overheard the council proposing violent measures; and I therefore rose and walked with them to the waggon. They entreated me to give up the point in dispute, as they saw clearly, they said, that it was bringing us into danger. Muchunka and Adam* strongly advised that I should not reject what was offered, but rather let them have the gun at any price, as it was to be feared that otherwise bad consequences might ensue.

Whether this advice was well-founded or not, I had no time for examining; but as I perceived, at this instant, reason for believing that my men would desert me if I increased their alarm by pushing the affair farther, I desired the interpreter to tell the assembly that although I considered the gun as worth much more than the price at which they had rated it, yet, as I desired nothing so much as their friendship, I should dispute with them no longer on the subject. To this, moved, as I supposed, by the conciliatory manner in which I spoke, they replied that six oxen should be given.

Immediately they all rose; and Mattivi then said he should wish to see the gun fired off. This was a request which I could find no pretext for refusing, although I saw too clearly that all these transactions were tending towards a point which I was endeavouring to avoid; that of getting it into their possession before the time which had been agreed on.

We therefore proceeded to an open place on the outside of the town, attended by a numerous crowd of spectators. A part of my men being left to guard the waggons, I ordered the rest to follow me with their muskets loaded. When the gun in question was discharged, the Chief desired that the others might also be fired.

In complying with this request, the one which had been loaded by Stuurman could not by any means be made to explode; and on examination it was found that he had rammed in the cartridge with the ball downwards. A failure of this kind, while exhibiting to the natives the power of our arms, was the more unlucky, as it led them to believe that my party was not entirely composed of men who were properly skilled in the use of them; for they watched all our motions with the most prying attention.

Mattivi then requested that Molaala might be allowed to fire off one of the guns. Neither could this be refused; but as soon as he had discharged it, instead of returning it to the Hottentot, as it was not the musket which had been intended for him, he was ordered by the Chief to take it home to his house. At so flagrant an act of bad faith, I loudly expressed my dissatisfaction, as it was an open breach of our agreement; but he, in his turn, pretended to be equally dissatisfied with me for wishing to detain what he had now bought and made his own; the whole party at the same time crying out that they ought not to give it out of their possession. At this moment I felt exceedingly irritated at their conduct, so deficient in honour and every just principle; but I suppressed my feelings as well as I was able, since a glance at the crowd, and at my own men, showed me too truly that I was completely in their power, and that my gun was irrecoverably gone. They must have read in my countenance what I thought of their dealings; but they walked away, exulting in the success of their cunning, and even, perhaps, inwardly proud of their superiority over a white man in this essential qualification, the possession of which seems in their eyes, and, I am ashamed to confess, in the eyes of many Europeans, to constitute a man of talents.

PART IV

THE CARIBBEAN

ENGLISHMEN began to migrate to the tropics in the 1620s, the decade when they also settled New England. From subsistence farming, cacao, and tobacco, interest moved to sugar, already turning a profit for the Portuguese in Brazil. By the 1640s England's island colonies began the conversion to a plantation system organized around this one lucrative crop. Labour-intensive sugar cultivation called for more workers, since few Indians remained in the wake of Spanish exploitation and imported disease. From white indentured servants, planters turned increasingly to slaves imported from Africa by the so-called Triangle Trade. English goods went to Africa to be traded for slaves, who were shipped to the West Indies (the infamous Middle Passage) and sold. Ships loaded with sugar and tropical products re-crossed the Atlantic to England. The population balance in the region shifted dramatically; by the 1780s blacks outnumbered whites ten to one on some islands. Guarded by British garrisons, white colonists lived in suppressed fear of the slave revolts that periodically erupted, drawing bloody reprisals.

The modern image of the Caribbean as a region of beach resorts, rum punch, and exotic flora has antecedents in eighteenth-century travel writing. Although most travellers came to the region on business, their reports often highlight the islands' exotic or aesthetic features. The eighteenth-century discourses of natural history and landscape aesthetics permeate Caribbean travel writing, often upstaging the region's less attractive features, in particular slavery. But slavery can never be entirely ignored, even by writers like Janet Schaw or William Beckford who would much rather dwell on tropical scenery. Whether the writer is of African or European descent, these selections all reveal aspects of the slave system. A half-century of political controversy over slavery was fought out partly in travel writing and the closely related genre of the 'slave narrative', examples of which we include. Slaves travelled too, though their travel was often (not always) coerced. Although the abolitionist movement was formally organized in 1787, the slave trade was not abolished until 1807. British slaves were freed in 1833, but then labelled 'apprentices' until full emancipation in 1838. By then profits from slaveholding and trade with the colonial Caribbean had declined; this, with generous government compensation, helped reconcile slave owners to the epochal change.

1. NATURAL HISTORY AND AESTHETICS

HANS SLOANE, *A Voyage to the Islands Madera, Barbados,*
Nieves, S. Christopher and Jamaica, with the Natural History of
the Herbs and Trees, Four-footed Beasts, Fishes, Birds, Insects,
Reptiles etc. of the last of those Islands; to which is prefixed an
Introduction wherein is an account of the inhabitants, air, waters,
diseases, trade, etc. (1707/1725)

Hans Sloane (1660–1753) travelled to the West Indies in 1687 as physician
to the new Governor of Jamaica. He was already a Fellow of the Royal
Society and would become its President in 1727, succeeding Sir Isaac
Newton. Sloane's interest in natural history led him to describe and draw
a wide range of Caribbean species and bring back a collection that he
would bequeath to the nation, forming the nucleus of the British
Museum. He published his observations in the islands in two volumes in
1707 and 1725. Sloane's conception of natural history includes the human
inhabitants of Jamaica, described in terms that combine taxonomy with
what we would call ethnography. He takes slavery for granted, listing
'Negroes' among the commodities of Jamaican trade and describing their
grisly punishments in a detached tone. Natural histories of West Indian
islands adorned with copious engravings and posh subscription lists were
a popular avocation for colonial professionals like the Revd Griffith
Hughes (*Natural History of Barbados*, 1750) or Patrick Browne, MD
(*Civil and Natural History of Jamaica*, 1789). Scientific interest helped
legitimize the pursuit of profit that drove Caribbean colonialism.

To Her Most Excellent Majesty, The QUEEN: this Natural History
of Jamaica, one of the Largest and most Considerable of Her
Majesty's Plantations in America, is with all Humility Dedicated, by
Her Majesty's most dutiful and most obedient Subject, Hans Sloane.

Introduction

The inhabitants of Jamaica are for the most part Europeans, some
Creolians,* born and bred in the Island Barbados, the Windward
Islands, or Surinam, who are the masters, and Indians, Negroes,
Mulattos, Alcatrazes, Mestizes, Quarterons,* etc. who are the slaves.

   The Indians are not the natives of the island, they being all destroyed by the Spaniards, of which I have said something before, but

are usually brought by surprise from the Musquitos* or Florida, or such as were slaves to the Spaniards, and taken from them by the English. They are very often very much chequered in their skin, by cupping with calabashes, are of an olive colour, have long black lank hair, and are very good hunters, fishers, or fowlers, but are nought at working in the fields or slavish work, and if checked or drubbed are good for nothing, therefore are very gently treated, and well fed.

The Negroes are of several sorts, from the several places of Guinea, which are reckoned the best slaves, those from the East Indies or Madagascins, are reckoned good enough, but too choice in their diet, being accustomed in their own countries to flesh meat, etc., and do not well here, but very often die. Those who are Creolians, born in the island, or taken from the Spaniards, are reckoned more worth than others in that they are seasoned to the island.

Clothing of the island is much as in England, especially of the better sort, that of the Indians and Negroes is a little canvas jacket and breeches, given them for Christmas. It seems to me the Europeans do not well, who coming from a cold country, continue here to clothe themselves after the same manner as in England, whereas all inhabitants between the tropics go even almost naked, and Negroes and Indians live almost so here, their clothes serving them but a very small part of the year.

When they sleep they untie their breeches, and loosen their girdles, finding by experience this custom healthy, and there is good reason for it, for by that means the circulation of the blood is not interrupted, and so consequently humours are not deposited in the several parts of the body, which ever follows such interruption.

The buildings of the Spaniards on this island were usually one storey high, having a porch, parlour, and at each end a room, with small ones behind for closets, etc. They built with posts put deep in the ground, on the sides their houses were plastered up with clay on reeds, or made of the split trunks of cabbage-trees nailed to one another, and covered with tiles, or palmetto thatch. The lowness, as well as fixing the posts deep in the earth, was for fear their houses could be ruined by earthquakes, as well as for coolness.

The houses built by the English are for the most part brick, and after the English manner, which are neither cool, nor able to endure the shocks of earthquakes. The kitchens, or cook-rooms here, are always at a small distance from their houses, because of the heat and smell, which are both noisome and troublesome.

There are no chimneys or fireplaces in their houses, but in the cook-room, this word is used to signify their kitchen, and is a sea word, as many others of that country.

The houses of considerable planters are usually removed from their sugar, or other works, that they may be free from the noise and smells of them, which are very offensive.

The Negroes' houses are likewise at a distance from their masters', and are small, oblong, thatched huts, in which they have all their movables or goods, which are generally a mat to lie on, a pot of earth to boil their victuals in, either yams, plantains, or potatoes, with a little salt mackerel, and a calabash or two for cups and spoons.

There are very good bricks and pots made here of the clay of the country, to the easy making of which the few rains, as well as plenty of firewood conduces much.

The air here being so hot and brisk as to corrupt and spoil meat in four hours after 'tis killed, no wonder if a diseased body must be soon buried. They usually bury twelve hours after death at all times of the day and night.

The burial place at Port Royal is a little way out of town, in a sandy soil, because in the town or church it is thought unhealthy for the living. Planters are very often buried in their gardens, and have a small monument erected over them, and yet I never heard of any of them who walked after their deaths for being buried out of consecrated ground.

An amputated member buried there, and dug up some days after, was found eaten by the ants all but the bones. In the caves where the Indians used to bury, the ants would eat the whole flesh off of the bodies, and would perforate the bones, and eat up the marrow, of which I have a proof, having brought with me from thence the bone of the arm of an Indian so perforated, and its marrow eaten by them.

The Negroes from some countries think they return to their own country when they die in Jamaica, and therefore regard death but little, imagining they shall change their condition, by that means from servile to free, and so for this reason often cut their own throats. Whether they die thus, or naturally, their country people make great lamentations, mournings, and howlings about them expiring, and at their funeral throw in rum and victuals into their graves, to serve them in the other world. Sometimes they bury it in gourds, at other times spill it on the graves.

They have every one his wife, and are very much concerned if they prove adulterous, but in some measure satisfied if their masters punish the man who does them the supposed injury, in any of his hogs, or other small wealth. The care of the masters and overseers about their wives is what keeps their plantations chiefly in good order, whence they ever buy wives in proportion to their men, lest the men should go wandering to neighbouring plantations, and neglect to serve them. The Negroes are much given to venery, and although hard wrought, will at nights, or on feast days, dance and sing; their songs are all bawdy, and leading that way. They have several sorts of instruments in imitation of lutes, made of small gourds fitted with necks, strung with horse hairs, or the peeled stalks of climbing plants or withes. These instruments are sometimes made of hollowed timber covered with parchment or other skin wetted, having a bow for its neck, the strings tied longer or shorter, as they would alter their sounds. The figures of some of these instruments are hereafter graved. They have likewise in their dance rattles tied to their legs and wrists, and in their hands, with which they make a noise, keeping time with one which makes a sound answering it on the mouth of an empty gourd or jar with his hand. Their dances consist in great activity and strength of body, and keeping time, if it can be. They very often tie cows' tails to their rumps, and add such other odd things to their bodies in several places, as gives them a very extraordinary appearance. . . .

The trade of Jamaica is either with Europe or America. That of Europe consists in bringing thither flour, biscuit, beef, pork, all manner of clothing for masters and servants, as Osnabrigs,* blue cloth, liquors of all sorts, etc. Madeira wine is also imported in great quantities from the island of that name, by vessels sent from England on purpose, on all which the merchant is supposed to gain generally 50 per cent profit. The goods sent back again, or exported from the island, are sugars, most part muscavados,* indigo, cotton-wool, ginger, pimento, all-spice or Jamaica-pepper, fustic-wood, prince-wood, lignum vitae, arnotto, log-wood,* and the several commodities they have from the Spaniards of the West Indies (with whom they have a private trade), as sarsaparilla, cacao-nuts, cochineal,* etc. on which they get considerable profit. There is about 20 per cent in exchange between Spanish money and gold in Jamaica, and English money paid in England. . . .

When the trade of the Asiento* for furnishing the Spanish West Indies with Negroes was in this island, it was not only very beneficial to the African Company and their factors, but to the governors of this island, as well as the captains of the frigates who conveyed them to Portobello, and on their delivery there had immediately paid them the money agreed on by the head.

The religion of those of the island, either Europeans, or descended from them Creolians, is as in England, and the same proportion of Dissenters are there as in England.

The Indians and Negroes have no manner of religion by what I could observe of them. 'Tis true they have several ceremonies, as dances, playing, etc. but these for the most part are so far from being acts of adoration of a god that they are for the most part mixed with a great deal of bawdry and lewdness.

The Negroes are usually thought to be haters of their own children, and therefore 'tis believed that they sell and dispose of them to strangers for money, but this is not true, for the Negroes of Guinea being divided into several captainships, as well as the Indians of America, have wars, and besides those slain in battles many prisoners are taken, who are sold for slaves, and brought hither. But the parents here, although their children are slaves forever, yet have so great a love for them that no master dare sell or give away one of their little ones, unless they care not whether their parents hang themselves or no.

Many of the Negroes, being slaves, and their posterity after them in Guinea, they are more easily treated by the English here, than by their own country-people, wherefore they would not often willingly change masters.

The punishments for crimes of slaves are usually for rebellions, burning them, by nailing them down on the ground with crooked sticks on every limb, and then applying the fire by degrees from the feet and hands, burning them gradually up to the head, whereby their pains are extravagant. For crimes of a lesser nature gelding, or chopping off half the foot with an axe. These punishments are suffered by them with great constancy.

For running away they put iron rings of great weight on their ankles, or pottocks about their necks, which are iron rings with two long necks riveted to them, or a spur in the mouth.

For negligence, they are usually whipped by the overseers with lance-wood switches, till they be bloody, and several of the switches broken, being first tied up by their hands in the mill-houses. Beating with manatee straps* is thought too cruel, and therefore prohibited by the customs of the country. The cicatrices are visible on their skins forever after; and a slave, the more he have of those, is the less valued.

After they are whipped till they are raw, some put on their skins pepper and salt to make them smart; at other times their masters will drop melted wax on their skins, and use several very exquisite torments. These punishments are sometimes merited by the blacks, who are a very perverse generation of people, and though they appear harsh, yet are scarce equal to some of their crimes, and inferior to what punishments other European nations inflict on their slaves in the East Indies, as may be seen by Moquet,* and other travellers. . . .

I went to Liguanea,* and crossed from Passage-Fort, the arm of the sea which comes in by Port Royal.

The greatest part of the shore of this island, and particularly of this bay, are full of a tree called mangrove, of which I shall speak hereafter. In the mean time, I think fit not only to take notice that oysters grow or stick to these trees, not upon them like fruit, as is vulgarly conceived, but only to so much of the root of the mangrove tree, as is under water: the tree-oysters stick and fasten themselves, and afterwards several of them stick together, the lower down they are the bigger; so that at low water the best is taken. They cause the flux and fevers when eaten in excess, and taste somewhat like ours. When through any accident these oysters die, they corrupt, stink, and infect the air and wind, and are noisome to the places about them, on this account the land-winds are thought to bring Port Royal no good air.

Sloops may, if they know the passage or canal, go to Passage-Fort from Port Royal, otherwise they cannot for the shoals. Men-of-war birds, so called, appear in this bay, they fly like kites, look black, are very large winged in proportion to the body, they fight with sea gulls (which are to be found here, and are like ours) for their prey.

Pelicans fish in this bay, likewise in blowing weather, when they cannot fish abroad, and in the calm mornings they dive after their prey. Spanish mackerel are taken in this bay in plenty. They are like ours, only made like a bonito. I here observed a small shoal of small fishes to leap out of the water, being pursued by greater fishes.

The whole shoals between Port Royal and Passage-Fort are covered with coral of several sorts, and *Alga angustifolia vitrariorum* or sea-grass. There are also star-fishes of several sorts, large and five-pointed, as well as small, and several sorts of the *Echinus marinus*. Alligators are often drawn on shore in the seine-nets by the fishermen, whose nets are generally broken by them. These alligators are so called from the word *alagarta*, in Spanish, signifying a lizard, of which this is an amphibious sort. When I was in Jamaica there was one of these used to do abundance of mischief to the people's cattle in the neighborhood of this bay, having his regular courses to look for prey. One of the inhabitants there, as I was told, tied a long cord to his bedstead, and to the other end of the cord fastened a piece of wood and a dog, so that the alligator swallowing the dog and piece of wood, the latter came cross his throat, as it was designed, and after pulling the bedstead to the window, and awaking the person in bed, he was caught. Alligators love dogs extremely, but prey also on cattle. This alligator was nineteen feet long.

There are also sharks to be found in the sea hereabouts. A man bathing in the sea by Port Royal had part of the flesh of his arm and breast at one mouthful torn off by a shark, of which he immediately died. I was told that one Rockey a privateer used to go and fight with them in the water, and so do some divers, killing them with bodkins run into their bellies, while they turn themselves to prey.

I saw in this harbour and bay a ship come from Guinea, loaded with blacks to sell. The ship was very nasty with so many people on board. I was assured that the Negroes feed on pindals, or Indian earth-nuts, a sort of pea or bean producing its pods underground. Coming from Guinea hither, they are fed on these nuts, or Indian corn boiled whole twice a day, at eight o'clock and four in the afternoon, each having a pint of water allowed him. The Negroes from Angola and Gambia are not troubled with worms, but those from the Gold Coast very much.

I was informed here that ewes bring forth twice in fifteen months, without any regard to the time of the year; but cows bring forth their young according to the seasons of Europe.

I saw some Guinea-sheep, they were brought from a ship from that country, being provided by the commander to eat at sea, but when the ship arrived they were presented to a planter in Liguanea. They are like goats in every respect, having for the most part black and white short hair, like that of a six weeks or a month old calf. They are much less than goats, multiply very fast, and are very sweet meat.

At some plantations bordering on this bay many whites die, as believed by the ill air, some of them lying in bottoms, bordering on marshes near the sea. On the other hand, plantations that are seated high are very healthy, and the people are not sickly. Colonel Barry's house, all galleried round, was formerly, when the Spaniards possessed the island, the only place in Liguanea inhabited. A very rich widow had here a sugar-work, and abundance of cattle in the savannas, near forty thousand.

JAMES HAKEWILL, *A Picturesque Tour of the Island of Jamaica, from Drawings Made in the Years 1820 and 1821* (1825)

James Hakewill (1778–1843), artist and architect, visited Jamaica in the early 1820s and painted the series of views published in 1825, in an expensive book with colour plates, as *A Picturesque Tour of the Island of Jamaica*. The title-page advertises his earlier *Picturesque Tour of Italy*: representations of exotic locales according to the fashionable aesthetics of the picturesque apparently sold well. The volume is dedicated 'to the noblemen and gentlemen, proprietors of estates in the West Indies . . . and to the merchants of the United Kingdom, connected with those valuable colonies'. The connection between landscape aesthetics and planter interests is apparent in several of our other selections as well (Schaw, Beckford, Lewis).

Introduction

The title of 'Picturesque Tour' has been appropriated to any work intended to convey a general idea of the surfaces and external appearances of a country, without undertaking to develop its moral and political institutions. The Tour which is here submitted to the attention of the public was professedly and exclusively picturesque, and it is hoped that the conditions of the Prospectus* will be found to have been fulfilled in the execution of the work. But a residence of nearly two years in the island of Jamaica must be pleaded as the author's apology for offering, also, a few remarks on the moral condition of some parts of its inhabitants; first, the negroes. As slaves these are, undoubtedly, subject to be sold; but large purchases of negroes, unless with the estate on which they are settled, and which would be useless without them, are not often made. Except what are called jobbing gangs, which sometimes, though rarely, may amount to from twenty to twenty-five in number, the only transfers which take place are of domestic or tradesman negroes, and no man would venture to buy a slave that had not previously agreed to live with him. If he did, the slave would inevitably run away; for while the purchaser requires a good character with the negro, the latter is equally alive to obtaining a knowledge of the habits and disposition of his future master. One or two facts will illustrate the nature and manner of these transfers. While the author was on the Montpelier estates, the resident carpenter, Mr Thomas, had ten negroes, of whom, as he intended to leave Jamaica, he was desirous of disposing. He desired them to find themselves a master, proposing only to negotiate a sale with a person with whom they could place themselves to their satisfaction. After some time they came to him with information that they were willing to serve Dr Pierce, of Belle Vue, who was desirous of engaging them, and with him Mr Thomas afterwards concluded the bargain. The negroes had previously arranged with Dr Pierce their provision, grounds, clothing, days of rest, and all the particulars of their allowances. And this is not confined to sales by private contract: the author was present at a public sale of negroes at Kingston, where a gentleman, accompanied by a friend, came up to a negro about to be submitted to the hammer, and (in the author's hearing) after a few preliminary questions, asked him if he would be disposed to live with him, described the nature of his work, the situation of his coffee plantation in Liguanea, and every inducement that occurred to him. His friend calling to the negro's recollection an old acquaintance, suggested that he must remember him lean and sickly, he was now on the same plantation healthy and fat. The negro consented to live on the plantation, and the gentleman purchased him.

With regard to their comforts it is to be remarked that nearly the whole of the markets of Jamaica are supplied with every species of vegetable and fruit by the overplus of the negroes' produce, by which traffic they acquire considerable riches. On Holland estate, in St Thomas in the East, the negroes keep a boat, which trades regularly between that place and Kingston, and these grumble as much at the low price of yams and plantain as an English farmer at the fall of corn.

Cascade on the Windward Road

The Cane River discharges itself into the sea, at about the distance of seven miles from Kingston, on the Windward Road. The road runs for some way on the sea-beach, passing Rock Fort, where there is a fine head of spring-water, from which the shipping is supplied, and from whence it is in contemplation to supply Up-park Camp and Kingston. Rock Fort is in its situation very like the Torre dei Confini, near Terracina,* forming the boundary-mark between the dominions of the Pope and the King of Naples; on the right the same brilliant sea, on the left the same almost inaccessible mountains; the Fort guarding the narrow pass. Leaving his carriage at the Pall Tavern, a small well served inn, on the road-side, the traveller proceeds on horseback, through a deep ravine, between mountains of so great a height as scarcely to admit the rays of the sun. At the bottom the Cane River takes its devious way, sometimes stretching in a broad even bed, sometimes urging its impetuous course among rocks of considerable magnitude which impede its progress. The distance from the high road to the Fall is about two miles, and the river is crossed and re-crossed more than twenty times.

The Fall is formed by the junction at its head of the Cane and Lucky Valley Rivers, which unite within a hundred yards of the spot, from whence they are precipitated into the gulf beneath, from a height of somewhat more than 200 feet. The road is tolerably good, having been formed with much labour for the traffic of the mules, for the supply and convenience of the estates and coffee mountains, which abound in its neighbourhood. For this purpose the rocks have been in two instances pierced and give a good miniature resemblance of the celebrated galleries of the Simplon.*

2. WORKING TRAVELLERS

JOHN GABRIEL STEDMAN, *Narrative of a Five Years Expedition against the Revolted Negroes of Surinam* (1790; ed. Richard Price and Sally Price; Baltimore, 1988)

John Gabriel Stedman (1744–97) joined the Scots Brigade of the Dutch army (in which his father had also served) at the age of sixteen. In 1772

Stedman embarked for the Dutch colony of Suriname, on the Caribbean coast of South America, as part of an army of 800 men sent to reinforce local troops in a campaign against marauding bands of escaped slaves known as 'maroons'. Living nomadically in the bush, the maroons had been raiding plantations on and off since the late seventeenth century. Despite peace treaties concluded in the 1760s, new maroon groups had pushed the colony to the edge of survival. Captain Stedman led his men on boat patrols up Suriname's rivers and on paralysing slogs through the bush, seldom finding their elusive enemies (he fought just one battle during his four-year stay). Loss of life among Europeans was enormous: of 1,650 soldiers sent over, only about 200 lived to return. Stedman formed a relationship with a slave woman, Joanna, and had a child by her, although she refused to return to Europe. Stedman wrote his narrative after his return and it was published in 1796, with engravings by William Blake and others from Stedman's own drawings. Unfortunately the publisher, Joseph Johnson, thought it necessary to bowdlerize the book, outraging its author. We reprint selections from Stedman's 1790 manuscript, edited in 1988 by Richard Price and Sally Price, anthropologists who have worked with the maroons' present-day descendants. Our selections feature Stedman's arrival in the colony; a combat with a giant anaconda; the aftermath of the battle of Gado Saby, with an exchange of taunts between Stedman's commanding officer, Colonel Fourgeoud, and the maroons; and the brutal execution of a free black man.

NOVEMBER 1772. A most dangerous revolt having broke out in the colony of Surinam amongst the negro-slaves who were armed and assembled in the woods threatening immediate destruction to that settlement, determined the states of the United Provinces to send out a fresh corps of 500 volunteers in 1772 to act conjointly with the troops already there, in quelling the insurrection and preventing a general massacre. At this time I was Lieutenant in the Hon. General Stuart's regiment of the Scots Brigade in the service of Holland when impressed by the prospect of preferment usually annexed to so hazardous a service and in the hopes of gratifying my curiosity in exploring a country so little known, I offered myself to be one of the party and had the honour to be accepted by his Serene Highness the Prince of Orange who immediately advanced me to the rank of Captain by brevet in the new corps intended for the expedition under Colonel Fourgeoud, a Swiss gentleman from Geneva near the Alpine mountains, who was invested with the supreme authority and appointed to be our Commander in Chief.

Having taken the oaths of fidelity on the 12th of November, provided myself with a case of pistols and otherwise prepared for the voyage, I took my last farewell from my old regiment and other friends and repaired to the Island of Texel where many of the troops were already assembled to be put on board.

2–3 FEBRUARY 1773. The fleet entered the beautiful River Surinam with a fine breeze, and at 3 o'clock p.m. dropped anchor before the new fortress called Amsterdam where the *Vigilance* transport had arrived 2 days before us, and which place I shall afterwards describe. The fortress immediately saluted the ships from the batteries and got the compliment returned when a long boat with one of our captains was dispatched to Paramaribo to give the Governor notice of the troops being arrived in the Colony.

Here the air was perfumed with the most odoriferous smell in nature by the many lemons, oranges, shaddocks* etc. with which this country abounds.

During this the companies walked on shore, and in the fortress, to refresh themselves, where I accompanied them and waited on the Commandant Colonel De Ponchera of the Society or Colony troops.

Now all were got safe on *terra-firma* prayers and hymns were laid aside as useless baubles while swearing and cursing became their substitute, If this is generally the custom I know not, but that it ought not to be such I dare maintain, since either to be a hypocrite, or altogether abandoned is equally despisable.

When stepping on land the first object I met was a most miserable young woman in chains simply covered with a rag round her loins, which was like her skin cut and carved by the lash of the whip in a most shocking manner. Her crime was in not having fulfilled her task to which she was by appearance unable. Her punishment to receive 200 lashes and for months to drag a chain of several yards in length the one end of which was locked to her ankle and to the other end of which was a weight of 3 score pounds or upwards. She was a beautiful negro maid and while I was meditating on the shocking load of her irons I myself nearly escaped being riveted by fascination—I now took a draft of the wretched creature upon paper which I here present to the sympathizing reader and which inspired me with a very unfavourable opinion of the humanity of the planters residing in this colony towards their negro slaves.

Here I found the grass very long and very coarse, which covered us all over with most disagreeable insects—by the colonists called *pattat* and *scrapat* lice—the first is so small that they are scarcely visible—the second are something larger and have the form of a tick or dog's louse; they both stick fast to the skin, and occasion the most disagreeable itching. In the rainy season they are reckoned the most numerous, and to walk barefooted is supposed the best way to avoid them, they adhering generally to the clothes with greater ease, and of course in greater numbers, from which they immediately find their way to the quick. From this inconveniency we only got rid at our return on board, by washing the parts infested, with the juice of lemons or limes, which gave us great consolation.

3rd. Several officers of the society or colony troops, with a number of other gentlemen came to visit us on board, and to welcome us into the colony, who complimented us with a great quantity of fruits, vegetables and other refreshments. They were rowed in most elegant barges or tent boats by 6 or 8 negroes, mostly accompanied with flags and small bands of music, which vessels I shall afterwards more amply describe.

But what astonished me most of anything was to see the barge men all as naked as when they were born, a small strip of check or other linen cloth excepted, which passed through between their thighs to cover what decency forbids us to expose, and was simply drawn (before and behind) over a thin cotton string that is tied around their loins. These men looked very well—being healthy, strong and young, their skin shining and almost as black as ebony, the colonists generally using their handsomest slaves to row their boats, serve at table etc.—but wide different from these were 1 or 2 canoes filled with half starved emaciated wretches that came alongside our ships, begging bits of salt-beef or dried fish from the soldiers and who would even fight for the value of a bone.

26 AUGUST 1773. Resting in my hammock between the paroxysms of my fever about half way between Coermoetibo and Barbacueber* while the *Charon** was floating down, the sentinel called to me that he had seen and challenged something black and moving in the brushwood on the beach which gave no answer and which from its thickness he concluded must be a man. I immediately dropped anchor and having manned the canoe, ill as I was, I stepped into it, when we

rowed up to the place mentioned by the sentinel; here we all stepped ashore to reconnoitre, I suspecting this to be no other than a rebel spy, or straggling party detached by the enemy—when one of my slaves named David declared it was no negro, but a large amphibious snake which could not be far from the beach, and I might have an opportunity to shoot it if I pleased but to this I had not the smallest inclination from its uncommon size, from my weakness, and the difficulty of getting through the thicket, which seemed impenetrable to the water's edge and I ordered to return on board; the negro then asked me liberty to step forwards and shoot it himself, assuring me it could not be at any distance, and warranting me against all danger; this spirited me so much that I determined to take his first advice, and kill it myself, providing he was to point it out to me, and bail the hazard by standing at my side, from which I swore that if he dared to move I should level the piece at himself, and blow out his brains without judge or jury, and to which he agreed; thus having loaded my gun with a ball cartridge we proceeded, David this was his name cutting away a path with the bill-hook—and a marine following with 3 more loaded firelocks to keep in readiness; we had not gone above 20 yards through mud and water (the negro looking every way with an uncommon degree of archness and attention) when starting behind me he called out, *me see Snakee*, viz, that he saw the snake coiled under the fallen leaves and rubbish of the trees. 'D——n you rascal,' said I, 'then stand before me till I also see him or you are dead this instant,' and this he did, when with very much difficulty I perceived the head of this monster distant from me not above 16 feet moving its forked tongue, while its eyes seemed to emit fire by their brightness. I now resting my piece upon a branch to take a proper aim fired, but missing the head the ball went through the body, when the animal struck around and, with such astonishing force, as cut away all the underwood around him with the facility of a scythe mowing grass, and by flouncing his tail made the glare* and dirt fly over our heads at a considerable distance, during which manoeuvre we all ran to the river and crowded into the canoe. The negro now entreated me to renew the charge, assuring me he would be quiet in a few minutes, and at any rate persisting in the snake's neither being able or inclined to pursue us (which he undertook to prove by walking before me till I should be ready to fire); I again did undertake to make the trial, the more while he said that his first starting backwards, had only proceeded to make room for myself. I now found him a little removed from his former station but very quiet, with his head as before out amongst the fallen leaves, rotten bark, and old moss; I fired at it immediately, but with no better success than the other time, the snake sending up such a cloud of dust and dirt as I never saw but in a whirlwind, and made us once more all betake to our heels for the canoe, where now being heartily tired of the exploit I gave orders to paddle for the barge; but the slave still entreating me to let him kill the animal, I was actually induced to make one third and last attempt in company with himself. Thus having once more discovered the snake we discharged both our pieces at once (not unlike the story told of Robinson Crusoe with Friday),* however with this good effect that he was now by one of us shot through the head, when David the slave, leaping with joy before the monster as his namesake the King had done before the Ark, fetched the painter or boat-rope in order to drag him to the canoe—but this again was a difficult job since the creature notwithstanding its being mortally wounded still continued to make such twists and writhes as made it dangerous for anyone to come very near him, however, the negro having made a running noose, threw it over his head with much dexterity, after a few fruitless attempts to make an approach—and now all taking hold of the rope we hauled him to the beach and tied him to the stern of the canoe to take him in tow, being still alive, where he kept swimming like an eel and I having no relish for taking such a ship mate on board—whose length notwithstanding to my astonishment all the negroes declared it to be but a young one, come to about its half-growth. I measured to be 22 feet and some inches, and its thickness like that of my black boy Quacoo, who might then be about 12 years old, and around whose waist I since measured the creature's skin.

Being arrived alongside of the *Charon* the next thing was what now to do with this huge animal, when it was determined to bring him ashore at Barbacoeba to have him skinned, and take out the oil etc. This we did, when the negro David having climbed up a tree with the end of the rope, let it down over a strong forked branch, and the other negroes hoisted the snake up in suspense. This done, David with a sharp knife between his teeth now left the tree, and clung fast upon the monster which was still twisting, and began his operations by ripping it up and stripping down the skin as he descended, which though the animal could now do him no hurt, I acknowledge had a terrible appearance, viz, to see a man stark naked, black and bloody, clung with arms and legs around the slimy and yet living monster—however, his labour was not in vain since he not only dextrously finished the operation, but provided me with (besides the skin) above 4 gallons of fine clarified fat or rather oil, losing perhaps as much more, which I delivered to the surgeons at Devils Harwar* for the use of the wounded men in the hospital and for which I received their hearty thanks, it being deemed, particularly for bruises, a very excellent remedy. At signifying my surprise to see the snake still living after he was deprived of his intestines and skin, Cramaca the old negro assured me, he would not die till after sunset; the negroes now cut him in slices in order to dress him and eat part of him, they all declaring he was exceedingly good and healthy, which to their great mortification, I refused giving my assent to—and we rowed down with the skin to Devils Harwar.

Having thus described the manner in which he was killed I shall now give some account of the animal itself, which is mentioned by many different authors, and of which several skins are preserved in the British and Mr Parkinson's Museums.* It is called by Mr Westley *Lyboija* and *Boa* in the British Encyclopedia, to where I refer the reader for a perfect account and an excellent engraving of this wonderful creature, which is in the colony of Surinam called *aboma*. Its length when full grown is sometimes 40 feet and more than 4 feet in circumference; its colour is a greenish black on the back, a fine brownish yellow on the sides, and a dirty white under the belly—the back and sides being spotted with irregular black rings, of a pure white in the middle. Its head is broad and flat, small in proportion to the body, with a large mouth beset with a double row of teeth, a forked tongue, and two bright prominent eyes; it is all covered over with large scales, some about the size of a shilling and under the body near the tail armed with two strong claws like cockspurs, to help its seizing its prey. It is an amphibious animal, that is to say, it delights in low and marshy places where it lies coiled up like a rope and concealed under all kinds of moss, rotten timber, and dried leafs to seize its prey by surprise, which from its great bulk it has no activity to pursue. This consists when hungry in anything that comes within its reach, no matter what, a sloth, a wild boar, a stag, or even a tiger, around which having twisted itself by the help

of its claws, so that it cannot escape, it next breaks by its irresistible
force every bone in the animal's body, which it then covers over with
a kind of slime or saliva from its mouth to make it slide, and at last
gradually sucks it in till it disappears. After this the *aboma* cannot
shift his station on account of the great knob or knot, which the
swallowed prey occasions in that part of the body where it rests, till
it is digested, which would hinder him from sliding alongst the
ground, and during which time the *aboma* wants no other subsistence. I have been told of negroes being devoured by this animal, to
which I willingly give credit should they chance to come within his
reach during the time of his affamation* and which proprieties of
seizing their prey long fasting etc. I believe to be common in many
(if not in most) other snakes nor do I apprehend that its flesh is in
any ways pernicious to the stomach which looked beautifully white,
had the appearance of fish, and I should never have refused the
negroes from eating it had I not observed a kind of dissatisfaction
amongst the remaining marines for going to give the negroes the
use of the kettle to boil it. The bite of this snake is said not to be
venomous, nor do I believe it bites at all from any other impulse
than hunger.

I shall only add that having nailed its skin on the bottom of a
canoe, and dried it in the sun (sprinkling it over with wood ashes to
prevent it from corruption) I sent it to a friend at Paramaribo from
where it was since sent to Holland as a curiosity.

[Stedman and his men, under the command of Colonel Fourgeoud, have
fought a battle (Stedman's only real battle in over four years in Suriname)
against the maroons of the village of Gado Saby, who have ended the
combat by setting fire to their own village and fleeing.]

20–1 AUGUST 1775. It was now about 3 o'clock p.m. and we as I said
were busied slinging our hammocks, when we were suddenly surprised by an attack from the enemy but who after exchanging a few
shot were soon repulsed. This unexpected visit however put us upon
our guard during the whole night, by allowing no fires to be lighted
and doubling the sentinels all around the camp. Thus situated I,
being excessively fatigued (besides several others), ventured in my
hammock, where I soon fell asleep; but not longer than the space of
an hour; when my faithful black boy Qwacco awaked me in pitch
darkness crying, *Massera Massera Boosee Negro, Boosee Negro.* And

hearing at the same time a brisk firing, while the balls rustled through the branches about me, I imagined no other than that the enemy was in the middle of our camp. In this surprise, and not perfectly awaked, I started up with my fusee* cocked, and (I not knowing where I run) overset Qwacco, and next fell myself over two or three bodies that lay on the ground and which I took to be shot; but one of which damning me for a son of a bitch told me if I moved I was a dead man. Colonel Fourgeoud with all his troops lying flat on their bellies, and who had issued orders no more to fire, the men having spent most of their ammunition the preceding day—I took his advice and soon discovered him to be one of our grenadiers, called Thompson. In this situation we continued to lie prostrate on our arms till next morning, when the sun rose and during which time a most abusive dialogue ensued between the rebels, and the rangers,* both parties cursing and menacing each other at a terrible rate, the first reproaching the others as being poltroons, and betrayers of their countrymen, whom they challenged the next day to single combat, swearing they only wanted to wash their hands in the blood of such scoundrels who had been the capital hands in destroying their fine settlement; while the rangers damned the rebels for a parcel of pitiful skulking rascals whom they would fight one to two in the open field, if they dared to show their ugly faces, that they had deserted their masters being too lazy to do their work, while they (the rangers) would stand by the Europeans till they died. After which they insulted each other by a kind of war whoop, then sang victorious songs, and sounded their horns in defiance. After which once more the popping began. And thus *ad perpetuum* the whole night till break of day, the music of their manly voices etc. resounding amidst the echoing solitude and surrounding woods with redoubled force. And which being already dark and gloomy added much to an awful scene of pleasing dreadfulness; while according to me the *tout ensemble* could not but inspire the brave with thoughts of fortitude and heroism and stamp the trembling coward for what he is.

At last poor Fourgeoud entered in the conversation, by the help of myself and Sergeant Fowler, who spoke the language, as his interpreters but which created more mirth than I before heard in the Colony. He promised them life, liberty, meat, drink, and all they wanted, but they replied with a loud laugh that they wanted nothing from him who seemed a half starved Frenchman, already run away from his own country; that if he would venture to give them a visit in person, he should not be hurt, and might depend on not returning with an empty belly. They called to us that we were more to be pitied than themselves, who were only a parcel of white slaves, hired to be shot at, and starved for 4 pence a day; and that they scorned to expend much of their powder upon such scarecrows, who had not been the aggressors by driving them in the forest and only obeying the command of their masters; but if the planters and overseers dared to enter the woods themselves not a soul of such scoundrels should ever return, no more than the rangers, some of whom might depend on being massacred that very day, or the next. And concluded by swearing that Bony should soon be the governor of all the Colony. After this they tinkled their billhooks, fired a volley, gave three cheers which were answered by the rangers, and all dispersed with the rising sun, to our great satisfaction, being heartily tired of such company. Whatever small our loss, while our fatigues were such that only the hardships suffered since by the British troops at Gibraltar* could be compared to them, where also (notwithstanding the contest lasted such a length of time) the loss of men by the enemies' fire was but very inconsiderate. However the mystery of our escape (which in Gibraltar was owing to fortification) was this morning unrevealed by the surgeons, who dressing the wounded extracted in place of lead bullets only pebbles, coat buttons, and silver coin, which could do us little harm, penetrating scarce more than skin deep, while even gold could do themselves as little good in a wild forest where they had nothing to buy for it. We also observed that several of the poor rebel negroes who had been shot had their pieces supplied only with the shard of a spa water can in place of a flint, which could not so well answer the effect etc. And this must account for their little execution on the bodies of their cruel beseigers, who nevertheless were pretty well peppered with small scars and contusions. Inconceivable are the many shifts which these people make in the woods—

> Inventas qui vitam excoluere per artes;
> Who by invented arts have life improved*

and where in a state of tranquillity they seemed as they had said to us to want for nothing—being plump and fat at least such we found those that had been shot. For instance game and fish they catch in great abundance by artificial traps and springs and which they preserve by barbecuing, while with rice, cassava, yams, plantains, and so on, their fields are ever over stocked. Salt they make with the ashes of the palm trees like the Gentoos* in the East Indies, or use red pepper. We even discovered concealed near the trunk of an old tree a case bottle with excellent butter, which the rangers told me they made by melting and clarifying the fat of the palm-tree worms and which fully supplied the above ingredient, while I absolutely found it more delicious. The pistachio or pinda nuts they also convert in butter, by their oily substance and frequently use them in their broths. The palm tree wine they are never in want of, and which they make by cutting deep incisions of a foot over square in the fallen trunk, where the juice being gathered it soon ferments by the heat of the sun, when it is not only a cool and agreeable beverage but strong sufficient to intoxicate—and soap they have from the dwarf[?] aloes. To build their houses the manicole or pinda tree answers the purpose; their pots they fabricate with clay found near their dwellings, while the gourd or calebas tree gives them cups etc., the silk grass plant and maureecee tree provides them in hammocks, and even a kind of caps grow natural upon the palm trees as well as brooms. The various kinds of nebees* supply the want of ropes, fuel for fire they have for the cutting, while a wood called *Bee Bee* serves for tinder to light it by rubbing two pieces on each other, and which by its elasticity makes excellent corks. Neither do they want candles, being well provided with fat and oil, while the bees also afford them wax and a great deal of excellent honey. As for clothes they scorn to wear them, preferring to go naked in a climate where the mildness of the weather protects them from that cursed encumbrance. The rebel negroes might breed hogs and fowls etc. for their supply and keep dogs for hunting and watching them, but this they decline from the apprehension of being discovered by their noise, even the crowing of a cock being heard in the forest at a considerable distance; after this digression I shall return once more to my journal.

Colonel Fourgeoud now made it his next business to destroy the surrounding harvest, when I was ordered this morning to begin the devastation with 80 marines, and 20 rangers by cutting all the rice etc. that (as I have said) was plentifully growing in the two above fields, which I did and during which time I discovered a third field

south from the first, when I also demolish[ed] and made report of to
Fourgeoud to his great satisfaction.

16 AUGUST 1776. The next morning early (while musing on all the
different dangers and chastisements that the lower class of people
are subjected to) I heard a crowd pass under my window. Curiosity
made me start up, dress in a hurry, and follow them when I discovered 3 negroes in chains surrounded by a guard going to be
executed in the savannah. Their undaunted look however averse
to cruelties fascinated my attention and determined me to see the
result, which was viz, that the sentence being read (in Low Dutch
which they did not understand), one was condemned to have his
head chopped off with an axe for having shot a slave who had
come to steal plantains on the estate of his mistress, while his
accomplice was flogged below the gallows. The truth was however
that this had been done by the mistress's absolute command, but
who being detected and preferring the loss of the negro to the
penalty of 500 florins, allowed the poor man to be sacrificed; he
laid down his head on the block with uncommon deliberation and
even stretched out his neck when with one blow it was severed
from his body.

The third negro whose name was Neptune was no slave, but his
own master, and a carpenter by trade. He was young and handsome—but having killed the overseer of the estate Altona in the Para
Creek in consequence of some dispute he justly lost his life with his
liberty. However the particulars are worth relating, which briefly
were that he having stole a sheep to entertain some favourite women,
the overseer had determined to see him hanged, which to prevent he
shot him dead amongst the sugar canes. This man being sentenced to
be broke alive upon the rack,* without the benefit of the *coup de
grâce*, or mercy stroke, laid himself down deliberately on his back
upon a strong cross, on which with arms and legs expanded he was
fastened by ropes. The executioner (also a Black) having now with a
hatchet chopped off his left hand, next took up a heavy iron crow or
bar, with which blow after blow he broke to shivers every bone in his
body till the splinters, blood and marrow flew about the field, but the
prisoner never uttered a groan, or a sigh. The ropes being now
unlashed I imagined him dead and felt happy till the magistrates
moving to depart he writhed from the cross till he fell in the grass,

and damned them all for a pack of barbarous rascals, at the same time removing his right hand by the help of his teeth, he rested his head on part of the timber and asked the bystanders for a pipe of tobacco, which was infamously answered by kicking and spitting on him, till I with some Americans thought proper to prevent it.

He then begged that his head might be chopped off, but to no purpose; at last seeing no end to his misery, he declared that though he had deserved death, he had not expected to die so many deaths, 'However you Christians (said he) have missed your aim, and I now care not were I to lay here alive a month longer,' after which he sung two extempore songs, with a clear voice taking leave from his living friends and acquainting his deceased relations that in a little time more he should be with them to enjoy their company for ever. This done he entered in conversation with two gentlemen concerning his process, relating every one particular with uncommon tranquillity, but said he abruptly, 'By the sun it must be eight o'clock, and by any longer discourse I should be sorry to be the cause of your losing your breakfast'. Then turning his eyes to a Jew whose name was De Vries, 'Apropos, Sir' (said he) 'Won't you please to pay me the 5 shillings you owe me.' For what to do? 'To buy meat and drink to be sure: don't you perceive that I am to be kept alive?' which (seeing the Jew look like a fool) he accompanied with a loud and hearty laugh. Next observing the soldier who stood sentinel over him biting occasionally on a piece of dry bread, he asked him, 'How it came that he, a white man, should have no meat to eat along with it?' 'Because I am not so rich,' said the soldier. 'Then I will make you a present: first pick my hand that was chopped off clean to the bones sir. Next begin to myself till you be glutted and you'll have both bread and meat which best becomes you', and which piece of humour was followed by a 2nd laugh and thus he continued when I left him, which was about 3 hours after the execution, but to dwell more on this subject my heart

Disdains
Lo! tortures, racks, whips, famine, gibbets, chains
Rise on my mind, appall my tear stain'd eye
Attract my rage, and draw a soul felt sigh,
I blush, i shudder, at the bloody theme.*

. . . Now how in the name of Heaven human nature can go through so much torture, with so much fortitude, is truly astonishing, without it be a mixture of rage, contempt, pride, and hopes of going to a better place or at least to be relieved from this, and worse than which I verily believe some Africans know no other Hell. Nay even so late as 1789 on October 30 and 31 (at Demerary) thirty-two wretches were executed, sixteen of whom in the above shocking manner, without so much as a single complaint was heard amongst them, and which days of martyr are absolutely a feast to many planters.

OLAUDAH EQUIANO, *The Interesting Narrative of the Life of Olaudah Equiano, or Gustavus Vassa, the African, Written by Himself* (1789)

On Olaudah Equiano (Gustavus Vassa) (1745?–1797) see Part III, Section 1. These excerpts emphasize the involuntariness of slave travel: the unexpected sale that sent Equiano to the Caribbean, his arrival there, and his sale to the Quaker merchant King.

In pursuance of our orders we sailed from Portsmouth for the Thames, and arrived at Deptford the 10th of December,* where we cast anchor just as it was high water. The ship was up about half an hour, when my master ordered the barge to be manned; and all in an instant, without having before given me the least reason to suspect anything of the matter, he forced me into the barge, saying I was going to leave him, but he would take care I should not. I was so struck with the unexpectedness of this proceeding, that for some time I could not make a reply, only I made an offer to go for my books and chest of clothes, but he swore I should not move out of his sight; and if I did he would cut my throat, at the same time taking his hanger.* I began, however, to collect myself: and, plucking up courage, I told him I was free, and he could not by law serve me so. But this only enraged him the more; and he continued to swear, and said he would soon let me know whether he would or not, and at that instant sprung himself into the barge from the ship, to the astonishment and sorrow of all on board. The tide, rather unluckily for me, had just turned downward, so that we quickly fell down the river along with it, till we came among some outward-bound West-

Indiamen;* for he was resolved to put me on board the first vessel he could get to receive me. The boat's crew, who pulled against their will, became quite faint at different times, and would have gone ashore; but he would not let them. Some of them strove then to cheer me, and told me he could not sell me, and that they would stand by me, which revived me a little, and encouraged my hopes, for as they pulled along he asked some vessels to receive me, and they would not. But, just as we had got a little below Gravesend, we came alongside of a ship which was going away the next tide for the West Indies; her name was the *Charming Sally*, Captain James Doran; and my master went on board and agreed with him for me; and in a little time I was sent for into the cabin. When I came there, Captain Doran asked me if I knew him. I answered that I did not; 'Then,' said he, 'you are now my slave.' I told him my master could not sell me to him, nor to anyone else. 'Why,' said he, 'did not your master buy you?' I confessed he did. But I have served him, said I many years, and he has taken all my wages and prize-money,* for I only got one sixpence during the war; besides this I have been baptized; and by the laws of the land no man has a right to sell me: and I added, that I had heard a lawyer, and others at different times, tell my master so.* They both then said that those people who told me so were not my friends: but I replied—It was very extraordinary that other people did not know the law as well as they. Upon this Captain Doran said I talked too much English; and if I did not behave myself well, and be quiet, he had a method on board to make me. I was too well convinced of his power over me to doubt what he said: and my former sufferings in the slave-ship presenting themselves to my mind, the recollection of them made me shudder. However, before I retired, I told them that as I could not get any right among men here, I hoped I should hereafter in Heaven; and I immediately left the cabin, filled with resentment and sorrow. . . .

Thus, at the moment I expected all my toils to end, was I plunged, as I supposed, in a new slavery: in comparison of which all my service hitherto had been perfect freedom; and whose horrors, always present to my mind, now rushed on it with tenfold aggrava-tion. I wept very bitterly for some time: and began to think that I must have done something to displease the Lord, that he thus punished me so severely. This filled me with painful reflections on my past conduct; I recollected that on the morning of our arrival at Deptford I had rashly sworn that as soon as we reached London I would spend the day in rambling and sport. My conscience smote me for this unguarded expression: I felt that the Lord was able to disappoint me in all things, and immediately considered my present situation as a judgement of Heaven on account of my presumption in swearing: I therefore, with contrition of heart, acknowledged my transgression to God, and poured out my soul before him with unfeigned repentance, and with earnest supplications I besought him not to abandon me in my distress, nor cast me from his mercy for ever. In a little time my grief, spent with its own violence, began to subside; and after the first confusion of my thoughts was over, I reflected with more calmness on my present condition: I considered that trials and disappointments are sometimes for our good, and I thought God might perhaps have permitted this in order to teach me wisdom and resignation; for he had hitherto shadowed me with the wings of his mercy, and by his invisible but powerful hand brought me the way I knew not. These reflections gave me a little comfort, and I rose at last from the deck with dejection and sorrow in my countenance, yet mixed with some faint hope that the Lord would appear for my deliverance.

Soon afterwards, as my new master was going ashore, he called me to him, and told me to behave myself well, and do the business of the ship the same as any of the rest of the boys, and that I should fare the better for it; but I made him no answer. I was then asked if I could swim, and I said, No. However I was made to go under the deck, and was well watched. The next tide the ship got under way, and soon after arrived at the Mother Bank, Portsmouth; where she waited a few days for some of the West India convoy. While I was here I tried every means I could devise among the people of the ship to get me a boat from the shore, as there was none suffered to come alongside of the ship; and their own, whenever it was used, was hoisted in again immediately. A sailor on board took a guinea from me on pretence of getting me a boat; and promised me, time after time, that it was hourly to come off. When he had the watch upon deck I watched also; and looked long enough, but all in vain; I could never see either the boat or my guinea again. . . .

On the 13th of February 1763, from the mast-head, we described our destined island Montserrat; and soon after I beheld those

> Regions of sorrow, doleful shades, where peace
> And rest can rarely dwell. Hope never comes
> That comes to all, but torture without end
> Still urges.*

At the sight of this land of bondage, a fresh horror ran through all my frame, and chilled me to the heart. My former slavery now rose in dreadful review to my mind, and displayed nothing but misery, stripes, and chains; and, in the first paroxysm of my grief, I called upon God's thunder, and his avenging power, to direct the stroke of death to me, rather than permit me to become a slave, and to be sold from lord to lord.

In this state of my mind our ship came to an anchor, and soon after discharged her cargo. I now knew what it was to work hard; I was made to help to unload and load the ship. And, to comfort me in my distress in that time, two of the sailors robbed me of all my money, and ran away from the ship. I had been so long used to a European climate that at first I felt the scorching West-India sun very painful, while the dashing surf would toss the boat and the people in it frequently above high-water mark. Sometimes our limbs were broken with this, or even attended with instant death, and I was day by day mangled and torn.

About the middle of May, when the ship was got ready to sail for England, I all the time believing that Fate's blackest clouds were gathering over my head, and expecting their bursting would mix me with the dead, Captain Doran sent for me ashore one morning, and I was told by the messenger that my fate was then determined. With trembling steps and fluttering heart I came to the captain, and found with him one Mr Robert King, a quaker* and the first merchant in the place. The captain then told me my former master had sent me there to be sold; but that he had desired him to get me the best master he could, as he told him I was a very deserving boy, which Captain Doran said he found to be true, and if he were to stay in the West Indies he would be glad to keep me himself; but he could not venture to take me to London, for he was very sure that when I came there I would leave him. I at that instant burst out a crying, and begged much of him to take me to England with him, but all to no purpose. He told me he had got me the very best master in the whole island, with whom I should be as happy as if I were in England, and for that reason he chose to let him have me, though he could sell me to his own brother-in-law for a great deal more money than what he got from this gentleman. Mr King, my new master, then made a reply, and said the reason he had bought me was on account of my good character; and, as he had not the least doubt of my good behaviour, I should be very well off with him. He also told me he did not live in the West Indies, but at Philadelphia, where he was going soon; and, as I understood something of the rules of arithmetic, when we got there he would put me to school, and fit me for a clerk. This conversation relieved my mind a little, and I left those gentlemen considerably more at ease in myself than when I came to them; and I was very thankful to Captain Doran, and even to my old master, for the character they had given me; a character which I afterwards found of infinite service to me. I went on board again, and took my leave of all my shipmates; and the next day the ship sailed. When she weighed anchor I went to the waterside and looked at her with a very wishful and aching heart, and followed her with my eyes until she was totally out of sight. I was so bowed down with grief that I could not hold up my head for many months; and if my new master had not been kind to me, I believe I should have died under it at last. And indeed I soon found that he fully deserved the good character which Captain Doran had given me of him; for he possessed a most amiable disposition and temper, and was very charitable and humane. If any of his slaves behaved amiss, he did not beat or use them ill, but parted with them. This made them afraid of disobliging him; and as he treated his slaves better than any other man on the island, so he was better and more faithfully served by them in return. By this kind treatment I did at last endeavour to compose myself; and with fortitude, though moneyless, determined to face whatever fate had decreed for me. Mr King soon asked me what I could do; and at the same time said he did not mean to treat me as a common slave. I told him I knew something of seamanship, and could shave and dress hair pretty well; and I could refine wines, which I had learned on shipboard, where I had often done it; and that I could write, and understood arithmetic tolerably well as far as the Rule of Three. He then asked me if I knew anything of gauging; and, on my answering that I did not, he said one of his clerks should teach me to gauge.*

Mr King dealt in all manner of merchandise, and kept from one to six clerks. He loaded many vessels in a year; particularly to Philadelphia, where he was born, and was connected with a great mercantile house in that city. He had besides many vessels and droggers* of different sizes, which used to go about the island and other places to collect rum, sugar, and other goods. I understood pulling and managing those boats very well; and this hard work, which was the first that he set me to, in the sugar seasons, used to be my constant employment. I have rowed the boat, and slaved at the oars, from one hour to sixteen in the twenty-four; during which I had fifteen pence sterling per day to live on, though sometimes only tenpence. However, this was considerably more than was allowed to other slaves that used to work often with me, and belonged to other gentlemen on the island: these poor souls had never more than ninepence a day, and seldom more than sixpence, from their masters or owners, though they earned them three or four pisterines* a day: for it is a common practice in the West Indies, for men to purchase slaves, though they have not plantations themselves, in order to let them out to planters and merchants, at so much apiece by the day, and they give what allowance they choose out of this produce of their daily work to their slaves for subsistence; this allowance is often very scanty. My master often gave the owners of those slaves two and a half of these pieces per day, and found the poor fellows in victuals himself, because he thought their owners did not feed them well enough according to the work they did. The slaves used to like this very well, and as they knew my master to be a man of feeling,* they were always glad to work for him in preference to any other gentleman; some of whom, after they had been paid for these poor people's labours, would not give them their allowance out of it. Many times have I seen these unfortunate wretches beaten for asking for their pay; and often severely flogged by their owners if they did not bring them their daily or weekly money exactly to the time; though the poor creatures were obliged to wait on the gentlemen they had worked for, sometimes more than half the day, before they could get their pay; and this generally on Sundays, when they wanted the time for themselves.

MARY PRINCE, *The History of Mary Prince, A West Indian Slave. Related by Herself* (1831)

Mary Prince (b. 1788) was born a slave in Bermuda. Kind owners during her childhood did not prepare her for the brutality of Captain I—— and his wife, to whom she was sold around 1800, separating her from her mother and sisters. Eventually Prince could stand the abuse no longer. She ran away to her mother, but her father brought her back, presumably to avoid worse punishment. Five years later Prince was happy to be shipped 900 miles to Turks Island and sold to a Mr D——, but found that 'it was but going from one butcher to another'. Our selections include the trip to Turks Island, labour in the salt ponds, and Prince's return to Bermuda, where her owner probably molested her (this is handled tactfully for prudish readers). When Prince heard that John Wood was going to Antigua, she asked to be sold to him. Antigua allowed free black men to vote, a symbolic recognition that all slaves might deserve civil rights. But Mr and Mrs Wood were as cruel as her previous owners. Prince turned to Christianity for solace and in 1826 married a free black man, Daniel James, without her owner's permission. Two years later she went to England with the Woods. Their continuing cruelty led her to exercise her right under the 1772 Mansfield Decision to walk away from them. She accepted help from the Anti-Slavery Society, who recorded and published her life story in the final phase of the political struggle over emancipation. Her step out of the Woods' house and into freedom is Mary Prince's last known journey. She surfaces once more in the written record (during a libel trial occasioned by her *History*); it is not known when she died, or whether she ever returned to her husband in Antigua.

Some little time after this, one of the cows got loose from the stake, and ate one of the sweet-potato slips. I was milking when my master found it out. He came to me, and without any more ado, stooped down, and taking off his heavy boot, he struck me such a severe blow in the small of my back, that I shrieked with agony, and thought I was killed; and I feel a weakness in that part to this day. The cow was frightened at his violence, and kicked down the pail and spilt the milk all about. My master knew that this accident was his own fault, but he was so enraged that he seemed glad of an excuse to go on with his ill usage. I cannot remember how many licks he gave me then, but he beat me till I was unable to stand, and till he himself was weary.

After this I ran away and went to my mother, who was living with Mr Richard Darrel. My poor mother was both grieved and glad to see me; grieved because I had been so ill used, and glad because she had not seen me for a long, long while. She dared not receive me into the house, but she hid me up in a hole in the rocks near, and brought me food at night, after everybody was asleep. My father, who lived at

Crow Lane, over the salt-water channel, last heard of my being hid up in the cavern, and he came and took me back to my master. Oh I was loth, loth to go back; but as there was no remedy, I was obliged to submit.

When we got home, my poor father said to Captain I——, 'Sir, I am sorry that my child should be forced to run away from her owner; but the treatment she has received is enough to break her heart. The sight of her wounds has nearly broke mine. I entreat you, for the love of God, to forgive her for running away, and that you will be a kind master to her in future.' Captain I—— said I was used as well as I deserved, and that I ought to be punished for running away. I then took courage and said that I could stand the floggings no longer; that I was weary of my life, and therefore I had run away to my mother; but mothers could only weep and mourn over their children, they could not save them from cruel masters—from the whip, the rope, and the cow-skin. He told me to hold my tongue and go about my work, or he would find a way to settle me. He did not, however, flog me that day.

For five years after this I remained in his house, and almost daily received the same harsh treatment. At length he put me on board a sloop, and to my great joy sent me away to Turks Island.* I was not permitted to see my mother or father, or poor sisters and brothers, to say goodbye, though going away to a strange land, and might never see them again. Oh the Buckra people* who keep slaves think that black people are like cattle, without natural affection. But my heart tells me it is far otherwise.

We were nearly four weeks on the voyage, which was unusually long. Sometimes we had a light breeze, sometimes a great calm, and the ship made no way; so that our provisions and water ran very low, and we were put upon short allowance. I should almost have been starved had it not been for the kindness of a black man called Anthony, and his wife, who had brought their own victuals, and shared them with me.

When we went ashore at the Grand Quay, the captain sent me to the house of my new master, Mr D——, to whom Captain I—— had sold me. Grand Quay is a small town upon a sandbank; the houses low and built of wood. Such was my new master's. The first person I saw, on my arrival, was Mr D——, a stout sulky looking man, who carried me through the hall to show me to his wife and children.

Next day I was put up by the vendue master* to know how much I was worth, and I was valued at one hundred pounds currency.

My new master was one of the owners or holders of the salt ponds,* and he received a certain sum for every slave that worked upon his premises, whether they were young or old. This sum was allowed him out of the profits arising from the salt works. I was immediately sent to work in the salt water with the rest of the slaves. This work was perfectly new to me. I was given a half barrel and a shovel, and had to stand up to my knees in the water, from four o'clock in the morning till nine, when we were given some Indian corn boiled in water, which we were obliged to swallow as fast as we could for fear the rain should come on and melt the salt. We were then called again to our tasks, and worked through the heat of the day; the sun flaming upon our heads like fire, and raising salt blisters in those parts which were not completely covered. Our feet and legs, from standing in the salt water for so many hours, soon became full of dreadful boils, which eat down in some cases to the very bone, afflicting the sufferers with great torment. We came home at twelve; ate our corn soup, called *blawly*, as fast as we could, and went back to our employment till dark at night. We then shovelled up the salt in large heaps, and went down to the sea, where we washed the pickle from our limbs, and cleaned the barrows and shovels from the salt. When we returned to the house, our master gave us each our allowance of raw Indian corn, which we pounded in a mortar and boiled in water for our suppers.

We slept in a long shed, divided into narrow slips, like the stalls used for cattle. Boards fixed upon stakes driven into the ground, without mat or covering, were our only beds. On Sundays, after we had washed the salt bags, and done other work required of us, we went into the bush and cut the long soft grass, of which we made trusses for our legs and feet to rest upon, for they were so full of the salt boils that we could get no rest lying upon the bare boards.

Though we worked from morning till night, there was no satisfying Mr D——. I hoped, when I left Capt. I——, that I should have been better off, but I found it was but going from one butcher to another. There was this difference between them: my former master used to beat me while raging and foaming with passion; Mr D—— was usually quite calm. He would stand by and give orders for a slave to be cruelly whipped, and assist in the punishment, without moving a muscle of his face; walking about and taking snuff with the greatest composure. Nothing could touch his hard heart—neither sighs, nor tears, nor prayers, nor streaming blood; he was deaf to our cries, and careless of our sufferings. Mr D—— has often stripped me naked, hung me up by the wrists, and beat me with the cow-skin, with his own hand, till my body was raw with gashes. Yet there was nothing very remarkable in this; for it might serve as a sample of the common usage of the slaves on that horrible island. . . .

When we were ill, let our complaint be what it might, the only medicine given to us was a great bowl of hot salt water, with salt mixed with it, which made us very sick. If we could not keep up with the rest of the gang of slaves, we were put in the stocks, and severely flogged the next morning. Yet, not the less, our master expected, after we had thus been kept from our rest, and our limbs rendered stiff and sore with ill usage, that we should still go through the ordinary tasks of the day all the same. Sometimes we had to work all night, measuring salt to load a vessel; or turning a machine to draw water out of the sea for the salt-making. Then we had no sleep—no rest—but were forced to work as fast as we could, and go on again all next day the same as usual. Work—work—work—Oh that Turks Island was a horrible place! The people in England, I am sure, have never found out what is carried on there. Cruel, horrible place!

Mr D—— had a slave called old Daniel, whom he used to treat in the most cruel manner. Poor Daniel was lame in the hip, and could not keep up with the rest of the slaves; and our master would order him to be stripped and laid down on the ground, and have him beaten with a rod of rough briar till his skin was quite red and raw. He would then call for a bucket of salt, and fling upon the raw flesh till the man writhed on the ground like a worm, and screamed aloud with agony. This poor man's wounds were never healed, and I have often seen them full of maggots, which increased his torments to an intolerable degree. He was an object of pity and terror to the whole gang of slaves, and in his wretched case we saw, each of us, our own lot, if we should live to be as old.

Oh the horrors of slavery! How the thought of it pains my heart! But the truth ought to be told of it; and what my eyes have seen I think it is my duty to relate; for few people in England know what slavery is. I have been a slave—I have felt what a slave feels, and I know what a slave knows; and I would have all the good people in

England to know it too, that they may break our chains, and set us free. . . .

I think it was about ten years I had worked in the salt ponds at Turks Island, when my master left off business, and retired to a house he had in Bermuda, leaving his son to succeed him in the island. He took me with him to wait upon his daughters; and I was joyful, for I was sick, sick of Turks Island, and my heart yearned to see my native place again, my mother, and my kindred.

I had seen my poor mother during the time I was a slave in Turks Island. One Sunday morning I was on the beach with some of the slaves, and we saw a sloop come in loaded with slaves to work in the salt water. We got a boat and went aboard. When I came upon the deck I asked the black people, 'Is there anyone here for me?' 'Yes,' they said, 'your mother.' I thought they said this in jest—I could scarcely believe them for joy; but when I saw my poor mammy my joy was turned to sorrow, for she had gone from her senses. 'Mammy,' I said, 'is this you?' She did not know me. 'Mammy,' I said, 'what's the matter?' She began to talk foolishly, and said that she had been under the vessel's bottom. They had been overtaken by a violent storm at sea. My poor mother had never been on the sea before, and she was so ill that she lost her senses, and it was long before she came quite to herself again. She had a sweet child with her—a little sister I had never seen, about four years of age, called Rebecca. I took her on shore with me, for I felt I should love her directly; and I kept her with me a week. Poor little thing! hers has been a sad life, and continues so to this day. My mother worked for some years on the island, but was taken back to Bermuda some time before my master carried me again thither.

After I left Turks Island, I was told by some negroes that came over from it, that the poor slaves had built up a place with boughs and leaves, where they might meet for prayers, but the white people pulled it down twice, and would not allow them even a shed for prayers. A flood came down soon after and washed away many houses, filled the place with sand, and overflowed the ponds: and I do think that this was for their wickedness; for the Buckra men there were very wicked. I saw and heard much that was very very bad at that place.

I was several years the slave of Mr D—— after I returned to my native place. Here I worked in the grounds. My work was planting and hoeing sweet-potatoes, Indian corn, plaintains, bananas, cab-bages, pumpkins, onions, etc. I did all the household work, and attended upon a horse and cow besides—going also upon all errands. I had to curry the horse—to clean and feed him—and sometimes to ride him a little. I had more than enough to do—but still it was not so very bad as Turks Island.

My old master often got drunk, and then he would get in a fury with his daughter, and beat her till she was not fit to be seen. I remember on one occasion, I had gone to fetch water, and when I was coming up the hill I heard a great screaming; I ran as fast as I could to the house, put down the water, and went into the chamber, where I found my master beating Miss D—— dreadfully. I strove with all my strength to get her away from him; for she was all black and blue with bruises. He had beat her with his fist, and almost killed her. The people gave me credit for getting her away. He turned round and began to lick me. Then I said, 'Sir, this is not Turks Island.' I can't repeat his answer, the words were too wicked—too bad to say. He wanted to treat me the same in Bermuda as he had done in Turks Island.

He had an ugly fashion of stripping himself quite naked, and ordering me then to wash him in a tub of water. This was worse to me than all the licks. Sometimes when he called me to wash him I could not come, my eyes were so full of shame. He would then come to beat me. One time I had plates and knives in my hand, and I dropped both plates and knives, and some of the plates were broken. He struck me so severely for this, that at last I defended myself, for I thought it was high time to do so. I then told him I would not live longer with him, for he was a very indecent man—very spiteful, and too indecent; with no shame for his servants, no shame for his own flesh. So I went away to a neighbouring house and sat down and cried till the next morning, when I went home again, not knowing what else to do.

After that I was hired to work at Cedar Hills and every Saturday night I paid the money to my master. I had plenty of work to do there—plenty of washing; but yet I made myself pretty comfortable. I earned two dollars and a quarter a week, which is twenty pence a day.

During the time I worked there, I heard that Mr John Wood was going to Antigua. I felt a great wish to go there, and I went to Mr D——, and asked him to let me go in Mr Wood's service. Mr Wood did not then want to purchase me; it was my own fault that I came under him, I was so anxious to go. It was ordained to be, I suppose; God led me there. The truth is, I did not wish to be any longer the slave of my indecent master.

Mr Wood took me with him to Antigua,* to the town of St John's, where he lived. This was about fifteen years ago. He did not then know whether I was to be sold; but Mrs Wood found that I could work, and she wanted to buy me. Her husband then wrote to my master to enquire whether I was to be sold? Mr D—— wrote in reply, 'that I should not be sold to anyone that would treat me ill'. It was strange he should say this, when he had treated me so ill himself. So I was purchased by Mr Wood for 300 dollars, (or £100 Bermuda currency). . . .

I had not much happiness in my marriage, owing to my being a slave. It made my husband sad to see me so ill-treated. Mrs Wood was always abusing me about him. She did not lick me herself, but she got her husband to do it for her, whilst she fretted the flesh off my bones. Yet for all this she would not sell me. She sold five slaves whilst I was with her; but though she was always finding fault with me, she would not part with me. However, Mr Wood afterwards allowed Daniel to have a place to live in our yard, which we were very thankful for.

After this, I fell ill again with the rheumatism, and was sick a long time; but whether sick or well, I had my work to do. About this time I asked my master and mistress to let me buy my own freedom. With the help of Mr Burchell, I could have found the means to pay Mr Wood; for it was agreed that I should afterwards serve Mr Burchell a while, for the cash he was to advance for me. I was earnest in the request to my owners; but their hearts were hard—too hard to consent. Mrs Wood was very angry—she grew quite outrageous—she called me a black devil, and asked me who had put freedom into my head. 'To be free is very sweet,' I said: but she took good care to keep me a slave. I saw her change colour, and I left the room.

About this time my master and mistress were going to England to put their son to school, and bring their daughters home; and they took me with them to take care of the child. I was willing to come to England: I thought that by going there I should probably get cured of my rheumatism, and should return with my master and mistress, quite well, to my husband. My husband was willing for me to come away, for he had heard that my master would free me—and I also hoped this might prove true; but it was all a false report.

The steward of the ship was very kind to me. He and my husband were in the same class in the Moravian Church. I was thankful that he was so friendly, for my mistress was not kind to me on the passage; and she told me, when she was angry, that she did not intend to treat me any better in England than in the West Indies—that I need not expect it. And she was as good as her word.

When we drew near to England, the rheumatism seized all my limbs worse than ever, and my body was dreadfully swelled. When we landed at the Tower,* I showed my flesh to my mistress, but she took no great notice of it. We were obliged to stop at the tavern till my master got a house; and a day or two after, my mistress sent me down into the wash-house to learn to wash in the English way. In the West Indies we wash with cold water—in England with hot. I told my mistress I was afraid that putting my hands first into the hot water and then into the cold, would increase the pain in my limbs. The doctor had told my mistress long before I came from the West Indies, that I was a sickly body and the washing did not agree with me. But Mrs Wood would not release me from the tub, so I was forced to do as I could. I grew worse, and could not stand to wash. I was then forced to sit down with the tub before me, and often through pain and weakness was reduced to kneel or to sit down on the floor, to finish my task. When I complained to my mistress of this, she only got into a passion as usual, and said washing in hot water could not hurt any one; that I was lazy and insolent, and wanted to be free of my work; but that she would make me do it. I thought her very hard on me, and my heart rose up within me. However I kept still at that time, and went down again to wash the child's things; but the English washerwomen who were at work there, when they saw that I was so ill, had pity upon me and washed them for me.

After that, when we came up to live in Leigh Street, Mrs Wood sorted out five bags of clothes which we had used at sea, and also such as had been worn since we came on shore, for me and the cook to wash. Elizabeth the cook told her, that she did not think that I was able to stand to the tub, and that she had better hire a woman. I also said myself, that I had come over to nurse the child, and that I was sorry I had come from Antigua, since mistress would work me so hard, without compassion for my rheumatism. Mr and Mrs Wood, when they heard this, rose up in a passion against me. They opened the door and bade me get out. But I was a stranger, and did not know one door in the street from another, and was unwilling to go away. They made a dreadful uproar, and from that day they constantly kept cursing and abusing me. I was obliged to wash, though I was very ill. Mrs Wood, indeed once hired a washerwoman, but she was not well treated, and would come no more.

My master quarrelled with me another time, about one of our great washings, his wife having stirred him up to do so. He said he would compel me to do the whole of the washing given out to me, or if I again refused, he would take a short course with me: he would either send me down to the brig in the river, to carry me back to Antigua, or he would turn me at once out of doors, and let me provide for myself. I said I would willingly go back, if he would let me purchase my own freedom. But this enraged him more than all the rest: he cursed and swore at me dreadfully, and said he would never sell my freedom—if I wished to be free, I was free in England,* and I might go and try what freedom would do for me, and be d——d. My heart was very sore with this treatment, but I had to go on. I continued to do my work, and did all I could to give satisfaction, but all would not do.

Shortly after, the cook left them, and then matters went on ten times worse. I always washed the child's clothes without being commanded to do it, and anything else that was wanted in the family; though still I was very sick—very sick indeed. When the great washing came round, which was every two months, my mistress got together again a great many heavy things, such as bed-ticks,* bed-coverlets, etc., for me to wash. I told her I was too ill to wash such heavy things that day. She said, she supposed I thought myself a free woman, but I was not; and if I did not do it directly I should be instantly turned out of doors. I stood a long time before I could answer, for I did not know well what to do. I knew that I was free in England, but I did not know where to go, or how to get my living; and therefore, I did not like to leave the house. But Mr Wood said he would send for a constable to thrust me out; and at last I took course and resolved that I would not be longer thus treated, but would go and trust to Providence. This was the fourth time they had threatened to turn me out, and, go where I might, I was determined now to take them at their word; though I thought it very hard, after I had lived with them for thirteen years, and worked for them like a horse, to be driven out in this way, like a beggar. My only fault was being sick, and therefore unable to please my mistress, who thought she never could get work enough out of her slaves; and I told them so: but they only abused me and drove me out. This took place from two to three months, I think, after we came to England.

When I came away, I went to the man (one Mash) who used to black the shoes of the family, and asked his wife to get somebody to go with me to Hatton Garden to the Moravian Missionaries: these were the only persons I knew in England. The woman sent a young girl with me to the mission house, and I saw there a gentleman called Mr Moore. I told him my whole story, and how my owners had treated me, and asked him to take in my trunk with what few clothes I had. The missionaries were very kind to me—they were sorry for my destitute situation, and gave me leave to bring my things to be placed under their care. They were very good people, and they told me to come to the church.

When I went back to Mr Wood's to get my trunk, I saw a lady, Mrs Pell, who was on a visit to my mistress. When Mr and Mrs Wood heard me come in, they set this lady to stop me, finding that they had gone too far with me. Mrs Pell came out to me, and said, 'Are you really going to leave, Molly? Don't leave, but come into the country with me.' I believe she said this because she thought Mrs Wood would easily get me back again. I replied to her, 'Ma'am, this is the fourth time my master and mistress have driven me out, or threatened to drive me—and I will give them no more occasion to bid me go. I was not willing to leave them, for I am a stranger in this country, but now I must go—I can stay no longer to be so used.' Mrs Pell then went upstairs to my mistress, and told that I would go, and that she could not stop me. Mrs Wood was very much hurt and frightened when she found I was determined to go out that day. She said, 'If she goes the people will rob her, and then turn her adrift.' She did not say this to me, but she spoke it loud enough for me to hear; that it might induce me not to go, I suppose. Mr Wood also asked me where I was going to. I told him where I had been, and that I should never have gone away had I not been driven out by my owners. He had given me a written paper some time before, which said that I had come with them to England by my own desire; and that was true. It said also that I left them of my own free will, because I was a free woman in England; and that I was idle and would not do my work—which was not true. I gave this paper afterwards to a gentleman who inquired into my case.*

I went into the kitchen and got my clothes out. The nurse and the servant girl were there, and I said to the man who was going to take out my trunk, 'Stop, before you take up this trunk, and hear what I have to say before these people. I am going out of this house, as I was ordered; but I have done no wrong at all to my owners, neither here nor in the West Indies. I always worked very hard to please them, both by night and day; but there was no giving satisfaction, for my mistress could never be satisfied with reasonable service. I told my mistress I was sick, and yet she has ordered me out of doors. This is the fourth time; and now I am going out.'

And so I came out, and went and carried my trunk to the Moravians. I then returned back to Mash the shoe-black's house, and begged his wife to take me in. I had a little West Indian money in my trunk; and they got it changed for me. This helped to support me for a little while.

3. PLANTERS

WILLIAM BECKFORD, *A Descriptive Account of the Island of Jamaica, With Remarks upon the Cultivation of the Sugar-cane, Throughout the Different Seasons of the Year, and Chiefly Considered in a Picturesque Point of View* (1790)

William Beckford (1744–99), first cousin of the author of the oriental tale *Vathek* (1782), was an illegitimate offshoot of one of Jamaica's wealthiest planter families and himself a planter there for thirteen years. After his return to England Beckford spent several years in the Fleet prison for debt (possibly due at least in part to property damage from a hurricane). There he wrote *Remarks on the Situation of the Negroes in Jamaica* (1788) and *A Descriptive Account of the Island of Jamaica* (1790). Beckford's tactics in the former are meliorist: he advocates humane plantation management and slave baptism but defends slavery itself, arguing that slaves are no worse off than British labourers and that abolition will only result in other nations taking Britain's share of the trade, with no benefit to Africans. The *Descriptive Account* intersperses practical advice on 'plantership' with painterly descriptions of Jamaican scenes; the aesthetics of the picturesque and the sublime, extravagantly pursued for over 600 pages, seems intended to set the stage for the defence of slavery that concludes the second volume. Our selections include a sublime cane-field fire, a picturesque harvest scene, and thoughts on the consequences of abolition and emancipation.

A cane-piece on fire is a most tremendous object: no flame is more alarming, none more rapid; and the fury and velocity with which it burns and communicates, cannot possibly be described, excepting by those who have been interested and disappointed witnesses of its destruction. If a fire happen in a cane-piece that has been lately cut, shall catch, and spread upon hilly land, and be observable at night, it will be seen to run in circular lines corresponding to the direction of the banks between which the canes have been regularly planted; and as the stream of flame is uncommonly brilliant, and when increased by the wind, is, by intenseness of heat, become pale, it partakes much of the colour and appearance of liquid lava, when it bursts in torrents from the side of a volcanic mountain, and presents a scene with which even the enthusiasm of Sir William Hamilton* could not fail to be pleased, and which might possibly awaken a curiosity which has been so often tried in the examination and description of the dangerous magnificence of Etna, or the more humble and less terrific eruptions of Vesuvius.

To attempt a description of that tremendous scenery of Nature which Brydone* has immortalized would be an insult to language; and to dwell upon the simple operations of fire, where he has dived into the chymic* operations of lava, and its extraordinary accompaniments, would argue a presumption which I hope I do not possess, and detract from that science before which I have a pleasure to bend.

A trash-house* in flames, from its size and contiguity to other buildings, is certainly a most dreadful and alarming sight; but has not (if I may venture to use the expression) so much of the picturesque scenery of destruction as the cane-piece in flames: as the mass is more ponderous and concentered, the fire is more confined, and of consequence does not admit of so sudden a blaze. It is the celerity of communication that brightens the fire-work, or that gives variety and surprise to an illumination.

So soon as a fire is observed upon a plantation, the shell resounds,* and the listening echoes receive and return the blast; the neighbouring estates and settlements imbibe, and constantaneously repeat, the shrill alarm: every ear is attentive, and every voice is silent. It continues its complaint upon the hills: it now declines and dies away; but, alas! to swell with a louder note, to supplicate assistance, or forbode despair. Every neighbour hears, is alert, and flies: if he come in time to assist, he is happy; if too late, his intention was good, his conscience acquits, and he can only console. Upon such occasions, the philanthropy of the Island is very commendably notorious. A man cannot suffer a signal calamity in Jamaica without pity at least, if not assistance: and this principle pervades every part of the Island, and every community of men.

The rolling of the smoke, the spreading of the flames, and the cracking of the canes, combine their dreadful influence with that of the raging element; and should the fire happen in the night, which is accompanied with particular terrors of its own, it is truly sublime,* and might be contemplated, with some degree of pleasing horror, did not reflection awaken at the melancholy scene, and the compassionate idea of the sufferings of another, engulf every principle but what might be directed to the alleviation of his misfortune, to the reparation of his loss, and to the dread lest a similar accident should befall himself. The shells upon such an occasion, and at such a time, have a very awful effect; and the appearance of the negroes amidst the flames, their fears and exertions, contrasted with the noisy impatience of the looks of the white people, and the groups of horses and mules in the background, together with that general motion and confusion that attend destruction, are striking particulars in this dreadful scenery.

Amidst the appearance of this calamity, should any of the cane-pieces happen to be on the side of hills, and near a river, the reflections therein of the clouds that roll in black and fiery volumes, the pale light that shoots out at the communication of every blaze, and the umbered* appearance of the negroes, that in a certain manner help to darken the shade, are seen to double, as it were, the dreadful landscape, and to add the picturesque of horror to the destruction that is blazing round.

Should the moon happen, at such a time, to be in her meridian, and a flitting cloud discharge a shower, the temporary conflict of the opposing elements would add very considerably to the romantic appearance of the night, and would in some measure resemble those awful contrasts of fire and water that are frequently observed in the eruptions of a volcano, and which I had once in my life the pleasure to observe.

Of this uncommonly sublime, and the more sublime as it is a destructive, scenery, the effect would be truly awful, if committed to the canvas of an intelligent and enthusiastic genius, and expressed in the forcible manner that Mr Deane* has described Vesuvius; and which exhibition cannot help bringing back to the mind the remembrance of a man whose talents might have afforded amusement to others, and profit to himself; but whose abilities were lost to the world, and whose life was closed at an early period, in disappointment and neglect, and in bodily feeling and mental distress.

When a fire in a piece of standing canes is perceived in the time of crop, the common practice is to cut through a particular portion of the field, to prevent the spark of communication from increasing a more general conflagration: and it is amazing with what celerity and skill this service of danger is commonly effected.

If a fire shall happen among the trash,* after the canes shall be removed, and shall spread with any violence, the most expeditious and certain method of extinguishing it is found to be the heaping of it up on the extremities of the piece; and thus, by making a counter-fire, and accumulating the combustible matter around that spot, to give a contrary direction to the rapidity of the flames. The intervals that are purposely left between the different pieces will sometimes serve as a barrier to the progress of the conflagration; but as the grass that grows upon them is often as dry as the trash itself, very great caution should be used, that they do not catch the neighbouring blaze; and which it would, at all events, be very difficult to prevent, if there be not water at hand, or plantain or other succulent leaves by which the sparks that catch may be easily extinguished.

After a sharp and continued drought, a sky in flames, and the sublunary earth on fire, it is astonishing to see how sudden a revolution will melt the first into rain, and cause vegetation to spring from the embers of the last! The late tremendous and afflicting scenes have soon their contrast: the rains no sooner fall, than Nature is instantaneously and visibly revived, and a cheerful verdure is observed to arise, and is shortly seen to triumph over defoliation and despair. It is in this sudden change that the elements of water and of fire seem to labour to obtain and support a transcendency; and that the sky puts on its most magnificently aërial, and the earth her most picturesque and splendid forms.

The man who can contemplate the rolling of the clouds that pace the mountains with gigantic strides, with the idea of representations in his mind; can ruminate upon their masses, and expatiate upon their forms; who can take pleasure in the beautiful varieties of vapours and of fogs, of ideal caverns and imaginary hills, of dotted forests and of silver lakes, of shadowy valleys and of open plains, of bounded islands and extensive seas—the man, I say, who can take delight in these objects of Nature, and range over their alternate and concentered beauties, with a painter's eye, and is willing to treasure them up in his mind for future imitation, will hardly find a spot, I should imagine, upon the habitable globe, in which these objects may be studied with greater effect, than in the clouds, the fogs, and moonlights of that Island which I have feebly endeavoured to describe. . . .

The labourers are now prepared for the expected harvest: they hold themselves in readiness in their respective houses to obey the lively summons: the shell is heard with a shrill alarm to call them forth; it echoes among the hills, and resounds across the plains; it seems to swell with a cheerful blast, and to invite to profit and abundance. The overseer is anxious to give his orders to commence the crop; he is the first in the field: the driver follows with his knotted stick, and his whip flung carelessly across his shoulder: the latter walks briskly to the place of labour; the negroes follow, and he shows them upon what part of the piece to begin.

The tops of the canes are now in a constant tremor; the yellow swarths* are strewed upon the ground; and vigour and dispatch are observed in everybody, and apparent in every land.

The driver, with an authoritative voice, cautions them to cut the canes close, and not to waste too much of the top; to separate those that are tainted, and to discard those joints that have been injured by the rats: he keeps them in a regular string before him, and takes care to chequer the able with the weak, that the work may not be too light for the first, nor too heavy for the last. He intimidates some, and encourages others; and too often, perhaps, a tyrant in authority, he imposes upon the timid, and suffers the sturdy to escape.

There is something particularly picturesque and striking in a gang of negroes, when employed in cutting canes upon the swelling projections of a hill; when they take a long sweep, and observe a regular discipline in their work: indeed the surrounding accompaniments of the field afford a very singular and interesting variety.

As the pieces upon hilly estates are in themselves uncommonly romantic, so are the minutiae of which they are composed not less various and pleasing. The colour of the negroes, when bending beneath the verdant canopies of the canes, and these softened by the branching shadows of the majestic cotton-tree* which rises in all the pride of vegetation and of height, from the lowly glen in which its ample roots have taken earth, and which defraud the minor products of the glade of genial moisture and sustentation, contribute to the moving landscape.

Behind the cutters are observed the rows of canes that glow with a bright and golden yellow; the tiers proceed, and bind them up: the mules now traverse to collect or carry off their heavy loads; the cattle are spread over the lower parts of the hill, and feed upon the tops that are left behind, while the wains* remain at bottom in quiet expectation of that freight which is to reward the avarice of the master, by the labour of his oxen; and what this labour is, their reduced and lank situation will too often, I fear, sufficiently explain.

The common practice at the beginning of crop* is to set in all the able hands for one or two days previously to the putting about the mill, to cut as many canes as possible, that it may continue, when once set in motion, a large and regular weekly execution; which, if the estate be not well handed, and abundant in cattle, it will be found very difficult to do.

Whenever the mill shall stand idle for want of a supply of canes, the negroes from the works* are then sent out to assist the operations of the field: the business of the coppers* becomes stagnant; they get cool; the liquor soddens; and every delay of this kind is of course attended with loss.

When the mill is therefore put about, it should, if possible, be kept to steady work; the feeders and the boilers* would be then confined to their particular provinces, and would not lose their time in being alternately ordered from the works to the field, and again from the field to the works.

The time of crop, particularly the commencement of it, exhibits a very lively and a pleasing scene, and every living creature seems to be in spirits and in expectation: the negroes are not only alert and cheerful, but the cattle and the mules, having recovered the fatigues of the planting-season, appear to be fresh and vigorous: nor do they seem to require the encouragement of the voice, nor to dread the thunders of the whip: for this instrument of correction in Jamaica, whether it be in the hands of the cart-man, the mule-boy, or the negro-driver, is heard, in either case, to resound among the hills and upon the plains, and to awaken the echoes wherever the reverberations of the lash shall pass.

There is something extremely animating in the prospect of the roads between the pieces upon which the canes are carted, and the mill: the wain that is piled up with its golden bundles, the slow and steady motion of the oxen, the more nimble step of the mules, and the seeming urgency of their sable* drivers, give interest and variety to the moving scene, and which are of course augmented according to the numbers of either that pass and repass upon the resounding and the dusty roads. . . .

If abolition,* unconditional, unqualified abolition shall take place, our interest in the West-India islands must be at an end, seventy millions of property will wear away with time, and be sunk at last: the revenue will suffer an annual diminution of three millions at least; the price of sugar, which is now become a necessary article of life,* must be immediately enhanced; discontentment and dissatisfaction may dismember the empire, from which too large a jewel* has been lately torn; the necessity of additional taxes may puzzle the minister, divide the legislature, and distress the people, who, indignant perhaps at exactions at home, which might have been provided for by foreign resource, may become disaffected to government, renounce their country, and take refuge in a neighbouring kingdom,* which may profit from our weaknesses and combat, and lastly overpower us with our own strength.

Next to abolition, emancipation comes as the second innovation upon the list; for it is natural to suppose that the same ideas of benevolence that will cut off the communication between Africa and the Islands will extend to the latter; and that the negroes, all at once, whether they will or no, or without the adduction of any proof that liberty will make them happy, are to be enfranchised, and independent of labour and of men, let what will be the consequence to those whose property they are, under whose government they live, and by whom alone they can be protected and safe. . . .

What will be the first consequence of emancipation? The indiscriminate sacrifice, in all probability, of the white inhabitants; or at best, some may be retained to expiate former servitude; the customs of ages will be inverted; and the people of our own colour and religion will become the degraded and the useless slaves of those who formerly looked up to them for protection, food, and comfort.

What would, in the second place, become of the negroes? Driven as they would be from their native homes, their hereditary grounds, and stripped at once of their personal possessions and domestic joys, they would set fire to their houses, destroy their provisions, live in open war and defiance of each other, and after having exterminated those of another colour, would by degrees extirpate those of their own; and those few who shall have survived the general massacre, must ultimately starve; and this gradation of horror, all those who are at all acquainted with the disposition of negroes must be convinced would eventually follow.

MATTHEW GREGORY LEWIS, *Journal of a West India Proprietor, Kept during a Residence in the Island of Jamaica* (1834)

Matthew Gregory Lewis (1775–1818), educated for the diplomatic service, attained notoriety at the age of 19 with the publication of *The Monk* (1796), a lurid, bestselling Gothic romance vilified by moralists. In 1812 Lewis inherited two Jamaican plantations with nearly 600 slaves and decided to visit his property to inspect the slaves' living conditions. Lewis was no emancipationist, believing slaves would be worse off if no one were responsible for their welfare, but his liberal innovations on his Cornwall plantation drew his neighbours' ire. On the voyage home from his second visit he died of yellow fever contracted in Jamaica. The *Journal of a West India Proprietor* was not published until 1834. Lewis's humorous, allusive style uneasily masks the tensions of his interaction with his slaves. Here Lewis arrives in Jamaica, witnesses a slave New Year's festival, and travels to his plantation. Picturesque excursions to Montego Bay and Spanish Town are followed by a brief, unhappy visit to Lewis's second plantation, Hordley.

1 JANUARY 1816. At length the ship has squeezed herself into this champagne bottle of a bay! Perhaps, the satisfaction attendant upon our having overcome the difficulty, added something to the illusion of its effect; but the beauty of the atmosphere, the dark purple mountains, the shores covered with mangroves of the liveliest green down to the very edge of the water, and the light-coloured houses with their lattices and piazzas completely embowered in trees, altogether made the scenery of the Bay wear a very picturesque appearance. And, to complete the charm, the sudden sounds of the drum and banjee, called our attention to a procession of the John-Canoe,* which was proceeding to celebrate the opening of the new year at the town of Black River. The John-Canoe is a Merry-Andrew dressed in a striped doublet, and bearing upon his head a kind of pasteboard house-boat, filled with puppets, representing, some sailors, others soldiers, others again slaves at work on a plantation, etc. The negroes are allowed three days for holidays at Christmas, and also New Year's day, which being the last is always reckoned by them as the festival of the greatest importance. It is for this day that they reserve their finest dresses, and lay their schemes for displaying their show and expense to the greatest advantage; and it is then that the John-Canoe is considered not merely as a person of material consequence, but one whose presence is absolutely indispensable. Nothing could look more gay than the procession which we now saw with its train of attendants, all dressed in white, and marching two by two (except when the file was broken here and there by a single horseman), and its band of negro music, and its scarlet flags fluttering about in the breeze, now disappearing behind a projecting clump of mangrove trees, and then again emerging into an open part of the road, as it wound along the shore towards the town of Black River.

> Magno telluris amore
> Egressi optata Troes potiuntur arena.*

I had determined not to go on shore, till I should land for good and all at Savannah la Mar. But although I could resist the 'telluris amor', there was no resisting John-Canoe; so, in defiance of a broiling afternoon's sun, about four o'clock we left the vessel for the town.

It was, as I understand, formerly one of some magnitude; but it now consists only of a few houses, owing to a spark from a tobacco-pipe or a candle having lodged upon a mosquito-net during dry weather; and although the conflagration took place at midday, the whole town was reduced to ashes. The few streets (I believe there were not above two, but those were wide and regular, and the houses looked very neat) were now crowded with people, and it seemed to be allowed, upon all hands, that New Year's day had never been celebrated there with more expense and festivity.

It seems that, many years ago, an Admiral of the Red was super-seded on the Jamaica station by an Admiral of the Blue,* and both of them gave balls at Kingston to the 'Brown Girls';* for the fair sex elsewhere are called the 'Brown Girls' in Jamaica. In consequence of these balls, all Kingston was divided into parties: from thence the division spread into other districts: and ever since, the whole island, at Christmas, is separated into the rival factions of the Blues and the Reds (the Red representing also the English, the Blue the Scotch), who contend for setting forth their processions with the greatest taste and magnificence. This year, several gentlemen in the neigh-bourhood of Black River had subscribed very largely towards the expenses of the show; and certainly it produced the gayest and most amusing scene that I ever witnessed, to which the mutual jealousy and pique of the two parties against each other contributed in no slight degree. The champions of the rival Roses—the Guelphs and the Ghibellines*—none of them could exceed the scornful animosity and spirit of depreciation with which the Blues and the Reds of Black River examined the efforts at display of each other. The Blues had the advantage beyond a doubt; this a Red girl told us that she could not deny; but still, 'though the Reds were beaten, she would not be a Blue girl for the whole universe!' On the other hand, Miss Edwards (the mistress of the hotel from whose window we saw the show), was rank Blue to the very tips of her fingers, and had, indeed, contributed one of her female slaves to sustain a very important character in the show; for when the Blue procession was ready to set forward, there was evidently a hitch, something was wanting; and there seemed to be no possibility of getting on without it—when suddenly we saw a tall woman dressed in mourning (being Miss Edwards herself) rush out of our hotel, dragging along by the hand a strange uncouth kind of a glittering tawdry figure, all feathers, and pitchfork, and painted pasteboard, who moved most reluctantly, and turned out to be no less a personage than Britannia herself, with a pasteboard shield covered with the arms of Great Britain, a trident in her hand, and a helmet made of pale blue silk and silver. The poor girl, it seems, was bashful at appearing in this conspicuous manner before so many spectators, and hung back when it came to the point. But her mistress had seized hold of her, and placed her by main force in her destined position. The music struck up; Miss Edwards gave the Goddess a great push forwards; the drumsticks and the elbows of the fiddlers attacked her in the rear; and on went Britannia willy-nilly!

The Blue girls called themselves 'the Blue girls of Waterloo'.* Their motto was the more patriotic; that of the Red was the more gallant: 'Britannia rules the day!' streamed upon the Blue flag; 'Red girls for ever!' floated upon the Red. But, in point of taste and invention, the former carried it hollow. First marched Britannia; then came a band of music; then the flag; then the Blue King and Queen—the Queen splendidly dressed in white and silver (in scorn of the opposite party, her train was borne by a little girl in red); his Majesty wore a full British Admiral's uniform, with a white satin sash, and a huge cocked hat with a gilt paper crown upon the top of it. These were immediately followed by 'Nelson's Car', being a kind of canoe decorated with blue and silver drapery, and with 'Trafalgar'* written on the front of it; and the procession was closed by a long train of Blue grandees (the women dressed in uniforms of white, with robes of blue muslin), all Princes and Princesses, Dukes and Duchesses, every mother's child of them.

The Red girls were also dressed very gaily and prettily, but they had nothing in point of invention that could vie with Nelson's Car and Britannia; and when the Red throne made its appearance, language cannot express the contempt with which our landlady eyed it. 'It was neither one thing nor t'other,' Miss Edwards was of opinion. 'Merely a few yards of calico stretched over some planks—and look, look, only look at it behind! You may see the bare boards! By way of a throne, indeed! Well, to be sure, Miss Edwards never saw a poorer thing in her life, that she must say!' And then she told me that somebody had just snatched at a medal which Britannia wore round her neck, and had endeavoured to force it away. I asked her who had done so? 'Oh, one of the Red party, *of course*!' The Red party was evidently Miss Edwards's Mrs Grundy.* John-Canoe made no part of the procession; but he and his rival, John-Crayfish (a personage of whom I heard, but could not obtain a sight), seemed to act upon quite an independent interest, and go about from house to house, tumbling and playing antics to pick up money for themselves. . . . I never saw so many people who appeared to be so unaffectedly happy. In England, at fairs and races, half the visitors at least seem to have been only brought there for the sake of traffic, and to be too busy to be amused; but here nothing was thought of but real pleasure; and that pleasure seemed to consist in singing, dancing, and laughing, in seeing and being seen, in showing their own fine clothes, or in admiring those of others. There were no people selling or buying; no servants and landladies bustling and passing about; and at eight o'clock, as we passed through the market-place, where was the greatest illumination, and which, of course, was most thronged, I did not see a single person drunk, nor had I observed a single quarrel through the course of the day; except, indeed, when some thoughtless fellow crossed the line of the procession, and received by the way a good box of the ear from the Queen or one of her attendant Duchesses. Everybody made the same remark to me; 'Well, sir, what do you think Mr Wilberforce* would think of the state of the negroes, if he could see this scene?' and certainly, to judge by this one specimen, of all beings that I have yet seen, these were the happiest. As we were passing to our boat, through the market-place, suddenly we saw Miss Edwards dart out of the crowd, and seize the Captain's arm— 'Captain! Captain!' cried she, 'for the love of Heaven, only look at the *Red* lights! Old iron hoops, nothing but old iron hoops, I declare! Well! for my part!' and then, with a contemptuous toss of her head, away frisked Miss Edwards triumphantly.

2 JANUARY 1816. Soon after nine o'clock we reached Savannah la Mar, where I found my trustee, and a whole cavalcade, waiting to conduct me to my own estate; for he had brought with him a curricle and pair for myself, a gig* for my servant, two black boys upon mules, and a cart with eight oxen to convey my baggage. The road was excellent, and we had not above five miles to travel; and as soon as the carriage entered my gates, the uproar and confusion which ensued sets all description at defiance. The works were instantly all abandoned; everything that had life came flocking to the house from all quarters; and not only the men, and the women, and the children,

but, 'by a bland assimilation', the hogs, and the dogs, and the geese, and the fowls, and the turkeys, all came hurrying along by instinct, to see what could possibly be the matter, and seemed to be afraid of arriving too late. Whether the pleasure of the negroes was sincere may be doubted; but certainly it was the loudest that I ever witnessed: they all talked together, sang, danced, shouted, and, in the violence of their gesticulations, tumbled over each other, and rolled about upon the ground. Twenty voices at once enquired after uncles, and aunts, and grandfathers, and great-grandmothers of mine, who had been buried long before I was in existence, and whom, I verily believe, most of them only knew by tradition. One woman held up her little naked black child to me, grinning from ear to ear; 'Look, Massa, look here! him nice lilly neger for Massa!' Another complained, 'So long since none come see we, Massa; good Massa, come at last.' As for the old people, they were all in one and the same story: now they had lived once to see Massa, they were ready for dying tomorrow, 'them no care'.

The shouts, the gaiety, the wild laughter, their strange and sudden bursts of singing and dancing, and several old women, wrapped up in large cloaks, their heads bound round with different-coloured handkerchiefs, leaning on a staff, and standing motionless in the middle of the hubbub, with their eyes fixed upon the portico which I occupied, formed an exact counterpart of the festivity of the witches in Macbeth. Nothing could be more odd or more novel than the whole scene; and yet there was something in it by which I could not help being affected; perhaps it was the consciousness that all these human beings were my *slaves*; to be sure, I never saw people look more happy in my life; and I believe their condition to be much more comfortable than that of the labourers of Great Britain; and, after all, slavery, in *their* case, is but another name for servitude, now that no more negroes can be forcibly carried away from Africa, and subjected to the horrors of the voyage, and of the seasoning after their arrival: but still I had already experienced, in the morning, that Juliet was wrong in saying 'What's in a name?' For soon after my reaching the lodging-house at Savannah la Mar, a remarkably clean-looking negro lad presented himself with some water and a towel: I concluded him to belong to the inn; and, on my returning the towel, as he found that I took no notice of him, he at length ventured to introduce himself, by saying, 'Massa not know me; *me your slave*!'—and really the sound made me feel a pang at the heart. The lad appeared all gaiety and good humour, and his whole countenance expressed anxiety to recommend himself to my notice; but the word 'slave' seemed to imply that, although he did feel pleasure then in serving me, if he had detested me he must have served me still. I really felt quite humiliated at the moment, and was tempted to tell him, 'Do not say that again; say that you are my negro, but do not call yourself my slave.'

Altogether, they shouted and sang me into a violent headache. It is now one in the morning, and I hear them still shouting and singing. I gave them a holiday for Saturday next, and told them that I had brought them all presents from England; and so, I believe, we parted very good friends.

3 JANUARY 1816. I have reached Jamaica in the best season for seeing my property in a favourable point of view; it is crop time,* when all the laborious work is over, and the negroes are the most healthy and merry. This morning I went to visit the hospital, and found there only eight patients out of three hundred negroes, and not one of them a serious case. Yesterday I had observed a remarkably handsome Creole* girl, called Psyche, and she really deserved the name. This morning a little brown girl made her appearance at breakfast, with an orange bough, to flap away the flies, and, on enquiry, she proved to be an emanation of the aforesaid Psyche. It is evident, therefore, that Psyche has already visited the palace of Cupid; I heartily hope that she is not now upon her road to the infernal regions: but, as the ancients had two Cupids, one divine and the other sensual, so am I in possession of two Psyches; and on visiting the hospital, *there* was poor Psyche the second. Probably this was the Psyche of the sensual Cupid.*

I passed the morning in driving about the estate: my house is frightful to look at, but very clean and comfortable on the inside; some of the scenery is very picturesque, from the lively green of the trees and shrubs, and the hermitage-like appearance of the negro buildings, all situated in little gardens, and embosomed in sweet-smelling shrubberies. Indeed, everything appears much better than I expected; the negroes seem healthy and contented, and so perfectly at their ease that our English squires would be mightily astonished at being accosted so familiarly by their farmers. This delightful north wind keeps the air temperate and agreeable. I live upon shaddocks and pine-apples. The dreaded mosquitoes are not worse than gnats, nor as bad as the Sussex harvest-bugs; and, as yet, I never felt myself in more perfect health. There was a man once, who fell from the top of a steeple; and, perceiving no inconvenience in his passage through the air, 'Come,' said he to himself, while in the act of falling, 'really this is well enough yet if it would but last.' Cubina, my young Savannah la Mar acquaintance, is appointed my black attendant; and as I had desired him to bring me any native flowers of Jamaica, this evening he brought me a very pretty one; the negroes, he said, called it 'John-to-Heal', but in white language it was *hoccoco-pickang*; it proved to be the wild Ipecacuanha.*

5 JANUARY 1816. As I was returning this morning from Montego Bay, about a mile from my own estate, a figure presented itself before me, I really think the most picturesque that I ever beheld: it was a mulatto girl, born upon Cornwall, but whom the overseer of a neighbouring estate had obtained my permission to exchange for another slave, as well as two little children, whom she had borne to him; but, as yet, he has been unable to procure a substitute, owing to the difficulty of purchasing single negroes, and Mary Wiggins is still my slave. However, as she is considered as being manumitted, she had not dared to present herself at Cornwall on my arrival, lest she should have been considered as an intruder; but she now threw herself in my way to tell me how glad she was to see me, for that she had always thought till now (which is the general complaint) that 'she had no massa'; and also to obtain a regular invitation to my negro festival tomorrow. By this universal complaint, it appears that, while Mr Wilberforce is lamenting their hard fate in being subject to a master, *their* greatest fear is the not having a master whom they know; and that to be told by the negroes of another estate that 'they belong to no massa', is one of the most contemptuous reproaches that can be cast upon them. Poor creatures, when they happened to hear on Wednesday evening that my carriage was ordered for Montego Bay the next morning, they fancied that I was going away for good and all, and came up to the house in such a hubbub that my agent was obliged to speak to them, and pacify them with the assurance that I should come back on Friday without fail.

But to return to Mary Wiggins: she was much too pretty not to obtain her invitation to Cornwall; on the contrary, I *insisted* upon her coming, and bade her tell her husband that I admired his taste very much for having chosen her. I really think that her form and features were the most statue-like that I ever met with: her complexion had no yellow in it, and yet was not brown enough to be dark—it was more of an ash-dove colour than anything else; her teeth were admirable, both for colour and shape; her eyes equally mild and bright; and her face merely broad enough to give it all possible softness and grandness of contour: her air and countenance would have suited Yarico;* but she reminded me most of Grassini in 'La Vergine del Sole',* only that Mary Wiggins was a thousand times more beautiful, and that, instead of a white robe, she wore a mixed dress of brown, white, and dead yellow, which harmonised excellently well with her complexion; while one of her beautiful arms was thrown across her brow to shade her eyes, and a profusion of rings on her fingers glittered in the sunbeams. Mary Wiggins and an old cotton-tree* are the most picturesque objects that I have seen for these twenty years.

On my arrival at home, my agent made me a very elegant little present of a scorpion and a couple of centipedes: the first was given to him, but the large centipede he had shaken out of a book last night, and having immediately covered her up in a phial of rum, he found this morning that she had produced a young one, which was lying drowned by her side.

4 MARCH 1817. I arrived without difficulty at Port Morant, where I found horses sent by my trustee to convey me to Hordley. The road led up to the mountains, and was one of the steepest, roughest, and most fatiguing that I ever travelled, in spite of its picturesque beauties. At length I reached my estate, jaded and wearied to death; here I expected to find a perfect paradise, and I found a perfect hell. Report had assured me that Hordley was the best managed estate in the island, and as far as the soil was concerned, report appeared to have said true; but my trustee had also assured me that my negroes were the most contented and best disposed, and here there was a lamentable incorrectness in the account. I found them in a perfect uproar; complaints of all kinds stunned me from all quarters: all the blacks accused all the whites, and all the whites accused all the blacks, and as far as I could make out, both parties were extremely in the right. There was no attachment to the soil to be found *here*; the

negroes declared, one and all, that if I went away and left them to groan under the same system of oppression without appeal or hope of redress, they would follow my carriage and establish themselves at Cornwall. I had soon discovered enough to be certain that, although they told me plenty of falsehoods, many of their complaints were but too well founded; and yet how to protect them for the future or satisfy them for the present was no easy matter to decide. Trusting to these fallacious reports of the Arcadian state of happiness upon Hordley, I supposed that I should have nothing to do there but grant a few indulgences, and establish the regulations already adopted with success on Cornwall; distribute a little money, and allow a couple of play-days for dancing; and under this persuasion I had made it quite impossible for me to remain above a week at Hordley, which I conceived to be fully sufficient for the above purpose. As to grievances to be redressed, I was totally unprepared for any such necessity; yet now they poured in upon me incessantly, each more serious than the former; and before twenty-four hours were elapsed I had been assured that, in order to produce any sort of tranquillity upon the estate, I must begin by displacing the trustee, the physician, the four white book-keepers, and the four black governors, all of whom I was modestly required to remove and provide better substitutes in the space of five days and a morning. What with the general clamour, the assertions and denials, the tears and the passion, the odious falsehoods, and the still more odious truths, and (worst of all to me) my own vexation and disappointment at finding things so different from my expectations, at first nearly turned my brain; and I felt strongly tempted to set off as fast as I could, and leave all these black devils and white ones to tear one another to pieces, an amusement in which they appeared to be perfectly ready to indulge themselves. . . .

Of all the points which had displeased me at Hordley, none had made me more angry for the time than the lie told me by the chief governor, which occasioned my displacing him. This fellow, who for the credit of our family (no doubt) had got himself christened by the name of John Lewis, had the impudence to walk into my parlour just as I was preparing to go to bed, and inform me that he could not get the business of the estate done. Why not? He could get nobody to come to the night-work at the mill, which he supposed was the consequence of my indulging the negroes so much. Indeed! and where were the people who ought to come to their night-work? in the negro village? No; they were in the hospital, and refused to come out to work. Upon which I blazed up like a barrel of gunpowder, and volleying out in a breath all the curses that I ever heard in my life, I asked him whether any person really had been insolent enough to select a whole night party from the sick people in the hospital, not one of whom ought to stir out of it till well? There stood the fellow, trembling and stammering, and unable to get out an answer, while I stamped up and down the piazza, storming and swearing, banging all the doors till the house seemed ready to tumble about our ears, and doing my best to out-Herod Herod,* till at last I ordered the man to begone that instant, and get the work done properly. He did not wait to be told twice, and was off in a twinkling. In a quarter of an hour I sent for him again, and enquired whether he had succeeded in getting the proper people to work at the mill? Upon which he had the assurance to answer that all the people were there, and that it was not of their not being at the mill that he had meant to complain. Of what was it then? 'Of their not being in the field.' When? 'Yesterday. He could not get the negroes to come to work, and so there had been none done all day.' And who refused to come? 'All the people.' But who? 'All.' But who, who, who?—their names, their names, their names? 'He could not remember them all.' Name one—well?— speak then, speak! 'There was Beck.' And who else? 'There was Sally, who used to be called Whanica.' And who else? 'There was . . . there was Beck.' But who else? 'Beck . . . and Sally' . . . But who else? who else? 'Little Edward had gone out of the hospital, and had not come to work.' Well! Beck and Sally, and little Edward; who else? 'Beck, and little Edward, and Sally.' But who else: I say, who else? 'He could not remember anybody else.' Then to be sure I was in such an imperial passion, as would have done honour to 'her majesty the queen Dolallolla'. Why, you most impudent of all impudent fellows that ever told a lie, have you really presumed to disturb me at this time of night, prevent my going to bed, tell me that you can't get the business done, and that none of the people would come to work, and make such a disturbance, and all because two old women and a little boy missed coming into the field yesterday! Down dropped the fellow in a moment upon his marrow bones: 'Oh, me good massa,' cried he (and out came the truth, which I knew well enough before he told me), 'me no come of my own head; me *ordered* to come; but me never tell massa lie more, so me pray him forgib me!' But his obeying any person on my own estate in preference to me, and suffering himself to be converted into an instrument of my annoyance, was not to be easily overlooked; so I turned him out of the house with a flea in his ear as big as a camel; and the next morning degraded him to the rank of a common field negro. The trustee pleaded hard for his being permitted to return to the waggons, from whence he had been taken, and where he would be useful. But I was obdurate. Then came his wife to beg for him, and then his mother, and then his cousin, and then his cousin's cousin: still I was firm; till on the day of my departure, the new chief governor came to me in the name of the whole estate, and begged me to allow John Lewis to return to the command of the waggons, 'for that all the negroes said, that it would be *too sad a thing* for them to see a man who had held the highest place among them degraded quite to be a common field negro'. There was something in this appeal which argued so good a feeling that I did not think it right to resist any longer; so I hinted that if the trustee should ask it again as a favour to himself, I might perhaps relent; and the proper application being thus made, John Lewis was allowed to quit the field, but with a positive injunction against his ever being employed again in any office of authority over the negroes.

4. LADIES

JANET SCHAW, *Journal of a Lady of Quality; Being the Narrative of a Journey from Scotland to the West Indies, North Carolina, and Portugal, in the Years 1774 to 1776* (ed. E. W. Andrews and C. Andrews, New Haven, 1921)

Janet Schaw (*c.*1731–*c.*1801) came from a prosperous Scottish family with property outside Edinburgh. Her older brother Robert was a North Carolina planter; another brother, Alexander, got a job in the 1770s with the customs service on the West Indian island of St Christopher (St Kitts). His sister accompanied him on his voyage, along with the three children of John Rutherfurd, another planter and a relative of the Schaws, who had sent them to Britain for their education. Caring for the three gave Janet Schaw, an unmarried woman of perhaps 35, an excuse to travel farther than most British ladies. Stopping in the islands, Schaw and the children continued to North Carolina on the eve of the American Revolution. Evacuated on board a Royal Navy man of war, they sailed home via Portugal, extending Schaw's travels, which she describes in the form of a letter-journal to a female friend—not published during her lifetime, but copied and shared with family and friends. Her lively, humorous writing and likeable persona may seem to modern sensibilities to conflict with her sympathy for slave owners. Our selections (taken from the first published edition of Schaw's journal) include the surprising shipboard discovery of a group of emigrants, Schaw's arrival in Antigua, and her impressions of its landscape and inhabitants. (Schaw sometimes narrates the events of several days under a single date heading.)

25 OCTOBER 1774. There is no such thing as being warm, do what we will, and though we have but little wind hitherto, yet we are jolted to death by the motion of the ship in these rough seas. Yet the Captain is every moment congratulating us on the smoothness of our vessel, which he declares is so soft in her motion that one may play at bowls on the deck. However, as I am like to beat out my teeth every time I try to drink, and often after all am not able to bring the cup to such a direction as to obtain my desire, I cannot help thinking he rather overrates the gentleness of her motions, though the mate in confirmation of what his Captain says, asserts, that last time he crossed the Atlantic, even in a calm, they were forced to lie flat on their faces, which the hogs stubbornly refusing, had their brains knocked out against the sides of the ship. How happy are we, who are only in danger of losing teeth and breaking limbs.

As I was amusing myself with my pen, and Fanny with her book, a little while ago, my brother came into the cabin, and informing us the weather was tolerable fair. He had provided watch-coats to secure us from the cold, and begged we would go with him upon deck, as he was sure a little fresh air would do us much good. We immediately accepted his invitation, and while we were preparing for this excursion, I asked my brother if he had seen all our crew, and what sort of hands they were; for that as I lay awake last night in bed, I heard a heavy groan (from that part of the steerage* which is only divided by a few boards from our stateroom), when presently a voice called out, 'What's the matter, man,' on which the groaner (as I supposed) replied, 'Alas! alas! this is a hard pillow for three score years to rest on.' My brother smiling took me by the hand, and reaching out the other to Fanny, bade us come along, and we would probably discover our groaning neighbour. We now ascended the companion or cabin stair, when, judge of my surprise, I saw the deck covered with people of all ages, from three weeks old to three score, men, women, children and suckling infants. For some time I was unable to credit my senses, it appeared a scene raised by the power of magic to bring such a crowd together in the middle of the sea, when I believed there was not a soul aboard but the ship's crew and our own family. Never did my eyes behold so wretched, so disgusting a sight. They looked like a cargo of Dean Swift's Yahoos* newly caught.

It was impossible to account for this strange apparition till the Captain informed me that they were a company of emigrants,* whom the owner had made him smuggle aboard privately, and had ordered to be kept close under the hatches till we were out at sea. He vindicated himself by declaring he was under the most absolute necessity of obeying the owner, whom he sincerely believed to be one of the greatest villains upon earth; that he and everyone was much surprised how we came to trust him, for that his character as a scoundrel was notorious wherever he had lived, that he himself had been ruined by him, and was now forced to serve him, as he had got his all into his possession, and put it out of his power to make bread in any other way. To this he added many other particulars, and summed up all by the comfortable intimation, that C——r, the supercargo,* was just such another, and put on board for the express purpose of cheating and deceiving us; he, the Captain, being thought too honest to perform this piece of duty. This tale he has also told my brother, which the goodness of his own heart induces him to believe: but for my own part, I take it to be a forged story altogether, and that they are all alike. The mate, however, notwithstanding the story of the hogs, seems an honest plain fellow, and I am inclined to think much better of him than of the others. Indeed he does not entertain a very high opinion of his messmates himself, nor appears much satisfied with his present berth, but says it is like Padie's candles, it will not mend. He so often mentioned Padie's candles that I became curious to know what sort of things they were, and found it was a favourite foremast joke of a teague,* who hung some candles before a fire to dry, and as they melted, swore, arrah, on my soul, now the more they dry the more they wet. This may be no joke to you, but has been such a one to us, that I am afraid the youngsters will make the poor man ashamed of his only piece of wit.

As I am resolved no more to encounter these wretched human beings, I will have the more time to write. Indeed you never beheld anything like them. They were fully as sensible of the motion of the vessel as we were, and sickness works more ways than one, so that the smell which came from the hole, where they had been confined, was sufficient to raise a plague aboard. I am besides not a little afraid, they may bestow upon me some of their livestock, for I make no doubt they have brought thousands alongst with them. Faugh! let me not think of it; it affects my stomach more than this smooth sailing vessel, or this shocking rough sea, in which we are tumbling about so, that I can hardly hold the pen. . . .

You remember I told you some days ago how much I had been surprised, as well as disgusted, at the appearance of a company of emigrants, who had been privately put aboard our ship. I was too much chagrined at their being with us to give myself the trouble of inquiring who they were, but now find they are a company of hapless exiles, from the Islands we have just passed, forced by the hand of oppression from their native land.

The Islands* were now full in sight, and they had all crowded to that side of the ship next to them, and stood in silent sorrow, gazing fondly on the dear spot they were never more to behold. How differently did the same sight affect them and me! What chilled my blood and disgusted my eye, filled their bosoms and warmed their hearts with the fondest, the most tender sensations, while sweet remembrance rushed on their minds and melted the roughest into tears of tenderness. The rude scene before us, with its wild rocks and snow-covered mountains, was dear to them, far more dear than the most fertile plains will ever appear. It was their native land, and how much is contained in that short sentence, none but those who have parted with their own can be judge of. Many, whom I now beheld, had passed year after year in peace and sweet contentment; they wished, they imagined nothing beyond what it afforded, and their grey hairs seemed a security that they should mingle their dust with that of their fathers, when the cruel hand of oppression seized on their helpless age, and forced them (at that late season) to seek a foreign grave across the stormy main.

Hard-hearted little tyrant of yonder rough domains, could you have remained unmoved, had you beheld the victims of your avarice, as I have done, with souls free from guilt, yet suffering all the pangs of banished villians; oh! had you seen them, their hands clasped in silent and unutterable anguish, their streaming eyes raised to heaven in mute ejaculations, calling down blessings, and pouring the last benedictions of a broken heart on the dear soil that gave them being; perhaps even a prayer for the cruel author of all their woes mixed in this pious moment. 'Lord require not our blood at his hands, he is the descendant of our honoured, our loved master, the son of him I followed to the field of same in my happy youthful days, of that loved Lord, who diffused peace, plenty and content around him.' The eager eye now went forth in search of particular spots marked by more tender remembrance; there a loved wife reared with fond maternal pride a blooming offspring. 'Yonder is my paternal cottage, where my cheerful youthful hours were passed in sweet content-ment. Ah! little then did I think of braving the wide Atlantic, or of seeking precarious bitter bread in a foreign land.'

In this general group of sorrow, there was one figure that more particularly engaged my attention. It was that of a female, who sup-ported with one arm an infant about a month old, which she suckled at her breast; her head rested on the other, and her hand shaded her face, while the tears that streamed from under it bedewed her breast and the face of the infant, who was endeavouring to draw a scanty nourishment from it. At her knee hung a little cherub about two years old, who looked smiling up into her face, as if courting her notice, and endeavouring to draw her from her melancholy reflec-tions; while a most beautiful little girl about eight years old stood by, and wept at the sight of her mother's tears. I wished for Miss Forbes, with her pencil of Sensibility,* to have done justice to this group of heart-affecting figures. I longed to address the mother, but there is a dignity in sorrow and I durst not intrude, but respectfully waited, till she gave me an opportunity. In a few minutes she raised her head from her hand and showed me a face that had once been beautiful, was still lovely, but had a broken heart impressed on every feature. When she observed me looking at her, she stood up and curtseyed. I returned her civility and moved towards her. 'You are from one of these islands,' said I. 'Yes, madam,' returned she, 'from that one we have just passed.' She looked abashed, and added with a heart-breaking smile, 'You, no doubt, wondered to see me so much affected, but I was just then within view of my father's house, he is the best of men as well as fathers, and I could not help thinking that perhaps, at that moment, he was pouring out his aged soul in prayers, for a lost and darling daughter'; but her words were choked; something too seemed to choke myself; so I relieved both by speaking to her of her children, who are indeed extremely lovely. She told me two were left with her father, and that she had one more on board. Just then a neat pretty girl about eighteen came up to take the child. 'Is that your daughter?' said I. 'No, madam,' returned she, 'that is an orphan niece of my husband, whom, in better days, he bred with a father's fondness. The poor child had no occasion to leave her own country. Many of her friends would gladly have taken her, but she would not leave us in our misery.' I looked at Marion, for so she is called. I thought I never beheld anything so beautiful. I wish to learn the history of this woman, which I will easily do, as they all know each other. I hope it will prove worth your reading and will give it a letter by itself. Though it be a hundred to one you never see these letters, yet as they give an idea of conversing with you, they afford myself infinite satisfaction.

Pity, thou darling daughter of the skies, what a change do you produce in the hearts where you vouchsafe to enter; from thee the fairest social virtues derive their being; it is you who melt, soften and humanize the soul, raising the man into a God. Before the brightness of thy heavenly countenance every dirty passion disappears—pride, avarice, self-love, caution, doubt, disdain, with all which claim Dame Prudence for their mother; and how different a set appears in thy train, those gently-smiling Goddesses—charity, meekness, gentle tenderness with unaffected kindness. What a change has she wrought on me since my last visit to the deck. Where are now the cargo of Yahoos? They are transformed into a company of most respectable sufferers, whom it is both my duty and inclination to comfort, and do all in my power to alleviate their misfortunes, which have not sprung from their guilt or folly, but from the guilt and folly of others.

I have made many friendships since these last two days, and was not a little vain, on my coming on deck this morning, to hear the children with infantine joy, call to each other: 'O there come the Ladies.' We rewarded their affection with some apples, which we gave the young Rutherfurds to bestow, a task which, they declared, afforded them more pleasure than the best apple-pie would have given them.

ST JOHN'S: 12 DECEMBER 1774. I write now on land, but my head is so giddy that I can't believe I am yet on shore, nor can I stand more than I did on shipboard; every thing seems to move in the same manner it did there. They tell me however, I will get the better of this in twenty-four hours.

My brother came on board this morning with some gentlemen, and carried us ashore. Everything was as new to me, as if I had been but a day old. We landed on a very fine wharf belonging to a Scotch gentleman, who was with us. We proceeded to our lodgings through a narrow lane; as the gentleman told us no ladies ever walk in this country. Just as we got into the lane, a number of pigs ran out at a door, and after them a parcel of monkeys. This not a little surprised me, but I found what I took for monkeys were Negro children, naked as they were born. We now arrived at our lodgings, and were received by a well behaved woman, who welcomed us, not as the mistress of a hotel, but as the hospitable woman of fashion would the guests she was happy to see. Her hall or parlour was directly off the street. Though not fine, it was neat and cool, and the windows all thrown open. A Negro girl presented us with a glass of what they call Sangarie, which is composed of Madeira, water, sugar and lime juice, a most refreshing drink. . . .

Our dinner consisted of many dishes, made up of kid, lamb, poultry, pork and a variety of fishes, all of one shape, that is flat, of the flounder or turbot kind, but differing from each other in taste. The meat was well dressed, and though they have no butter but what comes from Ireland or Britain, it was sweet and even fresh by their cookery. There was no turtle, which she regretted, but said I would get so much, that I would be surfeited with it. Our desert was superior to our dinner, the finest fruits in the world being there, which we had in profusion. During dinner, our hostess who presided at the head of her table (very unlike a British landlady) gave her hob and nob* with a good grace. I observed the young ladies drank nothing but lime-juice and water. They told me it was all the women drank in general. Our good landlady strongly advised us not to follow so bad an example—that Madeira and water would do nobody harm, and that it was owing to their method of living that they were such spiritless and indolent creatures. The ladies smiling replied that the men indeed said so, but it was custom and everybody did it in spite of the advices they were daily getting. What a tyrant is custom in every part of the world. The poor women, whose spirits must be worn out by heat and constant perspiration, require no doubt some restorative, yet as it is not the custom, they will faint under it rather than transgress this ideal law. I will however follow our good landlady's advice, and as I was resolved to show I was to be a rebel to a custom that did not appear founded on reason, I pledged her in a bumper of the best Madeira I ever tasted. Miss Rutherfurd followed my example; the old lady was transported with us, and young Mrs Dunbar politely said that, if it was in the power of wine to give her such spirits, and render her half so agreeable, she was sorry she had not taken it long ago; but would lose no more time, and taking up a glass mixed indeed with water, drank to us.

Just as we were preparing for tea, my brother, Dr Dunbar, Mr Halliday, the collector, and Mr Baird, the comptroller, and a very pretty young man called Martin came to us. Here was a whole company of Scotch people, our language, our manners, our circle of friends and connections, all the same. . . .

As I am now about to leave them, you, no doubt, will expect me to give my opinion as fully on the inhabitants, as I have done on their island and manners, but I am afraid you will suspect me of partiality, and were I to speak of individuals, perhaps you might have reason, but as to the characters in general I can promise to write without prejudice, and if I only tell truth, they have nothing to fear from my pen. I think the men the most agreeable creatures I ever met with, frank, open, generous, and I dare say brave; even in advanced life they retain the vivacity and spirit of youth; they are in general hand-some, and all of them have that sort of air that will ever attend a man of fashion. Their address is at once soft and manly; they have a kind of gallantry in their manner, which exceeds mere politeness, and in some countries, we know, would be easily mistaken for something more interesting than civility, yet you must not suppose this the politeness of French manners, merely words of course. No, what they say, they really mean; their whole intention is to make you happy, and this they endeavour to do without any other view or motive than what they are prompted to by the natural goodness of their own natures. In short, my friend, the woman that brings a heart here will have little sensibility if she carry it away.

I hear you ask me, if there is no alloy to this fine character, no reverse to this beautiful picture. Alas! my friend, though children of

the sun, they are mortals, and as such must have their share of
failings, the most conspicuous of which is, the indulgence they give
themselves in their licentious and even unnatural amours, which
appears too plainly from the crowds of mulattos, which you meet in
the streets, houses and indeed everywhere; a crime that seems to
have gained sanction from custom, though attended with the greatest inconveniences not only to individuals, but to the public in general. The young black wenches lay themselves out for white lovers, in
which they are but too successful. This prevents their marrying with
their natural mates, and hence a spurious and degenerate breed,
neither so fit for the field, nor indeed any work, as the true bred
Negro. Besides these wenches become licentious and insolent past all
bearing, and as even a mulatto child interrupts their pleasures and is
troublesome, they have certain herbs and medicines that free them
from such an encumbrance, but which seldom fails to cut short their
own lives, as well as that of their offspring. By this many of them
perish every year. I would have gladly drawn a veil over this part of a
character, which in everything else is most estimable.

As to the women, they are in general the most amiable creatures
in the world, and either I have been remarkably fortunate in my
acquaintance, or they are more than commonly sensible; even those
who have never been off the island are amazingly intelligent and able
to converse with you on any subject. They make excellent wives,
fond attentive mothers, and the best housewives I have ever met with.
Those of the first fortune and fashion keep their own keys and look
after everything within doors; the domestic economy is entirely left
to them, as the husband finds enough to do abroad. A fine house, an
elegant table, handsome carriage, and a crowd of mulatto servants are
what they all seem very fond of. The sun appears to affect the sexes
very differently. While the men are gay, luxurious and amorous, the
women are modest, genteel, reserved and temperate. This last virtue
they have indeed in the extreme; they drink nothing stronger in
general than sherbet, and never eat above one or two things at table,
and these the lightest and plainest. The truth is, I can observe no
indulgence they allow themselves in, not so much as in scandal, and
if I stay long in this country, I will lose the very idea of that innocent
amusement; for since I resided amongst them, I have never heard
one woman say a wrong thing of another. This is so unnatural that
I suppose you will (good naturedly) call it cunning; but if it is so, it is

the most commendable cunning I ever met with, as nothing can give them a better appearance in the eyes of a stranger.

As we became better acquainted, their reserve wore off, and I now find them most agreeable companions. Jealousy is a passion with which they are entirely unacquainted, and a jealous wife would be here a most ridiculous character indeed. Let me conclude this by assuring you that I never admired my own sex more than in these amiable creoles. Their sentiments are just and virtuous; in religion they are serious without ostentation, and perform every duty with pleasure from no other motive but the consciousness of doing right. In their persons they are very genteel, rather too thin till past thirty, after that they grow plump and look much the better for it. Their features are in general high and very regular, they have charming eyes, fine teeth, and the greatest quantity of hair I ever saw, which they dress with taste, and wear a great deal of powder. In short, they want only colour to be termed beautiful, but the sun who bestows such rich taints on every other flower, gives none to his lovely daughters, the tincture of whose skin is as pure as the lily, and as pale. Yet this I am convinced is owing to the way in which they live, entirely excluded from proper air and exercise. From childhood they never suffer the sun to have a peep at them and to prevent him are covered with masks and bonnets,* that absolutely make them look as if they were stewed. Fanny, who just now is blooming as a new blown rose, was prevailed on to wear a mask while we were on our tour, which in a week changed her colour, and if she had persevered I am sure a few months would have made her as pale as any of them. As to your humble servant, I have always set my face to the weather, wherever I have been. I hope you have no quarrel at brown beauty. . . .

I had a walk this morning that you would hardly believe me able to have taken, as it was no less than two miles, and up hill. This was truly a British frolic, and what no creole would ever dream of. The ascent however is not steep, and we set off several hours before the sun rose to a high plantation where breakfast was provided for us. The first part of the way was through cane pieces, which are just now in their greatest glory; but though they excluded the sun, they also prevented the breeze from giving us air, and we were a good deal incommoded, till we reached what is first called the mountain, which is one of the greatest beauties in nature, and I will take this opportunity to describe it. Properly speaking the whole island forms its base, as the ascent begins from the sea and rises from all sides to the top. It is covered with canes for about the third of the way up, then with myrtles, tamarinds, oranges and fruits of various kinds. Above that is a great variety of trees, whose verdure is not inferior to those in Britain, and I am told the climate there approaches to cold; and that further up, the air is so cold, that those who have tried it were instantly seized with pleurisies, and this I can easily believe, for as we were a good deal warmed with walking, the sudden change was very perceptible, and I was shivering with cold all the time we were at breakfast.

I could not however forbear lengthening my walk, by taking a more particular survey of the mountain. My brother and I accordingly walked a good way up along one of the streams of water which comes down from it. It was at present only a scanty rill, but by the appearance of its bed is at times a large fall. It divides the mountain for a good way up, and resembles one of our highland burns; its source as well as the burns being on the top. But how different is the appearance of its banks, where everything most beautiful in nature is mixed in delightful confusion. Oranges, limes, shaddocks, cherries, citron, papa trees* are all at once covered with flowers and fruit; besides a profusion of vines and flowers out of number we also saw cotton in plenty, which here is a shrub, as is coffee. But they are generally raised in cultivated plantations, for though they are all indigenous, they are much the better of culture. I formerly said that the seasons were united, which is the case all over the islands, and just now they are planting, reaping and bruising, in which I include distilling. But though perhaps there is no such rich land in the world as in this island, they use manure in great abundance, and would be as glad of the rakes* of Edinburgh streets as the Lothian farmers. No planter is above attending to this grand article, which is hoarded up with the utmost care, and I everywhere saw large dunghills of compound manure, composed of the ashes from the boiling kettle, the bruised canes, the spilt leaves of the cane, the cleaning of the houses and dung of the stables. These are turned up and kept till proper for use, and no infant cane is placed in its pit without a very sufficient quantity of this to bed and nurse it up.

The Negroes who are all in troops are sorted so as to match each other in size and strength. Every ten Negroes have a driver, who walks behind them, holding in his hand a short whip and a long one.

You will too easily guess the use of these weapons; a circumstance of all others the most horrid. They are naked, male and female, down to the girdle, and you constantly observe where the application has been made. But however dreadful this must appear to a humane European, I will do the creoles the justice to say, they would be as averse to it as we are, could it be avoided, which has often been tried to no purpose. When one comes to be better acquainted with the nature of the Negroes, the horror of it must wear off. It is the suffering of the human mind that constitutes the greatest misery of punishment, but with them it is merely corporeal. As to the brutes, it inflicts no wound on their mind, whose natures seem made to bear it, and whose sufferings are not attended with shame or pain beyond the present moment. When they are regularly ranged, each has a little basket, which he carries up the hill filled with the manure and returns with a load of canes to the mill. They go up at a trot, and return at a gallop, and did you not know the cruel necessity of this alertness, you would believe them the merriest people in the world.

Since I am on the chapter of Negroes' feelings, I must tell you that I was some days ago in town, when a number for market came from on board a ship. They stood up to be looked at with perfect unconcern. The husband was to be divided from the wife, the infant from the mother; but the most perfect indifference ran through the whole. They were laughing and jumping, making faces at each other, and not caring a single farthing for their fate. This is not however without exception; and it behoves the planter to consider the country from whence he purchases his slaves; as those from one coast are mere brutes and fit only for the labour of the field, while those from another are bad field Negroes, but faithful handy house-servants.

MARIA NUGENT, *Lady Nugent's Journal of her Residence in Jamaica from 1801 to 1805* (ed. Philip Wright; Kingston, Jamaica, 1966)

Maria Skinner (1771–1834), daughter of a prominent New Jersey loyalist family, married Major-General George Nugent, illegitimate grandson of an Irish peer, who helped put down the United Irishmen Rebellion in 1798. Nugent was rewarded with the prestigious and lucrative appointment of Lieutenant-Governor of Jamaica. During their time in Jamaica

(1801–6) the Nugents' two eldest children were born; the later part of her diary documents Maria Nugent's increasing anxiety about her own and her infants' health and her preoccupation with getting off the island alive. The years of her diary, 1801–5, saw the French reinvasion of neighbouring St Domingue (present-day Haiti), taken over by ex-slaves and mulattos in the island-wide rebellion of 1793–4. Defeat of the French by the new Haitian Republic in 1804 augmented the Nugents' fears. Our selections include the Nugents' arrival on the island, a visit to a spa and a plantation, and some remarks on the creoles, or island inhabitants. The Governor's Lady narrates her *faux pas* at a slave ball and vents her fear of slave revolt.

APRIL 1801. I must preface my intended journal by saying that it commences immediately after we had terminated a residence of some years in Ireland, of which we were both heartily sick, tired, and disgusted; having witnessed during the Rebellion,* which broke out in 1798, all the horrors of a civil war, during which my dear husband had the command in the north; so that he was not only obliged to meet the poor, infatuated, misguided people in the open field, but, after defeating them there, had also the distressing task of holding courts martial, and signing the death warrants of very many, which was indeed heart-breaking to us both.

After the suppression of the Rebellion, we wished to refresh ourselves and recruit our spirits, by returning to England; but Lord Cornwallis so earnestly desired that General Nugent would remain, and act as his Adjutant-General, that we took up our residence in Dublin, where we were aiding and abetting in all the odious *tracasseries* of the union between the two countries, till that point was carried. A change of Ministry then enabled General N. to resign his situation, and, to our great joy, on the 5th of April, 1801, we arrived once more in dear England.

A few days after our return, General Nugent was surprised by his appointment as Lieutenant-Governor and Commander-in-Chief of the island of Jamaica. We were neither of us over well pleased; but, like good soldiers, we made up our minds to obey.

As I had a cough, and was otherwise unwell from the anxieties of our Irish campaign, the doctors advised that I should not sleep in town. General N. accordingly took a little place at Hampstead, where we spent a most agreeable time, till the first week in May, when we took up our abode at Reddish's Hotel in St James's Street. Our little

home at Hampstead was so nice, that we regretted it very much. We
had there dear Miss Acheson, and many visitors that I loved; and, in
short, I enjoyed my little abode so much, I should greatly have
preferred remaining, instead of playing the Governor's lady to the
blackies: but we are soldiers, and must have no will of our own.

28–31 MAY 1801. Come in sight of Jamaica. We were all up, and on
the look-out by 6 o'clock. It appears beautiful. Such hills, such
mountains, such verdure; everything so bright and gay, it is delightful! Not much wind; it is now 7 o'clock in the evening, and we have
only just anchored in Port Royal Harbour. Thank God for all his
mercies. An express is just sent off to the Governor, in Spanish
Town. Colonel Ramsay of the Artillery, and Captain Coates of the
69th regiment, with a Navy officer from Lord Hugh Seymour, came
on board immediately. I am disappointed—I hoped to have landed
instantly, but there is so much etiquette about it, that it is settled we
are not to stir till tomorrow morning.

29th. General N. landed at 6 o'clock, under salutes from the forts
and all the ships of war in the harbour. The *Ambuscade* fired on his
leaving the deck, and I lay down in my cot, with a pillow over my
ears, the noise was so stunning.

30th. Up at 6 o'clock, and much amused till 8 (when we breakfasted) at seeing the black population, and the odd appearance of
everything from my windows. The King's House,* which is now our
residence, is a large brick building, of two storeys high, forming one
side of a square; opposite is the House of Assembly; the two other
sides are formed by a Guard House and Public Buildings. Our
apartments are very spacious, but very dirty. Immediately after
breakfast, Margaret Clifford set the black ladies to work, that our
rooms may be a little less filthy before we go to bed again.

Lord Balcarres, and a large party of gentlemen, at breakfast. I then
retired to make my little arrangements, and Lord B. and General N.
began their discussions, which lasted the greatest part of the morning. At 5 o'clock we found a numerous party assembled in the drawing-room. There were only two ladies, Mrs Rodon and Mrs Drew,
the first old and plain, the other the reverse. Lord Hugh Seymour
came for about half an hour, but could not remain for dinner. All the
gentlemen, civil and military, were introduced to me before we sat
down; I scarcely recollect the name or visage of any of them, only

they all looked very bilious and very warm. One gentleman seemed to suffer exceedingly: for, in spite of his constant mopping, the perspiration stood like drops of crystal on his face the whole time we were at dinner. All took their leave soon after nine. No suppers are given in this country, and I am glad of it, for I have neither strength nor inclination for late hours.

31st. I could not help laughing at a reply of Lord Balcarres, when I went down to breakfast. I remarked to him that it was a very fine day; to which he answered, Yes, it is, but I assure you, Mrs Nugent, you will be tired of saying this before many weeks are over. Captain Halkett and Captain Loring, of the Navy, at breakfast, in addition to the staff. I wish Lord B. would wash his hands, and use a nail-brush, for the black edges of his nails really make me sick. He has, besides, an extraordinary propensity to dip his fingers into every dish. Yesterday he absolutely helped himself to some fricassée with his dirty finger and thumb. Lord B. and General N. were discussing affairs all the morning. Another large dinner party at 6. Mrs Rodon again, and Mrs W. Bullock. The ladies told me strange stories of the influence of the black and yellow women, and Mrs Bullock called them serpents. The table today was loaded with large joints of meat, turtle, turkeys, hams, etc. I must not omit to mention here an extraordinary pet of Lord B.'s, which makes its appearance every day in the dining-room. It is a little black pig, that goes grunting about to everyone for a tit-bit. The first day his staff appeared very much shocked; but, seeing me rather amused with the novelty of it, they seemed reconciled.

4 AUGUST 1801. This day we have kept to ourselves, and the house is put into as good order as we could prevail upon the poor blackies to do it. They are all so good-humoured, and seem so merry, that it is quite comfortable to look at them. I wish, however, they would be a little more alert in clearing away the filth of this otherwise nice and fine house. Only our own staff at dinner, and as we were up at 6, and very busy all day, we took the liberty of going to bed at 9.

9–10 MARCH 1802. Devoured by mosquitoes all night. Set off for Bath immediately after breakfast, with an immense cavalcade of gentlemen on horseback, or in kittareens, sulkies* etc. etc. in addition to our own party. Stopped at Mr Baillie's Penn, just above Morant Bay. General N. etc. crossed over to see a fort and block-house, and

I proceeded, with the rest of the party, to Bath. A most beautiful and romantic drive over mountains, on the ledges of precipices, through fertile valleys, etc. Bath is truly a lovely village, at the bottom of an immense mountain. The houses are surrounded with gardens and coconut trees, and there is an immense row of cotton trees in front, most magnificent, and like our finest oaks. General N. came at 4. Dined at 6. Mr Cuthbert and Mr Chief Justice are here, for drinking the waters. They joined our party, and drank punch made of the Bath stream. I tasted it, and it is sickly, nauseous stuff. To bed before ten.

10th. Up at 5. Set off on horseback, in my night-cap, dressing gown, and poke bonnet, with General N. and a party of gentlemen. The road is the most beautiful thing I ever saw, narrow, and winding for two or three miles up a mountain. A dreadful precipice is on one side, at the bottom of which runs a river; but bamboos, etc. growing thickly up the sides of the mountain, lessened one's fears for the narrowness and height of the road.

The bathing-house is a low West India building, containing four small rooms, in each of which there is a marble bath. Then there is another house for infirm negroes, etc. In fact, a kind of public hospital with baths, and they tell you of wonderful cures performed by the waters.* I drank a glass of it first, which was really so warm that it almost scalded my throat. I then went in for twenty minutes, and had the heat increased till I got familiarized to the bath, which I really found most delightful and refreshing. I must, however, mention an adventure of the Governor's Lady. The old woman attending the bath was very anxious to see her, but her poke bonnet covered her face, and her dressing-gown concealed her person; but as the lady was stepping out of the bath, in a perfectly undisguised state, she heard a voice near her, and perceived, under the door, a pair of black eyes, and indeed a whole black face, looking earnestly at her; for the door was half a yard too short, and the old woman's petticoat had been applied to the breach; this she had slyly removed, and laid herself down on her stomach to peep. The Governor's Lady gave a great squall, and away ran the old woman.

After I came out of the bath, I drank another glass, and then proceeded down the mountain, at the bottom of which is a botanical garden. We rode, and were really much gratified, in seeing the variety of plants, shrubs, and trees, all so new to a European eye. The breadfruit, cabbage tree, jack-fruit, cinnamon, etc. were in great perfection; as likewise were the sago, and in short a number of beautiful shrubs I can't describe, and some of them as curious and extraordinary as they are beautiful. The leaf of the star-apple tree is like gold on one side, and bright green on the other. Another tree, the name of which I can't recollect, was purple on one side, and also green on the other. The Otaheite apple is a beautiful tree, bearing a bright pink blossom, like a tassel; but it is impossible for me to describe all the beautiful plants I saw. Besides, we were obliged to hurry home, a shower of rain coming on, which prevented our beginning our journey till 10 o'clock, when we proceeded to Golden Grove, another estate of Mr Simon Taylor's. I cannot here avoid mentioning that Mr Taylor is an old bachelor, and detests the society of women, but I have worked a reform, for he never leaves me an instant, and attends to all my wants and wishes. He recollects what I have once commended, and is sure to have it for me again. Every one of the party is astonished at this change; but I believe he takes me for a boy, as I constantly wear a habit, and have a short cropped head.

The road today was bad and intricate, so that we were obliged to have a guide to Golden Grove. After fording Sulphur and the Devil's River, we arrived safe there. It is an excellent house, surrounded by sugar works, coconut trees, etc. We drove up just at the dinner hour of the negroes. Never in my life did I see such a number of black faces together. We went into the sugar works, ate sugar, talked to the negroes, etc.; but another shower of rain coming on, obliged us to go to our own apartments. I put on my dressing-gown, and attempted to rest, but was every instant interrupted by mulatto ladies, with one curiosity or another in the eating way. A conch was first brought to me. It was a delicate white on the outside, and a beautiful pink in the inside. It was just caught, and the women told me that they put a little fire to the shell, and it instantly left its dwelling, poor little fish. A turtle, and several curious fish were also introduced for my inspection. So, as I found I could get no rest, and was uncommonly well after bathing this morning, I dressed, and walked about the house till dinner time. A little mulatto girl was sent into the drawing-room to amuse me. She was a sickly delicate child, with straight light-brown hair, and very black eyes. Mr T. appeared very anxious for me to dismiss her, and in the evening the house-keeper told me she was his own daughter, and that he had a numerous family, some almost on every one of his estates.

24 APRIL 1802. I will conclude my tour through the island with a few remarks. In this country it appears as if everything were bought and sold. Clergymen make no secret of making a traffic of their livings,* but General N. has set his face against such proceedings, and has refused many applications for the purpose. He is determined to do all he can towards the reformation of the church, and thus rendering it respectable. It is indeed melancholy to see the general disregard of both religion and morality, throughout the whole island. Everyone seems solicitous to make money, and no one appears to regard the mode of acquiring it. It is extraordinary to witness the immediate effect that the climate and habit of living in this country have upon the minds and manners of Europeans, particularly of the lower orders. In the upper ranks, they become indolent and inactive, regardless of everything but eating, drinking, and indulging themselves, and are almost entirely under the dominion of their mulatto favourites. In the lower orders, they are the same, with the addition of conceit and tyranny considering the negroes as creatures formed merely to administer to their ease, and to be subject to their caprice; and I have found much difficulty to persuade those great people and superior beings, our white domestics, that the blacks are human beings, or have souls. I allude more particularly to our German and our other upper men-servants. It was curious to observe, when we were entering any town, the number of trunks, band-boxes, etc. that were hurrying to the different houses, and the same at our departure, all going back to the country again, and all on negroes' heads; for whenever the ladies go to town, or are to appear in society, their black maids and other attendants start off with their finery in cases, or tin boxes, on their heads. Trunks of any size are carried in the same manner. In short, every thing is put upon the head, from the largest to the smallest thing; even a smelling-bottle, I believe, would be carried in the same way. I have often, on our tour, seen twelve or fourteen negroes in one line of march, each bearing some article for the toilette on his head. The Creole language is not confined to the negroes. Many of the ladies, who have not been educated in England, speak a sort of broken English, with an indolent drawling out of their words, that is very tiresome if not disgusting. I stood next to a lady one night, near a window, and, by way of saying something, remarked that the air was much cooler than usual; to which she answered, 'Yes, ma-am, *him rail-ly too fra-ish.*'

26 MAY 1803. A note from my dear N. to say that he will certainly be at home by 7 or 8 this evening. Order the servants a fête in consequence, and, with the assistance of the Misses Murphy, make all my preparations in the best manner. Dined with the gentlemen of the family, before 3, and immediately after take our stations in the piazza, to see the blackies enjoy themselves.

A long table was spread on the green, with all their most favourite dishes, of barbecued hog, jerked hog, pepper-pot, yams, plantains, etc. There were tubs of punch, and each of them had three glasses of Madeira, to drink three toasts—'Massa Gubernor, and Missis, and little Massa'—all of which were drank with three times three, by the men, women and children, and their sweethearts. The little children were all allowed a little sip, out of the grown up people's glasses.

As soon as that ceremony was over, I began the ball with an old negro man. The gentlemen each selected a partner, according to rank, by age or service, and we all danced. However, I was not aware how much I shocked the Misses Murphy by doing this; for I did exactly the same as I would have done at a servants' hall birthday in England. They told me, afterwards, that they were nearly fainting, and could hardly forbear shedding a flood of tears, at such an unusual and extraordinary sight; for in this country, and among slaves, it was necessary to keep up so much more distant respect! They may be right. I meant nothing wrong, and all the poor creatures seemed so delighted, and so much pleased, that I could scarcely repent it. I was, nevertheless, very sorry to have hurt their feelings, and particularly too as they seemed to think the example dangerous; as making the blacks of too much consequence, or putting them at all on a footing with the whites, they said, might make a serious change in their conduct, and even produce a rebellion in the island.

But to proceed with my fête. I had people on the look-out for the arrival of my dear N., and about 8 o'clock his approach was announced. I then marched at the head of the whole party, with little George in my arms, to meet him; the music playing, 'God save the King'. As he got out of his carriage to join us, we saluted him, with three cheers. Dear Georgy was at first a little frightened with the noise and bustle, but he soon began to laugh, and appeared to enjoy all that was going forwards, as if he understood the whole thing. We had a little supper in the piazza. The blackies resumed their dancing, and kept up their gaiety the greatest part of the night.

13–14 DECEMBER 1803. I spent half an hour in the chapel alone, and comfortably. Christmas Day, Easter, and Whitsuntide, are the only days in the year for the Communion, and I am anxious to be well prepared to take it the next time, if I live, please God! In the evening, many unpleasant and alarming reports, respecting the French prisoners on parole and the negroes in this town. One of the black men, a Dutch negro, had absented himself from prayers, and it was observed, by one of the staff, that he was seen making signs to one of the sentries, from a window. This, together with the rumours all day, of an understanding between the French prisoners and the free blacks, and their tampering with the negro slaves, was indeed most frightful. Before we went to bed, General N. sent to the officer of the guard, and made enquiry respecting the two sentries, placed at the front door of the King's House, during prayers; and found that they are Irish convicts, of notoriously bad character, and the rest of the guard chiefly recruits, from the French prisoners.* I cannot describe the anxiety I suffered, nor the thousand horrid ideas that pressed upon my mind; and, especially, as there has appeared of late a general apprehension throughout the country, and various reports have been made, within the last few weeks, of the alarming state of the negro population, etc. Before we went to bed, General N. secured his own arms. All the staff, too, were on the alert, and, as the nursery door did not lock well, I begged to have it nailed up for the night.

14th. The alarm continued, though secretly, all day. French prisoners coming in constantly, and it is suggested that the best plan will be to disarm them. Many members of assembly closeted with General N., but he tells me that, with the precautions taken, nothing is to be feared. The Murphy family at dinner.

PART V

NORTH AMERICA

BY 1700 the British colonies on the eastern seaboard of North America, settled in the early seventeenth century, were booming. Their population was over 250,000 (in 1670 it had been 111,000). By 1760 it had reached 1,600,000 and the settled area had tripled. Trade with England and the Caribbean drove colonial economies—shipbuilding in New England, tobacco, rice, and indigo further south—and immigration was ethnically diverse, including Dutch and Germans, French Protestants, and Jewish merchants and artisans as well as Britons seeking a cheaper, healthier, and more autonomous existence, and of course shiploads of African slaves. Although life remained difficult in many regions, colonists no longer faced the extreme hardships that had challenged early settlers. More and more of them, especially along the coast, were able to emulate metropolitan London culture. Colonists absorbed Enlightenment ideas and preoccupations like the passion for natural history that propelled William Bartram into the Florida bush. But cultural growth brought with it a consciousness of American difference. By the 1760s the colonies were ripe for political awakening, and of course it came. The dates of our anthology encompass the last half of the colonial period along with the post-Revolutionary decades, which saw curious Britons cross the Atlantic to inspect and report—often superciliously—on manners and customs in the breakaway republic.

Exploration and westward expansion continued throughout this period. (The most famous of the transcontinental expeditions, that of Meriwether Lewis and William Clark (1804–6), is not represented here, since we have restricted our selection to British travellers.) Canadian explorers such as Samuel Hearne, Alexander Mackenzie, and David Thompson wrote vividly of their experience in the continent's vast uncharted territory and their interactions with its Indian inhabitants. Seventeenth-century English-language accounts of American Indians have been characterized as 'thin', often relying on hearsay, with none of the detailed, first-hand descriptions found in the writings of French Jesuit missionaries. The early English accounts are often coloured by outrage at wartime atrocities and a shrill sense of Providential mission. John Lawson's *New Voyage to Carolina*, excerpted below, was one of the first accounts based on actual contact with Indians and informed by a more objective attitude. If the eighteenth century saw the rise of a primitivism exemplified by Bartram's gushy idealizing of the Seminole, the image of the 'noble savage' none the less did not displace his unregenerate antitype, vividly exemplified in Hearne's account of an inter-aboriginal massacre.

1. SURVEYORS AND EXPLORERS

JOHN LAWSON, *A New Voyage to Carolina; Containing the Exact Description and Natural History of that Country: Together with the Present State thereof* (1709)

John Lawson (d. 1711) arrived in North Carolina in 1700, worked as a deputy to the colony's Surveyor-General, and succeeded to the office in 1708. He took part in an early skirmish of the Virginia–North Carolina boundary dispute (resolved by William Byrd and his fellow Commissioners in 1728) and played a prominent role in the founding of North Carolina's two oldest towns, Bath and New Bern. Lawson was tortured and killed in 1711 by Tuscarora Indians who resented the new settlements in their territory.

The Congerees* are kind and affable to the English, the Queen being very kind, giving us what rarities her cabin afforded, as loblolly* made with Indian corn, and dried peaches. These Congerees have abundance of storks and cranes in their savannas. They take them before they can fly, and breed them as tame and familiar as a dunghill fowl. They had a tame crane at one of these cabins that was scarce less than six foot in height, his head being round, with a shining natural crimson hue, which they all have.* These are a very comely sort of Indians, there being a strange difference in the proportion and beauty of these heathens. Although their tribes or nations border one upon another, yet you may discern as great an alteration in their features and dispositions, as you can in their speech, which generally proves quite different from each other, though their nations be not above 10 or 20 miles in distance. The women here being as handsome as most I have met withal, being several fine-fingered brunettos amongst them, these lasses stick not upon hand long, for they marry when very young, as at 12 or 14 years of age. The English traders are seldom without an Indian female for his bed-fellow, alleging these reasons as sufficient to allow of such a familiarity. First, they being remote from any white people, that it preserves their friendship with the heathens, they esteeming a white man's child much above one of their getting, the Indian mistress ever securing her white friend provisions whilst he stays amongst them. And lastly, this correspondence makes them learn the Indian tongue much the sooner, they being of the Frenchman's opinion, how that an English wife teaches her husband more English in one night than a school-master can in a week. . . .

The mould here is excessive rich, and a country very pleasing to the eye, had it the convenience of a navigable river, as all new colonies (of necessity) require. It would make a delightful settlement.

We went eight miles farther, and came to the Wateree Chickanee Indians.* The land holds good, there being not a spot of bad land to be seen in several days going.

The people of this nation are likely tall persons, and great pilferers, stealing from us anything they could lay their hands on, though very respectful in giving us what victuals we wanted. We lay in their cabins all night, being dark smoky holes, as ever I saw any Indians dwell in. This nation is much more populous than the Congerees, and their neighbours, yet understand not one another's speech. They are very poor in English effects, several of them having no guns, making use of bows and arrows, being a lazy idle people, a quality incident to most Indians, but none to that degree as these, as I ever met withal.

Their country is wholly free from swamps and quagmires, being high dry land, and consequently healthful, producing large corn-stalks, and fair grain.

Next morning, we took off our beards with a razor, the Indians looking on with a great deal of admiration. They told us they had never seen the like before, and that our knives cut far better than those that came amongst the Indians. They would fain have borrowed our razors, as they had our knives, scissors, and tobacco-tongs, the day before, being as ingenious at picking of pockets as any, I believe, the world affords; for they will steal with their feet . . .

Next morning we set out early, breaking the ice we met withal, in the stony runs, which were many. We passed by several cottages, and about 8 of the clock came to a pretty big town, where we took up our quarters, in one of their state houses, the men being all out, hunting in the woods, and none but women at home. Our fellow traveller of whom I spoke before at the Congerees, having a great mind for an Indian lass for his bed-fellow that night, spoke to our guide, who soon got a couple, reserving one for himself. That which fell to our companion's share was a pretty young girl. Though they could not understand one word of what each other spoke, yet the female Indian, being no novice at her game, but understanding what she came thither for, acted her part dexterously enough with her cully, to make him sensible of what she wanted: which was to pay the hire, before he rode the hackney. He showed her all the treasure he was possessed of, as beads, red cadis,* etc. which she liked very well, and permitted him to put them into his pocket again, endearing him with all the charms which one of a better education than Dame Nature had bestowed upon her, could have made use of, to render her consort a surer captive. After they had used this sort of courtship a small time, the match was confirmed by both parties, with the approbation of as many Indian women as came to the house, to celebrate our Winchester-Wedding.* Every one of the bridesmaids were as great whores as Mrs Bride, though not quite so handsome. Our happy couple went to bed together before us all, and with as little blushing as if they had been man and wife for 7 years. The rest of the company being weary with travelling, had more mind to take their rest than add more weddings to that hopeful one already consummated; so that though the other virgins offered their service to us, we gave them their answer, and went to sleep. About an hour before day, I awaked, and saw somebody walking up and down the room in a seemingly deep melancholy. I called out to know who it was, and it proved to be Mr Bridegroom, who in less than 12 hours, was bachelor, husband, and widower, his dear spouse having picked his pocket of the beads, cadis, and what else should have gratified the Indians for the victuals we received of them. However that did not serve her turn, but she had also got his shoes away, which he had made the night before, of a dressed buckskin. Thus dearly did our spark already repent his new bargain, walking bare-foot, in his penitentials, like some poor pilgrim to Loretto.*

After the Indians had laughed their sides sore at the figure Mr Bridegroom made, with much ado, we mustered up another pair of shoes, or moggisons,* and set forward on our intended voyage, the company (all the way) lifting up their prayers for the new married couple, whose wedding had made away with that which should have purchased our food.

GEORGE SHELVOCKE, *A Voyage Round the World by the Way of the Great South Sea, Performed in the Years 1719, 20, 21, 22, in the Speedwell of London* (1726)

George Shelvocke (fl. 1690–1728) took part in the last of the buccaneer circumnavigations. Two English ships, *Speedwell* and *Success*, set out in 1719 to capture Spanish treasure ships carrying Peruvian silver along the western coast of South America. The voyage was plagued by major and minor catastrophes, including drunkenness (Shelvocke's), bad leadership and infighting between the two captains, sickness, starvation, shipwreck and mutiny, not to mention the slaughter of an albatross and ensuing bad luck fictionalized by the poet Coleridge in 'The Rime of the Ancient Mariner'. Our brief excerpt finds Shelvocke stopping for water on the coast of Baja California.

On Sunday, August 13, 1721. At daybreak we found ourselves near Puerto Seguro.* . . .

[I shall] give an account of the behaviour of the inhabitants upon our approach to them; some of whom came out on bark-logs* to meet us, whilst others got upon the tops of the hills and rocks near the sea-side, making fires for us. There was an universal joy spread through the whole body of them; those that were near the rocks to see us come in, incessantly running up and down to one another, and those who came out to us on bark-logs, paddled with all their strength, impatient to have a nearer view of us. Thus we entered Puerto Seguro, surrounded by these small embarkations, and the shore, on all sides, crowded with the Indians, whose number increased by multitudes which flocked from the adjacent parts.

Our anchor was no sooner down than they came off to us in shoals, some few on their bark-logs, but most of them swimming, talking and calling out to one another in a confused manner. Our ship was in an instant full of these swarthy gentlemen quite naked; amongst the rest was their King, or Chief-man, whom we could not distinguish by any particular ornament, nor by any deference that was paid to him more than to the rest; the only ensign of sovereignty which he bore about him was a black round stick made of a hard

wood, of about two foot and an half in length; this being observed by
some of my people, they brought him to me; upon which he, concluding that I was the chief of the ship, in a very handsome manner
delivered his black sceptre to me, which I immediately returned to
him. This man, notwithstanding his savage appearance, had a good
countenance, and his behaviour had something of the genteel in it.
I was, at first, at a loss to know how to entertain our numerous
guests, but soon found out a way to regale them, for we had a great
quantity of liquid sweetmeats; I therefore ordered what deep dishes
I had to be brought on the deck, the jars were broached, and the
dishes we filled with the choicest of Peruvian conserves; they were
every one accommodated with spoons, and though they could not sit
very regularly to their entertainment, because of their numbers, who
had all an equal welcome to the good cheer, yet, as we kept continually replenishing their empty dishes, they were all satisfied with as
much as they cared to eat; their food they liked extremely well, if
I may have leave to affirm it from the eagerness wherewith they ate
it; and the spoons, which were mostly silver, they returned with
great honesty, which they would doubtless have done had they been
gold, the value of those metals being (and perhaps always will be)
unknown to them.

Having thus commenced a friendship with them, I thought it
would not be unsafe to send an officer ashore to view the watering
place; but to make him the more welcome, I sent with him some
coarse blue baize, and some sugar, as a present to the women,
amongst whom it was to be equally distributed. The King seeing our
boat ready to put off, was for waiting on her with his bark-log, but
I (as well as I could) entreated him to take a passage in our boat,
which he seemed to be mightily pleased with.

The remainder of the day was spent in an interview between
us and our wild visitors, who behaved themselves in general very
quietly and peaceably. The officer returning with an account of his
civil reception, we prepared our casks to send ashore the next morning. Indeed from some accounts which I had read concerning these
people, I did not apprehend any molestation from them in wooding
and watering, though a first view of the country and inhabitants
would dishearten one a little from venturing freely amongst them;
they even appeared so terrible to our Negroes, who had been born
in Guinea (where they are not very polite) that one of them who

was sent with the officer on shore, was afraid to stir from the boat, and all the while kept an axe in his hand to defend himself from any that might attack him; but this dread perhaps proceeded from the contempt which the two first that came off to us had expressed towards our Negroes, in driving them from the Whites. As soon as the night approached, all the Indians swam ashore again, so that we had the pleasure of a clear ship to rest ourselves in after the fatigue of the day.

By daybreak the next morning our boat went ashore with those designed to cut the wood, and fill the water, and before the sun was up, we were again crowded with our former guests, who seemed as if they never could be tired with gazing at us and our ship. But that nothing should be wanting in us to keep up the amity we had already contracted, I ordered a great boiler to be carried ashore, with good store of flour and sugar, and a Negro cook to be continually boiling hasty pudding,* for the numerous spectators on the beach; and it really behoved us to endeavour to keep in their favour, since, whether in the ship, or on the strand, we were wholly in their power, those on shore being perpetually surrounded by multitudes, and we in the ship were from morning till night so incommoded by them that we could hardly move fore and aft through the throng of them.

They, at first, proved to be idle lookers on, till their natural compassion for the few of my men, whom they saw rolling of great casks of water over the heavy sand in the sultry heat of the day, inclined them to help us, together with the kind treatment they met with from us, and the particular readiness of their Chief to serve us, by showing his people a good example; for, after Mr Randall, my Lieutenant, he took up the second log of wood to carry to the boat, and was immediately followed by two or three hundred of them, so that they eased my men of a great fatigue, and shortened the time we should have occasion to stay at this place; they likewise rolled our cask down to the boat, but always expected a white face to assist them, who, if he did but touch it with his finger, it was sufficient encouragement for them to persevere in their labour.

WILLIAM BYRD, *History of the Dividing Line betwixt Virginia and North Carolina Run in the Year of Our Lord 1728* (1841)

William Byrd (1674–1744), the second of his name in the colony of Virginia, was the son of a wealthy planter and Indian trader who arrived in the New World before 1670. In 1728 Byrd was appointed head of a commission to settle the long-standing boundary dispute between Virginia and North Carolina. His account of the survey, *History of the Dividing Line*, informed by his broad reading and frequently off-colour wit, was not published until 1841. Our selections begin with the first meeting and quarrel between the Virginia and Carolina commissioners. Byrd goes on to ridicule North Carolinians, revel in a camp-out under the stars, and recommend intermarriage as the best solution to the colonists' relations with the Indians.

6 MARCH 1728. About three in the afternoon the two lag* commissioners arrived and, after a few decent excuses for making us wait, told us they were ready to enter upon business as soon as we pleased. The first step was to produce our respective powers, and the commission from each governor was distinctly read and copies of them interchangeably delivered.

It was observed by our Carolina friends that the latter part of the Virginia commission had something in it a little too lordly and positive. In answer to which we told them 'twas necessary to make it thus peremptory lest the present commissioners might go upon as fruitless an errand as their predecessors. The former commissioners were tied down to act in exact conjunction with those of Carolina and so could not advance one step farther or one jot faster than they were pleased to permit them. The memory of that disappointment, therefore, induced the government of Virginia to give fuller powers to the present commissioners by authorizing them to go on with the work by themselves, in case those of Carolina should prove unreasonable and refuse to join with them in carrying the business to execution. And all this was done lest His Majesty's gracious intention should be frustrated a second time.

After both commissions were considered, the first question was where the dividing line was to begin. This begat a warm debate, the Virginia commissioners contending, with a great deal of reason, to begin at the end of the spit of sand, which was undoubtedly the north shore of Currituck Inlet. But those of Carolina insisted strenuously that the point of high land ought rather to be the place of beginning, because that was fixed and certain, whereas the spit of sand was ever shifting and did actually run out farther now than formerly. The contest lasted some hours with great vehemence, neither party receding from their opinion that night. But next morning Mr. M[oseley], to convince us he was not that obstinate person he had been represented, yielded to our reasons and found means to bring over his colleagues.

Here we began already to reap the benefit of those peremptory words in our commission, which in truth added some weight to our reasons. Nevertheless, because positive proof was made by the oaths of two credible witnesses that the spit of sand had advanced two hundred yards toward the inlet since the controversy first began, we were willing for peace's sake to make them that allowance. Accordingly we fixed our beginning about that distance north of the inlet and there ordered a cedar post to be driven deep into the sand for our beginning.

While we continued here, we were told that on the south shore not far from the inlet dwelt a marooner that modestly called himself a hermit, though he forfeited that name by suffering a wanton female to cohabit with him. His habitation was a bower covered with bark after the Indian fashion, which in that mild situation protected him pretty well from the weather. Like the ravens, he neither ploughed nor sowed but subsisted chiefly upon oysters, which his handmaid made a shift to gather from the adjacent rocks. Sometimes, too, for change of diet, he sent her to drive up the neighbour's cows, to moisten their mouths with a little milk. But as for raiment, he depended mostly upon his length of beard and she upon her length of hair, part of which she brought decently forward and the rest dangled behind quite down to her rump, like one of Herodotus' East Indian Pygmies.* Thus did these wretches live in a dirty state of nature and were mere Adamites,* innocence only excepted.

8 MARCH 1728. All the people in the neighbourhood flocked to John Heath's to behold such rarities as they fancied us to be. The men left their beloved chimney corners, the good women their spinning wheels, and some, of more curiosity than ordinary, rose out of their sickbeds to come and stare at us. They looked upon us as a troop of knights-errant who were running this great risk of our lives, as they

imagined, for the public weal; and some of the gravest of them questioned much whether we were not all criminals condemned to this dirty work for offences against the state. What puzzled them most was what could make our men so very light-hearted under such intolerable drudgery. 'Ye have little reason to be merry, my masters,' said one of them, with a very solemn face. 'I fancy the pocosin* you must struggle with tomorrow will make you change your note and try what metal you are made of. Ye are, to be sure, the first of human race that ever had the boldness to attempt it, and I dare say will be the last. If, therefore, you have any worldly goods to dispose of, my advice is that you make your wills this very night, for fear you die intestate tomorrow.' But, alas, these frightful tales were so far from disheartening the men that they served only to whet their resolution.

9 MARCH 1728. The surveyors entered early upon their business this morning and ran the line through Mr Eyland's plantation, as far as the banks of North River. They passed over it in the piragua* and landed in Gibbs's marsh, which was a mile in breadth and tolerably firm. They trudged through this marsh without much difficulty as far as the high land, which promised more fertility than any they had seen in these lower parts. But this firm land lasted not long before they came upon the dreadful pocosin they had been threatened with. Nor did they find it one jot better than it had been painted to them. The beavers and otters had rendered it quite impassable for any creatures but themselves.

10 MARCH 1728. The only business here is raising of hogs, which is managed with the least trouble and affords the diet they are most fond of. The truth of it is, the inhabitants of North Carolina devour so much swine's flesh that it fills them full of gross humours. For want, too, of a constant supply of salt, they are commonly obliged to eat it fresh, and that begets the highest taint of scurvy. Thus, whenever a severe cold happens to constitutions thus vitiated, 'tis apt to improve into the yaws, called there very justly the country distemper. This has all the symptoms of the pox, with this aggravation, that no preparation of mercury will touch it. First it seizes the throat, next the palate, and lastly shows its spite to the poor nose, of which 'tis apt in a small time treacherously to undermine the foundation. This calamity is so common and familiar here that it ceases to be a scandal, and in the disputes that happen about beauty the noses

have in some companies much ado to carry it. Nay, 'tis said that once, after three good pork years, a motion had like to have been made in the House of Burgesses that a man with a nose should be incapable of holding any place of profit in the province; which extraordinary motion could never have been intended without some hopes of a majority.

Thus, considering the foul and pernicious effects of eating swine's flesh in a hot country, it was wisely forbid and made an abomination to the Jews, who lived much in the same latitude with Carolina.

11 MARCH 1728. We ordered the surveyors early to their business, who were blessed with pretty dry grounds for three miles together. But they paid dear for it in the next two, consisting of one continued frightful pocosin, which no creatures but those of the amphibious kind ever had ventured into before. This filthy quagmire did in earnest put the men's courage to a trial, and though I can't say it made them lose their patience, yet they lost their humour for joking. They kept their gravity like so many Spaniards, so that a man might then have taken his opportunity to plunge up to the chin without danger of being laughed at. However, this unusual composure of countenance could not fairly be called complaining.

Their day's work ended at the mouth of Northern's Creek, which empties itself into Northwest River; though we chose to quarter a little higher up the river near Mossy Point. This we did for the convenience of an old house to shelter our persons and baggage from the rain, which threatened us hard. We judged the thing right, for there fell a heavy shower in the night that drove the most hardy of us into the house. Though indeed our case was not much mended by retreating thither, because, that tenement having not long before been used as a pork store, the moisture of the air dissolved the salt that lay scattered on the floor and made it as wet within doors as without. However, the swamps and marshes we were lately accustomed to had made such beavers and otters of us that nobody caught the least cold.

We had encamped so early that we found time in the evening to walk near half a mile into the woods. There we came upon a family of mulattos that called themselves free, though by the shyness of the master of the house, who took care to keep least in sight, their freedom seemed a little doubtful. It is certain many slaves shelter themselves in this obscure part of the world, nor will any of their righteous neighbours discover them. On the contrary, they find their account in settling such fugitives on some out-of-the way corner of their land to raise stocks for a mean and inconsiderable share, well knowing their condition makes it necessary for them to submit to any terms. Nor were these worthy borderers content to shelter runaway slaves, but debtors and criminals have often met with the like indulgence. But if the government of North Carolina have encouraged this unneighbourly policy in order to increase their people, it is no more than what ancient Rome did before them, which was made a city of refuge for all debtors and fugitives and from that wretched beginning grew up in time to be mistress of great part of the world. And, considering how Fortune delights in bringing great things out of small, who knows but Carolina may, one time or other, come to be the seat of some other great empire?

12 MARCH 1728. Everything had been so soaked with the rain that we were obliged to lie by a good part of the morning and dry them. However, that time was not lost, because it gave the surveyors an opportunity of platting off their work and taking the course of the river. It likewise helped to recruit the spirits of the men, who had been a little harassed with yesterday's march. Notwithstanding all this, we crossed the river before noon and advanced our line three miles. It was not possible to make more of it by reason good part of the way was either marsh or pocosin. The line cut two or three plantations, leaving part of them in Virginia and part of them in Carolina. This was a case that happened frequently, to the great inconvenience of the owners, who were therefore obliged to take out two patents and pay for a new survey in each government.

In the evening we took up our quarters in Mr Ballance's pasture, a little above the bridge built over Northwest River. There we discharged the two piraguas, which in truth had been very serviceable in transporting us over the many waters in that dirty and difficult part of our business. Our landlord had a tolerable good house and clean furniture, and yet we could not be tempted to lodge in it. We chose rather to lie in the open field, for fear of growing too tender. A clear sky, spangled with stars, was our canopy, which, being the last thing we saw before we fell asleep, gave us magnificent dreams. The truth of it is, we took so much pleasure in that natural kind of lodging that I think at the foot of the account mankind are great losers by the luxury of feather beds and warm apartments.

The curiosity of beholding so new and withal so sweet a method of encamping brought one of the Senators of North Carolina to make us a midnight visit. But he was so very clamorous in his commendations of it that the sentinel, not seeing his quality either through his habit or behaviour, had like to have treated him roughly. After excusing the unseasonableness of his visit and letting us know he was a parliament man, he swore he was so taken with our lodging that he would set fire to his house as soon as he got home and teach his wife and children to lie like us in the open field.

13 MARCH 1729. Early this morning our chaplain repaired to us with the men we had left at Mr Wilson's. We had sent for them the evening before to relieve those who had the labour oar from Currituck Inlet. But to our great surprise, they petitioned not to be relieved, hoping to gain immortal reputation by being the first of mankind that ventured through the Great Dismal. But the rest being equally ambitious of the same honour, it was but fair to decide their pretensions by lot. After Fortune had declared herself, those which she had excluded offered money to the happy persons to go in their stead. But Hercules would have as soon sold the glory of cleansing the Augean stables,* which was pretty near the same sort of work.

7 APRIL 1728. I am sorry I can't give a better account of the state of the poor Indians with respect to Christianity, although a great deal of pains has been and still continues to be taken with them. For my part, I must be of opinion, as I hinted before, that there is but one way of converting these poor infidels and reclaiming them from barbarity, and that charitably to intermarry with them, according to the modern policy of the Most Christian King in Canada and Louisiana.* Had the English done this at the first settlement of the colony, the infidelity of the Indians had been worn out at this day with their dark complexion and the country had swarmed with people more than it does with insects. It was certainly an unreasonable nicety that prevented them entering into so good-natured an alliance. All nations of men have the same natural dignity, and we all know that very bright talents may be lodged under a very dark skin. The principal difference between one people and another proceeds only from the different opportunities of improvement. The Indians

by no means want understanding and are in their figure tall and well proportioned. Even their copper-coloured complexion would admit of blanching, if not in the first, at the farthest in the second, generation. I may safely venture to say, the Indian women would have made altogether as honest wives for the first planters as the damsels they used to purchase from aboard the ships. 'Tis strange, therefore, that any good Christian should have refused a wholesome, straight bedfellow, when he might have had so fair a portion with her as the merit of saving her soul.

8 APRIL 1728. We rested on our clean mats very comfortably, though alone, and the next morning went to the toilet of some of the Indian ladies, where, what with the charms of their persons and the smoke of their apartments, we were almost blinded. They offered to give us silk-grass baskets of their own making, which we modestly refused, knowing that an Indian present, like that of a nun, is a liberality put out to interest and a bribe placed to the greatest advantage. Our chaplain observed with concern that the ruffles of some of our fellow travellers were a little discoloured with puccoon,* wherewith the good man had been told those ladies used to improve their invisible charms.

14 OCTOBER 1728. This was the first time we had ever been detained a whole day in our camp by the rain and therefore had reason to bear it with the more patience.

As I sat in the tent, I overheard a learned conversation between one of our men and the Indian. He asked the Englishman what it was that made that rumbling noise when it thundered. The man told him merrily that the god of the English was firing his great guns upon the god of the Indians, which made all that roaring in the clouds, and that the lightning was only the flash of those guns. The Indian, carrying on the humour, replied very gravely he believed that might be the case indeed, and that the rain which followed upon the thunder must be occasioned by the Indian god's being so scared he could not hold his water.

30 OCTOBER 1728. We encamped on Crooked Creek near a thicket of canes. In the front of our camp rose a very beautiful hill that bounded our view at about a mile's distance, and all the intermediate space was covered with green canes. Though to our sorrow, firewood was scarce, which was now the harder upon us because a northwester blew very cold from the mountains.

The Indian killed a stately, fat buck, and we picked his bones as clean as a score of turkey buzzards could have done. By the advantage of a clear night, we made trial once more of the variation and found it much the same as formerly. This being His Majesty's birthday, we drank all the loyal healths in excellent water, not for the sake of the drink (like many of our fellow subjects), but purely for the sake of the toast. And because all public mirth should be a little noisy, we fired several volleys of canes, instead of guns, which gave a loud report. We threw them into the fire, where the air enclosed betwixt the joints of the canes, being expanded by the violent heat, burst its narrow bounds with a considerable explosion.

In the evening one of the men knocked down an opossum, which is a harmless little beast that will seldom go out of your way, and if you take hold of it will only grin and hardly ever bite. The flesh was well tasted and tender, approaching nearest to pig, which it also resembled in bigness. The colour of its fur was a goose grey, with a swine's snout and a tail like a rat, but at least a foot long. By twisting this tail about the arm of a tree, it will hang with all its weight and swing to anything it wants to take hold of. It has five claws on the forefeet of equal length, but the hinder feet have only four claws and a sort of thumb standing off at a proper distance. Their feet, being thus formed, qualify them for climbing up trees to catch little birds, which they are very fond of. But the greatest particularity of this creature, and which distinguishes it from most others that we are acquainted with, is the false belly of the female, into which her young retreat in time of danger. She can draw the slit, which is the inlet into this pouch, so close that you must look narrowly to find it, especially if she happen to be a virgin. Within the false belly may be seen seven or eight teats, on which the young ones grow from their first formation till they are big enough to fall off like ripe fruit from a tree. This is so odd a method of generation that I should not have believed it without the testimony of mine own eyes. Besides, a knowing and credible person has assured me he has more than once observed the embryo opossums growing to the teat before they were completely shaped, and afterwards watched their daily growth till they were big enough for birth. And all this he could the more easily pry into because the dam was so perfectly gentle and harmless that he could handle her just as he pleased.

I could hardly persuade myself to publish a thing so contrary to

the course that nature takes in the production of other animals
unless it were a matter commonly believed in all countries where that
creature is produced and has been often observed by persons of
undoubted credit and understanding. They say that the leather-
winged bats produce their young in the same uncommon manner;
and that young sharks at sea and young vipers ashore run down the
throats of their dams when they are closely pursued.

31 MAY The frequent crossing of Crooked Creek and mounting the
steep banks of it gave the finishing stroke to the foundering our
horses, and no less than two of them made a full stop here and would
not advance a foot farther, either by fair means or foul. We had a
dreamer of dreams amongst us who warned me in the morning to
take care of myself or I should infallibly fall into the creek; I thanked
him kindly and used what caution I could but was not able, it seems,
to avoid my destiny, for my horse made a false step and laid me down
at my full length in the water. This was enough to bring dreaming
into credit, and I think it much for the honour of our expedition that
it was graced not only with a priest but also with a prophet. We were
so perplexed with this serpentine creek, as well as in passing the
branches of the Irvin, which were swelled since we saw them before,
that we could reach but five miles this whole day.

In the evening we pitched our tent near Miry Creek, though an
uncomfortable place to lodge in, purely for the advantage of the
canes. Our hunters killed a large doe and two bears, which made all
other misfortunes easy. Certainly no Tartar ever loved horseflesh or
Hottentot guts and garbage better than woodsmen do bear. The
truth of it is, it may be proper food perhaps for such as work or ride
it off, but, with our chaplain's leave, who loved it much, I think it not
a very proper diet for saints, because 'tis apt to make them a little too
rampant. And, now, for the good of mankind and for the better
peopling an infant colony, which has no want but that of inhabitants,
I will venture to publish a secret of importance which our Indian
disclosed to me. I asked him the reason why few or none of his
countrywomen were barren. To which curious question he answered,
with a broad grin upon his face, they had an infallible secret for that.
Upon my being importunate to know what the secret might be, he
informed me that if any Indian woman did not prove with child at a
decent time after marriage, the husband, to save his reputation with

the women, forthwith entered into a bear diet for six weeks, which in that time makes him so vigorous that he grows exceedingly impertinent to his poor wife, and 'tis great odds but he makes her a mother in nine months. And thus much I am able to say besides for the reputation of the bear diet, that all the married men of our company were joyful fathers within forty weeks after they got home, and most of the single men had children sworn to them within the same time, our chaplain always excepted, who, with much ado, made a shift to cast out that importunate kind of devil by dint of fasting and prayer.

WILLIAM BARTRAM, *Travels Through North and South Carolina, Georgia, East and West Florida, the Cherokee Country, the Extensive Territories of the Muscogulges or Creek Confederacy, and the Country of the Chactaws* (1791)

William Bartram (1739–1823), an American naturalist, was the son of John Bartram of Philadelphia, dubbed by Linnaeus 'the greatest natural botanist in the world'. Bartram's *Travels* describes his journey (1773–7) from the foothills of the Appalachian Mountains to Florida and through the south-eastern interior all the way to the Mississippi River. The book quickly became a classic, praised by one scholar as 'the most astounding verbal artifact of the early Republic'. Bartram describes the plants and wildlife of the country, listing 215 native birds. Seminole, Creek, and Cherokee Indians are depicted in a vein of Romantic primitivism that influenced Wordsworth, Coleridge, Chateaubriand, and other writers.

[An encounter with a Seminole warrior]

I had now passed the utmost frontier of the white settlements on that border. It was drawing on towards the close of day, the skies serene and calm, the air temperately cool, and gentle zephyrs breathing through the fragrant pines; the prospect around enchantingly varied and beautiful; endless green savannas, chequered with coppices of fragrant shrubs, filled the air with the richest perfume. The gaily attired plants which enamelled the green had begun to imbibe the pearly dew of evening; nature seemed silent, and nothing appeared to ruffle the happy moments of evening contemplation; when, on a sudden, an Indian appeared crossing the path, at a considerable distance before me. On perceiving that he was armed with a rifle, the first sight of him startled me, and I endeavoured to elude his sight, by stopping my pace, and keeping large trees between us; but he espied me, and turning short about, sat spurs to his horse, and came up on full gallop. I never before this was afraid at the sight of an Indian, but at this time, I must own that my spirits were very much agitated: I saw at once, that being unarmed, I was in his power; and having now but a few moments to prepare, I resigned myself entirely to the will of the Almighty, trusting to his mercies for my preservation: my mind then became tranquil, and I resolved to meet the dreaded foe with resolution and cheerful confidence. The intrepid Seminole stopped suddenly, three or four yards before me, and silently viewed me, his countenance angry and fierce, shifting his rifle from shoulder to shoulder, and looking about instantly on all sides. I advanced towards him, and with an air of confidence offered him my hand, hailing him, brother; at this he hastily jerked back his arm, with a look of malice, rage, and disdain, seeming every way discontented; when again looking at me more attentively, he instantly spurred up to me, and with dignity in his look and action, gave me his hand. Possibly the silent language of his soul, during the moment of suspense (for I believe his design was to kill me when he first came up) was after this manner: 'White man, thou art my enemy, and thou and thy brethren may have killed mine; yet it may not be so, and even were that the case, thou art now alone, and in my power. Live; the Great Spirit forbids me to touch thy life; go to thy brethren, tell them thou sawest an Indian in the forests, who knew how to be humane and compassionate.' In fine, we shook hands, and parted in a friendly manner, in the midst of a dreary wilderness; and he informed me of the course and distance to the trading-house, where I found he had been extremely ill-treated the day before.

I now sat forward again, and after eight or ten miles riding, arrived at the banks of St Mary's, opposite the stores, and got safe over before dark. The river is here about one hundred yards across, has ten feet water, and, following its course, about sixty miles to the sea, though but about twenty miles by land. The trading company here received and treated me with great civility. On relating my adventures on the road, particularly the last with the Indian, the chief replied, with a countenance that at once bespoke surprise and pleasure, 'My friend, consider yourself a fortunate man: that fellow,' said he, 'is one of the greatest villains on earth, a noted murderer, and outlawed by his countrymen. Last evening he was here, we took his gun from him, broke it in pieces, and gave him a severe drubbing: he, however, made his escape, carrying off a new rifle gun, with which, he said, going off, he would kill the first white man he met.'

On seriously contemplating the behaviour of this Indian towards me, so soon after his ill treatment, the following train of sentiments insensibly crowded in upon my mind.

Can it be denied, but that the moral principle, which directs the savages to virtuous and praiseworthy actions, is natural or innate? It is certain they have not the assistance of letters, or those means of education in the schools of philosophy, where the virtuous sentiments and actions of the most illustrious characters are recorded, and carefully laid before the youth of civilized nations: therefore this moral principle must be innate, or they must be under the immediate influence and guidance of a more divine and powerful preceptor, who, on these occasions, instantly inspires them, and as with a ray of divine light, points out to them at once the dignity, propriety, and beauty of virtue.

[Adventures with alligators]

About one hundred yards above my harbour began a cove or bay of the river, out of which opened a large lagoon. The mouth or entrance from the river to it was narrow, but the waters soon after spread and formed a little lake, extending into the marshes: its entrance and shores within I observed to be verged with floating lawns of the pistia and nymphea and other aquatic plants; these I knew were excellent haunts for trout.

The verges and islets of the lagoon were elegantly embellished with flowering plants and shrubs; the laughing coots with wings half spread were tripping over the little coves and hiding themselves in the tufts of grass; young broods of the painted summer teal, skimming the still surface of the waters, and following the watchful parent unconscious of danger, were frequently surprised by the voracious trout; and he, in turn, as often by the subtle greedy alligator. Behold him rushing forth from the flags and reeds. His enormous body swells. His plaited tail brandished high, floats upon the lake. The waters like a cataract descend from his opening jaws. Clouds of smoke issue from his dilated nostrils. The earth trembles with his thunder. When immediately, from the opposite coast of the lagoon, emerges from the deep his rival champion. They suddenly dart upon each other. The boiling surface of the lake marks their rapid course, and a terrific conflict commences. They now sink to the bottom folded together in horrid wreaths. The water becomes thick and discoloured. Again they rise, their jaws clap together, re-echoing through the deep surrounding forests. Again they sink, when the contest ends at the muddy bottom of the lake, and the vanquished makes a hazardous escape, hiding himself in the muddy turbulent waters and sedge on a distant shore. The proud victor exulting returns to the place of action. The shores and forests resound his dreadful roar, together with the triumphing shouts of the plaited tribes around, witnesses of the horrid combat.

My apprehensions were highly alarmed after being a spectator of so dreadful a battle. It was obvious that every delay would but tend to increase my dangers and difficulties, as the sun was near setting, and the alligators gathered around my harbour from all quarters. From these considerations I concluded to be expeditious in my trip to the lagoon, in order to take some fish. Not thinking it prudent to take my fusee* with me, lest I might lose it overboard in case of a battle, which I had every reason to dread before my return, I therefore furnished myself with a club for my defence, went on board, and penetrating the first line of those which surrounded my harbour, they gave way; but being pursued by several very large ones, I kept strictly on the watch, and paddled with all my might towards the entrance of the lagoon, hoping to be sheltered there from the multitude of my assailants; but ere I had half-way reached the place, I was attacked on all sides, several endeavouring to overset the canoe. My situation now became precarious to the last degree: two very large ones attacked me closely, at the same instant, rushing up with their heads and part of their bodies above the water, roaring terribly and belching floods of water over me. They struck their jaws together so close to my ears, as almost to stun me, and I expected every moment to be dragged out of the boat and instantly devoured. But I applied my weapons so effectually about me, though at random, that I was so successful as to beat them off a little; when, finding that they designed to renew the battle, I made for the shore, as the only means left me for my preservation; for, by keeping close to it, I should have my enemies on one side of me only, whereas I was before surrounded by them; and there was a probability, if pushed to the last extremity, of saving myself, by jumping out of the canoe on shore, as it is easy to outwalk them on land, although comparatively as swift as lightning in the water. I found this last expedient alone could fully answer my expectations, for as soon as I gained the shore, they drew off and kept aloof. This was a happy relief, as my confidence was, in some degree, recovered by it. On recollecting myself, I discovered that I had almost reached the entrance of the lagoon, and determined to venture in, if possible, to take a few fish, and then return to my harbour, while daylight continued; for I could now, with caution and resolution, make my way with safety along shore; and indeed there was no other way to regain my camp, without leaving my boat and making my retreat through the marshes and reeds, which, if I could even effect, would have been in a manner throwing myself away, for then there would have been no hopes of ever recovering my bark, and returning in safety to any settlements of men. I accordingly proceeded, and made good my entrance into the lagoon, though not without opposition from the alligators, who formed a line across the entrance, but did not pursue me into it, nor was I molested by any there, though there were some very large ones in a cove at the upper end. I soon caught more trout than I had present occasion for, and the air was too hot and sultry to admit of their being kept for many hours, even though salted or barbecued. I now prepared for my return to camp, which I succeeded in with but little trouble, by keeping close to the shore; yet I was opposed upon re-entering the river out of the lagoon, and pursued near to my landing (though not closely attacked), particularly by an old daring one, about twelve feet in length, who kept close after me; and when I stepped on shore and turned about, in order to draw up my canoe, he rushed up near my feet, and lay there for some time, looking me in the face, his head and shoulders out of water. I resolved he should pay for his temerity, and having a heavy load in my fusee, I ran to my camp, and returning with my piece, found him with his foot on the gunwale of the boat, in search of fish. On my coming up he withdrew sullenly and slowly into the water, but soon returned and placed himself in his former position, looking at me, and seeming neither fearful nor any way disturbed. I soon dispatched him by lodging the contents of my gun in his head, and then proceeded to cleanse and prepare my fish for supper; and accordingly took them out of the boat, laid them down on the sand close to the water, and began to scale them; when, raising my head, I saw before me, through the clear water, the head and shoulders of a very large alligator, moving slowly towards me. I instantly stepped back, when, with a sweep of his tail, he brushed off several of my fish. It was certainly most providential that I looked up at that instant, as the monster would probably, in less than a minute, have seized and dragged me into the river. This incredible boldness of the animal disturbed me greatly, supposing there could now be no reasonable safety for me during the night, but by keeping continually on the watch: I therefore, as soon as I had prepared the fish, proceeded to secure myself and effects in the best manner I could. In the first place, I hauled my bark upon the shore, almost clear out of the water, to prevent their oversetting or sinking her; after this, every moveable was taken out and carried to my camp, which was but a few yards off; then ranging some dry wood in such order as was the most convenient, I cleared the ground round about it, that there might be no impediment in my way, in case of an attack in the night, either from the water or the land. . . .

It was by this time dusk, and the alligators had nearly ceased their roar, when I was again alarmed by a tumultuous noise that seemed to be in my harbour, and therefore engaged my immediate attention. Returning to my camp, I found it undisturbed, and then continued on to the extreme point of the promontory, where I saw a scene, new and surprising, which at first threw my senses into such a tumult, that it was some time before I could comprehend what was the matter; however, I soon accounted for the prodigious assemblage of crocodiles* at this place, which exceeded every thing of the kind I had ever heard of.

How shall I express myself so as to convey an adequate idea of it to the reader, and at the same time avoid raising suspicions of my veracity. Should I say, that the river (in this place) from shore to shore, and perhaps near half a mile above and below me, appeared to be one solid bank of fish, of various kinds, pushing through this narrow pass of St Juan's into the little lake, on their return down the river, and that the alligators were in such incredible numbers, and so close together from shore to shore, that it would have been easy to have walked across on their heads, had the animals been harmless? What expressions can sufficiently declare the shocking scene that for some minutes continued, whilst this mighty army of fish were forcing the pass? During this attempt, thousands, I may say hundreds of thousands, of them were caught and swallowed by the devouring alligators. I have seen an alligator take up out of the water several great fish at a time, and just squeeze them betwixt his jaws, while the tails of the great trout flapped about his eyes and lips, ere he had swallowed them. The horrid noise of their closing jaws, their plunging amidst the broken banks of fish, and rising with their prey some feet upright above the water, the floods of water and blood rushing out of their mouths, and the clouds of vapour issuing from their wide nostrils, were truly frightful. This scene continued at intervals during the night, as the fish came to the pass. After this sight, shocking and tremendous as it was, I found myself somewhat easier and more reconciled to my situation; being convinced that their extraordinary assemblage here was owing to this annual feast of fish; and that they were so well employed in their own element, that I had little occasion to fear their paying me a visit. . . .

To pursue my voyage up the river, and be obliged every evening to pass such dangerous defiles, appeared to me as perilous as running the gauntlet betwixt two rows of Indians armed with knives and firebrands. I however resolved to continue my voyage one day longer, if I possibly could with safety, and then return down the river, should I find the like difficulties to oppose. Accordingly I got everything on board, charged my gun, and set sail cautiously, along shore. As I passed by Battle lagoon, I began to tremble and keep a good look out; when suddenly a huge alligator rushed out of the reeds, and with a tremendous roar came up, and darted as swift as an arrow under my boat, emerging upright on my lee quarter, with open jaws, and belching water and smoke that fell upon me like rain in a hurricane. I laid soundly about his head with my club and beat him off; and after plunging and darting about my boat, he went off on a straight line through the water, seemingly with the rapidity of lightning, and entered the cape of the lagoon. I now employed my time to the very best advantage in paddling close along shore, but could not forbear looking now and then behind me, and presently perceived one of them coming up again. The water of the river hereabouts was shoal and very clear; the monster came up with the usual roar and menaces, and passed close by the side of my boat, when I could distinctly see a young brood of alligators, to the number of one hundred or more, following after her in a long train. They kept close together in a column without straggling off to the one side or the other; the young appeared to be of an equal size, about fifteen inches in length, almost black, with pale yellow transverse waved clouds or blotches, much like rattlesnakes in colour. I now lost sight of my enemy again.

Still keeping close along shore, on turning a point or projection of the river bank, at once I beheld a great number of hillocks or small pyramids, resembling hay-cocks, ranged like an encampment along the banks. They stood fifteen or twenty yards distant from the water, on a high marsh, about four feet perpendicular above the water. I knew them to be the nests of the crocodile, having had a description of them before; and now expected a furious and general attack, as I saw several large crocodiles swimming abreast of these buildings. These nests being so great a curiosity to me, I was determined at all events immediately to land and examine them. Accordingly, I ran my bark on shore at one of their landing-places, which was a sort of nick or little dock, from which ascended a sloping path or road up to the edge of the meadow, where their nests were; most of them were deserted, and the great thick whitish egg-shells lay broken and scattered upon the ground round about them.

The nests or hillocks are of the form of an obtuse cone, four feet high and four or five feet in diameter at their bases; they are constructed with mud, grass, and herbage. At first they lay a floor of this kind of tempered mortar on the ground, upon which they deposit a layer of eggs, and upon this a stratum of mortar seven or eight inches in thickness, and then another layer of eggs, and in this manner one stratum upon another, nearly to the top. I believe they commonly lay from one to two hundred eggs in a nest: these are hatched, I suppose, by the heat of the sun; and perhaps the vegetable substances mixed with the earth, being acted upon by the sun, may cause a small degree of fermentation, and so increase the heat in those hillocks. The ground for several acres about these nests shewed evident marks of a continual resort of alligators; the grass was every where beaten down, hardly a blade or straw was left standing; whereas, all about, at a distance, it was five or six feet high, and as thick as it could grow together. The female, as I imagine, carefully watches her own nest of eggs until they are all hatched; or perhaps while she is attending her own brood, she takes under her care and protection as many as she can get at one time, either from her own particular nest or others: but certain it is, that the young are not left to shift for themselves; for I have had frequent opportunities of seeing the female alligator leading about the shores her train of young ones, just as a hen does her brood of chickens; and she is equally assiduous and courageous in defending the young, which are under her care, and providing for their subsistence; and when she is basking upon the warm banks, with her brood around her, you may hear the young ones continually whining and barking, like young puppies. I believe but few of a brood live to the years of full growth and magnitude, as the old feed on the young as long as they can make prey of them.

The alligator when full grown is a very large and terrible creature, and of prodigious strength, activity, and swiftness in the water. I have seen them twenty feet in length, and some are supposed to be twenty-two or twenty-three feet. Their body is as large as that of a horse; their shape exactly resembles that of a lizard, except their tail, which is flat or cuneiform, being compressed on each side, and gradually diminishing from the abdomen to the extremity, which, with the whole body is covered with horny plates or squammae, impenetrable when on the body of the live animal, even to a rifle ball, except about their head and just behind their fore-legs or arms, where it is said they are only vulnerable. The head of a full grown one is about three feet, and the mouth opens nearly the same length; their eyes are small in proportion and seem sunk deep in the head, by means of the prominency of the brows; the nostrils are large, inflated and prominent on the top, so that the head in the water resembles, at a distance, a great chunk of wood floating about. Only the upper jaw moves, which they raise almost perpendicular, so as to form a right angle with the lower one. In the fore-part of the upper jaw, on each side, just under the nostrils, are two very large, thick, strong teeth or tusks, not very sharp, but rather the shape of a cone: these are as white as the finest polished ivory, and are not covered by any skin or lips, and always in sight, which gives the creature a frightful appearance: in the lower jaw are holes opposite to these teeth, to receive them: when they clap their jaws together it causes a surprising noise, like that which is made by forcing a heavy plank with violence upon the ground, and may be heard at a great distance.

But what is yet more surprising to a stranger is the incredible loud and terrifying roar which they are capable of making, especially in the spring season, their breeding time. It most resembles very heavy distant thunder, not only shaking the air and waters, but causing the earth to tremble; and when hundreds and thousands are roaring at the same time, you can scarcely be persuaded, but that the whole globe is violently and dangerously agitated.

[Description of a savanna]

The extensive Alachua savanna is a level green plain, above fifteen miles over, fifty miles in circumference, and scarcely a tree or bush of any kind to be seen on it. It is encircled with high, sloping hills, covered with waving forests and fragrant orange groves, rising from an exuberantly fertile soil. The towering Magnolia grandiflora and transcendent palm stand conspicuous amongst them. At the same time are seen innumerable droves of cattle; the lordly bull, lowing cow, and sleek capricious heifer. The hills and groves re-echo their cheerful, social voices. Herds of sprightly deer, squadrons of the beautiful fleet Seminole horse, flocks of turkeys, civilized communities of the sonorous watchful crane mix together, appearing happy and contented in the enjoyment of peace, till disturbed and affrighted by the warrior man. Behold yonder, coming upon them through the darkened groves, sneakingly and unawares, the naked red warrior, invading the Elysian fields and green plains of Alachua. At the terrible appearance of the painted, fearless, uncontrolled, and free Seminole, the peaceful innocent nations are at once thrown into disorder and dismay. See the different tribes and bands, how they draw towards each other! as it were deliberating upon the general good. Suddenly they speed off with their young in the centre; but the roebuck fears him not: here he lays himself down, bathes and flounces in the cool flood. The red warrior, whose plumed head flashes lightning, whoops in vain; his proud ambitious horse strains and pants; the earth glides from under his feet, his flowing mane whistles in the wind, as he comes up full of vain hopes. The bounding roe views his rapid approaches, rises up, lifts aloft his antlered head, erects the white flag,* and fetching a shrill whistle, says to his fleet and free associates, 'follow'; he bounds off, and in a few minutes distances his foe a mile; suddenly he stops, turns about, and laughing says, 'how vain! go chase meteors in the azure plains above, or hunt butterflies in the fields about your towns.'

We approached the savanna at the south end by a narrow isthmus of level ground, open to the light of day, and clear of trees or bushes, and not greatly elevated above the common level, having on our right a spacious meadow, embellished with a little lake, one verge of which was not very distant from us; its shore is a moderately high, circular bank, partly encircling a cove of the pond, in the form of a half moon; the water is clear and deep, and, at the distance of some hundred yards, was a large floating field (if I may so express myself) of the Nymphaea nelumbo, with their golden blossoms waving to and fro on their lofty stems. Beyond these fields of Nymphaea were spacious plains, encompassed by dark groves, opening to extensive pine forests, other plains still appearing beyond them.

This little lake and surrounding meadows would have been alone sufficient to surprise and delight the traveller; but being placed so near the great savanna, the attention is quickly drawn off, and wholly engaged in the contemplation of the unlimited, varied, and truly astonishing native wild scenes of landscape and perspective there exhibited: how is the mind agitated and bewildered, at being thus, as it were, placed on the borders of a new world! On the first view of such an amazing display of the wisdom and power of the supreme author of nature, the mind for a moment seems suspended, and impressed with awe.

This isthmus being the common avenue or road of Indian travellers, we pitched our camp at a small distance from it, on a rising knoll near the verge of the savanna, under some spreading live oaks: this situation was open and airy, and gave us an unbounded prospect over the adjacent plains. Dewy evening now came on; the animating breezes, which cooled and tempered the meridian hours of this sultry season, now gently ceased; the glorious sovereign of day, calling in his bright beaming emanations, left us in his absence to the milder government and protection of the silver queen of night, attended by millions of brilliant luminaries. The thundering alligator had ended his horrifying roar; the silver plumed gannet and stork, the sage and solitary pelican of the wilderness, had already retired to their silent nocturnal habitations, in the neighbouring forests; the sonorous savanna cranes, in well disciplined squadrons, now rising from the earth, mounted aloft in spiral circles, far above the dense atmosphere of the humid plain; they again viewed the glorious sun, and the light of day still gleaming on their polished feathers, they sung their evening hymn, then in a straight line majestically descended, and alighted on the towering palms or lofty pines, their secure and peaceful lodging places. All around being still and silent, we repaired to rest.

[The Indians' dread of the rattlesnake]

An occurrence happened this day, by which I had an opportunity of observing [the Seminoles'] extraordinary veneration or dread of the rattle snake. I was in the forenoon busy in my apartment in the council-house, drawing some curious flowers, when, on a sudden, my attention was taken off by a tumult without, at the Indian camp. I stepped to the door opening to the piazza, where I met my friend the old interpreter, who informed me that there was a very large rattle snake in the Indian camp, which had taken possession of it, having driven the men, women and children out, and he heard them saying that they would send for Puc-Puggy (for that was the name which they had given me, signifying the Flower Hunter) to kill him or take him out of their camp. I answered that I desired to have nothing to do with him, apprehending some disagreeable consequences; and desired that the Indians might be acquainted that I was engaged in business that required application and quiet, and was determined to avoid it if possible. My old friend turned about to carry my answer to the Indians. I presently heard them approaching and calling for Puc-Puggy. Starting up to escape from their sight by a back door, a party consisting of three young fellows, richly dressed and ornamented, stepped in, and with a countenance and action of noble simplicity, amity and complaisance, requested me to accompany them to their encampment. I desired them to excuse me at this time; they pleaded and entreated me to go with them, in order to free them from a great rattle snake which had entered their camp; that none of them had freedom or courage to expel him; and understanding that it was my pleasure to collect all their animals and other natural productions of their land, desired that I would come with them and take him away, that I was welcome to him. I at length consented and attended on them to their encampment, where I beheld the Indians greatly disturbed indeed. The men with sticks and tomahawks, and the women and children collected together at a distance in affright and trepidation, whilst the dreaded and revered serpent leisurely traversed their camp, visiting the fire places from one to another, picking up fragments of their provisions and licking their platters. The men gathered around me, exciting me to remove him: being armed with a lightwood knot, I approached the reptile, who instantly collected himself in a vast coil (their attitude of defence). I cast my missile weapon at him, which luckily taking his head, dispatched him instantly, and laid him trembling at my feet. I took out my knife, severed his head from his body, then turning about, the Indians complimented me with every demonstration of satisfaction and approbation for my heroism, and friendship for them. I carried off the head of the serpent bleeding in my hand as a trophy of victory; and taking out the mortal fangs, deposited them carefully amongst my collections. I had not been long retired to my apartment, before I was again roused from it by a tumult in the yard; and hearing Puc-Puggy called on, I started up, when instantly the old interpreter met me again, and told me the Indians were approaching in order to scratch me. I asked him for what? He answered for killing the rattle snake within their camp. Before I could make any reply or effect my escape, three young fellows singing, arm in arm, came up to me. I observed one of the three was a young prince who had, on my first interview with him, declared himself my friend and protector, when he told me that if ever occasion should offer in his presence, he would risk his life to defend mine or my property. This young champion stood by his two associates, one on each side of him: the two affecting a countenance and air of displeasure and importance, instantly presenting their scratching instruments, and flourishing them, spoke boldly, and said that I was too heroic and violent, that it would be good for me to lose some of my blood to make me more mild and tame, and for that purpose they were come to scratch me. They gave me no time to expostulate or reply, but attempted to lay hold on me, which I resisted; and my friend, the young prince, interposed and pushed them off, saying that I was a brave warrior and his friend; that they should not insult me; when instantly they altered their countenance and behaviour: they all whooped in chorus, took me friendly by the hand, clapped me on the shoulder, and laid their hands on their breasts in token of sincere friendship, and laughing aloud, said I was a sincere friend to the Seminoles, a worthy and brave warrior, and that no one should hereafter attempt to injure me. They then all three joined arm in arm again and went off, shouting and proclaiming Puc-Puggy was their friend, etc. Thus it seemed that the whole was a ludicrous farce to satisfy their people and appease the manes* of the dead rattle snake.

SAMUEL HEARNE, *A Journey from Prince of Wales's Fort, in Hudson's Bay, to the Northern Ocean. Undertaken by order of the Hudson's Bay Company. For the discovery of copper mines, a North West passage, etc. In the Years 1769, 1770, 1771, and 1772* (1795)

Samuel Hearne (1745–92) entered the navy as a boy of 11 to serve as midshipman in the Seven Years' War. He then joined the Hudson's Bay Company, expanding its fur trade with journeys of exploration in the Canadian north-west—a vast expanse unknown to Europeans before the efforts of explorers in the late eighteenth and early nineteenth centuries, including Hearne, Mackenzie, and Thompson by land and Cook and Vancouver by sea. In 1771, on his third try, Hearne reached the Coppermine River after a journey of 1,300 miles on foot with his Indian guides. Proceeding to the Great Slave Lake, he made his way back to Prince of Wales's Fort after extreme privation in 1772. Hearne mistakenly thought he had reached the northern coast of North America and stood on the shores of the 'Hyperborean Sea'. Though his surveying was often poor, he did prove, as he put it, that 'the Continent of North America is much wider than many people imagine'. Our selections begin as Hearne meets his Chipewyan Indian guide Matonnabe, who tells him why he thinks his first two attempts to get to the Coppermine River have failed. A description of Indian women and their treatment is followed by Hearne's account of a massacre of an Inuit camp by his guides and their subsequent purification ritual.

20 SEPTEMBER–OCTOBER 1770. In the evening of the twentieth, we were joined from the westward by a famous leader, called Matonab-bee;* mentioned in my instructions; who, with his followers, or gang, was also going to Prince of Wales's Fort,* with furs, and other articles for trade. This leader, when a youth, resided several years at the above Fort, and was not only a perfect master of the southern Indian language, but by being frequently with the company's servants, had acquired several words of English, and was one of the men who brought the latest accounts of the Coppermine River;* and it was on his information, added to that of one I-dot-le-ezey (who is since dead), that this expedition was set on foot.

The courteous behaviour of this stranger struck me very sensibly. As soon as he was acquainted with our distress, he got such skins as we had with us dressed for the southern Indians, and furnished me with a good warm suit of otter and other skins: but, as it was not in his power to provide us with snow-shoes (being then on the barren ground), he directed us to a little river which he knew, and where there was a small range of woods, which, though none of the best would, he said, furnish us with temporary snow-shoes and sledges, that might materially assist us during the remaining part of our journey. We spent several nights in company with this leader, though we advanced towards the Fort at the rate of ten or twelve miles a day; and as provisions abounded, he made a grand feast for me in the southern Indian style, where there was plenty of good eating, and the whole concluded with singing and dancing, after the southern Indian style and manner. . . .

During my conversation with this leader, he asked me very seriously if I would attempt another journey for the discovery of the copper-mines? And on my answering in the affirmative, provided I could get better guides than I had hitherto been furnished with, he said he would readily engage in that service, provided the Governor at the Fort would employ him. In answer to this, I assured him his offer would be gladly accepted; and, as I had already experienced every hardship that was likely to accompany any future trial, I was determined to complete the discovery, even at the risk of life itself. Matonabbee assured me that by the accounts received from his own countrymen, the southern Indians, and myself, it was very probable I might not experience so much hardship during the whole journey as I had already felt, though scarcely advanced one third part of the journey.

He attributed all our misfortunes to the misconduct of my guides, and the very plan we pursued, by the desire of the Governor, in not taking any women with us on this journey, was, he said, the principal thing that occasioned all our wants: 'for', said he, 'when all the men are heavy laden, they can neither hunt nor travel to any considerable distance; and in case they meet with success in hunting, who is to carry the produce of their labour? Women', added he, 'were made for labour; one of them can carry, or haul, as much as two men can do. They also pitch our tents, make and mend our clothing, keep us warm at night; and, in fact, there is no such thing as travelling any considerable distance, or for any length of time, in this country, without their assistance. Women,' said he again, 'though they do everything, are maintained at a trifling expense; for as they always

stand cook, the very licking of their fingers in scarce times is sufficient for their subsistence.' This, however odd it may appear, is but
too true a description of the situation of women in this country; it is
at least so in appearance; for the women always carry the provisions,
and it is more than probable they help themselves when the men are
not present.

18 APRIL 1771. Having a good stock of dried provisions, and most of
the necessary work for canoes all ready, on the eighteenth we moved
about nine or ten miles to the north north west, and then came to a
tent of northern Indians who were tenting on the north side of
Thelewey-aza River.* From these Indians Matonabbee purchased
another wife; so that he had now no less than seven, most of whom
would for size have made good grenadiers. He prided himself much
in the height and strength of his wives, and would frequently say, few
women would carry or haul heavier loads; and though they had, in
general, a very masculine appearance, yet he preferred them to those
of a more delicate form and moderate stature. In a country like this,
where a partner in excessive hard labour is the chief motive for the
union, and the softer endearments of a conjugal life are only considered as a secondary object, there seems to be great propriety in
such a choice; but if all the men were of this way of thinking, what
would become of the greater part of the women, who in general are
but of low stature, and many of them of a most delicate make, though
not of the exactest proportion, or most beautiful mould? Take them
in a body, the women are as destitute of real beauty as any nation
I ever saw, though there are some few of them, when young, who are
tolerable; but the care of a family, added to their constant hard
labour, soon make the most beautiful among them look old and
wrinkled, even before they are thirty; and several of the more ordinary ones at that age are perfect antidotes to love and gallantry. This,
however, does not render them less dear and valuable to their
owners, which is a lucky circumstance for those women, and a certain proof that there is no such thing as any rule or standard for
beauty. Ask a northern Indian, what is beauty? He will answer, a
broad flat face, small eyes, high cheek-bones, three or four broad
black lines across each cheek, a low forehead, a large broad chin, a
clumsy hook-nose, a tawny hide, and breasts hanging down to the
belt. Those beauties are greatly heightened, or at least rendered

more valuable, when the possessor is capable of dressing all kinds of skins, converting them into the different parts of their clothing, and able to carry eight or ten stone in summer, or haul a much greater weight in winter. These, and other similar accomplishments, are all that are sought after, or expected, of a northern Indian woman. As to their temper, it is of little consequence; for the men have a wonderful facility in making the most stubborn comply with as much alacrity as could possibly be expected from those of the mildest and most obliging turn of mind; so that the only real difference is, the one obeys through fear, and the other complies cheerfully from a willing mind; both knowing that what is commanded must be done. They are, in fact, all kept at a great distance, and the rank they hold in the opinion of the men cannot be better expressed or explained, than by observing the method of treating or serving them at meals, which would appear very humiliating, to a European woman, though custom makes it sit light on those whose lot it is to bear it. It is necessary to observe that when the men kill any large beast, the women are always sent to bring it to the tent: when it is brought there, every operation it undergoes, such as splitting, drying, pounding, etc. is performed by the women. When anything is to be prepared for eating, it is the women who cook it; and when it is done, the wives and daughters of the greatest captains in the country are never served till all the males, even those who are in the capacity of servants, have eaten what they think proper; and in times of scarcity it is frequently their lot to be left without a single morsel. It is, however, natural to think they take the liberty of helping themselves in secret; but this must be done with great prudence, as capital embezzlements of provisions in such times are looked on as affairs of real consequence, and frequently subject them to a very severe beating. If they are practised by a woman whose youth and inattention to domestic concerns cannot plead in her favour, they will forever be a blot in her character, and few men will choose to have her for a wife.

Finding plenty of good birch growing by the side of Theley-aza River, we remained there for a few days, in order to complete all the woodwork for the canoes, as well as for every other use for which we could possibly want it on the barren ground, during our summer's cruise. On the twentieth, Matonabbee sent one of his brothers, and some others, ahead, with birch-rind and woodwork for a canoe, and gave them orders to proceed to a small lake near the barren ground called Clowey, where they were desired to make all possible haste in building the canoe, that it might be ready on our arrival.

Having finished such woodwork as the Indians thought would be necessary, and having augmented our stock of dried meat and fat, the twenty-first was appointed for moving; but one of the women having been taken in labour, and it being rather an extraordinary case, we were detained more than two days. The instant, however, the poor woman was delivered, which was not until she had suffered all the pains usually felt on those occasions for near fifty-two hours, the signal was made for moving, when the poor creature took her infant on her back and set out with the rest of the company; and though another person had the humanity to haul her sledge for her (for one day only), she was obliged to carry a considerable load beside her little charge, and was frequently obliged to wade knee-deep in water and wet snow. Her very looks, exclusive of her moans, were a sufficient proof of the great pain she endured, insomuch that although she was a person I greatly disliked, her distress at this time so overcame my prejudice, that I never felt more for any of her sex in my life; indeed her sighs pierced me to the soul, and rendered me very miserable, as it was not in my power to relieve her.

16 JULY 1771. Early in the morning of the sixteenth, the weather being fine and pleasant, I again proceeded with my survey, and continued it for ten miles farther down the river,* but still found it the same as before, being everywhere full of falls and shoals. At this time (it being about noon) the three men who had been sent as spies met us on their return, and informed my companions that five tents of Esquimaux were on the west side of the river. The situation, they said, was very convenient for surprising them; and, according to their account, I judged it to be about twelve miles from the place we met the spies. When the Indians received this intelligence, no farther attendance or attention was paid to my survey, but their whole thoughts were immediately engaged in planning the best method of attack, and how they might steal on the poor Esquimaux the ensuing night, and kill them all while asleep. To accomplish this bloody design more effectually, the Indians thought it necessary to cross the river as soon as possible; and, by the account of the spies, it appeared that no part was more convenient for the purpose than that where we

had met them, it being there very smooth, and at a considerable distance from any fall. Accordingly, after the Indians had put all their guns, spears, targets, etc. in good order, we crossed the river, which took up some time. . . .

The number of my crew was so much greater than that which five tents could contain, and the warlike manner in which they were equipped so greatly superior to what could be expected of the poor Esquimaux, that no less than a total massacre of every one of them was likely to be the case, unless Providence should work a miracle for their deliverance.

The land was so situated that we walked under cover of the rocks and hills till we were within two hundred yards of the tents. There we lay in ambush for some time, watching the motions of the Esquimaux; and here the Indians would have advised me to stay till the fight was over, but to this I could by no means consent; for I considered that when the Esquimaux came to be surprised, they would try every way to escape, and if they found me alone, not knowing me from an enemy, they would probably proceed to violence against me when no person was near to assist. For this reason I determined to accompany them, telling them at the same time, that I would not have any hand in the murder they were about to commit, unless I found it necessary for my own safety. The Indians were not displeased at this proposal; one of them immediately fixed me a spear, and another lent me a broad bayonet for my protection, but at that time I could not be provided with a target; nor did I want to be encumbered with such an unnecessary piece of lumber.

While we lay in ambush, the Indians performed the last ceremonies which were thought necessary before the engagement. These chiefly consisted in painting their faces; some all black, some all red, and others with a mixture of the two; and to prevent their hair from blowing into their eyes, it was either tied before and behind, and on both sides, or else cut short all round. The next thing they considered was to make themselves as light as possible for running; which they did, by pulling off their stockings, and either cutting off the sleeves of their jackets, or rolling them up close to their armpits; and though the muskettoes* at that time were so numerous as to surpass all credibility, yet some of the Indians actually pulled off their jackets and entered the lists quite naked, except their breechcloths and shoes. Fearing I might have occasion to run with the rest,

I thought it also advisable to pull off my stockings, and cap, and to tie my hair as close up as possible.

By the time the Indians had made themselves thus completely frightful, it was near one o'clock in the morning of the seventeenth; when finding all the Esquimaux quiet in their tents, they rushed forth from their ambuscade, and fell on the poor unsuspecting creatures, unperceived till close at the very eaves of their tents, when they soon began the bloody massacre, while I stood neuter in the rear.

In a few seconds the horrible scene commenced; it was shocking beyond description; the poor unhappy victims were surprised in the midst of their sleep, and had neither time nor power to make any resistance; men, women, and children, in all upward of twenty, ran out of their tents stark naked, and endeavoured to make their escape; but the Indians having possession of all the landside, to no place could they fly for shelter. One alternative only remained, that of jumping into the river; but, as none of them attempted it, they all fell a sacrifice to Indian barbarity!

The shrieks and groans of the poor expiring wretches were truly dreadful; and my horror was much increased at seeing a young girl, seemingly about eighteen years of age, killed so near me, that when the first spear was stuck into her side she fell down at my feet, and twisted round my legs, so that it was with difficulty that I could disengage myself from her dying grasps. As two Indian men pursued this unfortunate victim, I solicited very hard for her life; but the murderers made no reply till they had stuck both their spears through her body, and transfixed her to the ground. They then looked me sternly in the face, and began to ridicule me, by asking if I wanted an Esquimaux wife; and paid not the smallest regard to the shrieks and agony of the poor wretch, who was twining round their spears like an eel! Indeed, after receiving much abusive language from them on the occasion, I was at length obliged to desire that they would be more expeditious in dispatching their victim out of her misery, otherwise I should be obliged, out of pity, to assist in the friendly office of putting an end to the existence of a fellow creature who was so cruelly wounded. On this request being made, one of the Indians hastily drew his spear from the place where it was first lodged, and pierced it through her breast near the heart. The love of life, however, even in this most miserable state, was so predominant, that though this might justly be called the most merciful act that could be done for the poor creature, it seemed to be unwelcome, for though much exhausted by pain and loss of blood, she made several efforts to ward off the friendly blow. My situation and the terror of my mind at beholding this butchery cannot easily be conceived, much less described; though I summed up all the fortitude I was master of on the occasion, it was with difficulty that I could refrain from tears; and I am confident that my features must have feelingly expressed how sincerely I was affected at the barbarous scene I then witnessed; even at this hour I cannot reflect on the transactions of that horrid day without shedding tears.

The brutish manner in which these savages used the bodies they had so cruelly bereaved of life was so shocking that it would be indecent to describe it; particularly their curiosity in examining, and the remarks they made, on the formation of the women; which, they pretended to say, differed materially from that of their own. For my own part I must acknowledge that, however favourable the opportunity for determining that point might have been, yet my thoughts at the time were too much agitated to admit of any such remarks; and I firmly believe, that had there actually been as much difference between them as there is said to be between the Hottentots and those of Europe, it would not have been in my power to have marked the distinction. I have reason to think, however, that there is no ground for the assertion; and really believe that the declaration of the Indians on this occasion was utterly void of truth, and proceeded only from the implacable hatred they bore to the whole tribe of people of whom I am speaking. . . .

It ought to have been mentioned in its proper place that, in making our retreat up the river, after killing the Esquimaux on the west side, we saw an old woman sitting by the side of the water, killing salmon, which lay at the foot of the fall as thick as a shoal of herrings. Whether from the noise of the fall, or a natural defect in the old woman's hearing, it is hard to determine, but certain it is, she had no knowledge of the tragical scene which had been so lately transacted at the tents, though she was not more than two hundred yards from the place. When we first perceived her, she seemed perfectly at ease, and was entirely surrounded with the produce of her labour. From her manner of behaviour, and the appearance of her eyes, which were as red as blood, it is more than probable that her sight was not very good; for she scarcely discerned that the Indians were enemies, till they were within twice the length of their spears of her. It was in vain that she attempted to fly, for the wretches of my crew transfixed her to the ground in a few seconds, and butchered her in the most savage manner. There was scarcely a man among them who had not a thrust at her with his spear; and many in doing this aimed at torture, rather than immediate death, as they not only poked out her eyes, but stabbed her in many parts very remote from those which are vital.

30 SEPTEMBER 1771. Among the various superstitious customs of those people, it is worth remarking, and ought to have been mentioned in its proper place, that immediately after my companions had killed the Esquimaux at the Copper River, they considered themselves in a state of uncleanness, which induced them to practise some very curious and unusual ceremonies. In the first place, all who were absolutely concerned in the murder were prohibited from cooking any kind of victuals, either for themselves or others. As luckily there were two in company who had not shed blood, they were employed always as cooks till we joined the women. This circumstance was exceedingly favourable on my side; for had there been no persons of the above description in company, that task, I was told, would have fallen on me; which would have been no less fatiguing and troublesome than humiliating and vexatious.

When the victuals were cooked, all the murderers took a kind of red earth, or ochre, and painted all the space between the nose and chin, as well as the greater part of their cheeks, almost to the ears, before they would taste a bit, and would not drink out of any other dish, or smoke out of any other pipe, but their own; and none of the others seemed willing to drink or smoke out of theirs.

We had no sooner joined the women, at our return from the expedition, than there seemed to be a universal spirit of emulation among them, vying who should first make a suit of ornaments for their husbands, which consisted of bracelets for the wrists, and a band for the forehead, composed of porcupine quills and moose-hair, curiously wrought on leather.

The custom of painting the mouth and part of the cheeks before each meal, and drinking and smoking out of their own utensils, was strictly and invariably observed, till the winter began to set in; and during the whole of that time they would never kiss any of their wives or children. They refrained also from eating many parts of the deer and other animals, particularly the head, entrails, and blood; and during their uncleanness, their victuals were never sodden in water, but dried in the sun, eaten quite raw, or broiled, when a fire fit for the purpose could be procured.

ALEXANDER MACKENZIE, *Voyages from Montreal through the Continent of North America to the Frozen and Pacific Oceans in 1789 and 1793* (1801)

Alexander Mackenzie (1755?–1820), born in Scotland, joined the North-west Fur Company in the 1780s as it set out to break the Hudson's Bay Company's monopoly. The local knowledge and experience he gained during several years at Fort Chipewyan, a trading post with the Chipewyan Indians, got Mackenzie appointed to lead an exploration party to the north-west in 1789. They reached the Great Slave Lake and followed a river flowing north-west from it—later named after the explorer—to the Arctic Ocean. In July 1792 Mackenzie set out again for the Pacific, travelling west along the Peace River; a year later he would be the first European to achieve this goal. He returned to London, flush with fur-trade profits, and published his *Voyages* in 1801 with a dedication to George III. Our selections from Mackenzie's 1792–3 expedition highlight his often tense interactions with Indians, including his guides as well as those he meets on the way. At the coast he meets some who tell him of previous encounters with Europeans, probably the explorer Vancouver and his naturalist Menzies. Mackenzie writes his name on a rock to memorialize his expedition and has a narrow escape.

SATURDAY, 6 JULY 1793. At four this morning I arose from my bed, such as it was. As we must have been in a most unfortunate predicament, if our guides should have deserted us in the night, by way of security, I proposed to the youngest of them to sleep with me, and he readily consented. These people have no covering but their beaver garments, and that of my companions was a nest of vermin. I, however, spread it under us, and having laid down upon it, we covered ourselves with my camlet* cloak. My companion's hair being greased with fish-oil, and his body smeared with red earth, my sense of smelling as well as that of feeling, threatened to interrupt my rest;

but these inconveniences yielded to my fatigue, and I passed a night of sound repose.

I took the lead in our march, as I had done yesterday, in order to clear the branches of the wet which continued to hang upon them. We proceeded with all possible expedition through a level country with but little underwood; the larger trees were of the fir kind. At half past eight we fell upon the road, which we first intended to have taken from the Great River, and must be shorter than that which we had travelled. The West-road river was also in sight, winding through a valley. We had not met with any water since our encampment of last night, and though we were afflicted with violent thirst, the river was at such a distance from us, and the descent to it so long and steep, that we were compelled to be satisfied with casting our longing looks towards it. There appeared to be more water in the river here than at its discharge. The Indian account, that it is navigable for their canoes, is, I believe, perfectly correct.

Our guides now told us that, as the road was very good and well traced, they would proceed to inform the next tribe that we were coming. This information was of a very unpleasant nature; as it would have been easy for them to turn off the road at a hundred yards from us, and, when we had passed them, to return home. I proposed that one of them should remain with us, while two of my people should leave their loads behind and accompany the other to the lodges. But they would not stay to hear our persuasions, and were soon out of sight. . . .

We accordingly followed our guides with all the expedition in our power, but did not overtake them till we came to a family of natives, consisting of one man, two women, and six children, with whom we found them. These people betrayed no signs of fear at our appearance, and the man willingly conversed with my interpreter, to whom he made himself more intelligible than our guides had been able to do. They, however, had informed him of the object of our journey. He pointed out to us one of his wives, who was a native of the sea coast, which was not a very great distance from us. This woman was more inclined to corpulency than any we had yet seen, was of low stature, with an oblong face, grey eyes, and a flattish nose. She was decorated with ornaments of various kinds, such as large blue beads, either pendant from her ears, encircling her neck, or braided in her hair: she also wore bracelets of brass, copper, and horn. Her garments consisted of a kind of tunic, which was covered with a robe of matted bark, fringed round the bottom with skin of the sea otter. None of the women whom I had seen since we crossed the mountain wore this kind of tunic, their blankets being merely girt round the waist. She had learned the language of her husband's tribe, and confirmed his account, that we were at no great distance from the sea.

21 JULY 1793. Under the land* we met with three canoes, with fifteen men in them, and laden with their moveables, as if proceeding to a new situation, or returning to a former one. They manifested no kind of mistrust or fear of us, but entered into conversation with our young man, as I supposed, to obtain some information concerning us. It did not appear that they were the same people as those we had lately seen, as they spoke the language of our young chief, with a different accent. They then examined everything we had in our canoe, with an air of indifference and disdain. One of them in particular made me understand, with an air of insolence, that a large canoe had lately been in this bay, with people in her like me, and that one of them, whom he called Macubah, had fired on him and his friends, and that Bensins* had struck him on the back, with the flat part of his sword. He also mentioned another name, the articulation of which I could not determine. At the same time he illustrated these circumstances by the assistance of my gun and sword; and I do not doubt but he well deserved the treatment which he described. He also produced several European articles, which could not have been long in his possession. From his conduct and appearance, I wished very much to be rid of him, and flattered myself that he would prosecute his voyage, which appeared to be in an opposite direction to our course.

However, when I prepared to part from them, they turned their canoes about, and persuaded my young man to leave me, which I could not prevent.

We coasted along the land at about west-south-west for six miles, and met a canoe with two boys in it, who were dispatched to summon the people on that part of the coast to join them. The troublesome fellow now forced himself into my canoe, and pointed out a narrow channel on the opposite shore that led to his village, and requested us to steer towards it, which I accordingly ordered. His

importunities now became very irksome, and he wanted to see everything we had, particularly my instruments, concerning which he
must have received information from my young man. He asked for
my hat, my handkerchief, and in short, everything that he saw about
me. At the same time he frequently repeated the unpleasant intelligence that he had been shot at by people of my colour. At some
distance from the land a channel opened to us, at south-west by west,
and pointing that way, he made me understand that Macubah came
there with his large canoe. When we were in mid-channel, I perceived some sheds; or the remains of old buildings on the shore; and
as from that circumstance I thought it probable that some Europeans
might have been there, I directed my steersman to make for that
spot. The traverse is upwards of three miles north-west. . . .

Another canoe soon arrived, with seven stout, well-looking men.
They brought a box, which contained a very fine sea-otter skin, and a
goat skin that was beautifully white. For the former they demanded
my hanger, which, as may well be supposed, could not be spared in
our present situation, and they actually refused to take a yard and a
half of common broad cloth, with some other articles, for the skin,
which proves the unreflecting improvidence of our European
traders. The goat skin was so bulky that I did not offer to purchase it.
These men also told me that Macubah had been there, and left his
ship behind a point of land in the channel, south-west from us; from
whence he had come to their village in boats, which these people
represented by imitating our manner of rowing. When I offered
them what they did not choose to accept for the otter skin, they
shook their heads, and very distinctly answered, 'No, no.' And to
mark their refusal of anything we asked from them, they emphatically
employed the same British monosyllable.

22 JULY 1793. While I was taking a meridian, two canoes, of a larger
size, and well manned, appeared from the main south-west channel.
They seemed to be the forerunners of others, who were coming to
co-operate with the people of the village, in consequence of the
message sent by the two boys, which has been already mentioned;
and our young Indian, who understood them, renewed his entreaties
for our departure, as they would soon come to shoot their arrows,
and hurl their spears at us. In relating our danger, his agitation was
so violent that he foamed at the mouth. Though I was not altogether

free from apprehensions on the occasion, it was necessary for me to disguise them, as my people were panic-struck, and some of them asked if it was my determination to remain there to be sacrificed? My reply was the same as their former importunities had received, that I would not stir till I had accomplished my object; at the same time, to humour their fears, I consented that they should put everything into the canoe, that we might be in a state of preparation to depart. The two canoes now approached the shore, and in a short time five men, with their families, landed very quietly from them. My instruments being exposed, they examined them with much apparent admiration and astonishment. My altitude, by an artificial horizon, gave 52° 21′ 33″; that by the natural horizon was 52° 20′ 48″ North latitude.

These Indians were of a different tribe from those which I had already seen, as our guide did not understand their language. I now mixed up some vermilion in melted grease, and inscribed, in large characters, on the south-east face of the rock on which we had slept last night, this brief memorial*—Alexander Mackenzie, from Canada, by land, the twenty-second of July, one thousand seven hundred and ninety-three.

As I thought that we were too near the village, I consented to leave this place, and accordingly proceeded north-east three miles, when we landed on a point, in a small cove, where we should not be readily seen, and could not be attacked except in our front.

23 JULY 1793. Our guide directed us to draw the canoe out of the reach of the tide and to leave it. He would not wait, however, till this operation was performed, and I did not wish to let him go alone. I therefore followed him through a bad road encumbered with underwood. When we had quitted the wood, and were in sight of the houses, the young man being about fifteen or twenty paces before me, I was surprised to see two men running down towards me from one of the houses, with daggers in their hands and fury in their aspect. From their hostile appearance, I could not doubt of their purpose. I therefore stopped short, threw down my cloak, and put myself in a posture of defence, with my gun presented towards them. Fortunately for me, they knew the effect of firearms, and instantly dropped their daggers, which were fastened by a string to their wrists, and had before been held in a menacing attitude. I let my gun

also fall into my left hand, and drew my hanger.* Several others soon joined them, who were armed in the same manner; and among them I recognized the man whom I have already mentioned as being so troublesome to us, and who now repeated the names of Macubah and Bensins, signifying at the same time by his action, as on a former occasion, that he had been shot at by them. Until I saw him my mind was undisturbed; but the moment he appeared, conceiving that he was the cause of my present perilous situation, my resentment predominated, and if he had come within my reach, I verily believe that I should have terminated his insolence forever.

The rest now approached so near that one of them contrived to get behind me, and grasped me in his arms. I soon disengaged myself from him; and, that he did not avail himself of the opportunity which he had of plunging his dagger into me, I cannot conjecture. They certainly might have overpowered me, and though I should probably have killed one or two of them, I must have fallen at last.

One of my people now came out of the wood. On his appearance they instantly took to flight, and with the utmost speed sought shelter in the houses from whence they had issued. It was, however, upwards of ten minutes before all my people joined me; and as they came one after the other, these people might have successively dispatched every one of us. If they had killed me, in the first instance, this consequence would certainly have followed, and not one of us would have returned home to tell the horrid fate of his companions.

DAVID THOMPSON, *David Thompson's Narrative of his Explorations in Western America, 1784–1812* (ed. J. B. Tyrrell, Toronto: Champlain Society, 1916)

Apprenticed to the Hudson's Bay Company, David Thompson (1770–1857) sailed to Canada in 1784. The 1780s were a period of intense competition between the Company and its new rival from Montreal, the Northwest Company, Alexander Mackenzie's employers. When Thompson arrived at Churchill Factory (a 'factory' is a trading post) the governor was Samuel Hearne, whom the Company instructed to guard the teenage boy's morals—which was ironic, since Hearne, like the previous governor, probably kept a harem of Indian women. Thompson's morals survived unscathed—he never smoked, drank, or swore, although he was cantankerous and self-righteous—but he hated Hearne all his life. In 1797 Thompson left the Hudson's Bay Company to join the 'Nor'Westers', bringing them his experience as a surveyor, wilderness traveller, and speaker of several Indian languages. In 1810–11 he led an expedition to the Pacific in a failed race with John Jacob Astor's American party to secure the mouth of the Columbia River. Despite his impressive geographical achievements, Thompson ended his life in obscurity and indigence. Thompson's fat and fascinating *Narrative*, written late in his long life, was not published until 1916. Our selections begin with reminiscences of early trading-post life, then take up the Pacific expedition and encounters with Indians along the way. The uncanny game of draughts was not included in published versions of the *Narrative* until 1962; we thank the Champlain Society for permission to reprint this excerpt from Richard Glover's recent edition (*David Thompson's Narrative 1784–1812*. Toronto: Champlain Society, 1962, 43–4).

[Life at a Hudson's Bay Company trading post]

Winter soon sets in;* the geese hunters return, and out of them are formed two parties of three or four men, each for grouse shooting, snaring hares etc. Each party has a canvas tent, like a soldier's bell tent with the top cut off to let the smoke out. Fowling pieces, ammunition, fish hooks and lines, steel traps and three weeks of salted provisions, with our bedding of blankets etc. completes our equipment. The shore ice of the river is now frozen to the width of half a mile, or more; the current of the river has much drift ice, it is time for the hunters to be off, the boats are ready, and we are placed on the ice, with four flat sleds, and a fine large Newfoundland dog; the boats return and we are left to our exertions. Our party consisted of four men and an Indian woman. We loaded the sleds with the tent, our baggage and some provisions, leaving the rest for another trip, each of us hauled about seventy pounds and the fine dog 100 pounds weight. We proceeded to a large brook, called French Creek, up which we went about a mile to where the pines of the forest were of some size and clean growth; the tent poles were now cut, and placed to form a circular area of about 12 to 14 feet diameter and 12 feet in height; the door poles are the strongest, about these poles we wrapped our tents, the fire place is in the centre, and our beds of pine branches, with a log next to the fire. Our furniture was a three gallon brass kettle, with a lesser one for water, two, or three tin dishes, spoons etc. A hoard is next made of logs well notched into each other of about eight feet in length, six feet wide at the bottom, five feet in height, and the top narrowed to two feet covered with logs to secure our provisions and game from the carnivorous animals. Our occupations were angling of trout, snaring of hares, shooting white grouse, trapping of martens, foxes and wolverines. Our enemy the polar bear was prowling about, the sea not being sufficiently frozen to allow him to catch seals.

By the latter end of November we had procured sufficient game to load three flat sleds, for the factory, hauled by two of us and our dog. To arrive at the factory, took us the whole of the day. The same evening William Budge, a fine handsome man, John Mellam, and the Indian woman were frying pork and grouse for supper, when the smell attracted a polar bear, who marched to the tent, and around it; his heavy tread was heard, and no more cooking thought of. As usual in the evening, the fowling pieces were being washed and cleaned, and were then not fit for use, but there was a loaded musket. At length Bruin found the door, and thrust in his head and neck; the tent poles prevented further entrance. Budge climbed up the tent poles and left Mellam and his Indian woman to fight the bear. The former snatched up the musket; it snapped. Seizing it by the muzzle he broke off the stock on the head of the bear, and then with hearty blows applied the barrel and lock to his head; the Indian woman caught up her axe on the other side of the door, and in like manner struck Bruin on the head, such an incessant storm of blows, as made him withdraw himself; he went to the hoard and began to tear it in pieces, for the game; a fowling piece was quickly dried, loaded with two balls, and fired into him. The wound was mortal: he went a few paces and fell, with a dreadful growl. Budge now wanted to descend from the smoky top of the tent, but the woman with her axe in her hand (2½ lbs) heaped wood on the fire, and threatened to brain him if he came down. He begged hard for his life; she was determined. Fortunately Mellam snatched the axe from her, but she never forgave him, for the Indian woman pardons man for everything but want of courage. This is her sole support and protection; there are no laws to defend her. The next morning on examining the head of the bear, the skin was much bruised and cut, but the bone had not a mark on it. We had two steel traps of double springs, with strong iron teeth, weighing each seventy pounds, and five feet in length, for wolves and wolverines: one of these was baited with a grouse, and placed on the ice at the mouth of the brook; a polar bear took the bait, the iron teeth closed on his head. He went about half a mile and then lay down; the next morning we traced the bear, he rose up, a curious looking figure with a trap of five feet across his nose. He went directly for the sea, and we respectfully followed; our guns had only small shot; when arrived at the edge of the ice, Bruin made a halt, and no doubt thought such a trap across his nose would be an impediment to swimming and catching seals, so wisely determined to get rid of it, turning round and looking at us, he bent his head and the trap on the ice, and placing his heavy fore paws on each of the springs, he loosened himself from the trap, and looking at us with an air of contempt, dashed into the sea, and swam away. We got the trap, but his heavy paws had broken one of the springs and rendered the trap useless. The other hunting party about three miles to the east-ward of us had also the visit of a polar bear; one evening from the smell of fried pork and grouse, he came to the tent, marched round and round it, but found no entrance; his heavy tread warned the inmates to be on their guard. The bear reared himself up on the tent, he placed the claws of his fore paws through the canvas, the man opposite ready with his gun, guided by his paws, fired and mortally wounded him; but in falling the bear brought down the tent and tent poles, under which, with the bear were three men and one woman, whom the bear, in the agonies of death, sadly kicked about, until relieved by the man who had shot the bear, the tent was drawn over his head, and he was free. . . .

The summer months pass away without regret, the myriads of tormenting flies allow no respite, and we see the cold months advance with something like pleasure, for we can now enjoy a book, or a walk. October and November produce their ice and snow, the rivers freeze over and form a solid bridge to cross where we please, our winter clothing is ready, and gloomy December is on us. The cold increases continually, with very little relaxation, the snow is now as dry as dust, about two feet in depth; it adheres to nothing, we may throw a gun into it and take it up as free of snow as if in the air, and no snow adheres to our snow shoes. The Aurora Borealis is seen only to the northward, sometimes with a tremulous motion, but seldom bright; haloes of the sun also appear. The month of January comes, and continues with intense cold; from the density of the air, the haloes, or mock suns, at times appear as bright as the real sun; but when in this state, betokens bad weather. The haloes of the moon are also very pleasing.

A curious formation now takes place called rime, of extreme thinness, adhering to the trees, willows and everything it can fasten on, its beautiful, clear spangles forming flowers of every shape, of a most brilliant appearance, and the sun shining on them makes them too dazzling to the sight. The lower the ground, the larger is the leaf, and the flower; this brilliant rime can only be formed in calm clear weather and a gale of wind sweeps away all this magic scenery, to be re-formed on calm days; it appears to be formed of frozen dew. The actual quantity of snow on the ground is not more than 2½ feet in depth in the woods, clear of drift, very light and dry; almost every fall of snow is attended with a gale of NE wind. The falling snow with the movable snow on the ground causes a drift and darkness in which the traveller is bewildered, and sometimes perishes. The months of February and March have many pleasant clear days, the gaudy, spangled rime is most brilliant, and requires a strong eye to look upon it. The climate is more moderate, there are a few fine days, the sun is bright with a little warmth, the snow lower, but does not thaw. In the months of March and April, the snow too often causes snow blindness, of a most painful nature. As I never had it, I can only describe the sensations of my companions. Accustomed to march in all weathers, I had acquired a power over my eyelids to open, or contract them as circumstances required, and to admit only the requisite quantity of light to guide me, and thus I prevented the painful effects of snow blindness. In the case of those affected the blue eye suffers first and most, the grey eye next, and the black eye the least; but none are exempt from snow blindness; the sensations of my companions, and others, were all the same; they all complained of their eyes, being, as it were, full of burning sand; I have seen hardy men crying like children after a hard march of four months in winter. Three men and myself made for a trading post in the latter part of March. They all became snow blind, and for the last four days I had to lead them with a string tied to my belt, and they were so completely blind that when they wished to drink of the little pools of melted snow, I had to put their hands in the water. They could not sleep at night. On arriving at the trading post, they were soon relieved by the application of the steam of boiling water as hot as they could bear it, this is the Indian mode of cure, and the only efficient cure yet known, but all complained of weakness of sight for several months after. Black crape is sometimes used to protect the eyes from the dazzling light of the snow, but the hunter cannot long make use of it: the chase demands the whole power of his eyesight. When thirsty a mouthful of snow wets the mouth but does not relieve thirst; the water of snow melted by the sun has a good taste, but snow melted in a kettle over a fire has a smoky taste, until made to boil for a few minutes; this takes away the smoky taste, and snow being put in, makes good water. . . .

During the winter at times we had much leisure and we employed it in playing at draughts for which we had two chequerboards, one with twelve, the other with twenty-four men on each side; it is a game of skill and I became expert at it. Having nothing to do, it was my constant employment; and for want of a companion frequently played by myself. A strange incident now happened to me and which sometimes happens to mankind which brings with it a strong influence on their conduct for the rest of their lives. I was sitting at a small table with the chequerboard before me, when the devil sat down opposite to me. His features and colour were those of a Spaniard, he had two short black horns on his forehead which pointed forwards; his head and body down to his waist (I saw no more) was covered with glossy black curling hair, his countenance mild and grave; we began playing, played several games and he lost every game, kept his temper but looked more grave; at length he got up or rather disappeared. My eyes were open, it was broad daylight; I looked around, all was silence and solitude; was it a dream or was it reality? I could not decide. Young and thoughtless as I was, it made a deep impression on my mind. I made no vow but took a resolution from that very hour never to play a game of chance, or skill or anything that had the appearance of them, and I kept it. It is now upwards of sixty-three years since and yet the whole of this strange incident is plain before me.*

[Down the Columbia River to the Pacific, July 1811]

6 JULY. A rainy morning; early several men with a few women came and smoked a while, the women had bracelets of shells and fillets of the same round the head. At 6½ a.m. we embarked and in less than four hours came to a tribe and village called Smeathhowe; as usual we put ashore, and I sent the Simpoils to invite them to come and

smoke with us. They found them consulting what they should make a present of, for the stranger must have a present made to him or them. My reason for putting ashore and smoking with the natives is to make friends with them, against my return, for in descending the current of a large river, we might pass on without much attention to them; but in returning against the current, our progress will be slow and close along the shore, and consequently very much in their power; whereas staying a few hours, and smoking with them, while explaining to them the object of my voyage makes them friendly to us. The men, women and children now came dancing, and singing a mild, plaintive song to which they kept time, when close to us, they twice said Oy Oy and sat down around us; one of them directed the women and children to sit near the men; the pipes were lighted, and they all smoked with avidity, the men taking from three to six whiffs, some swallowing the smoke, but the women were allowed only one whiff. They now gave us three well roasted salmon, and half a bushel of arrow wood berries, very acceptable to us, for which I paid them. I learned that from the time of the arrival of the salmon, all the fish that are taken for a certain time must be roasted, not boiled; the Chiefs then assemble, and after some ceremonies, the salmon are allowed to be boiled, or cooked for the rest of the season, as the people choose. The appearance of this tribe is the same as the last, except the women being more profusely ornated with shells: their knowledge of the river extended no farther than to the next village, where we would learn the state of the river beyond them. At noon we left them and soon came to a bold rapid of two miles in length, the waves being too high for our canoe we had to carry; the Chief and four young men came with horses and helped us to the foot of the rapid, for which I gave them eight inches of tobacco, which was thankfully accepted; this carrying place took us to 2½ p.m. We then descended a strong current for full three and a half hours, and camped on the left for the first time, the right being steep rocks. The country and banks of the river high, bold hills, very rude, with steep cliffs; we could have passed hours in viewing the wild scenery, but these romantic cliffs always indicated danger to us from the stream being contracted and forming whirlpools, very disagreeable companions on a river: on a cliff we saw a mountain sheep looking down on us, which we longed to eat, but he could not be approached. We had to kill two rattle snakes that would not get out of our way.

7 JULY. Having descended ten miles, we saw several men on horse-back proceeding to the westward; two of them rode to the riverside, we went too, and smoked with them, and each of us held on our ways. I learned that they were sent from a village to apprise them of our coming. Having continued for four miles, we came to two long lodges of the same structure as those we have passed, sufficiently well covered with rush mats; one of these lodges was two hundred and forty feet in length; the other sixty feet in length; each by thirty feet in breadth; all these measurements are by stepping the lengths at three feet each step. By their account the name of this tribe is Sinkowarsin:* they are about one hundred and twenty families, and from the women and children must be about eight hundred souls: the language is still a dialect of the Salish, but my Simpoil inter-preters find several words they did not understand; when we passed, and put ashore below them, they were all dancing in their lodges, to the sound of their songs, for hitherto we have not seen a musical instrument even of the most rude kind along this river. We sent to them to come and smoke, five steady looking men came, sat down near us and smoked, but although many of the natives we had passed viewed us with some suspicion, as at a loss what to make of us, these men much more so, nor could their countenances conceal that they did not know what to make of us; all the other villagers had been apprised of us by some who had smoked with us, these had only heard of us by report; except what they learned from the two horsemen; no speech, as usual, was made, and the Simpoil Indians who accompanied us explained to them all they saw with us. After smoking a few pipes, I requested all the other men to come, which they did, but in an irregular manner, and it was twenty minutes before they could be made to sit down. Smoking com-menced, and they offered us a small present of roots and berries. Their attention was strongly fixed on our persons, especially on those who had let their beards grow; on our dresses which were wholly of woollen or cotton, their clothing being of leather; on our guns, axes, knives and making of a fire, to which last they paid great attention. They appeared delighted with the use of the axe in cut-ting and splitting of the driftwood; I now explained to them by the interpreters the object of my voyage down the river, that it was to procure for them articles and clothing such as they saw with us, besides many other things, equally wanted by them. All this passed

in conversation with one and another; there was no Chief to speak to them; a fine looking man came and sat close to me with strong curiosity in his face; after eyeing me all over, he felt my feet and legs to be sure that I was something like themselves, but did not appear sure that I was so. A very old man now came to thank me for visiting them, and that he had the pleasure of smoking good tobacco before he died; at length being satisfied that we came as friends, and with the intention of doing them good, they brought to us two salmon, for which I paid them; they then lifted up their arms and hands towards the skies praying for our safety and to return to them: their appearance was much the same as those we had passed, but having more nourishment their persons were more full in form, and many of the men were handsome, with a manly look; the women I could not call any beautiful, but many were pretty, good looking with mild features, the children well formed and playful, and respect with kind attention to each other pervaded the whole; though at present poor in provisions, they were all in good health, and except the infirmities of old age, we have not seen a sick person, partly from using much vegetable food, and partly from a fine dry temperate climate.

They describe their country to the southward to be high, dry and barren, without animals; to the northward the lands are good with antelopes, mountain sheep (Big Horn) and goats, of which their clothing is made, and of the fine long wool of the latter they make good rude blankets. They had also a few bison robes which they must have traded from other tribes; all these things allowed them to be better clothed than any tribe we had yet seen. We saw no weapons of war with them, and like all the other tribes they may be said to be unarmed: and like them also they were all as cleanly as people can be without the use of soap, an article not half so much valued in civilized life as it ought to be. What would become of the belle and the beau without it. And also all linen, and cotton; I have often known the want of it, and had to use fine blue clay as a substitute.

As we were about to leave this people with their prayers for our safety, a fine looking man came to us and requested a passage in our canoe for himself and wife, to a tribe below us of which he was a Chief. He remarked to us that the Simpoil Indians could not inter- pret for us much farther down the river, as the natives spoke a different language, which both himself and his wife well understood, and that he would then become our interpreter; glad of the offer we gave them a passage with their little baggage. . . .

We embarked* and proceeded thirty-two miles down the river, and passed about eighty families in small straggling lodges; at one of which of ten families we put ashore to smoke with them, but they were terrified at our appearance. My men stayed on the beach, and I went forward a few paces unarmed, and sat down with a pipe and stem in my hand; they sent forward two very old men, who lying flat on the ground in the most pitiful manner, crawling slowly, frequently lifted their heads a little as if imploring mercy; my native interpreter would not speak to them, and all the signs I could make gave them no confidence; close behind the men three women crawled on their knees, lifting up their hands to me as if supplicating for their lives; the men were naked and the women nearly the same, the whole, a scene of wretched destitution; it was too painful. They did not smoke with us, I gave to each of the men two inches of tobacco, and left them. They appeared as if outcasts from the others; all those we have passed today appeared idle, we saw none of them employed with the seine; when I spoke to the interpreter when we camped to learn the state of these people, he gave me no answer, and both himself and his wife did not wish to be spoken to about them.

In the afternoon, when the river ran to the WSW a high mountain, isolated, of a conical form, a mass of pure snow without the appearance of rock, appeared, which I took to be Mount Hood, and which it was; from the lower part of the river this mountain is in full view, and with a powerful achromatic telescope I examined it; when clear, the snow always appeared as fresh fallen. It stands south of the Columbia River, near the shores of the Pacific Ocean, and from six thousand feet and upwards is one immense mass of pure snow; what is below the limit of perpetual snow appears to be continually renewed by fresh falls of snow; its many streamlets form rivers, one of which the Wilarmet, a noble river through a fine country, falls into the Columbia River.

14 JULY. We continued our journey, amused with the seals playing in the river; on the 15th near noon we arrived at Tongue Point, which at right angles stretches its steep rocky shores across the river for a full half a mile, and brought us to a full view of the Pacific Ocean,

which to me was a great pleasure, but my men seemed disappointed; they had been accustomed to the boundless horizon of the great lakes of Canada, and their high rolling waves; from the ocean they expected a more boundless view, a something beyond the power of their senses which they could not describe; and my informing them that directly opposite to us, at the distance of five thousand miles was the Empire of Japan added nothing to their ideas, but a map would. The waves being too high for us to double the point, we went close to the river bank where there is a narrow isthmus, of one hundred yards, and carried across it; from thence near two miles to the fur trading post of Mr J. J. Astor of the city of New York; which was four low log huts, the far famed Fort Astoria of the United States;* the place was in charge of Messrs McDougall and Stuart who had been clerks of the Northwest Company; and by whom we were politely received. They had been here but a few months, and arriving after a long voyage round Cape Horn, in the rainy season without sufficient shelter from tents, had suffered from ague and low fever, from which most of them had recovered.

This place was about seven miles from the sea, and too much exposed to the undulations of the waves; the quality of their goods for trade very low, but good enough for the beggarly natives about them, of the same race I have described, and with few exceptions, they appeared a race of worthless, idle, impudent knaves, without anything to barter, yet begging everything they saw. They were all accustomed to trade with the ships, mostly of the United States, and had learned a great part of the worst words of their language. The next day in my canoe with my men I went to Cape Disappointment, which terminates the course of this river, and remained until the tide came in; at ebb tide we noticed the current of the river riding in waves over the surface to the sea for about four miles; on all the shores of this ocean the agitation of the sea is constantly breaking against the rocky shore with high surges, and my men now allowed the great volume of water forming these high surges to be far superior to those of any lake.

Thus I have fully completed the survey of this part of North America from sea to sea, and by almost innumerable astronomical observations have determined the positions of the mountains, lakes and rivers, and other remarkable places on the northern part of this continent; the maps of all of which have been drawn, and laid down in geographical position, being now the work of twenty-seven years. . . .

On the 22nd July, in company with Mr David Stuart and three small wood canoes, with eight men, with an assortment of goods for trade with the natives, we left Astoria with a prayer to all merciful Providence to grant us a safe journey; with the exception of Coxe, my men were as before two Iroquois Indians, four Canadians, with Coxe, seven men. We were all eight well armed, each man had a gun and a long knife, except Coxe, who had one of my pistols, of Mortimer's make of eighteen inches barrel, carrying a ball of eighteen to the pound: for I remembered the menacing looks of many of the natives. On the contrary Mr David Stuart and his men were in a manner unarmed, and the natives who were all well armed viewed them with a kind of contempt.

28 JULY. A fine morning; to my surprise, very early, apparently a young man, well dressed in leather, carrying a bow and quiver of arrows, with his wife, a young woman in good clothing, came to my tent door and requested me to give them my protection; somewhat at a loss what answer to give, on looking at them, in the man I recognized the woman who three years ago was the wife of Boisverd, a Canadian and my servant; her conduct then was so loose that I had then requested him to send her away to her friends, but the Kootanaes were also displeased with her; she left them, and found her way from tribe to tribe to the sea. She became a prophetess, declared her sex changed, that she was now a man, dressed, and armed herself as such, and also took a young woman to wife, of whom she pretended to be very jealous: when with the Chinooks, as a prophetess, she predicted diseases to them, which made some of them threaten her life, and she found it necessary for her safety to endeavour to return to her own country at the head of this river.

Having proceeded half a mile up a rapid, we came to four men who were waiting for us, they had seven salmon, the whole of which they gave us as a present; I was surprised at this generosity and change of behaviour, as we were all very hungry, at the head of the rapid we put ashore, and boiled them; while this was doing, the four men addressed me; saying, when you passed going down to the sea, we were all strong in life, and your return to us finds us strong to live, but what is this we hear, casting their eyes with a stern look on her, is it true that the white men (looking at Mr Stuart and his men) have brought with them the smallpox to destroy us; and also two men of enormous size, who are on their way to us, overturning the ground, and burying all the villages and lodges underneath it: is this true and are we all soon to die? I told them not to be alarmed, for the white men who had arrived had not brought the smallpox, and the natives were strong to live, and every evening were dancing and singing; and pointing to the skies, said, you ought to know that the Great Spirit is the only master of the ground, and such as it was in the day of your grandfathers it is now, and will continue the same for your grandsons. At all which they appeared much pleased, and thanked me for the good words I had told them; but I saw plainly that if the man woman had not been sitting behind us they would have plunged a dagger in her.

2. MANNERS AND MORALS

ISAAC WELD, *Travels through the States of North America, and the Provinces of Upper and Lower Canada, during the years 1795, 1796, and 1797* (1799)

As a young man Isaac Weld (1774–1856) spent over two years travelling through the United States and Canada, returning home in 1797 'without entertaining the slightest wish to revisit' the continent. His *Travels* were published in 1799 to considerable acclaim, reaching a second edition within a year and appearing in French, German, and Dutch translations. They exhibit a spleen reminiscent of Smollett, but with less wit and intelligence. Here Weld comments on Americans' aversion to trees, compares them to the German settlers in Pennsylvania, and gives a lurid account of tavern recreations in Virginia.

The scenery in this neighbourhood is extremely interesting. From the top of the hills you meet with numberless bold and extensive prospects of the Chesapeake Bay and of the River Susquehannah; and scarcely do you cross a valley without beholding in the depths of the woods the waters of some little creek or rivulet rushing over ledges of rock in a beautiful cascade. The generality of Americans stare with astonishment at a person who can feel any delight at passing through such a country as this. To them the sight of a wheat field or a cabbage garden would convey pleasure far greater than that of the most romantic woodland views. They have an unconquerable aversion to trees; and whenever a settlement is made, they cut away all before them without mercy; not one is spared; all share the same fate, and are involved in the general havoc. . . .

From the face of the country being entirely overspread with trees, the eyes of the people become satiated with the sight of them. The ground cannot be tilled, nor can the inhabitants support themselves, till they are removed; they are looked upon as a nuisance, and the man that can cut down the largest number, and have the fields about his house most clear of them, is looked upon as the most industrious citizen, and the one that is making the greatest improvements* in the country. . . .

The Germans are a quiet, sober, and industrious set of people, and are most valuable citizens. They generally settle a good many together in one place, and, as may be supposed, in consequence keep up many of the customs of their native country as well as their own language. In Lancaster and the neighbourhood, German is the prevailing language, and numbers of people living there are ignorant of any other. The Germans are some of the best farmers in the United States, and they seldom are to be found but where the land is particularly good; wherever they settle they build churches, and are wonderfully attentive to the duties of religion. In these and many other respects the Germans and their descendants differ widely from the Americans, that is, from the descendants of the English, Scotch, Irish, and other nations, who from having lived in the country for many generations, and from having mingled together, now form one people, whose manners and habits are very much the same.

The Germans are a plodding race of men, wholly intent upon their own business, and indifferent about that of others: a stranger is never molested as he passes through their settlements with inquisitive and idle questions. On arriving amongst the Americans,* however, a stranger must tell where he came from, where he is going, what his name is, what his business is; and until he gratifies their curiosity on these points, and many others of equal importance, he is never suffered to remain quiet for a moment. In a tavern, he must satisfy every fresh set that comes in, in the same manner, or involve himself in a quarrel, especially if it is found out that he is not a native, which it does not require much sagacity to discover.

The Germans give themselves but little trouble about politics; they elect their representatives to serve in Congress and the state assemblies; and satisfied that deserving men have been chosen by the people at large, they trust that these men do what is best for the public good, and therefore abide patiently by their decisions: they revere the constitution, conscious that they live happily under it, and express no wishes to have it altered. The Americans, however, are for ever cavilling at some of the public measures; something or other is always wrong, and they never appear perfectly satisfied. If any great measure is before Congress for discussion, seemingly distrustful of the abilities or the integrity of the men they have elected, they meet together in their towns or districts, canvass the matter themselves, and then send forward instructions to their representatives how to act. They never consider that any important question is more likely to meet with a fair discussion in an assembly, where able men are collected together from all parts of the states, than in an obscure corner, where a few individuals are assembled, who have no opportunity of getting general information on the subject. Party spirit is for ever creating dissensions amongst them, and one man is continually endeavouring to obtrude his political creed upon another. If it is found out that a stranger is from Great Britain or Ireland, they immediately begin to boast of their own constitution and freedom, and give him to understand that they think every Englishman a slave, because he submits to be called a subject. Their opinions are for the most part crude and dogmatical, and principally borrowed from newspapers, which are wretchedly compiled from the pamphlets of the day; having read a few of which, they think themselves arrived at the summit of intellectual excellence, and qualified for making the deepest political researches.

The Germans, as I have said, are fond of settling near each other: when the young men of a family are grown up, they generally endeavour to get a piece of land in the neighbourhood of their relations, and by their industry soon make it valuable; the American, on the contrary, is of a roving disposition, and wholly regardless of the ties of consanguinity; he takes his wife with him, goes to a distant part of the country, and buries himself in the woods, hundreds of miles distant from the rest of his family, never perhaps to see them again. In the back parts of the country, you always meet numbers of men prowling about to try and buy cheap land; having found what they like, they immediately remove: nor having once removed, are these people satisfied; restless and discontented with what they possess, they are for ever changing. It is scarcely possible in any part of the continent to find a man, amongst the middling and lower classes of Americans, who has not changed his farm and his residence many different times. Thus it is that though there are not more than four millions of people in the United States, yet they are scattered from the confines of Canada to the farthest extremity of Georgia, and from the Atlantic to the banks of the Mississippi. Thousands of acres of waste land are annually taken up in unhealthy and unfruitful parts of the country, notwithstanding that the best settled and healthy parts of the middle states would maintain five times the number of inhabitants that they do at present. The American, however, does not change about from place to place in this manner merely to gratify a wandering disposition; in every change he hopes to make money. By the desire of making money, both the Germans and Americans of every class and description are actuated in all their movements; self-interest is always uppermost in their thoughts; it is the idol which they worship, and at its shrine thousands and thousands would be found, in all parts of the country, ready to make a sacrifice of every noble and generous sentiment that can adorn the human mind. . . .

Perhaps in no place of the same size in the world is there more gambling going forward than in Richmond. I had scarcely alighted from my horse at the tavern, when the landlord came to ask what game I was most partial to, as in such a room there was a faro table, in another a hazard table, in a third a billiard table, to any one of which he was ready to conduct me. Not the smallest secrecy is employed in keeping these tables; they are always crowded with people, and the doors of the apartment are only shut to prevent the rabble from coming in. Indeed, throughout the lower part of the country in Virginia, and also in that part of Maryland next to it, there is scarcely a petty tavern without a billiard room, and this is always full of a set of idle low-lived fellows, drinking spirits or playing cards, if not engaged at the table. Cock-fighting is also another favourite diversion. It is chiefly, however, the lower class of people that partake of these amusements at the taverns; in private there is, perhaps, as little

gambling in Virginia as in any other part of America. The circumstance of having the taverns thus infested by such a set of people
renders travelling extremely unpleasant. Many times I have been
forced to proceed much farther in a day than I have wished, in order
to avoid the scenes of rioting and quarrelling that I have met with at
the taverns, which it is impossible to escape as long as you remain in
the same house where they are carried on, for every apartment is
considered as common, and that room in which a stranger sits down
is sure to be the most frequented.

Whenever these people come to blows, they fight just like wild
beasts, biting, kicking, and endeavouring to tear each other's eyes out
with their nails. It is by no means uncommon to meet with those who
have lost an eye in a combat, and there are men who pride themselves upon the dexterity with which they can scoop one out. This is
called *gouging*. To perform the horrid operation, the combatant
twists his forefingers in the side locks of his adversary's hair, and
then applies his thumbs to the bottom of the eye, to force it out of
the socket. If ever there is a battle, in which neither of those engaged
loses an eye, their faces are however generally cut in a shocking
manner with the thumb-nails, in the many attempts which are made
at gouging. But what is worse than all, these wretches in their combat endeavour to their utmost to tear out each other's testicles. Four
or five instances came within my own observation, as I passed
through Maryland and Virginia, of men being confined in their beds
from the injuries which they had received of this nature in a fight. In
the Carolinas and Georgia, I have been credibly assured that the
people are still more depraved in this respect than in Virginia, and
that in some particular parts of these states, every third or fourth
man appears with one eye.

JOHN DAVIS, *Travels of Four Years and a Half in the United
States of America; during 1798, 1799, 1800, 1801, and 1802*
(1803)

John Davis (b. 1776) came to America at the age of 22 to try to make
a living as a private tutor. He travelled on foot through a great part of
the fifteen States, bringing a literary sensibility to his observations.
Davis dedicated his *Travels* to Thomas Jefferson, who wrote back, 'Such a

testimony of respect from an enlightened foreigner cannot but be flattering to me.' Our selections recount Davis's adventures in the Carolina
woods *en route* from Charleston to the plantation of Thomas Drayton,
where he worked as a tutor in the winter and spring of 1798–9. The idyll
was marred, in his view, by the slave labour that sustained it.

The place I had reached was Asheepo, a hamlet consisting of three or
more log-houses; and the inhabitants of every sex and age had collected round a huge elephant, which was journeying with his master
to Savannah.

Fortune had therefore brought me into unexpected company, and
I could not but admire the docility of the elephant, who, in solemn
majesty, received the gifts of the children with his trunk. But not so
the monkey. This man of Lord Monboddo* was inflamed with rage
at the boys and girls; nor could the rebukes of his master calm the
transports of his fury.

I entered the log-house which accommodated travellers. An old
negro-man had squatted himself before the fire. Well, old man, said
I, why don't you go out to look at the elephant? Hie! Massa, he calf!
In fact the elephant came from Asia, and the negro from Africa,
where he had seen the same species of animal, but of much greater
magnitude.

Travelling, says Shakespeare, acquaints a man with strange bed-
fellows;* and there being only one bed in the log-house, I slept that
night with the elephant driver. Mr Owen was a native of Wales, but
he had been a great traveller, and carried a map of his travels in his
pocket. Nothing shortens a journey more than good company on the
road; so I departed after breakfast from Asheepo, with Mr Owen, his
elephant, and his monkey.

Mr Owen related to me the wonders of his elephant, which at
some future day, I may perhaps publish in a separate treatise; but
they would be irrelevant to my present journey, which towards noon
I was left to prosecute alone. The elephant, however docile, would
not travel without his dinner; and Mr Owen halted under a pine-tree
to feed the mute companion of his toils.

For my own part, I dined at a solitary log-house in the woods,
upon exquisite venison. My host was a small planter, who cultivated
a little rice, and maintained a wife and four children with his rifled-
barrel-gun. He had been overseer to a Colonel Fishborne, and owned

half a dozen negroes; but he observed to me his property was running about at large, for four of them had absconded.

As I proposed to make Pocotaligo the end of my day's journey, I walked forward at a moderate pace; but towards evening I was roused from the reveries into which my walking had plunged me by a conflagration in the woods. On either side of the road the trees were in flames, which, extending to their branches, assumed an appearance both terrific and grotesque. Through these woods, belching flames and rolling smoke, I had to travel nearly a mile, when the sound of the negro's axe chopping of wood announced that I was near Pocotaligo.

At Pocotaligo I learned that the conflagration in the woods arose from the carelessness of some backwoods-men, who having neglected to extinguish their fires, the flames had extended in succession to the herbage and the trees.

I was somewhat surprised on entering the tavern at Pocotaligo to behold sixteen or more chairs placed round a table which was covered with the choicest dishes; but my surprise ceased when the Savannah and Charleston stage-coaches stopped at the door, and the passengers flocked to the fire before which I was sitting. In the Charleston coach came a party of comedians.* Of these itinerant heroes the greater part were my countrymen; and, as I was not travelling to see Englishmen, but Americans, I was not sorry when they retired to bed.

I was in a worse condition at Pocotaligo than Asheepo; for at Pocotaligo the beds were so small that they would hold only respectively one person. But I pity the traveller who takes umbrage against America, because its houses of entertainment cannot always accommodate him to his wishes. If he images no other happiness to himself in travelling but what is to be obtained from repasts that minister to luxury, and beds distinguished by softness, let him confine his excursions to the cities of polished Europe. The western continent can supply the traveller an employment more noble than a minute attention to the casualties of the road, which are afterwards to be enlarged upon with studied declamation. The world is called upon to sympathize with the sufferer; he who at home had been accustomed to the luxury of a bed, groaned the night out in America on the rack of a mattress; and for this the country is to be execrated, and the beautiful scenes of nature beheld with a jaundiced eye.

Finding there was no bed to be procured, I seated myself in a nook of the chimney, called for wine and cigars, and either attended to the conversation of the negro girls who had spread their blankets on the floor, or entertained myself with the half-formed notions of the landlord and coachman, who had brought their chairs to the fire, and were disputing on politics. Both Americans and English are subject to loquacious imbecility. Their subjects only differ. The American talks of his government, the Englishman of himself.

Early in the morning, I resumed my journey in the coach that was proceeding to Savannah; I had but a short distance more to go; for Coosohatchie is only ten miles from Pocotaligo. In journeying through America, the Indian names of places have always awakened in my breast a train of reflection; a single word will speak volumes to a speculative mind; and the names of Pocotaligo, and Coosohatchie, and Occoquan, have pictured to my fancy the havoc of time, the decay and succession of generations, together with the final extirpation of savage nations, who, unconscious of the existence of another people, dreamt not of invasions from foreign enemies, or inroads from colonists, but believed their power invincible and their race eternal.

I was put down at the post office of Coosohatchie. The postmaster was risen, expecting the mail. He invited me to partake of a fire he had just kindled, before which a negro boy was administering pap to a sickly infant, whom the man always addressed by the homeric title of My Son. . . .

An hour's ride through a forest of stately pines brought me to the plantation, where I was received with much affability by Mr Drayton and his lady, and where I was doomed to pass the winter in the woods of Carolina. . . .

The affability and tenderness of this charming family* in the bosom of the woods will be ever cherished in my breast, and long recorded, I hope, in this page. My wants were always anticipated. The family library was transported without entreaty into my chamber; paper and the apparatus for writing were placed on my table; and once, having lamented that my stock of cigars was nearly exhausted, a negro was dispatched seventy miles to Charleston for a supply of the best Spanish.

I conclude my description of this elegant family with an observation that will apply to every other that I have been domesticated in, on the western continent—that cheerfulness and quiet always predominated, and that I never saw a brow clouded, or a lip opened in anger.

One diminution to the happiness of a European in the woods of Carolina is the reflection that every want is supplied him by slaves. Whatever may be urged on the subject of negroes, as the voice of millions could lend no support to falsehood, so no casuistry can justify the keeping of slaves. That negroes are human beings is confessed by their partaking with the rest of mankind the faculty of speech, and power of combination. Now no man being born a slave, but with his original rights, the supposed property of the master in the slave is an usurpation and not a right; because no one from being a person can become a thing. From this conviction should every good citizen promote the emancipation of negroes in America.

The negroes on the plantation, including house-servants and children, amounted to a hundred, of whom the average price being respectively seventy pounds, made them aggregately worth seven thousand to their possessor.

Two families lived in one hut, and such was their unconquerable propensity to steal that they pilfered from each other. I have heard masters lament this defect in their negroes. But what else can be expected from man in so degraded a condition, that among the ancients the same word implied both a slave and a thief.

Since the introduction of the culture of cotton in the state of South Carolina, the race of negroes has increased. Both men and women work in the field, and the labour of the rice-plantation formerly prevented the pregnant negress from bringing forth a long-lived offspring. It may be established as a maxim that, on a plantation where there are many children, the work has been moderate.

It may be incredible to some that the children of the most distinguished families in Carolina are suckled by negro women. Each child has its Momma, whose gestures and accent it will necessarily copy, for children, we all know, are imitative beings. It is not unusual to hear an elegant lady say, Richard always grieves when Quasheehaw is whipped, because she suckled him. If Rousseau in his Emile could inveigh against the French mother, who consigned her child to a woman of her own colour to suckle,* how would his indignation have been raised to behold a smiling babe tugging with its roseate lips at a dug of a size and colour to affright a satyr?

Of genius in negroes many instances may be recorded. It is true that Mr Jefferson has pronounced the Poems of Phillis Whately below the dignity of criticism, and it is seldom safe to differ in judgment from the author of *Notes on Virginia*.* But her conceptions are often lofty, and her versification often surprises with unexpected refinement. Ladd, the Carolina poet,* in enumerating the bards of his country, dwells with encomium on 'Whately's polished verse'; nor is his praise undeserved, for often it will be found to glide in the stream of melody. Her lines on Imagination have been quoted with rapture by Imlay of Kentucky, and Stedman,* the Guiana traveller; but I have ever thought her happiest production the Goliah of Gath. . . .

It is, indeed, grating to an Englishman to mingle with society in Carolina; for the people, however well-bred in other respects, have no delicacy before a stranger in what relates to their slaves. These wretches are execrated for every involuntary offence; but negroes endure execration without emotion, for they say, when Massa curse, he break no bone. But every master does not confine himself to oaths; and I have heard a man say, By heaven, my Negurs talk the worst English of any in Carolina: that boy just now called a basin a round-something: take him to the driver! let him have a dozen!

Exposed to such wanton cruelty the negroes frequently run away; they flee into the woods, where they are wet with the rains of heaven, and embrace the rock for want of a shelter. Life must be supported; hunger incites to depredation, and the poor wretches are often shot like the beasts of prey. When taken, the men are put in irons, and the boys have their necks encircled with a 'pot-hook'.

The Charleston papers abound with advertisements for fugitive slaves. I have a curious advertisement now before me. 'Stop the runaway. Fifty dollars reward. Whereas my waiting fellow, Will, having eloped from me last Saturday, without any provocation (it being known that I am a humane master) the above reward will be paid to any one who will lodge the aforesaid slave in some jail or deliver him to me on my plantation at Liberty Hall. Will may be known by the incisions of the whip on his back; and I suspect has taken the road to Coosohatchie, where he has a wife and five children, whom I sold last week to Mr Gillespie.

                                                              A. Levi'

Thus are the poor negroes treated in Carolina. Indeed, planters usually consider their slaves as beings defective in understanding; an opinion that excites only scorn from the philosopher. The human soul possesses faculties susceptible of improvement, without any regard to the colour of the skin. It is education that makes the difference between the master and the slave. Shall the imperious planter say that the swarthy sons of Africa, who now groan under his usurpation of their rights, would not equal him in virtue, knowledge and manners, had they been born free, and with the same advantages in the scale of society? It is to civilization that even Europeans owe their superiority over the savage; who knows only how to hunt and fish, to hew out a canoe from a tree, and construct a wretched hut; and but for this, the inhabitants of Britain had still bent the bow, still clothed themselves in skins, and still traversed the woods.

ANNE GRANT, *Memoirs of an American Lady, With Sketches of Manners and Scenes in America as they Existed Previous to the Revolution* (1807)

Anne Grant (1755–1838) was born Anne MacVicar at Glasgow. Her farmer father joined the army and sailed for America in 1757, followed by his wife and daughter. They settled at Albany, New York, until the family's return to Scotland in 1768. In 1779 Anne married a clergyman named Grant in Inverness-shire, where she learnt Gaelic, studied Highland folklore, and relieved the poor. After her husband's death in 1801 Grant turned to literature to support herself and her eight children, publishing volumes of poetry and Highland ethnography. In *Memoirs of an American Lady* (Grant's hostess Margaret Schuyler, widow of an Albany colonel) Grant recalls her sojourn in pre-revolutionary New York, during years when the Indian tribes were still formidable and independence was on the horizon.

[An exchange of prisoners]

The Indian war* was now drawing to a close, after occasioning great disquiet, boundless expense, and some bloodshed. Even when we had the advantage which our tactics and artillery in some instances gave, it was a warfare of the most precarious and perplexing kind. It was something like hunting in a forest at best; could you but have supposed the animals you pursued armed with missile weapons, and ever ready to start out of some unlooked for place. Our faithful Indian confederates, as far as I can recollect, were more useful to us on this occasion than all the dear bought apparatus, which we collected for the purpose of destroying an enemy too wise and too swift to permit us to come in sight of them; or, if determined to attack us, sufficiently dextrous to make us feel before we saw them. We said, however, that we conquered Pontiac, at which no doubt he smiled; for the truth of the matter was, the conduct of this war resembled a protracted game of chess. He was as little able to take our forts, without cannon, as we were able without the feet, the eyes, and the instinctive sagacity of Indians, to trace them to their retreats. After delighting ourselves for a long while with the manner in which we were to punish Pontiac's presumption, 'could we but once catch him', all ended in our making a treaty,* very honourable for him, and not very disadvantageous to ourselves. We gave both presents and promises, and Pontiac gave—permission to the mothers of those children who had been taken away from the frontier settlements to receive them back again, on condition of delivering up the Indian prisoners.

The joyful day when the congress was held for concluding peace I never shall forget. Another memorable day is engraved in indelible characters upon my memory. Madame,* being deeply interested in the projected exchange, brought about a scheme for having it take place at Albany, which was more central than any other place, and where her influence among the Mohawks could be of use in getting intelligence about the children, and sending messages to those who had adopted them, and who, by this time, were very unwilling to part with them. In the first place because they were growing very fond of them; and again, because they thought the children would not be so happy in our manner of life, which appeared to them both constrained and effeminate. This exchange had a large retrospect. For ten years back there had been, every now and then, while these Indians were in the French interest, ravages upon the frontiers of the different provinces. In many instances these children had been snatched away while their parents were working in the fields, or after they were killed. A certain day was appointed, on which all who had lost their children, or sought those of their relations, were to come to Albany in search of them; where, on that day, all Indians possessed of white children were to present them. Poor women, who had travelled some hundred miles from the back settlements of Pennsylvania and

New England, appeared here, with anxious looks and aching hearts, not knowing whether their children were alive, or how exactly to identify them if they should meet them. I observed these apprehensive and tender mothers were, though poor people, all dressed with peculiar neatness and attention, each wishing the first impression her child should receive of her might be a favourable one. On a gentle slope near the fort, stood a row of temporary huts, built by retainers to the troops; the green before these buildings was the scene of these pathetic recognitions; which I did not fail to attend. The joy of even the happy mothers was overpowering, and found vent in tears; but not like the bitter tears of those who, after long travel, found not what they sought. It was affecting to see the deep and silent sorrow of the Indian women, and of the children, who knew no other mother, and clung fondly to their bosoms, from whence they were not torn without the most piercing shrieks; while their own fond mothers were distressed beyond measure at the shyness and aversion with which these long lost objects of their love received their caresses. I shall never forget the grotesque figures and wild looks of these young savages; nor the trembling haste with which their mothers arrayed them in the new clothes they had brought for them, as hoping that, with the Indian dress, they would throw off their habits and attachments. It was in short a scene impossible to describe, but most affecting to behold.

[Description of the breaking up of the ice on the Hudson River]

Soon after this I witnessed, for the last time, the sublime spectacle of the ice breaking up on the river; an object that fills and elevates the mind with ideas of power, and grandeur, and, indeed, magnificence; before which all the triumphs of human art sink into contemptuous insignificance. This noble object of animated greatness, for such it seemed, I never missed: its approach being announced, like a loud and long peal of thunder, the whole population of Albany were down at the riverside in a moment; and if it happened, as was often the case, in the morning, there could not be a more grotesque assemblage. No one who had a night-cap on waited to put it off; as for waiting for one's cloak, or gloves, it was a thing out of the question; you caught the thing next you, that could wrap round you, and ran. In the way you saw every door left open, and pails, baskets, etc., without number, set down in the street. It was a perfect saturnalia.

People never dreamt of being obeyed by their slaves, till the ice was past. The houses were left quite empty: the meanest slave, the youngest child, all were to be found on the shore. Such as could walk, ran; and they that could not, were carried by those whose duty it would have been to stay and attend them. When arrived at the show place, unlike the audience collected to witness any spectacle of human invention, the multitude with their eyes all bent one way, stood immovable, and silent as death, till the tumult ceased, and the mighty commotion was passed by; then everyone tried to give vent to the vast conceptions with which his mind had been distended. Every child, and every negro, was sure to say, 'Is not this like the day of judgment?' and what they said everyone else thought. Now to describe this is impossible, but I mean to account, in some degree, for it. The ice, which had been all winter very thick, instead of diminishing, as might be expected in spring, still increased, as the sunshine came, and the days lengthened. Much snow fell in February; which, melted by the heat of the sun, was stagnant, for a day, on the surface of the ice; and then by the night frosts, which were still severe, was added, as a new accession to the thickness of it, above the former surface. This was so often repeated, that in some years the ice gained two feet in thickness, after the heat of the sun became such, as one would have expected should have entirely dissolved it. So conscious were the natives of the safety this accumulation of ice afforded, that the sledges continued to drive on the ice, when the trees were budding, and everything looked like spring; nay, when there was so much melted on the surface that the horses were knee deep in water, while travelling on it; and portentous cracks, on every side, announced the approaching rupture. This could scarce have been produced by the mere influence of the sun, till midsummer. It was the swelling of the waters under the ice, increased by rivulets, enlarged by melted snows, that produced this catastrophe; for such the awful concussion made it appear. The prelude to the general bursting of this mighty mass was a fracture, lengthways, in the middle of the stream, produced by the effort of the imprisoned waters, now increased too much to be contained within their wonted bounds. Conceive a solid mass, from six to eight feet thick, bursting for many miles in one continued rupture, produced by a force inconceivably great, and, in a manner, inexpressibly sudden. Thunder is no adequate image of this awful explosion, which roused all the sleepers within reach of the sound, as completely as the final convulsion of nature, and the solemn peal of the awakening trumpet, might be supposed to do. The stream in summer was confined by a pebbly strand, overhung with high and steep banks, crowned with lofty trees, which were considered as a sacred barrier against the encroachments of this annual visitation. Never dryads dwelt in more security than those of the vine-clad elms, that extended their ample branches over this mighty stream. Their tangled nets laid bare by the impetuous torrents formed caverns ever fresh and fragrant; where the most delicate plants flourished, unvisited by scorching suns, or snipping blasts; and nothing could be more singular than the variety of plants and birds that were sheltered in these intricate safe recesses. But when the bursting of the crystal surface set loose the many waters that had rushed down, swollen with the annual tribute of dissolving snow, the islands and low lands were all flooded in an instant; and the lofty banks, from which you were wont to overlook the stream, were now entirely filled by an impetuous torrent, bearing down, with incredible and tumultuous rage, immense shoals of ice; which, breaking every instant by the concussion of others, jammed together in some places, in others erecting themselves in gigantic heights for an instant in the air, and seemed to combat with their fellow giants crowding on in all directions, and falling together with an inconceivable crash, formed a terrible moving picture, animated and various beyond conception; for it was not only the cerulean ice, whose broken edges, combating with the stream, refracted light into a thousand rainbows, that charmed your attention, lofty pines, large pieces of the bank torn off by the ice with all their early green and tender foliage, were drove on like travelling islands, amid this battle of breakers, for such it seemed. I am absurdly attempting to paint a scene, under which the powers of language sink. Suffice it, that this year its solemnity was increased by an unusual quantity of snow, which the last hard winter had accumulated, and the dissolution of which now threatened an inundation.

Solemn indeed it was to me, as the memento of my approaching journey, which was to take place whenever the ice broke, which is here a kind of epoch.

WILLIAM COBBETT, *A Year's Residence in the United States of America* (1818)

Cobbett first visited North America as a soldier in 1791, when his regiment was stationed in Nova Scotia. After his return, his involvement in a legal case against former officers—the first of many times Cobbett would fall foul of the law—caused him to flee to France and then America. He settled in Delaware and got involved in US politics, writing as 'Peter Porcupine'. Sued for defamation, he returned to England to publish in 1802 the first issue of Cobbett's *Weekly Political Register*, which continued publication until his death. By 1806 his conservatism had given way to reformist zeal. He spent two years in prison on seditious libel charges provoked by an article about flogging in the army. A government roundup of suspected radicals after a reformist mass meeting turned into the Spa Fields Riot of 1816 sent him fleeing to America once again. This time Cobbett lived on Long Island, New York, with his wife and five children, pursuing his lifelong passion for farming. When he returned to England he brought with him the bones of Thomas Paine. In these selections Cobbett praises Americans' work ethic but deplores their excessive drinking.

Labour is the great article of expense upon a farm; yet it is not nearly so great as in England, in proportion to the amount of the produce of a farm, especially if the poor-rates be, in both cases, included.

It is, too, of importance to know, what sort of labourers these Americans are; for, though a labourer is a labourer, still there is some difference in them; and, these Americans are the best that I ever saw. They mow four acres of oats, wheat, rye, or barley in a day, and, with a cradle, lay it so smooth in the swarths that it is tied up in sheaves with the greatest neatness and ease. They mow two acres and a half of grass in a day, and they do the work well. And the crops, upon an average, are all except the wheat, as heavy as in England. The English farmer will want nothing more than these facts to convince him, that the labour, after all, is not so very dear.

The causes of these performances, so far beyond those in England, is first, the men are tall and well built; they are bony rather than fleshy; and they live, as to food, as well as man can live. And, secondly, they have been educated to do much in a day. The farmer here generally is at the head of his 'boys', as they, in the kind language of the country, are called. Here is the best of examples. My old and beloved friend, Mr James Paul,* used, at the age of nearly sixty to go at the head of his mowers, though his fine farm was his own, and though he might, in other respects, be called a rich man; and, I have heard that Mr Elias Hicks,* the famous Quaker preacher, who lives about nine miles from this spot, has this year, at seventy years of age, cradled down four acres of rye in a day. I wish some of the preachers of other descriptions, especially our fat parsons in England, would think a little of this, and would betake themselves to 'work with their hands the things which be good, that they may have to give to him who needeth', and not go on any longer gormandizing and swilling upon the labour of those who need.

Besides the great quantity of work performed by the American labourer, his skill, the versatility of his talent, is a great thing. Every man can use an axe, a saw, and a hammer. Scarcely one who cannot do any job at rough carpentering, and mend a plough or a waggon. Very few indeed who cannot kill and dress pigs and sheep, and many of them oxen and calves . . .

So that our men, who come from England, must not expect that, in these common labours of the country, they are to surpass, or even equal, these 'Yankees', who, of all men that I ever saw, are the most active and the most hardy. They skip over a fence like a greyhound. They will catch you a pig in an open field by racing him down; and they are afraid of nothing. This was the sort of stuff that filled the frigates of DECATUR, HULL, and BRAINBRIDGE.* No wonder that they triumphed when opposed to poor pressed creatures, worn out by length of service and ill-usage, and encouraged by no hope of fair-play. My LORD COCHRANE* said in his place in parliament, that it would be so; and so it was. Poor CASHMAN,* that brave Irishman, with his dying breath, accused the government and the merchants of England of withholding from him his pittance of prize money! Ought not such a vile, robbing, murderous system to be destroyed?

Of the same active, hardy, and brave stuff, too, was composed the army of JACKSON,* who drove the invaders into the Gulf of Mexico, and who would have driven into the same Gulf the army of Waterloo, and the heroic gentleman, too, who lent his hand to the murder of Marshal Ney.* This is the stuff that stands between the rascals, called the Holy Alliance,* and the slavery of the whole civilized world. This is the stuff that gives us Englishmen an asylum; that gives us time to breathe; that enables us to deal our tyrants blows, which, without the existence of this stuff, they never would receive. This America, this scene of happiness under a free government, is the beam in the eye, the thorn in the side, the worm in the vitals, of every despot upon the face of the earth.

An American labourer is not regulated, as to time, by clocks and watches. The sun, who seldom hides his face, tells him when to begin in the morning and when to leave off at night. He has a dollar, a whole dollar for his work; but then it is the work of a whole day. Here is no dispute about hours. 'Hours were made for *slaves*,' is an old saying; and, really, they seem here to act upon it as a practical maxim. This is a great thing in agricultural affairs. It prevents so many disputes. It removes so great a cause of disagreement. The American labourers, like the tavern-keepers, are never servile, but always civil. Neither boobishness nor meanness mark their character. They never creep and fawn, and are never rude. Employed about your house as day-labourers, they never come to interlope for vict- uals or drink. They have no idea of such a thing: their pride would restrain them if their plenty did not; and, thus would it be with all labourers, in all countries, were they left to enjoy the fair produce of their labour. Full pocket or empty pocket, these American labourers are always the same men: no saucy cunning in the one case, and no base crawling in the other. This, too, arises from free institutions of government. A man has a voice because he is a man, and not because he is the possessor of money. And, shall I never see our English labourers in this happy state?

Let those English farmers, who love to see a poor wretched labourer stand trembling before them with his hat off, and who think no more of him than of a dog, remain where they are; or go off, on the cavalry horses, to the devil at once, if they wish to avoid the tax- gatherer; for, they would, here, meet with so many mortifications, that they would, to a certainty, hang themselves in a month. . . .

There is one thing in the Americans which, though its proper place was further back, I have reserved, or rather kept back, to the last moment. It has presented itself several times; but I have turned from the thought, as men do from thinking of any mortal disease that is at work in their frame. It is not covetousness; it is not niggardli- ness; it is not insincerity; it is not enviousness; it is not cowardice, above all things: it is DRINKING. Aye, and that too, amongst but too many men, who, one would think, would loathe it. You cannot go into hardly any man's house, without being asked to drink wine, or spirits, even in the morning. . . .

The Americans preserve their gravity and quietness and good-humour even in their drink; and so much the worse. It were far better for them to be as noisy and quarrelsome as the English drunkards; for then the odiousness of the vice would be more visible, and the vice itself might become less frequent. Few vices want an apology, and drinking has not only its apologies but its praises; for, besides the appellation of generous wine, and the numerous songs, some in very elegant and witty language, from the pens of debauched men of talents, drinking is said to be necessary, in certain cases at least, to raise the spirits, and to keep out cold. Never was anything more false. Whatever intoxicates must enfeeble in the end, and whatever enfeebles must chill. It is very well known, in the Northern countries, that, if the cold be such as to produce danger of frost-biting, you must take care not to drink strong liquors.

To see this beastly vice in young men is shocking. At one of the taverns at Harrisburgh there were several as fine young men as I ever saw. Well-dressed, well educated, polite, and every thing but *sober*. What a squalid, drooping, sickly set they looked in the morning!

FRANCES TROLLOPE, *Domestic Manners of the Americans* (1832)

Frances Trollope (1780–1863), mother of the novelist Anthony Trollope, was herself a novelist as well as a travel writer, though she published nothing before her fifty-third year. Her husband, Thomas Anthony Trollope, was dogged by failure (and probably depression) all his life. He tried law and farming, and then, in 1827, invested what was left of his money to open a bazaar for the sale of fancy goods in Cincinnati. Frances and three of her children had travelled to America (December 1827) with the charismatic reformer Fanny Wright to found a utopian community in Tennessee. Appalled by conditions there, they moved to Cincinnati, where Thomas joined them. The bazaar proved a fiasco. On her return to England (July 1831), in an attempt to recoup the family's losses, Trollope published *Domestic Manners of the Americans*. The book was an immediate and resounding success. Our selections support one critic's comment: 'Mrs. Trollope was personally entirely exempt from vulgarity, but she

knew her forte to lie in depicting it.' Riverboat 'gentlemen' and an evan-
gelical camp meeting are the targets of her satiric skill. Visits to the
Bureau of Indian Affairs in Washington, DC, and to slave owners in
Virginia occasion more political comment. Trollope's condemnation of
slavery, generally accepted in the United States, was one reason why many
Americans hated her book.

Preface

Although much has already been written on the great experiment,
as it has been called, now making in government, on the other
side of the Atlantic, there appears to be still room for many
interesting details on the influence which the political system of the
country has produced on the principles, tastes, and manners, of its
domestic life.

The author of the following pages has endeavoured, in some
degree, to supply this deficiency, by carefully recording the observations she had an opportunity of making during a residence of three
years and six months in different parts of the United States.

She leaves to abler pens the more ambitious task of commenting
on the democratic form of the American government; while, by
describing, faithfully, the daily aspect of ordinary life, she has
endeavoured to show how greatly the advantage is on the side of
those who are governed by the few, instead of the many. The chief
object she has had in view is to encourage her countrymen to hold
fast by a constitution that ensures all the blessings which flow from
established habits and solid principles. If they forgo these, they will
incur the fearful risk of breaking up their repose by introducing the
jarring tumult and universal degradation which invariably follow
the wild scheme of placing all the power of the state in the hands of
the populace.

Company on Board the Steam Boat

The weather was warm and bright, and we found the guard of the
boat, as they call the gallery that runs round the cabins, a very
agreeable station;* here we all sat as long as light lasted, and sometimes wrapped in our shawls, we enjoyed the clear bright beauty of
American moonlight long after every passenger but ourselves had
retired. We had a full complement of passengers on board. The deck,
as is usual, was occupied by the Kentucky flat-boat men, returning

from New Orleans, after having disposed of the boat and cargo which they had conveyed thither . . .

The gentlemen in the cabin (we had no ladies) would certainly neither, from their language, manners, nor appearance, have received that designation in Europe; but we soon found their claim to it rested on more substantial ground, for we heard them nearly all addressed by the titles of general, colonel, and major. On mentioning these military dignities to an English friend some time afterwards, he told me that he too had made the voyage with the same description of company, but remarking that there was not a single captain among them; he made the observation to a fellow-passenger, and asked how he accounted for it. 'Oh, sir, the captains are all on deck,' was the reply.

Our honours, however, were not all military, for we had a judge among us. I know it is equally easy and invidious to ridicule the peculiarities of appearance and manner in people of a different nation from ourselves; we may, too, at the same moment, be undergoing the same ordeal in their estimation; and, moreover, I am by no means disposed to consider whatever is new to me as therefore objectionable; but, nevertheless, it was impossible not to feel repugnance to many of the novelties that now surrounded me.

The total want of all the usual courtesies of the table, the voracious rapidity with which the viands were seized and devoured, the strange uncouth phrases and pronunciation; the loathsome spitting, from the contamination of which it was absolutely impossible to protect our dresses; the frightful manner of feeding with their knives, till the whole blade seemed to enter into the mouth; and the still more frightful manner of cleaning the teeth afterwards with a pocket knife, soon forced us to feel that we were not surrounded by the generals, colonels, and majors of the old world; and that the dinner hour was to be anything rather than an hour of enjoyment.

The little conversation that went forward while we remained in the room was entirely political and the respective claims of Adams and Jackson to the presidency* were argued with more oaths and more vehemence than it had ever been my lot to hear. Once a colonel appeared on the verge of assaulting a major, when a huge seven-foot Kentuckian gentleman horse-dealer asked of the heavens to confound them both, and bade them sit still and be d—d. We too thought we should share this sentence; at least sitting still in the cabin seemed very nearly to include the rest of it, and we never tarried there a moment longer than was absolutely necessary to eat.

The unbroken flatness of the banks of the Mississippi continued unvaried for many miles above New Orleans; but the graceful and luxuriant palmetto, the dark and noble ilex, and the bright orange, were everywhere to be seen, and it was many days before we were weary of looking at them. We occasionally used the opportunity of the boat's stopping to take in wood for a ten minutes' visit to the shore; we in this manner explored a field of sugar canes and loaded ourselves with as much of the sweet spoil as we could carry. Many of the passengers seemed fond of the luscious juice that is easily expressed from the canes, but it was too sweet for my palate. We also visited, in the same rapid manner, a cotton plantation. A handsome spacious building was pointed out to us as a convent, where a considerable number of young ladies were educated by the nuns.

At one or two points the wearisome level line of forest is relieved by *bluffs*, as they call the short intervals of high ground. The town of Natchez is beautifully situated on one of these high spots; the climate here, in the warm season, is as fatal as that of New Orleans; were it not for this, Natchez would have great attractions to new settlers. The beautiful contrast that its bright green hill forms with the dismal line of black forest that stretches on every side, the abundant growth of pawpaw, palmetto and orange, the copious variety of sweet-scented flowers that flourish there, all make it appear like an oasis in the desert.

Camp-Meeting

It was in the course of this summer* that I found the opportunity I had long wished for, of attending a camp-meeting, and I gladly accepted the invitation of an English lady and gentleman to accompany them in their carriage to the spot where it is held; this was in a wild district on the confines of Indiana.

The prospect of passing a night in the backwoods of Indiana was by no means agreeable, but I screwed my courage to the proper pitch, and set forth determined to see with my own eyes, and hear with my own ears, what a camp-meeting really was. I had heard it said that being at a camp-meeting was like standing at the gate of heaven, and seeing it opening before you; I had heard it said that being at a camp-meeting was like finding yourself within the gates of hell; in either case there must be something to gratify curiosity, and compensate one for the fatigue of a long rumbling ride and a sleepless night.

We reached the ground about an hour before midnight, and the approach to it was highly picturesque. The spot chosen was the verge of an unbroken forest, where a space of about twenty acres appeared to have been partially cleared for the purpose. Tents of different sizes were pitched very near together in a circle round the cleared space; behind them were ranged an exterior circle of carriages of every description, and at the back of each were fastened the horses which had drawn them thither. Through this triple circle of defence we distinguished numerous fires burning brightly within it; and still more numerous lights flickering from the trees that were left in the enclosure. The moon was in meridian splendour above our heads.

We left the carriage to the care of a servant, who was to prepare a bed in it for Mrs B. and me, and entered the inner circle. The first glance reminded me of Vauxhall,* from the effect of the lights among the trees, and the moving crowd below them; but the second showed a scene totally unlike anything I had ever witnessed. Four high frames, constructed in the form of altars, were placed at the four corners of the enclosure; on these were supported layers of earth and sod, on which burned immense fires of blazing pine-wood. On one side a rude platform was erected to accommodate the preachers, fifteen of whom attended this meeting, and with very short intervals for necessary refreshment and private devotion, preached in rotation, day and night, from Tuesday to Saturday.

When we arrived, the preachers were silent; but we heard issuing from nearly every tent mingled sounds of praying, preaching, singing, and lamentation. The curtains in front of each tent were dropped, and the faint light that gleamed through the white drapery, backed as it was by the dark forest, had a beautiful and mysterious effect, that set the imagination at work; and had the sounds which vibrated around us been less discordant, harsh, and unnatural, I should have enjoyed it; but listening at the corner of a tent, which poured forth more than its proportion of clamour, in a few moments chased every feeling derived from imagination, and furnished realities that could neither be mistaken nor forgotten.

Great numbers of persons were walking about the ground, who

appeared like ourselves to be present only as spectators; some of these very unceremoniously contrived to raise the drapery of this tent, at one corner, so as to afford us a perfect view of the interior.

The floor was covered with straw, which round the sides was heaped in masses, that might serve as seats, but which at that moment were used to support the heads and the arms of the close-packed circle of men and women who kneeled on the floor.

Out of about thirty persons thus placed, perhaps half a dozen were men. One of these, a handsome looking youth of eighteen or twenty, kneeled just below the opening through which I looked. His arm was encircling the neck of a young girl who knelt beside him, with her hair hanging dishevelled upon her shoulders, and her features working with the most violent agitation; soon after they both fell forward on the straw, as if unable to endure in any other attitude the burning eloquence of a tall grim figure in black, who, standing erect in the centre, was uttering with incredible vehemence an oration that seemed to hover between praying and preaching; his arms hung stiff and immovable by his side, and he looked like an ill-constructed machine, set in action by a movement so violent as to threaten its own destruction, so jerkingly, painfully, yet rapidly, did his words tumble out; the kneeling circle ceasing not to call in every variety of tone, on the name of Jesus; accompanied with sobs, groans, and a sort of low howling inexpressibly painful to listen to. But my attention was speedily withdrawn from the preacher, and the circle round him, by a figure which knelt alone at some distance; it was a living image of Scott's Macbriar,* as young, as wild, and as terrible. His thin arms, tossed above his head, had forced themselves so far out of the sleeves that they were bare to the elbow; his large eyes glared frightfully, and he continued to scream without an instant's intermission the word 'Glory!' with a violence that seemed to swell every vein to bursting. It was too dreadful to look upon long, and we turned away shuddering.

We made the circuit of the tents, pausing where attention was particularly excited by sounds more vehement than ordinary. We contrived to look into many; all were strewed with straw, and the distorted figures that we saw kneeling, sitting, and lying amongst it, joined to the woeful and convulsive cries, gave to each the air of a cell in Bedlam.*

One tent was occupied exclusively by Negroes. They were all

full-dressed, and looked exactly as if they were performing a scene on the stage. One woman wore a dress of pink gauze trimmed with silver lace; another was dressed in pale yellow silk; one or two had splendid turbans; and all wore a profusion of ornaments. The men were in snow white pantaloons, with gay coloured linen jackets. One of these, a youth of coal-black comeliness, was preaching with the most violent gesticulations, frequently springing high from the ground, and clapping his hands over his head. Could our missionary societies have heard the trash he uttered, by way of an address to the Deity, they might perhaps have doubted whether his conversion had much enlightened his mind.

At midnight a horn sounded through the camp, which, we were told, was to call the people from private to public worship; and we presently saw them flocking from all sides to the front of the preachers' stand. Mrs B. and I contrived to place ourselves with our backs supported against the lower part of this structure, and we were thus enabled to witness the scene which followed without personal danger. There were about two thousand persons assembled.

One of the preachers began in a low nasal tone, and, like all other Methodist preachers, assured us of the enormous depravity of man as he comes from the hands of his Maker, and of his perfect sanctification after he had wrestled sufficiently with the Lord to get hold of him, etc. The admiration of the crowd was evinced by almost constant cries of 'Amen! Amen!' 'Jesus! Jesus!' 'Glory! Glory!' and the like. But this comparative tranquillity did not last long: the preacher told them that 'this night was the time fixed upon for anxious sinners to wrestle with the Lord', that he and his brethren 'were at hand to help them', and that such as needed their help were to come forward into 'the pen'. The phrase forcibly recalled Milton's lines*—

> Blind mouths! that scarce themselves know how to hold
> A sheep-hook, or have learned aught else, the least
> That to the faithful herdsman's art belongs!
> —But when they list their lean and flashy songs,
> Grate on their scrannel pipes of wretched straw:—
>   The hungry sheep look up, and are not fed!
> But swoln with wind, and the rank mist they draw,
>   Rot inwardly—and foul contagion spread.

'The pen' was the space immediately below the preachers' stand; we were therefore placed on the edge of it, and were enabled to see and hear all that took place in the very centre of this extraordinary exhibition.

The crowd fell back at the mention of the pen, and for some minutes there was a vacant space before us. The preachers came down from their stand and placed themselves in the midst of it, beginning to sing a hymn, calling upon the penitents to come forth. As they sang they kept turning themselves round to every part of the crowd, and, by degrees, the voices of the whole multitude joined in chorus. This was the only moment at which I perceived anything like the solemn and beautiful effect which I had heard ascribed to this woodland worship. It is certain that the combined voices of such a multitude, heard at dead of night, from the depths of their eternal forests, the many fair young faces turned upward, and looking paler and lovelier as they met the moonbeams, the dark figures of the officials in the middle of the circle, the lurid glare thrown by the altar-fires on the woods beyond, did altogether produce a fine and solemn effect, that I shall not easily forget; but ere I had well enjoyed it, the scene changed, and sublimity gave place to horror and disgust.

The exhortation nearly resembled that which I had heard at 'the Revival',* but the result was very different; for, instead of the few hysterical women who had distinguished themselves on that occasion, above a hundred persons, nearly all females, came forward, uttering howlings and groans so terrible that I shall never cease to shudder when I recall them. They appeared to drag each other forward, and on the word being given, 'let us pray', they all fell on their knees; but this posture was soon changed for others that permitted greater scope for the convulsive movements of their limbs; and they were soon all lying on the ground in an indescribable confusion of heads and legs. They threw about their limbs with such incessant and violent motion that I was every instant expecting some serious accident to occur.

But how am I to describe the sounds that proceeded from this strange mass of human beings? I know no words which can convey an idea of it. Hysterical sobbings, convulsive groans, shrieks and screams the most appalling, burst forth on all sides. I felt sick with horror. As if their hoarse and overstrained voices failed to make noise enough, they soon began to clap their hands violently. The scene described by Dante was before me:

Quivi sospiri, pianti, ed alti guai
Risonavan per l'aere—
—Orribili favelle
Parole di dolore, accenti d'ira
Voci alti e fioche, *e suon di man con elle.**

Many of these wretched creatures were beautiful young females. The preachers moved about among them, at once exciting and soothing their agonies. I heard the muttered 'Sister! dear sister!' I saw the insidious lips approach the cheeks of the unhappy girls; I heard the murmured confessions of the poor victims, and I watched their tormentors, breathing into their ears consolations that tinged the pale cheek with red. Had I been a man, I am sure I should have been guilty of some rash act of interference; nor do I believe that such a scene could have been acted in the presence of Englishmen without instant punishment being inflicted; not to mention the salutary discipline of the treadmill, which, beyond all question, would, in England, have been applied to check so turbulent and so vicious a scene.

After the first wild burst that followed their prostration, the moanings, in many instances, became loudly articulate; and I then experienced a strange vibration between tragic and comic feeling.

A very pretty girl, who was kneeling in the attitude of Canova's Magdalene* immediately before us, amongst an immense quantity of jargon, broke out thus: 'Woe! woe to the backsliders! hear it, hear it Jesus! when I was fifteen my mother died, and I backslided, oh Jesus, I backslided! take me home to my mother, Jesus! take me home to her, for I am weary! Oh John Mitchell! John Mitchell!' and after sobbing piteously behind her raised hands, she lifted her sweet face again, which was as pale as death, and said, 'Shall I sit on the sunny bank of salvation with my mother? my own dear mother? oh Jesus, take me home, take me home!'

Who could refuse a tear to this earnest wish for death in one so young and so lovely? But I saw her, ere I left the ground, with her hand fast locked, and her head supported by a man who looked very much as Don Juan* might, when sent back to earth as too bad for the regions below.

One woman near us continued to 'call on the Lord', as it is termed, in the loudest possible tone, and without a moment's interval, for the two hours that we kept our dreadful station. She became frightfully hoarse, and her face so red as to make me expect she would burst a blood-vessel. Among the rest of her rant, she said, 'I will hold fast to Jesus, I never will let him go; if they take me to hell, I will still hold him fast, fast, fast!'

The stunning noise was sometimes varied by the preachers beginning to sing; but the convulsive movements of the poor maniacs only became more violent. At length the atrocious wickedness of this horrible scene increased to a degree of grossness that drove us from our station; we returned to the carriage at about three o'clock in the morning, and passed the remainder of the night in listening to the ever increasing tumult at the pen. To sleep was impossible. At daybreak the horn again sounded, to send them to private devotion; and in about an hour afterwards I saw the whole camp as joyously and eagerly employed in preparing and devouring their most substantial breakfasts as if the night had been passed in dancing; and I marked many a fair but pale face that I recognized as a demoniac of the night, simpering beside a swain, to whom she carefully administered hot coffee and eggs. The preaching saint and the howling sinner seemed alike to relish this mode of recruiting their strength.

After enjoying abundance of strong tea, which proved a delightful restorative after a night so strangely spent, I wandered alone into the forest, and I never remember to have found perfect quiet more delightful.

We soon after left the ground; but before our departure we learnt that a very satisfactory collection had been made by the preachers, for Bibles, Tracts, and all other religious purposes.

Indian Affairs

The bureau for Indian affairs contains a room of great interest: the walls are entirely covered with original portraits of all the chiefs who, from time to time, have come to negotiate with their great father, as they call the President. These portraits are by Mr King,* and, it cannot be doubted, are excellent likenesses, as are all the portraits I have ever seen from the hands of that gentleman. The countenances are full of expression, but the expression in most of them is extremely similar; or rather, I should say that they have but two sorts of expression; the one is that of very noble and warlike daring, the other of a gentle and naïve simplicity, that has no mixture of folly in it, but which is inexpressibly engaging, and the more touching, perhaps, because at the moment we were looking at them, those very hearts which lent the eyes such meek and friendly softness, were wrung by a base, cruel, and most oppressive act of their *great father*.

We were at Washington at the time that the measure for chasing the last of several tribes of Indians from their forest homes was canvassed in congress, and finally decided upon by the fiat of the President.* If the American character may be judged by their conduct in this matter, they are most lamentably deficient in every feeling of honour and integrity. It is among themselves, and from themselves, that I have heard the statements which represent them as treacherous and false almost beyond belief in their intercourse with the unhappy Indians. Had I, during my residence in the United States, observed any single feature in their national character that could justify their eternal boast of liberality and the love of freedom, I might have respected them, however much my taste might have been offended by what was peculiar in their manners and customs. But it is impossible for any mind of common honesty not to be revolted by the contradictions in their principles and practice. They inveigh against the governments of Europe, because, as they say, they favour the powerful and oppress the weak. You may hear this declaimed upon in Congress, roared out in taverns, discussed in every drawing-room, satirized upon the stage, nay, even anathematized from the pulpit: listen to it, and then look at them at home; you will see them with one hand hoisting the cap of liberty, and with the other flogging their slaves. You will see them one hour lecturing their mob on the indefeasible rights of man, and the next driving from their homes the children of the soil, whom they have bound themselves to protect by the most solemn treaties . . .

There were many objects of much interest shown us at this Indian bureau; but, from the peculiar circumstances of this most unhappy and ill-used people, it was a very painful interest.

The dresses worn by the chiefs when their portraits were taken are many of them splendid, from the embroidery of beads and other ornaments; and the room contains many specimens of their ingenuity, and even of their taste. There is a glass case in the room, wherein are arranged specimens of worked muslin, and other needlework, some very excellent handwriting, and many other little productions of male and female Indians, all proving clearly that they are perfectly capable of civilization. Indeed, the circumstance which renders their expulsion from their own, their native lands, so peculiarly lamentable, is that they were yielding rapidly to the force of example; their lives were no longer those of wandering hunters, but they were becoming agriculturists, and the tyrannical arm of brutal power has not now driven them, as formerly, only from their hunting grounds, their favourite springs, and the sacred bones of their fathers, but it has chased them from the dwellings their advancing knowledge had taught them to make comfortable; from the newly-ploughed fields of their pride; and from the crops their sweat had watered. And for what? To add some thousand acres of territory to the half-peopled wilderness which borders them.

The Possession of Slaves

It is not among the higher classes that the possession of slaves produces the worst effects. Among the poorer class of landholders, who are often as profoundly ignorant as the negroes they own, the effect of this plenary power over males and females is most demoralizing; and the kind of coarse, not to say brutal, authority which is exercised furnishes the most disgusting moral spectacle I ever witnessed. In all ranks, however, it appeared to me that the greatest and best feelings of the human heart were paralysed by the relative positions of slave and owner. The characters, the hearts of children, are irretrievably injured by it. In Virginia we boarded for some time in a family consisting of a widow and her four daughters, and I there witnessed a scene strongly indicative of the effect I have mentioned. A young female slave, about eight years of age, had found on the shelf of a cupboard a biscuit, temptingly buttered, of which she had eaten a considerable portion before she was observed. The butter had been copiously sprinkled with arsenic for the destruction of rats, and had been thus most incautiously placed by one of the young ladies of the family. As soon as the circumstance was known, the lady of the house came to consult me as to what had best be done for the poor child; I immediately mixed a large cup of mustard and water (the most rapid of all emetics) and got the little girl to swallow it. The desired effect was instantly produced, but the poor child, partly from nausea, and partly from the terror of hearing her death proclaimed by half a dozen voices round her, trembled so violently that I thought she would fall. I sat down in the court where we were standing, and, as a matter of course, took the little sufferer in my lap. I observed a general titter among the white members of the family, while the black stood aloof, and looked stupefied. The youngest of the family, a little girl about the age of the young slave, after gazing at me for a few moments in utter astonishment, exclaimed, 'My! If Mrs Trollope has not taken her in her lap, and wiped her nasty mouth! Why I would not have touched her mouth for two hundred dollars!'

The little slave was laid on a bed, and I returned to my own apartments; some time afterwards I sent to enquire for her, and learnt that she was in great pain. I immediately went myself to enquire farther, when another young lady of the family, the one by whose imprudence the accident had occurred, met my anxious enquiries with ill-suppressed mirth—told me they had sent for the doctor—and then burst into uncontrollable laughter. The idea of really sympathizing in the sufferings of a slave, appeared to them as absurd as weeping over a calf that had been slaughtered by the butcher. The daughters of my hostess were as lovely as features and complexion could make them; but the neutralizing effect of this total want of feeling upon youth and beauty must be witnessed, to be conceived.

There seems in general a strong feeling throughout America that none of the negro race can be trusted, and as fear, according to their notions, is the only principle by which a slave can be actuated, it is not wonderful if the imputation be just. But I am persuaded that were a different mode of moral treatment pursued, most important and beneficial consequences would result from it. Negroes are very sensible to kindness, and might, I think, be rendered more profitably obedient by the practice of it towards them, than by any other mode of discipline whatever. To emancipate them entirely throughout the Union cannot, I conceive, be thought of, consistently with the safety of the country; but were the possibility of amelioration taken into the consideration of the legislature, with all the wisdom, justice, and mercy that could be brought to bear upon it, the negro population of the Union might cease to be a terror, and their situation no longer be a subject either of indignation or of pity.

I observed everywhere throughout the slave states that all articles which can be taken and consumed are constantly locked up, and in large families where the extent of the establishment multiplies the number of keys, these are deposited in a basket, and consigned to the care of a little negress, who is constantly seen following her mistress's steps with this basket on her arm, and this, not only that the keys may be always at hand, but because should they be out of sight one moment, that moment would infallibly be employed for purposes of plunder. It seemed to me in this instance, as in many others, that the close personal attendance of these sable shadows must be very annoying; but whenever I mentioned it, I was assured that no such feeling existed, and that use rendered them almost unconscious of their presence.

I had, indeed, frequent opportunities of observing this habitual indifference to the presence of their slaves. They talk of them, of their condition, of their faculties, of their conduct, exactly as if they were incapable of hearing. I once saw a young lady who, when seated at table between a male and a female, was induced by her modesty to intrude on the chair of her female neighbour to avoid the indelicacy of touching the elbow of *a man*. I once saw this very young lady lacing her stays with the most perfect composure before a negro footman. A Virginian gentleman told me that ever since he had married, he had been accustomed to have a negro girl sleep in the same chamber with himself and his wife. I asked for what purpose this nocturnal attendance was necessary? 'Good heaven!' was the reply, 'if I wanted a glass of water during the night, what would become of me?'

PART VI

AUSTRALIA AND THE PACIFIC

AT the beginning of the eighteenth century access to the Pacific was effectively controlled by the Spanish Empire in South America and the Dutch in the East Indies. English privateers such as William Dampier, George Shelvocke, and Woodes Rogers ventured around Cape Horn to raid Spanish colonies and shipping, but a more systematic British penetration of the South Seas did not take place until the geopolitical decline of Spain and the ascendancy of Britain and France as rival superpowers in the second half of the eighteenth century. Official naval expeditions, most famously the three voyages led by James Cook, invested themselves with scientific purpose as they mapped potential trade routes and claimed new lands for the crown. Cook mapped the coasts of New Zealand and eastern Australia and explored constellations of islands, many of them new to Europeans—such as Hawaii, where Cook was killed in a skirmish with the inhabitants in 1779.

The Pacific voyages enthralled a growing reading public. Privateer narratives fuelled speculation in a South Sea Company, founded in 1711 on the delusory prospect of a booming Pacific trade. When the 'South Sea Bubble' burst in 1720, so did the national credit. Jonathan Swift parodied Dampier's matter-of-fact accretion of exotic detail in *Gulliver's Travels*, while Rogers's account of the castaway Alexander Selkirk, further popularized by Richard Steele, became the basis for Defoe's *Robinson Crusoe*. Commodore Anson's mid-century circumnavigation inspired such diverse writers as Smollett, Cowper, and Rousseau. The Cook voyages generated the media sensation of the age. Dr Johnson treated his Scottish hosts to an imitation of the hopping kangaroo, discovered (and devoured) by Cook and Joseph Banks. The Pacific islander Omai, brought back to London from the second voyage, was presented at court, charmed fashionable society with his affable manners, and had his portrait painted by Sir Joshua Reynolds.

Scientific ideology endorsed a genuine, however limited, openness to what these new worlds might offer, evident in Cook's recognitions of cultural difference and reflections on his own anomalous presence in other people's territory. The arrival of evangelical missions in the islands and the convict settlement in New South Wales, in the last decade of the eighteenth century, portend the closing of that epistemological space, and the devotion of the new world to modern regimes of spiritual and penal discipline.

1. PRIVATEERS, 1680–1744

WILLIAM DAMPIER, *A New Voyage Round the World* (1697–1703)

William Dampier (1652–1715) joined a crew of privateers in the Spanish Main and crossed the Isthmus of Darien to the Pacific, a wider field for plunder, in 1679. In his series of travel memoirs we read the gestation of a modern scientific sensibility within the older buccaneer tradition. After a botched raid on Guayaquil, on the Ecuadorean coast, Dampier sighs over 'Golden Dreams' of an era of private empire-building that is receding into the past. Dampier recorded detailed observations of the natural productions of the shores he visited, very much in the spirit of the typical institution of the new age, the Royal Society. While not the first European to make landfall on Australia, he gave the first account of it in English. Swift (as Jonathan Lamb has suggested) drew upon Dampier's resonantly negative evocation of New Holland for his account of Houyhnhnm-land and its degraded human inhabitants, the Yahoos.

[1684: the privateers' attempt on Guayaquil]

It was to this town of Guayaquil that we were bound, therefore we left our ships off Cape Blanco, and ran into the Bay of Guayaquil with our barque and canoes, steering in for the island Santa Clara, where we arrived the next day after we left our ships, and from thence we sent away two canoes the next evening to Point Arena. At this Point there are abundance of oysters, and other shellfish, as cockles and mussels; therefore the Indians of Puna often come hither to get these fish. Our canoes got over before day, and absconded in a creek, to wait for the coming of the Puna Indians. The next morning some of them, according to their custom, came thither on barque-logs, at the latter part of the ebb, and were all taken by our men. The next day, by their advice, the two watchmen of the Indian town Puna were taken by our men, and all its inhabitants, not one escaping. The next ebb they took a small barque laden with Quito-cloth. She came from Guayaquil that tide, and was bound to Lima, they having advice that we were gone off the coast, by the barque which I said we saw while we lay at the island Lobos. The master of this cloth-barque informed our men that there were 3 barques coming from Guayaquil, laden with Negroes: he said they would come from thence the next tide. The same tide of ebb that they took the cloth-barque, they sent a canoe to our barque, where the biggest part of the men were, to hasten them away with speed to the Indian town. The barque was now riding at Point Arena; and the next flood she came with all the men, and the rest of the canoes to Puna. The tide of flood being now far spent, we lay at this town till the last of the ebb, and then rowed away, leaving 5 men aboard our barque, who were ordered to lie still till 8 a clock the next morning, and not to fire at any boat or barque, but after that time they might fire at any object: for it was supposed that before that time we should be masters of Guayaquil. We had not rowed above 2 mile before we met and took one of the three barques laden with Negroes; the master of her said that the other two would come from Guayaquil the next tide of ebb. We cut her main-mast down, and left her at an anchor. It was now strong flood, and therefore we rowed with all speed towards the town, in hopes to get thither before the flood was down, but we found it farther than we did expect it to be, or else our canoes, being very full of men, did not row so fast as we would have them. The day broke when we were two leagues from the town, and then we had not above an hour's flood more; therefore our captains desired the Indian pilot to direct us to some creek where we might abscond all day, which was immediately done, and one canoe was sent toward Puna to our barque, to order them not to move nor fire till the next day. But she came too late to countermand the first orders; for the two barques before-mentioned, laden with Negroes, came from the town the last quarter of the evening tide, and lay in the river, close by the shore on one side, and we rowed upon the other side and missed them; neither did they see nor hear us. As soon as the flood was spent, the two barques weighed and went down with the ebb, towards Puna. Our barque, seeing them coming directly towards them, and both full of men, supposed that we by some accident had been destroyed, and that the two barques were manned with Spanish soldiers, and sent to take our ships, and therefore they fired 3 guns at them a league before they came near. The two Spanish barques immediately came to an anchor, and the masters got into their boats, and rowed for the shore; but our canoe that was sent from us took them both. The firing of these 3 guns made a great disorder among our advanced men, for most of them did believe they were heard at Guayaquil, and that therefore it could be no profit to lie still in the creek; but either row away to the town, or back again to our ships. It was now quarter ebb, therefore we could not move upwards, if we had been disposed so to do. At length Captain Davis said he would immediately land in the creek where they lay, and march directly to the town, if but 40 men would accompany him: and without saying more words, he landed among the mangroves in the marshes. Those that were so minded followed him, to the number of 40 or 50. Captain Swan lay still with the rest of the party in the creek, for they thought it impossible to do any good that way. Captain Davis and his men were absent about 4 hours, and then returned all wet, and quite tired, and could not find any passage out into the firm land. He had been so far that he almost despaired of getting back again: for a man cannot pass through those red mangroves but with very much labour. When Captain Davis was returned, we concluded to be going towards the town the beginning of the next flood; and if we found that the town was alarmed, we purposed to return again without attempting anything there. As soon as it was flood we rowed away, and passed by the island through the N.E. channel, which is the narrowest. There are so many stumps in the river, that it is very dangerous passing in the night (and that is the time we always take for such attempts) for the river runs very swift, and one of our canoes stuck on a stump, and had certainly overset, if she had not been immediately rescued by others. When we were come almost to the end of the island, there was a musket fired at us out of the bushes on the main. We then had the town open before us, and presently saw lighted torches, or candles, all the town over; whereas before the gun was fired there was but one light: therefore we now concluded we were discovered. Yet many of our men said, that it was a Holy-day the next day, as it was indeed, and that therefore the Spaniards were making fireworks, which they often do in the night against such times. We rowed therefore a little farther, and found firm land, and Captain Davis pitched his canoe ashore and landed with his men. Captain Swan, and most of his men, did not think it convenient to attempt anything, seeing the town was alarmed; but at last, being upbraided with cowardice, Captain Swan and his men landed also. The place where we landed was about 2 miles from the town: it was all overgrown with woods so thick that we could not march through in the night; and therefore we sat down, waiting for the light of the day. We had two Indian pilots with us; one that had been with us a month, who having received some abuses from a gentleman of Guayaquil, to be revenged offered his service to us, and we found him very faithful. The other was taken by us not above 2 or 3 days before, and he seemed to be as willing as the other to assist us. This latter was led by one of Captain Davis's men, who showed himself very forward to go to the town, and upbraided others with faint-heartedness. Yet this man (as he afterwards confessed) notwithstanding his courage, privately cut the string that the guide was made fast with, and let him go to the town by himself, not caring to follow him; but when he thought the guide was got far enough from us, he cried out that the pilot was gone, and that somebody had cut the cord that tied him. This put every man in a moving posture to seek the Indian, but all in vain; and our consternation was great, being in the dark and among woods; so the design was wholly dashed, for not a man after that had the heart to speak of going farther. Here we stayed till day, and then rowed out into the middle of the river, where we had a fair view of the town; which, as I said before, makes a very pleasant prospect. We lay still about half an hour, being a mile, or something better, from the town. They did not fire one gun at us, nor we at them. Thus our design on Guayaquil failed: yet Captain Townley and Captain François Gronet took it a little while after this. When we had taken a full view of the town, we rowed over the river, where we went ashore to a beef estancion or farm, and killed a cow, which we dressed and ate. We stayed there till the evening tide of ebb, and then rowed down the river, and the 9th day in the morning arrived at Puna. In our way thither we went aboard the 3 barques laden with Negroes that lay at their anchor in the river, and carried the barques away with us. There were 1,000 Negroes in the 3 barques, all lusty young men and women. When we came to Puna, we sent a canoe to Point Arena, to see if the ships were come thither. The 12th day she returned again, with tidings that they were both there at anchor. Therefore in the afternoon we all went aboard of our ships, and carried the cloth-barque with us, and about 40 of the stoutest Negro men, leaving their 3 barques with the rest; and out of these also Captain Davis and Captain Swan chose about 14 or 15 apiece, and turned the rest ashore.

There was never a greater opportunity put into the hands of men to enrich themselves than we had, to have gone with these Negroes, and settled ourselves at Santa Maria, on the Isthmus of Darien, and employed them in getting gold out of the mines there. Which might have been done with ease: for about 6 months before this, Captain Harris (who was now with us) coming over land from the North Seas, with his body of privateers, had routed the Spaniards away from the town and gold-mines of Santa Maria, so that they had never attempted to settle there again since. Add to this, that the Indian neighbourhood, who were mortal enemies to the Spaniards, and had been flushed by their successes against them, through the assistance of the privateers, for several years, were our fast friends, and ready to receive and assist us. We had, as I have said 1,000 Negroes to work for us, we had 200 tons of flour that lay at the Galapagos, there was the river of Santa Maria, where we could careen and fit our ships; and might fortify the mouth, so that if all the strength the Spaniards have in Peru had come against us, we could have kept them out. If they lay with guard-ships of strength to keep us in, yet we had a great country to live in, and a great nation of Indians that were our friends. Beside, which was the principal thing, we had the North Seas to befriend us; from whence we could export ourselves, or effects, or import goods or men to our assistance; for in a short time we should have had assistance from all parts of the West Indies; many thousands of privateers from Jamaica and the French islands especially would have flocked over to us; and long before this time we might have been masters not only of those mines (the richest gold-mines ever yet found in America) but of all the coast as high as Quito. And much more than I say might then probably have been done.

But these may seem to the reader but golden dreams. To leave them therefore: the 13th day we sailed from Point Arena towards Plata, to seek our barque that was sent to the island Lobos, in search of Captain Eaton.

[1688: natives of New Holland]

New Holland is a very large tract of land. It is not yet determined whether it is an island or a main continent; but I am certain that it joins neither to Asia, Africa, nor America. This part of it that we saw is all low even land, with sandy banks against the sea; only the points are rocky, and so are some of the islands in this bay.

The land is of a dry sandy soil, destitute of water, except you make wells; yet producing divers sorts of trees; but the woods are not thick, nor the trees very big. Most of the trees that we saw are dragon-trees, as we supposed; and these too are the largest trees of any there. They are about the bigness of our large apple-trees, and about the same height: and the rind is blackish, and somewhat rough. The leaves are of a dark colour; the gum distils out of the knots or cracks that are in the bodies of the trees. We compared it with some gum dragon, or dragon's blood, that was aboard, and it was of the same colour and taste. The other sorts of trees were not known by any of us. There was pretty long grass growing under the trees; but it was very thin. We saw no trees that bore fruit or berries.

We saw no sort of animal, nor any track of beast, but once; and that seemed to be the tread of a beast as big as a great mastiff dog. Here are a few small landbirds, but none bigger than a blackbird; and but few seafowls. Neither is the sea very plentifully stored with fish, unless you reckon the manatee and turtle as such. Of these creatures there is plenty; but they are extraordinary shy; though the inhabitants cannot trouble them much, having neither boats nor iron.

The inhabitants of this country are the miserablest people in the world. The Hodmadods of Monomatapa,* though a nasty people, yet for wealth are gentlemen to these; who have no houses and skin garments, sheep, poultry, and fruits of the earth, ostrich eggs, etc. as the Hodmadods have: and setting aside their human shape, they differ but little from brutes. They are tall, straight-bodied, and thin, with small, long limbs. They have great heads, round foreheads, and great brows. Their eyelids are always half closed, to keep the flies out of their eyes, they being so troublesome here, that no fanning will keep them from coming to one's face; and without the assistance of both hands to keep them off, they will creep into one's nostrils, and mouth too, if the lips are not shut very close: so that from their infancy being thus annoyed with these insects, they do never open their eyes as other people: and therefore they cannot see far, unless they hold up their heads, as if they were looking at somewhat over them.

They have great bottle noses, pretty full lips, and wide mouths. The two fore-teeth of their upper jaw are wanting in all of them, men and women, old and young; whether they draw them out, I know not; neither have they any beards. They are long visaged, and of a very unpleasing aspect, having no one graceful feature in their faces. Their hair is black, short and curled, like that of the Negroes; and not long and lank like the common Indians. The colour of their skins, both of their faces and the rest of their body, is coal black, like that of the Negroes of Guinea.

They have no sort of clothes, but a piece of the rind of a tree tied like a girdle about their waists, and a handful of long grass, or 3 or 4 small green boughs full of leaves, thrust under their girdle, to cover their nakedness.

They have no houses, but lie in the open air, without any covering, the earth being their bed, and the heaven their canopy. Whether they cohabit one man to one woman, or promiscuously, I know not: but they do live in companies, 20 or 30 men, women, and children together. Their only food is a small sort of fish, which they get by making weirs of stone across little coves or branches of the sea; every tide bringing in the small fish, and there leaving them for a prey to these people who constantly attend there to search for them at low water. This small fry I take to be the top of their fishery. They have no instruments to catch great fish, should they come; and such seldom stay to be left behind at low water; nor could we catch any fish with our hooks and lines all the while we lay there. In other places at low water they seek for cockles, mussels, and periwinkles. Of these shellfish there are fewer still: so that their chiefest dependence is upon what the sea leaves in their weirs; which, be it much or little they gather up, and march to the places of their abode. There the old people that are not able to stir abroad by reason of their age, and the tender infants, wait their return; and what Providence has bestowed on them, they presently broil on the coals, and eat it in common. Sometimes they get as many fish as makes them a plentiful banquet; and at other times they scarce get everyone a taste. But be it little or much that they get, everyone has his part, as well the young and tender, the old and feeble, who are not able to go abroad, as the strong and lusty. When they have eaten they lie down till the next low water, and then all that are able march out, be it night or day, rain or shine, 'tis all one; they must attend the weirs, or else they must fast, for the earth affords them no food at all. There is neither herb, root, pulse nor any sort of grain for them to eat, that we saw; nor any sort of bird or beast that they can catch, having no instruments wherewithal to do so.

I did not perceive that they did worship anything. These poor creatures have a sort of weapon to defend their weir, or fight with their enemies, if they have any that will interfere with their poor fishery. They did at first endeavour with their weapons to frighten us, who lying ashore deterred them from one of their fishing-places. Some of them had wooden swords, others had a sort of lances. The sword is a piece of wood shaped somewhat like a cutlass. The lance is a long straight pole sharp at one end, and hardened afterwards by heat. I saw no iron, nor any other sort of metal; therefore it is probable they use stone-hatchets, as some Indians in America do.

How they get their fire I know not; but probably, as Indians do, out of wood. I have seen the Indians of Bon-Airy* do it, and have my self tried the experiment: They take a flat piece of wood that is pretty soft, and make a small dent in one side of it, then they take another hard round stick, about the bigness of one's little finger, and sharpening it at one end like a pencil, they put that sharp end in the hole or dent of the flat soft piece, and then rubbing or twirling the hard piece between the palms of their hands, they drill the soft piece till it smokes, and at last takes fire.

These people speak somewhat through the throat; but we could not understand one word that they said. We anchored, as I said before, January the 5th, and seeing men walking on the shore, we presently sent a canoe to get some acquaintance with them: for we were in hopes to get some provision among them. But the inhabitants, seeing our boat coming, ran away and hid themselves. We searched afterwards 3 days in hopes to find their houses; but found none: yet we saw many places where they had made fires. At last, being out of hopes to find their habitations, we searched no farther; but left a great many toys ashore, in such places where we thought that they would come. In all our search we found no water but old wells on the sandy bays.

WOODES ROGERS, *A Cruising Voyage Round the World* (1712)

Dampier sailed on the ship that marooned Scottish sailor Alexander Selkirk (1676–1721) on Juan Fernandez, off the southern coast of Chile, in 1704. He was back again, as pilot, when the privateer captain Woodes Rogers (1679–1732) rescued Selkirk four years later.

[2 February 1709: the rescue of Alexander Selkirk]

We sent our yall* ashore about noon, with Captain Dover, Mr Frye, and six men, all armed; meanwhile we and the *Dutchess* kept turning to get in, and such heavy flaws* came off the land that we were forced to let fly our topsail-sheet, keeping all hands to stand by our sails, for fear of the wind's carrying 'em away: but when the flaws were gone, we had little or no wind. These flaws proceeded from the land, which is very high in the middle of the island. Our boat did not return, so we sent our pinnace, with the men armed, to see what was the occasion of the yall's stay; for we were afraid that the Spaniards had a garrison there, and might have seized 'em. We put out a signal for our boat, and the *Dutchess* showed a French Ensign. Immediately our pinnace returned from the shore, and brought abundance of craw-fish, with a man clothed in goat-skins, who looked wilder than the first owners of them. He had been on the island four years and four months, being left there by Captain Stradling in the Cinque-Ports; his name was Alexander Selkirk, a Scotch man who had been Master of the *Cinque-Ports*, a ship that came here last with Captain Dampier, who told me that this was the best man in her; so I immediately agreed with him to be a mate on board our ship. 'Twas he that made the fire last night when he saw our ships, which he judged to be English. During his stay here, he saw several ships pass by, but only two came in to anchor. As he went to view them, he found 'em to be Spaniards, and retired from 'em; upon which they shot at him. Had they been French, he would have submitted; but chose to risk his dying alone on the island, rather than fall into the hands of the Spaniards in these parts, because he apprehended they would murder him, or make a slave of him in the mines, for he feared they would spare no stranger that might be capable of discovering the South-Sea. The Spaniards had landed, before he knew what they were, and they came so near him that he had much ado to escape: for they not only shot at him but pursued him into the woods, where he climbed to the top of a tree, at the foot of which they made water, and killed several goats just by, but went off again without discovering him. He told us that he was born at Largo in the county of Fife in Scotland, and was bred a sailor from his youth. The reason of his being left here was a difference betwixt him and his Captain; which, together with the ship's being leaky, made him willing rather to stay here, than go along with him at first; and when he was at last willing, the Captain would not receive him. He had been in the island before to wood and water, when two of the ship's company were left upon it for six months till the ship returned, being chased thence by two French South-Sea ships.

He had with him his clothes and bedding, with a firelock, some powder, bullets, and tobacco, a hatchet, a knife, a kettle, a Bible, some practical pieces, and his mathematical instruments and books. He diverted and provided for himself as well as he could; but for the first eight months had much ado to bear up against melancholy, and the terror of being left alone in such a desolate place. He built two huts with pimento trees, covered them with long grass, and lined them with the skins of goats, which he killed with his gun as he wanted, so long as his powder lasted, which was but a pound; and that being near spent, he got fire by rubbing two sticks of pimento wood together upon his knee. In the lesser hut, at some distance from the other, he dressed his victuals, and in the larger he slept, and employed himself in reading, singing psalms, and praying; so that he said he was a better Christian while in this solitude than ever he was before, or than, he was afraid, he should ever be again. At first he never ate anything till hunger constrained him, partly for grief and partly for want of bread and salt; nor did he go to bed till he could watch no longer: the pimento wood, which burnt very clear, served him both for firing and candle, and refreshed him with its fragrant smell.

He might have had fish enough, but could not eat 'em for want of salt, because they occasioned a looseness; except crawfish, which are there as large as our lobsters, and very good. These he sometimes boiled, and at other times broiled, as he did his goat's flesh, of which he made very good broth, for they are not so rank as ours; he kept an account of 500 that he killed while there, and caught as many more, which he marked on the ear and let go. When his powder failed, he took them by speed of foot; for his way of living and continual exercise of walking and running cleared him of all gross humours, so that he ran with wonderful swiftness through the woods and up the rocks and hills, as we perceived when we employed him to catch goats for us. We had a bulldog, which we sent with several of our nimblest runners, to help him in catching goats; but he distanced and tired both the dog and the men, catched the goats, and brought 'em to us on his back. He told us that his agility in pursuing a goat had once like to have cost him his life; he pursued it with so much eagerness that he catched hold of it on the brink of a precipice, of which he was not aware, the bushes having hid it from him; so that he fell with the goat down the said precipice a great height, and was so stunned and bruised with the fall that he narrowly escaped with his life, and when he came to his senses, found the goat dead under him. He lay there about 24 hours, and was scarce able to crawl to his hut, which was about a mile distant, or to stir abroad again in ten days.

He came at last to relish his meat well enough without salt or bread, and in the season had plenty of good turnips, which had been sowed there by Captain Dampier's men, and have now overspread some acres of ground. He had enough of good cabbage from the cabbage-trees, and seasoned his meat with the fruit of the pimento trees, which is the same as the Jamaica pepper, and smells deliciously. He found there also a black pepper called *Malagita*, which was very good to expel wind, and against griping of the guts.

He soon wore out all his shoes and clothes by running through the woods; and at last being forced to shift without them, his feet became so hard that he ran everywhere without annoyance: and it was some time before he could wear shoes after we found him; for not being used to any so long, his feet swelled when he came first to wear 'em again.

After he had conquered his melancholy, he diverted himself sometimes by cutting his name on the trees, and the time of his being left and continuance there. He was at first much pestered with cats and rats, that had bred in great numbers from some of each species which had got ashore from ships that put in there to wood and water. The rats gnawed his feet and clothes while asleep, which obliged him to cherish the cats with his goat's-flesh; by which many of them became so tame that they would lie about him in hundreds, and soon delivered him from the rats. He likewise tamed some kids, and to divert himself would now and then sing and dance with them and his cats: so that by the care of Providence and vigour of his youth, being now but about 30 years old, he came at last to conquer all the inconveniences of his solitude, and to be very easy. When his clothes wore out, he made himself a coat and cap of goat-skins, which he stitched together with little thongs of the same, that he cut with his knife. He had no other needle but a nail; and when his knife was wore to the back, he made others as well as he could of some iron hoops that were left ashore, which he beat thin and ground upon stones. Having some linen cloth by him, he sewed himself shirts with a nail, and stitched 'em with the worsted of his old stockings, which he pulled out on purpose. He had his last shirt on when we found him in the island.

At his first coming on board us, he had so much forgot his language for want of use, that we could scarce understand him, for he seemed to speak his words by halves. We offered him a dram, but he would not touch it, having drank nothing but water since his being there, and 'twas some time before he could relish our victuals.

[Rogers narrates other cases of marooned seamen.]

But whatever there is in these stories, this of Mr Selkirk I know to be true; and his behaviour afterwards gives me reason to believe the account he gave me how he spent his time, and bore up under such an affliction, in which nothing but the Divine Providence could have supported any man. By this one may see that solitude and retirement from the world is not such an unsufferable state of life as most men imagine, especially when people are fairly called or thrown into it unavoidably, as this man was; who in all probability must otherwise have perished in the seas, the ship which left him being cast away not long after, and few of the company escaped. We may perceive by this story the truth of the maxim that necessity is the mother of invention, since he found means to supply his wants in a very natural manner, so as to maintain his life, though not so conveniently, yet as effectually as we are able to do with the help of all our arts and society. It may likewise instruct us, how much a plain and temperate way of living conduces to the health of the body and the vigour of the mind, both which we are apt to destroy by excess and plenty, especially of strong liquor, and the variety as well as the nature of our meat and drink: for this man, when he came to our ordinary method of diet and life, though he was sober enough, lost much of his strength and agility. But I must quit these reflections, which are more proper for a philosopher and divine than a mariner, and return to my own subject.

RICHARD WALTER AND BENJAMIN ROBINS, *A Voyage Round the World in the Years MCCCL, I, II, III, IV, by George Anson* (1748; ed. Glyndwr Williams, 1974)

George Anson (1697–1762) is a transitional figure: commander of the first official naval expedition into the Pacific (1740–4), and effectively the last of the privateers. Ordered to molest Spanish interests along the western littoral of South America during the War of Jenkins' Ear, Anson sacked Paita and captured the Acapulco treasure-galleon. The prize redeemed what had threatened to be a disaster: by the time Anson reached Juan Fernandez he had lost half of his squadron of six ships to the stormy seas around Cape Horn and two-thirds of his men (1,400 out of 2,000) to scurvy. A few decades later Captain Cook would claim to have prevented scurvy by dosing his crew with malt and vinegar; it was not until the nineteenth century that the disease was diagnosed as a vitamin C deficiency, caused by a lack of fresh fruit and vegetables. In the narrative of Anson's voyage (compiled by Richard Walter and Benjamin Robins) the hardbitten style of Dampier and Rogers gives way to a polite, more plausibly civilized manner.

[April–June 1741: the ravages of scurvy]

Soon after our passing Straits Le Maire, the scurvy began to make its appearance amongst us; and our long continuance at sea, the fatigue we underwent, and the various disappointments we met with, had occasioned its spreading of such a degree, that at the latter end of April there were but few on board, who were not in some degree afflicted with it, and in that month no less than forty-three died of it on board the *Centurion*. But though we thought that the distemper had then risen to an extraordinary height, and were willing to hope that as we advanced to the northward its malignity would abate, yet we found, on the contrary, that in the month of May we lost near double that number. And as we did not get to land till the middle of June, the mortality went on increasing, and the disease extended itself so prodigiously, that after the loss of above two hundred men, we could not at last muster more than six foremast men in a watch capable of duty.

This disease so frequently attending all long voyages, and so particularly destructive to us, is surely the most singular and unaccountable of any that affects the human body. For its symptoms are inconstant and innumerable, and its progress and effects extremely irregular; for scarcely any two persons have the same complaints, and where there has been found some conformity in the symptoms, the order of their appearance has been totally different. However, though it frequently puts on the form of many other diseases, and is therefore not to be described by any exclusive and infallible criterions; yet there are some symptoms which are more general than the rest, and therefore, occurring the oftenest, deserve a more particular enumeration. These common appearances are large discoloured spots dispersed over the whole surface of the body, swelled legs, putrid gums, and above all, an extraordinary lassitude of the whole body, especially after any exercise, however inconsiderable; and this lassitude at last degenerates into a proneness of swoon on the least exertion of strength, or even on the least motion.

This disease is likewise usually attended with a strange dejection of the spirits, and with shiverings, tremblings, and a disposition to be seized with the most dreadful terrors on the slightest accident. Indeed, it was most remarkable, in all our reiterated experience of this malady, that whatever discouraged our people, or at any time damped their hopes, never failed to add new vigour to the distemper; for it usually killed those who were in the last stages of it, and confined those to their hammocks, who were before capable of some kind of duty, so that it seemed as if alacrity of mind, and sanguine thoughts, were no contemptible preservatives from its fatal malignity.

But it is not easy to complete the long roll of the various concomitants of this disease; for it often produced putrid fevers, pleurisies, the jaundice, and violent rheumatic pains, and sometimes it occasioned an obstinate costiveness, which was generally attended with a difficulty of breathing; and this was esteemed the most deadly of all the scorbutic symptoms. At other times the whole body, but more especially the legs, were subject to ulcers of the worst kind, attended with rotten bones, and such a luxuriancy of fungous flesh, as yielded to no remedy. But a most extraordinary circumstance, and what would be scarcely credible upon any single evidence, is that the scars of wounds which had been for many years healed, were forced open again by this virulent distemper. Of this, there was a remarkable instance in one of the invalids on board the *Centurion*, who had been wounded above fifty years before at the battle of the Boyne; for though he was cured soon after, and had continued well for a great number of years past, yet on his being attacked by the scurvy, his wounds, in the progress of his disease, broke out afresh, and appeared as if they had never been healed: nay, what is still more astonishing, the callus of a broken bone, which had been completely formed for a long time, was found to be hereby dissolved, and the fracture seemed as if it had never been consolidated. Indeed, the effects of this disease were in almost every instance wonderful; for many of our people, though confined to their hammocks, appeared to have no inconsiderable share of health, for they ate and drank heartily, were cheerful, and talked with much seeming vigour, and with a loud strong tone of voice; and yet on their being the least moved, though it was only from one part of the ship to the other, and that in their hammocks, they have immediately expired; and others, who have confided in their seeming strength, and have resolved to get out of their hammocks, have died before they could well reach the deck; and it was no uncommon thing for those who were able to walk the deck, and to do some kind of duty, to drop down dead in an instant, on any endeavours to act with their utmost vigour, many of our people having perished in this manner during the course of this voyage.

With this terrible disease we struggled the greatest part of the time of our beating round Cape Horn; and though it did not then rage with its utmost violence, yet we buried no less than forty-three men on board the *Centurion*, in the month of April, as has been already observed, but we still entertained hopes, that when we should have once secured our passage round the Cape, we should put a period to this, and all the other evils which had so constantly pursued us.

[June 1741: landfall on Juan Fernandez]

On the 9th of June, at day break, as is mentioned in the preceding chapter, we first descried the island of Juan Fernandez; bearing N. by E. ½ E, at eleven or twelve leagues distance. And though, on this first view, it appeared to be a very mountainous place, extremely ragged and irregular; yet as it was land and the land we sought for, it was to us a most agreeable sight: for at this place only we could hope to put a period to those terrible calamities we had so long struggled with, which had already swept away above half our crew, and which, had we continued a few days longer at sea, would inevitably have completed our destruction. For we were by this time reduced to so helpless a condition that, out of two hundred and odd men which remained alive, we could not, taking all our watches together, muster hands enough to work the ship on an emergency, though we included the officers, their servants, and the boys.

The wind being northerly when we first made the island, we kept plying all that day, and the next night, in order to get in with the land; and wearing the ship in the middle watch, we had a melancholy instance of the almost incredible debility of our people; for the lieutenant could muster no more than two quarter-masters, and six foremast men capable of working; so that without the assistance of the officers, servants and the boys, it might have proved impossible for us to have reached the island, after we had got sight of it; and even with this assistance they were two hours in trimming the sails. To so wretched a condition was a sixty-gun ship reduced, which had passed Straits Le Maire but three months before, with between four and five hundred men, almost all of them in health and vigour.

However, on the 10th in the afternoon, we got under the lee of the island, and kept ranging along it, at about two miles distance, in order to look out for the proper anchorage, which was described to be in a bay on the north side. And now being nearer in with the shore, we could discover that the broken craggy precipices, which had appeared so unpromising at a distance, were far from barren, being in most places covered with woods; and that between them there were everywhere interspersed the finest valley, clothed with a most beautiful verdure, and watered with numerous streams and cascades, no valley, of any extent, being unprovided of its proper rill. The water too, as we afterwards found, was not inferior to any we had ever tasted, and was constantly clear. So that the aspect of this country would, at all times, have been extremely delightful, but in our distressed situation, languishing as we were for the land and its vegetable productions (an inclination constantly attending every stage of the sea-scurvy), it is scarcely credible with what eagerness and transport we viewed the shore, and with how much impatience we longed for the greens and other refreshments which were then in sight, and particularly for the water, for of this we had been confined to a very sparing allowance for a considerable time, and had then but five tons remaining on board. Those only who have endured a long series of thirst, and who can readily recall the desire and agitation

which the ideas alone of springs and brooks have at that time raised
in them, can judge of the emotion with which we eyed a large cascade of the most transparent water, which poured itself from a rock
near a hundred feet high into the sea, at a small distance from the
ship. Even those amongst the diseased, who were not in the very last
stages of the distemper, though they had been long confined to their
hammocks, exerted the small remains of strength that was left them,
and crawled up to the deck to feast themselves with this reviving
prospect. Thus we coasted the shore, fully employed in the contemplation of this diversified landscape, which improved upon us the
farther we advanced. But at last the night closed upon us, before we
had satisfied ourselves which was the proper bay to anchor in; and
therefore we resolved to keep in soundings all night (we having then
from sixty-four to seventy fathom) and to send our boat next morning to discover the road: however, the current shifted in the night,
and set us so near the land that we were obliged to let go the best
bower in fifty-six fathom, not half a mile from the shore. At four in
the morning, the cutter was dispatched with our third lieutenant to
find out the bay we were in search of, who returned again at noon
with the boat laden with seals and grass; for though the island
abounded with better vegetables, yet the boats-crew, in their short
stay, had not met with them; and they well knew that even grass
would prove a dainty, and indeed it was all soon and eagerly
devoured. The seals too were considered as fresh provision; but as
yet were not much admired, though they grew afterwards into more
repute. For what rendered them less valuable at this juncture was the
prodigious quantity of excellent fish, which the people on board had
taken, during the absence of the boat.

The cutter, in this expedition, had discovered the bay where we
intended to anchor, which we found was to the westward of our
present station; and, the next morning, the weather proving favourable, we endeavoured to weigh, in order to proceed thither. But
though, on this occasion, we mustered all the strength we could,
obliging even the sick, who were scarce able to keep on their legs, to
assist us; yet the capstan was so weakly manned, that it was near four
hours before we hove the cable right up and down; after which, with
our utmost efforts, and with many surges and some purchases we
made use of to increase our power, we found ourselves incapable of
starting the anchor from the ground. However, at noon, as a fresh

gale blew towards the bay, we were induced to set the sails, which fortunately tripped the anchor; on which we steered along shore, till we came abreast of the point that forms the eastern part of the bay. On the opening of the bay, the wind, that had befriended us thus far, shifted and blew from thence in squalls; but by means of the headway we had got, we luffed* close in, till the anchor brought us up in fifty-six fathom. Soon after we had thus got to our new berth, we discovered a sail, which we made no doubt was one of our squadron; and on its nearer approach, we found it to be the *Tryal* sloop. We immediately sent some of our hands on board her, by whose assistance she was brought to an anchor between us and the land. We soon found that the sloop had not been exempted from those calamities which we had so severely felt; for her Commander, Captain Saunders, waiting on the Commodore, informed him, that out of his small complement, he had buried thirty-four of his men; and those that remained were so universally afflicted with the scurvy that only himself, his Lieutenant, and three of his men were able to stand by the sails. The *Tryal* came to an anchor within us, on the 12th, about noon, and we carried our hawsers on board her, in order to moor ourselves nearer in shore; but the wind coming off the land in violent gusts, prevented our mooring in the berth we intended, especially as our principal attention was now employed on business rather of more importance; for we were now extremely occupied in sending on shore materials to raise tents for the reception of the sick, who died apace on board, and doubtless the distemper was considerably augmented by the stench and filthiness in which they lay; for the number of the diseased was so great, and so few could be spared from the necessary duty of the sails to look after them, that it was impossible to avoid a great relaxation in the article of cleanliness, which had rendered the ship extremely loathsome between decks. But notwithstanding our desire of freeing the sick from their hateful situation, and their own extreme impatience to get on shore, we had not hands enough to prepare the tents for their reception before the 16th; but on that and the two following days we sent them all on shore, amounting to a hundred and sixty-seven persons, besides at least a dozen who died in the boats, on their being exposed to the fresh air. The greatest part of our sick were so infirm that we were obliged to carry them out of the ship in their hammocks, and to convey them afterwards in the same manner from the water-side to their tents, over a stony beach. This was a work of considerable fatigue to the few who were healthy, and therefore the Commodore, with his accustomed humanity, not only assisted herein with his own labour, but obliged his officers, without distinction, to give their helping hand. The extreme weakness of our sick may in some measure be collected from the numbers who died after they had got on shore; for it had generally been found that the land, and the refreshments it produces, very soon recover most stages of the sea-scurvy; and we flattered ourselves that those who had not perished on this first exposure to the open air, but had lived to be placed in their tents, would have been speedily restored to their health and vigour. But, to our great mortification, it was near twenty days after their landing before the mortality was tolerably ceased; and for the first ten or twelve days, we buried rarely less than six each day, and many of those who survived recovered by very slow and insensible degrees. Indeed, those who were well enough at their first getting on shore to creep out of their tents, and crawl about, were soon relieved, and recovered their health and strength in a very short time; but in the rest, the disease seemed to have acquired a degree of inveteracy which was altogether without example.

2. THE COOK EXPEDITIONS, 1768–1780

James Cook (1728–79), the son of a Yorkshire farm labourer, rose through the ranks of the Royal Navy. Appointed lieutenant of the *Endeavour*, he led the first of three famous expeditions to the Pacific (1768–71). Sailing with the ostensible purpose of observing the transit of Venus across the sun, Cook carried secret orders to verify rumours of a new continent south of New Holland. In all three voyages Cook made a base at Tahiti, which had been visited in 1767 by Samuel Wallis in the *Dolphin* and shortly afterwards by a French expedition under Louis-Antoine de Bougainville. Bougainville, in particular, established the myth of Tahiti as the 'New Cytheria', an aphrodisiac island paradise.

The journals of Cook and Joseph Banks were worked up into an official account of the first voyage by John Hawkesworth in 1773—a compilation that Cook himself found unsatisfactory for its interpolations and glosses. Cook kept journals of his second and third voyages with a view to publishing them himself; after his death the official record of the last voyage was compiled by his second lieutenant James King. We reprint extracts from

J. C. Beaglehole's four-volume edition for the Hakluyt Society of the original *Journals of Captain James Cook on his Voyages of Discovery*.

JAMES COOK, *The Voyage of the Endeavour, 1768–1771*, ed. J. C. Beaglehole (Cambridge, 1955)

Upon arrival at 'King George's Island' (Wallis's name; Cook soon uses the native 'Otaheite') Cook draws up rules of conduct to regulate traffic with the natives, only to see this orderly economy subverted by sexual promiscuity and theft. If Cook and his party bask in hospitable Tahiti, despite such irritants, their encounters with the warlike inhabitants of New Zealand soon fray into violence. Cook sanitized his account of the massacre at Poverty Bay; desperate to find interpreters after a series of clashes with the Maori, he resolved to take hostages—with bloody results. Making his way up the Australian coast the following spring, warily observed by native peoples, Cook names places and claims the territory for the crown.

[13 April 1769: arrival at Tahiti]

As our stay at this place was not likely to be very short, I thought it very necessary that some order should be observed in trafficking with the natives: that such merchandise as we had on board for that purpose might continue to bear a proper value, and not leave it to everyone's own particular fancy which could not fail to bring on confusion and quarrels between us and the natives, and would infallibly lessen the value of such articles as we had to traffic with. In order to prevent this the following rules were ordered to be observed, viz.

RULES to be observed by every person in or belonging to His Majesty's barque the Endeavour, for the better establishing a regular and uniform trade for provisions etc. with the inhabitants of George's Island.

1. *To endeavour by every fair means to cultivate a friendship with the natives and to treat them with all imaginable humanity.*

2. *A proper person or persons will be appointed to trade with the natives for all manner of provisions, fruit, and other productions of the earth; and no officer or seaman, or other person belonging to the ship, excepting such as are so appointed, shall trade or offer to trade for any sort of provisions, fruit, or other productions of the earth unless they have my leave so to do.*

3. *Every person employed ashore on any duty whatsoever is strictly to attend to the same, and if by neglect he loseth any of his arms or working tools, or suffers them to be stole, the full value thereof will be charged against his pay according to the custom of the Navy in such cases, and he shall receive such farther punishment as the nature of the offence may deserve.*

4. *The same penalty will be inflicted on every person who is found to embezzle, trade or offer to trade with any part of the ship's stores of what nature soever.*

5. *No sort of iron, or anything that is made of iron, or any sort of cloth or other useful or necessary articles are to be given in exchange for anything but provisions.*

J. C.

[May–June 1769: Tahiti]

FRIDAY, 12 MAY. Cloudy weather with showers of rain. This morning a man and two young women with some others came to the Fort* whom we had not seen before: and as their manner of introducing themselves was a little uncommon I shall insert it: Mr Banks was as usual at the gate of the Fort trading with the people, when he was told that some strangers were coming and therefore stood to receive them. The company had with them about a dozen young plantain trees and some other small plants; these they laid down about 20 feet from Mr Banks. The people then made a lane between him and them; when this was done the man (who appeared to be only a servant to the 2 women) brought the young plantains singly, together with some of the other plants, and gave them to Mr Banks, and at the delivery of each pronounced a short sentence, which we understood not; after he had thus disposed of all his plantain trees he took several pieces of cloth and spread them on the ground, one of the young women then stepped upon the cloth and with as much innocency as one could possibly conceive, exposed herself entirely naked from the waist downwards; in this manner she turned herself once or twice round, I am not certain which, then stepped off the cloth and dropped down her clothes; more cloth was then spread upon the former and she again performed the same ceremony; the cloth was then rolled up and given to Mr Banks and the two young women went and embraced him, which ended the ceremony.

SATURDAY, 13 MAY. Nothing worthy of note happened during the day; in the night one of the natives attempted to get into the Fort by climbing over the walls but being discovered by the sentinels he made off; the iron and iron tools daily in use at the armourers' forge are temptations that these people cannot possibly withstand.

SUNDAY, 14 MAY. This day we performed divine service in one of the tents in the Fort where several of the natives attended and behaved with great decency the whole time: this day closed with an odd scene at the gate of the Fort where a young fellow above 6 feet high lay with a little girl about 10 or 12 years of age publicly before several of our people and a number of the natives. What makes me mention this, is because it appeared to be done more from custom than lewdness,* for there were several women present particularly Obarea* and several others of the better sort and these were so far from showing the least disapprobation that they instructed the girl how she should act her part, who young as she was, did not seem to want it.

SUNDAY, 28 MAY. Winds southerly and clear weather. This morning, my self, Mr Banks and Dr Solander* set out in the pinnace to pay Tootaha* a visit who had moved from Apparra to the SW part of the island. What induced us to make him this visit was a message we had received from him some days ago importing that if we would go to him he would give us several hogs. We had no great faith in this yet we was resolved to try, and set out accordingly; it was night before we reached the place where he was and as we had left the boat about half way behind us we were obliged to take up our quarters with him for the night. The Chief received us in a very friendly manner and a pig was ordered to be killed and dressed for supper, but we saved his life for the present, thinking it would do us more service in another place and we supped on fruit and what else we could get: here was along with the Chief Obarea and many more that we knowed, they all seemed to be travellers like ourselves, for neither the canoes they had along with them nor the houses where they were were sufficient to contain the one half of them. We were in all six of us and after supper began to look out for lodgings. Mr Banks went to one place, Dr Solander to another, while I and the other three went to a third; we all of us took as much care of the little we had about us as possible, knowing very well what sort of people we were among, yet notwithstanding all the care we took before 12 o'clock the most of us had lost something or other. For my own part I had my stockings taken from under my head and yet I am certain that I was not asleep the whole time. Obarea took charge of Mr Banks's things and yet they were stolen from her as she pretended. Tootaha was acquainted with what had happened, I believe by Obarea herself, and both he and her made some stir about it but this was all mere show and ended in nothing; a little time after this Tootaha came to the hut where I and those with me lay and entertained us with a concert of music, consisting of three drums, four flutes and singing; this lasted about an hour and then they retired; the music and singing was so much of a piece that I was very glad when it was over. We stayed with them till near noon the next day in hopes of getting some of our things again, and likewise some hogs but we were at last obliged to come away with the one we had saved out of the fire last night, and a promise from Tootaha that he would come to the ship in a day or two with more and bring with him the things that we had lost, a promise that we had no reason to expect he will fulfil. Thus ended our visit and we got to the Fort late in the evening.

WEDNESDAY, 14 JUNE. Between 2 and 4 o'clock this morning one of the natives stole out of the Fort an iron rake made use of for the oven; it happened to be set up against the wall and by that means was visible from the outside and had been seen by them in the evening as a man had been seen lurking about the Fort some hours before the thing was missed. I was informed by some others of the natives that he watched an opportunity when the sentinel's back was turned and hooked it with a long crooked stick and hauled it over the wall; when I came to be informed of this theft in the morning, I resolved to recover it by some means or other and accordingly went and took possession of all the canoes of any value I could meet with and brought them into the river behind the Fort to the number of 22, and told the natives then present (most of them being the owners of the canoes) that unless the principal things they had stolen from us were restored, I would burn them every one, not that I ever intend to put this in execution, and yet I was very much displeased with them as they were daily either committing or attempting to commit one theft or other, when at the same time (contrary to the opinion of everybody) I would not suffer them to be fired upon, for this would have been putting it in the power of the sentinels to have fired upon them upon the most slightest occasions as I had before experienced, and I have a great objection to firing with powder only amongst people who know not the difference; for by this they would learn to despise firearms and think their own arms superior and if ever such an opinion prevailed they would certainly attack you, the event of which might prove as unfavourable to you as them.

About noon the rake was restored us, when they wanted to have their canoes again: but now as I had them in my possession I was resolved to try if they would not redeem them by restoring what they had stolen from us before; the principal things which we had lost were the marine musket, a pair of pistols belonging to Mr Banks, a sword belonging to one of the petty officers, and a water cask with some other articles not worth mentioning: some said that these things were not in the island, others that Tootaha had them, and those of Tootaha's friends laid the whole to Obarea and I believe the whole was between these two persons.

TUESDAY, 20 JUNE. Got the powder ashore to air all of which we found in a bad condition and the gunner informs me that it was very little better when it came first on board. Last night Obarea made us a visit who we have not seen for some time: we were told of her coming and that she would bring with her some of the stolen things, which we gave credit to because we knew several of them were in her possession, but we were surprised to find this woman put herself wholly in our power and not bring with her one article of what we had lost. The excuse she made was that her gallant, a man that used to be along with her, did steal them and she had beat him and turned him away; but she was so sensible of her own guilt that she was ready to drop down through fear—and yet she had resolution enough to insist upon sleeping in Mr Banks's tent all night and was with difficulty prevailed upon to go to her canoe, although no one took the least notice of her. In the morning she brought her canoe with everything she had to the gate of the Fort, after which we could not help admiring her for her courage and the confidence she seemed to place in us and thought that we could do no less than to receive her into favour and accept the presents she had brought us, which consisted of a hog, a dog, some breadfruit and plantains. We refused to accept of the dog as being an animal we had no use for, at which she seemed a little surprised and told us that it was very good eating and we very soon had an opportunity to find that it was so, for Mr Banks having bought a basket of fruit in which happened to be the thigh of a dog ready dressed, of this several of us tasted and found that it was meat not to be despised and therefore took Obarea's dog and had him immediately dressed by some of the natives in the following manner. They first made a hole in the ground about a foot deep in which they made a fire and heated some small stones; while this was doing the dog was strangled and the hair got off by laying him frequently upon the fire, and as clean as if it had been scalded off with hot water, his entrails were taken out and the whole washed clean, and as soon as the stones and hole was sufficiently heated, the fire was put out, and part of the stones were left in the bottom of the hole; upon these stones were laid green leaves and upon them the dog together with the entrails. These were likewise covered with leaves and over them hot stones, and then the whole was close covered with mould: after he had laid here about 4 hours, the oven (for so I must call it) was opened and the dog taken out whole and well done, and it was the opinion of everyone who tasted of it that they never ate sweeter meat; we therefore resolved for the future not to despise dog's flesh. It is in this manner that the natives dress, or bake, all their victuals that require it, flesh, fish and fruit.

I now gave over all thought of recovering any of the things the natives had stolen from us and therefore intend to give them up their canoes whenever they apply for them.

[9–11 October 1769: Poverty Bay, New Zealand]

In the morning seeing a good number of the natives at the same place where we saw them last night, I went ashore with the boats manned and armed and landed on the opposite side of the river: Mr Banks Dr Solander and myself at first only landed and went to the side of the river, the natives being got together on the opposite side. We called to them in the George Island language, but they answered us by flourishing their weapons over their heads and dancing, as we supposed the war dance; upon this we retired until the marines were landed which I ordered to be drawn up about two hundred yards behind us. We then went again to the riverside having Tupia, Mr Green and Dr Munkhouse* along with us. Tupia spoke to them in his own language and it was an agreeable surprise to us to find that they perfectly understood him. After some little conversation had passed, one of them swam over to us and after him 20 or 30 more; these last brought their arms with them which the first man did not. We made them every one presents but this did not satisfy them; they wanted but everything we had about us particularly our arms, and made several attempts to snatch them out of our hands. Tupia told us several times as soon as they came over to take care of ourselves for they were not our friends, and this we very soon found for one of them snatched Mr Green's hanger from him and would not give it up; this encouraged the rest to be more insolent and seeing others coming over to join them I ordered the man who had taken the hanger to be fired at, which was accordingly done and wounded in such a manner that he died soon after; upon the first fire, which was only two muskets, the others retired to a rock which lay nearly in the middle of the river, but upon seeing the man fall they returned, probably to carry him off or his arms, the last of which they accomplished and this we could not prevent unless we had run our bayonets into them, for upon their returning from off the rock we had discharged of our pieces which were load[ed] with small shot and wounded three more, but these got over the river and were carried off by the others who now thought proper to retire.

Finding that nothing was to be done with the people on this side and the water in the river being salt, I embarked with an intent to row round the head of the bay in search of fresh water, and if possible to surprise some of the natives and to take them on board and by good treatment and presents endeavour to gain their friendship; with this view on

TUESDAY 10th. PM I rowed round the head of the bay but could find no place to land, on account of the great surf which beat everywhere upon the shore; seeing two boats or canoes coming in from sea, I rowed to one of them in order to seize upon the people and came so near before they took notice of us that Tupia called to them to come alongside and we would not hurt them, but instead of doing this they endeavoured to get away, upon which I ordered a musket to be fired over their heads, thinking that this would either make them surrender or jump overboard, but here I was mistaken for they immediately took to their arms or whatever they had in the boat and began to attack us; this obliged us to fire upon them and unfortunately either two or three were killed,* and one wounded, and three jumped overboard, these last we took up and brought on board, where they were clothed and treated with all imaginable kindness and to the surprise of everybody became at once as cheerful and as merry as if they had been with their own friends; they were all three young, the eldest not above 20 years of age and the youngest about 10 or 12.

I am aware that most humane men who have not experienced things of this nature will censure my conduct in firing upon the people in this boat nor do I myself think that the reason I had for seizing upon her will at all justify me, and had I thought that they would have made the least resistance I would not have come near them, but as they did I was not to stand still and suffer either myself or those that were with me to be knocked on the head.

In the morning, as I intended to put our three prisoners ashore and stay here the day to see what effect it might have upon the other natives, I sent an officer ashore with the marines and a party of men to cut wood, and soon after followed myself accompanied by Mr Banks, Dr Solander and Tupia, taking the three natives along with us whom we landed on the west side of the river before mentioned; they were very unwilling to leave us pretending that they should fall into the hands of their enemies who would kill and eat them; however they at last of their own accords left us and hid themselves in some bushes. Soon after this we discovered several bodies of the natives marching towards us, upon which we retired across the river and joined the wooders and with us came the three natives we had just parted with, for we could not prevail upon them to go to their own people. We had no sooner got over the river than the others assembled on the other side to the number of 150 or 200 all armed. Tupia now began to parley with them and the three we had with us showed everything we had given them, part of which they laid and left upon the body of the man that was killed the day before; these things seemed so far to convince them of our friendly intentions that one man came over to us while all the others sat down upon the sand: we every one made this man a present and the three natives that were with us likewise presented him with such things as they had got from us, with which after a short stay he retired across the river. I now thought proper to take everybody on board to prevent any more quarrels and with us came the three natives, whom we could not prevail upon to stay behind and this appeared the more strange as the man who came over to us was uncle to one of them. After we had returned on board we saw them carry off the dead man but the one that was killed the first evening we landed remained in the very spot they had left him.

WEDNESDAY 11th. In the PM as I intended to sail in the morning we put the three youths ashore seemingly very much against their inclination, but whether this was owing to a desire they had to remain with us or the fear of falling into the hands of their enemies as they pretended I know not; the latter however seemed to be ill founded for we saw them carried across the river in a catamaran and walk leisurely off with the other natives.

[6 May 1770: Botany Bay]

In the evening the yawl returned from fishing having caught two sting rays weighing near 600 pounds. The great quantity of new plants etc. Mr Banks and Dr Solander collected in this place occasioned my giving it the name of Botany Bay. It is situated in the latitude of 34°0′ S, longitude 208°37′ West; it is capacious safe and commodious, it may be known by the land on the sea-coast which is of a pretty even and moderate height, rather higher than it is farther inland with steep rocky cliffs next the sea and looks like a long island lying close under the shore: the entrance of the harbour lies about the middle of this land, in coming from the southward it is discoverd before you are abreast of it which you cannot do in coming from the northward; the entrance is little more than a mile broad and lies in WNW. To sail into it keep the south shore on board until within a small bare island which lies close under the north shore, being within that island the deepest water is on that side 7, 6 and five fathom a good way up. There is shoaled water a good way off from the south shore from the inner south point quite to the head of the harbour, but over towards the north and NW shore is a channel of 12 or 14 feet water at low water 3 or 4 leagues up to a place where there is 3 and 4 fathom but here I found very little fresh water. We anchored near the south shore about a mile within the entrance for the conveniency of sailing with a southerly wind and the getting of fresh water but I afterwards found a very fine stream of fresh water on the north shore in the first sandy cove within the island before which a ship might lay almost landlocked and wood for fuel may be got everywhere: although wood is here in great plenty yet there is very little variety, the largest trees are as large or larger than our oaks in England and grows a good deal like them and yields a reddish gum; the wood itself is heavy, hard and black like Lignum Vitae; another sort that grows tall and straight something like pines; the wood of this is hard and ponderous and something of the nature of American live oaks. These two are all the timber trees I met with. There are a few sorts of shrubs and several palm trees, and mangroves about the head of the harbour. The country is woody low and flat as far inland as we could see and I believe that the soil is in general sandy, in the wood are a variety of very beautiful birds such as cockatoos, lorikeets, parrots etc. and crows exactly like those we have in England. Water fowl are no less plenty about the head of the harbour where there are large flats of sand and mud on which they seek their food. The most of these were unknown to us, one sort especially which was black and white and as large as a goose but most like a pelican. On the sand and mud banks are oysters, mussels, cockles etc. which I believe are the chief support of the inhabitants, who go into shoaled water with their little canoes and pick them out of the sand and mud with their hands and sometimes roast and eat them in the canoe, having often a fire for that purpose as I suppose, for I know no other it can be for. The natives do not appear to be numerous neither do they seem to live in large bodies but dispersed in small parties along by the waterside; those I saw were about as tall as Europeans, of a very dark brown colour but not black nor had they woolly frizzled hair, but black and lank much like ours. No sort of clothing or ornaments were ever seen by any of us upon any one of them or in or about any of their huts, from which I conclude that they never wear any. Some we saw that had their faces and bodies painted with a sort of white paint or pigment. Although I have said that shellfish is their chief support yet they catch other sorts of fish some of which we found roasting on the fire the first time we landed, some of these they strike with gigs and others they catch with hook and line; we have seen them strike fish with gigs and hooks and lines were found in their huts. Sting rays I believe they do not eat because I never saw the least remains of one near any of their huts or fire places. However we could know but very little of their customs as we never were able to form any connections with them, they had not so much as touched the things we had left in their huts on purpose for them to take away. During our stay in this harbour I caused the English colours to be displayed ashore every day and an inscription to be cut out upon one of the trees near the watering place setting forth the ship's name, date etc.

JOSEPH BANKS, *Journal of the Right Hon. Sir Joseph Banks, Bart., K.B., P.R.S.* (ed. Sir Joseph D. Hooker, 1896)

Joseph Banks (1744–1820) was chief naturalist on the first Cook expedition, which made him famous. In 1778 he would be elected president of the Royal Society, an office he held for forty-one years. Banks was Britain's most influential patron of scientific projects in the last two decades of the eighteenth century; enterprises he sponsored included the transplant of breadfruit from the South Pacific to the Caribbean, to serve as cheap food for slaves, and exploration of the interior of Africa.

[22 June–2 July 1770: Australia, Endeavour River]

In the morning I saw her leak, which was very large: in the middle was a hole large enough to have sunk a ship with twice our pumps, but here Providence had most visibly worked in our favour, for it was in a great measure plugged up by a stone as big as a man's fist. Round the edges of this stone had all the water come in, which had so nearly overcome us, and here we found the wool and oakum, or fothering, which had relieved us in so unexpected a manner.

The effect of this coral rock upon her bottom is difficult to describe, but more to believe; it had cut through her plank and deep into one of her timbers, smoothing the gashes still before it, so that the whole might easily be imagined to have been cut with an axe.

Myself employed all day in laying in plants; the people who were sent to the other side of the water to shoot pigeons saw an animal as large as a greyhound, of a mouse colour, and very swift; they also saw many Indian houses, and a brook of fresh water.

24th. Gathering plants, and hearing descriptions of the animal, which is now seen by everybody. A seaman who had been out in the woods brought home the description of an animal he had seen,* composed in so seamanlike a style that I cannot help mentioning it; 'it was (says he) about as large and much like a one-gallon cagg, as black as the devil, and had two horns on its head; it went but slowly, but I dared not touch it.'

25th. In gathering plants today I had the good fortune to see the beast so much talked of, though but imperfectly; he was not only like a greyhound in size and running, but had a tail as long as any greyhound's; what to liken him to I could not tell; nothing that I have seen at all resembles him.

26th. Since the ship has been hauled ashore the water has, of course, all gone backwards; and my plants, which for safety had been stowed in the bread room, were this day found under water. Nobody had warned me of this danger, which never once entered my head. The mischief, however, was now done, so I set to work to remedy it to the best of my power. The day was scarcely long enough to get them all shifted, etc.; many were saved, but some were entirely spoiled.

28th. We have ever since we have been here observed the nests of a kind of ant, much like the white ant in the East Indies, but to us perfectly harmless: they were always pyramidal, from a few inches to six feet in height, and very much resembled the Druidical monuments which I have seen in England. Today we met with a large number of them of all sizes ranged in a small open place, which had a very pretty effect. Dr Solander compared them to the runic stones on the plains of Uppsala in Sweden; myself to all the smaller Druidical monuments I had seen.

1st July. Our second lieutenant found the husk of a coconut full of barnacles cast up on the beach; it had probably come from some island to windward.

2nd. The wild plantain trees, though their fruit does not serve for food, are to us of a most material benefit. We made baskets of their stalks (a thing we had learned from the islanders), in which our plants, which would not otherwise keep, have remained fresh for two or three days; indeed, in a hot climate it is hardly practicable to manage without such baskets, which we call by the island name of *papa mija*. Our plants dry better in paper books than in sand, with the precaution that one person is entirely employed in attending them. He shifts them all once a day, exposes the quires in which they are to the greatest heat of the sun, and at night covers them most carefully up from any damp, always being careful, also, not to bring them out too soon in the morning, or leave them out too late in the evening.

[6–7 and 14–15 July 1770: Endeavour River]

Set out today with the second lieutenant, resolved to go a good way up the river, and see if the country inland differed from that near the shore. We went for about three leagues among mangroves: then we got into the country, which differed very little from what we had already seen. The river higher up contracted much, and lost most of its mangroves: the banks were steep and covered with trees of a beautiful verdure, particularly what is called in the West Indies *mohoe* or bark-tree (*Hibiscus tiliaceus*). The land was generally low, thickly covered with long grass, and seemed to promise great fertility, were the people to plant and improve it. In the course of the day Tupia saw a wolf, so at least I guess by his description, and we saw three of the animals of the country, but could not get one; also a kind of bat as large as a partridge, but these also we were not lucky enough to get. At night we took up our lodgings close to the banks of the river, and made a fire; but the mosquitoes, whose peaceful dominions it seems we had invaded, spared no pains to molest us as much as was in their power: they followed us into the very smoke, nay, almost into the fire, which, hot as the climate was, we could better bear the heat of than their intolerable stings. Between the hardness of our bed, the heat of the fire, and the stings of these indefatigable insects, the night was not spent so agreeably but day was earnestly wished for by all of us.

7th. At last it came, and with its first dawn we set out in search of game. We walked many miles over the flats and saw four of the animals, two of which my greyhound fairly chased; but they beat him owing to the length and thickness of the grass, which prevented him from running, while they at every bound leaped over the tops of it. We observed, much to our surprise, that instead of going upon all fours, this animal went only upon two legs, making vast bounds just as the jerboa (*Mus iaculus*) does.

We observed a smoke, but when we came to the place the people were gone. The fire was in an old tree of touchwood. Their houses were there, and branches of trees broken down, with which the children had been playing, were not yet withered; their footsteps, also, on the sands below high-water mark proved that they had very lately been there. Near their oven, in which victuals had been dressed since noon, were the shells of a kind of clam, and the roots of a wild yam which had been cooked in it. Thus were we disappointed of the only good chance we have had of seeing the people since we came here, by their unaccountable timidity. Night soon coming on, we repaired to our quarters, which were upon a broad sand-bank under the shade of a bush, where we hoped the mosquitoes would not trouble us. Our beds of plantain leaves spread on the sand, as soft as a mattress, our cloaks for bed-clothes, and grass pillows, but above all the entire absence of mosquitoes, made me and, I believe, all of us sleep almost without intermission. Had the Indians come they would certainly have caught us all napping; but that was the last thing we thought of.

14th. Our second lieutenant had the good fortune to kill the animal that had so long been the subject of our speculations. To compare it to any European animal would be impossible, as it has not the least resemblance to any one I have seen. Its fore-legs are extremely short, and of no use to it in walking; its hind again as disproportionally long; with these it hops seven or eight feet at a time, in the same manner as the jerboa, to which animal indeed it bears much resemblance, except in size, this being in weight 38 lbs., and the jerboa no larger than a common rat.

15th. The beast which was killed yesterday was today dressed for our dinner, and proved excellent meat.

GEORGE FORSTER, *A Voyage Round the World, in His Britannic Majesty's Sloop, Resolution, commanded by Capt. James Cook, during the years 1772, 3, 4, and 5* (1777)

Cook returned, as commander of the *Resolution*, on a second quest for the mysterious southern continent (1772–5). After twice venturing into the Antarctic Circle he concluded that no such land-mass was to be found, unless it consisted of ice. George Forster (1754–94), the son and gifted assistant of Banks's successor as ship's naturalist, Johann Reinhold Forster (1729–98), published his own account of the expedition. The return to New Zealand brought eyewitness proof of cannibalism among the Maori. (Later, after the ships became separated, the crew of a ship's boat from the *Adventure* was killed and eaten.) Through his aversion Forster strives to understand the cultural logic of a practice about which he had been inclined to be sceptical. Observing the prostitution of native women for iron and cloth, he reflects on the moral corruption brought by European contact. Forster goes further: the common sailors, ignorant, hardened, and licentious, are the true savages.

[29 May 1773: New Zealand]

About thirty natives surrounded us in several canoes the next morning, and brought a few of their tools and weapons to sell, for which they received great quantities of our goods in exchange, owing to the eagerness with which our crews outbid each other. There were a number of women among them, whose lips were of a blackish blue colour, by punctuation; and their cheeks were painted of a lively red, with a mixture of ruddle* and oil. Like those at Dusky Bay, they commonly had slender and bandy legs, with large knees; defects which evidently are deducible from the little exercise they use, and their mode of sitting cross-legged and cramped up almost perpetually in canoes. Their colour was of a clear brown, between the olive and mahogany hues, their hair jetty black, the faces round, the nose and lips rather thick but not flat, their black eyes sometimes lively and not without expression; the whole upper part of their figure was not disproportionate, and their assemblage of features not absolutely forbidding. Our crews, who had not conversed with women since our departure from the Cape, found these ladies very agreeable and from the manner in which their advances were received, it appeared very plainly that chastity was not rigorously observed here, and that the sex were far from being impregnable. However their favours did not depend upon their own inclination, but the men, as absolute masters, were always to be consulted upon the occasion; if a spike-nail, or a shirt, or a similar present had been given for their connivance, the lady was at liberty to make her lover happy, and to exact, if possible, the tribute of another present for herself. Some among them, however, submitted with reluctance to this vile prostitution; and, but for the authority and menaces of the men, would not have complied with the desires of a set of people who could, with unconcern, behold their tears and hear their complaints. Whether the members of a civilized society, who could act such a brutal part, or the barbarians who could force their own women to submit to such indignity, deserve the greatest abhorrence, is a question not easily to be decided. Encouraged by the lucrative nature of this infamous commerce, the New Zealanders went through the whole vessel, offering their daughters and sisters promiscuously to every person's embraces, in exchange for our iron tools, which they knew could not be purchased at an easier rate. It does not appear that their married women were ever suffered to have this kind of intercourse with our people. Their ideas of female chastity are, in this respect, so different from ours, that a girl may favour a number of lovers without any detriment to her character; but if she marries, conjugal fidelity is exacted from her with the greatest rigour. It may therefore be alleged that, as the New Zealanders place no value on the continence of their unmarried women, the arrival of Europeans among them, did not injure their moral characters in this respect; but we doubt whether they ever debased themselves so much as to make a trade of their women before we created new wants by showing them iron tools, for the possession of which they do not hesitate to commit an action that, in our eyes, deprives them of the very shadow of sensibility.

It is unhappy enough that the unavoidable consequence of all our voyages of discovery has always been the loss of a number of innocent lives; but this heavy injury done to the little uncivilized communities which Europeans have visited is trifling when compared to the irretrievable harm entailed upon them by corrupting their morals. If these evils were in some measure compensated by the introduction of some real benefit in these countries, or by the abolition of some other immoral customs among their inhabitants, we might at least comfort ourselves that what they lost on one hand, they gained on the other; but I fear that hitherto our intercourse has been wholly disadvantageous to the nations of the South Seas; and that those communities have been the least injured who have always kept aloof from us, and whose jealous disposition did not suffer our sailors to become too familiar among them, as if they had perceived in their countenances that levity of disposition, and that spirit of debauchery, with which they are generally reproached.

[23 November 1773: New Zealand]

At their return they were witnesses of an instance of the ferocity of manners of this savage nation. A boy about six or seven years old demanded a piece of broiled penguin, which his mother held in her hands. As she did not immediately comply with his demand, he took up a large stone and threw it at her. The woman, incensed at this action, ran to punish him, but she had scarcely given him a single blow, when her husband came forward, beat her unmercifully, and dashed her against the ground, for attempting to correct her unnatural child. Our people, who were employed in filling water, told my father they had frequently seen similar instances of cruelty among them, and particularly, that the boys had actually struck their unhappy mother, whilst the father looked on lest she should attempt to retaliate. Among all savage nations the weaker sex is ill-treated, and the law of the strongest is put in force. Their women are mere drudges, who prepare raiment and provide dwellings, who cook and frequently collect their food, and are requited by blows and all kinds of severity. At New Zealand it seems they carry this tyranny to excess, and the males are taught from their earliest age to hold their mothers in contempt, contrary to all our principles of morality. I leave this barbarity without a comment, in order to relate the remaining occurrences of this day, which was pregnant in discoveries relative to the New Zealanders. The captain, with Mr Wales,* and my father, went to Motu-Aro in the afternoon, where they looked after the plantations, collected greens for the ships, etc. In the mean while some of the lieutenants went to the Indian Cove, with a view to trade with the natives. The first objects which struck them were the entrails of a human corpse lying on a heap a few steps from the water. They were hardly recovered from their first surprise, when the natives showed them several limbs of the body, and expressed by words and gestures that they had eaten the rest. The head, without the lower jaw-bone, was one of the parts which remained, and from which it plainly appeared that the deceased was a youth about fifteen or sixteen years old. The skull was fractured near one of the temples, as it seemed by the stroke of a pattoo-pattoo.* This gave our officers an opportunity of enquiring how they came in possession of the body. The natives answered that they had fought with their enemies, and had killed several of them, without being able to bring away any of the dead besides this youth. At the same time they acknowledged that they had lost some of their friends, and pointed to several women who were seated apart, weeping and cutting their foreheads with sharp stones, in commemoration of the dead. Our former conjectures were now amply verified, our apprehensions that we were the innocent causes of this disaster increased, and the existence of anthropophagi confirmed by another strong proof. Mr Pickersgill* proposed to purchase the head, in order to preserve it till his return to England, where it might serve as a memorial of this voyage. He offered a nail, and immediately obtained the head for this price,* after which he returned on board with his company, and placed it on the taffarel.* We were all occupied in examining it, when some New

Zealanders came on board from the watering-place. At sight of the head they expressed an ardent desire of possessing it, signifying by the most intelligible gestures that it was delicious to the taste. Mr Pickersgill refused to part with it, but agreed to cut off a small piece from the cheek, with which they seemed to be well satisfied. He cut off the part he had promised, and offered it to them, but they would not eat it raw, and made signs to have it dressed. Therefore, in presence of all the ship's company, it was broiled over the fire; after which they devoured it before our eyes with the greatest avidity. The captain arriving the moment after with his company, the New Zealanders repeated the experiment once more in his presence. It operated very strangely and differently on the beholders. Some there were who, in spite of the abhorrence which our education inspires against the eating of human flesh, did not seem greatly disinclined to feast with them, and valued themselves on the brilliancy of their wit, while they compared their battle to a hunting-match. On the contrary, others were so unreasonably incensed against the perpetrators of this action that they declared they could be well pleased to shoot them all; they were ready to become the most detestable butchers, in order to punish the imaginary crime of a people whom they had no right to condemn. A few others suffered the same effects as from a dose of ipecacuanha.* The rest lamented this action as a brutal depravation of human nature, agreeably to the principles which they had imbibed. But the sensibility of Mahine,* the young native of the Society Islands, shone out with superior lustre among us. Born and bred in a country where the inhabitants have already emerged from the darkness of barbarism, and are united by the bonds of society, this scene filled his mind with horror. He turned his eyes from the unnatural object, and retired into the cabin, to give vent to the emotions of his heart. There we found him bathed in tears; his looks were a mixture of compassion and grief, and as soon as he saw us, he expressed his concern for the unhappy parents of the victim. This turn which his reflections had taken gave us infinite pleasure; it spoke a humane heart, filled with the warmest sentiments of social affection, and habituated to sympathize with its fellow-creatures. He was so deeply affected that it was several hours before he could compose himself, and ever after, when he spoke on this subject, it was not without emotion. Philosophers, who have only contemplated mankind in their closets, have strenuously maintained that all the assertions of authors, ancient and modern, of the existence of men-eaters are not to be credited; and there have not been wanting persons amongst ourselves who were sceptical enough to refuse belief to the concurrent testimonies in the history of almost all nations in this particular. But Captain Cook had already, in his former voyage, received strong proof that the practice of eating human flesh existed in New Zealand; and as now we have with our own eyes seen the inhabitants devouring human flesh, all controversy on that point must be at an end.

[25 December 1773: Christmas at sea]

On the 25th, the weather was clear and fair, but the wind died away to a perfect calm, upwards of ninety large ice-islands being in sight at noon. This being Christmas-day, the captain, according to custom, invited the officers and mates to dinner, and one of the lieutenants entertained the petty-officers. The sailors feasted on a double portion of pudding, regaling themselves with the brandy of their allowance, which they had saved for this occasion some months before-hand, being solicitous to get very drunk, though they are commonly solicitous about nothing else. The sight of an immense number of icy masses, amongst which we drifted at the mercy of the current, every moment in danger of being dashed to pieces against them, could not deter the sailors from indulging in their favourite amusement. As long as they had brandy left, they would persist to keep Christmas 'like Christians', though the elements had conspired together for their destruction. Their long acquaintance with a seafaring life had inured them to all kinds of perils, and their heavy labour, with the inclemencies of weather, and other hardships, making their muscles rigid and their nerves obtuse, had communicated insensibility to the mind. It will easily be conceived that as they do not feel for themselves sufficiently to provide for their own safety, they must be incapable of feeling for others. Subjected to a very strict command, they also exercise a tyrannical sway over those whom fortune places in their power. Accustomed to face an enemy, they breathe nothing but war. By force of habit even killing is become so much their passion that we have seen many instances during our voyage where they have expressed a horrid eagerness to fire upon the natives on the slightest pretences. Their way of life in general prevents their enjoying domestic comforts; and gross animal appetites fill the place of purer affections.

> At last, extinct each social feeling, fell
> And joyless inhumanity pervades
> And petrifies the heart.
>
> THOMPSON*

   Though they are members of a civilized society, they may in some measure be looked upon as a body of uncivilized men, rough, passionate, revengeful, but likewise brave, sincere, and true to each other.

JAMES COOK, *The Voyage of the Resolution and Adventure, 1772–1775*, ed. J. C. Beaglehole (Cambridge, 1961)

When otherwise friendly natives deter the explorers from penetrating inland to survey an active volcano, Cook reflects on his historical role as an invader of their country.

[14 August 1774: Tanna, New Hebrides]

Happening to turn out of the common path we came into a plantation where there was a man at work; he either out of good nature or to get us the sooner out of his territories, undertook to be our guide. We had not gone with him far before we met another fellow standing at the junction of two roads with a sling and a stone in his hand, both of which he thought proper to lay aside when a musket was pointed at him. The attitude we found him in and the ferocity which appeared in his looks and his behaviour after led us to think he meant to defend the path he stood in; he pointed to the other along which he and our guide led us, he counted us several times over and kept calling for assistance and was presently joined by two or three more one of which was a young woman with a club in her hand; they presently conducted us to the brow of a hill and pointed to a road which led down to the harbour and wanted us to go that way. We refused to comply and returned to the one we had left which we pursued alone, our guide refusing to go with us; after ascending another ridge as closely covered with wood as those we had come over, we saw still other hills between us and the volcano, which discouraged us from proceeding farther, especially as we could get no one to be our guide and therefore came to a resolution to return. We had but just put this into execution when we met twenty or thirty

of the natives collected together and were close at our heels; we
judged their design was to oppose our advancing into the country
but now they saw us returning they suffered us to pass unmolested
and some of them put us into the right road and accompanied us
down the hill, made us to stop in one place where they brought us
coconuts, plantains and sugar canes and what we did not eat on the
spot, brought down the hill for us; thus we found these people civil
and good natured when not prompted by jealousy to a contrary
conduct, a conduct one cannot blame them for when one considers
the light in which they must look upon us, it's impossible for them to
know our real design. We enter their ports without their daring to
make opposition; we attempt to land in a peaceable manner; if this
succeeds it's well; if, not, we land nevertheless and maintain the
footing we thus got by the superiority of our firearms. In what other
light can they at first look upon us but as invaders of their country?
Time and some acquaintance with us can only convince them of
their mistake.

JAMES COOK, *The Voyage of the Resolution and Discovery,
1776–1780*, ed. J. C. Beaglehole (Cambridge, 1967)

Cook's third and last expedition (1776–80) followed the coast of Alaska
up into the Arctic Sea in a vain search for a Northwest passage to the
Atlantic. Cook brought back a passenger to the South Sea islands: Omai
(Mai), a native of Huahine, who had sailed to England in 1774 with
Captain Tobias Furneaux on Cook's sister-ship the *Adventure*. Although
high-born, Omai had lost caste after finding himself on the losing side in
an inter-island war. Cook took care to supply him with European goods,
crops, and livestock so as to bolster his status back at Huahine.

[12 August 1777: Omai's first reception at Tahiti]

When we first drew near the island, several canoes came off to the
ships, each conducted by two or three men, but as they were only
common fellows Omai took no notice of them nor they of him; they
did not even seem to perceive he was one of their countrymen
although they conversed with him for some time. At length a Chief
whom I had known before named Ootie and Omai's brother-in-law,
who chanced to be here, came on board, and three or four more, all

of whom knew Omai before he embarked with Captain Furneaux; yet there was nothing either tender or striking in their meeting. On the contrary there seemed to be a perfect indifference on both sides, till Omai asked his brother down into the cabin, opened the drawer where he kept his red feathers and gave him a few. This being presently known to those on deck, the face of affairs were entirely turned and Ootie, who would hardly speak to Omai before, now begged they might be Tyo's* and change names. Omai accepted of the honour and confirmed it with a present of red feathers, and Ootie by way of return sent ashore for a hog but it was evident to everyone that it was not the man but his property they were in love with, for had he not showed them his red feathers, which is the most valuable thing that can be carried to the island, I question if they had given him a coconut. Such was Omai's first reception amongst his countrymen and such as I always expected, but I expected, that with the property he was master of he would have had prudence enough to have made himself respected and even courted by the first persons in the island, but instead of that he rejected the advice of those who wished him well and suffered himself to be duped by every designing knave.

[26 October–2 November 1777: farewell to Omai]

SUNDAY, 26 OCTOBER. On the 26th Omai's house being nearly finished many of his moveables were got ashore; amongst many other useless things was a box of toys which when exposed to public view seemed to please the gazing multitude very much; but as to his pots, kettles, dishes, plates, drinking mugs, glasses etc. etc. etc. hardly anyone so much as looked at. Omai himself now found that they were of no manner of use to him, that a baked hog ate better than a boiled one, that a plantain leaf made as good a dish or plate as pewter and that a coconut shell was as good to drink out of as a black-jack; and therefore he very wisely disposed of as many of these things as he could to the people of the ships for hatchets and other useful articles. In the evening of the 28th we exhibited some of Omai's fireworks, before a great concourse of people who beheld them with a mixture of pleasure and fear; what remained were put in order and left with him, agreeable to the intention for which they were put on board, but by far the greatest part were either already expended or rendered useless by keeping so long.

THURSDAY, 30 OCTOBER. As soon as Omai was settled in his new habitation, I began to think of leaving the island and with that view get everything off from the shore, except the horse and mare and a goat big with kid, which were left in the possession of Omai. I also gave him a boar and two sows of the English breed and he had got a sow or two of his own. The horse covered the mare while we were at Otaheite so that there is little fear but they will in time have a breed of horses. Omai had picked up at Otaheite four or five Toutous,* the two New Zealand youths* remained with him and his brother and some others joined him here, so that his family already consisted of eight or ten without ever a woman among them, nor did Omai seem at all disposed to take unto himself a wife. The house which we built him was 24 feet by 18 and 10 feet high; it was built of boards and with as few nails as possible, that there might be no inducement to pull it down. As soon as we were gone he was, with the assistance of some of the chiefs, to build after the country fashion a large house over it; if it cover the ground which he marked out it will be as large as most on the island. His armour consisted of a musket, bayonet and cartouche-box; a fowling piece, two pair of pistols and two or three swords and cutlasses. And I left him about twenty pound of powder, a few musket cartridges, musket and pistol balls; these made him quite happy, which was my only view for giving him them, for I was always of opinion he would have been better without firearms than with them. After Omai had got his things ashore he had most of the officers of both ships two or three times to dinner; his table was always well covered with the very best the island afforded. Before I left the island I had the following inscription cut out upon the one end of his house viz.

Georgius tertius Rex 2 Novembris 1777

Naves $\begin{cases} Resolution\ Fac.\ Cook\ P^r \\ Discovery\ Car.\ Clerke\ P^r \end{cases}$

SUNDAY 2 NOVEMBER. At 4 PM I took the advantage of a breeze which then sprung up at east and sailed out of the harbour. Most of our friends remained on board till the ships were under sail, when to gratify them I ordered five guns to be fired and then they all took leave, except Omai who remained till we were at sea. We had come to sail by a hawser we had fast to the shore; in casting the ship it parted (being cut by the rocks) and the outer end left behind, as those who cast it off did not perceive it was broke; so that we had a boat to send

for it. In this boat Omai went ashore, after taking a very affectionate
farewell of all the officers; he sustained himself with a manly resolution till he came to me; then his utmost efforts to conceal his tears
failed, and Mr King, who went in the boat, told me he wept all the
time in going ashore. Whatever faults this Indian had they were more
than over-balanced by his great good nature and docile disposition;
during the whole time he was with me I very seldom had reason to
find fault with his conduct. His grateful heart always retained the
highest sense of the favours he received in England, nor will he ever
forget those who honoured him with their protection and friendship
during his stay there. He had a tolerable share of understanding, but
wanted application and perseverance to exert it, so that his knowledge of things was very general and in many instances imperfect. He
was not a man of much observation: there were many little arts as
well as amusements amongst the people of the Friendly Islands
which he might have conveyed to his own, where they probably
would have been adopted, as being so much in their own way, but I
never found that he used the least endeavours to make himself master of any one. This kind of indifference is the true character of his
nation. Europeans have visited them at times for these ten years past,
yet we find neither new arts nor improvements in the old, nor have
they copied after us in any one thing. We are therefore not to expect
that Omai will be able to introduce many of our arts and customs
amongst them or much improve those they have got. I think however
he will endeavour to bring to perfection the fruits etc. we planted
which will be no small acquisition. But the greatest benefit these
islands will receive from Omai's travels will be in the animals that
have been left upon them, which probably they never would have got
had he not come to England; when these multiplies, of which I think
there is little doubt, they will equal, if not exceed, any place in the
known world for provisions. Omai's return occasioned a number of
volunteers to go to Pretane;* and he was so ambitious of being the
only great traveller that he frequently put me in mind that Lord
Sandwich told him no more were [to] come. If there had been the
most distant probability of any ship being sent again to New Zealand
I would have brought the two youths of that country home with me,
as they were both desirous of coming; Tiarooa, the eldest, was an
exceeding well disposed young man with strong natural parts and
capable of receiving any instructions. He seemed to be fully sensible

of the difference between his own country and these islands and resigned himself very contentedly to end his days upon them; but the other was so strongly attached to us that he was taken out of the ship and carried ashore by force; he was a witty, smart boy and on that account much noticed in the ship.

3. COLONIZING NEW SOUTH WALES, 1788–1791

HIRAM WOOD, *The Voyage of Governor Phillip to Botany Bay* (1790)

After the loss of the North American colonies in 1776, the new continent claimed by Cook presented a solution to the problem of Britain's burgeoning criminalized underclass. New South Wales would be developed as an Enlightenment gulag on the far side of the world. The first fleet of eleven ships set sail in May 1787, carrying the new governor, Captain Arthur Phillip (1738–1814), along with officers and marines, civil servants, surgeons, and clergymen, and some 760 convicts, roughly a quarter of whom were women. Eight months later the fleet disembarked at Sydney Cove (Port Jackson), Botany Bay having proved unsuitable. From the numerous extant records we reprint Hiram Wood's official account of the arrival of the fleet, blandly insistent on decorum and decency.

[18 January 1788]

At the very first landing of Governor Phillip on the shore of Botany Bay, an interview with the natives took place. They were all armed, but on seeing the Governor approach with signs of friendship, alone and unarmed, they readily returned his confidence by laying down their weapons. They were perfectly devoid of clothing, yet seemed fond of ornaments, putting the beads and red baize that were given them on their heads or necks, and appearing pleased to wear them. The presents offered by their new visitors were all readily accepted, nor did any kind of disagreement arise while the ships remained in Botany Bay. This very pleasing effect was produced in no small degree by the personal address, as well as by the great care and attention of the Governor. Nor were the orders which enforced a conduct so humane, more honourable to the persons from whom they originated, than the punctual execution of them was to the officers sent out: it was evident that their wishes coincided with their duty; and that a sanguinary temper was no longer to disgrace the European settlers in countries newly discovered.

The next care after landing was the examination of the bay itself, from which it appeared that, though extensive, it did not afford a shelter from the easterly winds: and that, in consequence of its shallowness, ships even of a moderate draught would always be obliged to anchor with the entrance of the bay open, where they must be exposed to a heavy sea, that rolls in whenever it blows hard from the eastward.

[Botany Bay proves an unsatisfactory location for a large settlement, and Governor Phillip resolves to examine Port Jackson, to the north.]

These arrangements having been settled, Governor Phillip prepared to proceed to the examination of Port Jackson: and as the time of his absence, had he gone in the *Supply*, must have been very uncertain, he went round with three boats, taking with him Captain Hunter and several other officers, that by examining several parts of the harbour at once the greater dispatch might be made. On the 22nd of January they set out upon this expedition, and early in the afternoon arrived at Port Jackson, which is distant about three leagues. Here all regret arising from the former disappointments was at once obliterated; and Governor Phillip had the satisfaction to find one of the finest harbours in the world, in which a thousand sail of the line might ride in perfect security.

The different coves of this harbour were examined with all possible expedition, and the preference was given to one which had the finest spring of water, and in which ships can anchor so close to the shore that at a very small expense quays may be constructed at which the largest vessels may unload. This cove is about half a mile in length, and a quarter of a mile across at the entrance. In honour of Lord Sydney, the Governor distinguished it by the name of Sydney Cove. . . .

In passing near a point of land in this harbour, the boats were perceived by a number of the natives, twenty of whom waded into the water unarmed, received what was offered them, and examined the boat with a curiosity which impressed a higher idea of them than any former accounts of their manners had suggested. This confidence and manly behaviour induced Governor Phillip, who was highly pleased with it, to give the place the name of Manly Cove. The same people afterwards joined the party at the place where they had landed to dine. They were then armed, two of them with shields and swords, the rest with lances only. The swords were made of wood, small in the grip, and apparently less formidable than a good stick. One of these men had a kind of white clay rubbed upon the upper part of his face, so as to have the appearance of a mask. This ornament, if it can be called such, is not common among them, and is probably assumed only on particular occasions, or as a distinction to a few individuals. One woman had been seen on the rocks as the boats passed, with her face, neck and breasts thus painted, and to our people appeared the most disgusting figure imaginable; her own countrymen were perhaps delighted by the beauty of the effect.

During the preparation for dinner the curiosity of these visitors rendered them very troublesome, but an innocent contrivance altogether removed the inconvenience. Governor Phillip drew a circle round the place where the English were, and without much difficulty made the natives understand that they were not to pass that line; after which they sat down in perfect quietness. Another proof how tractable these people are, when no insult or injury is offered, and when proper means are used to influence the simplicity of their minds.

JOHN HUNTER, *An Historical Journal of Transactions at Port Jackson and Norfolk Island* (1793)

Extracts from memoirs by Captain John Hunter (1737–1821), Phillip's second in command, and Watkin Tench (1758–1833), lieutenant-captain of marines, describe encounters with the native Eora. Governor Phillip wanted to maintain friendly relations with the Eora, but the colony brought an irreversible disruption of their way of life. Phillip instituted a policy of kidnapping natives to train as interpreters, the population was devastated by a smallpox epidemic, and the settlers depleted their fisheries and other resources.

As soon as the ship was secured, I went on shore to wait on the governor, whom I found in good health. He was sitting by the fire, drinking tea with a few friends, among whom I observed a native man of this country, who was decently clothed, and seemed to be as much at his ease at the tea-table as any person there; he managed his cup and saucer as well as though he had been long accustomed to such entertainment.

This man was taken from his friends, by force, by Lieutenant Ball, of the *Supply*, and Lieutenant George Johnston, of the marines, who were sent down the harbour with two boats for that purpose, the governor having found that no encouragement he could give the natives, would dispose them to visit the settlement of their own accord: this method he had therefore determined upon, to get one man into his possession, who, by kind treatment, might hereafter be the means of disposing his countrymen to place more confidence in us. This man, whose name was Ara-ba-noo, was taken, as I have already said, by force, and in the following manner.*

After having been a short time in conversation with some of the gentlemen, one of the seamen, who had been previously directed, threw a rope round his neck, and dragged him in a moment down to the boat; his cries brought a number of his friends into the skirts of the wood, from whence they threw many lances, but without effect. The terror this poor wretch suffered can better be conceived than expressed; he believed he was to be immediately murdered; but, upon the officers coming into the boat, they removed the rope from his neck to his leg, and treated him with so much kindness that he became a little more cheerful.

He was for some time after his arrival at the governor's house, ornamented with an iron shackle about his leg, to prevent his being able to effect his escape with ease; this he was taught to consider as *bang-ally*, which is the name given in their language to every decoration; and he might well believe it a compliment paid to him, because it was no uncommon thing for him to see several (of the most worthless of the convicts, who had merited punishment) every day shackled like him; the cause of which he could not of course understand. However, he was very soon reconciled to his situation by the very kind treatment he received from every person about him, and the iron growing uneasy, it was taken off, and he was allowed to go where he pleased.

He very soon learnt the names of the different gentlemen who took notice of him, and when I was made acquainted with him, he learnt mine, which he never forgot, but expressed great desire to come on board my *nowee*; which is their expression for a boat or other vessel upon the water.

The day after I came in, the governor and his family did me the honour to dine on board, when I was also favoured with the company of Ara-ba-noo, whom I found to be a very good-natured talkative fellow; he was about thirty years of age, and tolerably well looked.

I expressed, when at the governor's, much surprise at not having seen a single native on the shore, or a canoe as we came up in the ship; the reason of which I could not comprehend, until I was informed that the smallpox had made its appearance, a few months ago, amongst these unfortunate creatures, and that it was truly shocking to go round the coves of this harbour, which were formerly so much frequented by the natives; where, in the caves of the rocks, which used to shelter whole families in bad weather, were now to be seen men, women, and children, lying dead. As we had never yet seen any of these people who have been in the smallest degree marked with the smallpox, we had reason to suppose they have never before now been affected by it, and consequently are strangers to any method of treating it: and, if we consider the various attitudes, which the different dead bodies have been found in, we may easily believe, that when any of them are taken ill, and the malady assumes the appearance of the smallpox (having already experienced its fatality to whole families), they are immediately deserted by their friends, and left to perish, in their helpless situation, for want of sustenance. Some have been found sitting on their haunches, with their heads reclined between their knees; others were leaning against a rock, with their head resting upon it: I have seen myself, a woman sitting on the ground, with her knees drawn up to her shoulders, and her face resting on the sand between her feet.

Two children, a boy of six or seven years of age, and a girl about ten, were lately picked up, labouring under the same disease; two old men, whom we had reason to believe were the fathers of the two children, were picked up at the same time, and brought to the hospital, and much care taken of them: the two men lived but a few days, but the children both recovered, and seemed well satisfied with their very comfortable situation. Through the means of these children, if they should retain their native language, a more intimate and friendly intercourse with the people of this country may in time be brought about.

Five or six days after my arrival, poor Ara-ba-noo was seized with the smallpox, and although every possible means for his recovery were used, he lived only till the crisis of the disease. Every person in the settlement was much concerned for the loss of this man.*

I was exceedingly concerned on hearing of the death of Captain Shea, of the marines, which happened while we were absent; his disorder was a general decay, which I think must have taken place very suddenly, for he was apparently strong and healthy when the *Sirius* sailed from Port Jackson.

Several people had been lost in the woods during our absence, and had either been killed by the natives, or perished there.

Another melancholy piece of information which we received on our arrival was that six marines had been tried by a criminal court, and found guilty of robbing the public stores: they were sentenced to death, and executed accordingly. It appeared upon the trial of these infatuated men that they had carried on this iniquitous (and I may add from our situation) dangerous practice to the settlement at large, for several months; and all originally occasioned by some unfortunate connections they had made with women convicts.

The settlement had been, during our absence, remarkably healthy.

WATKIN TENCH, *A Complete Account of the Settlement at Port Jackson* (1793)

Watkin Tench tells the story of the most famous of the captives, Bennelong, who managed to escape but then returned to the colony after the Governor was wounded in a fracas with his people. Phillip took Bennelong back with him to England in 1792, where (like Omai before him) he was presented at court. Bennelong returned to Sydney in 1795 and died there, an alcoholic outcast, in 1813.

[November 1789]

Intercourse with the natives, for the purpose of knowing whether or not the country possessed any resources by which life might be prolonged,* as well as on other accounts, becoming every day more desirable, the governor resolved to make prisoners of two more of them.

Boats properly provided, under the command of Lieutenant

Bradley of the *Sirius*, were accordingly dispatched on this service and completely succeeded in trepanning and carrying off, without opposition, two fine young men, who were safely landed among us at Sydney.

Nanbaree and Abaroo welcomed them on shore, calling them immediately by their names, Baneelon and Colbee.* But they seemed little disposed to receive the congratulations or repose confidence in the assurances of their friends. The same scenes of awkward wonder and impatient constraint, which had attended the introduction of Arabanoo, succeeded. Baneelon we judged to be about twenty-six years old, of good stature and stoutly made, with a bold intrepid countenance which bespoke defiance and revenge. Colbee was perhaps near thirty, of a less sullen aspect than his comrade, considerably shorter and not so robustly framed, though better fitted for purposes of activity. They had both evidently had the smallpox; indeed Colbee's face was very thickly imprinted with the marks of it.

Positive orders were issued by the governor to treat them indulgently and guard them strictly; notwithstanding which, Colbee contrived to effect his escape in about a week, with a small iron ring round his leg. Had those appointed to watch them been a moment later, his companion would have contrived to accompany him.

But Baneelon, though haughty, knew how to temporise. He quickly threw off all reserve, and pretended, nay, at particular moments, perhaps felt satisfaction in his new state. Unlike poor Arabanoo, he became at once fond of our viands and would drink the strongest liquors, not simply without reluctance but with eager marks of delight and enjoyment. He was the only native we ever knew who immediately showed a fondness for spirits; Colbee would not at first touch them. Nor was the effect of wine or brandy upon him more perceptible than an equal quantity would have produced upon one of us, although fermented liquor was new to him.

In his eating, he was alike compliant. When a turtle was shown to Arabanoo he would not allow it to be a fish and could not be induced to eat of it. Baneelon also denied it to be a fish, but no common councilman in Europe could do more justice than he did to a very fine one that the *Supply* had brought from Lord Howe Island, and which was served up at the governor's table on Christmas Day.

His powers of mind were certainly far above mediocrity. He acquired knowledge, both of our manners and language, faster than his predecessor had done. He willingly communicated information, sang, danced and capered, told us all the customs of his country and all the details of his family economy. Love and war seemed his favourite pursuits, in both of which he had suffered severely. His head was disfigured by several scars; a spear had passed through his arm and another through his leg. Half of one of his thumbs was carried away, and the mark of a wound appeared on the back of his hand. The cause and attendant circumstances of all these disasters, except one, he related to us.

'But the wound on the back of your hand, Baneelon! How did you get that?'

He laughed, and owned that it was received in carrying off a lady of another tribe by force. 'I was dragging her away. She cried aloud, and stuck her teeth in me.'

'And what did you do then?'

'I knocked her down, and beat her till she was insensible, and covered with blood. Then . . .'

Whenever he recounted his battles, 'poised his lance, and showed how fields were won',* the most violent exclamations of rage and vengeance against his competitors in arms, those of the tribe called Cameeragal in particular, would burst from him. And he never failed at such times to solicit the governor to accompany him, with a body of soldiers, in order that he might exterminate this hated name.

Although I call him only Baneelon, he had besides several appellations, and for a while he chose to be distinguished by that of Wolarawaree. Again, as a mark of affection and respect to the governor, he conferred on him the name of Wolarawaree and sometimes called him *Beenena* (father), adopting to himself the name of governor. This interchange we found is a constant symbol of friendship among them. In a word, his temper seemed pliant, and his relish of our society so great that hardly anyone judged he would attempt to quit us were the means of escape put within his reach. Nevertheless it was thought proper to continue a watch over him.*

[7 September 1790]

On the 7th instant, Captain Nepean of the New South Wales corps, and Mr White, accompanied by little Nanbaree and a party of men, went in a boat to Manly Cove, intending to land there and walk on to Broken Bay. On drawing near the shore, a dead whale in the most disgusting state of putrefaction was seen lying on the beach, and at least two hundred Indians surrounding it, broiling the flesh on different fires and feasting on it with the most extravagant marks of greediness and rapture. As the boat continued to approach they were observed to fall into confusion and to pick up their spears, on which our people lay upon their oars and Nanbaree, stepping forward, harangued them for some time assuring them that we were friends.

Mr White now called for Baneelon who, on hearing his name, came forth and entered into conversation. He was greatly emaciated, and so far disfigured by a long beard that our people not without difficulty recognized their old acquaintance. His answering in broken English, and inquiring for the governor, however, soon corrected their doubts. He seemed quite friendly. And soon after Colbee came up, pointing to his leg to show that he had freed himself from the fetter which was upon him when he had escaped from us.

When Baneelon was told that the governor was not far off, he expressed great joy and declared that he would immediately go in search of him, and if he found him not, would follow him to Sydney. 'Have you brought any hatchets with you?' cried he. Unluckily they had not any which they chose to spare; but two or three shirts, some handkerchiefs, knives and other trifles were given to them, and seemed to satisfy. Baneelon, willing to instruct his countrymen, tried to put on a shirt, but managed it so awkwardly that a man of the name of McEntire, the governor's gamekeeper, was directed by Mr White to assist him. This man, who was well known to him, he positively forbade to approach, eyeing him ferociously and with every mark of horror and resentment. He was in consequence left to himself, and the conversation proceeded as before. The length of his beard seemed to annoy him much, and he expressed eager wishes to be shaved, asking repeatedly for a razor. A pair of scissors was given to him, and he showed he had not forgotten how to use such an instrument, for he forthwith began to clip his hair with it.

During this time, the women and children, to the number of more than fifty, stood at a distance and refused all invitations which could be conveyed by signs and gestures to approach nearer. 'Which of them is your old favourite, Barangaroo, of whom you used to speak so often?'

'Oh,' said he, 'she is become the wife of Colbee! But I have got *bulla murree deein* (two large women) to compensate for her loss.'

It was observed that he had received two wounds in addition to his former numerous ones since he had left us; one of them from a spear, which had passed through the fleshy part of his arm; and the other displayed itself in a large scar above his left eye. They were both healed, and probably were acquired in the conflict wherein he had asserted his pretensions to the two ladies.

Nanbaree, all this while, though he continued to interrogate his countrymen, and to interpret on both sides, showed little desire to return to their society, and stuck very close to his new friends. On being asked the cause of their present meeting, Baneelon pointed to the whale, which stunk immoderately, and Colbee made signals that it was common among them to eat until the stomach was so overladen as to occasion sickness.

Their demand of hatchets being reiterated, notwithstanding our refusal, they were asked why they had not brought with them some of their own. They excused themselves by saying that on an occasion of the present sort they always left them at home, and cut up the whale with the shell which is affixed to the end of the throwing-stick.

Our party now thought it time to proceed on their original expedition, and having taken leave of their sable friends, rowed to some distance, where they landed and set out for Broken Bay, ordering the coxswain of the boat in which they had come down to go immediately and acquaint the governor of all that had passed. When the natives saw that the boat was about to depart, they crowded around her, and brought down, by way of present, three or four great junks* of the whale, and put them on board of her, the largest of which Baneelon expressly requested might be offered, in his name, to the governor.

It happened that His Excellency had this day gone to a landmark, which was building on the South Head, near the flagstaff, to serve as a direction to ships at sea, and the boat met him on his return to Sydney. Immediately on receiving the intelligence he hastened back to the South Head, and having procured all the firearms which could be mustered there, consisting of four muskets and a pistol, set out attended by Mr Collins and Lieutenant Waterhouse of the navy.

When the boat reached Manly Cove the natives were found still busily employed around the whale. As they expressed not any consternation on seeing us row to the beach, Governor Phillip stepped out unarmed and attended by one seaman only, and called for

Baneelon, who appeared but, notwithstanding his former eagerness, would not suffer the other to approach him for several minutes. Gradually, however, he warmed into friendship and frankness and, presently after, Colbee came up. They discoursed for some time, Baneelon expressing pleasure to see his old acquaintance, and inquiring by name for every person whom he could recollect at Sydney; and among others for a French cook, one of the governor's servants, whom he had constantly made the butt of his ridicule by mimicking his voice, gait, and other peculiarities, all of which he again went through with his wonted exactness and drollery. He asked also particularly for a lady from whom he had once ventured to snatch a kiss and, on being told that she was well, by way of proving that the token was fresh in his remembrance, he kissed Lieutenant Waterhouse, and laughed aloud. On his wounds being noticed, he coldly said that he had received them at Botany Bay, but went no farther into their history.

Hatchets still continued to be called for with redoubled eagerness, which rather surprised us, as formerly they had always been accepted with indifference. But Baneelon had probably demonstrated to them their superiority over those of their own manufacturing. To appease their importunity, the governor gave them a knife, some bread, pork and other articles; and promised that in two days he would return hither and bring with him hatchets to be distributed among them, which appeared to diffuse general satisfaction.

Baneelon's love of wine has been mentioned; and the governor, to try whether it still subsisted, uncorked a bottle and poured out a glass of it, which the other drank off with his former marks of relish and good humour, giving for a toast, as he had been taught, 'The King'.

Our party now advanced from the beach but, perceiving many of the Indians filing off to the right and left, so as in some measure to surround them, they retreated gently to their old situation, which produced neither alarm nor offence. The others by degrees also resumed their former position. A very fine barbed spear of uncommon size being seen by the governor, he asked for it. But Baneelon, instead of complying with the request, took it away and laid it at some distance, and brought back a throwing-stick which he presented to His Excellency.

Matters had proceeded in this friendly train for more than half an hour, when a native with a spear in his hand came forward, and stopped at the distance of between twenty and thirty yards from the place where the governor, Mr Collins, Lieutenant Waterhouse and a seaman stood. His Excellency held out his hand and called to him, advancing towards him at the same time, Mr Collins following close behind. He appeared to be a man of middle age, short of stature, sturdy and well set, seemingly a stranger and but little acquainted with Baneelon and Colbee. The nearer the governor approached, the greater became the terror and agitation of the Indian. To remove his fear, Governor Phillip threw down a dirk, which he wore at his side. The other, alarmed at the rattle of the dirk, and probably mis-construing the action, instantly fixed his lance in his throwing-stick.*

To retreat His Excellency now thought would be more dangerous than to advance. He therefore cried out to the man, *weeree, weeree* (bad; you are doing wrong), displaying at the same time every token of amity and confidence. The words had, however, hardly gone forth when the Indian, stepping back with one foot, aimed his lance with such force and dexterity that, striking* the governor's right shoulder just above the collarbone, the point glancing downward, came out at his back, having made a wound of many inches long. The man was observed to keep his eye steadily fixed on the lance until it struck its object, when he directly dashed into the woods and was seen no more.

Instant confusion on both sides took place. Baneelon and Colbee disappeared and several spears were thrown from different quarters, though without effect. Our party retreated as fast as they could, calling to those who were left in the boat to hasten up with firearms. A situation more distressing than that of the governor, during the time that this lasted, cannot readily be conceived: the pole of the spear, not less than ten feet in length, sticking out before him and impeding his flight, the butt frequently striking the ground and lacerating the wound. In vain did Mr Waterhouse try to break it; and the barb which appeared on the other side forbade extraction until that could be performed. At length it was broken, and His Excellency reached the boat, by which time the seamen with the muskets had got up and were endeavouring to fire them, but one only would go off, and there is no room to believe that it was attended with any execution.

When the governor got home, the wound was examined. It had

bled a good deal in the boat and it was doubtful whether the sub-clavian artery might not be divided. On moving the spear, it was found, however, that it might be safely extracted, which was accordingly performed.

[15 September 1790]

From so unfavourable an omen as I have just related, who could prognosticate that an intercourse with the natives was about to commence! That the foundation of what neither entreaty, munificence or humanity could induce, should be laid by a deed which threatened to accumulate scenes of bloodshed and horror was a consequence which neither speculation could predict, or hope expect to see accomplished.

On the 15th, a fire being seen on the north shore of the harbour, a party of our people went thither, accompanied by Nanbaree and Abaroo. They found there Baneelon and several other natives, and much civility passed, which was cemented by a mutual promise to meet in the afternoon at the same place. Both sides were punctual to their engagement, and no objection being made to our landing, a party of us went ashore to them unarmed. Several little presents, which had been purposely brought, were distributed among them; and to Baneelon were given a hatchet and a fish. At a distance stood some children who, though at first timorous and unwilling to approach, were soon persuaded to advance and join the men.

A bottle of wine was produced, and Baneelon immediately prepared for the charge. Bread and beef he called loudly for, which were given to him, and he began to eat, offering a part of his fare to his countrymen, two of whom tasted the beef, but none of them would touch the bread. Having finished his repast, he made a motion to be shaved and, a barber being present, his request was complied with, to the great admiration of his countrymen, who laughed and exclaimed at the operation. They would not, however, consent to undergo it, but suffered their beards to be clipped with a pair of scissors.

On being asked where their women were, they pointed to the spot, but seemed not desirous that we should approach it. However, in a few minutes, a female appeared not far off, and Abaroo was dispatched to her. Baneelon now joined with Abaroo to persuade her to come to us, telling us she was Barangaroo, and his wife, notwithstanding he had so lately pretended that she had left him for Colbee.

At length she yielded, and Abaroo, having first put a petticoat on her, brought her to us. But this was the prudery of the wilderness, which her husband joined us to ridicule, and we soon laughed her out of it. The petticoat was dropped with hesitation, and Barangaroo stood 'armed cap-a-pee in nakedness'. At the request of Baneelon, we combed and cut her hair, and she seemed pleased with the operation. Wine she would not taste, but turned from it with disgust, though heartily invited to drink by the example and persuasion of Baneelon. In short, she behaved so well, and assumed the character of gentleness and timidity to such advantage that, had our acquaintance ended here, a very moderate share of the spirit of travelling would have sufficed to record that amidst a horde of roaming savages in the desert wastes of New South Wales might be found as much feminine innocence, softness and modesty (allowing for inevitable difference of education) as the most finished system could bestow, or the most polished circle produce. So little fitted are we to judge of human nature at once! And yet on such grounds have countries been described and nations characterized. Hence have arisen those speculative and laborious compositions on the advantages and superiority of a state of nature.

JOHN NICOL, *The Life and Adventures of John Nicol, Mariner*, ed. John Howell (Edinburgh, 1822)

In 1790 a second convict fleet arrived at Port Jackson in a miserable condition, largely due to government failure to regulate the private contractors who supplied the ships. Many convicts had died *en route* and more than half of the survivors were sick with scurvy. The remarkable memoir by Scots seaman John Nicol (1755–1825) gives us a rare below-decks view of the lives of the lower and criminal classes, including—uniquely— women: Nicol sailed on the *Lady Juliana*, which carried female convicts to the colony as breeding stock.

I was appointed steward of the *Lady Juliana*, commanded by Captain Aitkin, who was an excellent humane man and did all in his power to make the convicts as comfortable as their circumstances would allow. The government agent, an old lieutenant, had been discharged a little before I arrived for cruelty to the convicts. He had even begun to flog them in the river. Government, the moment they learned the fact, appointed another in his place.

We lay six months in the river before we sailed, during which time all the jails in England were emptied to complete the cargo of the *Lady Juliana*. When we sailed there were on board 245 female convicts.* There were not a great many very bad characters. The greater number were for petty crimes, and a great proportion for only being disorderly, that is, street-walkers, the colony at the time being in great want of women.

One, a Scottish girl, broke her heart and died in the river. She was buried at Dartford. Four were pardoned on account of His Majesty's recovery. The poor young Scottish girl I have never yet got out of my mind. She was young and beautiful, even in the convict dress, but pale as death, and her eyes red with weeping.

She never spoke to any of the other women or came on deck. She was constantly seen sitting in the same corner from morning to night. Even the time of meals roused her not. My heart bled for her—she was a countrywoman in misfortune. I offered her consolation but her hopes and heart had sunk. When I spoke she heeded me not, or only answered with sighs and tears. If I spoke of Scotland she would wring her hands and sob until I thought her heart would burst. I endeavoured to get her sad story from her lips but she was silent as the grave to which she hastened. I lent her my Bible to comfort her but she read it not. She laid it on her lap after kissing it, and only bedewed it with her tears. At length she sank into the grave of no disease but a broken heart. After her death we had only two Scottish women on board, one of them a Shetlander.

I went every day to the town to buy fresh provisions and other necessaries for them. As their friends were allowed to come on board to see them, they brought money; and numbers had it of their own, particularly a Mrs Barnsley, a noted sharper and shoplifter. She herself told me her family for one hundred years back had been swindlers and highwaymen. She had a brother, a highwayman, who often came to see her as well dressed and genteel in his appearance as any gentleman. She petitioned the government agent and captain to be allowed to wear her own clothes in the river, and not the convict dress. This could on no account be allowed, but they told her she might wear what she chose when once they were at sea.

The agent, Lieutenant Edgar, had been with Captain Cook, was a kind humane man and very good to them. He had it in his power to throw all their clothes overboard when he gave them the convict dress, but he gave them to me to stow in the after hold, saying, 'They would be of use to the poor creatures when they arrived at Port Jackson.'

Those from the country came all on board in irons, and I was paid half a crown a head by the country jailers, in many cases, for striking them off upon my anvil, as they were not locked but riveted. There was a Mrs Davis, a noted swindler, who had obtained great quantities of goods under false names and other equally base means. We had one Mary Williams, transported for receiving stolen goods. She and other eight had been a long time in Newgate where Lord George Gordon had supported them. I went once a week to him and got their allowance from his own hand all the time we lay in the river.

One day I had the painful task to inform the father and mother of one of the convicts that their daughter, Sarah Dorset, was on board. They were decent-looking people, and had come to London to inquire after her. When I met them they were at Newgate. The jailer referred them to me. With tears in her eyes the mother implored me to tell her if such a one was on board. I told them there was one of that name. The father's heart seemed too full to allow him to speak but the mother with streaming eyes blessed God that they had found their poor lost child, undone as she was.

I called a coach, drove to the river and had them put on board. The father, with a trembling step, mounted the ship's side, but we were forced to lift the mother on board. I took them down to my berth and went for Sarah Dorset. When I brought her the father said in a choking voice, 'My lost child!' and turned his back, covering his face with his hands. The mother, sobbing, threw her hands around her. Poor Sarah fainted and fell at their feet. I knew not what to do. At length she recovered and in the most heart-rending accents implored their pardon.

She was young and pretty and had not been two years from her father's house at this present time, so short had been her course of folly and sin. She had not been protected by the villain that ruined her above six weeks, then she was forced by want upon the streets and taken up as a disorderly girl, then sent on board to be transported. This was her short but eventful history. One of our men,

William Power, went out to the colony when her time was expired, brought her home and married her.

I witnessed many moving scenes, and many of the most hardened indifference. Numbers of them would not take their liberty as a boon. They were thankful for their present situation, so low had vice reduced them. Many of these from the country jails had been allowed to leave it to assist in getting in the harvest, and voluntarily returned.

When I inquired their reason, they answered, 'How much more preferable is our present situation to what it has been since we commenced our vicious habits? We have good victuals and a warm bed. We are not ill treated or at the mercy of every drunken ruffian as we were before. When we rose in the morning we knew not where we would lay our heads in the evening, or if we would break our fast in the course of the day. Banishment is a blessing for us. Have we not been banished for a long time, and yet in our native land, the most dreadful of all situations? We dared not go to our relations whom we had disgraced. Other people would shut their doors in our faces. We were as if a plague were upon us, hated and shunned.'

Others did all in their power to make their escape. These were such as had left their associates in rapine on shore and were hardened to every feeling but the abandoned enjoyments of their companions. Four of these made their escape on the evening before we left England through the assistance of their confederates on shore. They gave the man on watch gin to drink as he sat on the quarterdeck, the others singing and making fun. These four slipped over her bows into a boat provided for their escape. I never heard if they were retaken. We sailed without them.

Mrs Nelly Kerwin, a female of daring habits, banished for life for forging seamen's powers of attorney and personating their relations, when on our passage down the river, wrote to London for cash to some of her friends. She got a letter informing her it was waiting for her at Dartmouth. We were in Colson Bay when she got this letter. With great address she persuaded the agent that there was an express for him and money belonging to her lying at Dartmouth. A man was sent who brought on board Nell's money, but no express for the agent. When she got it she laughed in his face and told him he was in her debt for a lesson. He was very angry, as the captain often told him Kerwin was too many for him.

We had on board a girl pretty well behaved, who was called by her acquaintance a daughter of Pitt's.* She herself never contradicted it. She bore a most striking likeness to him in every feature and could scarce be known from him as to looks. We left her at Port Jackson.

Some of our convicts I have heard even to boast of the crimes and murders committed by them and their accomplices, but the far greater number were harmless unfortunate creatures, the victims of the basest seduction. With their histories, as told by themselves, I shall not trouble the reader.

When we were fairly out to sea, every man on board took a wife from among the convicts, they nothing loath. The girl with whom I lived, for I was as bad in this point as the others, was named Sarah Whitlam. She was a native of Lincoln, a girl of a modest reserved turn, as kind and true a creature as ever lived. I courted her for a week and upwards, and would have married her on the spot had there been a clergyman on board.

She had been banished for a mantle she had borrowed from an acquaintance. Her friend prosecuted her for stealing it, and she was transported for seven years. I had fixed my fancy upon her from the moment I knocked the rivet out of her irons upon my anvil, and as firmly resolved to bring her back to England when her time was out, my lawful wife, as ever I did intend anything in my life. She bore me a son in our voyage out.

What is become of her, whether she is dead or alive, I know not. That I do not is no fault of mine, as my narrative will show.

But to proceed. We soon found that we had a troublesome cargo, yet not dangerous or very mischievous—as I may say, more noise than danger. When any of them, such as Nance Ferrel who was ever making disturbance, became very troublesome we confined them down in the hold and put on the hatch. This, we were soon convinced, had no effect as they became in turns outrageous, on purpose to be confined. Our agent and the captain wondered at the change in their behaviour.

I, as steward, found it out by accident. As I was overhauling the stores in the hold I came upon a hogshead of bottled porter with a hole in the side of it and, in place of full, there were nothing but empty bottles in it. Another was begun and more than a box of candles had been carried off. I immediately told the captain, who now found out the cause of the late insubordination and desire of confinement.

We were forced to change the manner of punishing them. I was desired by the agent Lieutenant Edgar, who was an old lieutenant of Cook's, to take a flour barrel and cut a hole in the top for their head and one on each side for their arms. This we called a wooden jacket. Next morning, Nance Ferrel, as usual, came to the door of the cabin and began to abuse the agent and captain. They desired her to go away between decks and be quiet. She became worse in her abuse, wishing to be confined and sent to the hold, but to her mortification the jacket was produced, and two men brought her upon deck and put it on.

She laughed and capered about for a while, and made light of it. One of her comrades lighted a pipe and gave it her. She walked about strutting and smoking the tobacco, and making the others laugh at the droll figure she made. She walked a minuet, her head moving from side to side like a turtle.

The agent was resolved she should be heartily tired, and feel in all its force the disagreeableness of her present situation. She could only walk or stand—to sit or lie down was out of her power. She began to get weary and begged to be released. The agent would not until she asked his pardon, and promised amendment in future. This she did in humble terms before evening, but in a few days was as bad as ever. There was no taming her by gentle means. We were forced to tie her up like a man, and give her one dozen with the cat-o'-nine-tails, and assure her of a clawing every offence. This alone reduced her to any kind of order.

How great was the contrast between her and Mary Rose. Mary was a timid modest girl who never joined in the ribaldry of the rest, neither did she take up with any man upon the voyage. She was a wealthy farmer's daughter who had been seduced under promise of marriage by an officer, and had eloped with him from her father's house. They were living together in Lincoln when the officer was forced to go abroad and leave her. He, before he went, boarded her with their landlady, an infamous character, who, to obtain the board she had received in advance without maintaining the unfortunate girl, swore she had robbed her of several articles.

Poor Mary was condemned by her perjury and sentenced to be transported. She had disgraced her friends and dared not apply to them in her distress. She had set the opinions of the world at defiance by her elopement, and there was no one in it who appeared to befriend her, while in all its bitterness she drank the cup of her own mixing. After the departure of the *Lady Juliana* her relations had discovered the fate of their lost and ruined Mary. By their exertions the whole scene of the landlady's villainy was exposed, and she stood in the pillory at Lincoln for her perjury.

Upon our arrival we found a pardon lying at Port Jackson, and a chest of excellent clothes sent by the magistrates for her use in the voyage home. She lodged all the time I was there in the governor's house and every day I took her allowance to her. She was to sail in the first ship for London direct, the *Lady Juliana* being bound for China. During the tedious voyage out I took her under my protection. Sarah and she were acquaint before they saw each other in misfortune. Mary washed the clothes and did any little thing for Sarah when she was confined, which she was long before we reached Port Jackson.

The first place we stopped at was Santa Cruz in the island of Tenerife for water. As we used a great quantity the agent, at the captain's request, had laid in tea and sugar in place of beef or pork allowed by government. We boiled a large kettle of water that served the whole convicts and crew every night and morning. We allowed them water for washing their clothes, any quantity they chose, while in port. Many times they would use four and five boatloads in one day.

We did not restrain the people on shore from coming on board through the day. The captains and seamen who were in port at the time paid us many visits. Mrs Barnsley bought a cask of wine and got it on board with the agent's leave. She was very kind to her fellow convicts who were poor. They were all anxious to serve her. She was as a queen among them.

We had a number of Jewesses on board. One, Sarah Sabolah, had a crucifix, and the others soon got them and passed themselves for Roman Catholics, by which means they got many presents from the people on shore and laid up a large stock for sea.

We next stood for Sao Tiago, accompanied by two slave ships from Santa Cruz to Sao Tiago, who sailed thus far out of their course for the sake of the ladies. They came on board every day when the weather would permit. At length they stood for the coast to pick up their cargo of human misery. We watered again and made all clear for a new start. Our Jewesses played off the same farce with their crucifixes, and with equal success.

We then stood for Rio de Janeiro where we lay eight weeks taking in coffee and sugar, our old stock being now reduced very low. I was employed on shore repairing flour casks to receive it. The Jewesses made here a good harvest, and the ladies had a constant run of visitors. I had received fifty suits of child-bed linen for their use— they were a present from the ladies of England. I here served out twenty suits. Mrs Barnsley acted as midwife and was to practise at Port Jackson, but there was no clergyman on board. When in port the ladies fitted up a kind of tent for themselves.

In crossing the line* we had the best sport I ever witnessed upon the same occasion. We had caught a porpoise the day before the ceremony which we skinned to make a dress for Neptune with the tail stuffed. When he came on deck he looked the best representation of a merman I ever saw, painted, with a large swab upon his head for a wig. Not a man in the ship could have known him. One of the convicts fainted, she was so much alarmed at his appearance, and had a miscarriage after. Neptune made the boys confess their amours to him, and I was really astonished at the number. I will not describe the ceremony to fatigue the reader, as it has been often described by others. . . .

At length we sailed for Port Jackson. We made one of the convicts shepherdess, who was so fortunate in her charge of the flock as not to lose one. While we lay at the Cape we had a narrow escape from destruction by fire. The carpenter allowed the pitch-pot to boil over upon the deck, and the flames rose in an alarming manner. The shrieks of the women were dreadful, and the confusion they made running about drove everyone stupid. I ran to my berth, seized a pair of blankets to keep it down until the others drowned it with water. Captain Aitkin made me a handsome present for my exertions.

The captain had a quantity of linen on board, and during the voyage had kept above twenty of the convicts making shirts to sell at Port Jackson. He got them made cheap and sold them to great advantage upon our arrival as the people of the colony were in want of every necessity.

At length, almost to our sorrow, we made the land upon the 3rd of June 1790, just one year all but one day from our leaving the river.

We landed all our convicts safe. My charge as steward did not expire for six weeks after our arrival, as the captain, by agreement, was bound to victual them during that time.

It is a fine country and everything thrives well in it. A sergeant of marines supplied the *Lady Juliana* with potatoes and garden stuffs for half a crown a day. There were thirty-six people on board and we had as much as we could use. There were only two natives in the town at the time, a boy and a girl.* These had been brought in by a party of the settlers, having been left by their parents. I saw but little of the colony, as my time was fully occupied in my duties as steward, and any moments I could spare I gave them to Sarah.

The days flew on eagles' wings, for we dreaded the hour of separation which at length arrived. It was not without the aid of the military we were brought on board. I offered to lose my wages but we were short of hands, one man having been left sick at Rio de Janeiro, and we had lost our carpenter who fell overboard. The captain could not spare a man and requested the aid of the governor. I thus was forced to leave Sarah, but we exchanged faith. She promised to remain true, and I promised to return when her time expired and bring her back to England.*

I wished to have stolen her away, but this was impossible, the convicts were so strictly guarded by the marines. There were no soldiers in the colony at this time. With a heavy heart I bade adieu to Port Jackson, resolved to return as soon as I reached England.

MARY ANN PARKER, *A Voyage Round the World, in the Gorgon Man of War: Captain John Parker. Performed and Written by his Widow; for the Advantage of a Numerous Family* (1795)

The third fleet, 1791, produced another rare memoir, by a lady passenger, Mary Ann Parker (b. *c.*1760), whose husband was captain of the *Gorgon*. In admitting the natives to sentimental domesticity Parker at least tries to imagine a future for them.

The inhabitants of New South Wales, both male and female, go without apparel. Their colour is of a dingy copper; their nose is broad and flat, their lips wide and thick, and their eyes circular. From a disagreeable practice they have of rubbing themselves with fish-oil, they smell so loathsome, that it is almost impossible to approach them without disgust.

The men in general appeared to be from five feet six to five feet nine inches high, are rather slender, but straight and well made: they have bushy beards, and the hair on their heads is stuck full with the teeth of fish, and bits of shells: they also ornament themselves with a fish-bone fastened in the gristle of the nose, which makes them appear really frightful; and are generally armed with a stick about a yard long, and a lance which they throw with considerable velocity.

The stature of the women is somewhat less than that of the men— their noses are broad, their mouths wide, and their lips thick. They are extremely negligent of their persons, and are filthy to a degree scarcely credible: their faces and bodies are besmeared with the fat of animals, and the salutary custom of washing seems entirely unknown to them.

Their huts or habitations are constructed in the most rude and barbarous manner: they consist of pieces of bark laid together some-what in the form of an oven, with a small entrance at one end. Their sole residence, however, is not in these huts; on the contrary, they depend less on them for shelter than on the numerous excavations which are formed in the rocks by the washing of the sea; and it is no uncommon thing to see fifty or sixty of them comfortably lodged in one of these caves.

Notwithstanding the general appearance of the natives, I never felt the least fear when in their company being always with a party more than sufficient for my protection. I have been seated in the woods with twelve or fourteen of them, men, women, and children. Had I objected, or shown any disgust at their appearance, it would have given them some reason to suppose that I was not what they term their *damely*, or friend; and would have rendered my being in their company not only unpleasant, but unsafe.

Before I conclude my description of the natives, it is but justice to remark that, in comparison with the inhabitants of most of the South-Sea Islands, they appear very little given to thieving; and their confidence in the honesty of one another is so great that they will leave their spears and other implements on the sea-shore, in full and perfect security of their remaining untouched.

From the treatment which I invariably experienced, I am inclined to think favourably of them; and fully believe that they would never injure our people, were they not first offended by them.

I cannot help observing that one of the men had a most engaging deportment; his countenance was pleasing, and his manners far beyond what I could possibly have expected. He was pleased to seat himself by me, changed names with Captain Parker, and took particular notice of the travelling knife and fork with which I was eating, and which I did myself the satisfaction to give him: he paid us a visit on board the ensuing day, and showed me that he had not lost my present, but made use of it, though somewhat awkwardly, whilst he demolished *two* or *three* pounds of the ship's pork.

The natives very frequently surrounded our vessel with their canoes. The women often held up their little ones, as if anxious to have them noticed by us. Sometimes, for the sake of amusement, I have thrown them ribands and other trifles, which they would as frequently tie round their toes as any other part of their person.

Since my return to England, Banalong, one of the natives brought hither by Governor Phillip, came to see me. To describe the pleasure that overspread this poor fellow's countenance when my little girl presented to him the picture of her dear father, is impossible; it was then that the tear of sensibility trickled down his cheeks; he immediately recognized those features which will never be obliterated from my memory, and spoke, with all the energy of Nature, of the pleasing excursion which they had made together up the country. The above is one amongst many instances which I could relate of the natural goodness of their hearts; and I flatter myself that the time is hastening when they will no longer be considered as mere savages;—and wherefore should they?

> Fleecy locks, and black complexion,
>   Cannot forfeit Nature's claim:
> Skins may differ, but affection
>   Dwells in white and black the same.*

4. THE COMING OF THE MISSIONARIES, 1796–1824

WILLIAM WILSON, *A Missionary Voyage to the Southern Pacific Ocean* (1799)

In 1796 a ship chartered by the non-denominational London Missionary Society (founded the previous year) set sail for the South Sea islands, arriving at Tahiti in March 1797. The missionaries were at first beset by difficulties, including civil war, which forced them to flee to New South Wales with their patron King Pomare II. Pomare's conversion to Christianity (1812) and return to power in Tahiti (1815) ensured the triumph of the new religion in the Society Islands.

SUNDAY, 5 MARCH 1797. The morning was pleasant, and with a gentle breeze we had by seven o'clock got abreast of the district of Atahooroo, whence we saw several canoes putting off and paddling towards us with great speed; at the same time it fell calm, which being in their favour, we soon counted seventy-four canoes around us, many of them double ones, containing about twenty persons each. Being so numerous, we endeavoured to keep them from crowding on board; but in spite of all our efforts to prevent it, there were soon not less than one hundred of them dancing and capering like frantic persons about our decks, crying, 'Tayo!* tayo!' and a few broken sentences of English were often repeated. They had no weapons of any kind among them; however, to keep them in awe, some of the great guns were ordered to be hoisted out of the hold, whilst they, as free from the apprehension as the intention of mischief, cheerfully assisted to put them on their carriages. When the first ceremonies were over, we began to view our new friends with an eye of inquiry: their wild disorderly behaviour, strong smell of the coconut oil, together with the tricks of the arreoies,* lessened the favourable opinion we had formed of them; neither could we see aught of that elegance and beauty in their women for which they have been so greatly celebrated. This at first seemed to depreciate them in the estimation of our brethren; but the cheerfulness, good-nature, and generosity of these kind people soon removed the momentary prejudices. One very old man, Manne Manne, who called himself a priest of the Eatooa,* was very importunate to be tayo with the captain;

others, pretending to be chiefs, singled out such as had the appearance of officers for their tayos; but as they neither exercised authority over the unruly, nor bore the smallest mark of distinction, we thought proper to decline their proposals till we knew them and the nature of the engagement better. At this they seemed astonished, but still more when they saw our indifference about the hogs, fowls, and fruit, which they had brought in abundance. We endeavoured to make them understand, but I think in vain, that this was the day of the Eatooa, and that in it we durst not trade: but their women repulsed, occasioned greater wonder. They continued to go about the decks till the transports of their joy gradually subsided, when many of them left us of their own accord, and others were driven away by the old man, and one named Mauroa, who now exercised a little authority. Those who remained were chiefly arreoies from Ulietea, in number about forty; and being brought to order, the brethren proposed having divine service upon the quarterdeck. Mr Cover officiated; he perhaps was the first that ever mentioned with reverence the Saviour's name to these poor heathens. Such hymns were selected as had the most harmonious tunes; first, 'O'er the gloomy hills of darkness'; then, 'Blow ye the trumpet, blow'; and at the conclusion, 'Praise God from whom all blessings flow'. The text was from the first epistle general of John, chap. iii. ver. 23, 'God is love'. The whole service lasted about an hour and a quarter. During sermon and prayer the natives were quiet and thoughtful; but when the singing struck up, they seemed charmed and filled with amazement; sometimes they would talk and laugh, but a nod of the head brought them to order. Upon the whole, their unweariedness and quietness were astonishing; and, indeed, all who heard observed a peculiar solemnity and excellence in Mr Cover's address on that day.

WILLIAM ELLIS, *Narrative of a Tour through Hawaii, or Owhyhee; With Remarks on the History, Traditions, Manners, Customs, and Language of the Inhabitants of the Sandwich Island* (1826)

The missionaries begin a new era in Polynesian history. They came not as visitors but as settlers, with the express purpose of changing this world forever. The volatile, open-ended play of cultural encounter, bafflement, and exchange is replaced by a determination to root out 'the national idolatry' and rescue heathen souls. William Ellis (1792–1874) sailed with a second wave of missionaries in 1816. His *Polynesian Researches* (1829) describes the establishment of native printing presses and the diffusion of literacy across the islands. At the same time, the form of the encounter allows the natives, on occasion, to speak back—and the end of the conversation is not always conversion, as we find in Ellis's earlier account of a debate with a Hawaiian priestess of the old religion at Waiakea.

Dense fogs and heavy rains are more frequent at Waiakea, and over the whole division of Hiro, than in any other part of the island. We were, therefore, not surprised at beholding, on the morning of the 10th, the district and coast enveloped in mist, and experiencing frequent showers of rain through the earlier part of the day. Between nine and ten in the forenoon, however, the fog cleared off, and the sun shone brightly on the glowing landscape.

Shortly after ten o'clock, the chiefs, and people in considerable numbers, assembled in a large house adjacent to that in which we resided, agreeably to the invitation given them last evening. The worship commenced as usual, and I preached from the text 'Happy is that people whose God is the Lord'.* The attention was not so good as that generally given by the congregations we had addressed. Many, however, quietly listened till the service was over. As we arose to depart, an old woman, who, during the discourse, sat near the speaker, and had listened very attentively, all at once exclaimed, 'Powerful are the gods of Hawaii, and great is Pélé, the goddess of Hawaii, she shall save Maaro' (the sick chief who was present). Another began to chant a song in praise of Pélé, to which the people generally listened, though some began to laugh. We supposed they were intoxicated, and therefore took no notice of them, but on our leaving the house, some of our people told us they were not *ona i ka ruma* (intoxicated or poisoned with rum), but inspired by the *akua* (goddess) of the volcano; or that one of them was Pélé herself, in the form of one of her priestesses. On hearing this, I turned back into the house, and when the song was ended, immediately entered into conversation with the principal one, by asking her if she had attended to the discourse that had been delivered there? She answered that she had listened, and understood it. I then asked if she thought Jehovah was good, and those happy who made him their God? She answered, 'He is your good God (or best God), and it is right that you should worship him; but Pélé is my deity, and the great goddess of Hawaii. Kirauea is the place of her abode. Ohiaotelani (the northern peak of the volcano) is one corner of her house. From the land beyond the sky, in former times, she came.' She then went on with the song which she had thus begun, giving a long account of the deeds and honours of Pélé. This she pronounced in such a rapid and vociferous manner, accompanied by such violent gestures, that only here and there a word could be understood. Indeed, towards the close, she appeared to lose all command of herself. When she had done, I told her she was mistaken in supposing any supernatural being resided in the volcano; that Pélé was a creature of their own invention, and existed only in the imagination of her *kahu*, or devotees. Adding, that volcanoes, and all their accompanying phenomena, were under the powerful control of Jehovah, who, though uncreated himself, was the Creator and Supporter of heaven and earth, and everything she beheld. She replied that it was not so. She did not dispute that Jehovah was a God, but that he was not the only God. Pélé was a goddess, and dwelt in her, and through her would heal the sick chief then present. She wished him restored, and therefore came to visit him. I said I also wished Maaro to recover, but if he did recover, it would be by the favour of Jehovah, and that I hoped he would acknowledge him, and seek to him alone, as he was the only true Physician, who could save both body and soul, making the latter happy in another world, when this world, with all its volcanoes, mountains, and oceans, should cease to exist.

I then advised her, and all present, to forsake their imaginary deity, whose character was distinguished by all that was revengeful and destructive, and accept the offers Jehovah had made them by his servants, that they might be happy now, and escape the everlasting death that would overtake all the idolatrous and wicked.

Assuming a haughty air, she said, 'I am Pélé; I shall never die; and those who follow me, when they die, if part of their bones be taken to Kirauea (the name of the volcano) will live with me in the bright fires there.' I said, Are you Pélé? She replied, Yes: and was proceeding to state her powers, etc. when Makoa, who had till now stood silent, interrupted her, and said, 'It is true you are Pélé, or some of Pélé's party; and it is you that have destroyed the king's land, devoured his people, and spoiled all the fishing grounds. Ever since you came to the islands, you have been busied in mischief; you spoiled the greater part of the island, shook it to pieces, or cursed it with barrenness, by inundating it with lava. You never did any good; and if I were the king, I would throw you all into the sea, or banish you from the islands. Hawaii would be quiet if you were away.'

This was rather unexpected, and seemed to surprise several of the company. However, the pretended Pélé said, 'Formerly we did overflow some of the land, but it was only the land of those that were rebels, or were very wicked people.* Now we abide quietly in Kirauea.' She then added, 'It cannot be said that in these days we destroy the king's people.' She mentioned the names of several chiefs, and then asked who destroyed these? not Pélé, but the rum of the foreigners, whose God you are so fond of. Their diseases and their rum have destroyed more of the king's men than all the volcanoes on the island. I told her I regretted that their intercourse with foreigners should have introduced among them diseases to which they were strangers before, and that I hoped they would also receive the advantages of Christian instruction and civilization, which the benevolent in those countries by which they had been injured were now so anxious to impart: that intoxication was wholly forbidden by Jehovah, the God of Christians, who had declared that no drunkard should enter the kingdom of heaven. I then said I was sorry to see her so deceived, and attempting to deceive others; told her she knew her pretensions were false, and recommended her to consider seriously the consequences of idolatry, and cease to practise her fatal deceptions; to recollect that she would one day die; that God had given her an opportunity of hearing of his love to sinners in the gift of his Son; and that if she applied to him for mercy, although now an idolatrous priestess, she might be saved; but if she did not, a fearful doom awaited her. 'I shall not die,' she exclaimed, 'but *ora no*' (live spontaneously). After replying to this, I retired; but the spectators, who had manifested by their countenances that they were not uninterested in the discussion, continued in earnest conversation for some time. The name of the priestess we afterwards learned was Oani. She resided in a neighbouring village, and had, that morning, arrived at Waiakea on a visit to Maaro.

When the national idolatry was publicly abolished in the year 1819, several priests of Pélé denounced the most awful threatenings of earthquakes, eruptions, etc. from the gods of the volcanoes, in revenge for the insult and neglect then shown by the king and chiefs.

But no fires afterwards appearing in any of the extinguished volcanoes, no fresh ones having broken out, and those then in action
having since that period remained in a state of comparative quies-
cence, some of the people have been led to conclude that the gods
formerly supposed to preside over volcanoes had existed only in
their imagination. The fearful apprehensions which they had been
accustomed to associate with every idea of Pélé and her companions
have in a great measure subsided, and the oppressive power of her
priests and priestesses is consequently diminished. There are, however, many who remain in constant dread of her displeasure, and who
pay the most submissive and unhesitating obedience to the requisi-
tions of her priests. This is no more than was to be expected, particularly in this part of the island, where the people are far removed from
the means of instruction, the example and influence of the principal
chiefs, and more enlightened part of the population; and it appears
matter of surprise that, in the course of three years only, so many
should have relinquished their superstitious notions respecting the
deities of the volcanoes, when we consider their ignorance and their
early impressions, and recollect that, while resting at night, perhaps
on a bed of lava, they are occasionally startled from their midnight
slumbers by the undulating earthquake, and are daily reminded of
the dreadful power of this imaginary goddess by almost every object
that meets their view, from the cliffs which are washed by the waves
of the sea, even to the lofty craters, her ancient seat above the clouds,
and amid perpetual snows.

Until this morning, however, none of the servants of Pélé had ever
publicly opposed her pretended right to that homage and obedience
which it was our object to persuade and invite them to render to
Jehovah alone; and though it was encouraging to notice that, by
many of the people present, the pretensions of Oani were disregarded, it was exceedingly painful to hear an idolatrous priestess
declaring that the conduct of those by whom they had been sometimes visited from countries called Christian had been productive of
consequences more injurious and fatal to the unsuspecting and
unenlightened Hawaiians than these dreadful phenomena in nature,
which they had been accustomed to attribute to the most destructive
of their imaginary deities, and to know also that such a declaration
was too true to be contradicted.

EXPLANATORY NOTES

PART I. EUROPE AND ASIA MINOR

5 *what it once was*: a commonplace of the period; Isaak Vossius, *Variarum Observationum Liber* (1685), claimed that ancient Rome had a population of 14 million. See David Hume's sceptical account, 'Of the Populousness of Ancient Nations' (1754).

8 *Minus est gravis Appia tardis*: 'the Appian Way is less fatiguing if you go slowly': Horace, *Satires* 1. 5. 6.

Holy-Week: from Palm Sunday to Easter.

Anjou . . . Spain: Angevin kings ruled Naples from 1268 until 1503, when the city became a Spanish province. Juan Manuel Fernando Pacheco de Acuna, Duke of Escalona-Villena, was Viceroy from 1702 to 1707.

St Januarius: San Gennaro, patron saint of Naples; the miraculous lique-faction of his blood, kept in a reliquary in the Duomo, is still a major event in the Neapolitan calendar.

Paschal . . . marks of the true religion: Blaise Pascal, in *Pensées*, section XIII, 'Of Miracles', declares miracles to be one of the 'three marks of religion' inaccessible to heretics.

At Gnatia . . . not I: Addison's translation of Horace, *Satires* 1. 5. 97–101.

9 *Huguenots*: French Calvinist Protestants, granted liberty of conscience (and thus the possibility of participating in 'controversies') by the Edict of Nantes, 1598, until its revocation in 1685.

del Cani [properly, *del Cane*]: of the dog. A high concentration of carbon dioxide, heavier than air, accounted for the phenomenon.

10 *since printed in England*: Bernard Connor, *Dissertationes Medico-Physicae* (1695).

Stagnum: reservoir containing mercury ('quicksilver') in a barometer ('weatherglass').

stum: unfermented or partially fermented grape-juice.

11 *temple of Minerva*: the Parthenon. Minerva is the Roman name for Athena.

Lord Elgin: Thomas Bruce, seventh Lord Elgin, carried away sculptures from the Parthenon between 1801 and 1810; in 1816 they were sold to the British Museum.

the present war against the Russians: Napoleon's ill-fated 1812 campaign.

13 *Irish Romish Priests*: Catholic priests trained at the Irish College in Rome, founded 1628. British commentators took it for granted that they were Jacobites—supporters of the exiled Stuart dynasty.

15 *Caesar's relation*: Julius Caesar, *Bellum Gallicum*, 6. 13.

   Argonauts: legendary explorers, led by Jason, who sought the Golden Fleece.

   Bacchus, Hercules, Ammon: itinerant deities and semi-divine heroes.

   Maximus Tyrius . . . Homer: Maximus of Tyre, *Orations*, 16. 6: 'Homer's Odysseus gained wisdom through his long wanderings, as he "saw the cities of many men and came to know their character." . . . But as for the sights seen by the philosopher, to what can they ever be compared? To a dream, but a truthful dream that travels to every corner of the universe.'

   Herodotus . . . Homer: Pseudo-Herodotus, in the *Life of Homer*, Section 6, relates how a shipowner persuaded the youthful Homer to travel with him.

   Adrian . . . anything remarkable: Spartian, *De Vita Hadriani*, 17. 8.

   Tertullian . . . upon its milk: Tertullian, *Ad Nationes*, 2. 14.

19 *policies*: systems of government.

21 *the reigning Prince*: Leopold III of Anhalt-Dessau (1740–1817), absent during Boswell's visit. Dietrich had acted as regent during his minority.

   cornes de chasse: hunting horns.

   Prince Albert: Albrecht, Leopold's 14-year-old brother.

   Macfarlane: Boswell's friend Walter Macfarlane of Macfarlane, an antiquary and thus punctilious about titles.

   The Prince's mistress: F. A. Pottle tentatively identifies her as Johanna Eleonora von Neitschutz, who had borne the Prince a son a little over a year before.

22 *Auchinleck*: the Boswell estate in Ayrshire.

   By chase our long-lived fathers earned their food: John Dryden, 'Epistle the Fifteenth: To My Honoured Kinsman John Driden', l. 88.

   Munzesheim: Baron Friedrich August von Münzesheim, 'a genteel, lively young Gentleman of the Bedchamber' (Boswell).

   a worthy prince: Karl Friedrich, Margrave of Baden-Durlach (1728–1811).

23 *nice*: fastidious.

24 *a most excellent fellow*: Jacob Hänni, Boswell's manservant.

25 *Temple*: Boswell's old friend William Temple (1739–96).

   innovators: Johnson's remark (recorded by Boswell the previous year) was directed against David Hume and other 'sceptical innovators'.

   Mademoiselle Le Vasseur: Thérèse Le Vasseur, with whom Rousseau had been living for twenty years.

27 *figmagairies*: 'whigmaleeries'—whims, crotchets.

   Saint-Preux: sentimental hero of Rousseau's novel *Julie, ou la Nouvelle Héloïse* (1761).

28 *to the end of my days*: Boswell quotes from Rousseau's *Émile*, book II; Rousseau pretends not to recognize the allusion.

29 *Joseph*: the local driver, 'a sober, sagacious, intelligent fellow ... a sensible knave'.

    beccaficas, grieves: blackcaps, thrushes.

30 *Mandrin*: Louis Mandrin (1725–55); the following account of him is substantially accurate.

33 *succession of ideas*: the association of ideas, a key principle of empiricist philosophy, was developed by David Hume and became the basis for Scottish Enlightenment aesthetic theory.

    Nero's four horses appear: fourth-century group of bronze statues on top of the facade of St Mark's basilica, looted from Constantinople by the Crusaders in 1204.

    Henry Dandelo: Enrico Dandolo, Doge of Venice from 1192 until his death in 1205, marched at the head of the Fourth Crusade and established the 'empire of the Latins' in Constantinople ('the capital of Asia').

    garden of Eden: mosaics in the atrium of St Mark's.

    she plucks, she eats: Milton, *Paradise Lost*, ix. 780–1.

    winged lion ... Ducal palace: the winged lion is the symbol of St Mark, patron of Venice; its effigies adorn the Palazzo Ducale, grand palace of the Doges and administrative centre of the city, and the adjoining Piazza San Marco.

    lion's mouth gaping for accusations: slot by the door of the Sala della Bussola, in the Palazzo Ducale, into which anonymous denunciations were posted.

34 *Vauxhall or Ranelagh*: London pleasure gardens

    Titian ... Palladio: Tiziano Vecellio (c. 1490–1576), painter, and Andrea Palladio (1508–80), architect, both active in and around Venice.

    Cicerone: guide expert in antiquities.

    Palais Royal: residence of Louis-Philippe, Duke of Orleans, who opened its galleries to the public.

    Voyage Pittoresque de Paris: by Antoine-Nicolas Dézaillier d'Argenville (1749).

35 *Raphael*: Raffaello Sanzio (1483–1520), at that date the most prestigious of the Italian Old Masters.

36 *headquarters ... where art is at her acme*: i.e. Florence.

    azaroli: fruit of the Neapolitan medlar, a species of hawthorn.

    panther sits at the gate: the city's totem animal. An independent republic from 1369 until 1799, Lucca earned its reputation for liberty by excluding the Inquisition and tolerating a free press.

    nec vult panthera domari: 'That the panther never will be tamed' (Piozzi's trans.). See William Lily, *A Short Introduction of Grammar* (1731),

95. First published in the mid-sixteenth century, Lily's book remained a school text well into the nineteenth.

Howel: James Howell (1594?–1666), whose *Epistolae Ho-Elianae* (1645–55), recounting his travels in France and Italy, was reprinted throughout the eighteenth century.

37 *Rutlandshire*: the smallest county in England (incorporated into Leicestershire in 1974).

Ilam gardens: Ilam Hall, near Ashborn in Derbyshire, home of the Port family from the seventeenth century, was famous for its Italian garden.

the Emperor . . . Grand Duke of Tuscany: the Holy Roman Emperor, whose support kept Lucca from being absorbed by the Medici, Grand Dukes of Tuscany from the sixteenth century.

best church: the Cathedral, dedicated to St Martin.

38 *il mondo è bello perche è variabile*: 'The world is pleasant because it is various' (Piozzi's trans.).

confrairies: religious fraternities.

villeggiatura: holiday in the countryside; the 'delicious and salutary baths' are at Montecatini Terme.

Dame Lucchesi: ladies of Lucca.

39 *an old writer*: Sir Thomas Browne, in *Extracts from Christian Morals*, III. xi.

40 *the bastions of the town their Corso*: the city walls, fortified 1504–1645, were planted with plane and chestnut trees and are still used as a municipal promenade.

usquebaugh: whisky (Gaelic).

Si ce n'etait pas . . . la republique des rats et des souris: 'If it were not a dear little pretty commonwealth—this?' 'Faith, madam, I call it the republic of the rats and mice' (Piozzi's trans.).

41 *Grandval*: Granville.

42 *Chateaubriant*: René Auguste de Chateaubriand, Comte de Combourg: father of the famous writer François René (1768–1848), who spent part of his childhood here.

43 *a gorge deployé*: with gaping mouths.

44 *car les tailles et les droits nous écrasent*: 'because the taxes and duties are crushing us'.

hotel de ville: town hall.

45 *tiers etat*: 'third estate', commoners (as distinct from nobles and clergy).

46 *M. Necker's passing*: Louis Necker (1732–1804), the king's finance minister, was dismissed in 1788 for advising reform measures. Recalled from Switzerland to solve the present crisis, he rode through Befort (Belfort) on 25 July escorted by a citizen's army.

vingtièmes . . . tailles: property taxes.

47 *vive le tiers, sans impositions*: 'long live the people—no taxes'.

48 *affiche, or placard*: public notice.

49 *Federation*: Festival of the Federation, 14 July 1790, held to celebrate the first anniversary of the fall of the Bastille.

the people were the sight: Alexander Pope, 'First Epistle of the Second Book of Horace, Imitated' (1737), l. 323.

Champ de Mars: 'Field of Mars', parade-ground on the bank of the Seine (now the site of the Eiffel Tower).

50 *National Assembly*: revolutionary legislative body, established 17 June 1789.

Mons. de la Fayette: Marie Joseph, Marquis de Lafayette (1757–1834), fought against the British in the American War of Independence. Commander of the National Guard and a member of the National Assembly, he played a moderating role in the early stages of the Revolution.

Dauphin: heir to the French throne.

51 *'while memory holds her seat in my bosom'*: William Hayward Roberts, 'To G. A. S. Esq., On his Leaving Eaton School' (1774), l. 68 (slightly misquoted).

Nous sommes mouillés à la nation: 'We are wet for the nation' (Williams's trans.).

La révolution . . . au lieu de sang: 'The French revolution is cemented with water, instead of blood' (Williams).

d'une danse ronde: 'With dancing in a circle' (Williams).

the Bastille: notorious state prison, symbol of the Old Regime, stormed by a crowd on 14 July 1789.

52 *A la Bastille—mais nous n'y resterons pas*: 'To the Bastille—but we shall not remain there' (Williams).

As make the angels weep: Shakespeare, *Measure for Measure*, II. ii. 120–1, 124–5.

Sterne says: in *A Sentimental Journey* (1768), 'The Passport: Versailles' (I).

54 *decemvirs*: members of ruling council or committee ('body of ten').

decade: tenth days, marked by the Republican calendar of 1793, which divided the months into three 10-day periods.

Germinal: the months were renamed in the Republican calendar.

committee of public safety: established by the National Assembly in 1793 and controlled by Robespierre's Jacobins, it became the de facto governing body during the Terror (1793–4).

55 *mark of Cain*: see Genesis 4: 15.

certificate of civism: official document (*certificat de civisme*) attesting the holder's loyalty to the revolutionary government.

55 *cabriolets*: light two-wheeled chaise drawn by a single horse.

56 *breathed a browner horror over the woods*: Alexander Pope, 'Eloisa to Abelard', l. 170 (reading 'breathes . . . on the woods').

58 *entry of the French into Brussels*: on 14 November 1793; the French army laid siege to Maastricht in October 1794.

61 *Candide*: famous novella (1759) by Voltaire.

62 *looped and windowed wretchedness . . . pelting of the storm*: compare Shakespeare, *King Lear*, III. iv. 29–32.

63 *But when . . . night of the grave!*: James Beattie, *The Hermit* (1797), ll. 31–2.

   Nassau troops: members of the 2nd (Nassau) Brigade.

64 *this ruined and roofless abode*: compare Thomas Campbell, 'Lines Written on Visiting a Scene in Argyllshire' (1800), l. 5: 'All ruined and wild is their roofless abode'.

   dust returns to the earth . . . gave it: see Ecclesiastes 12: 7.

65 *Grand Lord*: the Duke of Wellington, commander of the British forces.

   pococurantés: careless or indifferent persons (Italian).

66 *à prix juste*: at a fair price.

   introuvable: not to be found.

   one of the heroes of the day: Captain Colin Campbell (1776–1847) or Major Pryse Gordon (1762–1845), who both accompanied Scott to the field.

67 *Shakespeare's mulberry-tree*: the Revd Francis Gastrell, proprietor of Shakespeare's New Place in Stratford, was so annoyed by tourists that he chopped down the famous tree in 1759. According to Washington Irving it generated more relics than the True Cross.

   one of our Scottish men of rhyme: Scott goes on to quote his own versions (presumably) of three poems.

   Cressy and Agincourt: famous English victories over the French (1346, 1415) in the Hundred Years War.

   sirventes and lais, and courts of Love: genres of twelfth–thirteenth-century Provençal troubadour poetry, and one of its chief topoi.

68 *Lady Mar*: Lady Mary's sister Frances (1699?–1761), one of her chief correspondents.

69 *Empress Mother*: Eleonore Magdalene (1655–1720), daughter of Prince-Elector Philipp Wilhelm von der Pfalz. The current Emperor of Austria was Charles VI (1685–1740).

   Empress Amalia: Wilhelmine Amalie (1673–1742).

70 *prize shooting . . . Virgil*: see *Aeneid* 5. 485–544.

71 *Prince Eugene*: Prince Eugene of Savoy (1663–1736), famous Austrian general; he had visited England in 1712.

Esseek: Osijek, Croatia.

the words of Moneses: in Nicholas Rowe's *Tamerlane* (1702), I. i.

Lady——: one of Lady Mary's anonymous correspondents, in the preceding 'Embassy Letter'.

Anthropophagi ... below their shoulders: marvels of distant lands: Shakespeare, *Othello*, I. ii.

Adrianople: now Edirne, on Turkey's border with Bulgaria.

72 *Bagnio*: public bath or *hamam*.

73 *Uzelle, pek uzelle* [i.e. *Güzel, pek güzel*]: very beautiful (Turkish).

 our General Mother: Eve in *Paradise Lost*, iv. 304–18.

 Guido or Titian: Guido Reni (1575–1642) and Tiziano Vecellio (*c.*1490–1576), painters.

 Mr Gervase: Charles Jervas (1675?–1739), fashionable portrait painter. He had painted Lady Mary as a shepherdess in 1710.

74 *Justinian's church*: St Sofia, built in the sixth century under the Emperor Justinian, after which the city of Sofia is named.

75 *Talpock*: kalpak or calpack.

 'tis just as 'tis with you: Aphra Behn, *The Emperor of the Moon* (1687), III. i.

76 *Indian Houses*: shops selling luxury articles imported from India.

 Divan: Ottoman privy council.

 Grand Signor ... a Bassa: the Sultan; Pasha, a high-ranking official, usually a military commander or provincial governor

78 *end of the carnival*: Shrovetide, preceding Lent.

80 *Pera*: suburb of Constantinople (present-day Istanbul) across the Golden Horn, where European ambassadors and merchants were obliged to reside.

 Capitan Pacha: chief admiral of the Ottoman fleet.

 Romelia: Rumeli, the European side of the Bosphorus.

81 *plaister*: plastron, a quilted breast-plate.

83 *Arendall*: in Norway.

86 *runs foul of*: becomes entangled with.

 golden age: mythical ideal state, imagined by the ancient Greeks and a frequent topic of Enlightenment philosophical conjecture.

87 *love in idleness*: Shakespeare, *A Midsummer Night's Dream*, II. i. 168. 'Heart's-ease' are wild pansies.

 the horrors I had witnessed in France: Wollstonecraft had watched Louis XVI driven to the guillotine in 1793. Pregnant with her daughter, she went into hiding during the subsequent Terror; several of her Girondist friends were executed.

502   *Explanatory Notes*

88 *sublime . . . beautiful*: an aesthetic opposition theorized by Edmund Burke
    in *A Philosophical Enquiry into the Origin of Our Ideas of the Sublime and
    Beautiful* (1759).

91 *sufficient for the day . . . evil*: compare Matthew 6: 34.

    cattegate: Kattegat, the sound between Sweden and Denmark.

    Laurvig: Larvik.

    Dr Franklin's plan: in 'Remarks Concerning the Savages of North
    America' (1748) Benjamin Franklin describes the curiosity of the colon-
    ists towards Indians who visit their settlements: 'they crowd round them,
    gaze upon them, and incommode them where they desire to be private.'
    He says nothing, however, about wearing his name on a placard.

92 *cabriole*: cabriolet, two-wheeled carriage drawn by a single horse.

93 *The mayor, my friend*: Judge Jacob Wulfsberg: one of the 'gentlemen with
    whom I had business to transact' on behalf of Gilbert Imlay.

94 *passing sweet*: William Cowper, *Retirement* (1782), l. 737: 'How sweet, how
    passing sweet is solitude!'

    friend of my youth: Fanny Blood, who died in childbed in 1785, in Mary's
    arms.

                    PART II. THE BRITISH ISLES

99 *lect.*: letters (*lecturae*), i.e. literature.

    Newtontony: Fiennes's home at Newton Toney, near Salisbury.

    Breackly: Berkley. 'Philip Norton' (below) is Norton St Philip.

102 *Emount*: the Eden; other rivers mentioned are the Esk ('Essex') and Sark
    ('Serke').

103 *plodds*: plaids.

    Adison Bank: Aitchison Bank.

    clapbread: oat-cakes.

104 *Kerk*: possibly Selkirk.

105 *culture*: agriculture.

    learned writers on the subject of antiquity: notably William Camden, a new
    edition of whose *Britannia* (1586) was published in 1695.

111 *common-shore*: common sewer.

112 *ab Inferis*: from the underworld.

    Cotton's Wonders . . . Chatsworth: Charles Cotton, *The Wonders of the Peake*
    (1681); Thomas Hobbes, 'De Mirabilibus Pecci: Being the Wonders of
    the Peak in Darby-shire' (1636), which opens with a panegyric on
    Chatsworth.

115 *tenter*: wooden frame for stretching newly milled cloth to dry or set.

    kersie . . . shalloon: coarse woollen cloth, often ribbed; closely woven
    woollen material, used for linings.

St Giles's . . . Seven Dials: in London.

119 *Whiteboys*: rural insurgency movement, beginning in Co. Tipperary in the 1760s, provoked by land enclosures.

121 *Steelboys, Oakboys, Peep-of-day-boys etc.*: agrarian insurgent movements, mainly in the northern counties, patterned after the Whiteboys.

124 *an Irish potato*: introduced into Ireland in the sixteenth century, the potato rapidly became a staple, supporting population increases over the next 200 years—although dependency on a single crop made the country vulnerable to blight and famine.

bere: barley.

Cadmus's teeth: according to legend Cadmus populated Thebes by sowing dragon's teeth, which sprouted an army.

125 *rebels . . . Dwyer and Hoult*: the United Irishmen rising (1798). Michael Dwyer and Joseph Holt were leaders of a guerrilla campaign in the Wicklow Mountains.

126 *Why dost . . . in thy empty court*: James Macpherson, 'Carthon' (1765).

127 *Mr TULL . . . headlands*: pioneering agricultural improver Jethro Tull (1674–1741), in his *Horse-hoeing Husbandry* (1733).

128 *Malthuses . . . Scarletts*: economists who attacked poor relief: William Malthus (1766–1834) in the second edition of *An Essay on the Principles of Population* (1803) and *Principles of Political Economy* (1820), James Scarlett (1769–1844) in a parliamentary bill for amending the poor laws (defeated 31 May 1822).

Scotch Economists . . . Edinburgh Reviewers: Henry Brougham was an editor of the *Edinburgh Review* (founded 1802), which promoted the economic theory of Adam Smith and other Scottish Enlightenment philosophers as the scientific platform of Whig party policy.

a garden indeed: ironical allusion to the traditional epithet for Kent, 'the garden of England'.

130 *my glass*: a 'landscape mirror' or 'Claude glass', an essential piece of equipment for the picturesque tourist. See West's description, p. 136.

131 *Non ragionam di lor; ma guarda, e passa!*: Virgil's advice to Dante in *Inferno*, III. 51: 'Let us not consider them, but look, and pass by.'

Smith: Thomas Smith (d. 1767), landscape artist, who engraved a set of his own paintings of the Lakes.

132 *one branch of a noble art*: landscape painting.

133 *Mr Gray . . . in 1772*: Gray made his tour in 1769; the Welsh naturalist and travel writer Thomas Pennant passed through the region on his Scottish tours of 1769 and 1772.

136 *pike*: peak.

landscape mirror: also called the 'Claude Lorrain glass'.

141 *I sit by the sounding shore, etc.*: James Macpherson, *Fragments of Ancient Poetry, Collected in the Highlands of Scotland* (1760), XI.

turbantibus aequora ventis: 'it is pleasant when the winds are churning the ocean waters' [to watch from dry land]: Lucretius, *De rerum natura* 2. 1.

be my retreat . . . cheer the gloom: James Thomson, *Winter* (1726), 426–8, 430–1.

fowls: gannets ('solan geese'), which nest in vast numbers on St Kilda.

142 *the Irish tongue*: Gaelic.

tormentil: see Johnson's description of the process, below, p. 160.

143 *the late Mack-Leod's death*: Norman Macleod (d. 1685), proprietor of the island.

stone-houses: pyramid-shaped stone sheds where harvested seabirds are hung to dry.

dulse, and slake: kinds of seaweed.

stoved: baked.

144 *sea-ware*: seaweed.

sowens (i.e. flummery): porridge made of semi-fermented meal.

148 *aqua-vitae*: whisky (Gaelic, *usquebaugh*)

150 *Cromwell . . . subdued Scotland*: in 1650.

151 *Deliciae Poetarum Scotorum . . . May's Supplement*: anthology compiled by Arthur Johnstone, *Delitiae Poetarum Scotorum* (1637); Thomas May's continuation of Lucan, *Supplementi Lucani Libri Septem* (1640).

the Erse language: Gaelic

153 *Joseph*: Joseph Ritter, Boswell's servant.

Lord Alemoor: one of the judges of the Scottish Court of Session.

154 *London . . . False Alarm*: poem (1738), pamphlet (1770), and weekly periodical (1750), all written by Johnson.

Archer in The Beaux' Stratagem: by Thomas Farquhar (1707), IV. i.

155 *Fort Augustus*: they had stayed at Fort Augustus on the preceding day.

156 *a Macdonald in rags*: Johnson's fantasies of life as a Highland chief, like Macdonald of Skye (whom they were riding to meet), provided one of the running jokes of the *Journal*: made piquant by Macdonald's failure to live up to the feudal image.

157 *Glenelg*: on the mainland coast, across from Skye.

Sir A. Macdonald: Sir Alexander Macdonald, ninth Baron of Sleat, later first Baron Macdonald (1761–95).

158 *Poor Tom's a-cold*: Shakespeare, *King Lear*, III. iv. 135.

159 *choice of difficulties*: General James Wolfe, leader of the British expedition against Quebec, in a letter written during the siege (2 September 1759).

Prince Charles first landed: on 25 July 1745, beginning the last Jacobite Rising.

162 *Braidwood*: Thomas Braidwood's academy, the first of its kind in Britain, was founded in 1760.

   Wallis and Holder . . . Mr Baker: John Wallis (1616–1703) and Thomas Holder (1616–98), authors of treatises on speech, engaged in a controversy over methods of teaching the deaf and dumb in the 1670s. Henry Baker (1698–1774) developed his own pedagogy but did not publish it.

   Burnet: Gilbert Burnet recounts the story of a Swiss girl, deaf from infancy, who taught herself lip-reading in *Some Letters, containing an account of what seemed most remarkable in Switzerland, Italy, etc.* (1686).

163 *Self-love, and social is the same*: Alexander Pope, *An Essay on Man*, iii. 318.

165 *present Duke of Argyle*: John, fifth Duke (1723–1806).

   wonderful and whimsical Colin: Colin, first Earl of Argyll (d. 1493).

   finished by the present: the new castle at Inveraray, founded in 1746 by Archibald, third Duke, was not completed until 1789. To make room for it the town was demolished and rebuilt at a new location half a mile down the banks of Loch Fyne.

   a learned and elaborate traveller: Samuel Johnson. Hanway quotes from *A Journey to the Western Islands of Scotland*, 'Anoch'.

166 *bend a keener eye . . . vacancy*: Hamlet, III. iv.

   nothing loth: Homeric tag, from Alexander Pope's translation of *The Odyssey* (1725–6), 8. 337.

167 *I may perhaps transcribe incorrectly*: Hanway concludes by quoting from lines 594–606 of James Thomson's *Summer* (1727).

174 *And then . . . a home in every glade*: William Wordsworth, 'Ruth; or The Influences of Nature' (1800), ll. 67–72, quoted (approximately) from memory. The heroine is courted by a young soldier who has seen service in North America. In the previous stanza he tells her of 'many an endless, endless lake | With all its fairy crowds | Of islands, that together lie | As quietly as spots of sky | Among the evening clouds'.

175 *biggin'*: building.

176 *go ben*: go inside.

177 *spence*: pantry.

178 *muster place of the Clan-Alpine*: see Walter Scott, *The Lady of the Lake* (1810), v. xii.

179 *Goblin of Corrie-Uriskin*: see Scott's note 41 to *The Lady of the Lake*.

   I traced every ravine . . . valley of Shinar: compare *The Lady of the Lake*, I. xi. The ancient pile is the tower of Babel (Genesis 11: 1–9).

PART III. AFRICA

182 *spoon-meats*: soft or liquid food (suitable for infants or invalids).

186 *under-factor*: assistant merchant.

187 *Gromettas*: Negro servants.

old *Cracker*: alias John Leadstane, 'the most thriving' of the local slave traders.

manatee strap: whip made from the hide of the manatee (dugong) or sea-cow.

dashee: present, bribe.

188 *Palaaver-Room*: conference room.

Jack pudding: clown, jester.

Culgee: figured Indian silk.

20 lib.: 20 pounds.

congees: rice-porridge.

flageolet: simple wind instrument, similar to the recorder.

patent: document conferring a title of nobility.

190 *hand-spike*: a type of crowbar used on shipboard.

temporals: worldly conditions.

191 *Hottentots*: the Khoisan people of south-west Africa (pejorative term).

194 *Sherbro*: in present-day Sierra Leone.

Purrow: (Poro) secret cult for men, widespread and socially powerful among tribes in Sierra Leone and Liberia.

196 *Spectacle de la Nature*: by Noël Antoine Pluche, a book of popular natural history translated into English in 1733 as *Nature Display'd*.

201 *core*: cowrie.

bound: enslaved.

uncircumcised: earlier in the book Equiano has established a set of analogies between Africans and the Jews, including shared customs (such as male circumcision) and a common destiny of bondage and (eventual) deliverance.

203 *windlass*: winch or crank, used to wind a heavy rope or chain.

205 *necessary tubs*: latrines.

206 *St George's Bay Company*: trading company set up by abolitionist leader Granville Sharp in 1790 for the first settlers.

207 *abolishing the slave trade*: the political debate over abolition continued from the 1780s until 1807, when the trade was abolished. Slavery continued until emancipation in 1833.

the fleet . . . for Botany Bay: this was the third convict fleet sent to the new British penal colony in New South Wales; see Part VI, Section 3, below, in particular Mary Ann Parker.

208 *delightful prospects*: Falconbridge is using the vocabulary of landscape aesthetics, popularized by the spread of picturesque tourism in regions such as England's Lake District. See Part II, Section 2, above.

Duke of Buccleugh [*Buccleuch*]: the name of the ship, after a Scottish nobleman.

209 *cutter*: small single-masted vessel.

211 *the gentlemen*: the resident slave traders.

factory: trading station.

212 *harlequined*: decorated in contrasting colours, like a harlequin's tights.

213 *palaver*: conference.

214 *ostensible*: answerable.

Pegininee: piccaninny, child of African ethnic origin (here incorrectly used).

raree-shows: sights, curiosities (from peep-shows exhibited at English fairs).

215 *Clara*: Elliote's wife.

216 *our country women*: i.e. British women.

Wapping: the London docks.

217 *Gothic*: 'medieval'—feudal, barbaric.

round house: cabin or set of cabins at the rear of the ship's quarter-deck.

nicest: most precise.

218 *Mr W—lb—ce and Tom Paine*: William Wilberforce (1759–1833), parliamentary leader of the anti-slave-trade movement; Thomas Paine (1737–1809), political writer who supported the American and French Revolutions.

221 *Polyphemus banquet*: in Homer's *Odyssey*, Polyphemus is a Cyclops who devours men raw.

Mosaical law: biblical guidelines on animal slaughter.

223 *Vive la Joye et la Jeunesse!*: Long live happiness and youth!

Bacchus . . . Venus: classical deities of wine and love, respectively. 'In this particular they resemble the Cynics of old, of whom it was said, "Omnia quae ad Bacchum et Venerum pertinueurent in publico facere." Diogenes Laertius in Vit. Diogen' (Bruce). Bruce's Latin version—'they are used to doing everything in public, the works of Bacchus and Venus alike'— puts a bawdy twist on the original Greek in *Lives of the Eminent Philosophers*, 6. 2. 69.

He: Shalaka Woldo, Bruce's guide to the source of the Nile.

224 *Geesh*: district where the source lies.

225 *Strates*: Bruce's escort to Geesh.

Don Quixote: protagonist of Miguel Cervantes' novel, who believes he is a knight travelling with his squire, Sancho Panza. Sancho is appointed governor of Barataria (or so he is led to believe) in book II (1615).

the 4th: of November 1770.

226 *What's Hecuba . . . weep for her?*: Shakespeare, *Hamlet*, II. ii. 561–2.

227 *detur dignissimo*: a gift [literally, 'let it be given'] to the worthiest; see Jonathan Swift's dedication to *The Tale of a Tub* (1704). The phrase is associated with Alexander the Great.

Ali: the Moorish chief, Park's captor.

229 *Bushreens*: Muslims.

hope deferred maketh the heart sick: Proverbs 13: 12.

231 *nankeen breeches*: yellow cotton trousers.

233 *Dooty*: provincial governor or village headman.

234 *Bammakoo*: Bamako, Mali.

237 *kraals*: native villages (Dutch).

Bosjesmans: Bushmen (Dutch) or San (their name for themselves), an aboriginal people of southern Africa.

238 *Hottentots*: one of the two subgroups of the Khoisanid people of southern Africa, the other being the so-called Bushmen. During Barrow's time 'Hottentot' was also used derogatorily to mean 'person of inferior intellect or culture', 'barbarian'.

242 *Kaffers*: Bantu people of South Africa (Arabic *kafir*, 'infidel').

243 *lethalis arundo*: 'deadly arrow' (*letalis harundo*): Virgil, *Aeneid* 4. 73.

245 *Mahomedans*: Muslims.

247 *foomoo*: gentleman.

fathoms: six feet (nautical measure). Tuckey and his crew paid their African workers in baft, a coarse printed cotton cloth, measured in fathoms.

fetished: tabooed, thought to be inhabited by a spirit.

248 *retreat from Moscow*: by Napoleon's army, decimated by the Russian winter as well as by enemy action, in the disastrous campaign of 1812.

Chenoo: district chief or governor.

249 *Gangam*: priest.

251 *picturesque spot*: suitable for painting, fit to be the subject of a striking or effective picture. The picturesque came into vogue in England in the 1770s as part of the fashion for scenic tourism: see Part II, Section 2, above.

253 *Afrikaander*: South Africans of Dutch descent. 'I here write this name as it is commonly pronounced, and as it was spoken by his own family, although it would be more correctly written, *Afrikaaner*' (Burchell).

255 *Speelman, Philip, and Gert . . . Muchunka and Adam*: Burchell's San (Hottentot) employees.

PART IV. THE CARIBBEAN

258 *Creolians*: creoles: persons (of any race) born in the islands.

Mulattos, Alcatrazes, Mestizes, Quarterons: i.e. mestizos, quadroons. Categories developed by the Spanish according to a person's proportion of 'African blood'.

259 *Musquitos*: the Miskito Coast of present-day Nicaragua.

261 *Osnabrigs*: coarse linen cloth originally made in Osnabrück, Germany, often used to clothe slaves.

muscavados: unrefined sugar obtained from the juice of the sugar cane.

fustic-wood ... log-wood: fustic-wood, wood of the *Cladrastis* (*Chlorophora, Maclura*) *tinctoria*, used for yellow dye; prince-wood, or Spanish elm, timber of the *Cordia gerascanthoides* and *Hamelia ventricosa*; lignum vitae, hard and heavy wood of the *Guaiacum officinale* or *G. sanctum*, used in medicine; arnotto (annatto), orange-red dye from the *Bixa orellana*; log-wood, the heartwood of *Haematoxylon Campechianum*, used in dyeing.

cochineal: scarlet dye made from dried insects (*Coccus cacti*).

262 *Asiento*: contract between Spain and Great Britain at the Peace of Utrecht (1713) for furnishing the Spanish dominions in America with slaves.

263 *manatee straps*: made from the hide of the manatee or sea-cow.

Moquet: unidentified.

Liguanea: a plain, part of present-day Kingston, Jamaica

265 *Prospectus*: an author publishing by subscription submitted an advance prospectus or description of his book to subscribers, who then paid part of the cost of their copies in advance.

267 *Terracina*: on the coast between Rome and Naples. 'Torre dei Confini' means 'boundary tower'.

galleries of the Simplon: a feature of the new road through the famous pass over the Swiss Alps, built by Napoleon 1801–5.

269 *shaddocks*: large pear-shaped citrus fruit similar to a grapefruit.

270 *Coermoetibo and Barbacueber*: Coermoetibo Creek and Barbacoeba, an outpost on the River Cottica.

the Charon: Stedman's barge; in Greek mythology Charon ferried dead souls across the River Styx to Hades. Naming his second barge the *Cerberus*, after the three-headed dog guarding the entrance to Hades, Stedman noted that 'sudden Death and willful Murder would not have been out of Character' as names for the boats.

271 *glare*: mud (Scots).

272 *Robinson Crusoe with Friday*: firing at the cannibals, in the novel by Daniel Defoe (1719; Oxford, 1998), p. 234.

273 *Devils Harwar*: outpost on the River Cottica.

Mr Parkinson's Museums: 'In 1795 Stedman presented "eighteen Surinam curiosities" to James Parkinson's Leverian Museum, which since the mid-1780s had been attracting crowds in London' (Price).

274 *affamation*: hunger.

275 *fusee*: a light musket or firelock.

rangers: black soldiers fighting for the Dutch colonial government against the maroons.

276 *Gibraltar*: the siege of Gibraltar by Spanish and French troops (1779–83) inflicted terrible suffering on the defending forces.

Inventas . . . improved: Virgil, *Aeneid* 6. 663. Stedman appears to have got the line from Henry Fielding's *Tom Jones*, book V, chapter 1.

277 *Gentoos*: Hindus.

nebees: vines.

278 *upon the rack*: 'Stedman's description of Neptune's death may seem derivative from the death of Aphra Behn's fictional Oroonoko, set in Surinam a hundred years earlier. Scholars familiar with the realities of eighteenth-century Surinam, however, will realize that the event Stedman describes as an eyewitness needed no literary precursor. From other contemporary sources, we know that such theatrical public executions—and the victim's stoic or defiant reaction—were relatively frequent during this period' (Price).

279 *Disdains . . . I shudder, at the bloody theme*: unidentified; perhaps these lines are by Stedman.

280 *10th of December*: 1762.

hanger: short sword hanging from the belt.

281 *West-Indiamen*: ships trading to the West Indies.

prize-money: the value of ships and cargoes captured in wartime, which was shared among the crew.

tell my master so: the Mansfield Decision, a judicial ruling that prohibited masters from taking slaves back from Britain to the West Indies against their will, would not be made until 1772, a decade later than this incident.

283 *Regions of sorrow . . . Still urges*: Milton, *Paradise Lost*, i. 65–8 (reading 'rest can never dwell').

a quaker: the Society of Friends (Quakers) pressured its members to withdraw from participation in slavery during the eighteenth century, and even threatened those owning or trading in slaves with expulsion.

284 *gauge*: ascertain a ship's capacity.

285 *droggers*: West Indian coasting vessels.

pisterines: 'These pisterines are of the value of a shilling' (Equiano).

man of feeling: one ready to sympathize with others, especially social inferiors or those in distress (compare Henry Mackenzie's 1771 novel of that title).

287 *Turks Island*: Grand Turk, the largest of the Turks and Caicos Islands, east of the southern tip of the Bahamas.

Buckra people: white men: from *backra*, master, in the black patois of Surinam (*OED*).

288 *Vendue master*: official in charge of a slave auction.

salt ponds: salt remained the main product of the Turk Islands until the 1960s. In the eighteenth century slaves raked the salt ponds and the salt was traded to North America.

292 *Antigua*: one of the Windward Islands, located between the Atlantic and the Caribbean; it became a British colony in 1667. St John's (below) is the capital.

293 *the Tower*: of London, on the River Thames.

294 *I was free in England*: according to the 1772 Mansfield Decision a slave who left her owner in England could not be recaptured or taken back to the colonies without her consent, but should she return on her own she would again be a slave.

bed-ticks: mattresses.

296 *gentleman who inquired into my case*: Thomas Pringle (1789–1834), secretary of the Anti-Slavery Society, for whom Prince worked as a servant after leaving her owners. Pringle edited and published Prince's *History*, which she dictated to Susanna Strickland, a guest in the Pringle household.

297 *Sir William Hamilton*: appointed British envoy to Naples in 1764, Hamilton (1730–1803) was a noted antiquarian and amateur vulcanologist who hiked up Mount Vesuvius twenty-two times in four years, and produced numerous descriptions and sketches of the mountain in all phases of eruption.

Brydone: Patrick Brydone, author of the popular *Tour through Sicily and Malta* (1773).

chymic: chemical.

trash-house: shed for storing the refuse of sugar canes after the juice has been expressed, used as fuel.

298 *the shell resounds*: a large conch shell was used as a horn to summon slaves.

sublime: inspiring an aesthetic sensation of 'pleasing horror'. Edmund Burke's 1757 *Philosophical Enquiry into the Origin of our Ideas of the Sublime and Beautiful* synthesized British aesthetic thought on the sublime and helped popularize the concept among educated Britons.

umbered: darkened—literally, tinted with umber, a dark brown earth used as a pigment.

299 *Mr Deane*: unidentified.

trash: (field trash) dried leaves and tops of the sugar cane plants, stripped off while still growing to allow canes to ripen.

300 *swarths*: rows or lines of the crop, fallen after reaping.

301 *cotton-tree*: the silk cotton or Ceiba, *Ceiba pentandra*, perhaps Jamaica's

largest and—with cacti, creepers, and lianas growing on it—most spectacular tree. Heights of 150 feet and a stump diameter of 40 feet were recorded in the nineteenth century.

301 *wains*: wagons.

crop: sugar cane harvest.

works: buildings on a plantation for processing cane juice into unrefined sugar.

coppers: copper kettles for boiling down the cane juice ('liquor').

the feeders . . . the boilers: slaves who feed canes into the presses that extract their juice; skilled slaves who oversee the boiling of the cane juice.

302 *sable*: black, in elevated poetic diction: see e.g. 'The Sable Venus', a poem printed in Bryan Edwards's *History, Civil and Commercial, of the British Colonies in the West Indies* (1793).

abolition: of the slave trade, not of slavery itself (referred to as emancipation).

a necessary article of life: Sidney Mintz documents the creation of the demand for sugar in *Sweetness and Power: The Place of Sugar in Modern History* (New York: Penguin, 1985).

a jewel: the North American colonies, which won their independence in 1783.

a neighbouring kingdom: Britain's traditional arch-enemy, France.

304 *John-Canoe*: festival (and word) of African (possibly Yoruba) origin, with elements assimilated from European popular tradition (mumming, morris dancing, etc.). These extended Christmas and New Year's festivities often gave slaves openings for subversive comment through songs and role-playing; occasionally they became a cover for organizing revolt. The lead dancer wore a headdress like the one Lewis describes (though not a canoe) or a horned mask (closer to the festival's African origins).

Magno telluris . . . arena: 'Longing for land, the Trojans disembarked and gained the desired shore': Virgil, *Aeneid*, 1. 171–2.

305 *Admiral of the Red . . . of the Blue*: until 1864 the Royal Navy fleet was organized in three squadrons, the red, the white, and the blue. But 'the rival factions of the Blues and the Reds' could also have represented the army (red-coats) and the navy (blue-jackets), according to Errol Hill in *The Jamaican Stage, 1655–1900* (Amherst, Mass.: University of Massachusetts Press, 1992), 239.

Brown Girls: 'brown' may signify, here as elsewhere, mixed race.

the rival Roses—the Guelphs and the Ghibellines: red and white roses were the badges that distinguished the houses of Lancaster and York, rivals for the English throne, in the 'Wars of the Roses' (1455–87). Guelphs and Ghibellines were warring factions in fourteenth-century Florence.

306 *Waterloo*: in Belgium, site of the climactic battle in which Britain and its allies defeated Napoleon, 1815.

Trafalgar: British naval victory in the Napoleonic wars (1805); the commander of the fleet, Lord Admiral Horatio Nelson (1758–1805), was killed in the action.

Mrs Grundy: 'a personification of the tyranny of social opinion' (*OED*), from Thomas Morton's play *Speed the Plough* (1798): usually invoked as the voice of conventional propriety rather than (as here) an object of contempt.

307 *Mr Wilberforce*: William Wilberforce (1759–1833), philanthropist and MP, led the parliamentary campaign to abolish the slave trade.

curricle and pair . . . gig: light two-wheeled vehicles, drawn by a pair of horses and by a single horse, respectively.

309 *crop time*: harvest time was in fact the busiest time of year on a sugar plantation.

Creole: born in the West Indies (of any race).

Psyche . . . Cupid: Psyche was a nymph beloved by Cupid, who visited her at night, in an episode of Apuleius' *The Golden Ass*; Lewis refers to the Neoplatonists' allegorical interpretation of the tale, in which Psyche represents the soul.

310 *Ipecacuanha*: plant used as an emetic.

311 *Yarico*: the story of Inkle and Yarico, first told in Richard Ligon's *History of Barbados* (1657), became hugely popular in the eighteenth century in versions by Richard Steele (in *The Spectator*, 1711) and George Colman (in his eponymous musical play, 1787). Shipwrecked Englishman Thomas Inkle is cared for by Indian maid Yarico; they fall in love, she gets pregnant, but when they are rescued Inkle sells her into slavery. (Colman substituted a happy ending with their marriage.) See Frank Felsenstein, *English Trader, Indian Maid: An Inkle and Yarico Reader* (Baltimore: Johns Hopkins University Press, 1999).

Grassini in 'La Vergine del Sole': Josephina Grassini (1773–1850), Italian contralto celebrated for her beautiful looks as well as voice, made her London debut in 1804 in Gaetano Andreozzi's opera *La vergine del sole*.

cotton-tree: see note to p. 301, above.

313 *out-Herod Herod*: to rant and rave like a stage tyrant: Shakespeare, *Hamlet*, III. ii.

315 *steerage*: space below decks.

316 *Swift's Yahoos*: vicious, degraded race of humanity in the fourth book of *Gulliver's Travels* (1728).

emigrants: the disintegration of traditional social structures and local economies in the Highlands and Islands, in the wake of government suppression of the 1745 Jacobite rising, drove thousands of Scots to emigrate to North America by the mid-1770s.

supercargo: officer responsible for the sale of the ship's cargo and other commercial business. Schaw elsewhere castigates this individual as 'a republican and a violent American'.

316 *teague*: pejorative nickname for an Irishman.

317 *the Islands*: the Orkneys.

318 *Miss Forbes, with her pencil of Sensibility*: Miss Forbes has not been identified. Sensibility is defined by the *OED* as a 'capacity for refined emotion; delicate sensitiveness of taste; also, readiness to feel compassion for suffering, and to be moved by the pathetic in literature or art'. For the educated classes of late eighteenth-century Britain, sensibility had become a status symbol, its ostentatious performance signifying innate nobility and high moral character.

320 *hob and nob*: a toast to the present company.

323 *masks and bonnets*: a colonial custom described in other accounts of the period. *A Brief Account of the Island of Antigua* (1789) comments, 'With you, this would be termed the greatest ill-manners, but here custom has established it, if not necessary as fashionable.'

324 *shaddocks . . . papa trees*: citrus trees with grapefruit-like fruit; papaya trees.

     rakes: rakings (of horse-dung, used as fertilizer).

326 *the Rebellion*: the United Irishmen Rising, 1798, put down with a slaughter of somewhere between 10,000 and 25,000 rebels and non-combatants.

327 *King's House*: the Governor's residence from 1762 until the removal of the capital to Kingston in 1872.

328 *kittareens, sulkies*: names for a one-horse chaise or buggy.

329 *performed by the waters*: the government acquired the sulphuric thermal spring at Bath, in St Thomas parish, in 1699; the waters (with temperatures up to 53°C) were deemed curative of a host of ailments, including cancer and syphilis.

331 *livings*: clerical appointments in the Church of England were obtained through patronage. The system was notoriously subject to abuses, such as clergymen who collected salaries from more than one living and hired low-paid curates to perform their duties, and others (as here) who sold the position for cash. General Nugent's concern reflects his position as head of the church in Jamaica.

333 *French prisoners*: more than 500 non-French nationals, former soldiers of the French army in Haiti, were recruited by the British from among their prisoners of war.

PART V. NORTH AMERICA

335 *Congerees*: or Congarees; a Siouan people who lived in the South Carolina Piedmont, around present-day Columbia.

     loblolly: thick gruel.

which they all have: judging by its size, a whooping crane (*Grus americana*); now extremely rare.

336 *Wateree Chickanee Indians*: like the Congarees and Waxhaw (below), a Siouan tribe in central South Carolina.

337 *cadis*: coarse cheap serge.

Winchester-Wedding: a kind of jig, hence an impromptu festival.

Loretto: near Ancona, Italy; site of the Virgin Mary's house, conveyed there by angels.

moggisons: moccasins.

338 *Puerto Seguro*: Cabo San Lucas, the southern tip of Baja California.

bark-logs: dug-out canoes.

340 *hasty pudding*: a pudding made of flour stirred into boiling milk or water to the consistency of a thick batter.

341 *lag*: late, delayed.

342 *Herodotus' East Indian Pygmies*: Herodotus locates the Pygmies in Libya. Byrd may be recalling Ctesus of Cnidos's account of East Indian Pygmies in his *History of India*, related by Thomas Browne in *Pseudodoxia Epidemica* (1646), IV. xi.

Adamites: in a state of primitive nakedness, like Adam before the Fall.

343 *pocosin*: coastal swamp or wetland.

piragua: canoe.

346 *cleansing the Augean stables*: one of the 'impossible' tasks accomplished by Hercules: proverbially, an arduous and filthy job.

Most Christian King in Canada and Louisiana: the King of France. Louisiana and Quebec were French colonies until 1763.

347 *puccoon*: red vegetable dye.

353 *fusee*: light musket.

355 *crocodiles*: here, synonymous with 'alligator'. Different species of American crocodile (*Crocodylus acutus*) and alligator (*Alligator mississippiensis*) are native to the Florida wetlands.

359 *the white flag*: his tail.

362 *manes*: spirit (Latin). 'These people never kill the rattle snake or any other serpent, saying if they do so, the spirit of the killed snake will excite or influence his living kindred or relatives to revenge the injury or violence done to him when alive' (Bartram).

363 *Matonabbee*: Chipewyan chief, Hearne's guide and friend; he committed suicide in 1782.

Prince of Wales's Fort: present-day Churchill, Manitoba.

Coppermine River: in the Northwest Territories.

365 *Thelewey-aza River*: the Thlewiaza River runs from Nueltin Lake, on the northern border of Manitoba, to Hudson Bay.

367 *the river*: the Coppermine.

368 *muskettoes*: mosquitoes.

372 *camlet*: 'king of stuff originally made by a mixture of silk and camel's hair
     . . . now made with wool and silk' (Johnson).

374 *Under the land*: Mackenzie has arrived at Queen Charlotte Sound,
     present-day British Columbia.

     Macubah . . . Bensins: Captain George Vancouver (1757–98) and the ship's
     botanist Archibald Menzies (1754–1842), who surveyed the Canadian
     Pacific coast 1792–3. The Indians were Bella Bellas, relatives of the
     Vancouver Island Kwakiutl.

376 *this brief memorial*: Mackenzie's words, subsequently carved into the
     rock, are still legible there at the Dean Channel near Bella Coola, BC.

377 *hanger*: sword hanging from belt.

378 *Winter soon sets in*: Thompson is based at York Factory, at the mouth of
     the Hayes River on Hudson's Bay, present-day Manitoba.

382 *During the winter . . . plain before me*: this incident is omitted from the
     1919 version of *Thompson's Narrative*.

384 *Sinkowarsin*: Wenatchee Indians, a branch of the Salish.

386 *We embarked*: on 9 July 1811.

387 *Fort Astoria of the United States*: founded in April 1811 by John Jacob
     Astor's Pacific Fur Company, rivals of the Northwest Company, who
     would purchase Astoria in 1813.

390 *improvements*: 'I have heard of Americans landing on barren parts of the
     north-west coast of Ireland, and evincing the greatest surprise and pleas-
     ure at the beauty and improved state of the country, "so clear of trees!!" '
     (Weld).

     the Americans: 'In speaking of the Americans here, and in the following
     lines, it is those of the lower and middling classes of the people which I
     allude to, such as are met with in the country parts of Pennsylvania'
     (Weld).

394 *Lord Monboddo*: James Burnett, Lord Monboddo (1714–99), Scottish
     judge and moral philosopher, argued in *The Origin and Progress of
     Language* (1773) that orang-utans belonged to the human race and could
     be taught language.

     strange bed-fellows: see *The Tempest*, II. ii. 241.

395 *comedians*: actors.

396 *this charming family*: the family of Thomas Drayton (d. *c.*1820), Davis's
     employer.

397 *Rousseau . . . suckle*: see *Émile* (1762), book I.

398 *Notes on Virginia*: Thomas Jefferson, *Notes on the State of Virginia*
     (1787), ch. 14: 'Religion indeed has produced a Phyllis Whately; but
     it could not produce a poet.' Wheatley (*c.*1750–84) was the first

African-American author of a published book, *Poems on Various Subjects* (London, 1773). The contents include 'Goliath of Gath' and 'On Imagination', mentioned below.

Ladd, the Carolina poet: Joseph Brown Ladd (1764–86).

Imlay ... Stedman: Gilbert Imlay (see above, p. 83) settled in Kentucky in 1784, before his sojourn in Europe and liaison with Mary Wollstonecraft; he cites Wheatley on p. 229 of a *Topographical Description of the Western Territory of North America* (1797; Johnson Reprint Corporation, 1968). John Gabriel Stedman (see above, pp. 267–79) refers to Wheatley in his *Narrative of a Five Years Expedition* (ed. Price and Price, 1988, p. 517).

399 *the Indian war*: Pontiac's War, 1763–6, an uprising against the expansion of colonial settlements in Ohio and western Pennsylvania.

400 *a treaty*: under the terms of the peace treaty (1766) Pontiac received a pardon and went home.

Madame: Margarita Schuyler (1701–82), Grant's hostess and patron, the ostensible subject of her memoir.

405 *Mr James Paul*: or Paull (1770–1808), India merchant turned Radical politician and a former ally of Cobbett, who admired his 'industry and pluck'.

Mr Elias Hicks: founder of a radical Quaker sect (1748–1830).

DECATUR, HULL, and BRAINBRIDGE: Stephen Decatur (1779–1820), Isaac Hull (1773–1843), and William Bainbridge (1744–1833): American naval officers who defeated British frigates in the War of 1812.

LORD COCHRANE: Thomas, Lord Cochrane, tenth Earl of Dundonald (1775–1860), heroic naval commander and ineffectual Radical politician.

CASHMAN: John Cashman, sailor, hanged for participation in the Spafield riots, 1817; he was owed five years' back pay by the Admiralty as well as a share of prize-money.

JACKSON: General Andrew Jackson (1767–1845) defeated the British at the Battle of New Orleans, 1815.

Marshal Ney: Michel Ney, duc d'Elchingen (1769–1815), shot for treason, allegedly with the Duke of Wellington's connivance, after the defeat of Napoleon at Waterloo.

Holy Alliance: treaty (1815) between the sovereigns of Austria, Prussia, and Russia to consolidate the restoration of the old religious and absolutist regimes after the defeat of Napoleon.

408 *a very agreeable station*: Trollope is ascending the Mississippi from New Orleans to Memphis on the steamer *Belvedere*, January 1828.

409 *the presidency*: John Quincy Adams had been elected president in 1824, after a rancorous contest with General Andrew Jackson. A corruption scandal helped Jackson defeat Adams in the 1828 election.

410 *this summer*: in 1829; Trollope was resident in Cincinnati.

411 *Vauxhall*: London pleasure-garden.

412 *Scott's Macbriar*: Ephraim Macbriar, fanatical Covenanting preacher in Walter Scott's *Old Mortality* (1816).

Bedlam: London insane asylum (originally the hospital of St Mary of Bethlehem).

413 *Milton's lines*: 'Lycidas' (1637), ll. 119–27.

414 *the Revival*: Trollope narrates her visit to a revival meeting in Cincinnati in an earlier chapter.

415 *Quivi ... suon di man con elle*: 'Here sighs, cries and loud lamentations resounded through the air ... horrible utterances, words of sorrow, accents of rage, voices shrill and hoarse, and sounds of beating hands': Dante, *Inferno*, iii. 22–7.

Canova's Magdalene: 'The Penitent Magdalene', statue by Antonio Canova (1809), now in the State Hermitage Museum, St Petersburg.

Don Juan: legendary libertine, dragged down to Hell by a statue: see Molière's play *Le Festin de pierre* (1665) and the Da Ponte/Mozart opera *Don Giovanni* (1787).

416 *Mr King*: Charles Bird King (1785–1862) painted more than 100 portraits of Native American chiefs and elders who came to Washington for treaty negotiations between 1821 and 1842. Most of the portraits were destroyed in a fire in 1865.

417 *by the fiat of the President*: Andrew Jackson's Indian Removal Act (1830) drove Native Americans west of the Mississippi, in violation of existing treaties.

PART VI. AUSTRALIA AND THE PACIFIC

427 *Hodmadods of Monomatapa*: Hottentots, the Khoi people of the South African Cape.

429 *Bon-Airy*: Bonaire, island in the Dutch Antilles.

430 *yall*: yawl, ship's boat.

flaws: sudden gusts of wind.

439 *luffed*: sailed nearer the wind.

442 *the Fort*: Fort Venus, site of the observatory.

443 *more from custom than lewdness*: the published report of this incident caused a sensation in Europe; see Neil Rennie, 'The Point Venus "Scene" ', *The Global Eighteenth Century* (ed. F. A. Nussbaum, 2003, 239–50).

Obarea: Purea, 'queen' (high chief) of Bora-Bora.

Dr Solander: Daniel Carl Solander (1732–82), Swedish pupil of Linnaeus; Banks's assistant on the voyage.

Tootaha: Tutaha (?1708–73), Tahitian high chief.

446 *Tupia, Mr Green and Dr Munkhouse*: Tupaia (d. 1770), chief and high priest of Raiatea; Charles Green (1735–71), the expedition's astronomer; William Monkhouse (d. 1770), ship's surgeon. Tupaia came on board the *Endeavour* as a guest in July 1769; he proved a skilled navigator as well as interpreter.

447 *two or three were killed*: Cook heavily revised this passage. According to Banks's journal, the seven men in the canoe rebuffed the boat's approach with stones and paddles; Cook's party opened fire and killed four of them.

451 *an animal he had seen*: probably a fruit bat ('cagg' = keg).

455 *ruddle*: red earth or ochre.

457 *Mr Wales*: William Wales (*c.*1734–98), the expedition's astronomer.

pattoo-pattoo: club.

Mr Pickersgill: Richard Pickersgill (1749–79), third lieutenant on the *Resolution*.

this price: 'The head is now deposited in the collection of Mr John Hunter, F.R.S.' (Forster).

taffarel: or taffrail—the upper part of the stern.

458 *ipecacuanha*: an emetic.

Mahine: or Odiddy (d. 1790), chief of Morea; he joined the *Resolution* at Raiatea in September and returned the following June.

460 *At last . . . THOMPSON*: James Thomson, *Spring* (1728), ll. 304–6.

462 *Tyo's*: friends, in a ritual sealed with gift-exchange. Red feathers from the Friendly Islands were prized in the Society Islands.

463 *Toutous*: servants.

New Zealand youths: Tiarooa and Koa (Coaa), taken on board in February 1777. Omai and the youths died of fever three or four years later.

464 *Pretane*: Britain.

468 *in the following manner*: Arabanoo was kidnapped in December 1788.

470 *the loss of this man*: Arabanoo died in May 1789.

life might be prolonged: 'One of the convicts, a Negro, had twice eloped with an intention of establishing himself in the society of the natives, with a wish to adopt their customs and to live with them, but he was always repulsed by them, and compelled to return to us from hunger and wretchedness' (Tench).

471 *Baneelon and Colbee*: Bennelong and Colbee were taken in November 1789. Nanbaree and Abaroo are the children who survived the smallpox outbreak, described in the selection from Hunter.

472 *how fields were won*: compare Oliver Goldsmith, *The Deserted Village* (1770), l. 158 (reading 'Shouldered his crutch . . .').

a watch over him: although shackled, Bennelong managed to escape in May 1790.

474 *junks*: chunks, possibly cut from 'the lump or mass of thick oily cellular tissue beneath the case and nostrils of a sperm-whale, containing spermaceti' (*OED*).

476 *fixed his lance in his throwing-stick*: 'Such preparation is equal to what cocking a gun, and directing it at its object, would be with us. To launch the spear, or to touch the trigger, only remains' (Tench).

striking: 'His Excellency described the shock to me as similar to a violent blow, with such energy was the weapon thrown' (Tench).

479 *245 female convicts*: the second fleet sailed in July 1789; there were 226 convicts on board the *Lady Juliana*.

482 *Pitt's*: William Pitt the Younger (1759–1806), British Prime Minister.

485 *crossing the line*: crossing the Equator, traditionally celebrated with carnivalesque ceremonies in which sailors dressed up as 'King Neptune' and his wife.

486 *a boy and a girl*: Abaroo and Nanbaree; see Hunter and Tench, above.

bring her back to England: Nicol never saw her again. Immediately after his departure (July 1790) Sarah Whitlam married a first-fleet convict, John Coen Walsh; the couple eventually returned to England.

488 *Fleecy locks ... in white and black the same*: William Cowper, 'The Negro's Complaint' (1788), ll. 13–16.

489 *Tayo*: friend.

arreoies: members of a religious cult (*arioi*) which put on theatrical performances throughout the Society Islands—involving licentious sexual displays, according to European observers.

Eatooa: God (*atua*).

491 *Happy is that people whose God is the Lord*: Psalm 144: 15.

493 *a very wicked people*: 'broke the restrictions of the tabu, or brought no offerings' (Ellis).